Lecture Notes in Computer Science 8029

Commenced Publication in 1973
Founding and Former Series Editors:
Gerhard Goos, Juris Hartmanis, and Jan van Leeuwen

A. Ant Ozok   Panayiotis Zaphiris (Eds.)

Online Communities and Social Computing

5th International Conference, OCSC 2013
Held as Part of HCI International 2013
Las Vegas, NV, USA, July 21-26, 2013
Proceedings

Volume Editors

A. Ant Ozok
The Johns Hopkins University, School of Medicine, Department of Anesthesiology
UMBC, Department of Information Systems
1000 Hilltop Circle, Baltimore, MD 21250, USA
E-mail: ozok@umbc.edu

Panayiotis Zaphiris
Cyprus University of Technology, Department of Multimedia and Graphic Arts
30 Archbishop Kyprianou Street, 3036 Lemesos, Cyprus
E-mail: panayiotis.zaphiris@cut.ac.cy

ISSN 0302-9743   e-ISSN 1611-3349
ISBN 978-3-642-39370-9   e-ISBN 978-3-642-39371-6
DOI 10.1007/978-3-642-39371-6
Springer Heidelberg Dordrecht London New York

Library of Congress Control Number: 2013941481

CR Subject Classification (1998): H.5, K.3, K.8, H.3, K.4, J.1, J.4

LNCS Sublibrary: SL 3 – Information Systems and Application,
incl. Internet/Web and HCI

Typesetting: Camera-ready by author, data conversion by Scientific Publishing Services, Chennai, India

Printed on acid-free paper

Springer is part of Springer Science+Business Media (www.springer.com)

Foreword

The 15th International Conference on Human–Computer Interaction, HCI International 2013, was held in Las Vegas, Nevada, USA, 21–26 July 2013, incorporating 12 conferences / thematic areas:

Thematic areas:

- Human–Computer Interaction
- Human Interface and the Management of Information

Affiliated conferences:

- 10th International Conference on Engineering Psychology and Cognitive Ergonomics
- 7th International Conference on Universal Access in Human–Computer Interaction
- 5th International Conference on Virtual, Augmented and Mixed Reality
- 5th International Conference on Cross-Cultural Design
- 5th International Conference on Online Communities and Social Computing
- 7th International Conference on Augmented Cognition
- 4th International Conference on Digital Human Modeling and Applications in Health, Safety, Ergonomics and Risk Management
- 2nd International Conference on Design, User Experience and Usability
- 1st International Conference on Distributed, Ambient and Pervasive Interactions
- 1st International Conference on Human Aspects of Information Security, Privacy and Trust

A total of 5210 individuals from academia, research institutes, industry and governmental agencies from 70 countries submitted contributions, and 1666 papers and 303 posters were included in the program. These papers address the latest research and development efforts and highlight the human aspects of design and use of computing systems. The papers accepted for presentation thoroughly cover the entire field of Human–Computer Interaction, addressing major advances in knowledge and effective use of computers in a variety of application areas.

This volume, edited by A. Ant Ozok and Panayiotis Zaphiris, contains papers focusing on the thematic area of Online Communities and Social Computing, and addressing the following major topics:

- User Behavior and Experience in Online Social Communities
- Learning and Gaming Communities
- Society, Business and Health
- Designing and Developing Novel Online Social Experiences

The remaining volumes of the HCI International 2013 proceedings are:

- Volume 1, LNCS 8004, Human–Computer Interaction: Human-Centred Design Approaches, Methods, Tools and Environments (Part I), edited by Masaaki Kurosu
- Volume 2, LNCS 8005, Human–Computer Interaction: Applications and Services (Part II), edited by Masaaki Kurosu
- Volume 3, LNCS 8006, Human–Computer Interaction: Users and Contexts of Use (Part III), edited by Masaaki Kurosu
- Volume 4, LNCS 8007, Human–Computer Interaction: Interaction Modalities and Techniques (Part IV), edited by Masaaki Kurosu
- Volume 5, LNCS 8008, Human–Computer Interaction: Towards Intelligent and Implicit Interaction (Part V), edited by Masaaki Kurosu
- Volume 6, LNCS 8009, Universal Access in Human–Computer Interaction: Design Methods, Tools and Interaction Techniques for eInclusion (Part I), edited by Constantine Stephanidis and Margherita Antona
- Volume 7, LNCS 8010, Universal Access in Human–Computer Interaction: User and Context Diversity (Part II), edited by Constantine Stephanidis and Margherita Antona
- Volume 8, LNCS 8011, Universal Access in Human–Computer Interaction: Applications and Services for Quality of Life (Part III), edited by Constantine Stephanidis and Margherita Antona
- Volume 9, LNCS 8012, Design, User Experience, and Usability: Design Philosophy, Methods and Tools (Part I), edited by Aaron Marcus
- Volume 10, LNCS 8013, Design, User Experience, and Usability: Health, Learning, Playing, Cultural, and Cross-Cultural User Experience (Part II), edited by Aaron Marcus
- Volume 11, LNCS 8014, Design, User Experience, and Usability: User Experience in Novel Technological Environments (Part III), edited by Aaron Marcus
- Volume 12, LNCS 8015, Design, User Experience, and Usability: Web, Mobile and Product Design (Part IV), edited by Aaron Marcus
- Volume 13, LNCS 8016, Human Interface and the Management of Information: Information and Interaction Design (Part I), edited by Sakae Yamamoto
- Volume 14, LNCS 8017, Human Interface and the Management of Information: Information and Interaction for Health, Safety, Mobility and Complex Environments (Part II), edited by Sakae Yamamoto
- Volume 15, LNCS 8018, Human Interface and the Management of Information: Information and Interaction for Learning, Culture, Collaboration and Business (Part III), edited by Sakae Yamamoto
- Volume 16, LNAI 8019, Engineering Psychology and Cognitive Ergonomics: Understanding Human Cognition (Part I), edited by Don Harris
- Volume 17, LNAI 8020, Engineering Psychology and Cognitive Ergonomics: Applications and Services (Part II), edited by Don Harris
- Volume 18, LNCS 8021, Virtual, Augmented and Mixed Reality: Designing and Developing Augmented and Virtual Environments (Part I), edited by Randall Shumaker

- Volume 19, LNCS 8022, Virtual, Augmented and Mixed Reality: Systems and Applications (Part II), edited by Randall Shumaker
- Volume 20, LNCS 8023, Cross-Cultural Design: Methods, Practice and Case Studies (Part I), edited by P.L. Patrick Rau
- Volume 21, LNCS 8024, Cross-Cultural Design: Cultural Differences in Everyday Life (Part II), edited by P.L. Patrick Rau
- Volume 22, LNCS 8025, Digital Human Modeling and Applications in Health, Safety, Ergonomics and Risk Management: Healthcare and Safety of the Environment and Transport (Part I), edited by Vincent G. Duffy
- Volume 23, LNCS 8026, Digital Human Modeling and Applications in Health, Safety, Ergonomics and Risk Management: Human Body Modeling and Ergonomics (Part II), edited by Vincent G. Duffy
- Volume 24, LNAI 8027, Foundations of Augmented Cognition, edited by Dylan D. Schmorrow and Cali M. Fidopiastis
- Volume 25, LNCS 8028, Distributed, Ambient and Pervasive Interactions, edited by Norbert Streitz and Constantine Stephanidis
- Volume 27, LNCS 8030, Human Aspects of Information Security, Privacy and Trust, edited by Louis Marinos and Ioannis Askoxylakis
- Volume 28, CCIS 373, HCI International 2013 Posters Proceedings (Part I), edited by Constantine Stephanidis
- Volume 29, CCIS 374, HCI International 2013 Posters Proceedings (Part II), edited by Constantine Stephanidis

I would like to thank the Program Chairs and the members of the Program Boards of all affiliated conferences and thematic areas, listed below, for their contribution to the highest scientific quality and the overall success of the HCI International 2013 conference.

This conference could not have been possible without the continuous support and advice of the Founding Chair and Conference Scientific Advisor, Prof. Gavriel Salvendy, as well as the dedicated work and outstanding efforts of the Communications Chair and Editor of HCI International News, Abbas Moallem.

I would also like to thank for their contribution towards the smooth organization of the HCI International 2013 Conference the members of the Human–Computer Interaction Laboratory of ICS-FORTH, and in particular George Paparoulis, Maria Pitsoulaki, Stavroula Ntoa, Maria Bouhli and George Kapnas.

May 2013   Constantine Stephanidis
                                    General Chair, HCI International 2013

Organization

Human–Computer Interaction

Program Chair: Masaaki Kurosu, Japan

Jose Abdelnour-Nocera, UK
Sebastiano Bagnara, Italy
Simone Barbosa, Brazil
Tomas Berns, Sweden
Nigel Bevan, UK
Simone Borsci, UK
Apala Lahiri Chavan, India
Sherry Chen, Taiwan
Kevin Clark, USA
Torkil Clemmensen, Denmark
Xiaowen Fang, USA
Shin'ichi Fukuzumi, Japan
Vicki Hanson, UK
Ayako Hashizume, Japan
Anzai Hiroyuki, Italy
Sheue-Ling Hwang, Taiwan
Wonil Hwang, South Korea
Minna Isomursu, Finland
Yong Gu Ji, South Korea
Esther Jun, USA
Mitsuhiko Karashima, Japan

Kyungdoh Kim, South Korea
Heidi Krömker, Germany
Chen Ling, USA
Yan Liu, USA
Zhengjie Liu, P.R. China
Loïc Martínez Normand, Spain
Chang S. Nam, USA
Naoko Okuizumi, Japan
Noriko Osaka, Japan
Philippe Palanque, France
Hans Persson, Sweden
Ling Rothrock, USA
Naoki Sakakibara, Japan
Dominique Scapin, France
Guangfeng Song, USA
Sanjay Tripathi, India
Chui Yin Wong, Malaysia
Toshiki Yamaoka, Japan
Kazuhiko Yamazaki, Japan
Ryoji Yoshitake, Japan
Silvia Zimmermann, Switzerland

Human Interface and the Management of Information

Program Chair: Sakae Yamamoto, Japan

Hans-Jorg Bullinger, Germany
Alan Chan, Hong Kong
Gilsoo Cho, South Korea
Jon R. Gunderson, USA
Shin'ichi Fukuzumi, Japan
Michitaka Hirose, Japan
Jhilmil Jain, USA
Yasufumi Kume, Japan

Mark Lehto, USA
Hiroyuki Miki, Japan
Hirohiko Mori, Japan
Fiona Fui-Hoon Nah, USA
Shogo Nishida, Japan
Robert Proctor, USA
Youngho Rhee, South Korea
Katsunori Shimohara, Japan

Michale Smith, USA
Tsutomu Tabe, Japan
Hiroshi Tsuji, Japan

Kim-Phuong Vu, USA
Tomio Watanabe, Japan
Hidekazu Yoshikawa, Japan

Engineering Psychology and Cognitive Ergonomics

Program Chair: Don Harris, UK

Guy Andre Boy, USA
Joakim Dahlman, Sweden
Trevor Dobbins, UK
Mike Feary, USA
Shan Fu, P.R. China
Michaela Heese, Austria
Hung-Sying Jing, Taiwan
Wen-Chin Li, Taiwan
Mark A. Neerincx, The Netherlands
Jan M. Noyes, UK
Taezoon Park, Singapore

Paul Salmon, Australia
Axel Schulte, Germany
Siraj Shaikh, UK
Sarah C. Sharples, UK
Anthony Smoker, UK
Neville A. Stanton, UK
Alex Stedmon, UK
Xianghong Sun, P.R. China
Andrew Thatcher, South Africa
Matthew J.W. Thomas, Australia
Rolf Zon, The Netherlands

Universal Access in Human–Computer Interaction

Program Chairs: Constantine Stephanidis, Greece, and Margherita Antona, Greece

Julio Abascal, Spain
Ray Adams, UK
Gisela Susanne Bahr, USA
Margit Betke, USA
Christian Bühler, Germany
Stefan Carmien, Spain
Jerzy Charytonowicz, Poland
Carlos Duarte, Portugal
Pier Luigi Emiliani, Italy
Qin Gao, P.R. China
Andrina Granić, Croatia
Andreas Holzinger, Austria
Josette Jones, USA
Simeon Keates, UK

Georgios Kouroupetroglou, Greece
Patrick Langdon, UK
Seongil Lee, Korea
Ana Isabel B.B. Paraguay, Brazil
Helen Petrie, UK
Michael Pieper, Germany
Enrico Pontelli, USA
Jaime Sanchez, Chile
Anthony Savidis, Greece
Christian Stary, Austria
Hirotada Ueda, Japan
Gerhard Weber, Germany
Harald Weber, Germany

Virtual, Augmented and Mixed Reality

Program Chair: Randall Shumaker, USA

Waymon Armstrong, USA
Juan Cendan, USA
Rudy Darken, USA
Cali M. Fidopiastis, USA
Charles Hughes, USA
David Kaber, USA
Hirokazu Kato, Japan
Denis Laurendeau, Canada
Fotis Liarokapis, UK

Mark Livingston, USA
Michael Macedonia, USA
Gordon Mair, UK
Jose San Martin, Spain
Jacquelyn Morie, USA
Albert "Skip" Rizzo, USA
Kay Stanney, USA
Christopher Stapleton, USA
Gregory Welch, USA

Cross-Cultural Design

Program Chair: P.L. Patrick Rau, P.R. China

Pilsung Choe, P.R. China
Henry Been-Lirn Duh, Singapore
Vanessa Evers, The Netherlands
Paul Fu, USA
Zhiyong Fu, P.R. China
Fu Guo, P.R. China
Sung H. Han, Korea
Toshikazu Kato, Japan
Dyi-Yih Michael Lin, Taiwan
Rungtai Lin, Taiwan

Sheau-Farn Max Liang, Taiwan
Liang Ma, P.R. China
Alexander Mädche, Germany
Katsuhiko Ogawa, Japan
Tom Plocher, USA
Kerstin Röse, Germany
Supriya Singh, Australia
Hsiu-Ping Yueh, Taiwan
Liang (Leon) Zeng, USA
Chen Zhao, USA

Online Communities and Social Computing

Program Chairs: A. Ant Ozok, USA, and Panayiotis Zaphiris, Cyprus

Areej Al-Wabil, Saudi Arabia
Leonelo Almeida, Brazil
Bjørn Andersen, Norway
Chee Siang Ang, UK
Aneesha Bakharia, Australia
Ania Bobrowicz, UK
Paul Cairns, UK
Farzin Deravi, UK
Andri Ioannou, Cyprus
Slava Kisilevich, Germany

Niki Lambropoulos, Greece
Effie Law, Switzerland
Soo Ling Lim, UK
Fernando Loizides, Cyprus
Gabriele Meiselwitz, USA
Anthony Norcio, USA
Elaine Raybourn, USA
Panote Siriaraya, UK
David Stuart, UK
June Wei, USA

Augmented Cognition

Program Chairs: Dylan D. Schmorrow, USA, and Cali M. Fidopiastis, USA

Robert Arrabito, Canada
Richard Backs, USA
Chris Berka, USA
Joseph Cohn, USA
Martha E. Crosby, USA
Julie Drexler, USA
Ivy Estabrooke, USA
Chris Forsythe, USA
Wai Tat Fu, USA
Rodolphe Gentili, USA
Marc Grootjen, The Netherlands
Jefferson Grubb, USA
Ming Hou, Canada

Santosh Mathan, USA
Rob Matthews, Australia
Dennis McBride, USA
Jeff Morrison, USA
Mark A. Neerincx, The Netherlands
Denise Nicholson, USA
Banu Onaral, USA
Lee Sciarini, USA
Kay Stanney, USA
Roy Stripling, USA
Rob Taylor, UK
Karl van Orden, USA

Digital Human Modeling and Applications in Health, Safety, Ergonomics and Risk Management

Program Chair: Vincent G. Duffy, USA and Russia

Karim Abdel-Malek, USA
Giuseppe Andreoni, Italy
Daniel Carruth, USA
Eliza Yingzi Du, USA
Enda Fallon, Ireland
Afzal Godil, USA
Ravindra Goonetilleke, Hong Kong
Bo Hoege, Germany
Waldemar Karwowski, USA
Zhizhong Li, P.R. China

Kang Li, USA
Tim Marler, USA
Michelle Robertson, USA
Matthias Rötting, Germany
Peter Vink, The Netherlands
Mao-Jiun Wang, Taiwan
Xuguang Wang, France
Jingzhou (James) Yang, USA
Xiugan Yuan, P.R. China
Gülcin Yücel Hoge, Germany

Design, User Experience, and Usability

Program Chair: Aaron Marcus, USA

Sisira Adikari, Australia
Ronald Baecker, Canada
Arne Berger, Germany
Jamie Blustein, Canada

Ana Boa-Ventura, USA
Jan Brejcha, Czech Republic
Lorenzo Cantoni, Switzerland
Maximilian Eibl, Germany

Anthony Faiola, USA
Emilie Gould, USA
Zelda Harrison, USA
Rüdiger Heimgärtner, Germany
Brigitte Herrmann, Germany
Steffen Hess, Germany
Kaleem Khan, Canada

Jennifer McGinn, USA
Francisco Rebelo, Portugal
Michael Renner, Switzerland
Kerem Rızvanoğlu, Turkey
Marcelo Soares, Brazil
Christian Sturm, Germany
Michele Visciola, Italy

Distributed, Ambient and Pervasive Interactions

Program Chairs: Norbert Streitz, Germany, and Constantine Stephanidis, Greece

Emile Aarts, The Netherlands
Adnan Abu-Dayya, Qatar
Juan Carlos Augusto, UK
Boris de Ruyter, The Netherlands
Anind Dey, USA
Dimitris Grammenos, Greece
Nuno M. Guimaraes, Portugal
Shin'ichi Konomi, Japan
Carsten Magerkurth, Switzerland

Christian Müller-Tomfelde, Australia
Fabio Paternó, Italy
Gilles Privat, France
Harald Reiterer, Germany
Carsten Röcker, Germany
Reiner Wichert, Germany
Woontack Woo, South Korea
Xenophon Zabulis, Greece

Human Aspects of Information Security, Privacy and Trust

Program Chairs: Louis Marinos, ENISA EU, and Ioannis Askoxylakis, Greece

Claudio Agostino Ardagna, Italy
Zinaida Benenson, Germany
Daniele Catteddu, Italy
Raoul Chiesa, Italy
Bryan Cline, USA
Sadie Creese, UK
Jorge Cuellar, Germany
Marc Dacier, USA
Dieter Gollmann, Germany
Kirstie Hawkey, Canada
Jaap-Henk Hoepman, The Netherlands
Cagatay Karabat, Turkey
Angelos Keromytis, USA
Ayako Komatsu, Japan

Ronald Leenes, The Netherlands
Javier Lopez, Spain
Steve Marsh, Canada
Gregorio Martinez, Spain
Emilio Mordini, Italy
Yuko Murayama, Japan
Masakätsu Nishigaki, Japan
Aljosa Pasic, Spain
Milan Petković, The Netherlands
Joachim Posegga, Germany
Jean-Jacques Quisquater, Belgium
Damien Sauveron, France
George Spanoudakis, UK
Kerry-Lynn Thomson, South Africa

Julien Touzeau, France
Theo Tryfonas, UK
João Vilela, Portugal

Claire Vishik, UK
Melanie Volkamer, Germany

External Reviewers

Maysoon Abulkhair, Saudi Arabia
Ilia Adami, Greece
Vishal Barot, UK
Stephan Böhm, Germany
Vassilis Charissis, UK
Francisco Cipolla-Ficarra, Spain
Maria De Marsico, Italy
Marc Fabri, UK
David Fonseca, Spain
Linda Harley, USA
Yasushi Ikei, Japan
Wei Ji, USA
Nouf Khashman, Canada
John Killilea, USA
Iosif Klironomos, Greece
Ute Klotz, Switzerland
Maria Korozi, Greece
Kentaro Kotani, Japan

Vassilis Kouroumalis, Greece
Stephanie Lackey, USA
Janelle LaMarche, USA
Asterios Leonidis, Greece
Nickolas Macchiarella, USA
George Margetis, Greece
Matthew Marraffino, USA
Joseph Mercado, USA
Claudia Mont'Alvão, Brazil
Yoichi Motomura, Japan
Karsten Nebe, Germany
Stavroula Ntoa, Greece
Martin Osen, Austria
Stephen Prior, UK
Farid Shirazi, Canada
Jan Stelovsky, USA
Sarah Swierenga, USA

HCI International 2014

The 16th International Conference on Human–Computer Interaction, HCI International 2014, will be held jointly with the affiliated conferences in the summer of 2014. It will cover a broad spectrum of themes related to Human–Computer Interaction, including theoretical issues, methods, tools, processes and case studies in HCI design, as well as novel interaction techniques, interfaces and applications. The proceedings will be published by Springer. More information about the topics, as well as the venue and dates of the conference, will be announced through the HCI International Conference series website: http://www.hci-international.org/

General Chair
Professor Constantine Stephanidis
University of Crete and ICS-FORTH
Heraklion, Crete, Greece
Email: cs@ics.forth.gr

Table of Contents

User Behaviour and Experience in On-Line Social Communities

Learning and Gaming Communities

Society, Business and Health

Designing and Developing Novel On-Line Social Experiences

Part I

User Behaviour and Experience in On-Line Social Communities

User Generated Content: An Analysis of User Behavior by Mining Political Tweets

Rocío Abascal-Mena, Erick López-Ornelas, and J. Sergio Zepeda-Hernández

Universidad Autónoma Metropolitana – Cuajimalpa
Departamento de Tecnologías de la Información
Avenida Constituyentes 1054, Col. Lomas Altas, Del. Miguel Hidalgo
11950, México D.F. México
{mabascal,elopez,jzepeda}@correo.cua.uam.mx

Abstract. With the emergence of smarthphones and social networks, a very large proportion of communication takes place on short texts. This type of communication, often anonymous, has allowed a new public participation in political issues. In particular, electoral phenomena all over the world have been greatly influenced by these networks. In the recent elections in Mexico, Twitter became a virtual place to bring together scientists, artists, politicians, adults, youth and students trying to persuade people about the candidate: Andrés Manuel López Obrador (AMLO). Our research is based on the collection of all tweets sent before, during and after the presidential elections of July 1, 2012 in Mexico containing the hashtag #AMLO. The aim of this study is to analyze the behavior of users on three different times. We apply SentiWordNet 3.0 in order to know how user behavior changes depending of the political situation and whether this is reflected on the tweets.

Keywords: user behavior, sentiment analysis, social web, Twitter, public participation, web 2.0, user generated content.

1 Introduction

The increasing participation in social media and networks has resulted in an explosion called user-generated content. Researchers use this information in order to answer interesting questions that were impossible to solve before as: how does an idea spreads across users? What topics attract more? What is the user behavior face to a certain event? Some studies have established that it exist a certain correlation between the analysis of sentiments and the public opinion polls for job approval ratings [1]. In this way, we find that the analysis of sentiments is fundamental to give some clues about how users can influence or persuade others, by using a kind of humor, in Twitter.

The aim of this article is to analyze, from the hashtag #AMLO or containing among its 140-character the word *"AMLO"* (acronym for *"Andrés Manuel López Obrador"* that was one of the four candidates with longer follow-up by young people

A.A. Ozok and P. Zaphiris (Eds.): OCSC/HCII 2013, LNCS 8029, pp. 3–12, 2013.
© Springer-Verlag Berlin Heidelberg 2013

in social networks), the interaction of the users during a political event. Our corpus is composed by the tweets coming from one day before the election (June 30, 2012), the day of the election (July 1, 2012), and one day after the election (July 2, 2012). This dataset should, therefore, provide a broad coverage of the discussions between users that were for or against the candidate. In our approach we created a computer program in order to extract, from Twitter, the 140-character tagged with the hashtag #AMLO. Our program extracts all the contributions done in one day and it makes a copy of the information into a text document that we used later in two different computer programs to analyze discursive elements. These elements are full of humor, most of the time, of the political interaction in Twitter. The first one is Tropes Semantic Knowledge (see: http://www.semantic-knowledge.com/tropes.htm) which is used to make a textual analysis. The second one used was SentiWordNet 3.0 (see: http://sentiwordnet.isti.cnr.it/), to analyze the extracted adjectives after making the proper English translation. It presents numerical indices that allow researchers to subjectively assess the opinions, feelings and sensitivities discharges in the tweets that refer to the candidate Andres Manuel Lopez Obrador. Our objective is to gain some insight of the Mexican election in order to make an interpretation of the attitude or mood expressed in the tweets.

In this paper, Section 2 describes some state of the art around the use of analysis of sentiments in political cyber participation. Section 3 explains a tweet and how our corpus was created. Section 4 presents details of the use of SentiWordNet 3.0 in order to analyze sentiments covered in the tweets and we illustrate our experiment results performed to examine user behavior patterns. In Section 5, we conclude this paper with suggestions for further work.

2   State of the Art

Social networks have become in recent years, an excellent media that works in parallel to the traditional ones. In many countries, social media like Twitter, blogs and Facebook, are playing important roles in politics. Specially, Twitter prompts the user to express their thoughts and feelings and share them instantly and globally by trying to condense information. This has been very attractive to many users in the way they can read rapidly and have an idea of what is happening by not spending many time. Twitter is increasingly attracting a lot of users all over the world and it has experienced an extraordinary growth over the past years becoming the number one microblogging tool.

We find that Twitter has been, also, used as an important social medium in some critical social actions such as the Mumbai terror and the post-election protests in Iran. In another example, in the absence of democratic elections, an estimated of 70 million bloggers in China have become the voice of the people [2]. Also, a growing number of Pakistanis turned to YouTube, Flickr, Facebook and short message service (SMS) text messages as alternative media during the *"Pakistan Emergency"* from 2007 to 2008. This began after Pakistani President General Pervez Musharraf suspended the chief justice of the Supreme Court and the government canceled cell phone networks and some news channels were blocked [3]. Similarly, in Arab countries like Iran large-scale protests were coordinated from Twitter. In the same way the Arab countries did the *"Arab Spring"*, Mexico had its *"Mexican Spring"* in 2012 during election campaigns for President of the Republic. In this way, the use of social digital media presents a new opportunity to study how the user interacts with others knowing that the anonymity has a great importance in free expression. It is important to say that, in one year, the social network Twitter, in Mexico, grew from 4.1 million users to 10.7 million, thus Mexico is among the 10 countries *"most twiteros"* such as the U.S., England, Japan and Brazil.[1].

In Mexico, as in many other countries, most politicians and opinion leaders have an Internet presence and make use of social networks, especially Facebook and Twitter. However, this has not led into a closer relationship between government and citizens, a better democracy or reliable information. The marginal social groups, minorities, and civic organizations have been the most benefited from the advantages that digital media offers. The youth organization *"yosoy132"* was born during the elections in Mexico in 2012, using social networks and bringing together youth universities groups from all the country regardless of their social conditions. Digital media helped these groups to have greater presence in public space because traditional media generally didn't pay much attention to them. They have learned to create collaboration networks, and to share information and knowledge.

Bollen presents the first work around the analysis of the use of humor in Twitter data [4]. In this research Bollen uses POMS (Profile of Mood States) to distill, from Twitter messages, 6 time series corresponding to different emotional attributes (for example, tension, depression, anger, vigor, fatigue and confusion). POMS is a psychometric instrument that provides a list of adjectives for which the patient has to indicate the level of approval. Each adjective is related to a state of mind and, therefore, the list can be exploited as the basis for a mood analyzer from textual data. It is important to mention that although the authors argue that the data from Twitter could be used to predict the future of an election campaign, they do not present any predictive method. Although this article used the 2008 presidential campaign and the election of Obama as a stage, we don't find inferred conclusions regarding the predictability of elections. On the other hand, O'Connor employs a subjective lexicon coming from the Opinion Finder in order to determine a positive and negative score from every tweet corresponding to each data set [1]. In this case, the relation between the number of positive and negative tweets about a given topic are used to calculate a confidence score. O'Connor et al., clearly indicates that for the simple manual inspection we can find many examples that have been incorrectly classified according to a feeling. This method is used, by the authors, to measure issues such as consumer

---

[1] El Economista, March 21, 2012. http://eleconomista.com.mx/tecnociencia/2012/03/21/twitter-alcanza-mexico-107-millones-usuarios

confidence, presidential approval and the 2008 presidential election in the United States. According to O'Connor et al., the consumer confidence and the approval of presidential elections exposed some correlation between the feelings analyzed from the data coming from Twitter. However, they didn't find a correlation between the polls and the sentiments contained in the data from Twitter. In this case, there was no evidence to say that it is possible to make a prediction about the presidential candidates by analyzing the preferences expressed in Twitter.

Tumasjan et al., presented at 2010 a work that consists of two distinct parts: the first one used LIWC (Linguistic Inquiry and Word Count) to make a superficial analysis of the tweets that are related with the different political parties that were competing for the German Federal election of 2009 [5]. Is in the second part, however, in which the authors claim that the count of tweets that mention one of the parties or any candidate, accurately reflects the election results. On the other hand, they contend that the MAE (Mean Absolute Error) of the *"prediction"* based on Twitter data was very close to the real surveys. The study of Twitter combined with politics is a field of research that is just beginning and that allows not only the envision of situations that were not very frequent before, like the participation of youth in politics, but it also provides a sea of information, from technology, that can be of great interest to the society.

In the next section we are going to explain the constitution of our corpus and the process done to analyze the data.

3   Extraction of Tweets in Order to Constitute the Corpus

The role of social media during the presidential campaign of 2012 in Mexico gained great importance because Twitter became the principal media for the youngest people. Our analysis is based on all the tweets collected before, during and after the 2012 presidential elections in Mexico.

3.1   What Is a Tweet and How It Is Composed?

In our approach we used tweets extracted from Twitter. A tweet is a little message of no more than 140 characters that users creates in order to communicate thoughts, feelings, or even participate in conversations. The tweet allows the communication of texts, videos or pictures by providing a link to it. Some words of the tweet are preceded by the pound sing # (hashtag). By using the hashtag, users can recover, reply (known as retweet) or follow conversations about a certain subject because this hashtag becomes automatically a hyperlink on Twitter. Everyone who clicks on a hashtag has the possibility to view the sear results of all other tweets that contains the same hashtag. In our case, we used the hashtag AMLO, #AMLO, to recover all the conversations, ideas, phrases that were produced during the Mexican elections of 2012.

The tweets that we recovered have different structures. For example:

- A simple phrase like: *"2012 AMLO even though the others"* (in Spanish *"¡AMLO 2012 le peje a quien le peje!"*)
- A phrase containing name(s) of the user(s). For example: *"The document of AMLO seems very real. What's your opinion @XochitlGalvez?"* (In Spanish: *"El documento de AMLO parece muy real. ¿Tú cómo ves? @XochitlGalvez"*)
- A phrase with links, for example: *"They disobey the IFE, the promotional against AMLO is still in the air http://t.co/kEEhosEA."* (In Spanish: *"Desobede-cen al IFE, promocional contra AMLO sigue al aire http://t.co/kEEhosEA"*)
- A phrase with retweet RT and the name of the user who originally sent the phrase. For example: *"RT @epigmenioibarra: @ IFEMexico has enabled that the lies of PAN against AMLO, that were reported and verified in the media, are still present on radio and TV. That is outrageous."* (In Spanish: *"RT @epigmenioibarra: Ha permitido @IFEMexico que mentiras del PAN vs AMLO, denunciadas y comprobadas en los medios, salgan al aire en radio y TV. Que indignante"*)
- A phrase with hashtag(s), like #elpejehaceturismoelectoral, #elecciones2012, #NiUnVotoAlPRI."

3.2 Extraction of Tweets and Constitution of the Corpus

Our corpus was composed with tweets recovered before, during and after the elections of 2012. In order to recover the tweets we have done a program using Processing (see: http://processing.org) which is an open source programming language and integrated development environment (IDE) built to teach the fundamentals of computer programming in a visual context. Our program recovers all the tweets containing a #AMLO, and produces a text were the tweets are listed. Part of the pseudocode is listed below:

```
1. Use of Twitter API to communicate with Processing by a
   statement indicating that the search is done by #AMLO and
   that we are going to get a maximum of 100 responses each
   time.
2. Generate the file in which the information is going to be
   saved by declaring a variable of type PrintWriter.
3. The information that is retrieved from Twitter is in XML
   format.
4. Assign a new element XMLElement to explore structures in
   XML and to save tweets in order to recover the xml struc-
   ture.
5. Start a loop to read the file and retrieve the contents
   of all output lines.
```

For this analysis, we used Tropes (see http://www.semantic-knowledge.com/tropes.htm) to extract the main concepts around one of the four candidates for President named Andrés Manuel López Obrador (AMLO). We have also made an English translation of tweets in order to apply a sentiment analysis using SentiWordNet 3.0. [6].

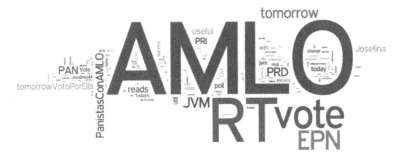

Fig. 1. Cloud of concepts for the corpus BEFORE the elections

Fig. 2. Cloud of concepts for the corpus AFTER the elections

This analyzer is a lexical resource in which each synset of WordNet [7] is associated with three numerical scores: O (how neutral the word is), P (how positive the word is), and N (how negative the word is). In the next section we are going to present some of the adjectives that were recovered by using Tropes and we are going to explain the process made in the use of SentiWordNet 3.0.

4   Analysis of Tweets by Using SentiWordNet 3.0

To analyze the tweets, our approach was based in the use of adjectives that were used in the tweets. In this case, first of all we extracted the adjectives by using Tropes which is a software that has been useful in the educational field, the discourse analysis, the anthropological and some others sciences. It is used to easily analyze written and oral texts from the semantics, grammar - especially the categories of words - and mainly the acts of speech. After the extraction made by Tropes we used Wordle (see: http://www.wordle.net) that exhibites by chromatic clouds of words, the most frequent words used in the discourse. They are differentiated by the size of the source. We selected the adjectives that appear in Tropes as well in Wordle. Examples of the clouds of concepts generated by Wordle are shown in Figure 1 (before elections) and Figure 2 (after elections). From the use of Wordle and Tropes we selected some of the adjectives that are more representative to our work. In table 1, we present the adjectives used for our analysis.

Table 1. Adjectives used to analyze each of the stages of the election process: before, during and after the elections

Before the elections	During the elections	After the elections
better	arrogant	absurd
crazy	awesome	perfect
honest	coherent	remarkable
intolerant	damn	sad
temperamental	disrespectful	true
tourist	gay	urgent
true	genius	visceral
worthy	liar	
	lost	
	militant	
	secret	
	serious	
	stupid	

Each of the adjectives presented above was analyzed by using SentiWordNet 3.0. This resource adds three numerical grades for each word: neutrality (how neutral is the word), positivity (how positive is the word) and negativity (how negative is the word). Each score is between 0 and 1 where the sum of the three should give 1. However, it is not as obvious to use SentiWordNet because the user has to carry out a disambiguation in order to know which of the interpretations or meanings of the words, shown in SentiWordNet, correspond with the sense that the user wants to give to the word found in the corpus. For example, if we search the adjective sad[2], in SentiWordNet, it has three senses. Between each of the senses there is a triangle showing a position with respect to the three scores. Below the triangle are the letters P (positive), O (neutral), N (negative) with their respective scores. For the sad example we have selected: *"sad#1 experiencing or showing sorrow or unhappiness; "feeling sad because his dog had died"; "Better by far that you should forget and smile / Than that you should remember and be sad"- Christina Rossetti."* The most important thing in our analysis is the numerical grades given by SentiWordNet 3.0 which we have used to compare the three corpus. In this case, for sad we have selected: P: 0.125 O: 0.125 N: 0.75.

---

[2] http://sentiwordnet.isti.cnr.it/search.php?q=sad

Table 2. Adjectives and numerical grade for the corpus *before* the elections

Before the elections	Numerical grade extracted from Senti-WordNet 3.0
better	P: 0.875 O:0.125 N: 0
crazy	P: 0 O: 0.5 N: 0.5
honest	P: 0.375 O: 0.625 N: 0
intolerant	P: 0.125 O: 0.125 N: 0.75
temperamental	P: 0 O: 0.75 N: 0.25
tourist	P: 0 O: 0.75 N: 0.25
true	P: 0.5 O:0.5 N:0
worthy	P: 0.875 O: 0.125 N: 0
AVERAGE	Positivity (P): 0.344 Neutrality (O):0.437 Negativity (N):0.219

Table 3. Adjectives and numerical grade for the corpus *during* the elections

During the elections	Numerical grade extracted from SentiWordNet 3.0
arrogant	P: 0.5 O: 0.125 N: 0.375
awesome	P: 0.875 O: 0 N: 0.125
coherent	P: 0.75 O: 0.25 N: 0
damn	P: 0.375 O: 0.25 N: 0.375
disrespectful	P: 0.5 O: 0.125 N: 0.375
gay	P: 0.375 O: 0.5 N: 0.125
genius	P: 0.75 O: 0.25 N: 0
liar	P: 0 O: 0.375 N: 0.625
lost	P: 0.125 O: 0.25 N: 0.625
militant	P: 0.5 O: 0.375 N: 0.125
secret	P: 0.25 O: 0.625 N: 0.125
serious	P: 0.25 O: 0.375 N: 0.375
stupid	P: 0 O: 0.25 N: 0.75
AVERAGE	Positivity (P): 0.404 Neutrality (O):0.288 Negativity (N):0.308

Table 4. Adjectives and numerical grade for the corpus *after* the elections

After the elections	Numerical grade extracted from SentiWordNet 3.0
absurd	P: 0.625 O: 0.375 N: 0
perfect	P: 0.625 O: 0.375 N: 0
remarkable	P: 0.375 O: 0.625 N: 0
sad	P: 0.125 O: 0.125 N: 0.75
true	P: 0.5 O: 0.125 N: 0.375
urgent	P: 0 O: 1 N: 0
visceral	P: 0.25 O: 0.75 N: 0
AVERAGE	Positivity (P): 0.357 Neutrality (O):0.482 Negativity (N):0.161

As we can see in the above tables, the average for each of the corpus reflects the tendency of the users in a political process. In this case, *during* the elections we have the adjectives that are more negative. The average of negativity *during* the election is 0.307 against 0.219 for *before* and 0.161 for *after*. Some of the adjectives that characterized the corpus *during* are: *arrogant, damn, disrespectful, liar* and *stupid*. All of these adjectives are supposed characteristics of the candidates. In this article we don't show examples of the tweets but they are, almost all of them, telling a story. In many cases, they tell the story of the user and his opinion. We can notice, also, that users are likely to attack and use strong words when the election is taking place in order to persuade electors.

After the elections, neutrality is the strongest attitude toward the result of the election and even if we find users that are not satisfied by the result they don't participate very much after they know the result of the election. Users who are satisfied are the ones that are making tweets in order to show their feeling. As we can notice one of the adjectives presented in the corpus *after* is: *sad*. Is in this last corpus that we find an adjective for a feeling. In the others two corpus, *before* and *during*, we don't find demonstrations about what the users are feeling and even more we find adjectives to emphasize characteristics of the candidates.

In all the tweets extracted we find the humor in order to persuade others users. When the users want to offend they do it by using the criticism showing cartoony defects. The user behavior is very particular in each of the stages of the election.

5   Conclusions and Further Work

Our paper presents a first interdisciplinary study which analyzes the political participation of young Mexicans during elections for President of the Republic through the tweets sent before, during and after the election of July 1, 2012. In this case, we visualize Mexican youth as social individuals who need others to make decisions, based on the presence of tweets, and instrument that empowers the users and affects the collective.

In our corpus we are able to find sequences than convey, in a remarkable way, mood traits like ethnographic, semantic and psychological elements that are constant throughout the corpus. Ingenuity and inventiveness emerge with particular communicative liberty. The users want to caricature and make ridiculous all the candidates. The criticism is open to everyone, and they do it. They write confidently, cheerfully most of the times, without fear of reprimand.

As in other countries, in Mexico the use of Twitter to create phrases and messages of 140 characters has encouraged the participation of young people creating movements like *"#yosoy132"* or *"#movimientoMx"*. These movements are a manifestation of young people belonging to groups with common interests. In this way, the increasing use of social networking has allowed to dilute geographical boundaries making closer the citizen to a greater democratic participation. Our interpretation through the application of Tropes, and SentiWordNet 3.0 confirms *"moments"* during the election period in which the representation and visualization of tweets reveals a reality of our Mexico: humor present in the political arena.

Further work, should include a comparison between political subjects and events that are produced everyday. Are the users writing tweets to persuade others? Can we compare the same situation (before, during and after elections) in other countries? One of our future works is also dedicated to the incorporation of geographic situation in order to know how this is reflected in the behavior of the users.

References

1. O'Connor, B., Balasubramanyan, R., Routledge, B.R., Smith, N.A.: From tweets to polls: linking text sentiment to public opinion time series. In: Proc. of 4th ICWSM, pp. 122–129. AAAI Press (2010)
2. Friedman, T.: Power to the (Blogging) People. New York Times (September 14, 2010), http://www.nytimes.com/2010/09/15/opinion/15friedman.html
3. Yusuf, H.: Old and New Media: Converging During the Pakistan Emergency (March 2007-February 2008). Massachusetts Institute of Technology, Center for Future Civic Media, Cambridge, Mass (2009), http://civic.mit.edu/blog/humayusuf/old-and-new-media-converging-during-the-pakistan-emergency-march-2007-february-2008
4. Bollen, J., Pepe, A., Mao, H.: Modeling public mood and emotion: Twitter sentiment and socio-economic phenomena. In: Proceedings of the Fifth International AAAI Conference on Weblogs and Social Media, pp. 450–453 (2011)
5. Tumasjan, A., Sprenger, T.O., Sandner, P.G., Welpe, I.M.: Predicting elections with twitter: What 140 characters reveal about political sentiment. In: Proceedings of the Fourth International AAAI Conference on Weblogs and Social Media, pp. 178–185 (2010)
6. Esuli, A., Sebastiani, F.: SENTIWORDNET: A Publicly Available Lexical Resource for Opinion Mining. In: Proceedings of the 5th Conference on Language Resources and Evaluation, LREC 2006, Genova, Italy, pp. 417–422 (2006)
7. Fellbaum, C.: WordNet: An Electronical Lexical Database. The MIT Press, Cambridge (1998)

Well-Being's Predictive Value

A Gamified Approach to Managing Smart Communities

Margeret Hall, Simon Caton, and Christof Weinhardt

Karlsruhe Service Research Institute, Karlsruhe Institute of Technology, Germany
{hall,simon.caton,weinhardt}@kit.edu

Abstract. Well-being is a multifaceted concept, having intellectual origins in philosophy, psychology, economics, political science, and other disciplines. Its presence is correlated with a variety of institutional and business critical indicators. To date, methods to assess well-being are performed infrequently and superficially; resulting in highly aggregated observations. In this paper, we present well-being as a predictive entity for the management of a smart community. Our vision is a low latency method for the observation and measurement of well-being within a community or institution that enables different resolutions of data, e.g. at the level of an individual, a social or demographic group, or an institution. Using well-being in this manner enables realistic, faster and less expensive data collection in a smart system. However, as the data needed for assessing well-being is highly sensitive personal information, constituents require incentives and familiar settings to reveal this information, which we establish with Facebook and gamification. To evaluate the predictive value of well-being, we conducted a series of surveys to observe different self-reported psychological aspects of participants. Our key findings were that neuroticism and extroversion seem to have the highest predictive value of self-reported well-being levels. This information can be used to create expected trends of well-being for smart community management.

Keywords: Smart community management, well-being, social computing, gamification, human flourishing.

1 Introduction

Individual well-being is evaluated in a variety of ways: as subjective well-being, psychological well-being, or via economic calculation [1-5]. While each domain has different strengths, when used as complimentary systems they create a fitting proxy of personal and institutional well-being [1]. The relationship between personal and communal well-being is the fundamental base for using well-being data in smart community management. At the basest level, communities are made by personal interactions with other individuals, groups, institutions and events. Perceptions of these interactions drive personal perceptions of well-being, which among other indicators is a predictor of social cohesion [6], a necessary condition for progressive smart communities. According to former European Commission Directorate-General

A.A. Ozok and P. Zaphiris (Eds.): OCSC/HCII 2013, LNCS 8029, pp. 13–22, 2013.

for Information Society and Media Erastos Filos, smart communities are "understood to be both, internetworked and knowledge-driven, therefore able to adapt to new organizational challenges rapidly, and sufficiently agile to create and exploit knowledge in response to opportunities of the digital age" [7, p1]. One information development for exploitation in digital societies is general institutional wellness. Forward-looking smart communities find it in their best interest to both satisfy and maintain their constituent base, which in turn helps the community develop sustainably.

We argue that constituents, decision makers, stakeholders as well as human resource divisions lack adequate measures to determine the state of psychological or social health in their institution. Without access to such information, it can be challenging to make decisions that affect members of their institution. It is also not possible to inspect the after effect(s) of such decisions. This knowledge gap hinders key actors in decision making scenarios. To circumvent potentially significant gaps in knowledge, digital well-being measurement is needed as a "best practice" mechanism for thriving smart communities.

Our research goal is to establish a low latency method for the observation and measurement of well-being within a community or institution. However, as the data needed to measure well-being is often private and highly sensitive, we proposed a gamified approach to incentivize participants to reveal this information in [7]. In this paper, we build upon this vision and make the first steps to validate its feasibility by investigating the predictive value of different measures and indicators for the assessment of individual well-being. Our study is based upon a series of weekly surveys in which we inspect different self-reported psychological aspects of participants to determine if they can predict or indicate specific aspects of well-being. As a baseline, we use the ten Human Flourishing constructs proposed in [8]. This is an important first step, as without such insights we cannot appropriately structure an application for the individualized measurement of institutional well-being.

2   Related Work

Multiple studies indicate that well-being is closely linked to health, longevity, and community belonging [10-13]. Well-being also has applications in organizational spheres, where organizational design and human resources are two examples. Healthier, happier employees have both lower incidences of absenteeism, are more productive, and have lower organizational health care related costs [10,14]. Dissatisfied employees have higher turnover levels – especially significant when considering that the cost of losing an employee can range between 1.5 and 2.5 times the departing employee's annual salary [15]. These studies show that well-being data is powerful: just as manifestations of increases in well-being act as a proxy for increased livability, systematic decreases in self-reported well-being signify deep-seated institutional issues. As such, personal well-being measurement can function as a strategic progress indicator for assisting institutional managers in resource allocation [14].

In gamifying well-being, leaders take proactive steps towards smart community management. Acting as a thermometer by which to gauge institutional health, well-being data serves not only as a feedback mechanism between various actors and policy makers, but as a forward-looking decision making tool [16,17]. Thus there is widespread interest in tracking mechanisms with high popular acceptance. Until recently, attempts to collect well-being data as an institutional feedback mechanism have been scarce. The most frequent method of collecting well-being information, the Daily Reconstruction Method, is formulated to reconstruct the events and affective state of individuals [18-20]. This important work establishes well-being data collection in a more frequent interval, although it is not in a near to real time environment.

Even though having been used earlier, the term "gamification" did not see widespread adoption before the second half of 2010 [21]. Since then it has been used with quite different scope and connotation. Antin and Churchill state that context sensitivity is often neglected with current, schematically imposed reward mechanisms [22]. Vessileva indicates that for gamification to work, it needs to take into account the users' different personalities [23]. However, this larger group of authors does not generally object gamification, but assumes that a reservoir of not yet used improvements does exist. Deterding subsumed "Gamification is the use of game design elements in non-game contexts [21]." Being generally more positive about its possible application, McGonigal proposes to construct games in the spirit of gamification that unlock the engagement and determination inherent in gaming to solve real-world problems [24]. She identifies gamers, while playing to be "super-empowered hopeful individuals" supported by an environment that provides superior abilities for blissful productivity, social fabric, urgent optimism, and epic meaning.

This too in turn is questioned by Huotari and Hamari who bring up that its perspective is too systemic [25]. They state that it depends on the individual perception of a user if a service is gameful, making it impossible for a service designer to identify the non-game context that is necessary for the above definition. Based on their background in service marketing, their suggestion to define gamification is as "a process of enhancing a service with affordances for gameful experiences in order to support user's overall value creation" – therefore setting priority on the goal of creating better experiences instead of the methods applied for achieving it.

2.1   Davies J-Curve and Social Disruption

In his book "Conditions of Happiness", Veenhoven wrote "The more healthy and active the citizens and the smoother their contacts, the greater the chance that society flourishes. Moreover, widespread dissatisfaction with life tends to act as a bomb under the social system [6, p 404]." We likewise hypothesize that significant issues of well-being manifest in (sub)groups of the population, and negative well-being will follow a Davies J-curve distribution [26]. This model indicates when social expectations have a large deviation from the actual outcomes of human well-being (relative deprivation), some form of social schism should be expected (Figure 1).

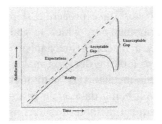

Fig. 1.   The Davies J-Curve

In other words, social unrest is a subjective response to a sudden reversal in fortunes after a long period of growth [26]. The strength of relative deprivation is evaluated by charting and changing the expected change of actual well-being levels against expected well-being figures. For a given attribute type, a lack of statistically significant differences between expected and actual well-being levels implies no discrepancy and no social unrest; significant differences implies the opposite.

2.2   Beyond the Vision: BeWell

In an endeavor to achieve near real time measurement of well-being with high user acceptance, a gamified survey collection method was proposed in Hall et al. [8]. Fully interactive, BeWell: a game of you, utilizes novel near real time data collection methods by using both the push method found in [18-20], and a gamified portal to entertain users [8] via smart devices. BeWell records personal well-being data over time as elicited in a series of responses based on gamified text and pictographs. Registration is completed with a series of short tests to assess users' personalities. This not only allows the program to assess the way the well-being levels are likely to change due to any given users baseline personality factors, but gives participants an additional facet with which to see their daily personal levels of flourishing holistically [8,9].

Badges and points gained through successful task completion can be used to level up, allow crowd-sourced (i.e. new) task suggestion, and permit community historical well-being badge achievement viewing rights [8]. Badging occurs in three states to incentivize further participation: low, moderate and exceptional mission completion. Anonymous data aggregation in turn allows smart community managers to use regionalized "well-being maps" in order to assist in decision-making when allocating resources, upgrading infrastructure, and/or engaging public political discourse.

3   Attributive Prediction and the J-Curve: A Use Case

To find expected and actual well-being, we propose that the historical characteristics of well-being create trends. From a combination of these trends and psychometric profiling, prediction of the aspects and existence of wellness can be completed. A proof of concept survey was propagated through the main authors' online social networks[1] in order to validate if attribute-based prediction can be used in conjunction with the measurement of well-being. Surveys were administered once per week for four weeks on Wednesdays, in order to control for variance in weekly activities, such as subjective preferences for weekends. All surveys were conducted in English. Ten identical questions covering varying aspects of human flourishing were posed to facilitate prediction of said dimension [9]. Demographic questions, the 44-item scale Big Five Inventory personality test, the Maximizer/Satisficer scale test, and a fairness scale [27-29] were also added as additional attributes. Each was administered for one week only to test prediction abilities of well-being based on pre-existing personality traits. These psychometric tests have low variance, and thus can be tested once and still are considered valid for the length of this one month survey. Respondents were given the option to review their results at the end of the four weeks.

3.1   Establishment of a Baseline

After four weeks, 65 of 85 participants completed all four iterations of the survey, with an overall loss of 14% of the participants across four weeks. Self-reported gender revealed a 50-50% female-male split, with one non-response. Three participants who completed the surveys self-reported being located in Asia; 22 from the United States; and 34 self-reported locations within Europe, with four declining to respond. 78% self-report being age 35 or under. 85% of respondents reported being currently employed. 81% of the respondents self-reported completing at least a master's degree. 86% of respondents refer to themselves as "moderately healthy" or "very healthy."

The self-defined subpopulations have telling normalized means which help to confirm the viability of this feasibility study. Perhaps unsurprisingly, there are not significant deviations between gender profiles and the normalized population mean across all human flourishing constructs. Overall, the regions of the United States and Europe are also quite similar, with the exception of the construct Resilience. In this area, Americans report higher average resiliency of 0.68, compared to the European mean of 0.62. Quite counter-intuitively, those whom report being unemployed score themselves significantly higher than the mean on the constructs Positive Emotion and Engagement, whereas those who reporting being employed are significantly higher for the constructs Positive Relationships and Vitality. Across the Health subcategory, those who rate themselves as "Very Healthy" are higher in almost all constructs than those who rate themselves in higher and lower health categories. Across age groups, there is an overall tendency towards growing less content through the middle-aged group, which is consistent with existing literature. We can expect that if the over 56 population engages the game, overall human flourishing trends for this group will rise again through the end of life. The effect is however unnoticeable for the construct Emotional Stability. A full listing of results can be seen in Table 1.

---

[1] Primarily the propagation was done with direct emails and Facebook, but also a smaller effort was place on LinkedIn and Google+.

Table 1. Human Flourishing Construct Means across Subpopulations

	Mean Male	Mean Female	Mean US	Mean EU	Mean Working	Mean Not Working	Mean Moderately Healthy	Mean Very Healthy	Mean Extremely Healthy	Mean Age 18-25	Mean Age 26-35	Mean Age 36-45	Mean Age 46-55	Mean All
Positive Emotion	0,70	0,74	0,72	0,73	0,71	0,77	0,69	0,75	0,71	0,72	0,72	0,75	0,67	0,72
Competence	0,71	0,70	0,70	0,70	0,71	0,69	0,62	0,72	0,70	0,73	0,68	0,69	0,63	0,70
Engagement	0,91	0,89	0,88	0,90	0,89	0,95	0,91	0,90	0,89	0,89	0,90	0,93	0,83	0,90
Positive Relationships	0,89	0,94	0,93	0,90	0,92	0,89	0,94	0,94	0,90	0,88	0,93	0,93	0,87	0,92
Meaning	0,73	0,76	0,74	0,73	0,75	0,76	0,69	0,77	0,75	0,76	0,74	0,72	0,68	0,75
Emotional Stability	0,65	0,63	0,65	0,62	0,65	0,63	0,61	0,69	0,63	0,65	0,64	0,64	0,63	0,64
Openness	0,75	0,75	0,73	0,74	0,75	0,76	0,74	0,80	0,72	0,77	0,75	0,77	0,57	0,75
Resilience	0,64	0,64	0,68	0,62	0,64	0,64	0,66	0,65	0,63	0,63	0,66	0,61	0,55	0,64
Self Esteem	0,74	0,75	0,74	0,73	0,74	0,76	0,74	0,78	0,73	0,77	0,73	0,76	0,65	0,75
Vitality	0,67	0,63	0,62	0,65	0,66	0,58	0,63	0,69	0,62	0,66	0,64	0,66	0,56	0,65

Overall, Positive Relationships and Engagement are the most highly rated constructs, meaning these are the areas in which people see themselves most fulfilled. This relationship is significant at the 0.01 level in a two-tailed Pearson correlation test, as seen in Table 2. Emotional Stability and Vitality are the lowest of the ten total constructs, which are also significantly correlated at the 0.01 level as seen in Table 3.

Table 2. Pearson correlation, Positive Emotion (PE) and Engagement (En);.

		PE	En
PE	Pearson Correlation	1	,372**
	Sig. (2-tailed)		,002
	N	65	65
En	Pearson Correlation	,372**	1
	Sig. (2-tailed)	,002	
	N	65	65

**. Correlation is significant at the 0.01 level (2-tailed).

Table 3. Emotional Stability (ES) and Vitality (V)

		ES	V
ES	Pearson Correlation	1	,664**
	Sig. (2-tailed)		,000
	N	65	65
V	Pearson Correlation	,664**	1
	Sig. (2-tailed)	,000	
	N	65	65

**. Correlation is significant at the 0.01 level (2-tailed).

3.2 Predicting Human Flourishing

When considering the seven attributes tested throughout the survey (fairness, maximization, extroversion, neuroticism, optimism, agreeableness, conscientiousness), we see much more varied results across subpopulations than are found throughout the human flourishing constructs (Table 4). This is encouraging, as the attributes here are the basis of how the gamified survey predicts wellness based on

Table 4. Attribute Predictor Means across Subpopulations

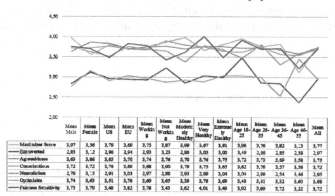

	Mean Male	Mean Female	Mean US	Mean EU	Mean Working	Mean Not Working	Mean Moderately Healthy	Mean Very Healthy	Mean Extremely Healthy	Mean Age 18-25	Mean Age 26-35	Mean Age 36-45	Mean Age 46-55	Mean All
Maximizer Score	3,97	3,56	3,79	3,60	3,75	3,87	3,90	3,67	3,81	3,96	3,76	3,82	3,23	3,77
Extroverted	2,83	3,12	2,96	2,94	2,93	3,23	2,85	3,03	3,00	3,49	2,86	2,85	2,38	2,97
Agreeableness	3,63	3,86	3,83	3,70	3,74	3,76	3,70	3,76	3,75	3,72	3,73	3,69	3,58	3,75
Conscientiousness	3,72	3,72	3,76	3,60	3,68	3,50	3,79	3,75	3,65	3,62	3,76	3,57	3,56	3,72
Neuroticism	2,76	3,15	2,91	3,03	2,97	2,88	2,93	2,89	3,04	3,04	2,99	2,54	3,46	2,95
Optimism	3,74	3,63	3,51	3,76	3,69	3,65	3,39	3,78	3,69	3,48	3,81	3,32	3,60	3,68
Fairness Sensitivity	3,75	3,70	3,48	3,82	3,78	3,43	3,62	4,01	3,49	3,92	3,69	3,72	3,22	3,72

subpopulations. After calculating human flourishing as based on the calculation of Huppert and So [8,9], we modeled a simple liner regression, with the human flourishing score as a dependent variable and the psychometric attributes as predictors.

With an R score of .727 and R Square of .528, we validate the feasibility of making predictions of human flourishing to be reasonably accurate. This is further confirmed by the results of an ANOVA on the linear model (Table 5) which confirms that at least one of the predictors has a highly significant correlation to human flourishing.

Table 5. Analysis of Variance (ANOVA), Human Flourishing and psychometric attributes

ANOVA^a

Model		Sum of Squares	df	Mean Square	F	Sig.
1	Regression	,899	7	,128	9,116	,000^b
	Residual	,803	57	,014		
	Total	1,701	64			

Of the seven predictors it was found that neuroticism and extroversion have the highest predictor importance. Neuroticism is the single most important predictor, representing 44% of the predictor weight. It is highly significant at 0.001 as an effect and a negative coefficient estimate. This indicates that higher levels of neuroticism predict lower flourishing levels. As an effect and a coefficient, extroversion is also highly significant at the 0.001 level with a positive coefficient estimate. As a single attribute, it contributes 27% of the prediction weight. High extroversion is predictive of high flourishing levels.

The strength of these two relationships to overall human flourishing scores is notable, as it suggests that inferences about the population can be made. This must however be further tested for interaction effects, which is to say that the existence of other attributes contribute to the overall human flourishing score and thus moderate the absolute impact of neuroticism and extroversion. This is especially noticeable in the case of gender per subpopulation (Table 4). Overall, women report lower human flourishing levels. Accordingly, this subpopulation rates itself with higher over overall levels of neuroticism. However, women also rate themselves to be more extroverted as a subpopulation than men. While this confounds the information above, this result also proves that a multi-faceted approach to defining and tracking well-being as an indicator is necessary, as the approach cannot be watered down into a pair of psychometric properties from which all attributes can be predicted.

3.3   Towards Validating the J-Curve

Our feasibility study has confirmed the ability of psychometric properties to predict levels of wellness. These results support the creation of attribute based tracking for the establishment of baseline well-being expectations. Using these attributes, we can create well-being profiles across subpopulations and use them to predict future well-being values; the expected trend line of the Davies J-Curve. By then considering current well-being information, we can inspect the deviation of reality from expectation. This can be performed either on an individual basis, institutional basis or somewhere in between, for example a social or demographic group. Per attribute group, these two lines are the measurement of policy impact, public debate, and institutional wellness. Manifestations of the absence of well-being or a change from its expected level are predictable when plotted, thus facilitating evaluation and stakeholder discussions. Our vision revolves around the use of smart devices, in the context of a familiar setting (Facebook), which should facilitate the construction of a smart community portfolio: a stakeholder feedback loop of community wellness and overall satisfaction. However, further research is needed to confirm if Facebook is a viable platform.

4   Conclusions and Future Work

This paper presents a methodology that utilizes attributive predications in order to analyze and evaluate data obtained in gamified human computer interaction systems for smart community management. We observed from our study, that two factors of the Big Five Inventory, namely neuroticism and extroversion, seem to have the highest predictive value. The outcomes from our analysis illustrate the ability to predict communal vigor for progressive and active management. These results aid in the realization of BeWell in that they provide a guideline for the development of future predictive models. This responsively tracks trends in noisy data of personal well-being, continually updates given new data points, and highlights otherwise hidden attribute-based well-being forecasting.

With respect to the calculation and measurement thereof, in the next instantiation machine-learning methodologies will be utilized to both calculate the current data input, and create a forecast of expected future input [30]. The real time community of BeWell could be further leveraged if combined with a data-mining approach that investigates the existence of positive or negative affect in data such as Facebook status updates, or Tweets. From the additional data points gained, more sensitive trending can be made in connecting the levels of well-being.

This aspect of popularly sourced well-being information is ripe for adaptation into the smart community spectrum. By utilizing this multi-faceted picture of the individual, BeWell encourages communities to proactively manage the components causing agency loss (e.g. cheating, lack of transparency, ill-health) as a form of adaptive people management. Such an elastic measure can be repurposed as both a diagnostic and predicative model for diverse participation-based movements and institutions when populated with well-being data. Well-being can be "mapped" to communities, regions, and institutions to illustrate policy effectiveness and enhance participative debates. Through the observation of a decrease in well-being, participatory approaches could be a reactive measure as a means to reengage previously content constituent-users, and engage new constituent-users throughout the community. Gamified well-being measurement is a progressive step in smart community management.

References

1. Diener, E., Suh, E.: Measuring quality of life: Economic, social, and subjective indicators. Social Indicators Research 40, 189–216 (1997)
2. Waterman, A.S.: Two conceptions of happiness: Contrasts of personal expressiveness (eudemonia) and hedonic enjoyment. Journal of Personality and Social Psychology 64(4), 678–691 (1993)
3. Ryan, R.M., Deci, E.L.: On happiness and human potentials: A review of research on hedonic and eudemonic well-being. Annual Review of Psychology 52, 141–166 (2001)
4. Samman, E.: Psychological and Subjective Well-being: A Proposal for Internationally Comparable Indicators. Oxford Development Studies 35(4), 459–486 (2007)
5. Frey, B., Stutzer, A.: Happiness and Economics: How the Economy and Institutions Affect Human Well-Being. Princeton UP, New Jersey (2001)
6. Veenhoven, R., Jonkers, T.: Conditions of happiness, vol. 2. D. Reidel, Dordrecht (1984)
7. Filos, E.: Smart Organizations in the Digital Age. In: Mezgar, I. (ed.) Integration of ICT in Smart Organizations, pp. 187–256. Idea Group Publishing, Hershey (2006), doi:10.4018/978-1-59140-390-6.ch007
8. Hall, M., Kimbrough, S.O., Haas, C., Weinhardt, C., Caton, S.: Towards the gamification of well-being measures. In: 2012 IEEE 8th International Conference on E-Science (e-Science), pp. 1–8 (2012)
9. Huppert, F., So, T.: Flourishing Across Europe: Application of a New Conceptual Framework for Defining Well-Being. Social Indicators Research, 1–25 (2012), http://dx.doi.org/10.1007/s11205-011-9966-7
10. Diener, E., Chan, M.: Happy People Live Longer: Subjective Well-Being Contributes to Health and Longevity. Applied Psychology: Health and Well-Being 3(1), 1–43 (2010)
11. Danner, D.D., Snowdon, D.A., Friesen, W.V.: Positive emotions in early life and longevity: findings from the nun study. Journal of Personality and Social Psychology 80, 804–813 (2001)
12. Chida, Y., Steptoe, A.: Positive psychological well-being and mortality: a quantitative review of prospective observational studies. Psychosomatic Medicine 70, 741–756 (2008)
13. Bray, I., Gunnell, D.: Suicide rates, life satisfaction and happiness as markers for population mental health. Social Psychiatry and Psychiatric Epidemiology 41, 333–337 (2006)

14. Harter, J.K., Schmidt, F.L., Keyes, C.L.: Well-being in the workplace and its relationship to business outcomes: a review of the Gallup studies. In: Flourishing: The Positive Person and the Good Life, pp. 205–224. American Psychological Association Press, Washington, D.C (2003)

15. Cascio, W.F.: Managing human resources: Productivity, quality of work life, profits, 6th edn. McGrawHill/Irwin, Burr Ridge (2003)

16. Frey, B., Stutzer, A.: Should National Happiness be Maximized? Working Paper No. 306 IEER, Zurich (2007)

17. Ahn, S.H., Choi, Y.J., Kim, Y.: Static Numbers to Dynamic Statistics: Designing a Policy-friendly Social Policy Indicator Network. Social Indicators Research 108(3), 387–400 (2011), doi:10.1007/s11205-011-9875

18. Kahneman, D., Krueger, A.B., Schkade, D.A., Schwartz, N., Stone, A.S.: A Survey Method for Characterizing Daily Life Experience: The Daily Reconstruction Method, vol. 306, pp. 1776–1780 (2004)

19. Killingsworth, M.: Track Your Happiness (2013),
    http://www.trackyourhappiness.org

20. Kroll, C., Pokutta, S.: Just a perfect day: Developing a happiness optimised day schedule. Journal of Economic Psychology (2012), doi:
    http://dx.doi.org/10.1016/j.joep.2012.09.015

21. Deterding, S., Khaled, R., Nacke, L.E., Dixon, D.: Gamification: Toward a Definition. Paper presented at CHI 2011, Vancouver, BC, Canada (2011)

22. Antin, J., Churchill, E.F.: Badges in Social Media: A Social Psychological Perspective. Paper presented at CHI 2011, Vancouver, BC, Canada (2011)

23. Vassileva, J.: Motivating participation in social computing applications: a user modeling perspective. User Modeling and User-Adapted Interaction 22, 177–201 (2012), doi:10.1007/s11257-011-9109-5

24. McGonigal, J., Gaming can make a better world (2010), TED Talk:
    http://www.ted.com/talks/jane_mcgonigal_gaming_can_
    make_a_better_world.html

25. Huotari, K., Hamari, J.: Defining Gamification - A Service Marketing Perspective. In: Proceedings of the 16th International Academic MindTrek Conference, Tampere, Finland (2012)

26. Davies, J.: Towards a Theory of Revolution. American Sociological Review 27(1), 5–19 (1962)

27. John, O.P., Donahue, E.M., Kentle, R.L.: The Big Five Inventory–Versions 4a and 54. University of California, Institute of Personality and Social Research, Berkeley, CA (1991)

28. Schwartz, B., Ward, A., Monterosso, J., Lyubomirsky, S., White, K., Lehman, D.R.: Maximizing versus satisficing: Happiness is a matter of choice. Journal of Personality and Social Psychology 83, 1178–1197 (2002)

29. Schmitt, M., Dörfel, M.: Procedural injustice at work, justice sensitivity, job satisfaction and psychosomatic well-being. European Journal of Social Psychology 29, 443–453 (1999)

30. Borgelt, C., Kruse, R.: Speeding up fuzzy clustering with neural network techniques. In: The 12th IEEE International Conference on Fuzzy Systems, vol. 2, pp. 852–856. IEEE Press, New York (2003)

You Are Not Alone Online: A Case Study of a Long Distance Romantic Relationship Online Community

Yurong He, Kari Kraus, and Jennifer Preece

School of Information Studies, University of Maryland, College Park
Human-Computer Interaction Lab, University of Maryland, College Park
{yrhe,kkraus,preece}@umd.edu

Abstract. Previous research on long distance romantic relationships (LDRRs) has tended to focus on the two people that make up the couple. With the advent of LDRR online communities, however, there is a need to expand the analysis to include larger social structures. Currently little is known about how and why individuals who are in LDRRs use LDRR online communities and what effect participating in this kind of public online space has on maintaining LDRRs. In this paper, we introduce a popular Chinese LDRR online community, the LDRR public page on Chinese Facebook, Renren, and report exploratory interviews conducted with users of this community to understand their behaviors and motivations for using it. We found that: 1) users lurk most of the time unless their strong empathy is aroused; 2) users' four major motivations are belonging, empathy, social support, and learning; 3) initial and continued motivations have different patterns; 4) perceived social support is the main benefit of participating in the LDRR public page.

Keywords: Long-distance romantic relationships, Online community, Renren, Public page, Motivation.

1 Introduction

"Another day has gone. I'm still all alone. How could this be? You're not here with me…Did you have to go? And leave my world so cold…" As Michael Jackson sang, long-distance romantic relationship (LDRR) couples have to face the harsh reality that they are separated from each other by physical distance most of the time in their daily life [1]. Today more and more couples worldwide are coping with LDRRs. By 2012, more than 14 million couples worldwide claimed they were in a LDRR [25]. Among all the people who are in LDRRs, college students predominate [22].

Because of lack of opportunities for face-to-face interaction, LDRR couples have to rely on various mediated forms of communication (e.g. cell phones, email, instant messaging tools, and social network sites) to maintain their relationships. Previous researchers have investigated the behaviors that contribute to maintaining LDRRs via mediated means (e.g. [13, 17, 18, 29, 33, 34]), and developed new technologies (e.g. [2, 8, 9, 14]) specifically for supporting LDRRs. These studies focus almost exclusively on the two members of a couple. This focus makes intuitive sense because

A.A. Ozok and P. Zaphiris (Eds.): OCSC/HCII 2013, LNCS 8029, pp. 23–32, 2013.
© Springer-Verlag Berlin Heidelberg 2013

romantic relationships are a special type of intimate interpersonal relationship, and the communication and interaction behaviors are often private and personal. However, public expression is also important in maintaining intimate relationships [7, 30]. We contend that the way people behave in maintaining their LDRRs via mediated forms of communication extends to larger groups of people in a public environment.

With the growing acceptance of online communities over the past thirty years, LDRR online communities have appeared in many countries to support LDRR couples. A large number of studies have investigated online social support communities covering many different kinds of topics (e.g. illness, social problems) [19], but LDRRs have not yet benefitted from such research. We know little about these kinds of online communities and their users. This is a new focus in studies of both LDRR maintenance and online support communities. This paper is an initial attempt to explore one LDRR online community and its users by taking advantage of grounded theory.

Our goal is to explore how and why users use a LDRR online community, and the benefits they derive from it. We conducted a semi-structured interview study in which we investigated one popular Chinese LDRR online community: the LDRR public page on Renren, the Chinese equivalent of Facebook.

Ultimately, our aim is to help researchers and designers better understand LDRR couples' needs and what will help them sustain their LDRRs. This paper makes three important contributions. First, we explore a case of an under-researched type of online social support community: an LDRR community. Second, we depart from the predominant approach of focusing on couple-oriented interaction, choosing instead to investigate the needs of individuals who are in LDRRs from a community-oriented perspective. Third, this exploratory study indicates the importance of the online community owner's role in sustaining and empowering the community.

2   Related Work

LDRR couples have fewer opportunities to interact with each other face-to-face and limited mediated interaction opportunities [24]. Furthermore, LDRR couples have other concerns that Geographically Close Romantic Relationship (GCRR) couples do not have, such as economic problems arising from telephone and travel expenses, coping with roller-coaster like emotions every time they meet and separate, and assessing the future of their relationships ([23], p.29; [31]). Consequently, LDRR couples are more likely to feel depressed, stressful and lonely than GCRR couples [10].

Among the technologies which have been widely adopted by the public, phones [e.g. 4] and video camera chatting [e.g. 33] are the most important and popular mediated means of communication for LDRR couples. However, they are insufficient for helping LDRR couples feel as emotionally close to each other as their GCRR counterparts. In the HCI field, researchers have developed innovative technologies for supporting LDRR couples' interaction (e.g. [14, 2]). These technologies often involve one half of a LDRR couple being made aware of the other half's presence by mimicking intimate forms of communication, such as Sensing Beds [9], which can sense the body position of one member of a LDRR couple in his or her bed, and then make the corresponding parts of the other half's bed warm, thus simulating co-presence.

Although a couple's private interaction has a direct bearing on the outcome of a relationship, the broader social environment is also important and can affect the nature of the couple's interaction [27]. In offline studies, researchers usually consider the influences of social networks on intimate relationships [27]. Furthermore, the effective provision of support probably springs from people who share similar social conditions and stressful experiences with the support recipients [28]. Having similar experiences increases a support provider's empathic understanding [11]. We believe the results of these offline studies are relevant to LDRR couples' online social networks.

The previous research summarized here provides us with important insights and background information. We are interested in a new type of public online support group. We want to explore why people join it, how they use it, and what they get from it. We have therefore chosen a popular LDRR online community that was built on the largest SNS in China. We opted for an open-ended and bottom-up approach in this exploratory study using Grounded Theory to help answer these questions.

3   Studying LDRR Online Community Practice

3.1   Research Site: LDRR Public Page on Renren

Chinese Facebook, Renren (Renren.com), was launched in 2005. It has now become the largest SNS in China with more than 200 million users to date. The public page, known simply as "Page," is one of the basic features on Renren. It allows individuals and organizations to build their public pages to establish closer relationships with their audience. Public pages have no privacy settings. Every Renren user can voluntarily follow any public page they are interested in, receive the latest updates from these pages, and communicate with the owners and the users of these pages.

The LDRR public page (异地恋, *yidilian*, a Chinese phrase that can be literally translated as "LDRRs"), is one of the most popular public pages on Renren (http://page.renren.com/600003160?checked=true). By February 2013, it already had more than 350,000 followers, and has become the fastest growing and largest LDRR online community in China. This number is increasing every day. The LDRR public page has basic features similar to those of Facebook including a Home Page, Wall, Comments, Information, Status, Photos, Diaries, Share, Message, Friends, etc. It also has exclusive and customizable features that include Video, Vote, Forum, Evaluation, Public Photos, Like, and Background Image. All followers have to have a Renren account before joining the public page.

Unlike many other online communities whose owners have less authority and control over their users, the owners of the LDRR public page have considerable authority and from their official position can control many of their followers' behaviors, in effect functioning as a super "guru" in this group. Only the owners can update the status; post diaries, photos, videos, and links; initiate voting and evaluation; and manage the forum on the Renren LDRR public page. The followers are only allowed to leave short comments, send private messages, and @ other Renren users (share content with specific users by using the "@" symbol to mention their names) and so forth. The content posted by the owners is more heavily emphasized on the public page than that contributed by the followers.

3.2   Data Collection

We conducted online semi-structured interviews in textual form in April and May of 2012. The interview questions included three sections: (1) demographic information; (2) LDRR status and conditions; and (3) users' behavior, motivation, and benefits. We used a Chinese online chatting tool, QQ, to conduct the interviews. Each interview lasted for 30 to 45 minutes. We recruited interviewees by using purposive sampling ([35]. p.145). We sent recruitment messages to 314 of the most recently active followers. The response rate was 6.69%. Twenty-one followers participated in the interview (Female=12, Male =9). They were all strangers to one another. Most interviewees' (15/21) partners are also LDRR public page followers, the rest of the interviewees' (6/21) partners are not. The interviewees' age range was from 18 to 28 (AVG=21.14, SD=2.17). Most of them (17/21) are undergraduate students and the rest (4/21) have jobs and bachelor degrees. All the interviewees were unmarried, and in stable heterosexual LDRRs. The duration of their romantic relationship ranges from 2 to 66 months (the median is 23 months), while the duration of their LDRR is from 2 to 36 months (the median is 10 months).

3.3   Data Analysis

We used grounded theory [5] and consensual qualitative research methods [12] to analyze interviewees' answers in the third interview section (e.g. [16]). Grounded theory allows researchers to find the concepts and themes that naturally arise from the data itself [5]. Consensual qualitative research methods emphasize that the decisions are made by multiple researchers' consensus [12]. One researcher first used microanalysis or "detailed line-by-line analysis" ([26], p. 57; e.g. [32]) to identify initial concepts and categories by conducting open coding to divide interviewees' answers into units of meaning. Then two researchers adjusted initial categories together and reached consensus on a coding scheme. The overall Cohen's Kappa was high (.75). In the end, we conducted axial coding based on the initial concepts and categories, which revealed the potential relationships between categories.

4   Findings

We first describe interviewees' LDRR public page use behavior, and then specify the key concepts and categories of motivation and benefits emerging from the interviews. An analysis of different patterns of initial and continued motivations is presented.

Finally we examine the interviewees' motivations and the benefits they gained from using the LDRR public page. Interviewees' numbers are noted after each quote ('I': individual followers, whose partners are not the LDRR public page followers; 'P': pair followers, they and their partners are both followers; 'F'=female; 'M'=male).

4.1 Use of the LDRR Public Page

Interviewees' time range for using the LDRR public page is from one month to 27 months. The median is four months. The frequency of use depends on the frequency of how often the owners of the public page update the contents. Interviewees read the update (i.e., status, photos, diaries, etc.) posted by the owners of the public page, but contribute to the content on the LDRR public page very infrequently. Previous research has defined this kind of behavior as "lurking" (e.g. [20]). All interviewees said they only left comments when they felt a specific status, story, picture, or comment aroused their strong empathy [15]. They left comments without necessarily intending to communicate with others. They did not expect a reply to their comments most of the time, but instead just wanted to reinforce and validate their own feelings.

4.2 Motivations for Participating in the LDRR Public Page

We asked interviewees about their initial motivations for following the LDRR public page, and then asked them a separate question about their continued reasons for participating once they had joined the community in order to see whether new motivations emerged. We first combined interviewees' initial and continued motivations together and identified four major categories of concepts: (1) Belonging; (2) Empathy; (3) Social Support; and (4) Learning. These major motivations are related to each other rather than mutually exclusive.

Belonging. The need to belong is a fundamental, powerful, and extremely pervasive motivation [3]. For the followers on the LDRR public page, the need to belong could be met to some degree from joining a group whose members are in a similar situation. Most interviewees (19/21) mentioned that either they were in a LDRR, or they thought the other followers on this public page are engaged in LDRRs like them and this motivated them to follow the public page.

"The followers on the LDRR public page are all LDRR couples, I felt a strong sense of belonging because we cherish the same ideals and follow the same path." [I-12-F]

Their answers indicated that belonging is the primary motivation for participating in the LDRR public page. Sharing the same characteristics with other LDRR followers on this public page allowed them to form a social group together.

Empathy. Social groups foster heightened empathy [15] between group members by leading to social interactions or social ties (see review in [6]). Empathy in turn could be a motivation for participating in an online social group. More than half of interviewees (13/21) expressed a shared understanding with other Renren followers engaged in LDRRs and viewed their own feelings as identical to theirs.

"Many status updates written by the owners of the public page expressed exactly what I was feeling, making me feel they are so close to my heart." [I-15-M]

"Other followers' comments made me feel that I have the same feelings as them. Their LDRR stories also happened to me." [I-1-F]

Empathic understanding is particularly relevant to the exchange of emotional support and instrumental and informational support [11]. In other words, feeling empathy is also related to the following third and fourth major motivations: social support and learning.

Social Support. Interviewees perceived the positive effects of emotional support from the LDRR public page on themselves and their LDRRs, providing a strong motivation to use it. These positive effects make interviewees (5/21) *"feel empowered" [P-2-M]*, and provides them *"with more confidence"[I-21-F]* to preserve their LDRRs; or allow interviewees (2/21) to adopt an optimistic outlook with respect to their LDRRs instead of focusing on the hardship of LDRRs. Other Interviewees also mentioned comfort (*"When I feel sad and helpless, I visit the public page and find comfort in it" [P-5-F]*); a reduced sense of loneliness (*"the owners' status and other followers' comments make me feel not that lonely" [I-6-F]*); and increased happiness (*"I want to see the positive aspects of LDRR from this public page, to make me feel that the LDRR is as sweet as a GCRR, and I am happy in the LDRR" [P-9-M]*). These and other comments all reflect the positive effects of social support on well-being.

Learning. Our interviewees expressed and confirmed the hardship of maintaining LDRRs. Half of the interviewees (11/21) mentioned that when they discovered the LDRR public page for the first time, they thought that it might be a place where they could learn from others how to maintain their LDRRs better.

"I use the public page because I want to learn how to build a better LDRR by understanding the LDRR-related information from the many perspectives provided on the public page." [I-7-M]

4.3   Different Patterns of Initial and Continued Motivations

After we identified four major motivations, we then analyzed initial and continued motivations separately and categorized them into the four major categories discussed above. We analyzed the number of the units of initial and continued motivations in each category (Fig. 1) and found that belonging was the dominant motivation when

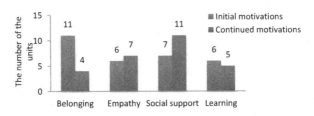

Fig. 1. Different patterns between initial and continued motivation

interviewees began to use the LDRR public page for the first time, while social support was the dominant motivation for continuing to use the public page. Empathy and learning played relatively equal roles in motivating interviewees to start participating in the public page for the first time, and for continuing to use it.

4.4   A Comparison of Motivations and Benefits

The motivations reflect interviewees' needs and reasons for participating in the LDRR public page. We applied the same codes to identify motivations and benefits. We also analyzed the units of total motivations (including initial and continued motivations) and benefits (Fig. 2) and found that the benefits are mostly reflected in the form of perceived social support for using the public page. The different patterns between motivations and benefits do not mean followers did not get what they wanted. Instead, it conveys a meaning that satisfying the need to belong and feel empathy transformed to receiving effective social support from the public page.

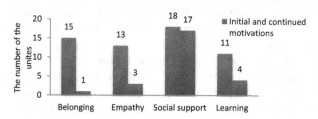

Fig. 2. Comparison of the total motivations and benefits

5   Discussion

One major characteristic of the LDRR public page on Renren is that it is a hierarchically organized online support community rooted in the culture of China. Our interview study has found that most of our interviewees are lurkers who initially participated in this online community because they were motivated by strong feelings of belonging, and they continued to use it for the perceived social support.

Since members in most online communities usually have greater input and influence than the people who oversee the communities [21], the survival of online communities strongly depends on members' voluntary participation and contributions. However, in our case, the people who run the community have hierarchical authority over their members. Members' participation is still crucial, but nonetheless subordinate to the role of the community leader, whose contribution becomes vital to the well-being of the online community. If the public owners were to quit their involvement with the LDRR public page, the community would quickly wane.

Most of our interviewees are lurkers. Previous research has found that concern for privacy is one of several reasons for lurking [e.g. 20]. Since the LDRR public page followers have to use their real-name Renren IDs, allowing others to trace them back to their personal pages on Renren, followers may be more likely to lurk out of concern for privacy, especially given that the topic under consideration on the LDRR page is one of personal intimate relationships. Another reason for lurking may be related to the design of the LDRR public page. One major design feature that fosters lurking: followers' limited ability to post and contribute to the content.

Although we chose an online community rooted in Chinese culture as our research site, many other culturally distinct and varied LDRR online communities exist. For example, there are popular LDRR online communities in the US, such as the LDRR public pages on Facebook. These show clear similarities to the LDRR public page on Renren in terms of purpose and content. The page designs and followers' behavior, however, are different in numerous respects. Their followers have greater authority than those on Renren. And the followers of the LDRR public page on Facebook are not exclusively from the US and are culturally more diverse than those on Renren. It may well be the case, then, that cultural differences play a role in helping explain the motivational and behavioral differences between users of the LDRR public page on RenRen and those on Facebook. This is an area that warrants further study.

People who are engaged in LDRRs need to know and feel they are not alone. The existence of LDRR public pages on SNS such as RenRen and Facebook allows them to satisfy these needs. We therefore suggest that designers have a critical role to play in creating systems, platforms, and devices that serve not only private communication between the two members of a couple, but also public communication among the individuals participating in these larger LDRR communities. Furthermore, the example of the LDRR public page on RenRen points to the need for design solutions that enhance the more expert- or owner-driven SNS model, for example by supplying better tools for owners to provide information, tell their stories, and curate content provided by followers. These features should be implemented with an eye to supporting the learning, sense of belonging, and empathic responses of users.

There are two major limitations to our study. First, we did not recruit both members of a couple. While we believe our interviewees' responses provide important insights, given our individual- and community-oriented (rather than couple-oriented) perspective, we would nonetheless like to recruit couples in the future, both members of whom follow the RenRen LDRR public page. Second, there are limitations to the sampling method that we used. In future studies we hope to conduct quantitative research and analysis based on random and large group members' data to extend and augment the results of our qualitative study that will provide more representative results.

6   Conclusions

Our study is an initial attempt to explore an influential LDRR online community in a Chinese SNS. In order to understand users' behaviors and motivations, we conducted an exploratory interview study. We found that: 1) users lurk most of the time unless their empathy is strongly aroused; 2) users' four major motivations for using the LDRR public page are belonging, empathy, social support, and learning; 3) initial and continued motivations have different patterns; 4) perceived social support is the main benefit of participating in the LDRR public page. The need to belong to a group of "similar others" held together largely by empathy and the desire for social support was particularly strong in this community.

Acknowledgments. We thank our interviewees, all publications support, and Chen Huang who helped code the data. We thank Professor Paul Resnick for his suggestions and comments.

References

1. Aylor, B.: Maintaining long-distance relationships. In: Canary, D.J., Dainton, M. (eds.) Maintaining Relationships Through Communication: Relational, Contextual, and Cultural Variations, pp. 127–140. Lawrence Erlbaum, Mahwah (2003)
2. Bales, E., Li, K.A., Griswold, W.: CoupleVIBE: Mobile implicit communication to improve awareness for (long-distance) couples. In: Proc. CSCW 2011. ACM Press (2011)
3. Baumeister, R.F., Leary, M.R.: The need to belong: Desire for interpersonal attachments as a fundamental human motivation. Psychological Bulletin 117, 497–529 (1995)
4. Bhandari, S., Bardzell, S.: Bridging gaps: affective communication in long distance relationships. Ext. Abstracts CHI 2008, pp. 2763–2768. ACM Press (2008)
5. Glaser, B.G., Strauss, A.L.: The Discovery of Grounded Theory: Strategies for Qualitative Research. Sociology Press, Chicago (1967)
6. Goette, L., Huffman, D., Meier, S.: The Impact of Social Ties on Group Interactions: Evidence from Minimal Groups and Randomly Assigned Real Groups. American Economic Journal: Microeconomics 4(1), 101–115 (2011)
7. Goffman, E.: The Presentation of Self in Everyday Life. Doubleday, New York (1959)
8. Gooch, D., Watts, L.: The Magic Sock Drawer project. Ext. Abstracts CHI 2011, pp. 243–252. ACM Press (2011)
9. Goodman, E., Misilim, M.: The Sensing Bed. In: Proc. UbiComp 2003 Workshop (2003)
10. Guldner, G.T.: Long-distance romantic relationships: Prevalence and separation-related symptoms in college students. Journal of College Student Development 37, 289–296 (1996)
11. Heaney, C.A., Israel, B.A.: Social networks and social support. In: Glanz, K., Rimer, B.K., Lewis, F.M. (eds.) Health Behavior and Health Education: Theory, Research, and Practice, 4th edn., pp. 185–209. Joseey-Bass, San Francisco (2008)
12. Hill, C.E., Thompson, B.J., Williams, E.N.: A guide to conducting consensual qualitative research. The Counseling Psychologist 25, 517–572 (1997)
13. Johnson, A.J., Haigh, M., Becker, J., Craig, E., Wigley, S.: College Students' Use of Relational Management Strategies in Email in Long-Distance and Geographically Close Relationships. Journal of Computer Mediated Communication 13, 381–404 (2008)
14. Kaye, J.J., Levitt, M.K., Nevins, J., Golden, J., Schmidt, V.: Communicating intimacy one bit at a time. Ext. Abstracts CHI 2005, pp. 1529–1532. ACM Press (2005)
15. Levenson, R.W., Ruef, A.M.: Empathy: A Physiological Substrate. Journal of Personality and Social Psychology 63, 234–246 (1992)
16. Marcus, M.A., Westra, H.A., Eastwood, J.D., Barnes, K.L.: What Are Young Adults Saying About Mental Health? An Analysis of Internet Blogs. Journal of Medical Internet Research 14(1) (2012)

17. Neustaedter, C., Greenberg, S.: Intimacy in Long-Distance Relationships over Video Chat Research Report 2011-1014-26, Department of Computer Science, University of Calgary, Calgary, AB, Canada T2N 1N4 (August 2011)

18. Neustaedter, C., Greenberg, S.: Intimacy in Long-Distance Relationships over Video Chat. In: Proc. CHI 2012. ACM Press (2012)

19. Pfeil, U.: Online support communities. In: Zaphiris, P., Ang, C.S. (eds.) Social Computing & Virtual Communities, Taylor and Francis, Boca Raton (2010)

20. Preece, J., Nonneke, B., Andrews, D.: The top five reasons for lurking: Improving community experience for everyone. Computers in Human Behavior 20, 201–223 (2004)

21. Ren, Y., Kraut, R., Kiesler, S.: Applying common identity and bond theory to design of online communities. Organization Studies 28(3), 377–408 (2007)

22. Stafford, L., Merolla, A.J., Castle, J.D.: When long-distance dating partners become geographically close. Journal of Social and Personal Relationships 23, 901–919 (2006)

23. Stafford, L.: Maintaining long-distance and cross-residential relationships. Lawrence Erlbaum Associates, Mahwah (2005)

24. Stafford, L., Merolla, A.J.: Idealization, reunions, and stability in long-distance dating relationships. Journal of Social and Personal Relationships 24, 37–54 (2007)

25. Statistic Brain. Long Distance Relationship Statistics (2012), http://www.statisticbrain.com/long-distance-relationship-statistics/

26. Strauss, A.L., Corbin, J.: Basics of Qualitative Research: Techniques and Procedures for Developing Grounded Theory, 2nd edn. Sage, Thousand Oaks (1998)

27. Sprecher, S., Felmlee, D., Orbuch, T.L., Willetts, M.C.: Social networks and change in personal relationships. In: Vangelisti, A., Reis, H.T., Fitzpatrick, M.A. (eds.) Stability and Change in Relationships, pp. 257–284. Cambridge University Press, New York (2002)

28. Thoits, P.: Stress, coping, and social support processes: where are we? What next? Journal of Health and Social Behavior, Extra Issue, 53–79

29. Utz, S., Beukeboom, C.: The role of social network sites in romantic relationships: Effects on jealousy and relationship happiness. Journal of Computer-Mediated Communication 16, 511–527 (2011)

30. Vetere, F., Gibbs, M.R., Kjeldskov, J., et al.: Mediating intimacy: technologies to support strongtie relationships. In: Proc. of CHI 2005, pp. 471–480. ACM Press (2005)

31. Westefeld, J.S., Liddell, D.: Coping with long-distance relationships. Journal of College Student Development 23, 550–551 (1982)

32. Xie, B.: Multimodal Computer-Mediated Communication and Social Support among Older Chinese. Journal of Computer-Mediated Communication 13(3), 728–750 (2008)

33. Yin, L.J.: Communication Channels, Social Support and Satisfaction in Long Distance Romantic Relationships. Communication Theses (2009), http://digitalarchive.gsu.edu/communication_theses/56

34. Zhao, X., Schwanda Sosik, V., Cosley, D.: It's complicated: how romantic partners use facebook. In: Proc. CHI 2012, pp. 771–780. ACM Press (2012)

35. Bernard, H.: Research Methods in Anthropology: Qualitative and Quantitative Methods, 5th edn. Altamira Press (2011)

Motivations of Facebook Users for Responding to Posts on a Community Page

Fei-Hui Huang

Department of Marketing and Distribution Management,
Oriental Institute of Technology,
Pan-Chiao, Taiwan 22061 R.O.C
kiki_huangs@yahoo.com

Abstract. This study used an Internet-based survey to understand what motivates Facebook users to like, share, or comment on the posts on a community page. This study investigates the classification of post content on a community page, the consumer–brand relationship, and motivations of users to identify how they influence user engagement with SNSs. This study used a Web-based survey to collect data on users' personal preferences, self-perceived relationships with brands, and motivation for responding to different forms of content. This empirical study explored the impact of consumer–brand relationships, post contents, gender, and motivation on users' response behavior to posts.

Keywords: User's motivation, Social networking sites, User-Web interaction, Virtual brand communities.

1   Introduction

The Internet has become a powerful tool and one of the most important communication channels worldwide. An increasing number of companies and organizations manage their brand communities by using free-of-charge social media platforms to establish relationships with consumers. Social media, especially social networking sites (SNSs), provide a new method of communicating to accelerate and escalate group formation, scope, and influence (Lin & Lu, 2011). The SNSs such as Facebook, MySpace, and Twitter are tremendously popular, with more and more people spending increasing amounts of time on SNS (Kaplan & Haenlein, 2010). Facebook, for example, has more than 800 million active users, and more than 50% of them log on to it on any given day. Facebook offers users with more than 900 million objects to interact with, and an average user is connected to 80 objects, including community pages, events, or groups (Facebook, 2010). This has led to users spending 700 billion minutes per month on Facebook (Facebook, 2010). Facebook tends to be characterized by greater social support and more trusting and closer relationships than do other SNSs (Keith et al., 2011). Marketers have also embraced Facebook, with a wide range of companies and organizations using this platform to share information about their brand through newsfeeds and posts. The key to a successful brand community on

A.A. Ozok and P. Zaphiris (Eds.): OCSC/HCII 2013, LNCS 8029, pp. 33–39, 2013.

SNS needs the users' interaction and involvement. The three objects Facebook offers—liking, sharing, and commenting—are examined in this study to investigate the interaction between a brand and its consumers and to understand users' motives for engaging with community pages. A greater number of users liking, sharing, or commenting on a post is likely to result in the success of the marketing. The more the users are willing to interact with posts on the fan pages, the more they are exposed to the information in the posts, leading to greater success for the brand in marketing terms. This study primarily investigates the classification of post content on a community page, the consumer–brand relationship, and motivations of users to identify how they influence user engagement with SNSs.

1.1   Consumer–Brand Relationships and Post Content

Companies are increasingly focusing on nurturing brand communities on SNSs as a vital part of their marketing and brand-building activities (Algesheimer, Dholakia & Herrmann, 2005). Marketers aim to form close relationships with their customers in an attempt to disseminate information, interact with highly loyal customers, bring consumers together, and thus increase their brand loyalty (Arnone, Colot & Croquet, 2010). The loyalty and trust in particular products, brands, or organizations may be reflected in participation in the virtual community (Casal et al., 2007; Koh & Kim, 2004). Also, consumers who experience a strong relationship with the brand are willing to recommend it to others, feel emotionally inclined toward it, and perceive themselves as part of it. Hence, consumer–brand relationships and post content may be important factors in motivating users to participate in and contribute to community pages.

1.2   Motivation in User Behavior

Identifying the factor that motivates the users' liking behavior is also an important issue for marketers. However, motivation is not a unitary concept. According to the self-determination theory (SDT), motivational drivers are generally subdivided into extrinsic and intrinsic motivation (Deci, & Ryan, 1985). Extrinsic motivation (e.g., to interact with Facebook friends or other fans on the community page and to gain rewards) and intrinsic motivation (i.e., to satisfy self-needs) are used in this study to find out what motivates user's response on the posts. Furthermore, several factors that drive user extrinsic motivation have been identified in previous studies. For instance, Yang et al. (2010) have noted the roles of entertainment value, perceived network externalities, interpersonal norms, and social norms in influencing YouTube users' intentions to share videos. Dholakia et al. (2004) identified four types of value—purposive, interpersonal, social enhancement, and entertainment—implicit in the motives of virtual community participants. These factors are also adapted in this study for eliciting specific user extrinsic motivation in responding to different category of post content. In addition, gender is one of the most common types of segmentation used in marketing practice. There are gender differences in motivations for Internet use. In this study, the effect of gender on Facebook users is also explored.

2   Methods

The study used a Web-based survey that comprised of (1) five questions to measure customer–brand relationships, (2) seven questions exploring user's motivation in his/her response to the brand posts, and (3) two questions on user demographics. Six Facebook pages (Traditional Chinese) for international brands were selected for the survey: Starbucks, MacDonald's, Apple, HTC, 7-Eleven, and Nike. The survey participants were 225 Facebook users who were familiar with Traditional Chinese. Among them, 123 (54.7%) were men and 102 (45.3%) women.

To explore the effect of post content on user responses, the study applied card-sorting techniques to identify the categories of the posts. Two social media managers, who have served in media and Internet companies and have more than two years' experience in curating Facebook fan pages, were asked to help in naming and classifying the posts. Through a bottom–up approach to naming, classifying, and grouping, the study categorized the posts into seven categories: (1) product and service news, (2) prizes and sale information, (3) charity and social services, (4) product- or service-related knowledge, (5) greetings and chat, (6) questions and voting, and (7) brand stories. A total of 42 posts (7 posts × 6 brands) were selected and displayed as snapshots in each questionnaire. The actual numbers of shares, likes, and comments on all posts were obscured to avoid influencing user response output. Furthermore, not every category of content could be found on the six brand pages, and therefore, the seven categories of posts were not counterbalanced in all selected pages. The study, hence, focuses only on discussing how the content categories, motivation, and customer–brand relationship affect users' output; it is unable to draw comparisons between different brands.

Customer–brand relationships were measured using a five-point Likert scale for five items adapted from the customer-brand relationship questions (Park et al., 2010). The response options were as follows: (1) I think the brand is part of me, (2) I think the brand can represent me, (3) I feel personally connected to the brand, (4) I feel emotionally bonded to the brand, and (5) I think the brand can tell people something about me. In addition, the survey included questions to identify factors that motivated user responses to the posts (liking, sharing, commenting, or doing nothing). The scale was adapted from questions developed by Dholakia et al. (2004). The participants were asked to select one option from the seven items or to select others and fill in the reason.

Finally, data analysis focused on examining the effects of customer–brand relationships, user motivation, and content categories on the responses to Facebook page posts. A multinomial logistic regression was conducted to model the level of user-brand relationships among the four types of user responses to the posts. A chi-square test was conducted to examine whether the type of motivations and content categories lead users to respond differently to the posts.

3   Results

3.1   Effects of Customer–Brand Relationship on User Responses to the Posts

Multinomial regression results indicated a significant relationship between customer-brand relationships and the four types of user response to the posts ($\chi2(12) = 79.45$, $p < .01$) with pseudo R-square values 0.049 (Cox and Shell) and 0.022 (Mc Fadden). The regression model shows 52.3% overall correct predicting percentage from 1,575 observed samples (225 participants x 7 responses). However, by looking into the observed frequencies, it revealed that the participants having low customer-brand relationships preferred to "do nothing" as their response to the posts. Other three types of responses cannot find a specific pattern.

3.2   Effects of User Motivation on User Responses to the Posts

A chi-square test indicated that there is a significant relationship between user motivation and their responses to posts ($\chi2(21) = 1089.69$, $p < .01$). A post-hoc Bonferroni corrected pairwise comparison revealed a significant difference in the effects of user motivation on their response. Overall, users who had one of the following three motivations were significantly more likely to make a response ("like", "share", or "comment") ($p < .01$), than "do nothing". These motivations are: "to share information or idea with friends;" "to disclose opinions, tastes, preferences, or interests;" or "to endorse and help promote the post."

More specifically, users who tended "to share information or ideas with friends" were found significantly more likely to "share" (52.5%, $p < .01$), compared to the other three response types (like, comment, and do nothing). Further, users who preferred "to interact with other fans on the page" were significantly more likely to comment (19.0%, $p < .01$) on the post. Furthermore, those who selected the "no special reason, just want to like, share or comment" option were significantly more likely to "like" (29.1%, $p < .01$) or "do nothing" (36.1%, $p < .01$). Users who reported having "other" motivations for responding to posts tended to "do nothing" (59.5%, $p < .01$) or "comment" (8.6%, $p < .01$). The following self-reported explanations were provided by those who noted "other" motivations: "I'm not interested in the topic"; "I don't like the post, the post doesn't touch my heart"; "I got the information but that's all; no idea in my mind."

3.3   Effects of Content Categories on User Responses

The chi-square test indicated a significant relationship between content categories and user responses ($\chi2(18) = 45.92$, $p < .01$). Post-hoc results showed that users tend to "like" both "product and service news" (17.8% > 10.4%, $p < .01$) and "brand stories"

(14.0% > 8.0%, p < .01), compare to "share" those two categories of posts. However, 14.6% users selected the "do nothing" option for the "brand stories" content, which is significantly higher proportion than that of users selecting the "share" option (14.6 > 8%, p < .01). The "question and voting" category was significantly likely to lead users to comment on the post, which was higher than the proportion of "likes" (29.3% > 15.1%, p < .01). This analysis did not find any significant content categories that were likely to drive users to "share" the posts.

3.4   Gender Difference

The surveyed responses to the posts showed that gender significantly affected user interaction with different posts ($\chi2(3) = 14.554$, p < .01). In general, compared to female users, males are significantly more likely to share (59.7% > 40.3%, p < .05) and comment on posts (67.2% > 32.8%, p < .05). On the other hand, more female than male users do not respond to posts (52.6% > 47.4%, p < .05). However, no significant gender difference was found for "Liking" posts (54.3 % and 45.7%, p >.05). Furthermore, a significant difference between genders ($\chi2(7) = 37.864$, p < .01) was found regarding the gender effects on user motivations. More specifically, more male users wanted to "share information or ideas with friends" (60.2% > 39.8%, p < .05) and "to interact with other fans on the page" (76.2% > 23.8%, p < .05) than did females. More female than male users, however, wanted to "collect or subscribe to the posts" (78.6% > 21.4%, p < .05) and responded to the post for "no special reason, just want to like, share, or comment" (55.0% > 45.0%, p < .05). Other motivations were not found to differ according to gender. Otherwise, no significant gender difference was found between content categories ($\chi2(6) = 37.864$, p > .5) and customer–brand relationship ($t(223) = 1.207$, p > .05).

4   Discussion and Conclusion

This empirical, survey-based study considered six different Facebook brand pages and asked participants to complete a questionnaire on their favorite page among the six. The study explored the impact of consumer–brand relationships, post content, and motivation on users' response behavior to posts.

The results revealed that the most popular response of Facebook users is "liking" the post (52.1%), followed by sharing (23.8%), doing nothing (20.4%), and commenting (3.7%). Furthermore, "liking" is a popular activity4 for both male and female Facebook users; however, gender differences were found in respect to other activities: Male users tended to share or comment on posts, while female users tended to do nothing. In addition, the consumer–brand relationship was found to explain a small part of user's response on posts.

The content and user motivation were found to be important factors affecting user responses. Most users simply like or share in response to the "product- or service-related knowledge" posts and like or to do nothing in response to the "brand stories" posts; however, many users are willing to follow and comment on "question and voting" content. Other types of post content including prizes and sale information, charity and social services, and greeting and chatting do not have significant different in terms of user responses. Furthermore, gender difference can be seen in responses to different types of posts. After reading "product and services news" or "question and voting" on the fan page, most male users clicked the like button while most female users chose not to respond.

The most important motivational factor that drives users to like or share posts is the desire to "share information/idea with friends" (maintaining interpersonal connectivity), followed by "endorsing and promoting the post" (social enhancement value). Another major motivational factors driving users to comment on posts are to "interact with other fans" (Social benefits) and "disclose opinions, tastes, preferences, or interests" (Self-presentation benefits). Users' liking or sharing activity is driven by the general need to maintain relationships, while the commenting activity is based on the specific need to express oneself or to make new contacts. Compared to female users, male users have a higher motivation to share information and interact with others. Thus, the major reason users, especially males, interact with brand posts through liking, sharing, or commenting activity is drove by extrinsic motivation for maintaining relationship and gaining social benefits, which accrue to Facebook friends or other brand page members. Finally, motivation characterized by "no special reason" can drive the users' liking activity or no responses, and "other" motivational factors drive users to do nothing because they are not interested in the post or they think that reading posts is enough. This study also found that the reasons female users interact with posts are for "collecting or subscribing to the posts" or "no special reason" (Intrinsic motivation). Compared to male users, female users have lower motivation to respond to posts. Many female users choose to do nothing with brand posts.

Many users liking or sharing the brand posts is to receive social support, and some of users commenting on the brand posts is to press self or interact with other users. The several previous study have showed that the users can through their friends and relatives to meet new friends and expand their social network on SNS (Powell, 2009; ledgianowski & Kulviwat, 2009) and join the brand communities to dispel their loneliness, meet like-minded others and receive companionship and social support (McKenna & Bargh, 1999; Wellman & Gulia, 1999). This shows that expanding social life, satisfying interpersonal needs, receiving social support, and maintaining friendship are the major reasons people spending time in and interacting with brand communities. Providing the posts with specific content and clear requirements is more important than strengthening consumer-brand relationships for enhancing user's intention of responding to the posts.

References

1. Algesheimer, R., Dholakia, U., Herrmann, A.: The social influence of brand communities: evidence from European car clubs. Journal of Marketing 69, 19–34 (2005)
2. Arnone, L., Colot, O., Croquet, M.: Company managed virtual communities in global brand strategy. Global Journal of Business Research 4(2), 97–112 (2010)

3. Casal, L., Flavin, C., Guinalu, M.: The impact of participation in virtual brand communities on consumer trust and loyalty: The case of free software. Online Information Review 31(6), 775–792 (2007)
4. Deci, E.L., Ryan, R.M.: Intrinsic motivation and self-determination in human behavior. Plenum, New York (1985)
5. Dholakia, U.M., Richard, P.B., Lisa, K.P.: A social influence model of consumer participation in network- and small-groupbased virtual communities. International Journal of Research in Marketing 21(3), 241–263 (2004)
6. Facebook: Press Room (2010), http://www.facebook.com/press/info.php?statistics (accessed July 26, 2010)
7. Kaplan, A.M., Haenlein, M.: Users of the world, unite! The challenges and opportunities of social media. Business Horizons 53(1), 59–68 (2010)
8. Keith, N.H., Lauren, S.G., Lee, R., et al.: Social networking sites and our lives. Pew Research Center's Internet & American Life Project 3 (2011)
9. Koh, J., Kim, D.: Knowledge sharing in virtual communities: an e-business perspective. Expert Systems with Applications 26, 155–166 (2004)
10. Lin, K.Y., Lu, H.P.: Why people use social networking sites: An empirical study integrating network externalities and motivation theory. Computers in Human Behavior 27, 1152–1161 (2011)
11. McKenna, K.Y.A., Bargh, J.A.: Causes and consequences of social interaction on the internet: A conceptual framework. Media Psychology 1, 249–269 (1999)
12. Park, C.W., MacInnis, D.J., Priester, J., et al.: Brand Attachment and Brand Attitude Strenght: Conceptual and Emperical Differentation of two Critical Brand Equity Drivers. Journal of Marketing 74, 1–17 (2010)
13. Powell, J.: 33 Million people in the room: How to create, influence and run a successful business with social networking. FT Press, NJ (2009)
14. Sledgianowski, D., Kulviwat, S.: Using social network sites: The effects of playfulness, critical mass and trust in a hedonic context. Journal of Computer Information Systems 49, 74–83 (2009)
15. Wellman, B., Gulia, M.: Net-surfers don't ride alone: Virtual communities as communities. In: Wellman, B. (ed.) Networks in the Global Village: Life in Contemporary Communities. Westview Press, Boulder (1999)
16. Yang, C., Hsu, Y.C., Tan, S.: Predicting the determinants of users' intentions for using YouTube to share video: moderating gender effects. Cyber Psychology & Behavior 13, 1–12 (2010)

Quantifying Cultural Attributes for Understanding Human Behavior on the Internet

Santosh Kumar Kalwar, Kari Heikkinen, and Jari Porras

Department of Software Engineering and Information Management,
Lappeenranta University of Technology, Lappeenranta, Finland
{santosh.kalwar,kari.heikkinen,jari.porras}@lut.fi

Abstract. Understanding human behavior on the Internet is a complex problem. One important part of the problem is measuring cultural attributes and their effect on human behavior. A clear understanding and comprehensive description of the link between human behavior and cultural attributes is essential for quantifying behavioral change. The objective of this paper is to introduce the result of a survey in which ($n = 152$) university participants participated in quantifying cultural attributes. The study results suggest that human behavior on the Internet can be linked to various cultural attributes. Notably the qualitative feedback and quantitative statistical results found following the cultural attributes to be important: safety, privacy, self, intuition and networking.

Keywords: Internet, human behavior, Internet anxiety, cultural attributes, HCI.

1 Introduction

"The only problem with Microsoft is they just have no taste. They have absolutely no taste. And I don't mean that in a small way, I mean that in a big way, in the sense that they don't think of original ideas, and they don't bring much culture into their products." - Steve Jobs (Triumph of the Nerds, 1996)

As boldly and beautifully stated by the late Steve Jobs, introducing *culture into products,* systems and design is vital for a product's success. Culture is presumed to be based on indicators such as race or ethnicity or sex. However, culture is a complex weave, a collection of not one cultural factor/attribute but a combination of various factors interwoven to set and affect our beliefs, values and behaviors. Academic research in computer science (CS) that investigates culture or its attributes is thus far limited in scope (Kamppuri, 2011). Therefore, the research question that we investigate in this paper is: *How can we quantify cultural attributes for understanding human behavior on the Internet?*

There is a vast amount of literature study on cultural theory, and this paper is narrowly focused on the issue of quantifying cultural attributes for understanding human behavior on the Internet. From measuring and developing cultural characteristics at individual level (Lee et al., 2010) to reconciling differences, improving physical environment and infrastructure, culture and its attributes plays an important role in society. Furthermore, there is a difference in how culture is perceived on the Internet (Marcus, A. & Gould, E., 2000).

A.A. Ozok and P. Zaphiris (Eds.): OCSC/HCII 2013, LNCS 8029, pp. 40–49, 2013.
© Springer-Verlag Berlin Heidelberg 2013

2   Literature Study

In software and application development, as well as an understanding of system requirements, data collection and effective implementation and testing, the cultural aspect is an important factor to study (Evers, 2001). In cultural psychology, culture comprises many variables such as age, ethnicity, occupation, and gender. The contributions of cultural psychology (Cole, 1998; McCrae, 2005) and cognitive sciences (Hutchins, 1995) to conceptualizing culture and cultural attributes are important as much experimental HCI research is based on the tradition of cultural psychological research. According to (Vatrapu, 2011), there are two types of cultural models; one that mainly deals with typologies and one that mainly deals with dimensions. The one that deals with typologies is easy to conceptualize. However, dealing with dimensions requires empirical validation. In their work a summary of empirical evidence regarding differences between East Asian and Western learner culture has been presented (Vatrapu, 2011; Nisbett, 2002). Thus, based on these existing literature sources we can derive cultural differences between East Asians and Western learners as shown in Table 1.

Table 1. Cultural differences between East Asians and Western learner

Westerns	East-Asians	Empirical evidence
Analytical in reasoning	Holistic in reasoning	(Vatrapu, 2011; Nisbett, 2002)
Individualism	Collectivism	(Hofstede, G. 1980; 1997)
Lower power distance index	Higher power distance index	(Hofstede, G. 1980; 1997)
Lesser difficulty in separating objects (more object-oriented)	Encountered difficulty in separating objects from surroundings (relation-oriented)	(Nisbett, 2002)
Application focused and analytical in logical grounds	Conceptual focused and willing on holistic grounds	(Vatrapu, 2011; Nisbett, 2002) (Hofstede, G. 1997)

Literature studies, e.g., (Hofstede, G., 1980; McCrae, R. R., 1992; Ebon, B., 1998), and (Terry Sullivan and Rebecca Matson. 2000; Kalwar, 2011) suggest that it is difficult to determine the self-reinforcing relationship between human behavior and cultural attributes. However, understanding culture and its attributes is important a) to overcome differences in understanding experiences of systems and products, especially in HCI, where the aim is mapping between human needs and technologies, and b) to overcome lack of consensus in understanding of cultural constructs. An interesting research paper (Tedre et al., 2006) highlights the importance of culture and its attributes for interface designs and describes CS and engineering majors' perception of culture as a neutral approach. Additionally, culture is important in the computing field not only because of globalization. Many studies (Vatrapu, 2011) (Kamppuri et al., 2006) show a growing interest for race and ethnicity factors as they pertain to digital life. In a doctoral thesis entitled, "Cultural Models in HCI: Hofstede, Affordance and Technology Acceptance," Lidia Oshlyansky points out cultural differences "do exist," and the Unified Theory of Acceptance and Use of Technology (UTAUT) model (Venkatesh et al., 2003) works cross-culturally (Oshlyansky 2007). On a similar note, user anxiety and phobia has been studied by (King and McNeese, 1998), whose paper outlines cognitive and clinical pitfalls by providing examples of affective computing for complex systems. Contributions from HCI (Cockton, 2006; Hvannberg and Cockton, 2008) especially in User experiences (McCarthy et al., 2006) have added importance to the value of cultural theory. In the study of culture and its attributes (Kalwar 2011; Alaoutinen, et al., 2012) the following cultural attributes in the given context require further investigation; intuition, privacy, security, networking and safety.

From the culture literature, we can conclude that there are wide-ranging views on cultural models, dimensions, factors/attributes, definitions, and usability issues that all should be considered in regard to a user's culture. This work aims to quantify these cultural attributes within the context of digital life, i.e., the Internet, for improved understanding of online human behavior. Based on the literature findings, the cultural attributes/dimensions of intuition, privacy, networking, safety and self are defined in Table 2.

Table 2. Cultural attributes within the context of digital life

Cultural attributes	*Definitions*	*Empirical evidence*	*Initial assumptions with Hofstede's dimensions*	*Initial assumptions with McCrae's "Big Five" dimensions*
Intuition	An act of knowing or sensing something based on personal, social and cultural experiences	(Brown, et al., 1989).	Long term vs. short term orientation	Openness to experience
Privacy	General concern on the Internet, where personal freedom should be cared, respected and taken seriously.	(Moore, 1984)	Power distance (PDI)	Neuroticism
Networking	An act by which users want/desire to collaborate with others on the Internet	(Castells, 2011)	Individualism vs. collectivism	Agreeableness
Safety	The method or technique to avoid uncertainties, security of data, and other cyber concerns	(Reason, 1990)	Uncertainty avoidance index (UAI)	Extraversion
Self	A self-less desires to perform better, learn and live	(Maslow, 1943)	Masculinity vs. Femininity	Conscientiousness

3   Methodology and Observations

The research methodology employed was to conduct a survey in which (n = 152) university participants participated in linking cultural attributes and human behavior on the Internet. Pre-testing with a small number (i.e. twelve users) was first carried out. Testing was carried out with 140 university participants. The testing was carried out in two phases because it was considered important that the respondents should understand the questions in a similar way as the researcher posited. In the test, the participants were asked to verify the importance of identified cultural attributes. Understanding cultural attributes has been carried out by classification of behavioral observations and by use of mixed research methodologies (i.e. both qualitative and quantitative) to enhance empirical results. Figure 1 below shows how the questions were organized. Open-ended questions were: 1) in your opinion, what is culture? 2) In your opinion, what is culture on the Internet? , and 3) what cultural issues affect your feelings on the Internet? Five-point Likert scale (5= of utmost importance, 1= very little or no importance) measures were used.

In your digital life, how important is each of the following?

	Of utmost importance	Very important	Of moderate importance	Of little importance	Of very little or no importance
Intuition (An act of knowing or sensing something)	O	O	O	O	O
Privacy (A general concern on the Internet)	O	O	O	O	O
Networking (The act by which users want/desire to collaborate)	O	O	O	O	O
Safety (A method or technique developed by a user to avoid uncertainties, security of data)	O	O	O	O	O
Self (A desire to perform better, learn, and live)	O	O	O	O	O

Fig. 1. Diagram illustrating measurement sheet/questions

4   Quantitative Results

The comparison data of the responses of the participants of Asian and Western ethnicity showed the results given in Figure 2 for the five cultural attributes considered. The survey gave quite surprising results in that Westerners ascribed "utmost importance" to "safety," and "privacy" (on the Internet). The results made us pause for reflection for two reasons. Firstly, on the present Internet, the safety cultural attribute is a critical issue and presents a key challenging requirement for building the future Internet. Secondly, the privacy cultural attribute is often assumed to be part of law or legal rights but here the study participants had a different opinion, conceiving it as a personal freedom, or cultural rights. Interestingly, Asians and others ethnicity gave utmost importance to "self" and "intuitions". For Africans and Asians, "networking" was of very greater importance than for other participants.

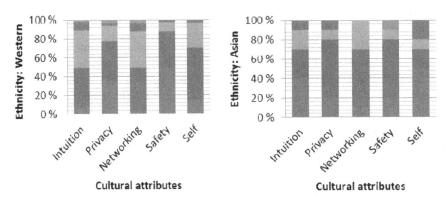

Of utmost importance ■ Of very important ■ Of moderate importance ■ Of little importance ■ Of very little or no importance

Fig. 2. Western and Asian ethnicity vs. cultural attributes

5   Qualitative Coding

As per the qualitative research methodology, the open-ended questions were coded based on qualitative feedback and criticism from the users. When asked the first question, "In your opinion, what is culture?" the following responses were received. For example, a user (1) had difficulty grasping the concept of "culture" and simply responded:

1.   *"Topic for discussion mainly, too abstract for me to really ponder..."*

Whereas, other users (2-5) came up with some serious answers:

2.   *"Culture is outcome of social needs and values."*
3.   *"Culture is manifested in all human actions, both immaterial and material, and dictates how we react to various situations and how we behave in interaction with other members of the community."*
4.   *"Culture is how we perceive the surrounding world and how we act in it according to the specific norms, traditions, and customs defined by the community."*
5.   *"Culture also guides our behavior towards people from other cultures."*

On a similar note, some users also reported that culture is "how we perceive," "manifested in all human," "way of doing," "guides our behavior," "beliefs," "group," "habit," and "people".

When asked for the second question, "In your opinion, what is culture on the Internet? Some users reported (6-8) that there is no culture on the Internet with the following responses; e.g.

6.   *"There isn't one. There are many, as there are in the world. The Internet is not (just one) 'thing'."*
7.   *"I haven't realized any identifiable culture on internet. I think behavior on internet is wild because of huge amount of users. Everybody follow her or him own approved rules."*

8. *"Internet represents only a part of the human culture; What is NOT on the Internet may be even more important than what is there."*

Similarly, other users (9-11) defined culture on the Internet as

9. *"Culture is something affecting how you use the Internet, how your idea about it, how you communicate with others through Internet."*

10. *"Culture on the Internet: don't touch and don't break down that not yours"*

11. *" It can be its contents; i.e., music, videos and pictures or on a larger perspective it's the defining characters of the internet that separates it from other medias, like you can't trust the contents of the internet on the same way you trust printed media or that anyone"*

However, other users also reported that culture on the Internet is "way one behaves," "how person uses, and act in internet," or even "same as normal culture," and "connections and reaction in online environment".

The questions were designed with the level of difficulty (i.e. easier, difficult, and very difficult) format. It was found that most users had experienced difficulty with the final question, "what cultural issues affect your feelings on the Internet?" In response, the users (12–14) responded:

12. *"Haven't thought about this."*

13. *"Good skills and attitude towards technology"*

14. *"I interact on internet only on very common level.*

The most frequent responses referred to "privacy", "security," and personal usage. For example, users (15-17) responded:

15. *"I am very careful with privacy on internet so, I do not reveal any private issues of my own or of my family on internet (in Facebook etc.)."*

16. *"Privacy, religion, language barriers, visual aspects of international sites."*

17. *"I think safety is really important to me and it comes from the culture that I live in, in our culture privacy is appreciated. Also, something that is always to be remembered is that in our culture people and things in general can be trusted, and in Internet that can't be done."*

For another user, the "excessive use of social networking sites" was among the cultural issue affecting her feelings on the Internet. For users (18, 19), personal feelings and symptoms (emphasis on "my," "impatient" in their responses) were important on the Internet.

18. *"My age and gender, definitely, which shape my attitudes and cultural interests; My education, job, and background; My family status (own kids and the Internet), my nationality, my hobbies; My beliefs and values..."*

19. *" Impatient (that is more personal than cultural issue), western individuality"*

Another user (20) indubitably believes that the Internet is "*spoiled*" by the accumulation of the number of users.

> 20. "*Internet has already been spoiled by the great mass of dumb and non-technical users. Self-aggrandizement and self-importance have flooded the internet making everything subjective, postmodern, and deconstructible. That is why I carefully choose what I view on the internet and choose not to comment anything...*"

As the observations from the data showed, most users felt on very little cultural issues and reported on more general level simply stating, "*same as in real world. Internet is just a tool*," "*ways of communication... things I am ready to reveal about myself e.g. in Facebook etc.*" In short, both quantitative and qualitative data suggested users being concerned on various cultural attributes as shown in Table 3.

Table 3. Some common observations based on qualitative and quantitative data

Westerns	East-Asians
The qualitative data supports empirical evidence that Westerns learners are individualistic, analytical and application focused.	The qualitative data supports empirical evidence that East-Asians learners are holistic, collectivist and conceptual focused.
According to *Hofstede's* dimensions and with regards to digital life, higher *power distance, uncertainty avoidance index* and lower *long-term orientation vs. short-term* and *masculinity vs. femininity* was visible.	According to *Hofstede's* dimensions and with regards to digital life, lower *power distance, uncertainty avoidance index* and higher *long-term vs. short-term* orientation and *masculinity vs. femininity* was visible.
According to *McCrae's "Big Five"* dimensions and with regards to digital life, lower *conscientiousness* and *openness to experience* was observed.	According to *McCrae's "Big Five"* dimensions and with regards to digital life, higher *conscientiousness*, and *openness to experience* was observed.
Safety and *Privacy* is utmost important	*Self* and *Intuition* is utmost important
Networking lesser important	*Networking* very important
Dreadful and anxious digital life	Interesting digital life
Symptoms of "self-aggrandizement," "narcissism," impatience," and "frustration," seems more likely.	Symptoms of "self-aggrandizement," "narcissism," impatience," and "frustration," seems less likely.

6   Discussion and Limitations

Previous study has shown that the significance of cultural attributes is important in understanding human behavior on the Internet (Clarke, R. 1999; Castells, 2011).

A recent paper (Proctor et al., 2011) discusses the effects of culture on user uptake of digital media and technology by building understanding of cultural differences that shape decision-making in the use and design of digital media (Apple-Computer, 1992). In addition, studies of (e.g., Davis, F., 1993; Evers, 2001; Shi, Q., 2010), show a close link between human behavior and cultural attributes. There was a difference between the initial assumption of *Hofstede's* and *McCrae's* dimensions and final outcome among various ethnicity and cultural attributes. *Hofstede's* dimensions are not useful in terms of quantifying cultural attributes with regards to digital life. Studies (Vatrapu, 2011; Shi, Q., 2010) indicate that cultural attributes are of utmost importance also for understanding human behavior (King and McNeese, 1998; Proctor et al., 2011); an insight which is confirmed here with quantifiable cultural attributes. The cultural models can be used to bridge the gaps between various cultures that affect not only user experience but also computer supportive collaborative work (CSCW) in learning environment. The result based on the literature, qualitative and quantitative statistics quantified importance to following cultural attributes: Safety-Privacy-Self-Intuition-Networking.

Overall, the study results suggest that understanding of human behavior on the Internet can be linked with various cultural attributes. The western ethnicity was relatively larger in the sample than other ethnicities, which means that no reliable forecast can be drawn from this result. Although the university participants consisted of students, researchers, teachers and other staff, the sample considered in this pool might have biased the findings of the study. Consequently, a limitation is that the present study does not consider a much larger and diverse sample representation. In addition, the imbalance in the number of participants from different ethnic backgrounds might have also affected on the validity of the results.

7   Conclusions and Lesson Learned

The present study suggests that analyzing and conceptualizing human behavior and cultural attributes may need some contextual linking. A possible alternative is to link cultural attributes with behavior on the Internet. In short, using this mixed research methodologies, we can claim that cultural attributes are significant in enhancing our understanding of human behavior on the Internet.

The beauty of the present inquiry is that by asking simple questions like: 1) In your opinion, what is culture? 2) In your opinion, what is culture on the Internet? , and 3) What cultural issues affect your feelings on the Internet? We can conclude that these cultural attributes can be measured. Interestingly, the quantitative findings stressed on the five-point Likert scale (5= of utmost importance, 1= very little or no importance) the following cultural attributes: Safety-Privacy-Self-Intuition-Networking. By placing emphasis on cultural attributes and self-assessing user behavior online, we can quantify cultural attributes effectively for understanding human behavior on the Internet. The lessons learned about studying user cultural attributes and human behavior on the Internet are as follows:

1. From the five cultural attributes given, most users highlight the importance of *"safety"* and *"privacy"* as the utmost important cultural attributes.
2. Although most of the participants' belonged to a western ethnic background, the cultural attribute, *"intuition"* is very important among the study participants.
3. Feelings and symptoms on the Internet are difficult to determine. However, some users did report general symptoms like *"impatient,"* and personal symptoms like *"self-aggrandizement"* and *"narcissism"*.
4. We can conceptualize human behavior on the Internet if we can link various cultural attributes and fulfill the user requirements by improving *safety*, *privacy*, and *self*.
5. The take-away message is that one should have an *intuitive* feeling to read, write, and learn stuff on the Internet for gaining broader cultural experiences.

Acknowledgments. This work has been partially supported by ECSE (East Finland Graduate School in Computer Science and Engineering), the Foundation of Nokia Corporation, LUT Foundation grant (Lauri ja Lahja Hotisen rahasto, Väitöskirjan viimeistelyapurahat), and the Finnish Foundation for Technology Promotion (Tekniikan edistämissäätiö).

Reference

1. Hofstede, G.: Culture's consequences: International differences in work related values. Sage, Beverly Hills (1980)
2. Hofstede, G.: Cultures and Organizations: Software of the Mind, Intercultural Cooperation and its Importance for Survival. McGraw-Hill (1997)
3. Davis, F.: User acceptance of information technology: system characteristics, user perception and Behavioral impacts. International Journal of Man Machine Studies 38, 475–487 (1993)
4. Marcus, A., Gould, E.: Cultural dimensions and global web user-interface design: What? So what? Now what? In: Sixth Conference on Human Factors and the Web, June 19 (2000)
5. Shi, Q.: An Empirical Study of Thinking Aloud Usability Testing From a Cultural Perspective. Samfundslitteratur, Frederiksberg (PhD Series; Nr. 30. 2010) (2010)
6. Kalwar, S.K.: Cultura: A two cultural model for understanding human behavior on the Internet. In: Proceedings of the IADIS International Conference Interfaces and Human Computer Interaction, MCCSIS 2011, pp. 321–326 (2011)
7. Ebon, B.: Internet or Outernet. Cyberghetto or Cybertopia? Preger, Westport (1998)
8. Sullivan, T., Matson, R.: Barriers to use: usability and content accessibility on the Web's most popular sites. In: Proceedings on the 2000 Conference on Universal Usability, CUU 2000, pp. 139–144. ACM, New York (2000)
9. Vatrapu, R.: Cultural considerations in learning analytics. In: Proceedings of the 1st International Conference on Learning Analytics and Knowledge (LAK 2011). ACM (2011)
10. Kamppuri, M., Bednarik, R., Tukiainen, M.: The expanding focus of HCI: case culture. In: NordiCHI 2006: Proceedings of the 4th Nordic Conference on Human-Computer Interaction: Changing Roles. ACM (2006)
11. Cole, M.: Cultural psychology. Belknap Press (1998)
12. Hutchins, E.: Cognition in the Wild (1995)

13. Cockton, G.: Designing worth is worth designing. In: NordiCHI 2006: Proceedings of the 4th Nordic Conference on Human-Computer Interaction: Changing Roles. ACM (2006)
14. Hvannberg, E.T., Cockton, G.: Maturing usability (2008)
15. McCrae, R.R., Oliver, P.J.: An introduction to the five-factor model and its applications. Journal of Personality 60(2), 175–215 (1992)
16. McCrae, R.R.: Personality profiles of cultures: aggregate personality traits. Journal of Personality and Social Psychology 89(3), 407 (2005)
17. McCarthy, J., Wright, P., Wallace, J.: The experience of enchantment in human–computer interaction. Personal and Ubiquitous Computing 10, 369–378 (2006)
18. Oshlyansky, L.: Swansea University. School of Physical Sciences. Computer Science. Cultural models in HCI (2007)
19. Proctor, R.W., Nof, S.Y., Yih, Y.: Understanding and Improving Cross-Cultural Decision Making in Design and Use of Digital Media: A Research Agenda. International Journal of Human-Computer Interaction 27(2), 151–190 (2011)
20. King, R.E., McNeese, M.D.: Human-computer anxiety and phobia: a consideration of foundations and interventions. In: Proceedings of the Fourth Annual Symposium on Human Interaction with Complex Systems, pp. 205–208. IEEE Computer Society (1998)
21. Nisbett, R.E., Norenzayan, A.: Culture and cognition. Stevens' handbook of experimental psychology (2002)
22. Tedre, M., Sutinen, E., Kähkönen, E., Kommers, P.: Ethnocomputing: ICT in cultural and social context. Communications of the ACM 49(1) (2006)
23. Lee, I., et al.: Measurement development for cultural characteristics of mobile Internet users at the individual level. Computers in Human Behavior 26(6), 1355–1368 (2010)
24. Evers, V.: Cross-Cultural Understanding of Interface Design, Doctoral Thesis, Institute of Educational Technology, Open University, UK (February 2001)
25. Apple-Computer. Human Computer Interface Guidelines. Addison Wesley, Reading (1992)
26. Venkatesh, V., Morris, Davis, Davis: User Acceptance of Information Technology: Toward a Unified View. MIS Quarterly 27, 425–478 (2003)
27. Kamppuri, M.: Theoretical and methodological challenges of cross-cultural interaction design. University of Eastern Finland (2011)
28. Maslow, A.H.: A theory of human motivation. Psychological Review 50(4), 370–396 (1943)
29. Moore, B.: Privacy: Studies in social and cultural history, vol. 73. ME Sharpe, Armonk (1984)
30. Castells, M.: The rise of the network society: The information age: Economy, society, and culture, vol. 1. Wiley-Blackwell (2011)
31. Reason, J.: Human Error. Cambridge University Press, New York (1990)
32. Brown, J.S., Collins, A., Duguid, P.: Situated cognition and the culture of learning. Educational Researcher 18(1), 32–42 (1989)
33. Clarke, R.: Internet privacy concerns confirm the case for intervention. Communications of the ACM 42(2), 60–67 (1999)
34. Alaoutinen, S., Heikkinen, K., Porras, J.: Experiences of learning styles in an intensive collaborative course. International Journal of Technology and Design Education, 1–25 (2012)

Assessing the Possibility of a Social e-Book by Analyzing Reader Experiences

Seyeon Lee, Jea In Kim, and Chung-Kon Shi

Graduate School of Culture Technology, KAIST
291 Daehak-ro(373-1 Guseong-dong), Yuseong-gu, Daejeon 305-701, South Korea
{birdkite,jeainkim86,chunkon}@kaist.ac.kr

Abstract. A social e-book provides not only the original text but also other readers' comments, and it enables social interactions inside the book. We posited that a social e-book could be a useful tool for collaborative learning, and it could provide new opportunities for classic humanities texts. The research objective is to find the tendencies of reader generated annotations during two social reading projects. For theoretical background, "the significance of the text - social interaction model" was used for the analysis conducted in this study, and we classified user generated annotations into three different types. As a result, participants had a tendency to make more annotations about their understanding and appreciation than regarding text interpretation. In addition, the result shows that the social e-book can promote fine-grained interactions. Regarding the comparison of the genres of the contents, the group of people who read the classic and humanities genre is more active than those who read the popular literature genre. For future study, more specific ways to improve interest and understanding will be examined for effective collaborative reading experiences through the social e-book.

Keywords: social reading, social media, e-book, collaborative learning, CMC.

1 Introduction

Social media such as Facebook and Twitter have permeated everyday life, and a combination of e-books and social media can provide new opportunities for social reading. Social reading involves sharing reader's thoughts and ideas with others during the reading process. A "social e-book" provides not only the original text but also other readers' comments, and it enables social interactions inside the book. Before we create this service, there are some questions we should resolve. Is a "social e-book" really helpful to promote reader's level of interest and understanding? What kind of content is proper for a social e-book? Which purpose is better for a social e-book – entertainment or education?

We posited that a "social e-book" could be a useful tool for collaborative learning, and it could provide new opportunities for books that ordinary people have turned away from because they consider them difficult and boring, such as classic humanities texts. We suggested that using a social e-book, readers who have different levels of knowledge can help each other to interpret difficult texts. We also assumed that if a

A.A. Ozok and P. Zaphiris (Eds.): OCSC/HCII 2013, LNCS 8029, pp. 50–57, 2013.

group of people set a common goal, members can be motivated to finish reading more than if they were reading individually.

There have been many attempts to combine e-books and SNS in both academic and industrial fields [1] [2] [3]; however, most efforts have on focused new service ideas from a technical approach without considering readers' text understanding process. Because most people consider reading as a personal activity, we need to observe readers' behavior very carefully before adding new social services to e-books. This paper focuses on the reader's experience and investigates the possibility of a social e-book as a useful reading tool, especially for learning difficult texts.

2   Research Objective

The research objective is to find the tendencies of reader generated annotations while reading books in the classic humanity genre using a social e-book. Through an analysis of two social reading projects, this research will prove how reader generated annotation can show the level of understanding and degree of fine-grained interaction. In addition, we will compare user-generated annotations during the social reading of the classic and humanities genre and the popular literature genre.

3   Research Method and Process

3.1   Social Reading Project 1 - "The Analects of Confucius"

We conducted two social reading projects. The reading material of the first project was the "Analects of Confucius." After the project, we analyzed reader generated annotations created during a social reading. Thirty people who were interested in Confucius participated voluntarily, and they read "the Analects of Confucius" together for 27 days. We used a web-based e-book "Readbuild" [4]. Using this tool, readers could make comments under each paragraph, highlight on sentences and make comments, and mark on the interesting paragraph (similar to 'like' button in Facebook). The number of people who wrote annotations was 22, and the total number of annotations was 298. After the project period, 16 people were interviewed to share their experience.

Fig. 1. A screen shot of the project main page (The web-based e-book service "Readbuild")

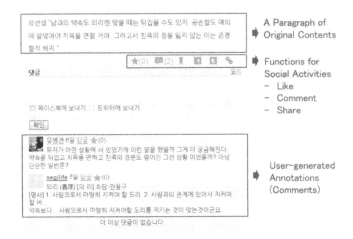

Fig. 2. A screen shot of the reading page & Composition of a social e-book service

3.2   Social Reading Project 2 – "Classic and Humanities vs. Popular Literature"

From the second project, we would like to determine if there is a difference in the reading activities depending on the genre of the reading materials. Thirty university students who were taking the same class participated in this project. We divided them into two groups, and each group read different reading materials for seven days. They used the same web-based e-book "Readbuild" used in the Project 1. One group read the classic and humanities genre, and the other group read popular literature genres such as SF and fantasy books. The participants were encouraged to read the given texts for 30 minutes per day during the seven days. Considering the period of the project, we chose short stories or an extracted chapter from a book. We started with 15 people in each group; however, two people in each group dropped out, leaving 13 people in each group. We collected 154 annotations from the project and analyzed them.

Table 1. Social Reading Project – "Classic & Humanities vs. Popular Literature"

Subject	Group A - Classic & Humanities	Group B – Popular Literature
Reading Materials (Author)	- Chapter 1 of "Confucius" - "Kriton" (Platon) - Chapter 1 of "Death" (Shelly Kagan)	- My father's Space Trip (Mi-hyun Yang) - Golem (Young-do Lee) - Murderers' Room (Ra-hyun Hwang)
Reading Quantity	11,688 words	15,538 words
Total Participants	13	13
Total Annotations	89	65
Total Like	146	106

3.3   The Significance of the Text – Social Interaction Model

For theoretical background, "the significance of the text – social interaction model" was used for the analysis conducted in this study. [5] In this model, there are three steps in the reading process: grasping the meaning of a text, interpreting significance, and understanding significance. This model separates the concepts of "interpreting" and "understanding". A reader first interprets the meaning of the text. The reader then finds underlying meaning, extends the idea, and applies it outside of the book: this is the "understanding" level. This theory suggests that the social interaction of readers is essential for moving up to the next level.

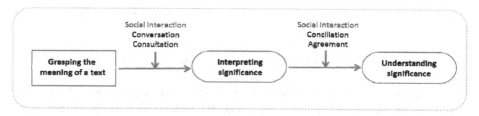

Fig. 3. The significance of the text – social interaction model

First, applying this model, we classified the user-generated annotations into three different types, as follows:

- **Interpretation level**: Annotations that show a reader's interpretation by means of facts, information and the reader's suppositions
- **Understanding level**: Annotations that show a reader's opinions, appreciation, and extended ideas after understanding
- **Other:** Comments that are not related to the original text (Chatting, how to use the service, etc.)

Second, among the annotations of the understanding level, we extracted short annotations that only combined the subject and verb and included simple expressions by the readers. If there was a difference in the percentage of these "short expressions" in the different genres of the texts, we assumed that this would show the tendencies of user-generated annotations.

Lastly, we compared the number of annotations that refer to a specific paragraph and the number of annotations that refer to the full text and general ideas. This comparison can show the degree of fine-grained interaction in the social e-book.

4   Results

4.1   Three-Pronged Analysis

Regarding the project 1 "the Analects of Confucius", annotations of "understanding level" were 69%, and annotations of "interpretation level" were 25%. Although the content was not easy to interpret, the interpretation level percentage was quite low.

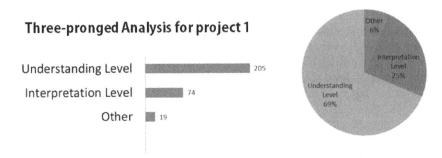

Fig. 4. Three-pronged Analysis for project 1 – "the Analects of Confucius"

It is assumed that readers tended to make more annotations about their understanding and appreciation than regarding text interpretation. However, we found that readers tried to find the correct interpretation and shared the information, especially when they did not know the meaning of a word or when they could not interpret the meaning because they did not have sufficient background information, such as knowledge about the characters, history, or region. They asked questions, and some of them copied the results that they found from online search engines.

When we compared the three-pronged analysis of "Classic & Humanities" and "Popular Literature" in project 2 regarding the annotations of the "interpretation level," we found seven annotations in the classic & humanities genre and no annotations in the popular literature genre. We assume that this transpired because when readers read popular literature, they can easily move to the understanding level and therefore did not need to make annotations regarding their interpretation.

Table 2. Three-pronged Analysis for project 2 – "Classic & Humanities vs. Popular Literature"

Subject	Group A - Classic & Humanities	Group B – Popular Literature
Interpretation Level	7	0
Understanding Level	56	50
etc.	26	15
total	89	65

4.2   Length of Annotation and Profundity of Thought

When we compared the average number of letters in the annotations, we found that group A (classic & humanities) made longer annotations than group B (popular literature). In order to determine the tendency of the annotations concretely, we extracted short annotations that only combined a subject and a verb and included the reader's simple expressions. Examples of annotations such as "That's so funny" "Interesting!" and "It's like a cautionary tale" belong to this category. As we supposed, the percentage of "short expressions" in group B (popular literature) was higher.

Table 3. Length of average length of annotation in each project & Number of annotation in category of "Short Expression"

Subject	Project 1	Project 2	
		Group A	Group B
Average number of letters in each Annotation	114.6	69.9	39.4
Number of "Short Expression"	27	6	17
Total Number of Annotations	298	89	65
Percentage of "Short Expression"	9%	7%	26%

In the interviews after the project, one participant reported that he read the popular literature genre for entertainment purposes and he did not have a reason to muse about the text and make long annotations. Another participant in the popular literature group said that he was anxious to find a spoiler from others' comments.

4.3 Degree of Fine-Grained Interactions

Regarding the degree of fine-grained interactions, almost 90% of annotations were based on a specific paragraph in the project 1. This result shows that the social e-book can promote fine-grained interactions. Realizing fine-grained interactions is difficult in previous methods of discussion such as book community websites and offline book clubs.

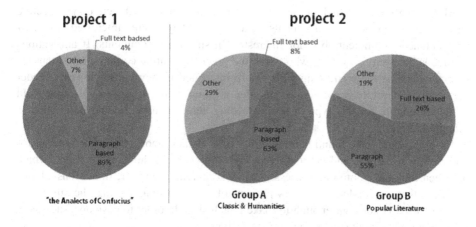

Fig. 5. Rates of Paragraph based annotation & Full text based annotation

When we compared group A (classic & humanities) and group B (popular literature) regarding the degree of fine-grained interactions, the rate of annotations that refer to the text overall was higher in group B. We found that readers have a tendency to make annotations after finishing reading and refer to their appreciation of the whole story when they read the popular literature genre.

5   Discussion

Among the 42 participants who were interviewed after the projects, 85% reported that they were willing to use the social e-book again and that they had positive responses regarding the use of the social e-books. However, six participants said that they did not want to use it anymore, and their reasons were various. One participant stated that because it is a web-based e-book, there were too many temptations to use other websites, also stating that it was difficult to concentrate on the book for this reason. Another participant reported eyestrain from electromagnetic waves. These are problems that all e-book services have to overcome. Another participant reported that social e-books had lower legibility than other types.

In addition, most participants indicated that the social reading experience raised their interest in the book. Participants said that they could learn about other people's thoughts from the social reading activity, but some were not sure if it was helpful to better understand the original text. When we started these two projects, we did not designate a group leader or 'information intellectual'. In order to promote more active participation, it may be helpful to have a group leader who can set up a reading schedule and encourage other members. Moreover, it may be even better if the group has an intellectual who has plenty of knowledge about a chosen book and who can therefore help other members to understand the book. During our projects, there were many questions and assumptions among the annotations, but it was unfortunate that there were not many people who gave correct answers.

Many participants had a tendency to write many subjective perspective annotations, and some participants stated that they were interested in their acquaintances' comments but not interested in stranger's comments. If annotations include subjectivity, knowing who wrote the given annotation could be important for other readers, as the readers might be more interested if they know the other reader personally. Therefore, we could assume that a group with a strong-tie relation would be more suitable for this type of social reading, and this aspect could be applied in school classes.

From this study, we found the possibility of a social e-book as an effective tool for collaborative learning and competitiveness in the classic & humanities genre, which has been thus far ignored as successful e-book content. However, limitations of this study are that we conducted too few projects of social reading and that the number of participants was not high enough to make conclusion. In order to develop a successful service, we need more studies using finer designs.

For future study, more specific ways to improve interest and understanding will be examined for effective collaborative reading experiences through the social e-book. Many experts feel that the end of printed books is not at hand, but we hold that various types of books will appear in the digital era. We expect that a social e-book can promote a reading culture and suggest new directions for future book clubs.

References

1. Ribière, M.: The sBook: towards Social and Personalized Learning Experiences. In: BooksOnline 2010, pp. 3–8 (2010)
2. Müller, H.: How to Carry Over Historic Books into Social Networks. In: BooksOnline 2011, pp. 25–34 (2011)
3. McFall, R.: Experiences Using a Collaborative Electronic Textbook: Bringing the "Guide on the Side" Home With You. In: SIGCSE 2006, pp. 339–343 (2006)
4. Readbuild, a web-based e-book service, http://www.readbuild.com
5. Kim, D.-N.: A study of view about the location of significance of text and the reading process. Korea Reading Association (2003)

Exploratory Study on Online Social Networks User from *SASANG* Constitution–
Focused on Korean Facebook Users

Joung Youn Lee[1], Hyun Suk Kim[2], Eun Jung Choi[3], and Soon Jung Choi[3]

[1] Newmedia Department, Korean German Institute of Technology, Korea
jylee@kgit.ac.kr
[2] Visual Communication, School of Design, Hong Ik University
kylekim@gmail.com
[3] Media Design, Korean German Institute of Technology, Korea
Choi2joy@gmail.com, soonjung89@naver.com

Abstract. This research seeks to adopt and implement *SASANG* Constitution to categorize usage of OSNs by a user's physiological type. An online survey (N=102) was conducted on a Facebook page and to identify Facebook users' *SASANG* Constitution, QSCC II was distributed. All results were collected through email. From the critical literature review, three hypotheses were established, and after a survey the following conclusions were drawn. So-Eum (SE), in comparison to its counterpart So-Yang (SY) who possesses more emotional stability, had less of Facebook usage time and frequency. The introverted So-Eum (SE) with high neuroticism placed more meaning on expression of oneself in their usage of the Facebook. The introverted So-Eum with high neuroticism documented their personal information with higher accuracy. This research focused on analyzing OSN usage patterns as seen through user's personality factors. This research was the first attempt in Korea to explore *SASANG* Constitution and OSN users' Constitution, thus had its innate research limits. Yet, nonetheless, it sheds light into the untapped area of researching a design as seen through OSN user's Constitution.

Keywords: *SASANG* Constitutional Theory, Five Factor Model, Personality, Online Social Networks.

1 Introduction

From broadcasting to interpersonal conversations, the modern internet has been presented as a combination of all previous technologies [4]. With these capabilities, the internet has created shift in paradigm of communication practices. One of consequences of the changes is various forms of computer mediated communication (CMC) has become one of major source of social interaction. Because online interactions generate more self-disclosure and fostered deeper personal questions than did face to face (FtF) conversations, CMC may results in a stronger relationship than might be possible through FtF methods [11].

A.A. Ozok and P. Zaphiris (Eds.): OCSC/HCII 2013, LNCS 8029, pp. 58–66, 2013.
© Springer-Verlag Berlin Heidelberg 2013

One of most famous OSNs in Korea, Facebook have users which account for about 18% of the entire Korean population. This growing new trend has prompted researchers to become interested in what types of people rely on online social media tools in their interactions with others [10, 18]. OSN, like Facebook, provides users with a unique CMC environment where individuals can disclose their thoughts, feelings, and experiences within their circle of personal-ties. Having access to the OSNs, however, is different from having access to the content that resides on it [23]. If people lack of motivation, appropriate skills, cognitive ability, and self-confidence assertively use the OSNs, a large portion of them may get left behind socially, economically and politically [19]. The arrival of OSNs population has shown the emergence of a new paradigm of digital divide.

In the beginning, the digital divide was conceptualized as a gap between those who do and those who do not have access to digital technologies. Since growth of social media usage, research on the digital divide is moving beyond physical access to a multifaceted concept of access that involves cognitive access, social access, and differentiated uses of the web. Although this new area has also focused on socio-demographic predictors, it has incorporated other factors that affect the usage, such as social and personality predictors [5].

The Five Factor Model, one of personality traits, which had been used in the management and psychology fields to predict user's attitudes and behavior, begun to examine the of psychological factors individual's use of technology, such as OSNs. The reason for personality predictor is growing dominant factor in OSNs research is OSNs' inherent interpersonal nature and self-disclosure aspects. But [1, 2] argues that many web designers perceive users as a homogeneous group and take no account of personality differences and this results rack of fulfilling individual needs and drives "second-level digital divide".

This research seeks to adopt and implement *SASANG* Constitution, which is proven to have high reproducibility that brings together physiological and pathological aspects. The purpose of this study is to examine the role of *SASANG* Constitution in Facebook usage.

2   Literature Review

2.1   Personality Traits and OSNs Uses

The personality theory considered by many to have the most relevance to the social aspects of the Internet is Five Factor Model [10]. This Big Five framework is model of personality that contains five factor representing personality traits as broad level: extraversion, neuroticism, openness to experiences, agreeableness, and conscientiousness. Each factor is bi-polar (e.g., extraversion vs introversion) and brief description of these traits is [10]:

— Neuroticism reflects a person's tendency to experience psychological distress and high levels of the trait are associated with sensitivity to threat.

- Extraversion reflects a person's tendency to be sociable and able to experience positive emotions.
- Openness to Experience represents an individual's willingness to consider alternative approaches, be intellectually curious and enjoy artistic pursuits.
- Agreeableness represents aspect of interpersonal behavior, reflecting a tendency to be trusting, sympathetic and cooperative.
- Conscientiousness reflects the degree to which an individual is organized, diligent and scrupulous

Early researches [1, 2] of examining personality and internet uses determined introversion and neuroticism were significantly related online activities. [4] concluded that people who are introverts or neurotic because of their difficulties in social interactions will locate "real me" through the internet; and extroverts and low non-neurotic people will locate their "real me" through traditional social interactions. Because it's anonymity of the internet environment at that time would made hypotheses more related to introvert and neurotic.

However after restriction on anonymity in many OSNs, researches have reflected a reversal association between personality and internet uses. Most people use OSNs to interact with people they already know [16]. As such OSNs may be more likely to interact in extravert way.

The meaningful personality traits of FFM that exert influence on OSNs can be sorted into three main traits-, neuroticism, extroversion and openness to experience [1, 2, 4]. In this research, we will only look into neuroticism and extroversion that have a positive correlation with *SASANG* Constitution.

Neuroticism explains emotional stability and anxiety and predicts a person's degree of sensitivity, it is stated that high neuroticism makes use of Internet out of loneliness and emotional instability [1, 2] and that individual depends on the Internet for communication purposes. People who exhibit high on neuroticism tend to spend more time on OSNs than extraverts [1, 21] or low level of Neuroticism [3], because they use OSNs to make themselves as attractive as possible [18] on online. Also people who exhibit neurotic tendencies like to use chat rooms [1] and instant messaging [11]. [3] found that highly neurotic people were more likely to post private information on their Facebook profile than those in the less neurotic group because more neurotic people for control over information[6].

Extraversion refers to the extent to which individuals are social, cheerful, optimistic, active and talkative. Individuals high in extraversion are expected to engage in high amounts of social interaction and approach others more easily [18]. [3] reported extraverts engaging in less divulgence of personal information on their Facebook profiles. These findings suggest that extraversion is more closely related to personal disclosure of one's current activities and thoughts as opposed to established interests, favorites and relationship status. A person with a strong tendency toward introversion possesses weaker self-regard and prefers to express individual true identity on line, whereas extroverts would prefer to express individual true identity in an off-line environment [1, 11]. [3] suggested that extraverts would see social networks as places to share information and opinions rather than as a substitute for real interaction. Studies also claim that introverted people with high levels of neuroticism document personal information more accurately [1, 13].

2.2   *SASANG* Constitution

According to SASANG Constitutional Theory, the individual differences in behavioral patterns, nature, physical characteristics, and susceptibility to certain diseases are based on people's bio-psychological traits. Despite its potential value in constructing personalized and integrative medicine, traits of *SASANG* types have not been studied in a quantitative and scientific manner, barring their development and propagation to other countries and cultures [8].

SASANG Constitution was systematically theorized in the book Dong-Yi-Soo-Bo-Won (The Principle of Life Preservation in Oriental Medicine) [17] by Jae Ma Lee in the field of traditional Korean Medicine. In *SASANG* Constitution, humans are classified into four *SASANG* types; Tae-Yang (TY), So-Yang (SY), Tae-Eum (TE), and So-Eum (SE). Each type has unique characteristics, as explained below [24].

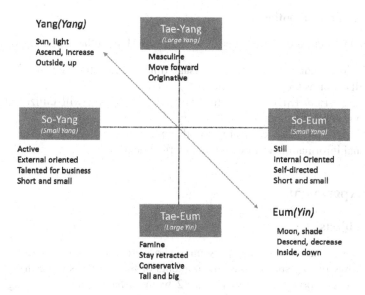

Fig. 1. SASANG Constitution

— T'ae-Yang (TY) types have large lungs and a small liver. They are usually creative, genuine, and visionary people who have good judgment, strong ambition, and charismatic leadership. Statistically, this type is quite rare (about 0.05% in population).

— T'ae-Eum (TE) types have large livers and small lungs. The personality is conservative and cautious, not outgoing, but reticent, quiet, in general. This type exhibits perseverant and outstanding leadership, and it has the largest portion among four types (about 50%).

— So-Yang (SY) types have large spleens and small kidneys. They tend to be extro-verts and progressive. This type is also passionate and inquisitive (about 30%).
— So-Eum (SE) types are generally short and small, and they usually have large kid-neys and a small spleen. Their personality is generally adorable, obedient, kind, prudent, and inactive (about 20%).

For the purpose of categorizing *SASANG* Constitution with Facebook users, the corre-lation between *SASANG* Constitution, neuroticism and extroversion are summarized through the literature review as below [8, 9].

Table 1. SASANG Constitution and Personlaity Traits(FFM)

	Extroversion	*Introversion*
High Neuroticism	Tea-Yang (TY)	So-Eum (SE)
Low Neuroticism	So-Yang (SY)	Tea-Yin (TE)

2.3   Research Hypothesis

Based on the literature review, the following research hypothesis can be posited.

H1. The frequency of Facebook usage time for So-Eum (SE) and So-Yang (SY) will differ as they are opposite to each other.
H2. So-Eum (SE), unlike other physiological types, will utilize Facebook to express his/her emotions and identity.
H3. So-Eum (SE), compared to other physiological types, will document per-sonal information accurately and in large quantities.

3   Experiment

3.1   Subjects

Surveys were conducted on 102 personnel who were a researcher's Facebook friends, which allows for the subjects and the contents of their profiles to be inspected. The sample was comprised of 60 men and 42 women, having an average age of 29.12 years (SD=5.81). An online survey was conducted on a Facebook page for the dura-tion of 20 days (Aug, 1 – 20, 2012). To identify Facebook users' *SASANG* Constitu-tion, QSCC II was distributed and results were collected through email.

3.2   Measures

QSCCII (Questionnaire for *SASANG* Constitution Classification II) is a *SASANG* Constitution-based inventory, which was developed by the Department of *SASANG* Medicine at Kyung Hee Medical Center (Seoul, Korea) in 1993. It has been also validated using 265 subjects from the Department of *SASANG* Constitutional

Medicine or Oriental Medicine & Western Medicine Cooperative Health Examination Center, Kyung Hee University Medical Center. The QSCC is composed of 121 forced-choice items. The internal consistency (Cronbach's alpha) of this inventory was 0.57, 0.59 and 0.63 for the SY, TE and SE types, respectively [4]. The *SASANG* Constitution of an individual was determined following two procedures. *SASANG* type was determined using PC-based software.

3.3   Facebook Questionnaire

The online Facebook Questionnaire was a 10-item questionnaire which was designed to measure basic Facebook use, motives of use and personal information posting on Facebook profile. Basic use items were designed to collect information about the use of common functions on Facebook, such as time spent using Facebook, frequency of visit, time spent on site and number of Facebook friends. From the previous research 6 items (social and contents investigation, communication, social connection, content gratification, self-expression or self-disclosure and social surfing) were used to assess the different motives towards Facebook. Participants were also asked to indicate what categories of personal information they had posted on their profiles. Response formats on this tool ranged from dichotomous item to five-point rating scales with a number of items requiring a numeric response.

4   Results

To determine whether Facebook usage time differs by physiological type, cross-tabulation was used. Table 2 below demonstrates that 41.7 % of So-Eum (SE) users were into the Facebook for more than an hour per day, scoring the highest.

Table 2. Facebook Time Spend

Time Spend	TE(%)	SY(%)	SE(%)
Less than 30 min	29.4	36.4	33.3
30min to 1hour	47.1	36.4	25.0
1hour to 2hours	17.6	9.1	16.7
2hours to 3hours	5.9	9.1	8.3
More than 3hours	0.0	9.1	16.7

As the Table 3 indicates, when looking at the frequency of site access, So-Eum (SE) scored the least in the category of 'less than five times', while scoring the highest in the category of 'almost continuously'. From this, we can interpret that, compared with So-Eum (SE), So-Yang (SY) spares less time for Facebook, hence validating Hypothesis 1.

Table 3. Frequecy of Facebook access

Frequency	TE(%)	SY(%)	SE(%)
Less than 5 times	35.3	36.4	25.0
5 to 10 times	35.3	22.7	33.3
10 to 15 times	5.9	22.7	8.3
15 to 20 times	17.6	18.2	8.3
Almost continuously	5.9	0.0	25.0

The second hypothesis aims to identify the differing purposes for using Facebook by physiological type. For analysis, we used ANOVA with 0.05 measure point. As Table 4 below suggests, Tae-Eum (TE) and So-Eum (SE) stated that they use Facebook to express themselves, but So-Yang (SY) scored less in that category (p = 0.009). This validates the claim that Tae-Eum (TE) and So-Eum (SE) with higher neuroticism make use of Facebook to express their emotional states and situations.

Table 4. Motivation of Facebook use

Time Spend	TE (average value)	SY (average value)	SE (average value)
Social Investigation	1.76	1.95	1.5
Communication*	4.11	3.59	4.25
Social Connection	3.94	3.81	4.0
Contents Gratification	2.47	2.36	2.33
Self-Expression/Disclosure***	3.29	2.22	3.41
To hang out*	3.29	2.68	3,33

$\cdot p<0.05, \cdot\cdot p<0.01, \cdot\cdot\cdot<0.001$

The Third Hypothesis aimed to determine whether there are differences in terms of filling in Facebook profile categories according to *SASANG* Constitution. Except for the 'living in' category, So-Eum (SE) scored the highest for filling in and writing most of the profile categories.

Table 5. Facebook Profile List

Profile List	TE(%)	SY(%)	SE(%)
About you	61.1	52.6	75.0
Basic Info	94.4	84.2	100.0
Contact Info	44.4	42.1	66.7
Living	66.7	31.6	58.3
Work & Education	33.3	52.6	75.0
Favorite Quotation	22.2	21.1	25.0
ETC	0.0	10.5	0.0

5   Conclusion

This research focused on analyzing OSN usage patterns as seen through user's personality factors. It sought to verify the hypotheses that were proposed to assess the correlation between *SASANG* Constitution and personality factors. From the critical literature review, three hypotheses were established, and after a survey the following conclusions were drawn.

1. So-Eum (SE), in comparison to its counterpart So-Yang (SY) who possesses more emotional stability, had less of Facebook usage time and frequency.
2. The introverted So-Eum (SE) with high neuroticism placed more meaning on expression of oneself in their usage of the Facebook.
3. The introverted So-Eum with high neuroticism documented their personal information with higher accuracy.

Realizing the limitations of this research, future research will take the following forms. First, the difference in usage of Facebook by *SASANG* type will spill over into looking not just at the Facebook but OSNs' other functions as well. For instance, interface design factors will be arranged in detail to suggest a design guideline and experiments for different physiological types.

This research was the first attempt in Korea to explore *SASANG* Constitution and OSN users' Constitution, thus had its innate research limits. Yet, nonetheless, it sheds light into the untapped area of researching a design as seen through OSN user's Constitution.

References

1. Amichai-Hamburger, Y., Ben-Artzi, E.: Loneliness and Internet use. Computers in Human Behavior 19(1), 71–80 (2003)
2. Amichai-Hamburger, Y., Vinitzky, G.: Social network use and personality. Computers in Human Behavior 26, 1289–1295 (2010)
3. Amiel, T., Sargent, S.: Individual differences in Internet usage motives. Computers in Human Behavior 20(6), 711–726 (2004)
4. Bargh, J.A., McKenna, K.Y.A.: Can you see the "real me"? A theory of relationship formation on the Internet. Journal of Social Issues 58(1), 33–48 (2002)
5. Boyd, D., Heer, J.: Profiles as conversation: Networked identity performance on Friendster. In: Proceedings of theThirty-Ninth Hawai'i International Conference on System Sciences. IEEE Press, Los Alamitos (2006)
6. Butt, S., Phillips, J.: Personality and self-reported mobile phone use. Computers in Human Behavior 24(2), 346–360 (2008)
7. Chae, H., Lyoo, I.K., Lee, S.J., Cho, S., Bae: An alternative way to individualized medicine: psychological and physical traits of Sasang typology. The Journal of Alternative and Complementary Medicine 9(4), 519–528 (2003)
8. Chae, H., Park, S.H., Lee, S.J., Kim, M.G., Wedding, D., Kwon, Y.K.: Psychological profile of SASANG Constitution: a systematic review. Evidence Based Complement Alternative Medicine (2009)

9. Chae, H., Park, S.H., Lee, S.J.: Hippocrates, Eysenck and the SASANG typology. European Psychiatry 26(1), 1013–1023 (2011)
10. Correa, T., Hinsley, A.W., Zuniga, H.: Who Interacts on Web?: The intersection of user's personality and socialmedia use. Computers in Human Behavior 26, 247–253 (2010)
11. Ehrenberg, A., Juckes, S., White, K.M., Walsh, S.P.: Personality and self-esteem as predictors of young people's technology use. Cyber-Psychology & Behavior 11(6), 739–741 (2008)
12. Ellison, N.B., Steinfeld, C., Lampe, C.: The benefits of Facebook "Friends:" Social capital and college students' use of online social network sites. Journal of Computer-Mediated Communication (2007)
13. Gross, R., Acquisti, A.: Information revelation and privacy in online social networks (The Facebook case). In: Proceedings of ACM Workshop on Privacy in the Electronic Society, pp. 71–80 (2005)
14. Hargittai, E.: Whose space? Differences among users and non-users of social network sites. Journal of Computer-Mediated Communication 13(1), article 14 (2007), http://jcmc.indiana.edu/vol13/issue1/hargittai.html
15. Kim, S., Ko, B., Song, I.: A study on the standardization of QSCC (Questionnaire for the SASANG Constitution Classification). J. Korean Orient. Med. Soc. 17, 337–393 (1996)
16. Lampe, C., Ellison, N., Steinfield, C.: The benefits of Facebook "friends": Social capital and college students' use of online social network sites. Journal of Computer-Mediated Communication 12(4), 1143–1168 (2007)
17. Lee, J.M.: Dong-Yi-Soo-Se-Bo-Won. Lee Jae Ma, Seoul, Korea (1894)
18. Moore, K., McElroy, J.C.: The influence of personality on Facebook usage, wall postings, and regret. Computers in Human Behavior 38(10), 267–274 (2012)
19. Newhagen, J.N., Bucy, E.P.: Routes to media access. In: Newhagen, J.N., Bucy, E.P. (eds.) Media Access: Social and Psychological Dimensions of New Technology Use. Lawrence Erlbaum Associates, Mahwah (2004)
20. Sheldon, P.: Student favorite: Facebook and motives for its use. Southwestern Mass Communication Journal 23(2), 39–53 (2008)
21. Tidwell, L.C., Walther, J.B.: Computer-mediated communication effects on disclosure, impressions, and interpersonal evaluations: Getting to know one another a bit at a time. Human Communication Research 28(3), 317–348 (2002)
22. Ross, C., Orr, E.S., Sisic, M., Arseneault, J.M., Simmering, M.G., Orr, R.R.: Personality and motivations associated with Facebook use. Computers in Human Behavior 25(2), 578–586 (2009)
23. Van Dijk, J.: Divides in succession: Possession, skills, and use of new media for social participation. In: Media Access: Social and Psychological Dimensions of New Technology Use, pp. 233–254. Lawrence Erlbaum Associates, Mahwah (2004)
24. The Association of Korean Oriental Medicine official Site, http://www.akom.org/eng/theory/tI12.html

Readability Assessment of Policies and Procedures of Social Networking Sites

Gabriele Meiselwitz

Department of Computer and Information Sciences,
Towson University
8000 York Road
Towson, MD, 21252, USA
gmeiselwitz@towson.edu

Abstract. Many internet users today are members of social network sites, building personal profiles and interacting with millions of users worldwide. These virtual environments are based on Web 2.0 technology and offer rich user interaction, personalized use of the environment, and the option for sophisticated user-created content. Some of these environments have developed into large communities with complex relationships within the community, which are covered by policies and procedures. Users accept these when they sign up with the site, and many find that these policies and procedures can be quite complex and difficult to read. A large number of participants in these environments are children or teenagers, making it even more important to ensure that all users fully understand what these policies and procedures entail. Even adult users often have trouble understanding and applying the policies and procedures, and in many cases users just accept the default when registering with the site. This paper addresses the readability of such statements and evaluates the comprehension difficulty of standard policies and procedures of selected social network sites. It concludes with a summary and suggestions for future research.

Keywords: Readability, Comprehension Difficulty, Policies, Procedures, Social Networking Sites.

1 Introduction

Social networking sites are very popular with teenagers and adults, and many internet users participate in more than one social network. The growth of social network users is part of a technological movement referred to as Web 2.0, which involves user participation, where users are actively producing and sharing information [9,11]. Expanding on the social connection in Web 2.0, the semantic web (sometimes referred to as Web 3.0) promotes structuring data on the web to enable better organization of web content and facilitate better information sharing and collaboration [11]. These trends of sharing personal and other information and organizing this information make it necessary to define relationships within and between online social communities, and most communities cover these in their online policies and procedures.

A.A. Ozok and P. Zaphiris (Eds.): OCSC/HCII 2013, LNCS 8029, pp. 67–75, 2013.
© Springer-Verlag Berlin Heidelberg 2013

The majority of teens (82%) who are online participate in social networks, and over 50% of adults have accounts on social networks, with many internet users having more than one account or profile and/or participating in several social networks [8]. Currently, most social networking sites have default policies that users agree to when signing up for participation in such sites. Although most sites offer changing of certain elements in their default policies and procedures, users tend not to change the default settings, experiencing changing of the defaults as a burden, and even perceiving them as authoritative recommendations [12]. In addition, many users experience difficulty when reading these policies; they find them overly complex, difficult to understand, and have little knowledge about how and when sites may change their policies and how these changes will be communicated to the user [5,6,10]. Users frequently decide not to read policies because it takes considerable time and efforts to locate, read, and analyze them. Studies have shown that it took users an average of 35 minutes to locate and analyze privacy policies of e-commerce sites, and that it can take analysts up to several hours to examine each policy [10].

In higher education, many instructors already are using Facebook groups, wikis, or blogs; and current Learning Management Systems like Blackboard offer synchronization with student Facebook accounts. New learning paradigms such as connectivism, distributed cognition, and communal constructivism address a shift to community knowledge and learning, making it a necessary for educators to consider social networking integration into their instruction and in support of departmental and faculty collaboration [9].

This project evaluates terms of service policies of twenty social networking sites with possible application in higher education. Policy accessibility is assessed by evaluating how users can locate the policy (e,g, is there a link easily accessible) and how the policy is presented to the user (e.g. one or several pages, downloadable as pdf). Readability is assessed by using several instruments to compute grade level readability scores.

2 Research Method

Twenty social networking sites are evaluated regarding the accessibility and readability of their site specific published policies and procedures. Accessibility of a site's policy for this study is defined as the ease of accessing the policy. Users must be able to find and access the site easily to enable them to read the policy. Frequently, the policy is presented at the time a user creates an account at the site. However, many users elect not to read the policy at all at this time, read only parts of it, or give the text a brief scan, ready to continue with the process of account creation [10]. Moreover, it is preferable to not tie the policy to the sign up process and give users the option to read the policy before they decide to sign up for an account. Therefore, accessibility of the policy was evaluated by assessing the location and presentation of the policy. For example, is the policy easily available on the homepage, does the user have to go through several clicks to access the policy, what is the length of the policy, and what is the file format of the policy (html, pdf, or other).

Readability of the policy assesses the degree to which a user understands and comprehends the content of policy. Several standardized tests are available to assess the readability of text; the most often used is the Flesch Reading Ease Score (FRES) [3]. The FRES computes a final reading score considering average sentence length and average number of syllables per word. Longer words and sentences are more difficult to read and produce a lower reading score. A higher score means an easier reading level [3]. FRES has been used for decades ubiquitously and now is often bundled into word processing software; it is used by the Department of Defense, educational institutions, and several states require that some of their legal documents are written at a particular reading level according to FRES [3,5]. The final score as computed with the FRES can then be translated into a Flesch Grade Level which maps the FRES score to a U.S. grade school level, making it easier to associate the readability level of a certain text with a grade school education level [3,5].

Although the Flesch Reading Ease Score is the most widely used method, other tests are available to assess the reading level. The Gunning-Fog and SMOG indices use a similar method as the FRES, and also compute a final score of grade level. FRES uses total syllables; FOG and SMOG are based on the use of complex words (words with three or more syllables). The Coleman-Liau (CL) index also produces a final score of grade level, however, it relies on numbers of characters rather than the syllable/word approach [3].

For the purpose of this study, multiple methods are used to evaluate the policies of social networking sites. Text will be evaluated using the Flesch grade level, Gunning-Fog, SMOG, and Coleman-Liau assessment to compute an average of the reading level.

One may want to assume that the majority of high school students entering college reads at a 12-th grade reading level, however, research indicates a different trend. The average reading level of adults in the U.S. is at a 7th grade reading level, and research shows that the average reading performance of 12th- grade high school students has been steadily declining [4]. Although female students outperform male students and the percentage of students with parents who graduated from college increased, reading levels have fallen since 1992 (actually since 1985) across all groups [4, 13]. Studies also show that textbooks used by college freshmen are often several grade levels above their reading ability; sometimes over 50% of students have a reading level of several grades below that of the text they are using [2, 7].

Sites for this project were selected using the Wikipedia/Alexa Top 500 social network compilation [14]. The following selection criteria have been applied: sites have to focus mainly on the U.S., must have applicability in higher education, and sites with a higher number of registered users were selected over sites with a lower number of registered users.

The program used to calculate the readability scores of social network site policies in this project is Text-Statistics, a public domain program providing several methods to compute readability scores. The tool was selected because it is available free of charge, calculates several scores, and is able to process HTML files (it will strip all html code from the text file) [1].

3   Results

Results include the evaluation of twenty sites, and evaluate the terms of service policies of the site. Results are discussed by a) evaluating the Flesch Reading Ease Score (FRES) and the Flesch Grade Level (FGL), b) evaluating the average of FGL, FOG, SMOG, and CL and c) comparing results achieved with FGL and FOG, SMOG, and CL.

3.1   Flesch Reading Ease Score and Flesch Grade Level

Table 1 displays the sample of social networking sites including URL, the total number of words, total number of pages, Flesch Reading Ease Score, and Flesch Grade Level. Since all documents were online in HTML format, the number of pages was calculated by allocating 500 words per single spaced page. The total numbers of pages reanges from 3-27, with an average of 9.5 pages per policy.

Table 1. Overview of Sites including URL and FRES and FGL

Site	URL	Words	Pages /500wds	FRES	FGL
Facebook	www.facebook.com	4583	9.17	55.9	8.7
Twitter	www.twitter.com	3504	7.01	42	13.9
Google+	plus.google.com	1699	3.40	53.7	10.5
Pinterest	www.pinterest.com	2290	4.58	49.3	10.6
Mylife	www.mylife.com	6643	13.29	49.4	10.1
Friendster	www.friendster.com	2969	5.94	31.5	16.4
Secondlife	www.secondlife.com	11600	23.20	39.3	14.5
Flickr	www.flickr.com	5656	11.31	47.1	10.2
Youtube	www.youtube.com	3828	7.66	43.7	12.9
Tumblr	www.tumblr.com	5202	10.40	41.4	13.7
Wikipedia	www.wikipedia.org	5817	11.63	38.5	13.9
Xanga (Blog)	www.xanga.com	2733	5.47	31.3	15.7
Blogger	www.blogger.com	1699	3.40	53.7	10.5
Livejournal	www.livejournal.com	5489	10.98	35.2	13.7
Blogspot	www.blogspot.com	1699	3.40	53.7	10.5
Edublogs	www.edublogs.org	2463	4.93	39.8	12.8
LinkedIn	www.linkedin.com	6424	12.85	35.1	13.5
Xing	www.xing.com	3728	7.46	48.7	10.6
Ziggs	www.ziggs.com	3273	6.55	35.9	15.9
Ning	www.ning.com	13654	27.31	37.4	15
Average		**4747.65**	**9.50**	**43.13**	**12.68**
Standard Deviation		**3140.60**	**6.28**	**7.82**	**2.29**

For the social networking sites evaluated, the average FGL was 12.68 (SD=2.29). The most difficult Terms of Service had a FGL of 15.9, roughly equivalent to some-one with an undergraduate college degree. The most readable policy required a read-ing grade level of 8.7, comparable to the reading level of a high school freshman.

All sites have their policies available on the main page, and have direct links to "Terms of Service" and "Privacy". Facebook, however, has a sophisticated structure for policies with several links to the main policy page, and some policies are linked to other policy pages. In addition, Facebook also uses a different naming convention than the other evaluated 19 sites; on the Facebook Site, Terms of Service are referred to as "Terms and Rights and Responsibilities", and Privacy policies are referred to as "Data Use Policy", and include several sections and links.

3.2 Reading Grade Level Using Average of Several Instruments

Table 2 summarized the grade level scores using FGL, FOG, SMOG, and CL. Using several instruments, the average of all surveyed sites is 13.02, representing the read-ing ability of a second year college student. The site with the highest average reading grade level is Friendster, with an average reading grade level of 15.20, the site with the most readable policy again is Facebook with a reading grade level of 10.23, representing the reading level of a college sophomore. Gunning-Fog produces the highest scores, with some scores ranging up to 18, which is comparable to a post graduate college education. This may possibly be due to the fact that the Gunning-Fog index does not take into account that not all multi-syllabic words are difficult, and thus may result in a higher score of difficulty.

Table 2. Average of Sites using FGL, FOG, SMOG, and Coleman-Liau

Site	FGL	FOG	SMOG	Coleman-Liau	AVG FGL/ FOG/SMOG/CL
Facebook	8.7	10.1	8.9	11.7	9.85
Twitter	13.9	16	12	13	13.73
Google+	10.5	12.7	10.1	13	11.58
Pinterest	10.6	11.7	10.3	13	11.40
Mylife	10.1	11.9	9.7	13.5	11.30
Friendster	16.4	18.4	13.6	13.6	15.50
Secondlife	14.5	16.1	12.3	12.9	13.95
Flickr	10.2	11.8	9.5	14	11.38
Youtube	12.9	14.3	11.4	13.2	12.95
Tumblr	13.7	16	12.5	13.8	14.00
Wikipedia	13.9	16.4	12.5	13.2	14.00
Xanga (Blog)	15.7	17.2	13.1	13.8	14.95
Blogger	10.5	12.7	10.1	13	11.58

Table 2. (*Continued*)

Livejournal	13.7	15.1	12.3	14.9	14.00
Blogspot	10.5	12.7	10.1	13	11.58
Edublogs	12.8	15.2	12.2	14.2	13.60
LinkedIn	13.5	14.7	12.7	14.5	13.85
Xing	10.6	12.9	10.1	12.5	11.53
Ziggs	15.9	18	13.6	13	15.13
Ning	15	16.8	12.6	13.9	14.58
Average	**12.68**	**14.54**	**11.48**	**13.39**	**13.02**
Standard Deviation	**2.29**	**2.35**	**1.47**	**0.73**	**1.60**

3.3   Categories

Figure 1 summarizes the readability status of the terms of service policies of all evaluated social networking sites. The figure illustrates the distribution of site readability across grade levels. Evaluation shows that most policies (55%) require users to read on a college level, 40% of evaluated sites require users to read on a high school $11^{th}/12^{th}$ grade reading level. Only one of the sites has a $9^{th}/10^{th}$ grade reading level, and no sites have a reading level below high school. It should also be considered that this assumes the best case that a graduating high school senior entering college actually reads on a 12th grade reading level. Unfortunately, this only applies to some students.

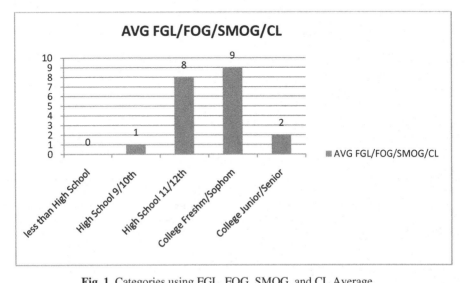

Fig. 1. Categories using FGL, FOG, SMOG, and CL Average

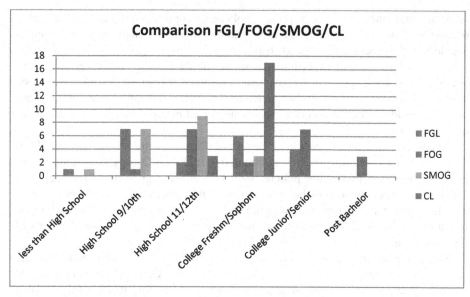

Fig. 2. Categories comparing FGL, FOG, SMOG, and CL

Figure 2 compares all of the used evaluation instruments, the Flesch grade level (FGL), Gunning-Fog (FOG), SMOG, and Coleman-Liau (CL). Comparing all four instruments shows that the majority of sites require an 11th/12th high school grade and college freshman/sophomore reading level. In contrast to FGL, FOG, and SMOG, who all show a somewhat even distribution across high school and college reading levels, the Coleman-Liau index shows a spike at the college freshman/sophomore level, in fact, 85% of all evaluated sites are in this category. Coleman-Liau relies on the total number of characters rather than the syllable/word approach, which may cause this different distribution.

4   Conclusion

This project evaluated the readability of policies of social networking sites. Twenty social networking sites were evaluated, and the evaluation points out that most social networking sites assume a reading grade level beyond a high school reading level. Over half of all sites (51% of the average scores) require a college level reading abili-ty. The average reading level of an adult in the U.S. is a 7th grade reading level, and although the college student population can be assumed to read at a higher level than 7th grade, reading levels of 12th grade high school students have steadily declined over the past years, and many high school seniors entering college read at a level below 12th grade. In addition, considering how many students sign up for social networks before they get to college, the grade level score is clearly beyond the reading abilities of many students at the time they sign up for a user account.

The evaluation concentrated on the main Policy page, the Terms of Services page. Unfortunately, if the main page is requiring a college reading level, it may be suspected that other sites such as privacy policies or copyright policies are at a similar reading level. If a user encounters a high reading level on the main policy page and is unable to fully process the contents, he/she may get discouraged and not even pursue reading other policies or procedures pages. It should also be considered that some policies are of substantial length, page length assumed 500 words per page (appr. one page single spaced), and ranges between 3 and 27 pages, with an average of 9.5 pages per policy, and reading and processing this amount of material may be quite a task for users to tackle.

Considering that all policies of social networking sites are online and in HTML format, the computer science HCI community could significantly contribute to improve the situation of lengthy policies with high reading grade level requirements. The user interface could possibly consider implementations allowing users to configure the presentation form, such as audio or visual image support on demand; or allow users to decide if they want to see the complete policy or view smaller parts of the policy at a time.

Policy creators may also consider software assisting policy makers in developing, writing, and posting policies for the World Wide Web. Online generators could be made available to assist inexperienced site owners in creating meaningful, readable policies. This project was a pilot study to assess readability of social networking site policies, it is planned to continue research on this project by evaluating additional policies on the site, as well as increasing the number of sites evaluated. It is also planned to conduct a more detailed statistical analysis to evaluate the difference between instruments.

References

1. Child, D.: Text-Statistics (2012),
   https://github.com/DaveChild/Text-Statistics
2. Cline, T.: Readability of Community College Textbooks and the Reading Ability of the Students Who Use Them. Journal of Literacy Research 5(2), 110–118 (1972)
3. DuBay, W.H.: The principles of readability. Impact Information, 1–76 (2004)
4. Grigg, W., Donahue, P., Dion, G.: The Nation's Report Card: 12th-Grade Reading and Mathematics. National Center for Education Statistics (2005),
   http://nces.ed.gov/pubsearch/pubsinfo.asp?pubid=2007468
5. Jensen, C., Potts, C.: Privacy Policies as Decision-Making Tools: An Evaluation of Online Privacy Notices. In: Proceedings of Computer Human Interaction (CHI). ACM (2004)
6. Kienle, H., Lober, A., Mueller, H.: Policy and Legal Challenges of Virtual Worlds and Social Network Sites. In: Proceedings of IEEE Conference of Requirements Engineering and Law (2008)
7. Kurzmann, M.: The Reading Ability of College Freshmen Compared to the Readability of Their Textbooks. Reading Improvement (1974)
8. Lenhart, A., Purcell, K., Smith, A., Zuckuhr, K.: Social Media & Mobile Internet Use Among Teens and Young Adults. PewResearch Center (2010),
   http://pewinternet.org/Reports/201/
   Social-Media-and-Young-Adults.aspx

9. Meiselwitz, G., Lazar, J.: Accessibility of Registration Mechanisms in Social Networking Sites. In: Stephanidis, C., et al. (eds.) 2009 Human Computer Interaction Conference Proceedings. ACM (2009)

10. Proctor, R., Ali, M., Vu, K.: Examining Usability of Web Privacy Policies. International Journal of Human-Computer Interaction 24(3), 307–328 (2008)

11. Thompson, J.: Is Education 1.0 ready for Web 2.0 Students? Journal of Online Education 3(4) (2007)

12. Toch, E., Sadeh, N., Hong, J.: Generating Default Privacy Policies for Online Social Networks. In: Proceedings of Computer Human Interaction (CHI). ACM (2010)

13. U.S. Department of Education. Adult Literacy in America. National Center for Education Statistics (2002), http://nces.ed.gov/pubs93/93275.pdf

14. Wikipedia: List of Social Networking Sites, http://en.wikipedia.org/wiki/List_of_social_networking_websites (retrieved online December 22, 2012)

Online Idea Contests:
Identifying Factors for User Retention

Stefan Richter[1], Stefan Perkmann Berger[1], Giordano Koch[2], and Johann Füller[3]

[1] Institute for Entrepreneurship and Innovation, Vienna University, Austria
mail@richter-stefan.info, stefan.perkmann-berger@wu.ac.at
[2] Chair of Public Management, University of Hamburg, Germany
giordano.koch@hyve.de
[3] Department of Strategic Management, Marketing and Tourism, Chair for Innovation
and Entrepreneurship, Innsbruck University School of Management, Austria
johann.fueller@uibk.ac.at

Abstract. Current literature about idea contests has emphasized individuals' motives for joining volunteer idea contests. However, explanation of why people stay or leave in the long run is rare. We identify factors that motivate users to participate repeatedly to sequential online idea contests. The research setting consists of three idea contests carried out by Swarovski, Austria. We accompanied Swarovski during the conceptualization of the idea contests, implementation and post processing activities. We distributed a questionnaire to participants (N= 117) to get insights about their motivation to participate, their experiences in the contest and willingness to participate again. Results not only highlight the importance of pre-contest expectations, but also the importance of the experiences made in previous contests such as the user's perceived fairness.

Keywords: Multiple Idea Contests, User Retention, Motivation, Open Innovation.

1 Introduction

"Given the necessity of generating creative ideas repeatedly, firms have traditionally relied on an internal staff of professional inventors" (Bayus 2010: 1). However, more firms are using the "wisdom of the crowd" to get fresh ideas. Recent examples include: Sony Ericsson Content Award 2008, A1 Innovation Days, Siemens Smart Grid Contest, Lufthansa Air Cargo Innovation Challenge, Swarovski Lifestyle Electronics Design Competition, etc. (cf. Bullinger and Moeslein 2010: 4). As a result firms get access to new ideas within a very short timeframe. Due to the positive results of previous idea contests (Poetz and Schreier 2012) it can be observed that firms (e.g. Siemens, Swarovski, Spar) begin to repeat such contests and consider implementing idea contests as a fixed instrument in their innovation management portfolio. Besides continuous access to innovative ideas repeating idea contests entail further benefits such as building up an innovation community potentially leading to significant cost-saving synergies and expanding the "crowd" which is per se limited to a

A.A. Ozok and P. Zaphiris (Eds.): OCSC/HCII 2013, LNCS 8029, pp. 76–85, 2013.
© Springer-Verlag Berlin Heidelberg 2013

number of individuals (Bullinger et al., 2009). However, establishing a self-sustaining community of innovators seems rather challenging. "Participants of an innovation contest are initially unrelated, come (seemingly) out of the void, are temporarily very active and communicative and then stop their activities and disappear again" (Bullinger et al. 2009: 4). In recent years valuable research was done to gain an understanding why users participate for a first time in such idea contests (e.g. see Bretschneider et al. 2012; Franke and Klausberger 2012). However, explanation of why people stay or leave in the long run is rare (Fang and Neufeld 2009). First insights have been gathered by Fueller (2006) but there is still a lack of understanding about why an individual would contribute repeatedly to virtual co-creation projects initiated by a firm leading us to the following research question: What are the factors that lead to repeated participation in sequential online idea contests hosted by the same firm?

2 Theoretical Background

Idea contests are a form of crowdsourcing, where "… a firm (seeker) … faced with an innovation problem sets up a solution contest involving a number of potential solution providers (solvers) …, in which a pre-announced reward is paid to the solver with the best solution" (Terwiesch and Xu 2008). It follows the same concept that "large groups of people are smarter than an elite few, no matter how brilliant they may be" (Surowiecki 2005: 1). Compared to traditional online market research, individuals are asked not only about their opinions, wants and needs, but also to come up with their own creative solutions, and thus eliminating the sticky information problem (Lilien et al. 2002). There are several studies that analyzed the motivational factors for one-time participation (e.g. Jeppesen and Frederiksen 2006, Fueller et al. 2008). A shared insight is that self-interest is a main driver of user participation (e.g. Franke and Klausberger 2012; Leimeister 2009). Regarding repeated participation, Fueller (2006) states that "initially, one may engage due to the expected value from one's own use of the developed solution; in the long run, enjoyment and fun may drive one's engagement" (Fueller 2010: 103). There are further studies showing that motivations are not stable but rather change over time (Fang and Neufeld, 2009; Shah 2006). For firms which want to retain users over several contests, changes in motivation are relevant to consider. It can be assumed that the majority of the motivational factors explaining one-time-contribution do also play a role for repeated participation. However, motives that attract new users might also be different from those that retain users. To come up with a good, holistic selection of relevant motivational factors, we follow the classification of Fueller (2010) of intrinsic, internalized extrinsic, and extrinsic factors. Two intrinsic motives that have repeatedly shown to influence user participation is the curiosity about such contests (Berlyne 1960; Fueller 2006) and having fun in developing new ideas (Organisciak 2008). Most relevant internalized factors have shown to be the opportunity to develop their skills and to gain new expertise (Amabile 1996; Brabham 2008b), to get recognized by the firm and other via promoting own ideas (Brabham 2010; Leimeister 2009) and the chance to get in contact with interesting people that have the same interest and are willing to share and discuss ideas (Kozinets 2002a). Additionally altruism has been identified as one important driver of user engagement in innovation contests (Bretschneider et al. 2012). Among the extrinsic motives personal need (Franke and Shah 2003; Bretschneider et al. 2012) and receiving monetary incentives (Lerner and Tirole 2000) seem to be important explanatory factors for user participation. However, it seems likely that users following these motives will not participate again as the probability that the firm realizes the idea or that the participant gets the monetary price is pretty low. This could potentially lead to dissatisfaction and with that refusing a repeated participation. These lead to the following hypotheses:

H1a:	*Users who are motivated by **curiosity** are more likely to participate again.*
H1b:	*Users who are motivated by **fun** are more likely to participate again.*
H2a:	*Users who are motivated to **develop their skills** are more likely to participate again.*
H2b:	*Users who are motivated to **promote their ideas** are more likely to participate again.*
H2c:	*Users who are motivated by **altruism** are more likely to participate again.*
H2d:	*Users who are motivated to **make friends** are more likely to participate again.*
H3a:	*Users who are motivated by their **personal need** are less likely to participate again.*
H3b:	*Users who are motivated to win the **prize money** are less likely to participate again.*

Following the expectation-confirmation theory it can be assumed that besides user's expectations or self-interest motives, experience with the contest of the particular firm significantly influence whether someone does something again or not (Bhattacherjee 2001). It has been shown that community functionalities such as social interactions can significantly influence the satisfaction of a user (Chen 2007). Individuals not only participate in idea contests because they are interested in the topic, but also to get in contact with like-minded others (Kozinets 2002b). Experiencing the community itself and social interactions within the community can have a lasting effect on the intention to be part of that community again in the future. Franke et. al (2012: 1) noted that besides self-interest also "fairness perceptions with regard to the distribution of outcomes between the firm and contributors (distributive fairness) and the fairness of the procedures leading to this distribution (procedural fairness) (...)" play an important role in defining user participation. It logically follows that the fairness perceptions through the experience of a user during the idea contest influences his or her decision to participate in future contests.

H4a:	*Users who feel to be **part of the community** are more likely to participate again.*
H4b:	*Users who have **meaningful social interactions** are more likely to participate again.*
H5a:	*Users who perceive the **contest jury** and its **decisions as fair** are more likely to participate again.*
H5b:	*Users who are **satisfied with the distribution of the benefits** between the company and the participants are more likely to participate again.*

3   Methodology

The hypotheses are tested with data generated by the latest two of the three idea contests that were initiated by the jewelry producer Swarovski to date. The second contest was about the creation of jewelry designs, while the third contest was about the creation of creative and innovative lifestyle electronics. Empirical data for this study was collected via an online questionnaire that was distributed to participants of the third design contest initiated by the jewelry producer. The item "I intend to actively participate in future contests by the firm" was included to measure the participant's intention to participate again. Even though the use of an *intention item* has certain limitations, a high correlation between intention and action can been observed in several studies (Chandon et al. 2005). The final sample consisted of 117 observations. 69% of respondents participated for the first time in one of the firm's contests, 21% participated in one previous contest of the firm and 10% participated in both previous contests. Measurement items for the 12 hypotheses were identified through an extensive literature review (Butler et al. 2002; Constant et al. 1996) and the convergent validity has been assessed following Fornell and Larcker (1981). All three conditions for convergent validity were met. Group differences were identified through T-Tests and one-way factorial ANOVA analyses. To investigate repeated participation a more in-depth regression analysis was conducted. We included gender and professional background as control variables. To validate the quality of our empirical model, we analyzed the goodness-of-fit by using the chi-square normalized divided by degrees of freedom (Λ^2/df), which should not exceed 5 (Bentler 1989), and the R^2. Λ^2/df was 2.45 ($\Lambda^2 = 51.402$; df = 21; p < 0.01), suggesting adequate model fit. R^2 was very high as well: 65% of the variance in y is explained by the explanatory variables. In addition to contest three data, we used survey data from the firm's second idea contest, too. This data contained the same motivational constructs as the data from contest three. Thus, by identifying those users who participated in contest two and contest three, we could explore potential differences among users' motivation over time by applying the Mann-Whitney U-Test and the Kolmogorov-Smirnov-Test.

4   Findings

The descriptive results show that while the means are rather low for the extrinsic motives and the community items (including the item *make friends*), they are overly high for all other factors (> 4 on a Likert scale of 1 to 5, with 5 being the highest). First-time participants initially join the contest out of curiosity (mean = 4.64), for fun (mean = 4.70), to develop skills (mean = 4.52), to promote their ideas (mean = 4.60), or due to altruistic reasons (mean = 4.53). In addition to the descriptive results and T-Tests, we established an empirical model that reflects the theoretical model we developed earlier, with factors that allow for testing all established hypotheses (see Table 1).

As can be seen in Table 1 the main motivational factors influencing the intention of first-time participants to participate again in online idea contests of the same firm are *altruism* and *skill development*. In terms of experiences *distributional* and *procedural fairness* significantly influence the intention to participate again. These findings show that community factors (i.e. *sense of community* and *interaction feedback*) do not play a significant role on the intention to participate again for first-time participants. Additionally data shows that taking part in an idea contest strongly shapes the motives of future participation. Repeaters that are taking part to *promote their ideas* and to *make friends* have a higher intention to participate again. In contrast those who are taking part to *develop* their *skills* or which are driven by *altruism* are significantly less likely to participate again. Interestingly the data indicates that participants who are driven by *distributive fairness* are also less likely to participate again.

Table 1. Linear regression results[1]

Independent variable	Beta / Sig.	
Motivation Curiosity	.077	
Motivation Fun *(removed due to multicollinearity issues)*		
Motivation Skill Development	.200	**
Motivation Promotion Ideas	-.163	
Motivation Altruism	.246	***
Motivation Make Friends	-.114	
Motivation Personal Need	-.074	
Motivation Rewards	.006	
Sense of Community	.015	
Interaction Feedback	-.044	
Fairness Procedural	.329	***
Fairness Distributive	.202	**
Gender	.184	*
Hobby Designers	-.385	***
Repeaters	-.025	
Repeaters * Motivation Skill Development	-.415	***
Repeaters * Motivation Promotion Ideas	.719	***
Repeaters * Motivation Altruism	-.446	***
Repeaters * Motivation Make Friends	.614	***
Repeaters * Fairness Distributive	-.537	***
N / R² / Adjusted R²	**117 / .646 / .577**	

The data indicates that motives are not static but rather change over time. To get a better idea about changes in an individual's motive structure on an absolute level we compared the motives of participation between users who participated in contest II and contest III (N= 15).

The results show that the intrinsic motivation for *skill development* and *curiosity* significantly decreases over time for the same individuals. The same holds for extrinsic motives (i.e. *rewards*) that decrease in the long run. Only the motivation of enjoying such challenges (*fun*) increases significantly.[2]

---

[1] Dependent variable: "I intend to actively participate in future contests" | * $p < 0.1$; ** $p < 0.05$; *** $p < 0.01$ | 'Repeaters' Dummy: 0 = First-time participants, 1 = Second and third-time participants.

[2] The factor *Promotion Ideas* has not been available in the questionnaire for contest two.

Table 2. Individual's motivation change over time[3]

Factor	Mean change	Mann-Whitney-U-Test	Kolmogorov-Smirnov-Test
Altruism	↓	ns	ns
Skill Development	↓	ns	**
Curiosity	↓	***	**
Fun	↑	**	***
Rewards	↓	***	**

Additionally we looked at participants of contest II who had a high intention to participate in contest III and compared the means of the motivational factors from those that actually took part in the subsequent contest III (N= 15) with those that did not participate (N= 101). Table 3 shows four significant group differences among those two groups. These results are in line with our empirical regression model as well as the descriptive results. Repeaters seem to be more *altruistic* and more motivated by the *joy of the task* itself. On the other side, repeaters show a lower motivation to *develop* their own *skills* and a lower *identification* with the (brand) *community*.

Thus, not only the comparison of the motivation of repeaters with the motivation of non-repeaters, but also the comparison of repeaters motivation during their first and later participation shows similar changes in motivation over time.

Summing-up, and as confirmed in Table 2 whose data is based on users who participated in contest two and contest three (N= 15), we find no support for H1a as *curiosity* is not significantly influencing the intention to participate again. We find mixed support for H1b, H2a and H2b as *fun* and to *promote ideas* become more important drivers to

Table 3. Binary regression results[4]

Factor	Beta	
Altruism	1.088	**
Fun	2.196	**
Skill Development	-2.292	**
Sense of Community	-0.785	*

participate again in the long-run, while *developing* the proper *skills* is initially important but gets significantly less important over time. *Altruism* is an important driver to participate at first but gets less important over time providing mixed support for H2c. To *make friends* does not influence the intention to participate again but becomes more important in the long-run, providing mixed support for H2d. In line with hypothesis H3a those that are motivated to take part because of their *personal need* are less likely to participate again. The same holds for the motive to *win the prize money*, which reduces the intention to participate again in the future, rejecting H3b. Furthermore, feeling part of a community as well as having meaningful interactions does not seem to lead to a higher intention to participate in the long term as shown in other studies. As there might be alternative explanations we would partially reject H4a and H4b. *Procedural fairness* is influencing the intention to participate again for first-time participants confirming H5a. *Distributional fairness* is negatively influencing the intention to participate in the long run, and with that rejecting H5b.

---

[3] ↓ Factor less important in contest three than in contest two | * p < 0.1; ** p < 0.05; *** p < 0.01 | ns = not significant.

[4] Nagelkerkes R-Q: 0.319 | Omnibus significance: 0.213/0.16/0.16 | * p < 0.1; ** p < 0.05; *** p < 0.01.

5   Discussion

There are a few motivational factors clearly dominating the intention to participate in future idea contests. In contrast to their important role for one-time contribution, extrinsic motives such as *personal need* and *rewards* are not influencing the decision to participate again or not. Even more, we have indications that participants who are highly motivated by extrinsic motives are more likely to not participate again. In contrast internalized extrinsic motives seem to be the most important drivers for the intention to repeatedly participation in idea contests. *Altruism* and *skill development* are both reasons to join the contest for the first time. When it comes to truly intrinsic motives (fun, curiosity) we observe mixed importance for future participation. *Curiosity* is a factor that rather attracts participants for a first-time and less for subsequent participation in idea contests. In contrast *fun* is high among all first-time participants and third-time participants still show a pretty high level of *fun*. In fact, the group comparison shows that those who participated more than once (i.e. contest II and III) are significantly higher motivated by fun than those that participated only in one contest. For those that perceive the participation in idea-contests fun in a first place perceive the participation also highly enjoyable in a second or third time. Thus, the joy of solving the design tasks seems to be an important explanatory variable.

While the *altruistic* motivation and the motivation to *develop your own skills* become less of a reason to participate again, the motives to *make friends* and to *promote ideas* become important drivers. Though the descriptive results indicate that users who join such contests repeatedly are still altruistically motivated, this motive loses its significant importance for future participations compared to other factors. This is similar to the motive to *develop own skills* that seems to get saturated rather quickly. This could be related to the limits of learning possibilities within idea contests. The more extrinsically-oriented motive, which is to *promote your own ideas*, gains importance over time. Users who want to be recognized by the firm for their ideas and creative work are those who are most likely to participate in future contests. Finally, while in the beginning the task provides enough personal satisfaction and is the reason for participating, the idea to *connect with like-minded people* and *make friends* with them becomes more important at a later stage, too.

In addition to the user's expectations or motivational factors, we observe that experience factors from previous contest(s) strongly influence the intention to participate in idea contests by the same firm repeatedly. The results show that while motivational factors change over time experience factors remain rather stable. In this contest, participants perceived the contest as fair and were overly satisfied with the outcomes. Both dimensions of fairness (i.e. procedural fairness and the distributive fairness), were highly significant for further participation in our regression model. However, it seems that the importance of the distributive fairness seems to decrease over time with further participations. Furthermore, community factors had no influence on the future participation intention. The relatively low means of the *sense of community* item and *interaction feedback* item indicate that participants were either not very satisfied with the community or not central for them.

5.1   Theoretical and Managerial Implications

The findings of this paper provide new and relevant insights to the research area about idea contests and extend the initial work of Fueller (2006). Several factors could be observed that drive the user's intention to participate repeatedly in sequential online idea contests hosted by the same firm. It seems that especially those who highly enjoy the creative task itself, who have a high brand passion, and who have a high motivation to get in contact with the firm by promoting their own ideas are not losing interest to take part in future contests. However, we raised attention of significant motivation differences among participants with different number of participations in previous contests. First-time participants might also be driven by altruistic reasons or the chance to further develop their skills to go for a second participation. Yet those motives seem to become less important with further participations. Our findings shed more light on the phenomenon of repeated participation in idea contests and draw interesting implications for firms who conduct idea contests. To ensure idea contests can be implemented as fixed tool for their innovation management, firms need to know how they can retain users over several contests as the crowd is a scarce resource and costly to acquire. It seems to be crucial to appreciate good ideas and stay in contact with the submitter after the contest if such users shall be retained successfully. Those users need to have the feeling that their input is taken seriously and that the firm appreciates their effort. They have most likely a high passion for the brand and are invigorating the community. In addition, users who joined for a second or third time highly enjoy the task itself. A firm needs to think about how it can make sure that this *fun level* is maximized during the contest. This includes aspects like: making the task challenging but fun, giving the user as much autonomy as possible, ensuring interesting discussions in the community, creating a friendly and funny atmosphere during the contest, supporting users whenever necessary, and implement activities (e.g. videos, social media actions) that make the contest *cool and fun*. All these mentioned aspects can help to achieve a critical mass for an idea contest more easily and thus reduce the risk of exhausting the available crowd, which would lead to a failure of future contests. In addition, firms need to understand that a fair contest setting regarding the distribution of the benefits and the selection of the winners are crucial for retaining users in the future. Otherwise users are likely to leave the community and do negative word-of-mouth (Hauer 2009). While for online communities and open source projects the identification with the community is crucial for a long-term user engagement, it seems to be less crucial for idea contests with the short-term existence of a more competitive community.

5.2   Limitations and Further Research

The underlying study contains a number of limitations and potential for further research. Firstly, the number of observations (N= 117) is rather small and with a high number of parameters vs. observations overfitting issues can occur. Even though the predictive performance for some of the factors is limited, we still believe that the main results we observed are reliable and not due to statistical errors. Multiple data points such as descriptive results and the analyses with contest two data helped to validate our main results. A second limitation is that the results are based on one case study only, thus they are industry-specific and might not be applicable for other contests. Thirdly, there might be other factors influencing repeated participation that have not been taken into consideration by our theoretical model e.g. interest in the task, brand passion, autonomy. It would be interesting to observe how motivational factors can also affect the perceived level of fairness or community factors. Additionally, instead of using the *intention level,* actual participation should be tested in a long-term study over several contests and studies in different industries and with different communities should be conducted to generate more insights into this fascinating phenomenon of repeated participations in online idea contests.

References

1. Amabile, T.: Creativity in Context. Westview Press, Boulder (1996)
2. Bayus, B.L.: Crowdsourcing and individual Creativity over Time: The detrimental Effects of past Success. Wired (2010)
3. Bentler, P.M.: EQS Structural Equations Program Manual, BMDP Statistical Software, Los Angeles (1989)
4. Berlyne, D.E.: Conflict, Arousal, and Curiosity. McGraw-Hill, New York (1960)
5. Bhattacherjee, A.: Understanding Information Systems Continuance: An Expectation-Confirmation Model. MIS Quarterly 25(3), 351–370 (2001)
6. Brabham, D.C.: Moving the Crowd At Threadless. Information, Communication & Society 13(8), 1122–1145 (2010)
7. Bretschneider, U., Rajagopalan, B., Leimeister, J.M.: Idea Generation in Virtual Communities for Innovation: The Influence of Participants' Motivation on Idea Quality. In: 45th Hawaii International Conference on System Sciences, Hawaii (2012)
8. Bullinger, A.C., Haller, J., Moeslein, K.M.: Innovation Mobs - Unlocking the Innovation Potential of Virtual Communities Innovation Mobs – Unlocking the Innovation Potential of Virtual Communities. In: AMCIS 2009 Proceedings (2009)
9. Bullinger, A.C., Moeslein, K.M.: Innovation Contests – Where are we? In: AMCIS 2010 Proceedings (2010)
10. Butler, B., Sproull, L., Kiesler, S., Kraut, R.: Community Effort in Online Groups: Who Does the Work and Why? In: Weisband, S., Atwater, L. (eds.) Leadership at a Distance (2002)
11. Chandon, P., Morwitz, V.G., Reinartz, W.J.: Do Intentions Really Predict Behavior? Self-Generated Validity Effects in Survey Research. Journal of Marketing 69(2), 1–14 (2005)
12. Chen, I.Y.L.: The factors influencing members' continuance intentions in professional virtual communities – a longitudinal study. Journal of Information Science 33(4), 451–467 (2007)
13. Constant, D., Sproull, L., Kiesler, S.: The Kindness of Strangers: The Usefulness of Electronic Weak Ties for Technical Advice. Organization Science 7(2), 119–135 (1996)
14. Draper, N., Smith, H.: Applied Regression Analysis. Wiley (1998)
15. Fang, Y., Neufeld, D.: Understanding Sustained Participation in Open Source Software Projects. Journal of Management Information Systems 25(4), 9–50 (2009)
16. Fornell, C., Larcker, D.F.: Evaluating structural equation models with unobservable variables and measurement error. Journal of Marketing Research 18, 39–50 (1981)

17. Franke, N., Klausberger, K.: Exploitation or fair deal? The impact of fairness on users' decision to contribute to "crowdsouring" business models (2012) (forthcoming)
18. Franke, N., Shah, S.: How Communities Support Innovative Activities: An Exploration of Assistance and Sharing Among Innovative Users of Sporting Equipment. Research Policy 32(1), 157–178 (2003)
19. Fueller, F.: Refining Virtual Co-Creation from a Consumer Perspective. California Management Review 52(2) (2010)
20. Fueller, F.: Why Consumers Engage in Virtual New Product Developments Initiated by Producers. Advances in Consumer Research 33, 639–646 (2006)
21. Fueller, F., Matzler, K., Hoppe, M.: Brand Community Members as a Source of Innovation. Journal of Product Innovation Management 25(6), 608–619 (2008)
22. Hauer, S.: Wie Fair Sind Online-Communities Für Ihre User? GRIN Verlag (2009)
23. Jeppesen, L., Frederiksen, L.: Why Do Users Contribute to Firm-Hosted User Communities? The Case of Computer-Controlled Music Instruments. Organization Science 17(1), 45–63 (2006)
24. Kozinets, R.: Can Consumers Escape the Market? Emancipatory Illuminations from Burning Man. Journal of Consumer Research 29(1), 20–38 (2002a)
25. Kozinets, R.: The Field Behind the Screen: Using Netnography for Marketing Research in Online Communications. Journal of Marketing Research 39(1), 61–72 (2002b)
26. Leimeister, J.M., Huber, M., Bretschneider, U., Krcmar, H.: Leveraging Crowd-sourcing: Activation-Supporting Components for IT-Based Ideas Competition. Journal of Management Information Systems 26(1), 197–224 (2009)
27. Lerner, J., Tirole, J.: The Simple Economics of Open Source. National Bureau of Economic Research Working Paper, Cambridge (2000)
28. Lilien, G.L., Morrison, P.D., Searls, K., Sonnack, M., von Hippel, E.: Performance Assessment of the Lead User Idea-Generation Process for New Product Development. Management Science 48(8), 1042–1059 (2002)
29. Organisciak, P.: Motivation of Crowds: The Incentives That Make Crowdsourcing Work (2008), http://crowdstorming.wordpress.com/2008/01/31/motivation-of-crowds-the-incentives-that-make-crowdsourcing-work/ (retrieved August 07, 2012)
30. Poetz, M.K., Schreier, M.: The Value of Crowdsourcing: Can Users really compete with Professionals in Generating New Product Ideas? Innovation. Journal of Product Innovation Management 29(2), 245–256 (2012)
31. Shah, S.: Motivation, Governance, and the Viability of Hybrid Forms in Open Source Software Development. Management Science 52(7), 1000–1014 (2006)
32. Surowiecki, J.: The Wisdom of Crowds. Random House, New York (2005)
33. Terwiesch, C., Xu, Y.: Innovation Contests, Open Innovation, and Multiagent Problem Solving. Management Science 54(9), 1529–1543 (2008)

What Motivates People Use Social Tagging

Ning Sa and Xiaojun Yuan

College of Computing and Information, University at Albany, SUNY, Albany, NY, US
{nsa,xyuan}@albany.edu

Abstract. Motivation for tagging is one of the topics in the research of social tagging systems. Most studies on motivations have focused on tag creators without consideration of tag consumers. In this study, we tried to address this issue with a survey. The survey was conducted through several tagging sites aiming to study the usage of tags on the internet, including why and how people use tags, as well as their perspectives of the existing tagging websites. The results revealed that most frequent tag creators use the tags very often. However, there are users who use others' tags frequently without bothering creating tags by their own. The results also indicate that search is the primary motivation of creating tags as well as using tags. Besides searching, more than half of the respondents selected other types of motivations like "organizing" and "navigation".

Keywords: social tagging, motivation, tag creator, tag consumer.

1 Introduction

Social tagging systems (e.g. decilious.com) enable users to organize their own resources and to search for new information. Related research has covered a broad range of topics, including vocabulary problems [5-7], motivation for tagging [4], [9], [11], [14], and presentations and functions of tags [2], [8], [10], [13].

Research has shown that social tagging system can be better designed to reflect user goals if their incentives of tagging were understood better. Marlow, Naaman, Boyd, and Davis [11] proposed six types of user incentives: future retrieval, contribution and sharing, attract attention, play and competition, self-presentation, and opinion expression. Ames and Naaman [1] further organized tagging motivations by tagging audience and tagging functions on Flickr, the public photo sharing website. They distinguished three categories of audiences: self, family and friends, and the general public. Similar research includes [12] and [3].

However, most of previous studies focused on investigating the user motivations of creating tags.

Tags are created to be used by the tag creators as well as the other users. There might also be users who do not frequently create tags but still use tags a lot for various purposes. Though research has been done on which kind of tasks users could perform with tags, the actual motivations of why users use tags were seldom mentioned. Kim and Rieh [9] investigated user perceptions of tags in an interview and separated "taggers" (tag creators) from non-taggers. They reported that the Web users

A.A. Ozok and P. Zaphiris (Eds.): OCSC/HCII 2013, LNCS 8029, pp. 86–93, 2013.
© Springer-Verlag Berlin Heidelberg 2013

were not certain about the nature and value of tags. However the participants of their interview were Internet users who reported "having seen tags" [9, p672] and were not necessarily frequent tag users.

In this study, we tried to address user motivations by covering both tag creation and tag consumption processes in a survey. The survey was distributed on several popular social tagging websites. We aim to study why and how people use tags, as well as their perspectives of the existing tagging websites. The tagging behavior of the users from different websites was also compared.

In the rest part of this article, we will describe the methodology, results, discussion and conclusions in sequence.

2   Methodology

2.1   Population and Sampling Method

The target population is the users of various social tagging websites. The existing tagging websites are different in terms of type of resources, source of materials, tagging rights, tag representations, etc. We believe that a better evaluation could be made by comparing different systems. As a result, the target tagging sites include flickr.com, last.fm, delicious.com, CiteULike.org, and movielens.umn.edu. These sites were selected based on their popularity and the ease of contacting their users. The survey was distributed by posting topics on the forum and by sending messages directly to the users. Fig. 1 shows the screenshots of some of these sites.

Fig. 1. Resource differences of the tagging websites

2.2   Survey Design

The survey is composed of demographic information and social tagging system use. In the first part, such information as age, job, education, user experiences in search engine usage and social network tool usage was elicited. In the second part, three types of questions were asked, including (1) the frequency of using social tagging system; (2) the motivation and behavior of the users in tag creation process and tag consumption process; and (3) user evaluation on the systems according to their various motivations as well as different tag representations. Table 1 lists some of the critical questions in the survey. It would take the participants around 15 minutes to complete the questionnaire. The survey was based on voluntary and the participants did not receive any compensation.

Table 1. Sample survey questions

Type of the questions	Question
Use frequency	Which is your favorite tagging website?
	How often do you log on to the website?
Tag creation	How often do you create tags?
	What is your purpose when creating tags?
	How often do you pick from your history tags when tagging a resource?
	How often do you choose from recommended tags/tags created by others when tagging a resource?
	How often do you apply your own new tags when tagging a resource?
Tag consumption	How often do you view/use tags created by yourself and others?
	What do you use tag for when using/viewing the tags?

3   Results and Discussion

3.1   Demographic Characteristics and Use Frequency

The survey has 63 completed responses in June through September, 2012. Table 2 summarizes the demographic characteristics of the participants. There are more males than females in the study. 47.6% of the participants are in their twenties and the others range from 30 to 50 and above. 74.6% of the participants have bachelors or higher degree.

Fig. 2 shows the frequency of using tagging websites. Most users (about 76%) used tagging sites very frequently. We further separated the process of tag creating and that of tag using. Table 3 indicates that most frequent tag creators use the tags very often. However, there are users who use others' tags frequently but did not bother creating tags by their own. Thus, a better designed social tagging system is important for these kinds of users. There is no significant difference among participants of different gender and different educational level. However, 87.9% of the participants of age 30+ are frequent tag creators while the rate for participants in their twenties is only 58.6%. This difference is significant (p=0.009).

Table 2. Demographic characteristics of the participants

characteristics	value	# subjects
Gender	Male	50
	Female	13
Age	18-29	30
	30-39	13
	40-49	11
	50-	9
Educational level	Middle school	2
	High school	11
	Bachelor	28
	Master	14
	PhD	5
	other	3

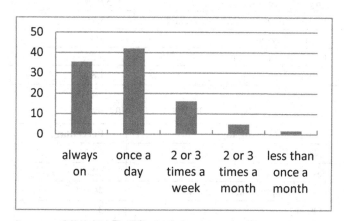

Fig. 2. Frequency of using the tagging websites

Table 3. Tag creators vs. Users

	Frequent user	Non-frequent user
Frequent tag creator	35	8
Non-frequent tag creator	10	6

3.2 User Motivations

In our study, we provided four options of tag creating motivations, i.e. "organize my stuff", "for future retrieval/finding/search", "share and express myself", and "comment or annotate resources provided by others". As shown in table 4, "for future retrieval/finding/search" is the primary motivation to tag (78.8%). After correlating the additional information provided by the users, we discovered that the "future retrieval" refers to the retrieval performed by the users themselves as well as by others. Some users also indicated that they would use their unique tags to make their resources easily retrievable from the crowd. These findings are consistent with the three types of motivation proposed by [11], that is, "future retrieval", "attract attention", and "self-representation". According to table 5, search is the primary motivation for users to use tags. About 82% users use tags for searching. No significant difference was found among participants of different gender, age, and educational degree.

Search is not the only tag creating motivation. Over 50% of users also selected "express myself" and "organize my stuff" as their motivations of creating tags. On the other hand, "navigation" and "get an impression of what the resource is about" are also important reasons of what users use tags for. These findings agree with the results of [11] that most users are motivated by a number of motivations.

Table 4. User motivation of creating tags

Purpose of creating tags	Percentage %
Organize my stuff	57.3%
For future retrieval/finding /search	**78.8%**
Express myself	**59%**
Comment or annotation	26.2%
Other	14.8%

Table 5. User motivation of using tags

Purpose of using tags	Percentage %
Navigation	**55.2%**
Search	**82.8%**
Get an impression of the resource	46.6%
Other	3.4%

3.3   Comparison of User Behavior on Different Websites

Creating Tags for Search

Among the 63 respondents, 46% indicated that their favorite tagging website is Flickr.com while 42.9% said that they visited Last.fm most frequently. Motivations of participants from the two websites were then compared. Participants from both websites put "for future retrieval/finding/search" as their primary purpose of creating tags. However, they responded differently when being asked of "do you think the tags help you in performing the tasks above? Why or why not?". It was observed from the answers that most Flickr users create tags to make their photos easily retrieved by themselves as well as by the others. For example, a Flickr user said:

> *"These tags make finding pictures much easier. I have so many, so it keeps everything straight".*

Another said:

> "*Yes... so others can find my images when they search*".

On the other hand, Last.fm users also use tags to organize, as one participant said:

> "*it makes it much faster to organize things*"

As to search, they are more likely to use tags to explore new music, as one users said:

> "*...it helps me to find similar artists that I may not have yet heard...*".

One possible reason which can be used to explain the difference is the different nature of these two websites. Flickr is a photo sharing website, which means the users upload their photos then share. When they create tags, they are trying to make their own resources retrievable from the thousands of photos. While on Last.fm, there might be fewer users who are there to share their own work. Most users may want to explore songs and bands which are similar to what they are familiar with.

Tagging Behavior

The differences found in tagging purpose may affect the way the users create tags. Table 6 and 7 compares the tagging behavior difference between these two sites. Compared to Last.fm user, Flickr users applied new tags more frequently and selected less recommended tags. Since Flickr users create tags mainly to aid search of their own photos, they may tend to apply unique tags. For Last.fm users, as they search for similar music based on other people's experiences, they may pay more attention to popular and general tags.

Table 6. How often do you apply new tags?

	Most of the time	often	sometimes	seldom	never
Flickr	46.4% (13)	35.7% (10)	10.7% (3)	3.6% (1)	3.6% (1)
Last.fm	24% (6)	8% (2)	56% (14)	8% (2)	4% (1)

Table 7. How often do you choose from recommended tags/tags created by others when tagging a resource?

	Most of the time	often	sometimes	Seldom	Not applicable
Flickr	3.6% (1)	14.3% (4)	50% (14)	14.3% (4)	17.9% (5)
Last.fm	12% (3)	60% (15)	24% (6)	0% (0)	4% (1)

4   Conclusions

In this study, a survey was conducted, aiming to find out the user motivations of creating tags as well as using tags. The survey was targeted at frequent users on several popular social tagging websites. The results indicate that besides frequent tag creators, there are frequent tag consumers who use tags frequently but do not create tags often. The needs of this type of users have been underestimated in the previous studies.   The result reveals that users create and use tags for multiple reasons. However, the primary reason of creating and using tags is "search". We also found that the different tagging behaviors among different website users could result from different interpretation of "search". The Flickr users create tags to facilitate future search for their own photos performed by themselves as well as by the others so they might want to apply more unique tags. The Last.fm users care more about exploring music similar to what they are familiar with so they might use more general and recommended tags.

This study generated some interesting findings. But limitations exist in terms of the limited number of participants and questions asked in the survey. Based on the results that most people create tags to facilitate future retrieval and use tags to search, our next step will be about how to better perform search with tags. The new study will involve user interface design for facilitating tag creation process and searching process.

References

1. Ames, M., Naaman, M.: Why we tag: motivations for annotation in mobile and online media. In: Proceedings of the SIGCHI Conference on Human Factors in Computing Systems, CHI 2007, pp. 971–980. ACM, New York (2007), doi:10.1145/1240624.1240772
2. Bateman, S., Gutwin, C., Nacenta, M.: Seeing things in the clouds: the effect of visual features on tag cloud selections. In: Proceedings of the Nineteenth ACM Conference on Hypertext and Hypermedia, HT 2008, pp. 193–202. ACM, New York (2008), doi:10.1145/1379092.1379130
3. Beenen, G., Ling, K., Wang, X., Chang, K., Frankowski, D., Resnick, P., Kraut, R.E.: Using social psychology to motivate contributions to online communities. In: Proceedings of the 2004 ACM Conference on Computer Supported Cooperative Work, CSCW 2004, pp. 212–221. ACM, New York (2004), doi:10.1145/1031607.1031642
4. Belkin, N.J.: Anomalous states of knowledge as a basis for information retrieval. Canadian Journal of Information Science 5, 133–143 (1980)
5. Furnas, G.W., Landauer, T.K., Gomez, L.M., Dumais, S.T.: The vocabulary problem in human-system communication. Commun. ACM 30(11), 964–971 (1987), doi:10.1145/32206.32212
6. Furnas, G.W., Fake, C., von Ahn, L., Schachter, J., Golder, S., Fox, K., Davis, M., et al.: Why do tagging systems work? In: CHI 2006 Extended Abstracts on Human Factors in Computing Systems, CHI EA 2006, pp. 36–39. ACM, New York (2006), doi:10.1145/1125451.1125462
7. Golder, S., Huberman, B.: Usage patterns of collaborative tagging systems. Journal of Information Science 32(2), 198–208 (2006)

8. Halvey, M.J., Keane, M.T.: An assessment of tag presentation techniques. In: Proceedings of the 16th International Conference on World Wide Web, WWW 2007, pp. 1313–1314. ACM, New York (2007), doi:10.1145/1242572.1242826

9. Kim, Y.-M., Rieh, S.Y.: User perceptions of the role and value of tags. In: Proc. CHI 2011, pp. 671–674. ACM, Vancouver (2011)

10. Kuo, B.Y.-L., Hentrich, T., Good, B.M., Wilkinson, M.D.: Tag clouds for summarizing web search results. In: Proceedings of the 16th International Conference on World Wide Web, WWW 2007, pp. 1203–1204. ACM, New York (2007), doi:10.1145/1242572.1242766

11. Marlow, C., Naaman, M., Boyd, D., Davis, M.: HT06, tagging paper, taxonomy, Flickr, academic article, to read. In: Proceedings of the Seventeenth Conference on Hypertext and Hypermedia, HYPERTEXT 2006, pp. 31–40. ACM, New York (2006), doi:10.1145/1149941.1149949

12. Moore, T.D., Serva, M.A.: Understanding member motivation for contributing to different types of virtual communities: a proposed framework. In: Proceedings of the 2007 ACM SIGMIS CPR Conference on Computer Personnel Research: The Global Information Technology Workforce, SIGMIS CPR 2007, pp. 153–158. ACM, New York (2007), doi:10.1145/1235000.1235035

13. Rivadeneira, A.W., Gruen, D.M., Muller, M.J., Millen, D.R.: Getting our head in the clouds: toward evaluation studies of tagclouds. In: Proceedings of the SIGCHI Conference on Human Factors in Computing Systems, CHI 2007, pp. 995–998. ACM, New York (2007), doi:10.1145/1240624.1240775

14. Yuan, X., Belkin, N.J.: Investigating information retrieval support techniques for different information-seeking strategies. Journal of the American Society for Information Science and Technology 61(8), 1543–1563 (2010)

Understanding Social Network Sites (SNSs) Preferences: Personality, Motivation, and Happiness Matters

Yuanyuan Shi, Xitong Yue, and Jin He

Institute of Psychology, Chinese Academy of Sciences
4A, Datun Road, Beijing, China
{Shiyy,Yuext,Hej}@Psych.ac.cn

Abstract. Chinese Social Network Sites (SNSs), such as Qzone, Renren, Weibo, have attracted millions of users, many of whom have integrated SNSs surfing into daily practices. In this research, we aimed to understand people's preferences for particular SNSs and some specific features of SNS, and explore the impacts of personality and motivations on SNSs usage. In Study 1, we compared the personalities, motivations and SNSs behaviors of Chinese major SNSs users. Study 2 focused on the relationship between motivation and happiness on SNSs. Finally, we drew a script on the way and reason for choosing a particular SNS and favoring specific features of each SNS.

Keywords: Social Network Site (SNS), Personality, Motivation, Subjective Well-being (SWB).

1 Introduction

Internet has introduced major changes in our social lives [1], and it is a leading social arena where people can meet and interact with others. Social network sites (SNSs) are defined as web-based services that allow individuals to construct a public or semi-public profile, sharing text, images, and photos, and to share connections with a certain list of other users on the Internet [2]. Since the first introduction, SNSs, such as MySpace, Facebook, Cyworld (in Korea), Bebo (in Britain) and Renren (in China) have attracted millions of users, many of whom have integrated SNSs surfing into daily practices.

1.1 SNSs Users' Motivations

In general, individuals flock to social network sites for maintaining relationships [2] but users' motivations might vary from site to site, and usually individual show obvious preference to particular SNS. Specifically, for Westerners, sites like MySpace and Facebook attract users with social motivations, while sites like LinkedIn are used by individuals looking forward to establishing professional or business contacts [3]. However, there are few researches on SNSs preferences and how they come into being.

A.A. Ozok and P. Zaphiris (Eds.): OCSC/HCII 2013, LNCS 8029, pp. 94–103, 2013.
© Springer-Verlag Berlin Heidelberg 2013

Researchers discovered that both internal (enjoyment) and external (usefulness) factors affect users' to continue using SNSs [4]. As an information technology, an SNS user cares about whether the SNS allows him (or her) to effectively build and maintain relationships among the mechanisms that allow strangers to become acquainted and keep in touch, and that provides for the individual to form profiles and enable people to reach out toward one another [5, 6]. As a pleasure-oriented information system, SNS users keep using with stronger motivation if they have more intense perceived enjoyment from it [7, 8].

According to recent research, enjoyment is the most influential factor affecting continued intention to use SNS for both men and women [4]. In the SNSs, both the rich and the poor would get richer [9]. That is to say, those have better social skills and more friends and those with social deficits and less friends may both satisfy their social needs [10]. By the further investigating users' motivations, satisfaction towards life and SNSs behaviors, we can get to know the role Internet serves in our real life.

1.2   Personality and SNSs Usage

In SNSs, people extend real life and communicate with their real personality [11], and profiles can be seen as a form of digital body where individuals write themselves into being[2]. Thus, social network sites provide rich sources of naturalistic behavioral data, and it's a good chance to explore people's personality in the cyber virtual world. Of the cast array of human personality traits, the majority can be subsumed within five broad domains ---- extraversion-introversion, antagonism-agreeableness, conscientiousness, neuroticism, and openness to experience, which has been known as the Big Five [12].

Collectively, the five dimensions predict most of the outcomes that truly matter in life [14]. Several of the Big Five personality factors are believed to be associated with the way individuals interact with each other and maintain their social relationships. Due to its relevance to social behavior, the Big Five factors have recently been employed to investigate the use of certain forms of online social media, such as social networking sites [15-18] and blogs [19]. Researchers have found that, compared to nonusers, SNSs users are more likely to be extraverted and narcissistic, less likely to be conscientious, shy, or socially lonely, but they also have stronger feelings of family loneliness [18]. However, few researches have explored the personality variance among different kinds of SNSs.

1.3   Aims of Current Study

In this research, we aimed to understand people's preferences for particular SNSs and particular SNS features, and explore the impacts of personality and motivations on SNSs usage. In Study 1, we compared the personalities, motivations and SNSs behaviors of users on different Chinese major SNSs. Study2 focused on the relationship between motivation and happiness on SNSs. Finally, we would draw a script on how and why people choose to use a particular SNS or a particular SNS feature. The expected findings would likely help SNS product designers to locate target market, and improve interacting designs and user experience. This is the first try to identify SNSs users with personality, motivation and life satisfaction.

2　Study 1: Personality, Motivations and SNSs Usage

In Study 1, we explored the different SNSs users' personality, motivations and their SNSs usage.

2.1　Participants

328 volunteers took part in Study 1, 198 of them are females, and the majority of them were students. Their age ranked from 17 to 45, and the average age was 22.73 (SD =3.36).

2.2　Methods

First of all, we conducted a pilot survey to identify the most popular SNSs in China. A list of SNSs both domestic and abroad were given, and participants were asked to choose the SNSs they had accounts and profiles. Thus, we got the top 3 Chinese SNSs: Qzone, Renren, and Sina Weibo.

In the formal study, Participants completed a package of questionnaires including the SNS behavior questionnaire, the motivations to use SNSs, and the Big Five Personality Inventory.

SNS Behaviors. We revised a Facebook Questionnaire [16] into 3 versions(Renren, Qzone , and Weibo) to measure participants SNSs behaviors, such as participant's frequency in updating their profiles, the degree they caring about visitors' comments and other necessary information. Participants were required to point one SNS they were using most frequently, recall their regular activities in this website, and complete only one questionnaire of the most frequently used SNS. Each item of the SNS questionnaire is on 4-point scale (1 = not at all, 4= very much).

Motivations. Participants were asked the reasons for visiting SNSs by multiple choices from a list of 11 items, namely, "I visit social network sites to keep in touch with my old friends", "I visit social network sites to relax", "I visit social network sites to get information", "I visit social network sites because I think it might be helpful for my work", "I visit social network sites to kill time", "I visit social network sites to communicate my hobbies", "I visit social network sites to record my life", "I visit social network sites to meet new friends", "I visit social network sites to keep in touch with my family", "I visit social network sites to show off and display myself", "I visit social network sites to get a sense of belonging". Besides multiple choices, an open-end question was added in the end.

Personality. Participants were asked to complete personality scale the 50-item Big Five Personality Inventory. The scale consisted of the following five personality factors: agreeableness (e.g., "I can understand the feelings of others"), neuroticism (e.g., "I'm moody"), extraversion (e.g., "I am talkative"), conscientiousness (e.g., "I work meticulously"), and openness to experience (e.g., "I am imaginative"). 10 items for each factor and each item was evaluated on a 6-point Likert scale, ranging from "strongly disagree" to "strongly agree". The internal consistency coefficient was good for both the whole Big Five scales ($\alpha = 0.86$) and each of the subscales: agreeableness ($\alpha = 0.74$), neuroticism ($\alpha = 0.86$), extraversion ($\alpha = 0.86$), conscientiousness ($\alpha = 0.79$), and openness to experience ($\alpha = 0.83$).

2.3 Results and Discussion

Popularity. When asking participants to name their favorite SNS, 40.18% users preferred Qzone, 36.50% said Renren, and 19.33% chose Weibo. As results showed, significantly, 1) Qzone users shared the longest SNS usage experience ($M_{SNS\text{-}age} = 5.05$), Renren the second ($M_{SNS\text{-}age} = 4.62$), and Weibo the shortest ($M_{SNS\text{-}age} = 2.86$), just in the same order that they were introduced to ordinary people; 2) Qzone had the youngest user group ($M_{age} = 22.2$), and Weibo users were more mature ($M_{age} = 23.72$), $F = 4.616$, $p = 0.011$; 3) Weibo users visited their sites more frequently, about 3.5 day a week, significantly higher than Renren ($M = 3.11$) and Qzone users ($M = 3.24$), $F = 3.03$, $p = 0.05$, and they also spent a little more time on the site, about 1.5 hours.

Motivations and SNSs Usage. According to the result of motivation questionnaire, we found people used SNSs to: 1) keep contact with old friends (90.08%) and family(33.33%); 2) relax(73.97%) and kill time(60.95%); 3) get more information(60.32%) and facilitate their work(62.86%); 4) communicate their hobbies(39.68%) and make new friends (35.56%); 5) record life events(50.16%), display themselves(27.30%), and finally find a sense of belonging(13.65%). In general, it consisted with a research conducted in Western country [3]. As mentioned above, this result also support that enjoyment (e.g. relax, killing time) and usefulness (e.g. contacting old friends, making new friends) are two main factors affecting people continue using SNSs [4].

Besides, we compared motivations variation between different genders, and found that: females would like to use SNSs to contact with their old friends(93.43%), significant higher than males(81.40%), $t = 3.41$, $p = 0.001$; more females thought SNSs would be helpful for their work(69.19%), significant higher than males(55.04%), $t = 2.62$, $p = 0.009$; females intended to believe they would get more information in SNSs(66.67%), significant higher than males(52.71%), $t = 2.55$, $p = 0.011$; besides, more female (56.06%) than males (40.31%) would like to use SNSs to record their life, $t = 2.81$, $p = 0.005$.

When making multiple comparisons among different SNSs' users, we found: people believed they could get more information in Weibo ($F = 3.65$, $p = 0.027$), and meet more new friends in Renren, $F = 1.45$, $p = 0.236$, and tie to their family more closely in Qzone, $F = 4.43$, $p = 0.013$. As consequence of this, the SNSs behaviors data properly proved the results of the motivation variation. Results showed, Renren users significantly had more friends ($F = 23.05$, $p < 0.001$), used more private message ($F = 37.54$, $p < 0.001$), and updated more photos($F = 7.58$, $p < 0.001$); although they'd like to search new friends, the acquaintance still took up a large part of their SNSs friends group. Whereas, Weibo users were also more likely to search strangers and add new friends, thus, they had more friends who they have no actual ties with ($F = 55.58$, $p < 0.001$); besides, they updated states more frequently ($F = 2.55$, $p = 0.079$) but updated fewer photos than Renren users. Qzone users had a significant large proportion of friends that they met in the reality, updated more blogs ($F = 2.35$, $p = 0.097$), and also cared more about the others' feedback.

Personality and SNSs Usage. Although multiple comparison of personality showed there was little difference among the personalities of different SNS users, but pairwise comparison indicated Renren users were more extroverts than Weibo ($F = 2.96$, $p = .049$).

We combined behavior data of different SNSs together, and for each behavior we performed a standard multiple regression analysis with gender, the Big Five Personality factors as the independent variables (see table 1). According to the regression analysis, in the dimensions of Big Five personality traits, the extroverts tended to be more active in the SNSs: they had more friends, updated their profiles more frequently, gave more feedback and also cared more about others' comments, and they were more likely to make new friends and share their profiles. Besides, those who scored higher on consciousness had more friends that they know in the reality, while net friends took up a larger proportion for people getting a high score in the openness. What's more, open people used more applications and spent more time in playing games. The agreeable tended to give more feedback. Meanwhile, the neuroticism gave less feedback, but care more about others comment towards themselves.

Table 1. Regression analyses of gender, age, Big Five personality factors on SNS usage

	NF	PF	PM	US	UB	UP	SP	GF	CF	SS	PG
GEN	0.08	-0.06	0.08	-0.13*	0.05	-0.07	-0.05	-0.09	-0.10$^+$	0.19***	0.02
AGE	-0.08	-0.15**	0.13*	0.05	0.23***	-0.07	0.11*	0.03	-0.10$^+$	0.11*	0.11$^+$
AGR	0.03	0.08	0.01	0.03	0.07	0.05	0.06	0.16**	0.01	-0.08	-0.10$^+$
NEU	-0.01	0.01$^+$	-0.09	0.01	0.00	0.05	-0.02	0.02	-0.18**	-0.01	-0.04
EXT	0.27***	0.07	0.13*	0.19***	0.15**	0.33***	0.21***	0.20***	0.24***	0.21***	0.09
CON	0.07	0.12*	-0.04	-0.05	-0.07	0.05	0.05	0.02	0.05	0.08	-0.02
OPE	0.05	-0.19***	0.06	0.08	0.06	-0.06	-0.03	-0.01	-0.07	0.01	0.15*
R^2	0.09***	0.07***	0.03*	0.06***	0.07***	0.12***	0.04**	0.08***	0.07***	0.08***	0.03*

Note: NF = number of friends; PF= proportion of friends; PM = private message; US = update states; UB = update blogs; UP = update photos; SI = self-image; SP = share profiles; GF = give feedback; CF = care feedback; SS = search strangers; PG = play games; GEN = gender; AGR = Agreeableness; NEU = neuroticism; EXT = Extraversion; CON = consciousness; OPE = openness; + $p <.1$; * $p < .05$; ** $p < .01$; *** $p < .001$.

The results consisted with former study, which suggested that agreeableness was positively related to favorably commenting on SNS [19], extraversion was correlated with the communicative features of SNS [15, 17], openness to experience was correlated with the use of a wide variety of SNSs features[14]. Besides, conscientious individuals upload significantly fewer profiles to SNS, and used less SNS features, which suggested that conscientious individuals tended to spent less time on SNS [17], because these sites promoted procrastination and served as a distraction from more important tasks [20].

2.4   Conclusions

In summary, our data suggest that, personality and motivation impact the preference for SNSs:

1. College students prefer Renren, which requires users to use real information; thus, they could make more friends that have actual ties with their real life. Renren provides a platform that helps users enhance their actual social relationships, which has attracted a lot of users who want to extend their social environment on the internet. Renren's real-name registration sets a limit to users behaviors, and users shall be responsible for every word they have typed. As a result, Renren users would use more private messages, and appear to be more extraverted.
2. Weibo appeals to more adults' appetite. Since anonymity means somewhat duty-free, Weibo users believe, they can get more information about society and social life. They are more likely to update states, and would like to communicate with people of different social backgrounds, as a result of which, they have more friends that have no actual tie. Weibo provides a platform to see the world in different views; thus, Weibo users seem to be more open, but have less interests in playing games.
3. Owing to the widely use of Tencent QQ (a popular instant messaging software service), Qzone has the widest range of user group. Although anonymity, Qzone users have a strong motivation to keep contract with old friends and family members; as a result, people met in real life still take up a large proportion of users' Qzone friends. Qzone provides a platform to record life, where users could seat alone and write in peace, that's why Qzone users are more likely to write blogs instead of short states.

3   Study 2: Happiness and SNSs Usage

In prior study, we find quite a lot of people seek fun in the SNSs, then, are people really happy in the SNSs? In the second study, we test the relationships between SNS behaviors and subjective well-being.

3.1   Participants

89 volunteers took part in Study2, 51 of them are females. The average age was 23.83 (SD =5.044).

3.2   Methods

Besides recoding participants' SNS behaviors and their motivations, we measured their happiness level.

SWB. Subjective well-being (SWB), which is often referred to more colloquially as happiness, reflects the extent to which people think and feel that their life is going well [21]. SWB, in fact, is "a broad category of phenomena that includes people's emotional responses, domain satisfactions, and global judgments of life satisfaction" [22, 23]. Specifically, reported SWB consists of two distinctive components [24]: an affective part, which refers to both the presence of positive affect and the absence of negative affect, and a cognitive part. The affective part is a hedonic evaluation guided by emotions and feelings, while the cognitive part is an information-based appraisal of one's life for which people judge the extent to which their life so far measures up to their expectations and resembles their envisioned "ideal" life.

As consequence of this, to measure the cognitive evaluations of life satisfaction, we used a 5-item Satisfaction With Life Scale (SWLS)[25]. This 7-piont Likert scale required subjects to view satisfaction with life as a whole, including past, current and future, and the internal consistency coefficient of the scale is good (α =0.88). To measure the affective aspects of SWB, we used an 8-item Affective Experience Scale (AES). In this 7-point Likert scale, 4 pleasant affects (happiness, contentment, joy, cheer) and 4 unpleasant affect(sadness, worry, anger, and unhappy) are included to measure participants' on-line evaluation of their mood or emotions. The internal consistency coefficient of the scale is also good (α =0.83).

3.3   Results and Discussion

We found that there was no differences on either cognition part or affection part of SWB among different SNSs users .

Motivations and SWB. We conducted correlations between SNSs users' motivation and their SWB level, and found that: a) those whose intention was contacting their family seemed to be more satisfied with their life (r =0.45, p < 0.001); b) and those whose motivation was making new friends appeared to have more positive emotions in SNSs (r =0.24, p = 0.027); c) however, those who wanted to kill time by using SNS feel less happy in the SNS(r = -0.26, p = 0.016). That is to say, people's happy experience would increase only when having a social motivation to maintain using SNSs, while those who want to seek pure fun would feel lonely and vanity instead.

SNS Usage and SWB. We computed correlations between SNSs usage and SWB level, and found that both cognition and affection part were significantly correlated with the time users had contacted with SNSs (r =0.23, p = 0.036; r = 0.27, p = 0.012), but no significant correlation with the frequency or time spend in SNSs (rs <0.06). That is to say, people may benefit more if they have used SNSs for enough years, when having constructed stable social networks and utilized certain SNS features with facility.

More importantly, there was a significantly correlation between certain SNSs usage and happiness, for example, the use of private message, updating blogs, and playing games were significantly correlated with cognition part of SWB, and updating photos and making comments were significantly correlated with both cognition and affection parts of SWB. To further analysis, for each part of SWB as the dependent variables we performed a standard multiple regression analysis with gender, age, and SNSs behaviors as the independent variables.   Results showed, in SNSs, frequency of updating photos and giving comments were impotent predictors of both cognition part (β =.29, t = 2.361, p =.021; β = .38, t =2.49, p =.015) and affection part of SWB(β =.29, t = 2.20, p =.031; β = .29, t =1.72, p =.089); however, caring others' comments could be a negative predictor of cognition part of SWB (β =-.26, t = -2.12, p =.038). However, other SNS behaviors were not significant predictors of either cognition part or affection part . This indicates the happiest SNSs users are those who have a larger proportion of acquaintance, update more photos, give more feedback, and care less about others' comments.

3.4   Conclusions

Different people surf different SNSs to make their ends meet, as consequence of which, users would feel equally both cognition part and affection part of SWB among different SNSs. However, it seems that a happy SNS users is the one who has a large proportion of acquaintance, updates photos and gives feedback frequently, and cares less about others' comments. Besides, people may benefit more if they have used SNSs for enough years, when they have constructed stable social networks and utilized certain SNS features with facility. What's more, people's happy experience would increase only when having a social motivation to maintain using SNSs, while those who want to seek pure joy would feel lonely and vanity instead.

4   General Conclusions

In the first study, after a series of surveys conducted among users of Chinese major SNSs, we carefully compared the similarities and differences between different SNS users, and explored the relationships among their personality, motivation and SNSs usage. The results suggest that, generally speaking, gender, age, and personality factors impact the choosing of SNS and provide clues for understanding their behaviors. This research recommends that SNS operators develop specific applications for the demands of different genders, different age groups, and different personality.

More importantly, our second study explores the happiness level of SNS users. Prior study has proved that people who have a larger number of self-defining identities are better prepared to face changes and stresses in life[26]. By interaction with others in the SNSs, people get new identities, which results in increased feelings of self-worth and acceptance. If defined properly, the "role rich" also experience better health [27, 28] and greater satisfaction with their real lives [29]. That is to say, when using properly, SNSs would increase people's positive emotions and satisfaction with life. These results would promote network externalities development and encourage more people to use such a platform, which of course make SNSs industry another booming.

References

1. Amichai-Hamburger, Y.: Internet and personality. Computers in Human Behavior 18(1), 1–10 (2002)
2. Ellison, N.B.: Social network sites: Definition, history, and scholarship. Journal of Computer-Mediated Communication 13(1), 210–230 (2007)
3. Lenhart, A.: Adults and social network websites. Pew Internet and American Life Project 14 (2009)
4. Lin, K.Y., Lu, H.P.: Why people use social networking sites: An empirical study integrating network externalities and motivation theory. Computers in Human Behavior 27(3), 1152–1161 (2011)
5. Pfeil, U., Arjan, R., Zaphiris, P.: Age differences in online social networking–A study of user profiles and the social capital divide among teenagers and older users in MySpace. Computers in Human Behavior 25(3), 643–654 (2009)
6. Li, C., Bernoff, J.: Groundswell. Winning in a World Transformed by Social Technologies. Harvard Business Press (2008)
7. Kang, Y.S., Lee, H.: Understanding the role of an IT artifact in online service continuance: An extended perspective of user satisfaction. Computers in Human Behavior 26(3), 353–364 (2010)
8. Sledgianowski, D., Kulviwat, S.: Using social network sites: The effects of playfulness, critical mass and trust in a hedonic context. Journal of Computer Information Systems 49(4), 74–83 (2009)
9. Amichai-Hamburger, Y., Kaplan, H., Dorpatcheon, N.: Click to the past: The impact of extroversion by users of nostalgic websites on the use of Internet social services. Computers in Human Behavior 24(5), 1907–1912 (2008)
10. Amichai-Hamburger, Y.: The social net: understanding human behavior in cyberspace. Oxford University Press (2005)
11. Back, M.D., Stopfer, J.M., Vazire, S., Gaddis, S., Schmukle, S.C., Egloff, B., Gosling, S.D.: Facebook profiles reflect actual personality, not self-idealization. Psychological Science 21(3), 372–374 (2010)
12. Goldberg, L.R.: An alternative "description of personality": the big-five factor structure. Journal of Personality and Social Psychology 59(6), 1216–1229 (1990)
13. Robins, R.W.: The nature of personality: Genes, culture, and national character. Science 310(5745), 62–63 (2005)
14. Amichai-Hamburger, Y., Vinitzky, G.: Social network use and personality. Computers in Human Behavior 26(6), 1289–1295 (2010)
15. Correa, T., Hinsley, A.W., De Zuniga, H.G.: Who interacts on the Web?: The intersection of users' personality and social media use. Computers in Human Behavior 26(2), 247–253 (2010)
16. Ross, C., Orr, E.S., Sisic, M., Arseneault, J.M., Simmering, M.G., Orr, R.R.: Personality and motivations associated with Facebook use. Computers in Human Behavior 25(2), 578–586 (2009)

17. Ryan, T., Xenos, S.: Who uses Facebook? An investigation into the relationship between the Big Five, shyness, narcissism, loneliness, and Facebook usage. Computers in Human Behavior 27, 1658–1664 (2011)
18. Guadagno, R.E., Okdie, B.M., Eno, C.A.: Who blogs? Personality predictors of blogging. Computers in Human Behavior 24(5), 1993–2004 (2008)
19. Wang, J.L., Jackson, L.A., Zhang, D.J., Su, Z.Q.: The relationships among the Big Five Personality factors, self-esteem, narcissism, and sensation-seeking to Chinese University students' uses of social networking sites (SNSs). Computers in Human Behavior 28, 2313–2319 (2012)
20. Butt, S., Phillips, J.G.: Personality and self reported mobile phone use. Computers in Human Behavior 24(2), 346–360 (2008)
21. Lucas, R.E., Diener, E.: Personality and subjective well-being. In: The Science of Subjective Well-Being, pp. 171–194 (2008)
22. Diener, E., Lucas, R.E.: Personality and subjective well-being. In: Kahneman, D., Diener, E., Schwarz, N. (eds.) Well-Being: The Foundations of Hedonic Psychology, pp. 213–229. Sage Foundation, New York (1999)
23. Diener, E., Suh, E.M., Lucas, R.E., Smith, H.L.: Subjective well-being: Three decades of progress. Psychological Bulletin 125(2), 276–302 (1999)
24. Diener, E.: Assessing subjective well-being: Progress and opportunities. Social Indicators Research 31(2), 103–157 (1994)
25. Diener, E., Emmons, R.A., Larsen, R.J., Griffin, S.: The satisfaction with life scale. Journal of Personality Assessment 49(1), 71–75 (1985)
26. McKenna, K.Y., Bargh, J.A.: Plan 9 from cyberspace: The implications of the Internet for personality and social psychology. Personality and Social Psychology Review 4(1), 57–75 (2000)
27. Verbrugge, L.M.: Multiple roles and physical health of women and men. Journal of Health and Social Behavior, 16–30 (1983)
28. Linville, P.W.: Self-complexity and affective extremity: Don't put all of your eggs in one cognitive basket. Social Cognition 3(1), 94–120 (1985)
29. Spreitzer, E., Snyder, E.E., Larson, D.L.: Multiple roles and psychological well-being. Sociological Focus 12(2), 141–148 (1979)

Influence of Monetary and Non-monetary Incentives on Students' Behavior in Blended Learning Settings in Higher Education

Stefan Stieglitz[1], Annika Eschmeier[1], and Michael Steiner[2]

[1] University of Münster, Department of Information Systems, Leonardo-Campus 11, 48149 Münster, Germany
{stefan.stieglitz,annika.eschmeier}@uni-muenster.de
[2] University of Münster, Marketing Center Münster, Am Stadtgraben 13-15, 48143 Münster, Germany
michael.steiner@uni-muenster.de

Abstract. Previous research shows that blended learning has the ability to increase the learners' motivation and learning success. However, motivational aspects in blended learning have not been sufficiently researched yet. We therefore investigated the influence of non-monetary and monetary incentives on learners' behavior. We selected "likes" as a non-monetary incentive and enabled students to rate other students' posts (similar to Facebook). In a second turn, a monetary incentive (a tablet PC or the cash equivalent, respectively) was raffled among the students of a top 10 "like"-ranking. Based on log-file data and survey results, we observe that both variations ((1) only "likes" and (2) "likes" & tablet PC prize) do not differ with respect of their influence on the overall activity of learners during the lecture. Thus, the additional monetary incentive did not increase activity. We conclude that monetary incentives do not seem to be efficient.

Keywords: blended learning, incentives, lecture, higher education.

1 Introduction

A well-known problem in higher education is that it is hardly possible to activate all students into learning content in mass lectures. This hampers knowledge inclusion since students can often hardly follow the course content at some point in time. Earlier studies show that blended learning has the potential to increase learners' motivation and learning success [1-3]. Furthermore, the increasing competition among universities forces them to provide better learning conditions. In this sense, support of blended learning could be an enabler to raise the attractiveness of universities for students [4].

Blended learning is understood as a combined approach of e-learning and presence learning. Social media, e.g., discussion forums or blogs, have been identified as appropriate platforms to support learners' interaction among each other or with lecturers

A.A. Ozok and P. Zaphiris (Eds.): OCSC/HCII 2013, LNCS 8029, pp. 104–112, 2013.
© Springer-Verlag Berlin Heidelberg 2013

[5,6]. These applications provide lecturers as well as students with new potentials to improve learning success. Students can, for example, discuss lecture content in a forum and solve problems on their own. Blended learning works best when integrated in a vivid community [7]. However, most learning communities only exist for a short period of time (e.g., during one semester) and are rather designed as a community of instruction and not "naturally" grown. Therefore, motivating students to participate in such settings voluntarily is a major challenge.

Despite their high relevance, motivational aspects in blended learning have not been sufficiently researched yet. We therefore address the following question: How do non-monetary and monetary incentives affect learners regarding their participation in blended learning approaches?

In order to contribute to this research question, we conducted a case study on a learning community consisting of 564 students. In this setting, we selected "likes" as a non-monetary incentive and implemented a functionality in a learning platform which allows students to rate other students' posts (similar to Facebook). These "likes" were publicly visible. Additionally, a public ranking of the students (based on the number of "likes") was published in the learning system. A tablet PC (or its monetary equivalent) was selected as monetary incentive. Common wisdom would suggest that both types of incentives potentially increase activity. However, monetary incentives may have little or no effect at all. Based on 5 surveys, we were better able to understand the impact of both types of incentives.

The remainder of the paper is structured as followed: First we discuss relevant academic literature in the field. We then explain the methodology we applied to answer our research question. In the next chapter we discuss the results. The article ends with a conclusion and some aspects of further research potentials.

2 Literature Review

2.1 Blended Learning

Over the last decade, blended learning gained much importance in higher education. Reasons for that are improvements of information and communication technology (ICT) solutions and a growing pressure on universities and lecturers to support new learning approaches [8-10]. Moore [11] presented a framework of three types of interaction that influence distance education: a) learner-content interaction, b) learner-instructor interaction, and c) learner-learner interaction.

E-learning systems are aimed at supporting students to interact across time and space, and foster the individuals' contribution to learning [5, 12]. E-learning systems generally comprise a set of tools to support e-learning such as Wikis, blogs, chats, file sharing etc. [13]. In contrast to e-Learning, blended learning combines face-to-face elements and online lectures/exercises [7, 14]. Heterick & Twigg [15] found that blended learning has the potential to be more effective and efficient than the traditional classroom model alone because students can continue to discuss content between the lectures. As stated above, blended learning works best when integrated in a vivid community of inquiry [7].

Communities of inquiry (CoI) commonly consists of three elements: cognitive, social, and teaching presence [16]. The learning model in CoI is based on constructivism that means that fostering self-education enables learning (i.e., students are able to construct their understanding of the context individually). Blended learning offers the possibility to engage students into CoIs for creating self-determined learning contexts.

2.2   Satisfaction and Incentives in E-Learning Environments

Previous research shows that motivating students to participate actively in e-learning environments is a major challenge in large scale lectures [17]. We therefore assess the influence of two types of extrinsic incentives on learners' activity and satisfaction with an e-learning environment. Namely, we assess the influence of a non-monetary incentive type (number of "likes") and a monetary incentive (a tablet PC or 500 € cash equivalent) within a learning contest.

Increasing learners' activity (posting and reading behavior) is our major goal. Moreover, overall satisfaction is another element for students' motivation [18]. Therefore and in line with previous research [17, 19-24], we also assess satisfaction with a lecture to evaluate the incentives' influence.

We selected "likes" as a non-monetary incentive as previous studies showed that such social learning components may strongly influence learners' motivation [23]. "Likes" (similar to those on Facebook) can be interpreted as peer-based ratings and may increase learning environments' efficiency [17]. Additionally, "likes" do not only influence learners' behavior (they are more likely to read texts that received more "likes") but also indicate a certain status of a learner within the community. Thus, "likes" are an option to gain social acceptance from peers [23].

Monetary incentives may also motivate students to participate actively and benefit from a learning environment. For example, cash prizes or products could be raffled among the students. Monetary incentives differ from non-monetary incentives with respect to two aspects. The most obvious difference is in their very nature (their financial value). Moreover, monetary incentives target different student groups. While everybody can get a "like" (i.e., the number of "likes" is "unlimited") only one or very few students can get the monetary incentive (i.e., the number of prizes within learning contests is usually limited to one or very few). While non-monetary incentives are targeted to any student in the e-learning community, monetary incentives are only relevant to very few (e.g., the 10% best) students. The majority of students might not be motivated by this kind of incentive as they might not expect to have a chance of winning the prize. Due to these specific characteristics, monetary incentives may have two opposite effects. They may motivate the best students to participate more actively in the E-learning community and to post more in a forum. Every other student would benefit from this specific knowledge. However, monetary incentives could also have negative effects. For example, students could try to manipulate a learning competition in order to increase their odds of winning the prize. If other students discover such manipulation, overall activity and satisfaction with the E-Learning environment may decrease.

In summary, we expect a positive influence from non-monetary incentives (e.g., social media components such as "likes") and positive as well as negative effects from monetary incentives on learners' satisfaction within an e-learning environment.

3   Empirical Study

In order to address our research question, we investigated the impact of different incentives in a blended learning scenario with 564 students. The lecture (marketing on bachelor level) was held at a major German university in April-June 2012 and consisted of two parts, each lasting for one month (moreover, the exam was one month after the last lecture).

We investigate two types of data: log files from the databases of the learning environment and survey data. We analyzed the number of pages viewed and students "likes" in detail. This quantitative data provides insights about usage patterns of the participating students. Moreover, we conducted five surveys in order to analyze the effects of incentives on learners' perceptions and satisfaction.

We tested the non-monetary incentive ("likes") in the first part of the lecture (i.e., over a period of one month). The first two surveys assess the effect of this incentive. At the beginning of the second part of the lecture, the monetary incentive was introduced and a tablet PC was raffled among the students from a top 10 "like" ranking from the first part (but students had not been aware of this incentive before this lecture). Afterwards, the lecturer explained that he would raffle a second tablet PC among the top 10 students at the end the second part of the lecture. Thus, from now on we assessed the combined effect of "likes" and a monetary incentive. A survey was conducted after this session to assess the immediate effect of this monetary incentive, followed by two additional surveys (one after the last lecture and one after the exam) to assess its long-term effect.

4   Results and Discussion

4.1   Descriptive Data

Overall, 564 students registered to the e-learning system. Figure 1 provides an overview of the forum's aggregated weekly number of page views. User activity increased two weeks after the start of the lecture and remained stable for the remainder of the lecture. There is one peak in Figure 1 after the end of the lecture and just before the exam, which might not come as a surprise as students start studying more intently close to the final exam.

The number of "likes" by students are presented in Figure 2. Clearly, we again observe a peak at the end of the lecture. The two peaks (in Figure 1 and 2) are close. However, they differ with respect to their timing. Students' "liking" activity increased in week 7, however, overall student activity (number of pages accessed, see Figure 1) peaks in week 8. Thus, "liking" behavior is not correlated with overall activity in the e-learning community. Figure 2 also shows that introducing the learning contest and the monetary incentive (that are based on the number of "likes" students received) increases the overall number of "likes" in the community.

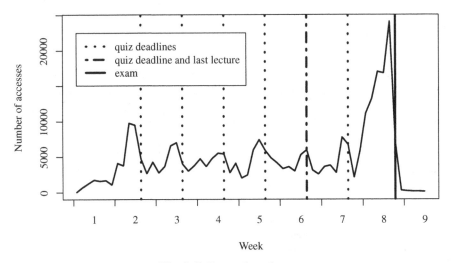

Fig. 1. Daily number of accesses

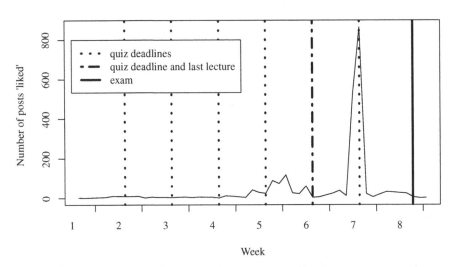

Fig. 2. Daily number of post "likes"

Based on the log file analysis, we conclude that monetary incentives do not increase overall activity in the forum. Moreover, an analysis of students' "liking" behavior indicates that at least some students were trying to influence the results of the learning contest just before its deadline by excessively "liking" their friends' posts.

4.2   Survey Data

Log file analysis indicates at least some attempt to manipulate the learning contest's results. But does such manipulation negatively influence overall satisfaction with the e-learning system? We analyze survey data to answer this research question. The students were asked to participate in five surveys as described above. An Apple iPod shuffle was raffled among the participants of each survey.

Before presenting and interpreting the survey results, it is important to provide some more information on the timing of these surveys. Survey 1 was conducted in a timeframe between the weeks 1 and 3. We therefore do not assume that students were already able to assess the benefits of the e-learning environment. Thus, this survey measures students' expectations and first impressions of the system. Survey 2 took place in week 4. We expect students already to have gained experience with the e-learning system at that time. Moreover, the monetary incentive had not been introduced to the students yet. Immediately after introducing the monetary incentive, we asked the students to participate in survey 3 (that took place in week 5 and 6). Survey 3 thus measures the immediate effect of introducing a monetary incentive. As stated in the theoretical section of this paper, we expected that some students might try to manipulate the learning contest. Survey 4 therefore started immediately after the deadline of the learning contest (both in week 7). We thus intended to survey the immediate influence of manipulation by some students on overall satisfaction with the lecture. Survey 5 was conducted after the exam (starting from week 8) and aimed at measuring the long term effect of non-monetary and monetary incentives.

Table 1 provides an overview of the total number of respondents in each of these studies.

Table 1. Number of respondents per survey

Survey	Number of respondents
1	298
2	312
3	336
4	281
5	257

Learners' satisfaction with the e-learning system is presented in Figure 3. Each of the five experimental studies was conducted anonymously. We are therefore not able to conduct common tests such as the repeated measures ANOVA. However, based on the reported mean values and standard deviation values, we conclude that differences are minor or non-existent. This is especially important for surveys 2, 3, and 4. By comparing surveys 2 and 3 we intended to assess the immediate effect of introducing a monetary incentive. Our results strongly indicate that introducing a learning contest and a monetary incentive does not have any effect on students' perceptions (mean values and standard deviation almost stay the same, see Figure 3). Moreover, manipulations of some students in order to increase their odds of winning the learning contest (they massively "liked" uninformative posts such as "good", "well done" etc.) did obviously also not influence students' satisfaction with the e-learning system (we again observe almost identical results, when comparing the mean values and standard deviation of survey 3 and 4). This result is surprising as attempts of some students to manipulate the learning contest were obvious. For example, 25 students complained about their peer's behavior in an open question in survey 4. We conclude that manipulative behavior of some students did not influence overall satisfaction with the E-Learning environment.

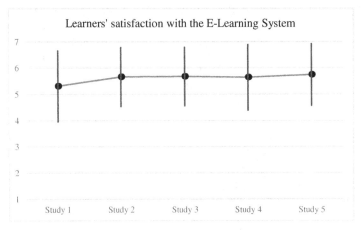

Fig. 3. Students' satisfaction with the e-learning system

Table 2. Statistical data on student satisfaction

Survey	Std. dev.	Mean
1	1.35	5.31
2	1.13	5.66
3	1.11	5.67
4	1.25	5.64
5	1.17	5.74

In survey 3, we also asked students to evaluate the monetary incentive directly on a 7-point rating scale (1 = not favorable, 7 = highly favorable). The results (mean = 4.02; standard deviation = 1.93) reveal that students' evaluations were above average but far from enthusiastic about the learning contest and the monetary incentive. Students' perceptions towards "likes" were also surveyed in survey 3. They were perceived to be more favorable (mean = 4.52, standard deviation = 1.55) than the monetary incentive. A dependent sample t-test reveals that this difference is highly significant (p-value = 0.000).

In summary, based on an analysis of students' perceived satisfaction with the e-learning system, we conclude that learning contests and monetary prizes are not efficient. They do not increase learners' satisfaction.

5   Conclusion

Motivating students to use e-learning systems actively is challenging. We therefore tested two types of incentives that might increase learners' satisfaction with the learning experience. Specifically, we compare a non-monetary ("likes") and a monetary incentive (a monetary prize that was raffled in a learning competition). We analyze log file data as well as results from five surveys to evaluate these incentives.

Our results indicate that students value both types (evaluations are above average); however, they significantly prefer the non-monetary incentive. Moreover, monetary incentives did not additionally increase learners' activity in the e-learning system nor did they improve learners' satisfaction. Instead, there might even be (minor) negative effects of monetary incentives due to some students that were trying to manipulate the learning contest to improve their odds of winning the prize (i.e. smaller groups of learners started "liking" each other's comments; even obviously trivial content got "likes"). As a next step, further research is needed to support our results, e.g., by analyzing case studies on a larger scale.

References

1. Dziuban, C., Moskal, P., Hartman, J.: Higher Education, Blended Learning and the Generations: Knowledge is Power—No More. In: Bourne, J.R., Moore, J.C. (eds.) Elements of Quality Online Education: Engaging Communities. Sloan Center of Online Education, Needham (2005)
2. Hughes, G.: Using blended learning to increase learner support and improve retention. Teaching in Higher Education 12(3), 349–363 (2007)
3. Klein, H.J., Noe, R.A., Wang, C.: Motivation to learn and Course Outcomes: the impact of delivery mode, learning goal orientation, and perceived barriers and enablers. Personnel Psychology 59(3), 665–702 (2006)
4. Rovai, A.P., Downey, J.R.: Why some distance education programs fail while others succeed in a global environment. Internet and Higher Education 13(3), 141–147 (2010)
5. Alrushiedat, N., Olfman, L., Kung, M., van der Pol, J.: Knowledge Sharing Motivations, Perceived Enjoyment and Anchoring Effects on Perceived Usefulness of Asynchronous Online Discussions. In: AMCIS 2010 Proceedings, Paper 326 (2010)
6. Wan, A.T., Sadiq, S., Li, X.: Exploratory Study on Learners' Experience in an eLearning System. In: AMCIS 2011 Proceedings - All Submissions, Paper 209 (2011)
7. Garrison, D.R., Kanuka, H.: Blended Learning: Uncovering its transformative potential in higher education. Internet and Higher Education 7(2), 95–105 (2004)
8. Garrison, R.: Implications of Online Learning for the Conceptual Development and Practice of Distance Education. Journal of Distance Education 23(2), 93–104 (2009)
9. Hillman, S.J., Corkery, M.G.: University infrastructural needs and decisions in moving towards online delivery programmes. Journal of Higher Education Policy and Management 32(5), 467–474 (2010)
10. Söderstrom, T., From, J., Lövquist, J., Törnquist, A.: The Transition from Distance to Online Education: Perspectives from the Educational Management Horizon. European Journal of Open, Distance and E-Learning (June 01, 2012)

11. Moore, M.G.: Editorial: Three types of interaction. American Journal of Distance Education 3(2), 1–7 (1989)
12. Du, Z., Fu, X., Zhao, C., Liu, Q., Liu, T.: Interactive and Collaborative E-Learning Platform with Integrated Social Software and Learning Management System. In: Lu, W., Cai, G., Liu, W., Xing, W. (eds.) ITSE 2012. LNEE, vol. 212, pp. 11–18. Springer, Heidelberg (2013)
13. Dalsgaard, C.: Social Software: E-learning beyond learning management systems. European Journal of Open, Distance and E-Learning (July 12, 2006)
14. Duhaney, D.C.: Blended learning in education, training, and development. Performance Improvement 43(8), 35–38 (2004)
15. Heterick, B., Twigg, C.: The Learning MarketSpace (February 1, 2003), http://www.thencat.org/Newsletters/Feb03.html
16. Garrison, D.R., Anderson, T., Archer, W.: Critical Inquiry in a Text-Based Environment: Computer Conferencing in Higher Education. Internet and Higher Education 2(2-3), 87–105 (1999)
17. Wegener, R., Leimeister, J.M.: Peer Creation of E-Learning Materials to Enhance Learning Success and Satisfaction in an Information Systems Course. In: Proceedings of the 20th European Conference on Information Systems, Paper 170 (2012)
18. Keller, J.: Motivation in Cyber Learning Environments. International Journal of Educational Technology 1(1), 7–30 (1999)
19. Anderson, T., Dron, J.: Learning technology through three generations of technology enhanced distance education pedagogy. European Journal of Open, Distance and E-Learning (February 2012)
20. Wegener, R., Leimeister, J.M.: Do Student-Instructor Co-Created eLearning Materials Lead To Better Learning Outcomes? Empirical Results from a German Large Scale Course Pilot Study. In: 45. Hawaii International Conference on System Sciences, HICSS, pp. 31–40 (2012)
21. Wegener, R., Menschner, P., Leimeister, J.M.: Design and evaluation of a didactical service blueprinting method for large scale lectures. In: ICIS 2012 Proceedings (2012)
22. Wu, J., Tennyson, R.D., Hsia, T.: A study of student satisfaction in a blended e-learning system environment. Computers & Education 55(1), 155–164 (2010)
23. Yu, A.Y., Tian, S.W., Vogel, D., Kwok, R.C.-W.: Embedded Social Learning in Online Social Networking. In: ICIS 2010 Proceedings, Paper 100 (2010)
24. Stieglitz, S., Lattemann, C., Fohr, G.: Learning Arrangements in Virtual Worlds. In: Proceedings of the 43rd Hawaii International Conference on System Sciences (2010)

Eye Tracking Analysis of User Behavior in Online Social Networks

Wan Adilah Wan Adnan, Wan Nur Hafizhoh Hassan,
Natrah Abdullah, and JamaliahTaslim

Faculty of Computer and Mathematical Sciences,
UniversitiTeknologi MARA, Malaysia
{Adilah,natrah,jamaliah}@tmsk.uitm.edu.my,
wnurhafizhoh@gmail.com

Abstract. Social network has become a global phenomenon which attracts a wide range of population from all around the world of different ages, and cultures. People are using online social networks for several purposes like sharing information, chatting with friends, sharing photos and commenting. However, the analysis of users' behavior in social networks received little attention. Therefore, the purpose of this study is to analyze user behavior in terms of users' activities in social network sites by adopting eye tracking techniques. Four main measurements were examined which includes the first place user looks, time spent on areas of interest, main activities and completion time. Results from eye tracking analysis based on the first place user looks and on the time duration have indicated that wall *post* recorded most users' attention. Results have shown that the main activity was reading friends' status on the *wall posts* area. The findings provide support for the effort to understand and to model user behavior using eye tracking technique.

Keywords: User Behavior, Eye Tracking Analysis, Social Networking, Eye Movement data, Experimental Study.

1   Introduction

Social networks sites are getting extensive popularity among internet users in recent years. It was becoming a popular medium for socializing online and tools to facilitate friendship. People are using online social networks for countless activities like sharing information, chatting with friends, sharing photos and commenting. Many social network studies have been reported in the literature. However, studies examining user's behavior in social networks have received little attention [1]. Furthermore, according to Ozturk and Rizvanoglu[2], there are a limited number of social network studies that adopt eye-tracking technique. Majority of prior user behavior studies are carried out through observations and surveys. Recent studies show that eye tracking provides valuable insights into how users perceive online content. According to Michailidou et al [3], investigating sighted users' web behavior using eye movement tracking methods gives a better understanding of users' page presentation perception and cognition. In addition, Ozturk and Rizvanoglu[2] states that integrating an eye

A.A. Ozok and P. Zaphiris (Eds.): OCSC/HCII 2013, LNCS 8029, pp. 113–119, 2013.

tracker would provide more precise information about user behavior which includes: the location where a user is looking at any given time, the time duration in viewing or reading at a particular area, and the sequence of location a user viewed in performing a particular action or activity.

This paper is aimed to understand users' behaviour in social network activities through the use of eye tracker. The users behaviour were analysed based on their eye movement data, which provides information about first location or area a user look, time spent on area of interest, main activities and time to complete a given task.

2   Existing Research on User Behaviour in Social Network

Social networking is one of the major phenomena of Web in recent years. According to Horng[4], the number of social network sites on Web 2.0 has been growing rapidly. Boyd and Ellison [5] defined social network sites as web-based services that allow users to share a public or private profile with common users and explore connections with others within the site.

In the last few years, the immense interest of the users towards the social network sites brought the emergence of various studies on this phenomenon. Fox and Naidu [6] evaluated the usability of three of the most popular social network sites known as Myspace, Facebook and Orkut. In this study, the usability test was conducted to evaluate first-time users' satisfaction, navigational efficiency and general preferences. Their finding concluded that Facebook is the best social network sites.

Many studies investigated the user behavior in social networking. Gyarmati and Trinh [1] stated that the success of a social network whether in short-term or in long-term, depending on the behavior of its users, in particular the users' activities. In addition, Acquisti et al. [7] emphasized that people use social networking services for countless activities which include connecting with existing networks for making and developing friendship or contacts, representing themselves online, creating and developing an online presence, viewing content and information, creating and customizing profiles, authoring and uploading their own content, adding and sharing third-party content, posting messages whether in private or public and also collaborating with other people.

Hampton et al. [8] also explored the user behavior or activities in Facebook. In his survey, he examined what people do on Facebook. Results from their survey, showed that on average day 15% of Facebook users update their own status, 22% comment on another's post or status, 20% comment on another user's photos, 26% "Like" another user's content and 10% send another user a private message.

Majority of prior user behavior studies have been conducted using survey and observation. There are limited studies that adopt eye tracking technique which have been highlighted in the literature could provide valuable insights into user behavior [2][3].

2.1   Eye Tracking Technique in User Behavior Studies

According to Lorigo et al. [9] the application of eye tracking has recently received significant attention from research scientists from various fields including search engine companies, marketing firms, and usability professionals. Regarding this context, Carlo and Marcos [10] used eye-tracking in their study to analyze the browsing behavior of users in the search engine result page (SERPs), as wells as to examine the differences in behavior for different kind of queries such as informational, navigational and transaction. In addition, many usability studies used eye tracking to investigate the usability of web pages. Ozturk and Rizvanoglu [2] adopted eye-tracking in their experimental study to explore the usability of the profile pages in social network sites. In their findings, they emphasized several ways to improve usability in profile pages such as only relevant information should be presented in profile pages as well as the content block need to be visually separated in order to make the content readable, scannable and easy to perceive. Their findings also had shown that mostly users pay attention to the profile picture and their recent activities in the profile page. Related to this context, Michailidou et al. [3] also presented an eye tracking study to investigate sighted users' browsing behavior in the context of web accessibility. In this study, nine web pages were investigated to determine how the page's visual clutter is related to sighted users' browsing patterns. The results showed that salient elements attract users' attention first, and users tend to spend more time on the main content of the page. This study also emphasized that common gaze patterns begin at the salient elements of the page, move to the main content, header, right column and left column of the page and finish at the footer area.

3 Method

This study adopted an experimental method, based on within-participants design approach. Eight postgraduate students participated in this study. All participants have Facebook account. The experiment was conducted at User Sciences and Engineering Laboratory (USELAB).There were four measurements of user behavior collected in this study: first place user look, time spent on area of interest, main activities performed and completion time. These user behavior measures, as shown in Table 1, are captured from eye tracker based on gaze plot, observation length, heat maps, and screen recording.

Table 1. User Behavior Measurement

What to measure	How to measure	Description of Outcome
First place the users look	Gaze plot	Point of Attraction
Time spend on Social Interaction Elements Layout	Heat Map Number of gaze per AOI (area of interest)	Level of importance of an elements
Completion time	Screen recording	User performance: Time taken to complete a given task.

A popular social network site, Facebook was selected in this study for analyzing user behavior. Facebook has been recognized as the most influential social network sites on the internet and equally familiar to all participants. For the purpose of analysis, the layout of the Facebook main page is categorized into six areas of interest, which are navigation bar, applications, groups, wall posts, advertisements and chatting rooms as shown in Figure 1.

Fig. 1. Layout of social network

The experiment was divided into two sessions. In the first session, participants were required to explore the Facebook for 5 minutes, and in the second session, participants were required to do a specific task and user performance based on completion time were recorded. User behavior data were captured and recorded using Tobii T60 Model eye tracker which used two infrared light sources. The reflections from retina were recorded by a camera. The data was analyzed by software named Tobii Studio 1.3.

4   Analysis and Results

Gaze plot was analyzed to determine the first place user looks. Gaze plot provides details of eye movements including order and duration of gaze fixations. Each fixation is illustrated by a dot with a number inside it. This number indicates the sequence in which the place is visited. The first area a participant looking at is given the number one, as shown in Figure 2. Results from the gaze plots have shown that, for all participants, wall posts area was the first place that they looked at. This finding indicated that participants' first attention was on the wall posts area.

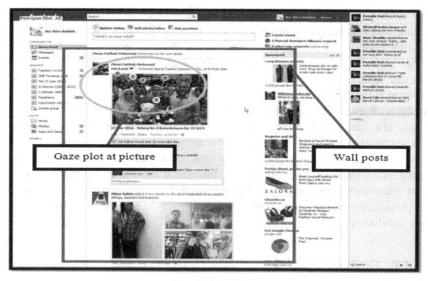

Fig. 2. Gaze Plot

In addition, based on the observation length analysis, that informed about the time spent on a particular area, majority of participants recorded the longest duration of time spent on the wall post area too.

Further analysis was conducted on the visual hotspots of heat map to identify the most attention grabbing area. These colored hotspots, from green to red, show the varying level of attention. The most attention area is denoted by a red circle at its center of attention as shown in the heat map in Figure 3. As expected, result showed that wall post received the most attention from all the participants. Thus, it can be concluded that wall post is the most important area in social network.

Fig. 3. Heat Map

For identifying the main wall post activity performed by the participants, screen recording data was analyzed. Result has revealed that the main wall post activity performed by majority of participants was reading their friends status. Other popular activities at wall post area were viewing photos and viewing links. The result has shown that updates from friends can drive one's attention to keep on reading other users status content.

Analysis on user behaviour based on participant's main activity and gender difference was also conducted. Result from correlation analysis showed that there is no significant relationship between gender and main activities of participants.

A correlation analysis was conducted to analyze the relationship between frequency of use and completion time. From this analysis, it has shown that there was a significant relationship between frequency of use and completion time. This indicates that experienced users perform faster than novice users in completing a given task due to their familiarity.

5   Conclusions

This paper examined user behavior in online social network using eye tracking data. Results showed that wall post area is the main area of interest. Wall post that is located at the center of the screen received the most attention based on the observation of the first place they looked, as well as on the duration of time recorded. Finding also showed that the main activity among users was reading friends' status on the wall posts area. The findings provide support for the effort to understand and to model user behavior. Further research is required to examine possible differences in user behavior for different type of demographics and culture.

References

1. Gyarmati, L., Trinh, T.A.: Measuring user behavior in online social networks. IEEE Network: The Magazine of Global Internetworking 24(5), 26–31 (2010)
2. Ozturk, O., Rizvanoglu, K.: A Close Look at the Phenomenon: An Eye Tracking Study on the Usability of the Profile Pages in Social Networking Sites. In: Proceedings of International Symposium of Interactive Media Design, pp. 1–12 (2010)
3. Michailidou, E., Harper, S., Bechhofe, S.: Investigating Sighted Users' Browsing Behaviour to Assist Web Accessibility. In: Proceedings of Tenth International ACM SIGACCESS Conference on Computers and Accessibility, ASSETS 2008, pp. 121–128 (2008)
4. Horng, S.M.: Analysis of Users' Behavior on Web 2.0 Social Network Sites: An Empirical Study. In: Proceedings of Seventh International Conference on Information Technology, pp. 454–459 (2010)
5. Boyd, D.M., Ellison, N.B.: Social Network Sites: Definition, History, and Scholarship. Journal of Computer-Mediated Communication, 1–12 (2007)
6. Fox, D., Naidu, S.: Usability Evaluation of Three Social Network Sites. Usability News, 1–11 (2009)

7. Acquisti, A., Bryce, J., Collier, A., Farmer, J., Grant, L., Kelly, B.: Young People and Social Networking Services. Childnet International 2008, United Kingdom (2008)
8. Hampton, K.N., Goulet, L.S., Rainie, L., Purcell, K.: Social networking sites and our lives. pewinternet. org. Washington (2011)
9. Lorigo, L., Haridasan, M., Brynjarsdottir, H., Xia, L., Pallacini, F., Granka, L., Pan, B.: Eye tracking and online search: Lessons learned and challenges ahead. Journal of the American Society for Information Science and Technology 59(7), 1041–1052 (2008)
10. Carlo, C.G., Marco, M.C.: Different Users and Intents: An Eye-tracking Analysis of Web Search. In: Proceedings of the Fourth ACM International Conference on Web Search and Data Mining (WSDM 2011), pp. 262–267 (2011)

Who Are Seeking Friends? The Portrait
of Stranger-Seeker in Social Network Sites

Xitong Yue, Yuanyuan Shi, and Huajian Cai

Institute of Psychology, Chinese Academy of Sciences,
People's Republic of China
Huajian.cai@gmail.com

Abstract. We aim to understand the stranger seeking behaviors on Social Network Sites (SNSs) and learn about the characteristics of these people who frequently seek strangers (stranger-seeker). By conducting two surveys, we obtain
an overall acknowledgement of stranger seeking behavior and give a portrait of
stranger-seekers in social network sites. We find: stranger-seekers are extroversive, narcissism, in poor family relationship, motivated to seek belongingness,
but without a larger proportion of strange friends. This finding may contribute
to personal attractiveness oriented online product design.

Keywords: Social Network Site (SNS), stranger seeking, personality, relation
quality.

1 Introduction

Internet has brought about great changes to human lives [1], and provides chances for
meeting and interacting in a virtue space. Social network sites (SNSs) are social networking tools to generate online relationship and serve as compensation for reality,
they are defined as web-based services that allow individuals to (1) construct a public
or semi-public profile within a bounded system, (2) articulate a list of other users with
whom they share a connection, and (3) view and traverse their list of connections and
those made by others within the system [2]. SNSs have gained great popularity among
the overall world since its birth. For example, Facebook, the largest SNS in the world,
declared that they share more than 900 million registered users by 30th, June 2012,
other popular SNSs include MySpace, Twitter, Google+, Renren (China), QQzone
(China), etc.

Individuals have integrated SNS surfing into their daily practices. They flocked to
social network sites for several reasons, among which a main one is to maintain the
established relationships [2]. According to a survey conducted by Lenhart in 2009,
nearly 90% of adults surveyed say they use online profiles to keep up with friends,
while 57% say they use them to make plan with their friends, and 49% say to meet
new friends. In a word, the success of SNSs in a large degree can be attributed to the
capability to enlarge one's social network and encourage social interaction.

There is a growing body of evidence indicating that individual differences on personality factors are associated with SNS usage[3]. Guadagno and his colleagues con-

A.A. Ozok and P. Zaphiris (Eds.): OCSC/HCII 2013, LNCS 8029, pp. 120–125, 2013.
© Springer-Verlag Berlin Heidelberg 2013

ducted two studies and indicate that people who are high in openness to new experience and high in neuroticism are likely to be bloggers[4]. Moreover, women high in neuroticism are more likely to be bloggers as compared to those low in neuroticism whereas no difference was found for men[4].While using SNSs, whereas neurotic individual hold an instrument orientation.

Extroversive people demonstrate more frequent SNSs use and communicative functions[5-6], have more friends, participant in more groups [5]. Individuals who scored higher on neuroticism are more willing to share personally-identifying information, spend more time in SNSs, be less likely to use private messages[5], and prefer the asynchronous methods of communication [6]. It has been found an interaction between agreeableness and gender. Female belong to low agreeableness group upload fewer pictures compared with those in high agreeableness group[7]. Individuals who scored higher on openness to experience tend to use Facebook as a communication tool and to use a greater number of features. Contrary to open people, conscientious people be more cautious in SNS activities (Ross, et al, 2009), reveal a larger number of friends due to high-target orientation[8].

Self-view and relationship quality may be another related factors. Naricissism indicates a over-high self-evaluation. The survey based on Facebook found that, compared to nonusers, Facebook users are more narcissistic, less likely to be conscientious, shy, or socially lonely, and they also have stronger feelings of family loneliness. In regards to narcissism, individuals with higher scores on exhibitionism also have higher preferences for Photos and Status Updates [6].

Besides family loneliness, family factors can also influence internet behavior. People with poorer family function cannot acquire proper emotion support and often involved in pathological internet use.

However, current research mainly focuses on the overall SNS behavior, and rarely exist research on some kind of SNS behavior, for example, there is lack of research on on-line friends seeking behavior. Meeting strangers on-line is among one of the most interesting experiences during SNSs usage. To meet netizen's needs of large social network and provide more chances for social interaction, some Chinese SNS service providers have expanded their market to mobile phone users and developed mobile APPs, such as Momo and KK-friend. Mobile APPs allow their users to search for strangers nearby and initiate close relationships immediately.

Given its market prospect and significance, it's a necessity to learn about the stranger seekers' behavior, motivation and characteristics. However, as far as we know, the knowledge of stranger-seekers is quite limited. We know little about (a) which types of people like to seek strangers; (b) how these people evaluate themselves; (c) their identification to SNSs; and (4) their ability of forming health relationship with others. Next, we will give an introduction of our exploration on stranger seeking behaviors and give a portrait of the stranger-seekers from the following perspectives: their personality, self-views, identification, relationship quality, etc. The expected findings will likely help SNS product designers to improve interaction designs and user experience. And this is the first try to make such an overall view of online friends seeking behavior.

2   Purpose

We categorized above factors into two types: personal factors and inter-personal factors. As to personal factors, we selected personality, self-view and identification as important elements. We examine the inter-personal factors from the family relation perspective. Prior research indicates family relation quality and family environments relates to unhealthy internet behavior, so we decide to explore whether stranger-seekers on-line come from families sharing high-quality or low-quality family relations.

3   Methods

We conducted two surveys. Survey one focused on personal factors while survey two continued to explore inter-personal factors.

3.1   Study One

There were 240 participants in survey one. All of them reported their SNS behaviors and identification on a revised Facebook Questionnaire[5], a 50-item Big Five Questionnaire [9] (α = 0.870) and the Narcissism Personality Inventory [10](α=0.791. Our subjects included users from the most popular Chinese SNSs including Renren, Weibo, QQzone, Douban.

Revised Facebook Questionnaire (RFQ)
The RFQ is used to measure personal identification to SNS and multiple SNSs behaviors. SNSs behaviors include participant's frequency of SNSs use, searching strangers, the proportion of strangers among friends, and other necessary information.

The Big Five Personality Inventory (BFPI)
The BFPI[11] is a 44-item measure that consists of the following five personality factors: extraversion (e.g., "I see myself as someone who is talkative"), agreeableness (e.g., "I see myself as someone who likes to cooperate with others"), conscientiousness (e.g., "I see myself as someone who does a thorough job"), neuroticism (e.g., "I see myself as someone who can be moody"), and openness to experience (e.g., "I see myself as someone who is inventive"). Each item was evaluated on a 5-point Likert scale, ranging from "Strongly Disagree" to "Strongly Agree". The BFPI has been shown to have satisfactory reliability and validity [12]. The internal consistency coefficient for each of the subscales is good: extraversion (a = .86), agreeableness (a = .79), conscientiousness (a = .82), neuroticism (a = .84), and openness to experience (a = .80).

Narcissism Personality Inventory
Narcissism reflects self-evaluation, especially a high evaluation, so we use the Narcissism Personality Inventory (NPI)-16 to measure self-view. NPI-16 has acceptable face, internal, discriminant, and predictive validity[13]. Example items include "I am

more capable than other people" and "There is a lot that I can learn from other people." Higher scores on the NPI indicate a more narcissistic personality. Overall, the NPI-16 is both a valid and reliable measure that captures a range of facets of this construct, particularly in situations in which the use of a longer measure is impractical. Higher scores one NPI indicate unhealthy self-view.

Result and Discussion

According to the result, we found a significant correlation between extraversion and stranger seeking behavior(r = 0.194***), that is, extroversive people are more likely to seek strangers. This result is consistent with prior findings which indicate that while using SNSs, extroversive people are more likely to use the communicative functions of SNS[14] .

We also found a positive correlation between narcissism and stranger seeking, which indicates that people who value themselves high show more interests to others. This finding suggests that narcissistic people are not as self-centered as thought.

3.2   Study Two

Procedure

In survey two, 151 participants   (57 males, 94 female; mean age= 21.98, SD= 1.995) answered the same Facebook questionnaire in study one and a revised Relationship Quality questionnaire (Bartholomew & Horowitz, 1991, Griffin & Bartholomew, 1994;α= 0.815).

Relationship Quality Scale composes 17 items. The items in the scale are selected from Hazan and Shaver's (1987) attachment measure, Bartholomew and Horowitz's (1991) Relationship Questionnaire, and Collins and Read's (1990) Adult Attachment Scale and Griffin and Bartholomew (1994) Relationship Scales Questionnaire and revised to measure family relationship quality. The revised questionnaire included items like "I find it difficult to depend on my family" and share a high reliability (α= 0.815). Participants need to indicate the proper description of their family relationships on a 7-point scale. Higher score indicates better family relation quality.

Result and Discussion

In study 2, we found a significant negative correlation(r = -0.262**) between family relationship quality and the frequency of stranger seeking. That is, the poorer the family relationship, the stronger willingness of seeking strangers. Surprisingly, stranger seekers didn't have more strange friends: the correlation between strange friend proportion and strangers seeking behavior was -0.071, and the percents of stranger friends do not vary according to strangers seeking behavior (X2=10.678, p=0.099).

This result suggests when family interactions cannot meet one's need for dependence and intimacy, individuals will turn to strangers for emotional support. The correlation between identification and seeking behavior also supported this conclusion. Stranger-seekers hold a higher identification to the SNSs and are more afraid to lose the connection (see Table 1).

Table 1. Correlations result of the main varibles

	1	2	3	4	5	6	7	8	9
1. SNS_searchstranger	1								
2. SNS_friends_know	-.071	1							
3. SNS_life	.071	.159*	1						
4. SNS_lost	.151*	-.162*	365***	1					
5. SNS_belong	.166*	.036	.533***	.477***	1				
6. SNS_sad	.104	-.040	370***	.537***	.548***	1			
7. NPI	.176**	.021	.127	.094	.192**	.166**	1		
8. Extraversion	.227***	.036	.132*	.148*	.226***	.190**	.577***	1	
9. Family relation quality	-.262***	.171*	.084	.068	.003	-.009	-.094	.077	1

Note: $* p < .05$; $*** p < .001$.

4   Conclusion

According to the two large surveys, we found those who are extroversive, narcissism, in poor family relationship, motivated to seek belongingness on the SNSs, are most intended to search strangers on SNS for friends-making, but unfortunately, such seeking behavior does not lead to a large proportion of strange friends in their friends list.

This result may due to the lack of actual friend applications or social attractiveness of stranger seekers. Although low relationship quality and extroversive individual did do more searching, but they may just search and scan others information but not submit friends application actually. So there is no difference between friends distribution. Another reason may be these individuals are less attractive. According to prior study, individual from dy-functional family often showed more psychological problems, such as passive, depressed, aggressive, sharing low self-esteem and subjective well-being. They are at a higher risk in communication disadvantage and are skilled in social interaction. So although they submit more friends' applications, they may also receive more rejection or fail to establish long-term connections.

In a word, stranger seekers are extroversive, narcissism, in poor family relationship, motivated to seek belongingness on the SNSs, but without a large proportion of strange friends. The SNSs product manager should take these into consideration and come up ideas on how to display personal characteristics attractively.

References

1. Amichai-Hamburger, Y.: Internet and personality. Computers in Human Behavior 18(1), 1–10 (2002)
2. Ellison, N.B.: Social network sites: Definition, history, and scholarship. Journal of Computer-Mediated Communication 13(1), 210–230 (2007)
3. Amichai-Hamburger, Y., Ben-Artzi, E.: Loneliness and Internet use. Computers in Human Behavior 19(1), 71–80 (2003)
4. Guadagno, R.E., Okdie, B.M., Eno, C.A.: Who blogs? Personality predictors of blogging. Computers in Human Behavior 24(5), 1993–2004 (2008)

5. Ross, C., Orr, E.S., Sisic, M., Arseneault, J.M., Simmering, M.G., Orr, R.R.: Personality and motivations associated with Facebook use. Computers in Human Behavior 25(2), 578–586 (2009)
6. Ryan, T., Xenos, S.: Who uses Facebook? An investigation into the relationship between the Big Five, shyness, narcissism, loneliness, and Facebook usage. Computers in Human Behavior 27(5), 1658–1664 (2011)
7. Amichai-Hamburger, Y., Vinitzky, G.: Social network use and personality. Computers in Human Behavior 26(6), 1289–1295 (2010)
8. Correa, T., Hinsley, A.W., de Zúñiga, H.G.: Who interacts on the Web?: The intersection of users' personality and social media use. Computers in Human Behavior 26(2), 247–253 (2010)
9. Costa Jr., P.T., McCrae, R.R.: Revised NEO Personality Inventory (NEO-PI-R) and NEO Five-Factor Inventory (NEO-FFI) professional manual. Psychological Assessment Resources, Odessa (1992)
10. Raskin, R., Hall, C.S.: The Narcissistic Personality Inventory: Alternative form reliability and further evidence of construct validity. J. Pers. Assess. 45(2), 159–162 (1981)
11. John, O.P., Donahue, E.M., Kentle, R.L. (eds.): The Big Five inventoryversions 4a and 54. University of California, Institute of Personality and Social Research, Berkeley, CA (1991)
12. Srivastava, S., John, O.P., Gosling, S.D., et al.: Development of personality in early and middle adulthood: set like plaster or persistent change? Journal of Personality and Social Psychology 84(5), 1041 (2003)
13. Ames, R.D., Rose, P., Anderson, P.C.: The NPI-16 as a short measure of narcissism. Journal of Research in Personality 40, 440–450 (2006)
14. Amichai-Hamburger, Y., Kaplan, H., Dorpatcheon, N.: Click to the past: The impact of extroversion by users of nostalgic websites on the use of Internet social services. Computers in Human Behavior 24(5), 1907–1912 (2008)

Part II
Learning and Gaming Communities

The Effect of Leaderboard Ranking
on Players' Perception of Gaming Fun

Charles Butler

The Norwegian School of Information Technology, Oslo, Norway
charlesabutler@gmail.com

Abstract. Although fun is desirable in nearly all commercial games, defining it and actually getting it into a game can prove difficult. Developers have added multiplayer features to their games since the beginning of the industry in an attempt to create fun, but to what extent does this actually affect a player's perception of a game's fun? This paper gives an overview of relevant research relating to fun and play before attempting to tackle the key issue of the effect of player success as measured by leaderboard rankings on the perception of a game's fun.

Keywords: fun, play, video games, computer games, game design.

1   Introduction

There are a number of difficulties when attempting to study fun or people's perception thereof. It seems problematic to attach a concrete definition to such an abstract concept. Additionally, since most people likely feel very familiar with the concept, finding a definition that all can agree on is even more challenging. Few studies tackle the concept directly, but there is a body of research concerning the concept of play. Since it seems logical to associate the activities of play with the concept of fun, it also seems valid to consider these activities as well. Much of this research involves attempting to classify or categorize various activities to form a model of play.

A common trend in many modern games is the addition of various multiplayer features. These often seem incidental to, or even entirely separate from, the main gameplay of the game, even though they can certainly add replay value and additional interest. A notable example of this is the Xbox Live functionality that integrates with Xbox 360 games. Of course, some games benefit tremendously from this added functionality, but do they all? Designers must be aware that certain features can both add and detract from the perception of fun if they are to make informed decisions about what features to add.

This project investigated the effect of one specific game alteration on the perceived fun of players. The testing process allowed testers to play a game that randomly selected one of three leaderboard versions to present to the player at the game's conclusion. One leaderboard version was non-populated, having only the player's score listed. The game dynamically populated another version with names and scores higher

A.A. Ozok and P. Zaphiris (Eds.): OCSC/HCII 2013, LNCS 8029, pp. 129–136, 2013.

than the player's score, and the last used names and scores lower than the player's score.

It may seem that a more successful player would perceive themselves to be having more fun than a less successful player and vice versa. However, this project set out to test whether or not leaderboard results would alter a player's perception of fun and to what extent. The concept of a leaderboard serves as a proxy for success relative to that of other players and could be of use to game designers in determining which multiplayer features to incorporate into their designs. While many different factors likely influence the feature set of a game, additional data concerning this specific factor could provide extra insight in certain situations, even if it is not the primary motivation.

2   Background

A review of the common background material related to fun and play investigated a number of different areas in an attempt to understand how players derive a sense of fun from games.

Salen and Zimmerman [8] examined a number of categorizations in an attempt to classify either the type of activity that leads to pleasure in play, or fun, or the resulting emotion. One common, and incredibly broad, definition of fun is offered:

> *"Game designer Hal Barwood organizes all of the varied emotions a game can produce under the heading of "fun." Fun games are what players want. A fun game makes for a pleasurable experience, which is why people play."*

However, game designer Marc LeBlanc [8] finds the term insufficient to fully describe the concept. He instead developed a categorization based on of the type of pleasure that players experience while playing games. Psychologist Michael J. Apter [8] offered a very similar categorization in his essay "A Structural-Phenomenology of Play" that focuses on the cognitive arousal that play provides.

Anthropologist Roger Caillois [8, 3] developed one of the more widely used categorizations of the different forms of play:

1. Agôn: competition and competitive struggle
2. Alea: submission to the fortunes of chance
3. Mimicry: role-playing and make believe
4. Ilinx: vertigo and physical sensation

Additionally, Caillois expands on these categories with the concepts of paida and ludus. Paida and ludus add additional depth to each of his four categories by providing a continuum from pure paida to pure ludus upon which the various games or play types fall.

> *"Paida represents wild, free-form, improvisational play, whereas ludus represents rule-bound, regulated, formalized play"*

However, while the type of play may give clues to the player's motivations, it does not specifically address it. Game designers should be interested in the types of play that people choose to participate as well as their reasons for doing so. Game designers Neal and Jana Hallford [8, 5] point out the importance of rewards in keeping the player satisfied, offering a categorization based on the types of rewards offered to players.

While those rewards may describe various ways that a designer can keep players interested by giving rewards to the players' avatars, individual players value various rewards to very differing extents. People play games for many reasons, and it seems logical to assume that they are predominately doing so because playing gives them some sort of reward. It also seems to follow that the game designer could do a far better job providing fun for the player if it was easy to tell what rewards a player values most. While many games are likely self-selecting (for example, racing games are likely to attract the type of player that feels most rewarded by ilinx types of play), the different categorizations of play presented above do not speak directly to what the player might enjoy. Richard Bartle [1] addresses the motivations behind various player actions and the things designers can do to reward them. After conducting an analysis of the responses to a long running debate about what players want from a game, Bartle categorized players into four quadrants, commonly known as the Bartle Player Types, consisting of Achievers, Socializers, Explorers, and Killers. Later, in an effort to further define variances he noticed within his player types, he expanded the graph to include an additional axis based on whether players interacted with the game world in an implicit or explicit manner.

By analyzing which features appeal to which groups, a game designer can more accurately predict how well a game fits with its intended target audience. The designer may also be able to broaden the appeal of the game by intentionally adding features that appeal to players outside of that audience. Bartle's types deal primarily with the motivations of the players, but he considers analysis of their actual behavior to also be worthy of comment. In regard to in-game behavior, he uses a study conducted by the system administrator of *Habitat*, F. Randall Farmer [1], which categorized players based specifically on their behavior. Farmer also noted that players tended to change behaviors over time. Players would start being primarily interested in the game, but as they became more experienced, they would begin to derive more and more of their fun from their interactions with the community. In a similar fashion, Bartle has noted the ways in which players seem to progress from one of his types to another as they become more experienced with the game [1].

Raph Koster [7] indicates that fun is essentially derived from the player's brain attempting to find patterns and succeeding in doing so, meaning that learning is really the mechanism that allows for fun. However, he sees the need to refine what people mean when they talk about having fun. He compares his categorization of the types of fun to Nicole Lazzaro's [7] four clusters of emotions: hard fun, easy fun, altered states, and the people factor. Koster also notes that we should be mindful of the positive emotions of interpersonal interactions that are often enjoyable even though they may not necessarily meet his definition of fun. While often overlooked by designers, these are consistent with Farmer's [1] notion of players becoming caretakers of other players as they grow. Allowing for the development of these emotions within a game could be crucial in keeping players satisfied and increasing the longevity of a game.

Koster [7] contends that much of what humans perceive as fun stems from activities that aid in survival and that games naturally evolve along with the needs of the players to serve them in the survival of their species. One notion that follows from the idea of games as an evolutionary teacher is that of the optimal arousal level theory [6]. This concept states that higher mammalian brains naturally pursue an equilibrium level of arousal, seeking out exciting activities when bored or relaxing activities when stressed. This could help explain the differences in what various players consider fun.

Howard Bloom [2] reinforces the need for a certain level of arousal. He argues against the trend of reducing stress and competition in our society. The popular belief is that stress causes health problems, but the benefits of actively engaging in competition, such as increasing one's social status, actually imparts significant health benefits such as lower blood pressure and enhanced emotional states.

Many of the previously cited individuals refer to the work of Mihaly Csikszentmihalyi [4]. His concept of flow is very relevant to fun and, as a result, is sought after by game designers who want their players to experience flow-like states (which could arguably be called synonymous to immersion) while playing games.

3   Method

3.1   The Project

This project involved the creation of a simple, web-based game created with Adobe Flash that has three different leaderboard versions. The game is a side-scrolling shooter that tracks the player's score and displays a leaderboard at the end of the game that manufactures the intended results regardless of the player's score. One version of the leaderboard indicated that the player had a higher score than any of the previous players. Another indicated that the player had a lower score than any of the previous players. The final version of the leaderboard displayed only the current player's score with all other slots being empty. Upon an initial play of the game, a leaderboard version was randomly selected. If a player chose to replay the game or returned to the site later, the page loaded the game with the same version of the leaderboard that the player previously encountered, although without the attached surveys or additional screens. However, even though the leaderboard encountered upon replay contained the same data as the initial version, the replay version was functional, and the player was able to place scores on it naturally.

While the scope of the game intended for this project was very limited, this was not detrimental to the data collection. The player only needed to play for a short time for the collection of data, so replayability was not a high priority. The quality of the game did not seem to dissuade many testers as the quality of both the visuals and gameplay were on par with Flash games commonly found on the internet.

3.2   Recruiting Testers

The testing used posts on online discussion forums to recruit participants. This method allowed the recruitment of a large number of testers with minimal effort, and it was highly scalable, allowing for the easy expansion of future testing sessions. To test the hypothesis, the only required data was the player's game version and the corresponding fun rating. However, additional data allowed for a more thorough analysis. Demographic data allowed the project to test for variances in extent of the effect on fun based on different groupings of people.

For this test, the recruitment posts focused specifically on forums that cater to video game players. This choice in recruiting assumed that individuals who frequent video game forums would be ideal initial testers for a number of reasons. First, they were assumed to be more likely to participate in the test than users of non-gaming forums. Second, they were assumed to be more comfortable with the technology, conventions, and terminology used in the test, improving the survey responses, and finally, they were assumed to be more capable of successfully handling any technical difficulties that might arise, reducing the abandonment rate.

3.3   Analysis

After filtering out invalid log entries (primarily due to abandoned surveys and technical problems encountered by the testers), complete surveys and accompanying gameplay data were collected on 132 unique testers (repeat players were tracked and filtered by IP address). Of these 132 participants, 54 players received the winning leaderboard version, 39 players received the losing version, and 39 players received the blank version.

There were three main areas of focus in the data analysis for this project. The first area was concerned with the relevant gameplay data collected during the testing sessions, including score, replay percentage, and difficulty rating. The second was an examination of the game ranking metrics and the distribution of those responses across the three different game types. This analysis attempted to detect any patterns or correlations between the game type and the ratings that the participants submitted on their surveys. The third segment of the analysis attempted to determine if any of the additional survey data collected about the participants related in any meaningful way to the fun ratings given to the game. This analysis broke the data down based on the different fun ratings given. (Readers should note that this analysis combined the results of the highest and second highest fun ranking due to their only being one response in the highest rank.)

The analysis first checked the data at a high level to see if any patterns or apparent inconsistencies emerged. Contingency tables served to help analyze the relationship between variables, and their use was appropriate here as the collected data contained a number of potentially related variables. A contingency table analysis using the chi-square statistic attempted (where applicable) to determine if there was a demonstrable relationship between the two nominal scale variables (i.e. the fun rating and the other rating specific to the test).

3.4   Potential Issues

It was impossible to avoid bias entirely, so a few of the potential biases of particular concern appear here. First, biases based on factors such as demographic differences, gameplay preferences, and the locations of the requests for testers were almost certain to occur. The analysis of the final data attempted to mitigate this bias by grouping similar players to identify any serious biases. Additionally, the chosen testers were of a very specific population for the reasons mentioned above, so to get results representative of the general population, much more extensive testing would need to be conducted.

The number of testers could be a problem as well. While 132 testers is a significant number of testers, once broken down into segments, the numbers are considerably less significant, making the chance of skewed results very high for some comparisons.

The intended perception of the losing condition was likely not communicated in many cases. Scoring high enough to even appear on a typical leader board could be seen as a sign of success and not at all like a negative condition. This may serve to make the results more about varying extents of success than winning versus losing.

When questioning players about the difficulty of the game, the intent of the question should be more specifically defined. It is possible that there was confusion as to whether the question addressed the complexity of the game or the difficulty in conquering the gameplay challenges.

4   Key Findings

- Winning, losing, or the lack of competition does affect the player, though not always in the expected way or in the same way for all players.
- The winning condition seemed to polarize the perception of fun, causing clusters of responses at the upper and lower bounds of the responses.
- The losing condition seemed to centralize the perceptions of fun, causing the responses to cluster in the middle of the scale.
- Players encountering competition (a winning or losing condition) replayed the game at least once approximately 50% more often than those with the neutral condition.
- Players who encountered the losing condition replayed the game at least once approximately 100% more often than those with the neutral condition.
- Even though it likely runs counter to the expectations of many game developers, fun ratings do not necessarily correlate with a player's likeliness of replaying a game (though there may be a threshold above which this changes).

- Measuring behavior is more reliable than measuring responses. The responses given to the replaying likeliness question were not strongly correlated to the measured replay data.
- Making a game too easy or too shallow can hurt its fun rating as judged by the player comments.
- Once a player decides that a game is too easy, it might be difficult to change that opinion, or alternatively, the player may be considering a different definition of difficulty.
- Higher scores do not necessarily correlate with more fun.

5   Conclusions

Presented here are a number of models describing various types of play, fun, and related emotions. While no single model is universally accepted, one can still find many useful and relevant points within the various approaches. In the search for fun, one is likely to benefit from viewing the problem from multiple perspectives, examining the ways in which people play, the motivations behind the desire to play, the specific features commonly cited as fun, and the emotions associated with each. All are valuable and provide insight into creating effective game designs.

The intent of this project was to examine a specific game mechanic for its effect on perceived fun. The hypothesis was that success relative to other players has a corresponding effect on the player's perception of fun. This work offers game designers quantitative evidence useful in determining what effect the addition of related multiplayer features might have on their game. The alteration of a high-score screen was appropriate because it is a feature that has very little, if anything, to do with the actual gameplay of a game, and yet, games have had these screens added to them since the early days of the industry. They add a mechanism for encouraging competition by quantifying "bragging rights" to a game. This is likely to appeal to a certain subset of players, but the potential to affect the other players is important to consider as well.

After the collection and analysis of the data, there were a number of findings. The first concerned the main hypothesis that success relative to other players has a corresponding effect on the player's perception of fun. The findings indicate that success relative to other players does affect the player's perception of fun, though not necessarily in a corresponding way (at least for all players). Success seems to affect players' perceptions in different ways, possibly depending on their expectations and any number of other factors. The results seem to indicate that success has a polarizing effect, increasing the number of high and low fun responses. Additionally, it seems that failure has a centering effect, encouraging more medium responses, and even though it appears to reduce high responses, it seems to reduce low responses by a similar amount.

One of the most telling outcomes was the number of players who replayed the game at least one additional time after completing the survey. As expected, a higher percentage of players receiving the losing version replayed the game than of those with the winning or blank versions. In fact, the losing version's replay percentage was more than double that of the blank version. A post-game survey question asked the players about the likeliness of playing again. The responses to this question indicate that players of the losing version are only slightly more likely to play again than the players of the other two versions (whose responses were practically equal). This supports the idea that what players say and what they actually do is not always the same. Additionally, the replay percentage did not seem directly correlated with the players' fun rating. The replay percentage of players who ranked the game highest was over 3.5 times higher than the overall average, but the lowest fun grouping replayed the game three times more often than the second and twice as often as the third. It is possible that until a player perceives a game as being "fun enough," any replay that occurs is for a reason other than fun, whereas above that threshold, fun may become more relevant.

One of the most significant unexpected results was the number of players who rated the game as too easy. This was surprising for a game that becomes practically impossible after a few short minutes. It seems likely that designing for accessibility past a certain point reduces the fun of your game to a certain number of players. One possible cause is that some players may quickly decide how easy or difficult a game is and stick to that decision no matter how difficult it becomes. Another possibility is that players may equate difficulty to the ease of learning and playing the game, causing players to rate games with simple mechanics as easy regardless of the difficulty of the overcoming the gameplay challenges.

One other unexpected result was that score seemed to have no significant effect on fun rating. It was an assumption that players better at the game would give it a higher fun score, and while players who played similar game types rated the game as more fun, playing similar games apparently was not correlated with achieving high scores.

References

1. Bartle, R.A.: Designing Virtual Worlds. New Rider Publishing, Indianapolis (2003)
2. Bloom, H.: The Lucifer Principle: A Scientific Expedition into the Forces of History. The Atlantic Monthly Press, New York (1995)
3. Caillois, R.: Man, Play, and Games. University of Illinois Press, Champaign (2001)
4. Csikszentmihalyi, M.: Flow: The Psychology of Optimal Experience. HarperCollins, New York (1991)
5. Hallford, Hallford: Swords and Circuitry: A Designer's Guide to Computer Role Playing Games. Prima Publishing, Roseville (2001)
6. Hebb, D.O.: Drives and the C.N.S (Conceptual Nervous System). Psychological Review 62, 243–254 (1955)
7. Koster, R.: A Theory of Fun for Game Design. Paraglyph Press, Inc., Scottsdale (2005)
8. Salen, Zimmerman: Rules of Play: Game Design Fundamentals. The MIT Press, Cambridge (2004)

Using Facebook for Collaborative Academic Activities in Education

Habib M. Fardoun[1], Bassam Zafar[1], and Antonio Paules Ciprés[2]

[1] King Abdulaziz University, Faculty of Computing and Information Systems,
Information Systems Department, 21589, Jeddah, Kingdom of Saudi Arabia
{hfardoun,bzafar}@kau.edu.sa
[2] University of Castilla-La Mancha, School of Advanced Computer Engineering,
Information Systems Department, 02071, Albacete, Spain
apcipres@gmail.com

Abstract. In this article we will try to use the services of Facebook, in a controlled environment, so that teachers can carry out their teaching. From the educational point of view, Facebook provides a new starting point, collaborative work, from plugins development tailored to the needs of teachers in schools. And this requires to take into account the hierarchical structure and the distribution of groups and students in the center, and, to have a system to monitor the work of the students for assessment and grading. With the work proposed here, we do not intend to create a social network, conceived as "Facebook", but including a plugin that allows the use of "Facebook" like a Learning Management System (LMS). These features would make the social network "Facebook", offer collaborative services for members of the educational community, and compete with other applications, like Google Apps Education. Moreover, being a LMS in a collaborative and education environment, facilitate the management, rating and monitoring of student activities. The justification for this system comes from the high number of students and teachers who already have an account on the social network, and they are already used to their patterns of communication and interaction. This adaptation may allow greater use of Information and Communication Technologies (ICT) and government resources that have been allocated to the project Escuela 2.0.

Keywords: Social Networks, Facebook, Educational Patterns, Educational Environments, LMS, Collaborative Educational systems.

1 Introduction

Social networks have recently been introduced in the lives of many people that were previously far from the Internet phenomenon. And, it is not uncommon to hear talks on the street about Facebook, and not necessarily among young people. The extraordinary ability to communicate and to connect people with networks has caused that a large number of people use them with very different purposes. They are used to find and engage with long ago lost friends, to discuss various subjects, all kinds of

A.A. Ozok and P. Zaphiris (Eds.): OCSC/HCII 2013, LNCS 8029, pp. 137–146, 2013.
© Springer-Verlag Berlin Heidelberg 2013

support causes, organize meetings of friends, former classmates or to publicize meetings and conferences, through which not only it provides details about the meeting, but people can confirm their attendance or absence of the event.

For that, the educational world cannot remain oblivious to like this social phenomenon, which is changing the way of communication between people. The education system works primarily with information, so there is no sense to use transmission systems and publication of the same based on those used in the early and mid-twentieth century, without incorporating what society already is using as part of their daily lives. Education must train people to what will work in ten years, not to emulate the way that worked for last ten years. Undoubtedly the potential communication of social networks is still to be discovered and should be studied more in depth [1]. It is in these moments when they begin to create networks for educational purposes and, without doubt, in the coming months there will be interesting developments in this regard.

Social networks have become a virtual environment where many people converge. The exponential growth of social networks today have turned these sites into an interesting analysis tool to find usages, customs and origin of many users that comprise them. Some of these social networking services like Facebook, among others, are used by many universities in the world to publish their works, videos, resources and projects, to be criticized and evaluated by the community, and this become of a great support to teachers. Using this tool is increasingly common among humans; hundreds of thousands of users worldwide have experienced the use of Facebook as a tool for the development of social communities. The impact of social networks like Facebook or Twitter is growing stronger worldwide. However, to think about the role of teachers in our time, it would be possible from a contextualization: insert the teacher's role in the context of the knowledge society.

The proper use of these social networks demonstrates a variety of tools and resources that can be used to improve the instruction and communication between students, teachers, administrators and tutors support teams, thus improving by this the teaching/learning process, about which Internet has positive effects. Education in relation to new technologies should be designed as a means to assist and collaborate with the method allowing improving teaching and thereby enabling the student to obtain a meaningful learning.

In this paper we propose a new concept of using the existent services of Facebook, in the educative system, without living this, to become by this a peer communication platform which immense repositories of knowledge universally accessible and constantly updated, thanks to its inclusion in the Cloud, within the CSchool system [2]. Thus, we believe that no self-respecting educational system should do without that resource. By incorporating the classroom networks, it requires us to make changes in the organizational culture of schools and pedagogical approaches; this is done by adopting a set of educational patterns [3], which helps in merging the use of Facebook services in adequate aspect.

2 Performed Work in Schools Related to Social Networks

Originally the reason for conducting this research is an image I found on the desktop of the computer of one of my students:

- *To my question: Why do you put this wallpaper?*
- *He replied: It is what I see every day.*

From here we begin to consider the possibility of including social media, network, in educational classroom, since students are accustomed to use them in any place, and in case of school the reason is distraction and to review their personal messages. As researchers, we must pay attention to the users, and in our case they are the teachers and. It is already exists a large number of social networks being used for educational purpose, between these:

- Ning: http://www.ning.com/
- Elgg: http://elgg.com/
- Mahara: https://mahara.org/
- Uimp2.0: http://redsocial.uimp20.es/
- Google Plus for Education:
- Auula: http://www.auula.com/

Where we can perform a collaborative work in the classroom, but our intention is not to design a social network for a specific use, so why to create our own social network when we have, for example, more than 1000 million of users in Facebook, where the probability that my students have account in it is high. So our intention is to use the services of Facebook Social network for our educational purpose making it more focused to the educational process.

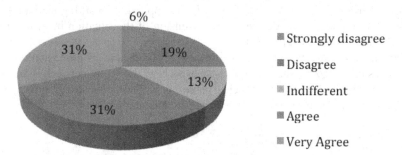

Fig. 1. Percentage of the answer of the question: Do ICTs provide flexibility in time and space, to communicate with your students

During the last academic year, 2011-2012, we conducted a set of surveys in order to obtain tangible data, about the relationship of social networks and the learning environment, because, there was a negative scope by teachers in the use of social networks. During our Learning/Teaching process in the classrooms, we found significant behavior aspects, from the students and teacher part, which make us think about the possibility of inclusion of social networks into the educational process in schools, next we present some questions, given to teachers, and which correspond to the use of social networks:

- To the question "Are you in favor of using social media in educational settings?" 65% answered positively.
- "Do ICTs provide flexibility in time and space, to communicate with your students?" 62% appreciated the inclusion of ICTs, see Figure 1
- "The ICTs do not allow students to exercise in the acquisition of some basic intellectual skills? The teachers observe that the use of ICT increases the acquisition of basic skills, with direct reference to the acquisition of basic skills. The 75% of them answered negatively to this use; see Figure 2.

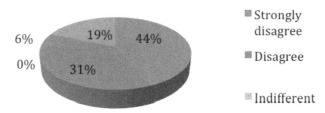

Fig. 2. Percentage of the answer of the question: The ICTs do not allow students to exercise in the acquisition of some basic intellectual skills.

We also raise a question for teachers, rate the type of work they do with the use of ICT in the classroom, as we can see in Figure 3. Teachers score very favorably the use of ICT for cooperative work on projects. After analyzing the survey, we found that the definition of social network from the analytical point of view, is a set of actors linked to a set of relationships that meet certain properties, which have a structure and characteristics defined by the social behavior [4] and hierarchical structure, which is extracted from the context in which it is being applied, so working methodologies, communication patterns are defined as an extension of the situation in which the actors perform their work [5] [6] [7] [8].

Teachers show a very high interest in tracking students to evaluate and qualification of the student, so the inclusion of these aspects of the social network is an important and very relevant, since the teacher bases his work in educational programming classroom with a structure and a very specific documentation [9].

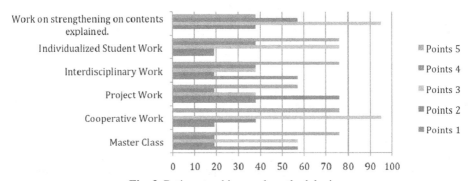

Fig. 3. Ratings teaching work methodologies

Next we present a set of questions, we made, focused on the organization of didactic content of the teacher, thus those do not perform only the teaching work:

- Is it useful to generate a report with the score of the level of achievement of the objectives and responsibilities of students, student group? 84% of teachers surveyed are in favor of reporting the objectives achieved by students during the teaching lessons; see Figure 4.
- Is the school organization reflected in the ICT in your daily work? 69.23% of teachers confirm this assertion.

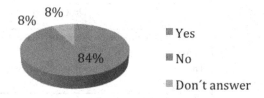

Fig. 4. Percentage of the answer of the question: Is it useful to generate a report with the score of the level of achievement of the objectives and responsibilities of students?

We are therefore faced with a scenario where the work of teachers is teaching and organizational work, where the daily work of the students should be collected for further analysis and to allow the teacher to perform the tasks of monitoring and evaluation of the student, and to prepare an inclusive education in the classroom appropriate to the group of pupils and students in particular. In our previous research we have defined several development methodologies, the use of patterns in classroom makes us think that the dual curriculum, that Pere Marques define in [10], is wrong to be applied in the Web 2.0 world, and that the social networks are tools that interrogates the teacher, of how to do things but does not provide the methods of analysis of all the information that he needs to do the monitoring, evaluation and qualification of the teaching-learning process. For that we have to be careful and not to define a new teaching methodology focused on social networking, but in the structuring of the social network itself to perform a flexible and dynamic space, for the teacher, in which he can integrate social teaching methodologies.

3   Educational Patterns Used in Social Networks

We have to be careful not in defining a new teaching methodology focused on social networking, but in the social network structure itself, by making it flexible and dynamic space for the teacher, to perform his teaching and learning process, to integrate his social teaching methodologies, and a system where the educational documentation is fully insured for its evaluation. Our experience with educational tools, shows us that there must be a set of patterns that guide the work within any educational and collaborative tool [11], for that here in our merge between the CSchool system and

Facebook, we apply a set of patterns, which we already define to cover the educational process in classroom, to ensure the correct function and work of this merge. Thus we found that the patterns provided by a social network for teachers, to interact with their students, are those of the social network, and we can apply them in an educational context to become valid. To this end we establish the comparative educational models with collaborative and learning objects, these patterns are taken from [11] (Figure 6-12. Systematizing Resource patterns under an e-learning System page 158).

Table 1. Coordination Patterns Presentation in Facebook and Description

e-Learning	Facebook	Description
Agenda	Calendar	Users can maintain communications with a close group of friends.
Calendar		The social network will tell you who read the group messages.
News	Wall	We add to the wall a description for the group.
Exam	Wall	Adding to wall information and calendar information to alert users.
Exercise		The system comes with a plugin for Dropbox [12] to send information to students as the statement or the practices they
Work		have to perform.

Our goal is to establish the equivalence between the social network and the e-learning patterns, so that we would have a platform with social networks that interacts with already established e-learning standards, see Table 1, Table 2 and Table 3.

Table 2. Coordination Patterns Presentation in Facebook and Description

e-Learning	Facebook	Description
Contact Professor	Wall, Email, Video Chat	The teacher can communicate privately to students with different social network options.
Discussion	Wall	The teacher can establish communication needs in the
Work group		Wall group members can interact and exchange
Debate		information to perform a pattern of communication.
FAQ		

Once the relationships are established, between the e-Learning patterns and the social network Facebook functionalities, we can observe that almost all of these options are representative of educational patterns, which we considered necessary. The system works through the exchange of information, which is in the cloud, but there are features that require a complete implementation for these functions. The next section will present a detailed description of these functions.

Table 3. Coordination Patterns Presentation in Facebook and Description

e-Learning	Facebook	Description
Presentation	Wall	The Professor can play all these educational patterns through the wall since students can perform all these patterns by including any type of file.
Video		
Material		
Bibliography		
Demonstration		

4   Architecture

This architecture present the social network Facebook as a key part of the proposed educative system integrated in the cloud, where Facebook is a Web 2.0 Service, one of our main goals is to push Spanish teachers to the inclusion of their activities and use of this social network in schools.

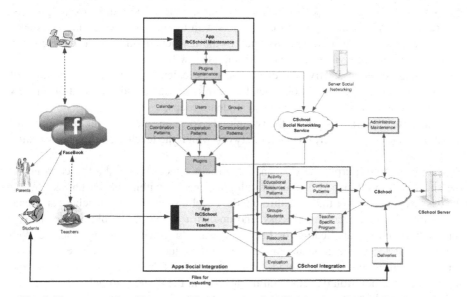

Fig. 5. The proposed architecture of the system, to join Facebook and educational process

Our approach is a mixed system, in which the teacher performs the management of the social network through an application that facilitates the management of content and the creation of all these educational patterns in social network, and control of the elements described above. Students communicate, with the teachers and with their classmates, through Facebook, while the students' deliveries and exams, to be corrected, are sent to the Document Management System (DMS), which controls all the educational management of the center, which also store the school curricular materials. The DMS also contains the students' official curriculum, to control the lessons and courses objectives, and to allow the assessment and grading of students. Next, we present the system architecture, as you can observe in Figure 6., the system has been integrated in the CSchool architecture [13].

The architecture is divided into two parts, very distinct, first we find the cloud of educational services, where the management system works; and on the other hand we have the cloud CSchool Social Networking Service, which manages all the needs for the integration of curricula and school activities in the Facebook social network. This integration has been made possible through the use of Facebook plugins, where we have invoked specific applications to allow this integration in the cloud. And then, we develop an application to manage the integration of both, the social networking and educational applications in our cloud "CSchool", presented in previous articles [2][13]. We divide these applications, for integration, into two parts: for teachers and for administrators.

4.1   Teachers FB Applications

The teacher through these applications can manage the patterns objects necessary for the correct use of Facebook in education, which is integrated thanks to the plugins, Figure 6, shows how this application interacts with the platform which manages educational content and curriculums assigned to the teacher, in addition to their groups, students areas and calendar. This application, also, will allow the teacher to integrate his teaching resources, activities, exercises, tests, calendar, etc. i.e. the creation of educational patterns in Facebook, social network, services, and the creation of new patterns through the necessary plugins in student groups.

This application interacts with the two clouds: form one side, we get the educational patterns; and in the other, the social network which the teacher configure according to his needs.

We highlight in purple the relevant plugins for education standards, according to the specification described above, this plugin generate within the Facebook content the desired pattern, after that, and through the Facebook service, the teacher can create a structure, learning/teaching process, and upload it to the Facebook; besides he can track it through the application or Facebook wall. In green color, we find the Web Services that access the educational services of the educative yields where the necessary information, interact and stored, for the operation of the management system, and to promote the inclusion of data from the teacher in the system, so helps the teacher's in his daily work, by monitoring his activities, and to improve the process of evaluation and monitoring of the student.

4.2   Administrators FB Applications

The administrator is responsible for managing and maintaining the user groups, this process involves a migration of users and groups, which is configured in the management platforms that schools have. Furthermore, the system administrator will have the necessary options for updating the Facebook page. Note that the system will accept the evaluable content entries, the students sent to the server, as deliverables, to avoid any posterior problems. The inclusion of an activity, on the server, for its revise and posterior delivery to the student, corresponds to the creation of Servlet that process the input of a new student. More services, have been added to the administrator to perform the maintenance tasks, between the two clouds: to create users and groups, and to verify the synchronization between the two educational clouds.

As first step, parents and students interact directly with the new educative Facebook, a controlled approach by the teacher of the use of these in the educational world. With the presented architecture, the plugins system, guarantees a dynamic system, thus, we can include other social networks depending on the needs of the teacher, and following a clear line since the beginning of the creation of an educational learning/teaching process.

5   Conclusion and Future Work

In this paper we have tried to simplify the use of social networks, in our case study "Facebook" in the educational world, for that we have established the teacher as the main focus point of the system, and not the student, as it usually done, because teachers are not familiar with these new social networks. By this we gave teachers the opportunity to share with students, through the use of social networks, some educational activities and to perform the evaluation process of these. By including another layer to the system, this allows the interaction with social networks from other management education applications, where it offers the teacher a lot of features. In this paper we have tried to work with the most used educational patterns [11], where we present their migration to work within social networks, but over the time, and with the increased use of social networks, new patterns will appear, because of the needs of teachers, as for the new features that offer advances in social networks.

As future work, we are studding to create and use of social networks in business and industrial environments, not just for marketing use, but as a collaborative online work place, depending on the needs and the type of management application that the small businesses have. This allows that bridge applications can be made, which do not involve a lot of time in its configuration and professionals training will not be high, when it depends on ICTs and social networks issues.

Acknowledgments. Thank for all teachers and students as to the school of Alcañiz for participating with us to try this system.

References

1. Fardoun, H.M., Alghazzawi, D.M., López, S.R., Penichet, V.M.R., Gallud, J.A.: Online Social Networks Impact in Secondary Education. In: Vittorini, P., Gennari, R., Marenzi, I., de la Prieta, F., Rodríguez, J.M.C. (eds.) International Workshop on Evidence-Based TEL. AISC, vol. 152, pp. 37–45. Springer, Heidelberg (2012)
2. Fardoun, H.M., Paules, A., Romero López, S., Zafar, B.: CSchool Interactive Design. In: 1st International Workshop on Interaction Design in Educational Environments (IDEE 2012), ICEIS 2012 Conference, Wroclaw, Poland, June 28 (2012)

3. Fardoun, H.M., Mashat, A.S., Alghazzawi, D.M.: Educative Resource Patterns Presentation in a Model-Based Instructional E-Learning System Design Environment. In: 1st international Workshop on Interaction Design in Educational Environments (IDEE 2012), ICEIS 2012 Conference, Wroclaw, Poland, June 28 (2012)
4. Santos, F.R.: Reis: Revista Española de Investigaciones Sociológicas (48), 137–152 (October-December 1989)
5. Las redes sociales como herramientas para el aprendizaje colaborativo: una experiencia con Facebook, http://dialnet.unirioja.es/servlet/dcfichero_articulo?codigo=3129947
6. Menéndez, L.S.: Consejo Superior de Investigaciones Científicas (CSIC). Unidad de Políticas Comparadas (UPC) Grupo de Investigación sobre Políticas de Innovación, Tecnología, Formación y Educación (SPRITTE) Apuntes de Ciencia y Tecnología (7) (Junio de 2003)
7. González, F.S.: Posibilidades pedagógicas. Redes sociales y comunidades educativas Social Networks and Educational Communities. Pedagogical Possibilities. Fundacion Telefonica (76) (Julio-Septiembre 2008),
   http://sociedadinformacion.fundacion.telefonica.com/telos/articulocuaderno.asp@idarticulo%3D7&rev%3D76.html
8. Fernández-Díaz, E., Gorospe, J.M.C.: Integración de las TIC en proyectos co-laboratios mediante apadrinamientos digitales. RELATEC: Revista Latinoamericana de Tecnología Educativa 7(2), 57–67 (2008) ISSN-e 1695-288X
9. Fardoun, H., Montero, F., López Jaquero, V.: eLearniXML: Towards a model-based approach for the development of e-Learning systems considering quality. Advances in Engineering Software 40(12), 1297–1305 (2009)
10. Marques, P.: (2013),
    http://peremarques.blogspot.com.es/2011/09/que-es-el-curriculum-bimodal-i.html (last access: June 2012)
11. Fardoun, H.: PhD Thesis. ElearniXML: towards a model-based approach for the development of e-learning systems. University Castilla-La; Mancha (2011)
12. Taylor, C.: Facebook Integrates With Dropbox To Power File-Sharing Within Facebook Groups (2012),
    http://techcrunch.com/2012/09/26/facebook-integrates-with-dropbox-to-power-file-sharing-within-facebook-groups/
13. Fardoun, H.M., Ciprés, A.P., Alghazzawi, D.M.: CSchool-DUI for Educational System using Clouds. In: 2nd Workshop on Distributed User Interfaces: Collaboration and Usability CHI 2012 Workshop, Austin, Texas, USA, May 05-10 (2012); Proceedings of the 2nd Workshop on Distributed User Interfaces: Collaboration and Usability. In conjunction with CHI 2012 Conference, Austin, Texas, USA, pp. 35–39 ISBN-10: 84-695-3318-5

Improvement of Students Curricula
in Educational Environments by Means
of Online Communities and Social Networks

Habib M. Fardoun[1], Abdulrahman H. Altalhi[1], and Antonio Paules Ciprés[2]

[1] Faculty of Computing and Information Systems, King Abdulaziz University,
21589 Jeddah, Saudi Arabia
{hfardoun,ahaltalhi}@kau.edu.sa
[2] School of Engineering, University of Castilla-La Mancha,
02071 Albacete, Spain
apcipres@gmail.com

Abstract. The school is part of our society, which increasingly uses more and more the social networks. Therefore, we must continue this momentum, not only by using them, but by also guiding the students of its proper use. Thus, most educators working with high and middle level schools are aware of the involvement of young people in social networks, but few of these educators are prepared to deal with them the issue. Experts discuss the risks and benefits of such sites, and the role of schools, to offer a comprehensive approach that addresses the needs of online students. This paper seeks a solution to the complex world of social networking in education, where users can belong to a social network not as such, but as a set of objects that define a necessity. This research work tries to redefine social networking of an online community, where objects that work on the same stage define the team. To do this we propose a school architecture, where objects define the curricular activities, with known characteristics.

Keywords: Educative systems, social networks, cloud computing, Web Services, systems architecture, Students Curriculum, Educative Curricula.

1   Introduction

In the current educational environment, students are heavy users of social networks, blogs, wikis, instant messaging, etc. On the other hand, not all teachers have much interest in the use of these tools for educational use. The idea is to define a system that unifies these users, in an environment that accommodates the concept of online community. Taking into account the scenarios in which teachers perform their work, and the active approach which can build on-line communities, to capture the attention of the students, and thereby achieve the learning/teaching objectives presented for each teaching unit. Therefore, we must continue this momentum, of using on-line communities, not only by using them, but also guiding the students to their proper use. We are going, to try, to understand the potential of on-line communities for learning, to create new learner-centered models. This idea proposes that students

A.A. Ozok and P. Zaphiris (Eds.): OCSC/HCII 2013, LNCS 8029, pp. 147–155, 2013.
© Springer-Verlag Berlin Heidelberg 2013

continue participating, within their education, in identifying routes more interesting and relevant to them. We are not offering just a wide range of options for on-line communities, but also designing learning networks. This aims to provide students a space, outside of the lifelong structured programming, to explore their passions supporting their peers and tutors. Thus, by involving students beyond the limitations of time and classes space, first it allows educators to continue working with them throughout the week, besides, it gives them the invaluable opportunity to share their experiences, which occurred outside the classroom with the learning community.

Therefore, the challenge that we are facing is to give them the opportunity to share their interests and activities constantly occurring elsewhere. If we do that, we will be able to know more about the profile of our students, and we can create new opportunities for all and thus we will facilitate their learning. As students have more connectivity and access to technology resources than ever, developing new practices and platforms to support them in how to manage their learning opportunities solves this challenge. The proposed architecture here, allow users, through online communities, to implement their curricula schedules. This architecture for educational environments with contemporary functional or structural didactic courses, is developed in the cloud, and defines how users can interact with each other under the same activity, through milestones for students.

- Didactic function: Emphasize teaching mental operations to analyze, induce, infer, evaluate, choose, encode.
- Didactic structure: teaches mental tools as notions, concepts, feelings, attitudes, words or gestures.

As we can see, these two types of teaching are generalists, and the aim of this paper is to address these needs, patterns, from the point of view of ICT applied on on-line communities.

2 State of Art

In addition to the equipment found in schools, the vast majority of students have mobile devices with 4G connection, 94% of the users, between 16 and 35 years, of "Tuenti" [1] has mobile, 84% of the users connect to internet through their mobile device, and 47% have contract 4G connection data service. By following the classification of social networks [2], and the pedagogical possibilities of these in the educational settings [3], and the collaborative tools [4], we found that:

D. Boyd and Nicole B. Ellison [5] define social networks as a set of Internet-based services that allows users to build a profile in the system, establish their own relationships and see their list of connections. It was observed, that there is an association between the social network definition and the relationships between adolescents. It's because students in-school space is bounded, and they establish their relations of friendship according to this environment, as it is demonstrated, the impact of social networks in these contexts is high [6]. Inclusive education means that members of a school community learn together, irrespective of their origin, including students with learning disabilities. This definition implies the same opportunities to participate, so student's can be benefit from an education adapted to their educational needs, not only to students requiring significant curricular adaptation. This approach about on-line communities, make us thing about the basis of the teachers within the education systems, *in other articles that have been treated*, in considering the curricular pro-grams, working sessions and the carried out evaluation of the students [7]. All this must be done with usability and quality criteria in the development of interfaces [8].

Currently, in the educational environments, there is no architecture that is adapted to these needs, where the stage is completely focused on school and the relationships between its users, and is done through the activities and specifications that teachers provide them. As mentioned previously, the work is collaborative, and not about creating a new social network, for teachers and students, it's about creating a social network that allows teachers to work the learning contents throughout the courses schedules. Final y the platform, in development, emulates the characteristics that the mobile devices and Smartphones, which students and teachers may possess and view the applications with.

3   System Needs and Definition

The rise of social networks and mobile devices, in youth groups, requires the creation of a system that allows the use of social networks for educational purposes *the problem comes from the high percentage of rejection to use these from parents and teachers.* Their reasons are usually associated with the loss of time, and the content that social networks might possess, making it in the major cause of their rejection to its use.

Usually, students move freely in these environments and, they are able to manage their own data and profile without facing difficulties. The proposed system, aims to make a direct link between the social network and the educational environment. Nor-mally, all educational environments contains a documentary system, related to a man-agement application that performs the maintenance of students, and their associated curricular functions, necessary for teachers, to monitor their educational process, this monitoring of work sessions schedules leads the student activities. The idea is to manage these activities as if it were a social network, by applying them for education-al use, the process that will bring out the information, monitored by the teacher who must assess his students, and must pay attention about what content they are visiting and consulting.

The educational process in a collaborative work for primary and secondary stu-dents, involves the following steps: (1) Data collection, (2) Information processing, (3) Share information, (4) Treat information, (5) Presentation of the contents and its application. To ensure, always, the correct application of these steps, a set of patterns in each of these phases, must be established. All of these patterns are already defined in social networks, but the inclusion of specific needs, is done, for the scenario in which it takes place. The scenario, will be a class session, in which a timeline is estab-lished to allow students to carry out guided activities, this timeline is related to the timing of their course, which in his turn is stored in the system, to create the set of objectives, and pedagogical data, achieved by each student during this process. This pedagogical information is stored, for its posterior use in reports, that teachers emit of these students over the time, and favor their educative improvement. Also, these patterns will facilitates, to teachers, the preparation of specific educational activities as needed, or assess the student group as a whole.

4   Educative Patterns Used within Online Community

The educational patterns, through which teachers and students interact with educative online community, are:

- **Data Collection:** The students collect the data, in the initial phase of the teaching-learning process, using different teaching methodologies within various search systems, to perform their activities. This trains the student to filter the educative content, make searching actions, and to collect the important, needed, data.
- **Processing of Information:** Once the data is collected, students can then specify which of these data are valid for the activity to be performed. The student structures this information, in order to achieve the objectives of the performed activity.
- **Sharing of Information:** Once the information, which students will share with their peer group, is processed, those can begin to have an overview of the different parts of the activity to complete his information, view.
- **Treatment of Information**: The student performs a process of information processing, structuring and formatting, to achieve the completion of the activity, and thus to make its presentation. In this process is where the student actually performs the synthesis, and study where he must integrate and adjust the information to achieve the specified objectives.
- **Presentation of Content and its implementation**: The student begins to execute the presentation of the activity to the group of students.

These educational patterns interact within an online community or social network in *Cloud Environment,* where these behave as objects that interact between each other. The reason of why we have defined a cloud of patterns is to have the possibility to include them in any educational platforms, placed in any placed, and thus, we can add these features to the curricular management tools of the schools.

5   System Architecture

The system that we propose here is flexible for deployment, and enables interoperability between platforms, that may depend on it, allowing interaction via mobile devices. For that, its architecture allows the inclusion of the needed items for its realization, since it is based on a Cloud system, thanks to its support of the CSchool [8]. The system architecture is integrated with management software for schools and, in turn, gives support to the official curriculum, which comes from central servers.

The first raised question was: how to make the inclusion of curriculum materials in a social network? This was the starting point, thus it covers how social network interact with the elements of the curriculum, so that teachers can develop their work in it, and prepare well their activities. The operation of this online community is based on using the patterns, for the activities, the teachers want to apply, and then they proceed with the publication of these in the cloud. These patterns are all identified and managed in the cloud, i.e. managing the relationships and how two patterns interact between each other. The users, teachers and students, are not registered or housed in the cloud, only the patterns and their relationships, based on the definition of object according to the patterns that the teacher can possess [9]. With this we achieved a flexible and dynamic system, which can be embedded into existing educational platforms, as an embedded object, composed of the data and academic curriculum that the teachers store.

This architecture allows schools to have similar functionality to those of social networks, thus these patterns list increase continuously, with the appearance of new features within the system. Where users, students and teachers increase their knowledge from the interaction of these patterns in the cloud and processing the activities. In the other hand, the system also offers a timing of the activities raised by the teacher, and those developed by the student. Also it contemplates the maintenance of the temporary teaching process, and it dispose of navigation task to go through the academic results, of each student, which goes through the life teaching activities, for each activity and each group within the system. As we are working with learning contents, which are didactic elements, each of them identified in the system with a unique identifier, they stores information needed for its composition, depending on the type of pattern or relationship with the task to perform. However, some properties are common to all of them, these are described below:

- ID: Identifies the full learning content in the system.
- Type: The type of learning content identification to allow its construction.
- Parent_ID: Identifies the ID of the parent upon which the pattern will traverse the entire sequence of learning contents associated with the initial pattern.
- Start_Date: Controls the start of the activity.
- Activity_Date: A data structure that stores a file editions.
- End_Date: Date of completion of the activity.
- Teaching Information: Stores information of the objectives, content and basic skills to work within this activity, in addition to the information required for student assessment.

Essentially this architecture is a data structure stored in XML, which can be accommodated in a database or in an XML document, which from SQL procedures, it is possible to interact directly with the system using APIs [10] [11]. The hosting of documents, with the educational content, is done in compressed files, that enables it's storage in any FTP server [12], accessible from most applications, using programmed functions packages for different languages, which convert it in a hybrid system that allows the inclusion of social networking features in educational environments, by specifying the relationships between the identified patterns. Such relationships are not based on personal criteria, such as conventional human friendly relations, but it is the curricular needs of students, or that the teachers require for each educative process. Fig. 1., shows the system architecture and how it is included within the educational platform, which also allows browsing the identified educational patterns through the objects defined in the cloud. The different elements that compose it are:

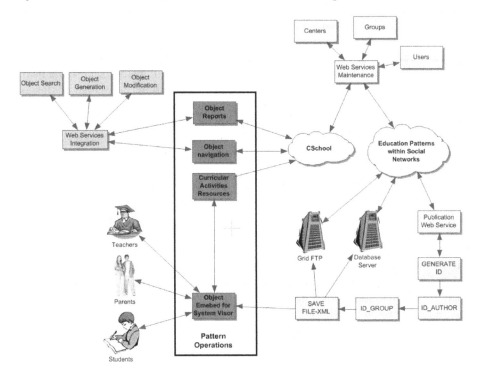

Fig. 1. System architecture, describe the creation of patterns related to the relationship educational system and social networks

- **Educative Patterns within Social Networks Cloud**, it hosts the objects of the patterns required for the teaching-learning process, in addition to their operations. It also stores the relationships and objects created for the users of the system. This cloud offer publishing services, for this we use Web Services, which will contain the business logic, required for storing the pattern information in the server. It is an XML file, which is identified by the ID fields, of the file, the Author and the Group.
- **CSchool** is an educational platform for schools management [DUI 2012]; it includes the basic needs of the educational curricula and activities. This platform communicates using Web Services for maintenance labors (yellow), and to keep the two systems synchronized with the users. Being a cloud system, we decided to create a composite bridge to facilitate the interoperability and communication between the different systems (orange).

- **Reports Object** produce a report patterns represented by the objects in the cloud, from there, depending on the user level, the reports that users have can be obtained.
- **Navigation Object**, it takes users to visualize the patterns represented by the search criteria, which they may determine, from here after selecting the object users can proceed to view and edit the data.
- **Embebed Object for System Visor** is the entry point from which users will see the objects in a session, activity or program.

This architecture can perform a deployment, depending on the conditions of the customer, as the specification and configuration of Web Services enable it to adapt quickly to any platform.

6   Case Study

The presented case study, defines the activity "Going to a Tour", provided by the teacher of the 5th grade, of the "Collegio publico juan XXIII" school (Spain), this activity treats the area of knowledge of the environment, while performing a trip in the countryside, the collected data, by the students, is about the local wildlife. This activity involves the following points: (1) Students must collect the data, i.e. making pictures of the animals and plants, they find during the trip. (2) Students must perform a search of the species, making a classification of the same, performing a scheme of the found species, and finally, adding its characteristics. (3) Students share their information, with their peers, to get the greatest number of species. (4) Students should perform a work, where they can include these features, and make a presentation of the most prominent and the curiosities of the journey.

Using the proposed system, the teacher defines the patterns associated to these points of the activity, these patterns are: (1) Starting the activity, information of the activity, objectives and core competencies to work with. (2) Data collection of animal/plant species. (3) Search for information of the collected data, using Internet (i.e. Wikipedia), students first identifies the species, and they complete it with the necessary information. (4) Sharing of information about animal/plant species. (5) Process of the information by, preparing, adding, and formatting animal/plant species. (6) Process the data as a whole, to structure the information processed earlier, giving the students the opportunity to analyze the environmental setting found in the tour. (7) Prepare the presentation of the content. (8) Final grade and report to parents.

Point 1 and 10, are common to all the activities, they come into two patterns, which do not really have any didactic work, they are management and administration patterns, which prepare students for the steps to be followed, the end report to be given to the parents, and the store of the done work, by the students. In each of these patterns added by the teacher, each activity goes through an evaluation and summative process, which corresponds to the level of achievement of the objectives, as the final grade result for each of these patterns. Each pattern contains a percentage value of the rating data, and a score of the achieved goals, based on the analysis of these data, the teacher views the evaluation of the educative process of the students. After the evaluation process, the teacher closed the student activity, storing it for future reference by the other members of the educational community, and classifying it as curricular structure, according to where it was created, and finally, generating a report to be sent to the parents.

7   Conclusions

The development of this document matches the needs that teachers have with the use of social networks. From the standpoint of teaching, these networks facilitate communication between users of the educative centers. From our experience in the creation of educative platforms, and our study of social networks, in the last few years [6, 9, 13, 14, 15, 16], we found that there is a really need to incorporate necessary materials into social networks, for educative staff who use them, and at the same time, these patterns should be easy to use. So in a scenario, that describes the educational world, these patterns will represent the curricular activities, which require the needs of social networks and their tools to be carried out by the users. The set of elements that are hosted in the cloud, provides a social networking aspect of the curricular patterns interrelate with each other, timed and monitored by the teacher. In the other hand, the teacher controls all elements within the proposed educative social network, which allows the implementation of activities, following the patterns that the relations of objects establish.

After launching this system, for its validation in an educational environment, the users with whom we have worked were teachers from primary and secondary school, the first problem we faced was when we named the words "social network", thus, most teachers only associated it to "Tuenti" and "Facebook", and the dangers that it entails. While in fact, we are presenting a networking of patterns, which will give users the feeling of being in a social network tailored to their working environment. Users define objects to interact with other unknown users, but the object itself is part of a community of objects that are defined by the users' needs, and these are the same for all system users. Relations between objects give full content to the provided patters to students and for its future growth.

As a future work, we are studding the possibility of the inclusion of these activities and their scores on the students' personal curricula, to improve the whole educational curricula. By making use of intelligent agents, the system can make a selection of what goals and what core competencies require modification, to help teachers in their teaching process.

References

1. Tuniti, Spanish social network, https://www.tuenti.com/?m=login
2. de Haro, J.J.: Redes Sociales en Educación (2010) ISBN: 9788441527966
3. Levis, D.: Redes educativas 2.1 Medios sociales, entornos colaborativos y procesos de enseñanza y aprendizaje. Facultad de Ciencias Sociales de la Universidad de Buenos Aires. RUSC vol. 8(1). Universitat Oberta de Catalunya, Barcelona (Enero de 2011) ISSN 1698-580X

4. González, F.S.: Herramientas colaborativas para la enseñanza usando tecnologías web: weblogs, wikis, redes sociales y web 2.0 (2005)
5. Boyd, D.M., Ellison, N.B.: Social Network Sites: Definition, History, and Scholarship. Journal of Computer-Mediated Communication 13(1) (2007a), http://jcmc.indiana.edu/vol13/issue1/boyd.ellison.html
6. Fardoun, H.M., Alghazzawi, D.M., López, S.R., Penichet, V.M.R., Gallud, J.A.: Online Social Networks Impact in Secondary Education. In: International Workshop on Evidenced-Based Technology Enhanced Learning, EBTEL 2012, Salamanca (Spain), March 28-30 (2012)
7. Ciprés, A.P., Fardoun, H.M., Mashat, A.: Cataloging Teaching Units: Resources, Evaluation and Collaboration. In: Proceedings of the Federated Conference on Computer Science and Information Systems, pp. 825–830, ISBN 978-83-60810-51-4
8. Fardoun, H.M., Paules, A., Alghazzawi, D.M.: CSchool: DUI for Educational System by means of Clouds. In: 2nd Workshop on Distributed User Interfaces: Collaboration and Usability CHI 2012 Workshop, Austin, Texas, USA (2012)
9. Fardoun, H.M.: PhD Thesis, ElearniXML: towards a model based approach for the development of e-learning systems. University of Castilla-La Mancha (2011)
10. Oracle Database: XML SQL Utility, http://docs.oracle.com/cd/B19306_01/appdev.102/b14252/adx_j_xsu.html (last access: June 2012)
11. Oracle Database: Oracle9i XML API Reference, http://docs.oracle.com/cd/A97630_01/appdev.920/a96616/arxml24.html (last access: June 2012)
12. Postel, J., Reynolds, J.: Protocolo de Tranferencia de Ficheros (FTP). Network Working Group (IEN 149) (1985)
13. Fardoun, H.M., López, S.R., Alghazzawi, D.M., Castillo, J.R.: Looking for Leaders: Reaching the Future Leaders in Education through Online Social Networks. Procedia - Social and Behavioral Sciences 47, 2036–2043 (2012), doi:10.1016/j.sbspro.2012.06.945, ISSN 1877-0428
14. Fardoun, H.M., López, S.R., Alghazzawi, D.M., Castillo, J.R.: Education System in the Cloud to Improve Student Communication in the Institutes of: C-LearniXML++. Procedia - Social and Behavioral Sciences 47, 1762–1769 (2012), doi:10.1016/j.sbspro.2012.06.897, ISSN 1877-0428
15. López, S.R., Fardoun, H., Alghazzawi, D.M.: Coaching for Students: Parents Tutoring Children as part of their Educational Process. In: Proceedings of the Federated Conference on Computer Science and Information Systems, pp. 863–870, ISBN 978-83-60810-51-4

Metaheuristic Entry Points for Harnessing Human Computation in Mainstream Games

Peter Jamieson, Lindsay Grace, Jack Hall, and Aditya Wibowo

Miami University
Oxford, OH
jamiespa@muohio.edu

Abstract. In this work, we describe a promising approach to harnessing human computation in mainstream video games. Our hypothesis is that one of the best approaches to seamlessly incorporating harnessing withing these games is by examining existing game mechanics and matching them to meta-heuristic algorithms. In particular, we believe that the best choices for early exploration of this problem are nature inspired meta-heuristic algorithms for combinatorial optimization problems. In this paper, we will describe the problem in more detail and describe two proof of concept games that demonstrate the viability of this approach. The first game is designed to be incorporated in Real-time Strategy games within the resource gathering aspects of these games, and the algorithm and problem that are used is related to Ant Colony Optimization and the Traveling Salesman Problem. The second game explores a racing game where the problem and algorithm are embedded in the numerical characteristics of the racer such as speed, agility, and jump power. These characteristics represent current solutions to different traveling salesman problems, and the solutions are modified through training and mating of racers; this is analogous to mutations and crossbreeding in genetic algorithms.

1 Introduction

Hybrid computation systems that can take advantage of computation (or problem solving) skills of both humans and computation machines have the potential to solve complex real-world problems that at present may be tedious human tasks, challenging unsolved problems, or are complex tasks that no computer algorithm has yet been created to solve. In the case of humans, we are able to make decisions based on observed patterns and understanding of the big picture, but we tire from monotonous tasks and are slow when dealing with low-level computational tasks. Computing machines, on the other hand, are tireless and accurate, but are hard to program/design to process high-level concepts. The challenge is merging these two entities so that humans enjoy the computation activity as a game, and the overall system provides better solutions to the real-world problems compared to an algorithm or human alone.

Ultimately, if we could harness human computation during the play of games, then we would recycle a massive amount of thought that, currently, is directed

A.A. Ozok and P. Zaphiris (Eds.): OCSC/HCII 2013, LNCS 8029, pp. 156–163, 2013.

purely to entertainment. With the linking of people via the web, we have a human cloud that many have tried to harness for a number of tasks. Popular crowd sourcing examples, such as Amazon's Mechanical Turk (MTurk), and human computing games (HCG [2]) such as Foldit [7] have shown some success in harnessing humans for tasks. Still, mainstream video games (including casual games) are played for at least an hour a week by 135 million people in the U.S.A. according to Macchiarella's white paper report [14]. That is a massive "thought" resource that to this day remains untapped.

In this work, we describe an approach to harnessing human computation in mainstream video games. Our hypothesis is that early approaches to incorporating harnessing withing games will happen by examining existing game mechanics and matching them to meta-heuristic algorithms. In particular, we believe that the best choices for early exploration of this problem are nature inspired meta-heuristic algorithms for combinatorial optimization problems.

To test our hypothesis we, first, explain the challenges associated with including HCGs in mainstream video games. Specifically, we identify how creating isomorphs of problems for games and puzzles is particularly challenging.

We then describe two proof-of-concept games that demonstrate the viability of our approach. The first game is designed to be incorporated in Real-time Strategy (RTS) games within the resource gathering aspects of these games. The algorithm and problem that are used as the HCG connection is related to Ant Colony Optimization (ACO) [4] and the Traveling Salesman Problem (TSP). The second game explores a racing game where the problem and algorithm are embedded in the numerical characteristics of the racer such as speed, agility, and jump power. These characteristics represent current solutions to different TSPs, and the solutions to these problems are modified through training and mating of racers; this is analogous to mutations and crossbreeding in genetic algorithms (GAs) [9].

2 Background and Definitions

The Human Cloud (HC) can be described as a network of intelligence, connected through existing systems like the Internet. Harnessing the HC has been done in a number of projects in a form of crowd-sourcing, which is defined in this paper as using the knowledge and effort of a large group of individuals. In particular, Human Computing Games (HCGs) have been used to harness the HC and include games such as protein folding [7], picture identification [5], and other types of human computation have been achieved without the game aspect such as security camera searches [10] and searching for space dust [19].

HCG's and other types of productive play fall under the greater domain of games with a purpose (GWAP) (defined by von Ahn) and the general and contested term serious games. Since von Ahn's original work on a ESP [5], over 40 HCGs have been presented at conferences and in journals by a growing number of researchers.

One of these games, Foldit has had tremendous success [7], it is a game developed to allow players to interact with complex proteins, attempting to solve one of the problems facing biological science - how to predict protein structure. Foldit presents 3D abstraction of proteins and simplifies the chemistry behind protein folding by making the problem into a game. It is clear to the user that they are folding proteins as no abstraction is made, but users are rewarded for their efforts by a driving goal to get to the top of the leader board. Foldit develops solutions that are better than those produced by machines by encouraging competition between the 50,000+ players of the game and has been successful.

Most HCGs are projects with real-world problems and these problems are presented in what we call the "direct form". Users are aware of the real-world problems since the game is presented in this manner, and the players are motivated to help by competing against others for status or other direct incentives such as money or recognition. The limitation of this approach is that only a specific problem can be solved in the direct approach, the game must be designed from the real-world problem, and the larger potential population of game players who just play for entertainment tends to be left untapped.

2.1   Isomorphs

Humans are able to make heuristic problem solving decisions based on observed patterns and an understanding of the big picture, but we tend to tire with monotonous tasks that are not motivated by intrinsic rewards, and we are slow when dealing with low-level computational tasks. One of the major challenges in incorporating HCG aspects into mainstream video games is how can we take a real-world computation problem and map it into the game. More, importantly, can this mapping be done in a way so that the problem being solved just seems part of the game.

To achieve this, we must address what is called an isomorph. More specifically, an isomorphic problem has multiple presentation formats at the surface level, but are the same problem underneath. For example, a problem like mowing the lawn requires that a mower be controlled to both efficiently cover the area that needs to be mowed and avoid any live obstacles that might enter the mowers path such as children or animals. An isomorph of the lawn mowing problems could be a coloring game where the goal is to draw in an area without lifting the crayon and avoiding random targets that might try to make you lift your crayon. A similar term to isomorphing in the field of computer science is reduction.

Isomorphic problems have been of interest to cognitive psychologists, and they have been used to help us understand strategical approaches people take to solving problems [18], [13]. An equivalent problem example that illustrates the basic concept of an isomorph is for tic-tac-toe. Zhang *et. al.* [22] show some common ways of presenting tic-tac-toe, and we have replicated one of these in figure 1. In figure 1, the number game is shown where players take turns at picking a number (by coloring in a circle) with the goal of picking three numbers to total fifteen exactly. This game is the same as tic-tac-toe, and the figure shows how these numbers can map to locations on the tic-tac-toe board.

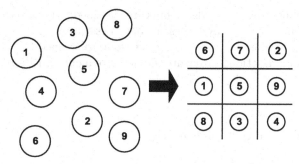

Fig. 1. How a number game of picking 3 numbers that make 15 is an isomorph of tic-tac-toe board

2.2 Meta-heuristics Algorithms and Combinatorial Problems

Meta-heuristic algorithms are one type of algorithm used to solve combinatorial optimization problems [15]. An excellent survey of some of these algorithms is described by Blum *et. al.* [1] and these algorithms can be considered as guiding a search through a search space with iterative improvements. Common meta-heuristic algorithms include algorithms such as Simulated Annealing [12], Tabu Search [8], Ant Colony Optimizations [4], Genetic Algorithms [9], and newer ones such as Firefly [21] and Bees algorithms [16].

Blum *et. al.* [1] try to classify many of these algorithms and use various categories. Of particular interest to this project is those that are classified as nature inspired versus non-nature inspired. We believe that the nature inspired algorithms may be easier to use as interfaces for good isomorphs. We think this may be true based on the connection between human actions in nature, game enjoyment and its relationship to our basic needs as described by Falstein in his game design article, "Natural Funativity" [6].

Regardless of the classification, we hypothesize that meta-heuristic algorithms are an excellent interface point to think of good game isomorphs that humans can work with computers to solve real-world problems. Meta-heuristics have been used to solve a number of classical problems such as the traveling salesman problem, the quadratic assignment problem, and the timetabling and scheduling problems. In terms of a tighter connection to real-world problems there are too many applications to list here. Recently, at CEC 2011 a report was prepared that lays out 15 problems to help evaluate evolutionary algorithms [3], and these problems are in areas such as energy and power distribution, chemical production, economics, antenna design, and aerospace.

The no-free-lunch theorem [20], suggests that there does not exist an algorithm for solving all optimization problems that is generally on average better than competitors. This means that choosing one algorithm over another is not that important, but since our algorithmic based games will be a combination of human and computer, we hypothesize that this theorem is still true, but the algorithms aspects, which include how visualizations of the cost function are presented to the gamer, will have an impact on the quality of solutions.

Finally, some meta-heuristic algorithms are classified as nature inspired versus non-nature inspired [1]. We hypothesize that these nature inspired algorithms may be easier to use as interfaces for good isomorphs since there is a connection between human actions in nature, game enjoyment and its relationship to our basic needs as described by Falstein in his game design article, "Natural Funativity" [6].

3   Proof-of-Concept Games

In this section, we describe two games that we have developed to study how well nature inspired meta-heuristic games fit within aspects of mainstream video games. The section following this one will provide discussion on what we have learned from these experiences.

3.1   Swarm-Miner for ACO in Games

Swarm-miner is a game that is inspired by the resource collection in RTS games. The basic idea of our game is to have the human interact with resource collectors in a game to improve the quantity of the collected resources (as reflected by minimizing the cost function of the TSP).

The Ant Colony Optimization (ACO) algorithm is utilized for solving the traveling salesman problem in this game. Without human assistance, the ACO algorithm solves the TSP problem by simulating agents, ants, that investigate paths with the simple heuristic that edges with higher pheromone levels are more likely to lead to improved paths and thus are more likely to be chosen by ants. As many ants investigate paths, the pheromone levels on those edges that correspond to a path segment that is shortest are increased.

The objective of our Swarm-Miner game is to mix the solution of shortest path with ACO and humans where the game player wants to find the shortest path for as many maps as possible, thus improving the resource collection. Each map represents, in theory, one of the areas that a resource collector in an RTS game would be harvesting resources. In the proof-of-concept game, rank is determined by those users who have found the current best solution to one of several puzzles hosted on a server. The game is intended to draw on human intuition in order to assist the ACO algorithm in solving this difficult problem. Users utilize various mechanics for altering the paths that will be searched and the likelihood that a path edge will be incorporated into the algorithm's search. Two of these mechanics include doping and re-routing. The doping mechanic allows users to change the pheromone level on an edge that is currently in the ACO optimal path. The re-routing mechanic allows users to re-order the sequence of nodes in which a continuous section of the optimal path follows.

While ACO is one of the most powerful algorithms that can be used to solve the TSP, we have observed during the development process that user solutions are usually equally or more optimal than those solutions that were found by the algorithm computing idly (i.e. without human assistance).

3.2 Monster Racer for GA in Games

Monster Racer is a third-person perspective video game where players control a monster that competes in races similar in nature to Mario Cart. In addition to racing, players interact with their monsters by training them to improve the monster's racing attributes, which includes speed, agility and jump power. This can be done by either training or breeding monsters which translates to steps within a Genetic Algorithm (GA) operations, mutation and crossover, respectively.

In the beginning of the game, a player's monster starts with certain attributes generated by the game. These attributes are actually directly related to the cost function of a solution to an instance of a Traveling Salesman Problem (TSP). For example, a specific TSP problem for speed is shared by all game players, and the initial speed for a player's monster is created by running a GA for a certain number of generations with a unique random seed. Therefore, for this game, three different GAs are run at the beginning, and each produces a solution to three distinct TSPs. The cost function for these solutions is then used to calculate the monsters attributes - agility, speed, and jumping.

As players compete in races, points are earned, which then can be used to either train or breed a player's monster. Training performs random mutations on the current solution for an attribute selected to be trained. If training is successful, in the back-end, the GA has found a better solution for the TSP problem, and translates this solution as an improved monster attribute.

Breeding can also be done to improve a player's monster. Players use allocated points to look at other player's monsters, and then the player chooses one of the other monsters to breed with. Breeding is actually a series of crossover operations using the genome of both monster's attributes. If any of the crossover operations produce a better solution, then the monsters attribute is increased accordingly.

As the game progresses, players compete in a traditional racing game, and at the same time, through competition try to improve the abilities of their monsters in a similar way that a GA behaves.

4 Discussion on Our Approach

Developing these two games has taught us a few important lessons about both how to incorporate meta-heuristics as an entry point for HCGs in mainstream video games and some ideas on how this field of research might move forward.

First, *the isomorph of meta-heuristics algorithms into games is a reasonable match*. The choice of GA and ACO are algorithms that fit well with traditional game mechanics. Though the isomorphs are not seamlessly integrated into games, they match well with game play. For example, Swarm-Miner replicates the resource gathering stages in a classical RTS, but no modern game requires micromanaging resource gathering. Similarly, monster racer incorporates the GA through avatar characteristics, and the cross-breeding and mutation are mechanics within the game, but the cross-breeding mechanic, in particular, is a rare mechanic in mainstream video games.

Second, *the granularity of the HCG is small in comparison to how it fits in the entire mainstream game.* This means that HCGs in mainstream video games will, likely, only be a subset of the entire game. This allows designers to consider sub-problems of the video game as harnessing points for mini-HCGs. For example, swarm-miner represents only the resource mining stage of a much larger RTS game.

Third, *the creation of HCGs and crowd sourcing systems lacks a framework to aid in the development, aggregation, and quality control of such solutions.* Both of these games took a significant time to create even in their proof-of-concept form. There appears to be a major opportunity to create a crowd sourcing framework that would allow researchers to quickly design their ideas and experiment with them. In particular, as these systems develop there are three issues that are interesting as research questions, but require significant infrastructure development.

– User action tracking: as we attempt to understand how hybrid systems solve problems differently from traditional computational methods there is a need for user behavior tracking. For example, Foldit observed users and created new and more efficient automated algorithms based on their solutions [11]
– Aggregation: as identified in Quinn *et. al.* [17], there is a need to collect answers into a global solution. The question remains, what are the most efficient methods to do this as these systems scale in terms of users?
– Quality control: also identified in Quinn *et. al.* [17], there is a need to regulate the solutions provided by users to protect the system from poor and bad behavior.

To test even one solution in this space is very difficult, and a framework that speeds up this development would provide a significant step forward in this area of research.

5   Conclusion

In this paper, we discussed the benefit of creating HCGs defined by meta-heuristic algorithms to harness human computation in mainstream video games. In particular, we described two proof-of-concept games we have developed that test out our ideas. From these experiences we have learned a few important lessons, and describe how a framework for crowd sourcing applications (both games and non-games) would benefit future research in this domain.

References

1. Blum, C., Roli, A.: Metaheuristics in combinatorial optimization: Overview and conceptual comparison. ACM Comput. Surv. 35, 268–308 (2003), http://doi.acm.org/10.1145/937503.937505
2. Cusack, C., Largent, J., Alfuth, R., Klask, K.: Online games as social-computational systems for solving np-complete problems. In: Meaningful Play (2010)

3. Das, S., Suganthan, P.: Problem definitions and evaluation criteria for CEC 2011 competition on testing evolutionary algorithms on real world optimization problems. Tech. rep. (2010), http://web.mysites.ntu.edu.sg/epnsugan/PublicSite/SharedDocuments/CEC2011-RWP/Tech-Rep.pdf
4. Dorigo, M., Maniezzo, V., Colorni, A.: Ant system: optimization by a colony of cooperating agents. IEEE Transactions on Systems, Man, and Cybernetics, Part B: Cybernetics 26(1), 29–41 (1996), http://ieeexplore.ieee.org/xpls/abs_all.jsp?arnumber=484436&tag=1
5. ESP Game: (2008), http://www.gwap.com/gwap/gamesPreview/espgame/
6. Falstein, N.: Natural Funativity. Gamasutra.com (2004), http://www.gamasutra.com/features/20041110/falstein_pfv.html
7. FoldIt: (2008) http://fold.it/portal/
8. Glover, F.: Future paths for integer programming and links to artificial intelligence. Comput. Oper. Res. 13, 533–549 (1986), http://dl.acm.org/citation.cfm?id=15310.15311
9. Goldberg, D.E.: Genetic Algorithms in Search, Optimization, and Machine Learning, 1st edn. Addison-Wesley Professional (January 1989), http://www.amazon.com/exec/obidos/redirect?tag=citeulike07-20&path=ASIN/0201157675
10. Internet Eyes: (2009), http://interneteyes.co.uk/
11. Khatib, F., Cooper, S., Tyka, M.D., Xu, K., Makedon, I., Popovic, Z., Baker, D., Players, F.: Algorithm discovery by protein folding game players. Proceedings of the National Academy of Sciences (2011), http://www.ts-si.org/files/doi101073pnas1115898108.pdf
12. Kirkpatrick, S., Gelatt, C.D., Vecchi, M.P.: Optimization by Simulated Annealing. Science 220(4598), 671–680 (1983)
13. Kotovsky, K., Hayes, J.R., Simon, H.A.: Tower of Hanoi - Problem Isomorphs and Solution Processes. Bulletin of the Psychonomic Society 22(4), 290 (1984)
14. Macchiarella, P.: Trends in Digital Gaming: Free-to-Play, Social, and Mobile Games. Tech. rep. (2012)
15. Papadimitriou, C.H., Steiglitz, K.: Optimization Algorithms and Complexity. Dover Publications, Inc., New York (1982)
16. Pham, D., Ghanbarzadeh, A., Koç, E., Otri, S., Rahim, S., Zaidi, M.: The bees algorithm, a novel tool for complex optimisation problems. In: Virtual International Conference on Intelligent Production Machines and Systems, pp. 454–459 (2006), http://www.bees-algorithm.com/modules/2/4.pdf
17. Quinn, A.J., Bederson, B.B.: Human computation: a survey and taxonomy of a growing field. In: Proceedings of the SIGCHI Conference on Human Factors in Computing Systems, pp. 1403–1412 (2011), http://doi.acm.org/10.1145/1978942.1979148
18. Simon, H.A., Hayes, J.R.: Understanding Process - Problem Isomorphs. Cognitive Psychology 8(2), 165–190 (1976)
19. Stradust@Home: (2009), http://stardustathome.ssl.berkeley.edu/
20. Wolpert, D.H., Macready, W.G.: No Free Lunch Theorems for Search, REPORT SFI-TR-95-02-010. Tech. rep. (1996)
21. Yang, X.S.: Nature-Inspired Metaheuristic Algorithms. Luniver Press (2008)
22. Zhang, J., Johnson, T., Wang, H.: Isomorphic Representations Lead to the Discovery of Different Forms of a Common Strategy with Different Degrees of Generality. In: Proceedings of the 20th Annual Conference of the Cognitive Science Society (1998), http://citeseerx.ist.psu.edu/viewdoc/download;jsessionid=93CB1A5E27B562C8B7BD109A1BF3A241?doi=10.1.1.139.9596&rep=rep1&type=pdf

Project Awareness System –
Improving Collaboration through Visibility

Daniel Kadenbach and Carsten Kleiner

University of Applied Sciences and Arts Hannover, Germany
{daniel.kadenbach,carsten.kleiner}@hs-hannover.de

Abstract. This paper proposes and describes the Project Awareness
System (PAS) which is designed to improve the awareness of projects
and project participants within and beyond organizational borders. The
aim of this system is to increase the visibility of projects, so that users
can easily find interesting ones and contact their participants to increase
communication, collaboration and reuse of project results. The system
enables an organizational unit to easily store project information at a
central place. It does not impose strict rules regarding what data about
projects can be stored. In this way strongly heterogeneous project environments can be mapped. The system offers its users extensive search
mechanisms to find the projects they are looking for. The PAS additionally supports federation of multiple instances. The user can browse
through the projects of multiple organizational units and organizations
at one place, while each unit stays in full control of its data.

Keywords: CSCW, collaboration, project awareness, virtual communities, education.

1   Introduction

Projects and their results are the essence of our work. They help us to proceed,
build upon established work, improve it and create something new. They serve
as sources of inspiration. They help us to learn and to develop, to gather and
share knowledge. In the best case, they create a durable value for the community.
Projects can only achieve most of these benefits if they are visible, accessible and
sustainable. With these attributes, the value of a project rises or falls. If it is not
possible for others to become aware of a project, find it and access its contents or
at least be able to contact its authors, it looses a great deal of its real potential.

For example, how do you find a master thesis, a scientific project or a capstone
project in your own department? What if you only have a few keywords for your
search? How can you find out if such or a similar project already exists at a
different institution so you could share knowledge, build upon existing results or
even work together? Only a fraction of active and finished projects have got a
website which could be indexed by a search engine. So how are we able to avoid
carrying out the same small projects again and again instead of working together
on something big and new, if there is no reliable way to find similar projects?

A.A. Ozok and P. Zaphiris (Eds.): OCSC/HCII 2013, LNCS 8029, pp. 164–173, 2013.
© Springer-Verlag Berlin Heidelberg 2013

Why do most projects start from scratch instead of building upon something which already exists or improving it? How much more could we accomplish if we knew what other institutions, staff members or students are working on, if we had the possibility to work together and learn from each other?

Our paper describes the so-called Project Awareness System (PAS) which we designed to answer these questions. The proposed system mainly focuses on academical and/or open-source environments for research or software engineering projects, but it may also be applicable to other environments and projects. Its primary aim is to make projects visible, accessible and sustainable to protect and enhance their value. The PAS therefore stores information about projects of an organizational unit at a central place and offers this information through well-defined interfaces. The PAS acts as an easy to use, uniform project portal, offering a project portfolio of the organizational unit independently of its internal project culture and infrastructure. It offers interfaces to store and access project information either manually or automatically. In its core we define a project description language to store the different project attributes. Using this representation, projects can be managed, assessed and found.

1.1 Motivation and Aims

There were three main motivations to create the PAS, partially contained in the aforementioned questions of the introduction:

1. Keeping Track of Your Own Projects. Over the years you will probably carry out a multitude of projects and it may be hard to keep track of them all. For example, just creating different folders in your file system to store your project information limits you in the way you sort your projects and therefore, in the way of finding one by special criteria. Usually, you will only be able to sort them by one criteria in different folders, e.g. their creation date. But you will have to search through all of them if you are searching a project which uses a special technology, or in which you worked with a specified person. Additionally no one else will be able to get to know what you have worked on.

2. Awareness for Projects of Your Organizational Unit. Apart from knowing and finding your own projects, there is probably a multitude of projects carried out at your organizational unit. Most of the time, apart from the project teams themselves and their "customers" there are not many persons who are aware of these projects, at least this has often been the case in our department. Projects may exist in quite different environments: Some may only exist on paper, some may use a Subversion or Git repository somewhere, some may use a project management service like Trac or Redmine and some projects may even be hosted on the Internet. Consequently it is impossible to be aware of many of them. But by not knowing which other projects exist or existed, great chances are lost. Being aware of the other projects may lead to more communication and collaboration. It may lead to more motivation, because projects are visible to others. It may also help to shape the spirit of the organizational unit, because everyone is able to see the achievements of her or his colleagues.

3. Finding Specific Projects in Your Organization and Beyond. Finally, the most important thing is finding projects. We cannot stress this point enough. There can hardly be any real progress if we are not able to easily find the projects of others. Every time someone starts a project, she or he has to look up if something similar has already been done or is being done at the moment. In both cases, synergetic effects could be utilized, efforts could be shared, help could be offered – but only if it is possible to find these projects. Again, some projects only exist on paper, some only on the computers of their participants, some are available on servers of their organizations and some are hosted at different Internet services[1]. How to keep track of all of them? At the moment our answer to that question is: You simply cannot. Even not in your own organization. You may conduct a search, but probably you will only find a fraction of the work, which has been done. And this has to be changed.

The aims of the PAS are therefore: Firstly, to be a central point of information for projects, offering a project portfolio of its organizational unit or organization and enabling its users to easily and extensively search for projects, to increase the visibility and sustainability of projects and to promote collaboration and reuse of results. Secondly, to be able to be used in a federation of systems, so that this single point of information may even exist for multiple organizational units, organizations or also at higher levels. And finally, to be able to be used with a minimum of effort and therefore being as simple as possible. This also means that everything has to be done to automatically keep the managed data up to date and valuable.

1.2   Related Work

Several authors have already done research in how to improve project awareness in project teams, like in [6] where dashboards and feeds are used or in [1], [2] and [3]. Our approach tries to increase the awareness also beyond project teams.

Majumdar and Krishna investigated in [4] how to utilize social computing implications for virtual teams, which is also a foundation for our work. Ohira et al. described a tool in [5] to improve knowledge collaboration on the base of project hosting sites, which is also an aim of us, while we use a different approach.

1.3   Structure

In Section 2, we are going to describe the architecture and functions of the PAS in more detail to show the challenges it faces and the benefits it may create. We will start by giving an overview of the system and its architecture. After that, we will look into the main features of the PAS – namely its data model, its interfaces and its federation support – and discuss aspects of their implementation. Finally, in Section 3, we will sum up our findings and critically review our proposed system: its weak points, potential and our future work.

---

[1] Services like e.g. Google Code, Sourceforge, GitHub, Gitorious, CodePlex, Alioth, GNU Savannah, Assembla and JavaForge just to mention a few of them.

2   Description of the PAS

In the following section we will describe the Project Awareness System. After discussing some general considerations, we will show an overview of the system architecture and explain the main ideas of the system in greater detail.

2.1   General Considerations

During the design of the system, we tried to follow two design goals: simplicity and usability. Like with many CSCW-systems, which are mainly used as a free choice by their users, the biggest challenge in implementing the PAS lies in the acceptance of its users. So from the beginning on, the system has to enthuse its users and give them a direct reward for the additional work they have just to use the system. Only in this way the accumulated data of projects can reach a critical mass at which it itself generates a surplus value for the users of the system. From this point on, the managed project data creates an appeal to use the PAS, as long as the quality of the data is high. We already identified two significant risks for the implementation: On the one hand, the system must not impose too much work for its users; in contrary, ideally users should not be forced to do any additional work at all. On the other hand, it has to be ensured that the managed data meets certain quality criteria. E.g. the data has to be accurate and up to date. Both points show how essential it is that project data can be managed by the system in an automated manner. Therefore it is crucial that the system comes with a well defined automation interface which can be used to automatically insert and update data.

To reach a high usability it is crucial to consider the most important factor of the system with much attention: humans. The user interface has to be simple, intuitively to learn and to use, and should return a direct surplus value to the user for every caused effort. The main user interaction, apart from creating and updating project data, will be the execution of searches. These searches must be very customizable to be able to search for projects through different criteria and considering that project data may be dynamic.

Finally, the system should not impose any constraints on the project data it manages. It has to be able to dynamically manage new data structures, because it would be impossible to describe all possible project attributes beforehand. Projects are too different by their definition. There may be useful templates for different project types (we specified a template for software engineering projects), but users of the PAS should not be limited by the use of such templates. Therefore users have to be able to add special data to their project descriptions. And users should not be forced by a template to provide data which does not make sense for their concrete projects. The system has to dynamically store and manage dynamically added data, making it as visible and easy to search for, as if it were a part of a well-defined template.

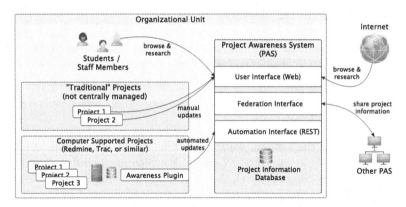

Fig. 1. PAS Architecture and Usage Overview

2.2   Overview of the PAS

The PAS can be seen as a specialized project database at a central well-known place in an organization, which offers easy to use interfaces. An overview of its architecture and usage is illustrated in Figure 1. As you can see, the system offers three different interfaces to realize its functions:

1. A user web-interface where human users have access to all the functions of the system, like searching for projects, creating new projects or updating them. The system can be accessed from inside of the organizational unit or, if desired, also from other networks or even the Internet. The web interface also acts as a project portfolio for the organization. Project teams which conduct traditional local or paper based projects can use this interface to publish and update their project data. In contrast to that, project teams which are already using CSCW support tools should use the automated approach, which is offered through the automation interface.

2. An automation interface, which enables automated clients to use the system. These clients can be used to automatically create and update project data from other project supporting systems. For example, a plugin for project management tools (like e.g. Redmine or Trac) can be written to automatically insert and update project data into the system at regular intervals, ensuring the actuality and correctness of the data while unburdening the users from all work. This interface can also be used to implement individual client software to further simplify the use of the system for special groups with common projects and to adapt even more to special requirements.

3. A federation interface which enables multiple PAS instances to be hierarchically tied together in a federation and synchronize their data. This makes it possible to offer a single point of information for multiple PAS instances while each of them retains its sovereignty.

We are currently in the process of developing a well-engineered default-implementation of the system after having finished a prototypical implementation as a proof-of-concept. The default implementation has to be ready to be easily deployed at other institutes and therefore has to meet very high quality criteria. We use simple standard technologies and methods for the implementation. In this way the deployment, operation, maintenance, adaption and further development of the system is not burdened with complex technologies or requirements:

- The PAS follows the well known three-tier client-server architecture. The PAS server is implemented as a servlet, which uses a MySQL-database to store all project data. The servlet may run in a standard servlet container like Apache Tomcat; it does not need a full enterprise application server.
- We use HTTPS as a transfer protocol for all interfaces. This ensures that all data is transferred encrypted and that the source of information can be trusted.
- The web user interface is realized with the Google Web Toolkit, which allows to write simple Java code for the client side which is compiled into JavaScript. In this way, the potential of dynamic JavaScript at the client can be utilized while only having to deal with simple Java code in the development. Using this approach a far more sophisticated user-interface could be implemented.
- The automation and federation interfaces use REST over HTTPS for their communication, data is encoded to JSON. This makes it easy to write other software (for example individual clients or plugins to update data) which is able to communicate with these interfaces in many different programming languages.
- User authentication is done via LDAP, so that we could reuse existing user-databases of the organization. This may be a point which has to be adapted for the use in other organizational units, where LDAP is not a choice.

After this overview of the system architecture and its implementation we are now looking at the heart of the system: the data model which is mainly used to store the heterogeneous project meta data.

Data Model. To begin with, each PAS instance is attached to the domain of the organizational unit for which it is used. In this way, every project created in an instance will share its domain. As mentioned before the PAS currently does not have a user-database for authentication itself and uses an existing one via LDAP to reduce the administrative work and complexity of the application.

The most special requirement in handling the actual project data is the fact that from the point of the PAS it is unclear which data will later be used to describe a project. This is because of the diversity of projects and project environments (like supportive tools and systems). So the PAS maps project data into so called project attributes, which are named with a dot-notation to structure them. Table 1 shows a simplified list of attributes for the default project template which the PAS currently offers. This template is meant to only be a help, just very few attributes are mandatory (like project name, description and status) for a project, and further attributes can be added is necessary and can also be structured with the dot-notation. The challenge is to process this additional data seamlessly in the application and intuitively integrate it in the user interface, which we will investigate further in the next subsection.

These attributes are stored in the MySQL-database for each project, along with some additional information:

- The database also stores a list of each known attribute together with a description of it. This description is shown to the user when she or he selects the attribute and enters an attribute value. For dynamically created attributes the users are able to enter descriptions themselves.
- Additionally, each project attribute instance is saved with a modification time. This becomes important for the realization of the federation function, because with this information only attributes have to be synchronized between PAS instances which actually changed since the last synchronization.
- Finally, category trees are saved in the database. They make it possible to create hierarchical ordered categories which can be used to classify the project. The user interface is then able to show which project belongs to a category or its subcategories and lets the user browse through them. As the concrete categories strongly depend on the conducted project types, these trees will probably differ from organisation to organisation.

One thing which is currently not implemented, but could be sensible for the future, would be to make it possible to store images and files directly in the PAS. At the moment only links to images and files can be stored. But it would probably improve the user experience if users would be able to upload project related images, icons and files directly. In this way, project results could also be preserved for the future, e.g. even if the project homepage goes down one day. On the other hand, it has to be weighted out if this functionality does not make the system to complex and if it is the duty of the awareness system to host files.

Table 1. Overview of the Main Attributes of the Default Project Template

Attribute-Group	Attribute
general	name, shortName, description, shortDescription, homepage, logo, screenshots, maintainer, team, licence, creationDate, language, news, identifier, visibility, federation
classification	domain, organization, status, tags, categories, operatingSystem, programmingLanguage, technologies, predecessorProject, successorProjects, dependencies
social	ratings, reviews, views, likes, followers
tools	vcs, downloads, wiki, forum, faq, mailinglist, tracker

In the following we will shed light on some of the interesting aspects of the three interfaces of the PAS. All of them have to deal with dynamically created data, which is especially a challenge in the web user interface to nonetheless create an intuitive user experience.

Web User Interface. The web user interface is realized with GWT to create a dynamic and rich user interface with the flexibility client-side JavaScript offers. However, this flexibility is really needed to realize different functions, for example:

– When creating a project, users are able to select attributes from the default project template and from dynamic attributes which were used in other projects. To do this efficiently, the possible attributes are ordered in a tree, which maps the structure of the dot-notation of the attribute names. In this way, the users can easily and quickly navigate to attributes. Every time an attribute in this tree is selected, its description is shown and the user is able to enter a value for the attribute and save it. Additionally, the user can use a filter through a text box if she or he knows a part of the attribute name, or can even add a new attribute to the project, which is not in the tree.

– The search also benefits from the possibilities of dynamic web pages. There the user can dynamically add filters to create complex searches with just a few clicks and keywords. The user can choose between the attributes and combine them with operators (equal, not equal, greater, lower than) and values to easily create queries. For example, she or he could search a project which contains a special keyword somewhere in its attributes, has an active status, was updated not more than a few days ago, uses a special technology and has a higher rating level than a specified amount. This can only be realized in an intuitive way with a smart and dynamic web page.

– The user has to be supported whenever possible. Therefore the system suggest possible values in a list for an attribute whenever the user is about to enter an attribute value and also tries to complete the users input. To do this in a sensible way, the PAS looks up the frequency of attribute values in managed projects and if this frequency is higher than a certain threshold, it proposes the value. This is meant to get more sensible input, because sometimes the user may have the possibility to express an attribute value in different ways. But if she or he can choose a value from this list, it is more likely to be the same when it should be.

– The system also has support for several social functions to increase the quality of the managed data and to enable more search options for its users. It counts how often a project has been viewed by users; it lets users comment, rate and like projects; and it enables users to follow a project, so that they will be informed of changes of the project meta data.

Finally, data privacy may be a concern of the web interface. To protect email addresses, they are not shown in the interface. Only a form is shown, where a message can be left. A user can only be contacted through the system, when the sender has a validated email address. The recipient may also mark messages as spam whereby the administrator of the system is contacted who can take care of further actions.

Automation Interface. The automation interface is offered via REST and has largely the same functionality as the web user interface. Its main purpose is to be

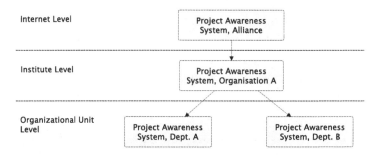

Fig. 2. Federation of Multiple PAS

used from plugins, which could be written for and installed into project supportive software like Trac, Redmine, Allura and others. These software tools already
manage projects for their users and could easily and automatically update the
project data at regular intervals to the PAS with such plugins.

Additionally, special clients for the PAS could be written using this interface
to further adapt the system to specific organisational needs.

Federation Interface. The federation interface allows multiple PAS instances
to hierarchically share their project information at different levels, which is illustrated in Figure 2. For example, a PAS at the institute level federated with
the PAS instances of its organizational units would be able to list all projects
from all its units, enabling its users to share a single point of information for all
projects. Ideally, the vision is that these federations grow as much as possible,
so that all projects of a kind are finally available at a single point.

The federation is realized through regular synchronisation of the project metadata databases. For example, if a PAS from a department A like in the figure is
the child of the PAS from organisation A, then a federation user has to be configured in the department PAS. With this user, the organisation PAS regularly
connects to the department PAS and synchronises a special part of its database
with it. This data is used to offer information about the department projects. In
the synchronisation process only projects which permit federation are processed.
From these projects only attributes are transmitted which have changed since
the last synchronisation to minimize bandwidth.

3   Conclusion

In this paper, we identified the need to be aware of other projects. We drafted
the possible benefits from being able to be more aware of the projects which are
carried out at your own organisation unit, organisation or even world wide. This
is especially true if the projects are academically or open-source and therefore,
want to create common values. Only if we have a reliable way to find these
projects, we will really be able to build upon each others work and to realize
even higher aims together.

To solve this problem, we introduced the PAS, which would enable organisations to collect their project metadata at a central place and even share them with others. It mainly depends on the acceptance of its users if the PAS is able to realize the aforementioned benefits. There still has to be done work to finish the default implementation and start to use the system. Many aspects of the system have to be further investigated and optimized using feedback from its users, so that everything is done to reach a high acceptance and to create a really useful and usable application. Usage studies have to be conducted with the first version. Other project supporting systems which offer portal functionality have to be investigated more closely, to further optimize the system and develop it into a form where it could become appealing for great accepted project supporting systems like GitHub, GoogleCode or SourceForge. Hopefully they will want to share their project metadata via a common interface, making them all together easily searchable instead of creating separated islands of information. And if that aim is finally reached someday, it probably will not matter if the used system is an successor of PAS or something else.

References

1. Anderson, K.M., Bouvin, N.O.: Supporting project awareness on the www with the iscent framework. SIGGROUP Bull. 21(3), 16–20 (2000),
   http://doi.acm.org/10.1145/605647.605650
2. Bharadwaj, V., Reddy, Y.V.R.: A framework to support collaboration in heterogeneous environments. SIGGROUP Bull. 24(3), 103–116 (2003),
   http://doi.acm.org/10.1145/1052829.1052852
3. Gutwin, C., Penner, R., Schneider, K.: Group awareness in distributed software development. In: Proceedings of the 2004 ACM Conference on Computer Supported Cooperative Work, CSCW 2004, pp. 72–81. ACM, New York (2004),
   http://doi.acm.org/10.1145/1031607.1031621
4. Majumdar, A., Krishna, S.: Social computing implications for technology usage and team interactions in virtual teams. In: 2011 7th International Conference on Collaborative Computing: Networking, Applications and Worksharing (CollaborateCom), pp. 443–450 (October 2011)
5. Ohira, M., Ohsugi, N., Ohoka, T., Matsumoto, K.: Accelerating cross-project knowledge collaboration using collaborative filtering and social networks. In: MSR 2005: Proceedings of the 2005 International Workshop on Mining Software Repositories, pp. 1–5. ACM, New York (2005)
6. Treude, C., Storey, M.A.: Awareness 2.0: Staying aware of projects, developers and tasks using dashboards and feeds. In: Proceedings of the 32nd ACM/IEEE International Conference on Software Engineering, ICSE 2010, vol. 1, pp. 365–374. ACM, New York (2010), http://doi.acm.org/10.1145/1806799.1806854

A Comparative Review of Research Literature on Microblogging Use and Risk in Organizational and Educational Settings

Soureh Latif Shabgahi[1], Nordiana Ahmad Kharman Shah[1,2], and Andrew M. Cox[1]

[1] Information School, University of Sheffield, United Kingdom
[2] Faculty of Computer Science and Information Technology, University of Malaya, Malaysia
{lip11sl,lip11na,a.m.cox}@sheffield.ac.uk, dina@um.edu.my

Abstract. Although the enterprise and education are very different sectors of activity and have diverse research traditions, this review argues that there is a benefit to be derived from comparing research work across the two settings. A thematic analysis of research literature collected for the two fields was undertaken, and a generic framework of uses and risks of microblogging produced, which is the main contribution of the paper. Two of the main aspects of microblogging in organisations are found to be communication and awareness; and in education the main aspect is learning. Some of the ideas about how to use microblogging are potentially useful for the other context, particularly the concept of awareness from the organisational literature. While the organisational literature has a major focus on risk, this appreciation is far less developed in the educational context, increasing such an emphasis would increase impact on employability.

Keywords: Microblogging, Enterprise microblogging, Microblogging in Higher Education, Twitter, Yammer.

1 Introduction

The number of active users on Twitter has increased beyond those predictions made by Bennett (2012), where it was suggested that Twitter would have more than 250 million active users by the end of 2012. Microblogging (MB), on Twitter and using other tools such as weibo and yammer, is the most recent social phenomena of Web 2.0 (Hauptmann and Gerlach 2010) enabling users to broadcast information about their activities, opinions and status, as well as to receive quick notifications (Günther et al. 2009; Java et al. 2007; Zhang et al. 2010). Users can stay connected to their friends, family members and co-workers through their computers and mobile phones (Huberman et al. 2008). Inevitably the phenomenon of microblogging has already attracted much research interest.

The use of microblogging has been investigated across a number of contexts by researchers, such as a learning tool (Ebner and Maurer 2009), describing phenomenon (Huberman et al. 2008), for facilitating collaborative processes among employees

A.A. Ozok and P. Zaphiris (Eds.): OCSC/HCII 2013, LNCS 8029, pp. 174–181, 2013.
© Springer-Verlag Berlin Heidelberg 2013

(Riemer et al. 2011a), as a form of electronic consumer word-of-mouth (Jansen and Zhang 2009) and in professional communities of practice (Dunlap and Lowenthal 2009). Some other research attempts to identify global patterns in Twitter usage, without recognizing differences between contexts (Java et al. 2007). But most research to date has been limited to a particular sector of use. Research that explores experiences across different sectors is rather lacking.

The present study explores the value of a comparative literature review. It compares the literature on microblogging applications in two different areas, namely, Enterprise Microblogging (EMB) and in Higher Education (MIHE) with a view to integrating understanding across the two domains, be that copying practices between sectors or emulating theoretical viewpoints.

More formally the research questions that the review sought to answer were:

1. What does the research literature tell us about how MB is being used in the two contexts?
2. Which practices in use could be borrowed between the sectors?
3. Which theoretical perspectives and methods might be borrowed between sectors?

2 Methodology

The review is based on a thematic analysis of peer reviewed research literature collected in October 2012. The collection comprised around 30 papers on enterprise microblogging (EMB), defined as use of microblogging primarily with internal audiences behind the firewall. Around 25 papers on microblogging in Higher Education (MIHE) made up the rest of the corpus. The literature was identified through specialized journals and conference proceedings database for research publications. For EMB these included the HCI conference, Information Systems conferences, International conference on Collaboration Technologies and Systems, Information security management conference, Business and information systems engineering, IEEE and ACM. For MIE, these included ERIC, Sage journals online, relevant e-learning conferences, such as ALT-C, ASCLITE. Additionally, web of sciences was used, using keyword searches on terms including: 'Microblogging' 'Twitter' 'Yammer' 'Social Media' 'Web 2.0' 'Higher Education' 'Enterprise'. The selection criteria included articles that contained the description, methodology, trials, results of the use of microblogging in EMB and MIHE.

For the EMB literature, the researchers found the first paper to be published in 2009. Most of the research to date has been published about examples from the USA and Europe and have been about uses in large organisations, often IT consultancies. They are typically of single case studies, rather than surveys of a number of organisations or a whole industry sector. Typically the research is the result of trials of microblogging tools internally. Much of the research in MIHE has centred on integration of microblogging in educational systems, particularly use of Twitter to support learning and teaching in higher education. Research on MIHE was mostly published in USA and Europe, with the first paper in 2008. Most of the publications have been experiments on the effects of microblogging in learning and classroom activities, and single case studies, rather than a comparison between several classrooms or activities.

Thematic analysis was carried out by the researchers. Relevant themes were identified from both literatures focusing on uses and risks. These themes were then analysed and cross-compared repeatedly for consistency and validity. The thematic analysis led to the development of a generic framework identifying themes of the uses and risks of microblogging in the two settings (Figures 1 and 2).

The two literatures from which the papers are drawn have their own distinctive theoretical traditions, methods and terminology and clearly the two sectors have very different underlying purposes, yet it is hoped that the common framework allows useful comparisons to be drawn between the two fields.

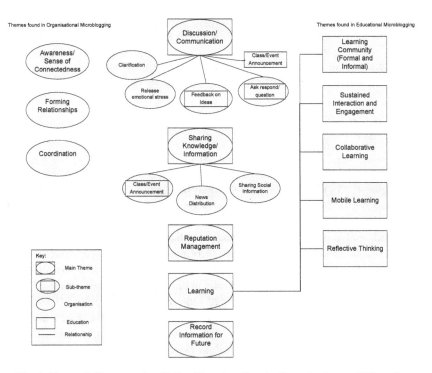

Fig. 1. Thematic Framework of Microblogging Uses in Organisation and Education

3   Discussion

The research reported in this paper made a comparison between companies' use of microblogging for business directed purposes (i.e. marketing, project management and collaboration) and higher education uses to improve quality education outcomes / enhance pedagogy system (i.e. teacher-student interaction, promoting social media tools, academic professional development). It demonstrated the falsity of the perception that most Web2.0 technologies are being used mainly for personal purposes such as for socialising, networking and interacting with friends. As Hannay and Fretwell (2011) have argued Web 2.0 has great potential to be implemented in higher education because these technologies provide substantial implications enable interactivity, excite learners, and foster greater student participation. Likewise, many companies are investing on Web 2.0 tools for internal employees' communication and collaboration (Faroughi 2011).

Given the very different contexts and differing theoretical traditions in the two areas there might be a view that a comparison would not be likely to be fruitful. It is argued here, however, that there is considerable benefit in comparing literatures from two different settings, although researchers in different fields tend to use different theoretical frameworks and methodologies and this may make comparison hard.

Making the comparison has led to the development and evaluation of two generic frameworks, which together are the main contribution of the paper. By placing a number of works in such a simple, visual generic framework differences and gaps in the literature can be identified. A number of benefits arise from such a comparison, both in identifying practices that could be transferred between contexts and theoretical and methodological approaches for researchers. The framework also could be expanded for a review across other contexts.

As regards Figure 1, and uses of microblogging, the framework identifies several areas which have been investigated in both literatures such as discussion/communication, knowledge sharing and reputation management (Riemer et al. 2011a; Zhao et al. 2011; 201; Kassens-Noor 2012; Grosseck and Holotescu 2008; Ross and Terras 2011; Valetsianos 2011). Themes only found in organisational microblogging are forming relationships and coordination. Awareness/sense of connectedness through microblogging has also been an influential concept in organisational contexts (Zhao et al. 2011; Günther et al. 2009) much more than in educational settings, but seems to be potentially applicable there too. This illustrates how in some areas similarities are masked by different terminology. Arguably, Dunlap and Lowenthal's (2009) exploration of social presence in the MIHE literature relates to the widely used concept of awareness from EMB literature. Nevertheless, on the whole the perspective of awareness seems to be under-developed in MIHE and could probably be usefully applied to a greater degree there.

The majority of published studies in education have focused on Twitter to support learning in higher education. Themes of uses found in educational microblogging, but not in the organisational context, are learning community (Dunlap and Lowenthal 2009, Ebner and Maurer 2009), sustained interaction and engagement (Dunlap and Lowenthal 2009), collaborative learning (McWilliams et al. 2011; Perifanou 2009), mobile learning (Holotescu and Grosseck 2011) and reflective thinking (Wright 2010). It might be beneficial for organisations, therefore, also to conceptualise microblogging as a learning tool. For instance in education, learning community (formal and informal) stresses the value of continuous communication about work regardless of the location and time. Mobile learning can also be encouraged in organisations more, for encouraging with employees to build a learning network. These microblogging uses might have applicability in the corporate sector too.

Risks (see Figure 2) identified in the enterprise microblogging litera-ture were difficulty/unfamiliarity in using microblogging (Grit 2009; Grosseck and Holotescu 2008), distraction and (Case and King 2010; Raeth et al. 2009) wasting time (Günther et al. 2009; Othman and Siew 2012), and noise- to-value ratio (Raeth et al. 2009), privacy of the users (Mayfield 2009), security concerns (Grosseck and Holotescu 2008; Zhang et al. 2010) and length restrictions (Ebner et al. 2010; Riemer et al. 2011). As regards risks, the analysis identified that there was less concern with risk in the literature of microblogging in education, compared to the preoccupation with the topic in the organisational literature. This may be because educational uses are in their early stages, but seems to reflect a greater all round consciousness of risk in organisations. This comparison suggests the argument that educators are not intro-ducing users enough to the possible risks of microblogging. The focus on positive uses does not expose users to the same sense of risk. In terms of future employability in organisations (Foroughi 2011), learners could be introduced to the risks of mi-croblogging as a more central issue, even if this was through creating exercises that explicitly place learners imaginatively in organisational contexts.

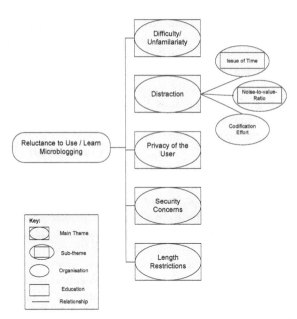

Fig. 2. Thematic Framework of Microblogging Risks in Organisation and Education

The review also identified a number of possible guidelines and policies to address such risk concerns, mainly developed within the organisational literature. For in-stance, continuously emphasizing the usefulness of internal systems (Othman and Siew 2012) and providing training for early adopters and users (Raeth et al. 2009) is proposed as a way to help reduce difficulty/unfamiliarity in using microblogging (Lowe and Laffey 2011), distraction (Case and King 2010) and issue of time (Müller and Stocker 2011; Ehrlich and Shami 2010; Günther et al. 2009). Also, in terms of security Mayfield (2009) suggested that there should be privacy restrictions on content, and documents and workspaces should be provided for users to only view activities they should have access to. These aspects could be introduced in the educational context too.

The review also points to some lessons for researchers in terms of methodology. On the whole the EMB literature uses a wider range of methods: logs, social network analysis, genre analysis, interviews and questionnaires. Sometimes information about staff members can be matched to their microblogging activity. MIHE tends to use a narrower range of methods. Small class room studies tend to have quite restricted sample sizes and duration. Reference to the EMB literature could inspire researchers to undertake larger scale more longitudinal studies. In fact, both literatures are relatively limited in these terms.

4   Conclusion

This has been the first review that we are aware of which has concentrated on the uses and risks of microblogging technologies in two different contexts of organisation and education. The comparison of literature on microblogging in the two sectors has led to the development and evaluation of a generic framework, which graphically presents its use and risks. The framework could also be a useful guide for other researchers to explore issues around microblogging in different settings, such as educators using microblogging for research or use in professional contexts. The framework is hospitable to expansion. Understanding of the ways microblogging can be used most effectively can lead to sharing of best practices. It is helpful to researchers to see how different theoretical concepts and research methods might be deployed in another context. The framework might also be used for comparing other technologies apart from web2.0/microblogging.

References

1. Bennett, S.: Twitter on track for 500 million total users by March, 250 million active users by end of 2012 (2012), http://www.mediabistro.com/alltwitter/twitter-active-total-users_b17655
2. Case, C.J., King, D.L.: Cutting Edge Communication: Microblogging at the Fortune 200, Twitter Implementation and Usage. Issues in Information Systems XI (1), 216–223 (2010)
3. Dunlap, J.C., Lowenthal, P.R.: Tweeting the night away: using Twitter to enhance social presence. Journal of Information Systems Education 20(2), 129–155 (2009)
4. Ebner, M., Maurer, H.: Can weblogs and microblogs change traditional scientific writing? Future Internet 1(1), 47–58 (2009)
5. Ebner, M., Lienhardt, C., Rohs, M., Meyer, I.: Microblogs in higher educaion—a chance to facilitate informal and process-oriented learning? Computers & Education 55(1), 92–100 (2010)
6. Ehrlich, K., Shami, N.S.: Microblogging Inside and Outside the Workplace. In: Proceedings of the Fourth International AAAI Conference on Weblogs and Social Media, pp. 42–49 (2010)

7. Foroughi, A.: A Research Framework for Evaluating the Effectiveness of Implementations of Social Media in Higher Education. Online Journal for Workforce Education and Development 5(1), 5 (2011)
8. Grit, J.W.: Stumble upon hidden Knowledge: Microblogging in Organizations, Master thesis Communication Studies, University of Twente, pp. 1–58 (2009)
9. Grosseck, G., Holotescu, C.: Can we use Twitter for educational activities? In: Proceedings of the 4th International Scientific Conference: eLearning and Software for Education, Bucharest (2008)
10. Günther, O., Krasnova, H., Riehle, D., Schöndienst, V.: Modeling Microblogging Adoption in the Enterprise. In: Americas Conference on Information Systems 2009 Proceedings, pp. 1–10. Association for Information Systems (2009)
11. Hannay, M., Fretwell, C.: The higher education workplace: Meeting the needs of multiple generations. Research in Higher Education Journal 10, 1–12 (2011)
12. Hauptmann, S., Gerlach, L.: Microblogging as a Tool for Networked Learning in Production Networks. In: Proceedings of the 7th International Conference on Networked Learning, pp. 176–182 (2010)
13. Holotescu, C., Grosseck, G.: Mobile learning through microblogging. In: Procedia-Social and Behavioral Sciences. 3rd World Conference on Educational Sciences, vol. 15, pp. 4–8 (2011)
14. Huberman, B.A., Romero, D.M., Wu, F.: Social networks that matter: Twitter Under the Microscope (2008)
15. Jansen, B.J., Zhang, M., et al.: Twitter power: Tweets as electronic word of mouth. Journal of the American Society for Information Science and Technology 60(11), 2169–2188 (2009)
16. Java, A., Song, X., Finin, T., Tseng, B.: Why we twitter: Understanding microblogging usage and communities. In: SNA-KDD Workshop on Web Mining and Social Network Analysis, pp. 56–65. ACM (2007)
17. Kassens-Noor, E.: Twitter as a teaching practice to enhance active and informal learning in higher education: The case of sustainable tweets. Active Learning in Higher Education 13(1), 9–21 (2012)
18. Lowe, B., Laffey, D.: Is Twitter for the birds?: using Twitter to enhance student learning in a marketing course. Journal of Marketing Education 33(2), 183–192 (2011)
19. Mayfield, R.: Enterprise Microblogging Whitepaper, Social text, pp. 1–11 (2009)
20. McWilliams, J., Hickey, D.T., Hines, M.B., Conner, J.M., Bishop, S.C.: Using collaborative writing tools for literary analysis: Twitter, fan fiction and the crucible in the secondary English classroom. Journal of Media Literacy Education 2(3), 238–245 (2011)
21. Perifanou, M.A.: Language micro-gaming: fun and informal microblogging activities for language learning. Communications in Computer and Information Science 49, 1–14 (2009)
22. Müller, J., Stocker, A.: Enterprise Microblogging for Advanced Knowledge Sharing: The References@BT Case Study. Journal of Universal Computer Science 17(4), 532–547 (2011)
23. Othman, S.Z., Siew, K.B.: Sharing knowledge through organization's blogs: The role of organization, individual and technology. In: 3rd International Conference on Business and Economic Research Proceeding, pp. 562–581 (2012)
24. Raeth, P., Smolnik, S., Nils, U., Butler, B.S.: Corporate Adoption of Web 2.0: Challenges, Success, and Impact, pp. 1–10 (2009)
25. Riemer, K., Diederich, S., Richter, A., Scifleet, P.: Tweet Talking - Exploring The Nature of Microblogging at Capgemini Yammer. Business and Information Systems, 1–15 (2011)

26. Riemer, K., Altenhofen, A., Richter, A.: What are you doing?- Enterprise Microblogging as Context Building. In: European Conference on Information Systems (ECIS) Proceedings, pp. 1–13 (2011a)
27. Ross, C., Terras, M., et al.: Enabled backchannel: conference Twitter use by digital humanists. Journal of Documentation 67(2), 214–237 (2011)
28. Veletsianos, G.: Higher education scholars' participation and practices on Twitter. Journal of Computer Assisted Learning (2011)
29. Wright, N.: Twittering in teacher education: reflecting on practicum experiences. Open Learning 25(3), 259–265 (2010)
30. Zhang, J., Qu, Y., Cody, J., Wu, Y.: A Case Study of Micro-blogging in the Enterprise: Use, Value, and Related Issues. In: Proceedings of the 28th International Conference on Human Factors in Computing Systems, Atlanta, USA, pp. 123–132 (2010)
31. Zhao, D., Rosson, M.B., Matthews, T., Moran, T.: Microblogging's Impact on Collaboration Awareness: a field study of microblogging within and between project teams. IEEE International Conference on Collaboration Technologies and Systems, Philadelphia, pp. 31–39 (2011)

Being Example: A Different Kind of Leadership, Looking for Exemplary Behaviors

Sebastián Romero López[1], Habib M. Fardoun[2], and Abdulfattah S. Mashat[2]

[1] University of Castilla-La Mancha, School of Engineering, Information Systems Department,
02071 Albacete, Spain
sebastian.romero@uclm.es
[2] King Abdulaziz University, Faculty of Computing and Information Technology,
Information Systems Department,
21589 Jeddah, Saudi Arabia
{hfardoun,amshat}@kau.edu.sa

Abstract. Creating applications that focus on students to make them understand the value of society, and to be an active member of it, is important, as it is needed to educate them correctly in academic environment, near to the formal learning process applied till now. For this in this paper we present a platform named "Being Example: A different kind of leadership" that encourage students to participate and communicate with all the school students to interchange and discuss educative problems they have. "Being example" platform is the extension of the presented platform "Looking for Leaders", it encourages students to be leaders, by performing good actions and promote their peers to follow them, and not to just because of the skills they have.

Keywords: Educational Systems, Social Networks, Human-Computer Interaction, Students Behaviors, Secondary Schools, Educational System Evaluation.

1 Introduction

Students often demonstrate their desire and ambition to succeed in their studies, in order to be rated by their teachers, parents or managers [1]. The idea of this paper is to improve the methodology for secondary schools to introduce online social networks as a part of their system, and to offer services to the educational community (students, parents and teachers) for the construction of a training school experience that allows the development of values, attitudes, socio-emotional skills, and ethical standards [2]. As a result, this creates a social life where all members of the educational environment participate, share and develop completely. From one side, students will learn to be citizens, how to vote, and to be responsible for the improvements and changes of their own educative system; under the supervision of the management team of the center and the school board. This methodology intends students to have responsibilities through their participation (voting, debate, leadership, etc.) in their own school system.

A.A. Ozok and P. Zaphiris (Eds.): OCSC/HCII 2013, LNCS 8029, pp. 182–190, 2013.
© Springer-Verlag Berlin Heidelberg 2013

The improvement comes to give answer to several surveys that were done after using the prototype presented in [2]. Its main improvement   reside in adding a new type of leadership concept, not by calling leader to some users but by pointing them as an example for one or some of the student's actions.

This article consists of 5 sections: starting with the introduction, followed by the state of art. Third, we discuss one of the surveys that were done to the students (looking for weaknesses). The fourth section presents the new added functionality. Finally, we end the paper with the conclusions and future work.

2   State of Art

According to Danah Boyd [3], social networks are Websites that give users a range of services based on Web technologies that allow individuals to: build a public or semi-public profile with relationships system, to have a list of other users with whom they share a connection, and finally, view and navigate through the list of users' connections with those who share a connection in the system. The shape and nomenclature of the connections listed above vary from one social network to another.

2.1   Social Networks in Secondary Schools

In education, the ability to keep in touch a large group of students is the first characteristic that high schools should take advantage of. When teachers make use of Internet technologies in their teaching process, especially when they have a large number of students; raise the effectiveness of the educational task, thus, this variety in the sources of information for teachers and students, since both groups are forced to visit a large number of resources (blogs, wikis, etc.) that contain all needed information and at the same time cross students data. For this, it is the perfect medium, for teaching / learning environment, which push these blogs to be widely used in education, and because of the multiplicity of subjects, teachers and students who live together in one or several schools [4].

The social networking phenomenon is growing, especially in recent years, in parallel with the development of services and tools called Web 2.0. What sets this system mainly from its predecessor, Web 1.0, is a communicative paradigm shift, where the user of the network goes from being a consumer of content to participate in building and developing them. For these reasons, in our case for students in education systems, we see that the use of social networks for the development of our proposal is fundamental, and presents a very promising solution for the future pillars of the system to learn the meaning and importance of their vote, how it affects in the system development, and finally students will learn the way they can make use of it.

2.2   Previous Works

Looking for Leaders [2] is a tool for participation, awareness and leadership within the educational systems of secondary education. The users of the platform can perform organizational activities, create and participate in the educational community events. It is based on the performance of social networks, adding a number of extra features to support active participation by students in their educational system. It has been taken into account that users of this platform are minors, and therefore decided that in principle it is an independent platform (per school) for the better management and control of the school. One of the main functions of the tool is to enhance participation in the daily activities that take place in school. For instance: reading workshops, sports clubs and so on. This is the platform that was improved during the work and research that is being shown in the paper.

The field study of [5] reflects the big use of the new technologies and social networks by high school students, this cheer up us to follow our social networks research at high schools. In this research work, says that 88% of the high school students use the Tuenti social network [6]. Also, it highlights a set of advantages for their application in teaching, where the field study focus on Tuenti and Facebook social networks. First, it presents the results obtained through an anonymous questionnaire given at three centers of the community Castilla-La Mancha, Spain (two secondary and one primary education centers). Next, it discusses the main findings of this field study conducted during the last two academic years and applied over 425 students (381 secondary education and 64 of primary one).

3   A Survey: Looking for Weaknesses

This section shows the features of "Looking for leaders" and the survey that was done to the students. The most significant result of performing this survey, was that, students felt they are important, and a real part of the system, as they can complain and propose changes.

3.1   Looking for Leaders Features

The features (before the improvement) related to leadership are as follows:

- Leadership by accumulation. Each student may delegate his or her vote to peers either because they have similar ideas, or because the student likes their way of leading, to be the class representative. Students who delegated their vote shall not vote until they revoke the delegation. For example, if a student is a voting delegate of three other students, his or her vote will count as four.
- Representatives of the group. All groups will include the following figures: the group representative/s and the rest of students. A manager coordinates and represents the group actions, can be a student or, in some occasions, several students from the group.
- Voting proposals. Everyone can open a voting form. If the proposal goes beyond 10% participation in its first four days, since its creation it will remain active, otherwise it will be closed.

- Academic timeline. Students can view their actions with respect to the system as a timeline. Viewing the activities in which they participated or the ones that were successful and the ones that were not.
- Proposals of change regarding system aspects. Made by the students themselves, each center may set a percentage of votes for a proposal that the school management may take into account. One possibility would be to evaluate the proposals, which reach more than 50% of votes.

Once the main features about leadership are presented the survey complete its meaning.

3.2   The Survey Description

The survey that was done had two parts. The first part was an anonymous questionnaire composed of ten questions that was filled by eighty-two students. Additionally to this, to obtain complete information of the survey, we made some face-to-face interviews with seven students. The anonymous questionnaire, performed by students, was done to look for the platform weaknesses, and to know its acceptance level. The most interesting results of it are:

- To the question: Would you add more features to the system? The 90.2% answered yes.
- Do you agree with the leadership's features of the system?

  o   The 30% answered yes,
  o   While the 33% answered no, and
  o   The rest answered don't know / don't answer (N/A).

The seven students who participated in the face-to-face interviews were picked by random. We couldn't interview the eighty-two who participated in filling the questionnaire because of the lack of time. Each interview was performed between ten and fifteen minutes, there weren't a script of questions so dependent. We let the students to speak freely about the platform, some interesting commentaries were:

- María said: "I am tired of how the society behaves; the acknowledgements are always for the same little group".
- Elena said: "I get tired of using the system when I realized that no one was interacting with me".
- Luis said: "Many social networks, many passwords sometimes this is messy".

In this paper are reflected just the negative commentaries that needed our attention. There were positive commentaries as well but the focus of the research, here, is to look for the negative points of the system.

3.3   Survey Consequences

After the surveys, it was clear that "Looking for Leaders" platform was in need to new functionalities, to correct what its weaknesses (like what "María" said), thus, this platform is not just for leaders, it is developed to serve the whole educative community. There were many questions, but the main one was: How we can make everyone feel the leadership means? Its answer is: by "Being Example".

4   Being Example

The process to improve Looking for Leaders, and the main changes done to it, are discussed in this section. The first step after the surveys, was proposing a vote on the website of the system, where every user could vote Agree or not agree. Why to propose a vote? One of the goals of this platform is to get the involvement of the students, so to follow the spirit of the platform the decision of change was given to the students. The results are shown at Fig. 1.

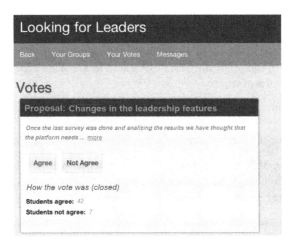

Fig. 1. The first step after the surveys, proposing a vote on the website of the system, where every user could vote Agree or not agree

So after the vote, and taking into account the results, the next step was to define the change to improve "Looking for Leaders", and this definition is as follows:

"Being Example" goal is to promote the possibility of young students of being a good example for their peers. Our own experience in educations, ensure us that it happens continuously in our centers, but they aren´t rewarded. It happened with bad examples as well ones. But in our case, we are not sociologists, so it is not our responsibility to judge if the examples are good or bad. Our aim, with this platform, is just to enhance the participation in the platform, and make more visible to the educative community the good examples that surround them. So, *how to get this visibility?*, Simple, by adding new features to the online community.

Once "Being Example" has been described in a short way, in the next sub-section the new needed features are discussed.

4.1   "Being Example" New Features

The new features were added, and developed over the platform "Looking for Leaders" [2], by re-using as the same code and maintaining all its functionalities. Table 1 shows the main features added to the system. Which all its users can use: admins, students and teachers.

Table 1. It shows the main features added to the Being Example" system, and which all its users can use them

Main Features Available		
Features	*Admin.*	*Users*
New proposal	Yes	Yes
Voting a proposal	Yes	Yes[a]
Accept a new proposal	Yes	No
Check the results of a proposal	Yes	Yes
Close a vote	Yes	No
Check the accepted proposal list	Yes	Yes
Check rewarded proposals	Yes	Yes
Select a proposal as the month or week winner	No[b]	No

a. Users cannot vote in a proposal if they are sanctioned.

b. The system is the responsible of selecting the winners.

The "Being Example" feature is presented, in the platform, with the functionality "New proposal": where registered users could add a new "Being Example" proposal. This proposal has to be accepted, first, by the system administrator "Accept a new proposal" feature. Once the proposal is accepted the rest of users can vote it, the default time for voting is one week. After this week the vote is closed automatically (there is another possibility, closing a vote by the administrator before it completes a week, for facing problems). After this process, a list with the most voted proposals are prized in a weekly and monthly way (a diploma).

4.2   Changes in the System

In Fig. 2 there are an example of "Being Example" proposal. A new button was added to the main menu of the website interface, named "Examples". The vote respect to a "Being Example" proposal is the same that we had before for the vote in the prototype of [2].

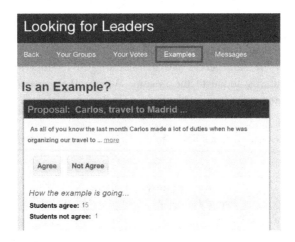

Fig. 2. An example of "Being Example" proposal, a new button was added to the main menu of the website interface, named "Examples"

Once the user acceded to the Examples section, he has different subsections:

- Closed Proposals: Represents the proposals situation once they were ended.
- Active Proposals: This subsection contains the proposals whose process of vote is still active.
- Rewarded Proposals: Once the vote of a proposal is closed and the week or the month ends, the proposal with more votes goes to this subsection, and a diploma is given to the person who proposed it.
- Adding new proposal: Where users can add new being example proposals.
- Proposal review: Only the administrators (teachers usually) of the system could access to this subsection.

The general aspect of the platform architecture remains equal. The Database has been changed as well to work with the data of the new features. The server schema (Fig. 3) suffers minor changes in the "Proposal" part where a new type was added: "Being Example" proposal.

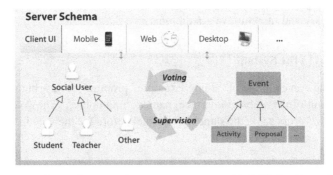

Fig. 3. The server schema changes, where a new type was added: "Being Example" proposal

Some of the aspects of the system remain equal, in order to keep the platform functionality properly, like the recommended rules for the system. There are three possible sanctions, by the team of teachers responsible of the students who make use of the platform in an inappropriate manner:

- When a student loses the representative position, he or she shall not be able to re-present his/her candidacy in the system for a certain period of time.
- Temporary voting ban. The student shall not be able to participate in any of the voting proposals. Advisable to take this measure with students who are using their vote unethically.
- Observer. In this case, the student adopts the observer role, and he shall not use any of the system features. This would be the most restrictive measure.

5   Conclusions

After improving Looking for Leaders we can observe that its deployment in the educational environment, where the prototype was being used, was successful. Even the students with commentaries on the website showed their happiness about being part of the process of the improvement of their own educative system. Now the platform allows more kinds of leadership, trying to make students feel important inside their environment.

The problem that "Luis" highlights during his interview: "Many social networks, many passwords sometimes this is messy" is being researched long time ago, like for example the work done in [7] with opened 2.0. But the reality is that each company wants to impose its user id. As a future work, we are already studding the way to implement the option of login by using user id of the biggest web companies (as Facebook, Google…).

The results and its application in secondary schools, shows that this platform is a very interesting tool to analyze data, from passive participation (early voting only), and active participation, of students in the secondary school, to assess the level of leaders, the level of discontent and a number of indicators. In futures research this data analysis will be shown. The points of leadership were future work in [2], but because of the obtained results of the survey, we decided to improve the system by adding other type of features, the ones presented in this paper.

Acknowledgments. We would like to thank Castilla-La Mancha Secondary schools for participate as end user to apply our prototype and participate on the survey to improve it.

References

1. Moridis, C.N., Economides, A.A.: Prediction of student's mood during an online test using formula-based and neural network-based method. Computers & Education (2009), doi:10.1016/j.compedu.2009.04.002

2. Fardoun, H.M., López, S.R., Alghazzawi, D.M., Castillo, J.R.: Looking For Leaders: Reaching the Future Leaders in Education through Online Social Networks. In: Cyprus International Conference on Educational Research, CY-ICER 2012, February 8-10. North Cyprus (2012)

3. Danah, B., Nicole, E.: Social Network Sites: Definition, History, and Scholarship. Journal of Computer-Mediated Communication 13(1), article (2007)

4. Danah, B.: Why Youth (Heart) Social Network Sites: The Role of Networked Publics in Teenage Social Life. In: Buckingham, D. (ed.) MacArthur Foundation Series on Digital Learning – Youth, Identity, and Digital Media. MIT Press, Cambridge (2007)

5. Fardoun, H.M., Alghazzawi, D.M., López, S.R., Penichet, V.M.R., Gallud, J.A.: Online Social Networks Impact in Secondary Education. In: International Workshop on Evidenced-Based Technology Enhanced Learning, EBTEL 2012, Salamanca (Spain), March 28-30 (2012)

6. Tuenti on-line social network, http://www.tuenti.com

7. Recordon, D., Reed, D.: OpenID 2.0: a platform for user-centric identity management. In: Proceedings of the Second ACM Workshop on Digital Identity Management, DIM 2006, pp. 11–16. ACM, New York (2006), doi:10.1145/1179529.1179532

WEB 2.0 Technologies Supporting Students and Scholars in Higher Education

Paula Miranda[1], Pedro Isaias[2], Carlos Costa[3], and Sara Pifano[2]

[1] Escola Superior de Tecnologia de Setúbal, IPS
Campus do IPS, Estefanilha, 2910-761 Setúbal, Portugal
[2] Universidade Aberta, Palácio Ceia, Rua da Escola Politécnica, 1269-001 Lisboa, Portugal
[3] DCTI/ISCTE, Lisboa, Portugal
paula.miranda@estsetubal.ips.pt, pisaias@uab.pt,
carlos.costa@iscte.pt

Abstract. As computers, notebooks and mobile phones update Facebook's statuses, search and contribute to different themes for Wikipedia and tweet the latest news, a generation and a unique manner of communication are born from this new terminology and philosophy of open and flexible access, shared knowledge, user-generated content and media richness. As many trends, Web 2.0 started by being an exclusivity of certain type of users and then a snowball-like effect made it one of the most popular techno-social phenomena of the 21st century. Word of mouth, user recommendation and the technology itself turned an innovation into a routine. Soon it was disseminated through the different sectors of society, reaching business, health and also education. This paper will examine the benefits that both students and scholars experience in using Web 2.0 in the higher education context.

Keywords: Web 2.0 technologies, higher education, teachers, students.

1 Introduction

Education is a central concern for any society. The responsibility to promote the dissemination of knowledge and to provide the highest quality curricula possible lies on universities. Despite this recognised role, universities and other higher education institutions are no longer the sole information providers particularly due to the exponential development of information and communication technology, namely the World Wide Web. The central role of education inside a society, leads to a constant need for improvement. Educators continuously seek for new methodologies to improve the educational experience, with a growing focus on social technologies [21].

The education sector has experimented with many different technologies with pedagogical value. Nonetheless, not all of these technologies have proven their actual learning benefits. In terms of Web 2.0 tools, the ambiguity felt by education is sometimes attributed to the central notion of user-as-author. This main concept of the Social Web means that everyone is encouraged to voice their opinions and contribute actively, independently of their knowledge in the subject [5].

A.A. Ozok and P. Zaphiris (Eds.): OCSC/HCII 2013, LNCS 8029, pp. 191–200, 2013.

Although students and teachers are partners in the academic setting and depend of one another to achieve their goals, their roles place them at different ends of the education system. They experience the learning process differently and when examining the advantages of any type of educational technology it is paramount to analyse both sides. Hence, the consideration of Web 2.0 advantages in higher education is not completed without an assessment of the benefits that students and scholars may experience. This paper will examine Web 2.0´s role as an educational resource in higher education from the perspective of both students and teachers. It will begin by providing an overview of the enthusiasm surrounding the implementation of Web 2.0 in higher education and it will then analyse its perks for teachers and students. To conclude it will provide a brief discussion on the shortcomings of the alliance between Web 2.0 and higher education.

2   Web 2.0 and Higher Education: Enthusiasm

Students and teachers stand as the two key elements of the education system. They each represent a different set of interests, objectives and obligations. Thus, it is evident that they experience the advantages that Web 2.0 brings to higher education in a significantly disparate manner. Since Web 2.0 has started to spread its influence in the several areas of society, more than a few new terms have emerged. It is common to use 2.0 as the suffix that indicates Web 2.0's influence or usage. Concepts such as Business 2.0, Health 2.0, and Education 2.0 have become common denominations for the implementation of Web 2.0's tools in each of these sectors. In this paper, both teachers 2.0 and students 2.0 are labels that stand for the teachers and students who use Web 2.0 tools. Both terms are to be understood under this general and extensive meaning.

In general, Web 2.0 potential advantages for higher education subsume the facilitation of collaboration, peer participation, promotion of an independent and autonomous manner of learning and teaching and serves as a connection between formal and informal methods of education delivery [15]. Web 2.0 allows access to open educational material and software. Furthermore, most of these resources are free of charge, which represents an advantage over conventional resources. Web 2.0 also benefits the higher education sector because it reduces bureaucracy and paperwork in the student-teacher relationship; it offers flexibility to the learning and teaching processes; it foments interactivity and collaboration both internally and externally; it liberates the learning community from any space and time restraints; and as a precursor of new technology, it brings the academia up to date with the more recent trends and news [3]. Jadu [11] reports that blogging and online forums are the two most used Web 2.0 tools by higher education entities internally. With regard to external resources, Twitter, Youtube and social networks (Facebook and MySpace) are the most popular among academic institutions.

3   The Teaching Process: Teachers 2.0

Research has shown that, despite their remaining scepticism with regard to the adoption of Web 2.0 tools and services in higher education institutions, there is an increasing number of scholars that are investing in the implementation of Web 2.0 as a valuable pedagogical resource. Table 1 shows the how higher education teachers are using the social media in their professional and personal lives.

Table 1. Teachers' preferred Social media platforms [13]

Social Media Platform	Professional Reasons	Personal Reasons
Facebook	30%	57%
YouTube	40%	49%
LinkedIn	17%	22%
Blogs	24%	21%
Wikis	17%	15%
Twitter	7%	11%
Flickr	5%	7%
Slideshare	3%	3%
MySpace	2%	3%

The table above demonstrates that by now social media has reached an acceptable level of confidence. Teachers seem to be widely adopting Web 2.0 tools both in their private and professional arenas. It is also possible to observe that Facebook and YouTube are the favourite Web 2.0 websites for personal and professional usage, which confirms their overall popularity. Also, only Blogs and Wikis had a higher percentage in the professional arena than in the personal, meaning that professionally speaking teacher give prevalence to Facebook, YouTube and Blogs. These three types of social media are the elected for educational purposes.

From scholars' point of view, the benefits of using social technology to assist the teaching process are manifold. The Social Web allows for an improvement of their teaching methodology, diversifying not only their approach but also their knowledge. Moreover, by promoting the exchange of information, Web 2.0 gives educators an important opportunity to share their teaching materials and benefit from their peers' resources as well. Also the reach of Web 2.0 means that this cooperation can take place in the same institution or between different institutions from different parts of the world [6]. The widespread use of Web 2.0 facilitates the communication and exchange of ideas and resources between scholars that can be as close as the department on the next building or be teaching in a university in a different continent. Web 2.0 has presented teachers with the opportunity to develop their own material more easily and also to share that material with their peers. The ease of use that characterises Web 2.0 tools facilitates the creation of content either by one teacher alone or by several teachers' collaboration [5]. The fact that content can be produced and manipulated constitutes an important tool as teachers can take the material that already exists and adapt it to suit the specific educational requirements of their students.

An immediate advantage that emerged from the use of Web 2.0 in education was the enhancement of cooperation between academic institutions. This collaboration has come as far as co-authoring. It is increasingly easy for academic educators to share their unique material for teaching and also to benefit from the material created by others [6]. In the case that the scholars prefer not to create their own material, there are unlimited resources online, that others have generated. This material is also available in a wide range of formats and has, therefore the flexibility to be incorporated with the other traditional materials that are used in lectures [14].

Since the application of Web 2.0 tools in higher education benefits scholars at many levels of the teaching process it is important to understand how they benefit the teacher's preparation for that process. The fact that more and more universities are adopting Web 2.0 tools as pedagogical instruments, places a considerable pressure on the higher education teaching community. Teachers are expected to be aware of these new technologies and they are being required to master them so they can be used in their classes. This situation leads to questions regarding teachers' preparation to do so. Web 2.0 has its own peculiar traits and if on the one hand it may constitute a problem for teachers who are less prepared for these social tools, it can, on the other hand, be a solution for the challenge of having to keep up with new technological trends. Albion [1] argues that the answer to the recent challenges emerging from the need to master Web 2.0 tools is the use of these tools to create learning communities. These communities would have the twofold purpose of enhancing teachers' preparation for the adoption of Web 2.0 and of providing actual experience. By engaging in these communities, scholars would be participating directly in a Web 2.0 platform and, by experiencing it firsthand, they would be able to derive knowledge from this practice. This knowledge could then assist them in the moment of incorporating Web 2.0 in their own lessons. This is crucial for professionals that will/are being required to implement them in their teaching practice.

There are also financial perquisites in using Web 2.0 as an auxiliary. Teachers using Web 2.0 to prepare their classes have the opportunity to benefit from a cost efficient tool. Some of the more conventional technologies used in education are expensive and require constant pricey updates. Web 2.0 provides services and tools which are, in their majority, free and independent of costly upgrades [14]. Moreover, they provide teachers with the support they require in order to make their teaching methods more adequate to the existing and dominant student-centric approaches. They become, therefore, empowered to recycle their lectures into more appealing, varied and encouraging lessons, with new ways of exposing the course content and developing their own professional aptitudes [15]. They benefit from new ways of delivering information and are able to support the evolution of their academic careers, by fomenting a diverse set of digital skills.

A great part of a teacher's work has to do with evaluation, with providing feedback on students work. Web 2.0 hosts a variety of services that helps to simplify this otherwise time consuming task. There are systems of voice recording, for example, that allow for a swift feedback from the teachers, minimizing the time spent on writing their assessments on students projects [14]. The interactivity that characterizes Web 2.0, not only helps to reach a wider audience and to be able to ask for advice from people from all over the world. The interactivity that most tools allow, grants the tutors with instruments that cultivate interaction almost on their own, this will free the teacher to do other important tasks. Also, it relieves a significant part of the strain that the tutors feel when trying to assure that interaction in their lessons reaches a high level of satisfaction for students [14].

4   Learning in the Social Web Age: Students 2.0

Students 2.0 are mainly characterized for their use of Web 2.0 in education. They are a new generation of learners that extend the social use of Web 2.0 in their private lives to the public domain of education. Huang & Yoo [9] conducted a survey on students' acceptance of Web 2.0 tools and one of the variables that they measured was the frequency with which different social media applications were used by students. Table 2 illustrates the differences between social media applications in terms of their frequency of use.

Table 2. Students' frequency of use of Web 2.0 applications (adapted from [9])

Frequency of use / Web 2.0 applications	Never used	Less than once a week	2-5 times per week	More than 5 times per week	Total responde nts
Blog	79	28	2	1	110
Wiki	138	18	2	2	160
Instant messengers	7	25	25	31	88
Social networks (ex. Facebook)	7	8	13	72	100
Video sharing (ex. YouTube)	39	39	21	9	108
Online games	126	30	6	7	169
Virtual environment (ex. Second Life)	239	3	0	2	244

Table 3. Students' utilization levels in Web 2.0 applications (adapted from [9])

	Blogs	Wikis	Instant messengers	Social networking	Online video sharing	Online games	Online virtual com.
Performance	4.30	4.79	4.43	4.93	5.08	4.09	4.54
Effort	4.98	4.88	6.95	7.18	5.63	5.09	4.64
Attitude	4.63	4.80	5.43	5.91	5.85	4.80	4.64
Social influence	4.27	4.65	5.16	5.40	5.30	4.53	4.55
Anxiety	4.85	4.84	3.00	3.02	4.19	4.36	4.97

Table 2 shows that wikis, social virtual environments and online games had the lowest frequency rates and social networks and instant messaging were rated as the most frequently used. This data shows a cleavage between the levels of familiarity that students have with the various social technologies. Their acceptance of the technology and the frequency with which they use it will also contribute to the benefits they can harvest. In the same way, how they perform in a technology equally dictates the profit they can take from them. Using a 9-point Likert scale, table 3, illustrates the results of Huang & Yoo [9] survey concerning students' utilization level in the afore-mentioned web 2.0 applications. There was nearly no effort put into the technology that students use more frequently and the anxiety they feel when using them is low. When compared with the anxiety that platforms such as Second Life provoke, it becomes evident that these are the tools they least use and are less comfortable with.

Web 2.0 offers a variety of platforms and services and its application in education varies accordingly. There are tools to accommodate a significant number of academic demands. The existing platforms allow students to create and share media. YouTube is an example of a host of media content, in this case video, that students can share among themselves. Also, communication and discussion can be easily facilitated by forums and discussion boards, which can also be a valuable resource in terms of searching for information and assignment material. Another way to connect is through social networks, where communities of students and teachers are assuming significant contours and asserting their presence. Web based games and virtual worlds can also be a way of connecting with other and another added benefit is the fact that some-times these environments are designed according to certain historical realities, hence combining entertainment with knowledge. Text is an option that was not left behind, despite the multiplicity of formats available. Wikis and blogs are two technologies that permit extensive text content. Students can use them to search for information and to add information. They have the technology to allow students to write exten-sively on different types of subjects. Wikis allow for co-creation and blogs are an advantageous tool for writing and receiving feedback on that writing [7].

With Web 2.0, learners assume a much more active part in the entirety of the learn-ing course of action. They are more able to interact with each other and be active participants at all levels and phases of their learning path. The peculiar features of Web 2.0 allows them to be editors of their own material, to share that material with their peers and even to evaluate their own content as well as their peers contributions. The options of contributing with original material, to edit existing content and to pro-vide feedback are unlimited and allow for a great latitude in terms of educational practices [2]. Authoring content and sharing it with their peers is one of the advan-tages that teachers and students have in common. The students have as well the power to produce their own content and share what they have created with others. Pedagogi-cally speaking this is a very effective manner of increasing the amount of information that a student learns. In order to create content for a project or task in the context of their course, students have to learn about what they are going to present and this is a valuable strategy to increase engagement with the curricula [5]. The content creation tools developed by Web 2.0 allow students to be at the origin new information. They have at their disposal, the tools to contribute with their own information and also to edit the information that is already available online. They are no longer dependent on conventional publishers. They can publish their own material or reprocess someone else's material and they can do that in a variety of formats. They are not solely limited to words, they can produce images, audio, video [4].

The around-the-clock availability of Web 2.0 is very important for the possibility it grants students to access information at anytime that they require it. This is particular-ly important for students who cannot attend classes or study only in a part-time regime. Additionally it provides a suitable alternative to conventional libraries, which operate on standard working hours and therefore limit access to publications needed to accomplish academic tasks. This flexibility equally applies to space. There are no space constraints with Web 2.0, since it can be accessed anywhere with an internet connection. Students have the possibility to work in the university or outside of its borders. This dynamic access promotes the creation of a learning community unbound by the academic campus [3].

The particular facets of Web 2.0 encourage students to be more focused in an open learning environment, where communities of practice can be created to potentiate learning and engage in more practical skills acquirement. Students have a less passive behavior and adopt, in most cases, a more participatory attitude. The Social Web also prepares them better for the reality of professional life by emphasizing problem solving approaches [2]. Moreover, students are already familiarized with Web 2.0 technologies and they can easily and swiftly adjust to them [3]. Unlike some educational technology, Web 2.0 tools are not time consuming in terms of training, not only because they are intuitive, but also due to their popularity among the younger generations. Web 2.0 is a valuable source of collaborative technologies. Research has shown that students tend to use these social tools to engage with their peers outside the classroom and to perform group work. These tools are basically used to share files between the members of the group and to assist the communication among members [18]. Web 2.0 is an empowering tool that provides students with both the opportunity and the means to develop a more independent form of study and also of doing research. The learner has new avenues of information and a wide range of tools to question and interact with them [7]. The learner finds new ways of posing questions and innovative methods of finding the answers.

5   Web 2.0 and Higher Education: Caution

The consideration of deploying any type of technology must be coupled with a meticulous reflexion about its potential demerits [12]. Despite the positive aspects that have been highlighted in the previous sections, it is imperative to analyse the elements of Web 2.0's application in higher education. Also, the in-depth knowledge of its shortcomings is important to the full enjoyment of its benefits. By weighting both the advantages and the tensions associated with the use of Web 2.0 in higher education it is possible to have a more complete depiction of this phenomenon.

As an endless source of information, the internet contains certain perils that have been exacerbated by the openness of Web 2.0, namely the many faces of cyberbullying and the widespread availability of all types of improper content [7]. Another aspect to consider in terms of content is copyright and the protection of the data that users generate. There are two main challenges here, on the one side, there is the perceived intricacy of assessing what content is reliable and on the other side, there is insufficient control in protecting original material [17]. Finally, it is important to highlight the fact that, since everyone can contribute, there is an increasing difficulty in distinguishing the voices of the experts from those of the amateurs [6]. In light of this amalgamation of opinions an information flow, it has become fundamental for students to cultivate a critical sense. Web 2.0 does not require editorial vetting and not all learners have developed the necessary aptitudes to select the most pertinent content. The same type of triage is necessary when choosing which platforms, services and tools to use for educational purpose. The rate, at which they emerge, makes the task of assessing their pedagogical potential a very complex one [17]. The adoption of technology that was initially created for social purposes implies that its application for other uses might be compromised by its entertaining nature. The overuse of Web 2.0 tools in education can constitute a distraction from the main point of learning [19]. The incapacity that the current assessment strategies have demonstrated in terms of providing a complete account of what the students have accomplished in using Web 2.0 tools remains an often cited argument for those who continue to doubt the pedagogical benefits of the Social Web [8].

The higher education sector is in terms of culture and organisation a very unique entity, with characteristics that are often divergent from the precepts of Web 2.0: academic hierarchy vs. a democratic bottom up viewpoint; scrupulous triage of academic material and curriculum vs. the lack of editorial control of Web 2.0; academic orientation vs. social and entertainment direction [20]. Also, some of the tools that are adopted inside the higher education entities are developed only for internal, which clearly contradicts the basic Web 2.0 precept of everyone, everywhere, anytime knowledge [17]. The widespread use of Web 2.0 does not necessarily translate into a universal use of these tools. The digital divide is still a contemporary challenge, since not all students have the same access to these platforms [16] and variables such as user's aptitudes and technology capability help to dictate the existing digital divide [10].

The impulsive character of Web 2.0 platforms means that sometimes certain tools and services are regarded as important pedagogical instruments and employed in academic practices, but they can abruptly change in format, content and/or purpose, rendering them ineffective in terms of their educational application. The rate at which Web 2.0 changes is much faster than the rate at which the universities can incorporate them [17]. This changeability is also a hindrance when attempting to create a coherent list of the required skills that students should have in order to thrive in the digital era. Since an agreement cannot be reached in terms of what these competences should be, it is very complicated to embody them in the curricula [12].

6   Conclusion

Students and scholars play important yet different roles in higher education. They seem to be positioned at opposite ends of the learning process. Nonetheless, the teaching and learning roles attributed to teachers and students respectively, seemed very clear in the past, but are nowadays more blended as a result of the increasing control of students over the learning process. Scholars have to teach, but they also have to learn. If this was true before, it is even more real now, that technology changes at a fast pace. Teachers are being faced with the need to keep an updated record of and to practice new educational technologies.

Despite that fact that this paper was organized to highlight the different perspectives of students and scholar when it comes to the profits of deploying Web 2.0 tools in higher education, it also becomes clear that there many similarities. Interaction, collaboration, user-generated content, editorial features, format variety and flexibility, openness, free services and worldwide reach are some of the core definitions, characterizing the Social Web and they are simultaneously the main advantages, common to students and teachers, for incorporating it in higher education. Since these concepts are more liberal than the conventional structure of formal academic institutions there are still some difficulties that prevent the full acceptance of Web 2.0's pedagogical value. Also, and more importantly, Web 2.0 in itself will not bring a magical solution for the challenges that today's education face, but depending on how it is implemented, it may be a valuable help in addressing them.

References

1. Albion, P.: Web 2.0 in teacher education: two imperatives for action. Computers in the Schools 25(3/4), 181–198 (2008), http://eprints.usq.edu.au/4553/1/Albion_Web_2.0_in_teacher_education.pdf (retrieved November 10, 2012)
2. An, Y., Williams, K.: Teaching with Web 2.0 Technologies: Benefits, Barriers and Lessons Learned. International Journal of Instructional Technology and Distance Learning 7(3), 41–48 (2010), http://www.itdl.org/Journal/Mar_10/Mar_10.pdf (retrieved November 14, 2012)
3. Armstrong, J., Franklin, T.: A review of current and developing international practice in the use of social networking (Web 2.0) in higher education. Franklin Consulting (2008), http://www.franklin-consulting.co.uk/LinkedDocuments/the%20use%20of%20social%20networking%20in%20HE.pdf (retrieved October 29, 2012)
4. Bennett, S., Bishop, A., Dalgarno, B., Kennedy, G., Waycott, J.: Implementing web 2.0 technologies in higher education: A collective case study. Computers & Education 59(2), 524–534 (2012)
5. Berger, E.J., Krousgrill, C.M.: HigherEd 2.0: Web 2.0 in Higher Education. In: Deliyannis, I. (ed.) Interactive Multimedia. InTech (2012), http://www.intechopen.com/books/interactive-multimedia/highered-2-0-web-2-0-in-higher-education (retrieved October 10, 2012)
6. Conole, G., Alevizou, P.: A literature review of the use of Web 2.0 tools in Higher Education. Higher Education Academy EvidenceNet (2010), http://www.heacademy.ac.uk/assets/EvidenceNet/Conole_Alevizou_2010.pdf (retrieved October 10, 2012)
7. Crook, C., et al.: Web 2.0 technologies for learning: The current landscape - opportunities, challenges and tensions. BECTA Research Report (2008), http://dera.ioe.ac.uk/1474/1/becta_2008_web2_currentlandscape_litrev.pdf (retrieved October 8, 2012)
8. Gray, K., Thompson, C., Sheard, J., Clerehan, R., Hamilton, M.: Students as Web 2.0 authors: Implications for assessment design and conduct. Australasian Journal of Educational Technology 26(1), 105–122 (2010), http://www.ascilite.org.au/ajet/ajet26/gray.pdf (retrieved October 11, 2012)
9. Huang, W., Yoo, S.J.: Correlation between College Students' Usage and Technology Acceptance Level on Web 2.0 Applications for Learning. Paper presented at the Annual Meeting of the AECT Convention, Hyatt Regency Orange County, Anaheim, CA, October 26 (2010)

10. Hughes, A.: Higher education in a Web 2.0 World. Report of an independent Committee of Inquiry into the impact on higher education of students' widespread use of Web 2.0 technologies. The Committee of Inquiry into the Changing Learner Experience (CLEX) (2009), http://www.jisc.ac.uk/media/documents/ publications/heweb20rptv1.pdf (retrieved October 30, 2012)

11. Jadu: An Investigation into the Challenges, Application and Benefits of Social Media in Higher Education Institutes (2010), http://www.jadu.co.uk/downloads/ file/ 18/research_into_the_challenges_usage_and_benefits_of_social_m edia_in_higher_education_institutions (retrieved October 29, 2012)

12. Johnson, L., Smith, R., Willis, H., Levine, A., Haywood, K.: The 2011 Horizon Report. The New Media Consortium, Austin, Texas (2011), http://net.educause.edu/ ir/library/pdf/hr2011.pdf (retrieved October 28, 2012)

13. Moran, M., Seaman, J., Tinti-Kane, H.: Blogs, Wikis, Podcasts and Facebook: How Today's Higher Education Faculty Use Social Media. Pearson Learning Solutions and Babson Survey Research Group, Boston (2012), http://www.pearsonlearningsolutions.com/assets/downloads/pdfs/ pearson-social-media-survey-2012-bw.pdf (retrieved November 20, 2012)

14. Odom, L.: Mapping Web 2.0 Benefits to Known Best Practices in Distance Education. DE Oracle at UMUC. Center for Support of Instruction (2010), http://instruction.blackhawk.edu/blackboard/pdf/ Mapping_Web_20_Benefits_LaddieOdom.pdf (retrieved November 14, 2012)

15. Ovelar, R.: Exploring How Faculties Use and Rate Web 2.0 for Teaching and Learning Purposes. In: Proceedings of the 5th Doctoral Consortium at the European Conference on Technology Enhanced Learning, vol. 709, pp. 49–54. CEUR-WS.org, Barcelona (2009), http://ceur-ws.org/Vol-709/paper09.pdf (retrieved November 14, 2012)

16. Selwyn, N.: Social media in higher education. In: The Europe World of Learning, 62nd edn. Routledge, London (2012), http://www.educationarena.com/ pdf/sample/sample-essay-selwyn.pdf (retrieved October 5, 2012)

17. Strawbridge, F.: Is there a case for Web 2.0 in Higher Education? Do the benefits outweigh the risks? – Assignment for Introduction to Digital Environments for Learning (2010), http://www.education.ed.ac.uk/e-learning/gallery/ strawbridge_web_2.pdf (retrieved October 12, 2012)

18. Vaughan, N., Nickle, T., Silovs, J., Zimmer, J.: Moving To Their Own Beat: Exploring How Students Use Web 2.0 Technologies To Support Group Work Outside of Class Time. Journal of Interactive Online Learning 10(3), 113–127 (2011), http://www.ncolr.org/jiol/issues/pdf/10.3.1.pdf (retrieved November 14, 2012)

19. Walker, D.: How many penguins does it take to sink an iceberg – the challenges and opportunities of web 2.0 in education. Web 2.0 in Education (UK) (2008), http://web2educationuk.wetpaint.com/page/Web+2.0 +Research+Project (retrieved October 12, 2012)

20. Weller, M.J., Dalziel, J.: On-line Teaching: Suggestions for Instructors. In: Cameron, L., Dalziel, J. (eds.) Proceedings of the 2nd International LAMS Conference 2007: Practical Benefits of Learning Design, November 26, pp. 76–82. LAMS Foundation, Sydney (2007), http://lamsfoundation.org/lams2007sydney/papers.html (retrieved October 10, 2012)

21. Wheeler, S.: Learning Space Mashups: Combining Web 2.0 Tools to Create Collaborative and Reflective Learning Spaces. Future Internet 1, 3–13 (2009), http://www.mdpi.com/1999-5903/1/1/3/pdf (retrieved November 10, 2012)

Empirical Study of Routine Structure in University Campus

Kingkarn Sookhanaphibarn[1] and Ekachai Kanyanucharat[2]

[1] School of Science and Technology, Bangkok University, Thailand
kingkarn.s@bu.ac.th
http://mit.science.bu.ac.th
[2] Information Network Department, Bangkok University, Thailand
ekachai.k@bu.ac.th

Abstract. This paper presents the use of wireless usage data as a research tool for analyzing the routine structure of people. The patterns of wireless usage can infer the routine of student life in campus. In our experiments, we discover the student routine structure from the volume and time of the wireless usage. Without following an individual trace for any particular person, we use the volume and time of the whole accesses for particular time and location in a university campus. The analysis is based on the large wireless LANs, one-year log data of the city campus of Bangkok University (August 2011 - July 2012), and the experiment is focused on the wireless access points provided in important places of student activity such as canteens, classrooms, libraries. The resulting outputs are the location preference vectors and a new calendar based on student routine structure. The results can support the computational and comparative analysis of space through the lens of service management and enhance user-driven facilitates of the university campus.

Keywords: Eigen-decomposition, Eigenplaces, Eigenbehaviors, Eigenvectors, Principal component analysis (PCA), Behavior research, Wireless networks, Segmentation, Classification.

1 Introduction

On university campuses, the need of wireless usage has been increasing with the number of use of mobile technology in higher education. This is due to the rapid adoption of cell phonesparticularly Blackberries, iPhones, and dual-mode phones. Students use PDAs not only to make calls, but also to perform a variety of tasks such as viewing class material, checking bus schedules, finding locations, monitoring laundry machines, and updating their Facebook status. As a results, they prefer to keep their mobile online whenever they are in wireless access area.

The merit of the investigation on wireless networks usage is for supporting campus communications, and providing reliable and competitively priced voice, data and video services. Surprisingly, student lifestyles, i.e. attending classrooms, self-studying, meals, outdoor activities, can be influenced with these

A.A. Ozok and P. Zaphiris (Eds.): OCSC/HCII 2013, LNCS 8029, pp. 201–209, 2013.

facilitates [1–6]. Contrasting to the unidirectional radio and television infrastructure, the bidirectional wireless data networks can act as probes, propagating data about their users environment back to a network observer. Assuming that the volume, timing, and distribution of packets across networks is able to let us study the student lifestyle in campus.

Unlike most campus Wi-Fi deployment studies have focused on network performance and management or inferred user mobility. For these few years ago, there were some interesting works such as Jong Hee Kang and his colleagues [7] incorporating the concept of place allows a more sophisticated analysis and understanding of wireless environments. Calabrese et al. [1] introduced a method to analyze and categorize wireless access points (APs) based on common usage characteristics that reflect real-world, place-based behaviors. Lastly, Eagle and Pentland [8] exploited the mobile usages for understanding the people mobility. In this paper, we will study the student routine structure from the volume and time of the wireless usage. Without following an individual trace for any particular person, we use the volume and time of the whole accesses for particular time and location.

This paper is organized as followings. Section 2 reviews the use of wireless technology in daily life as well as the description of an essentially increasing number of the Internet usage in university. Section 3 summarizes with a common framework for applying eigen-decomposition to analyze the campus life. Section 4 gives a case study in Bangkok University, Thailand, and shows the experiments and their results. Section 5 reports and discusses on the obtained results. Section 6 will conclude the paper.

2   Student Daily Life with Wireless Network

2.1   Wireless Network Technology

Wireless technologies can be categorized according to their coverage areas. Wireless Local Area Networks (WLANs) are designed to provide wireless access in areas with cell radius up to hundred meters and are used mostly in home and office environments. Wireless Metropolitan Area Networks (WMANs) cover wider areas, generally as large as entire cities.Wireless Wide Area Networks (WWANs) are designed for areas larger than a single city. Different network standards are designed for each of these categories. However, some of these standards fit into several of these categories.

As of today, WLAN is the most widely deployed wireless technology. The most notable WLAN standard is IEEE 802.11 family. Another WLAN standard is the HiperLAN family by ETSI. These two technologies are united under the Wireless Fidelity (WiFi) alliance. Both technologies serve a local area with a radius of 50100 m at most. A typical WLAN network consists of an Access Point (AP) in the center and Stations (STAs) connected to this AP. Communication to/from a STA is always carried over the AP. There is also a decentralized working mode of WLAN, in which all STAs can talk to each other directly in an ad-hoc fashion. While WiFi initially provided an aggregate throughput of 11 Mbps (per AP), the current standard provides a throughput of 54Mbps. Also, in the market there are WiFi devices that support data rates up to 108 Mbps using various additional techniques. With the emerging IEEE 802.11n standard, WiFi is expected to standardize these improvements and provide throughput values up to 540 Mbps.

2.2   Internet and Its Uses in Daily Life

Being reachable anywhere and at any time has obvious advantages, such as improved coordination and the elimination of wasted time when waiting for input from individuals who may be traveling, visiting, or wandering. Some people strongly agreed that mobility mean efficiency.. This is because, given that wireless phones are carried around by users, they may be able to fill time, implying the users can call someone, check email, or send text messages in time slots between other scheduled activities, while wandering from one point to another on campus or while traveling from home to work. Sometimes, the filling of time is equivalent to the killing of time when the individuals use the mobile devices merely to keep themselves engaged or entertained in a free time slot (or in a time slot that should have been put to more productive use); otherwise, mobile devices can enable shifting of time, for example, by checking email and reading/sending short messages during time slots between scheduled activities.

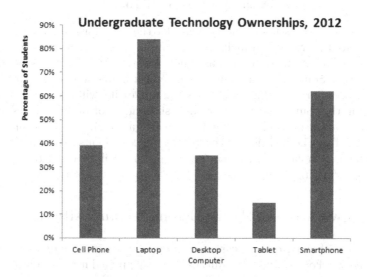

Fig. 1. Students show a need of technology use with the number of their own communication devices (Retrieved from [9])

Use for Studying. Mobile technology is also increasing the productivity of faculty members because they no longer need to go to their offices to set up meetings on their calendars, make phone calls, or use email to respond to student questions. Many professors use mobile devices to notify students of class updates, conduct quick quizzes or polls, and submit data while doing classroom field work. As shown in the statistic chart of technology ownership (Fig. 1), a full 86 percent of students own laptops and 62 percent own smart-phones; tablets and e-readers are not far behind. These devices can do so much more than serve as a word processor or a research tool.

The study found that 70 percent of students learn best in a blended environment consisting of face-to-face learning and an online supplement. The solutions such as WebEx and TelePresence are efficient e-learning tools that help improve productivity, decrease costs, and lower carbon emissions. University staff use TelePresence to hold administration and cabinet meetings, present dissertations, conduct campus interviews and recruit students, meet with professors outside the office, and provide distance learning.

For example, our campus also used the WebEx as an alternative way for a classroom. The WebEx is making inroads "inside" the classroom, simulating visual communications between students and teachers in the traditional classroom setting. For example, professors use the WebEx "attention indicator" feature to monitor whether students are giving the class their full attention. Professors can also require students participating in the WebEx session to turn on "desktop sharing" to ensure that the students are actively engaged in the class.

2.3 Wireless Access Data as a Research Tool

The knowledge of the student lifestyle can let the universities know their needs to improve and increase the facilities in campus. The universities, then, have a guideline for a new project such as a new location of cafeteria is required to serve the need. Sometimes, a change of cafeteria hours should be extended or not. Those are some possible arguments the university will be questioned after investigating the routine structure of their students. Not only students' routine but also the routine of faculty staff will be investigated. For faculty staff, this can be determined by the location of the wireless access points. To understand the people behaviors in campus, the wireless usage data will be exploited to explain the routine structure.

3 Framework of Applying Eigen-Decomposition

The technique of using decomposition was applied to the segmentation of campus universities. For example, the authors in [1, 5] applied it to the data of Wi-Fi network at the Massachusetts Institute of Technology (MIT) because correlating data is as a consequence of network activity with the physical environment. Their approach provides an instant survey of building use across the entire campus at a surprisingly fine-grained level. Their methodology can discover the important information about activity distribution across campus without recourse to any reference data. For example the particular area can be defined with their functions such as exclusively academic, incorporating classroom and administrative functions.

In conclusion for the campus universities, the resulting eigenvectors (namely eigenplaces) have implications for research across a range of wireless technologies as well as potential applications in network planning, traffic and tourism management, and even marketing.

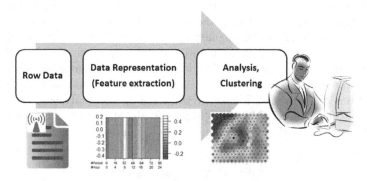

Fig. 2. Framework for applying eigendecomposition

From the aforementioned applications, their methodologies can be illustrated as shown in Fig. 2. We called it as "Framework of applying eigen-decomposition" before the employment. This framework shows three main steps:

1. Input data are scrupulously chosen to be an answer for the formulated questions. From the aforementioned applications, the input data are traces: ex., traces of avatars in MMORGs, traces of visitors in exhibitions, art galleries, and museums [10–12]. For acquisition of people movement, Wi-Fi access log files are one of most suitable sources because Wi-Fi access log recorded must be required under a computer crime law.
2. Intermediate data are the feeding input before analysis, i.e., data representation. The data representation is depended on the purpose of analysis. We will give two examples. First, for grouping APs based on the usage, we will use a matrix of Wi-Fi usage time for representing a particular AP. Second, for grouping people based on visited locations, we will track the people location and create a matrix of visiting time. This matrix is a representative of an individual routine.
3. Analysis and clustering are the final step before the employment. After preparing the intermediate data, we have a set of matrices each of which is a representative. Then, we start with transforming them to the zero-mean data, and computing their covariance matrix. After that, the eigen-decomposition is proceeded to the covariance matrix. For analysis, we interpret the characteristics of either places or people from the resulting eigenvectors. Also the classification is further applied to a set of the eigenvectors. The classification can be either supervising or unsupervised training techniques. For example, an unsupervised k-means clustering can be chosen.

4   Experiments

In this experiment, we firstly match the WiFi usage with the student activities in campus university. Then, we design three experiments based on the distinct functionality of places: canteen, library, and classrooms, and the summarization of WiFi usage is categorized into the activity places and the school calendar as shown in Fig. 3. In this experiments, we conduct the analysis on Bangkok University located in Bangkok Thailand and the map of university . The WiFi access data at areas of canteen, library and classroom were used for analysis. Because of the severe flooding disaster in Bangkok, the flooding period was not included from our analysis. Then, the duration of our analysis is for only the second semester (Jan. 4 - May 13, 2012). We also defined the number of time slots is 96 because the WiFi system generates the access log for every 15 minute.

Table 1. Academic Calendar

Semester	Academic Activity	Calendar Date
	Study	Jun 13, 2011 - Jul 31, 2011
	Midterm exam	Aug 1, 2011 - Aug 8, 2011
1/2011	Study	Aug 9, 2011 - Oct 4, 2011
	Final exam	Sep 27, 2011 - Oct 4, 2011
	School break	Oct 5, 2011 - Jan 3, 2011
	Study	Jan 4, 2012 - Mar 8, 2012
		Jan 4, 2012 - Apr 17, 2012
2/2011	Final Exam	Mar 8, 2012 - Mar 15, 2012
		Apr 18, 2012 - Apr 25, 2012
	School break	Apr 26, 2012 - May 13, 2012
	Study	May 14, 2012 - Jul 1, 2012
3/2011	Final exam	Jun 2, 2012 - Jul 4, 2012
	School break	Jun 5, 2012 - Aug 13, 2012

From the visualization, there are 4×3 eigenvectos for representing the routine structure of students at canteen, library, and classroom. The one-day routine is considered because it is a repeating structure. On weekdays, students at city campus will have the study time table between 9:00-16:30 for undergraduate programs but 18:00-21:00 for graduate programs (as shown in Table 1).

5   Results and Discussions

Following the proposed methodology in Section 3, the resulting eigenvectos of AP access data are shown in Fig. 4. The first eigenvectors are the most influenced routine. The second, third, and so on are in decreasing order. The tone-shading is the quantitative indicator. The brightest tone indicates the highest amount of people at particular place.

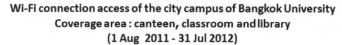

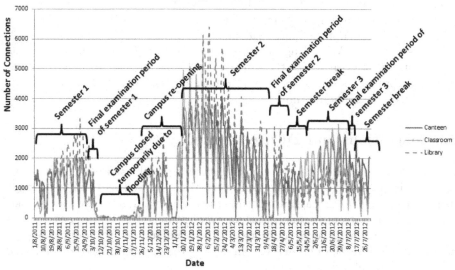

Fig. 3. Visualization of extracted routine structure at canteen, library, and classrooms

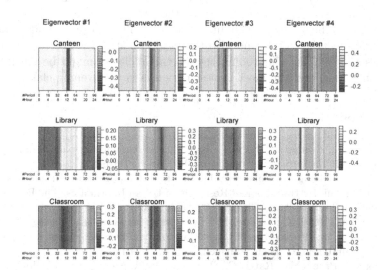

Fig. 4. Visualization of extracted routine structure at canteen, library, and classrooms

1. First primary routine structure at the following places:.
2. Canteen: Interestingly, students decided not to have a small talk or leisure time during lunch by 12:00-13:00. It is because the canteen was much very crowded.
3. Library: Basically, the library is full of students during 16:30-17:00 but very most crowded during 16:30-18:30. The reason is a transition period between undergraduate and graduate students.
4. Classroom: The WiFi usage at classrooms is mostly from graduate students because most of them use the tablets, notebooks for searching, typing their short note, etc. Comparing with the morning classes, the afternoon classes got busier than the morning.

6   Conclusions and Future Works

In the information age, the enormous data is around us. People can access through the Internet everywhere and every time, as well as connect through their family, friends, colleagues, and others. With the Moore's law, notebooks, net- books, and tablets are affordable for every people. The WiFi service area is extensively provided to serve the increasing demand and easily found in the public places. The WiFi log files of APs can infer to the number of people connected to APs at particular date and time.

This paper considered the patterns of wireless usage that can infer the routine of student life and developed a systematic approach for discovering the patterns. We also gave a case study of Bangkok university, Thailand. In this study, we found very interestingly patterns such as the canteen has least WiFi usage at noon. Library is the most crowded during 16:30-18:30 because the undergraduate students finished their class and also the graduate students are coming before their class at 18:00. For classrooms, the afternoon classes might be much busier than the morning, and the most busiest period is in the evening classes.

References

1. Calabrese, F., Reades, J., Ratti, C.: Eigenplaces: segmenting space through digital signatures. IEEE Pervasive Computing 9(1), 78–84 (2010)
2. Sevtsuk, A., Huang, S., Calabrese, F., Ratti, C.: Mapping the mit campus in real time using wifi. In: Handbook of Research on Urban Informatics: The Practice and Promise of the Real-Time City, pp. 326–338 (2008)
3. Sevtsuk, A., Ratti, C.: iSpots. how wireless technology is changing life on the mit campus. In: Proceedings of the 9th International Conference on Computers in Urban Planning and Urban Management, CUPUM (2005)
4. Huang, S., Proulx, F., Ratti, C.: iFind: a peer-to-peer application for real-time location monitoring on the mit campus (2007)
5. Hsu, W.J., Dutta, D., Helmy, A.: Mining behavioral groups in large wireless lans. In: Proceedings of the 13th Annual ACM International Conference on Mobile Computing and Networking, pp. 338–341. ACM (2007)
6. Sevtsuk, A., Ratti, C.: Urban activity dynamics. Economist (2007)

7. Kang, J.H., Welbourne, W., Stewart, B., Borriello, G.: Extracting places from traces of locations. In: Proceedings of the 2nd ACM International Workshop on Wireless Mobile Applications and Services on WLAN Hotspots, pp. 110–118. ACM (2004)

8. Eagle, N., Pentland, A.S.: Eigenbehaviors: Identifying structure in routine. Behavioral Ecology and Sociobiology 63(7), 1057–1066 (2009)

9. Magazine, E.: Important facts about college students and technology (retrieved on February 26, 2012)

10. Sookhanaphibarn, K., Thawonmas, R., Rinaldo, F., Chen, K.T.: Spatiotemporal analysis in virtual environments using eigenbehaviors. In: Proceedings of the 7th International Conference on Advances in Computer Entertainment Technology, pp. 62–65. ACM (2010)

11. Sookhanaphibarn, K., Thawonmas, R., Rinaldo, F.: Eigenplaces for segmenting exhibition space. In: Proc. of the 4th Annual Asian GAME-ON Conference on Simulation and AI in Computer Games (GAMEON ASIA 2012), Kyoto, February 24-25 (2012)

12. Sookhanaphibarn, K., Thawonmas, R.: Visualization and analysis of visiting styles in 3d virtual museums. In: Digital Humanities 2010, Conference Abstracts Book, London UK (2010)

Communication and Avatar Representation during Role-Playing in Second Life Virtual World

S. Tugba Tokel and Esra Cevizci

Department of Computer Education and Instructional Technology
Middle East Technical University, Turkey
stugba@metu.edu.tr,
esra.cevizci@metu.edu.tr

Abstract. This study investigated the use of verbal and nonverbal communication tools avatar representation in Second Life virtual world. Students' responses to a questionnaire and interviews were analyzed. Results showed that students found that discourse tools, such as private message and call, very useful to increase their communication with peers and get feedback from the instructor. Moreover, majority of the participants found the use of peers' gestures. Furthermore, results suggest that different avatars reflect peers' inner personalities increased students' communication with peers.

1 Introduction

The rapid development of new technologies has changed the way we communicate, collaborate, and learn. Three-dimensional (3D) virtual worlds have been one of these technologies that provide us new opportunities. Recently virtual worlds have been used for different purposes, including education, commerce, medicine, and military training. Development in wireless computing, audio and video technologies as well as the ubiquity of multimedia and Internet made the 3D virtual worlds more practical and usable (Dalgarno & Lee, 2010; Dickey, 2005; Warburton, 2010).

Second Life (Linden Lab, San Francisco) and Active Worlds (Active Worlds Inc., Las Vegas) are some of the examples for virtual worlds. Second Life is one of the popular one, and statistics showed that 30 million registered SL users as in July 2012 (Linden Research, 2012).

As the use of virtual worlds have been increasing, examining the experiences of individuals in virtual worlds and the way they communicated by using both verbal and nonverbal communication tools have become an important issue. The purpose of this study was to examine how the affordances of virtual worlds affected the experiences of preservice teachers during the learning of collaboration learning techniques in Second Life virtual world. Specifically, the study aimed to examine to how does verbal communication (voice, audio, chat), non-verbal communication (gestures), and avatar representation (unique identity) affected their experiences.

A.A. Ozok and P. Zaphiris (Eds.): OCSC/HCII 2013, LNCS 8029, pp. 210–215, 2013.
© Springer-Verlag Berlin Heidelberg 2013

2   The Study

The study involved 46 third-year pre-service teachers. The participants involved in the implementation of collaboration learning techniques in virtual classrooms in the Second Life METU Campus (Figure 1).

Fig. 1. Second life METU Campus

In order to collect data about the use of gestures and avatar representation, a questionnaire was used. It included two questions about the use of gestures: "How important for you to use gestures and expressions with your avatar?"; "How important for you that your friends avatars' use of gestures and expressions?".

For the avatar representation, it included four questions: "To what extend does your avatar resemble you?"; "To what extend does your avatar's behavior and personality similar to your real behavior and personality?"; "How important for you that your avatar look like to you": "How important for you that your friends' avatar resemble them?".

In addition to the questionnaires, 14 participants were randomly selected and were asked to volunteer for the interview. Interview included questions about the experiences of students.

3   Results

Interview results showed that, in general, there were positive reaction to the use of communication tools. Majority of the students, 85%, found discourse tools, especially private message and call very useful. Comparing to face-to-face classrooms, 70% of the students mentioned about the advantages of these discourse tools to communicate with their peers and to get feedback from them. They stated that even they were at the opposite side of the virtual classroom or at different place on the island, they could be able to easily communicate with each other with these communication tools.

One student said: "Even we were at the other side of the virtual classroom or island, we were still able to communicate with our peers. It was very good."

Although most of the students saw the benefits of discourse tools to increase communication, 20% of the students found it difficult to use. They said that especially the group chat deficit their attention and they found writing and following all the discussion at the same time difficult.

Students said that they had problems at first, but then they got used to it. One student said: "When one peer ask or make a comment on something in group chat, there were more than one answer or comment. This was a little bit chaotic. But, I think it was because we had just started using the tool in this kind of environment." On the other hand, 60% of the students did not have problems about discourse tools.

In terms of use of gestures, all of the participants used basics, including raising hand, clap, agreement, disagreement. As shown in figures, majority of the participants found the use of gestures important, 45% very much, and 22% extremely. However, 22% of them found it somewhat important, and 11% of them found a little important. Participants' ratings for the importance of the peers' avatars use of gestures showed similar results. Majority of the participants found the use of peers' gestures 35% very much, 26% somewhat. On the other hand, 26% of them found it somewhat important, and 11% of them found a little important, and %2 of the found not important at all.

In terms of avatar resemblance, results showed that almost half of the participants' avatar resemble to themselves. Moreover, while 37% of the participants' avatar behavior and personality resemble to their real behavior and personality very much, 13 % does not resemble at all. While 35% of the participants found resemblance of their avatar is important for them, 35% percent found it is not important at all.

Questionnaire results of the importance of the use gesture and expressions and avatar representation is shown in Figure 2, 3, 4, 5, 6 and 7.

How important for you to use gestures and expressions with your avatar?

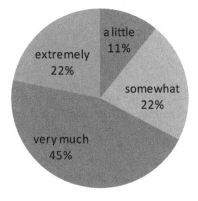

Fig. 2. Importance of the use of gestures and expressions

How important for you that your friends avatars' use gestures and expressions?

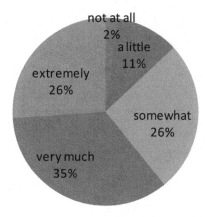

Fig. 3. Importance of the use of peers' gestures and expressions

To what extent does your avatar resemble you?

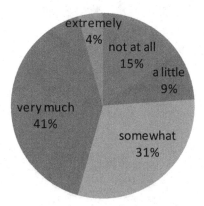

Fig. 4. Avatar resemblance

**To what extent does your avatar's
behavior and personality similar
to your real behavior and personality?**

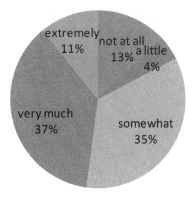

Fig. 5. Avatar behavior and personality

**How important for you that
your avatar look like to you?**

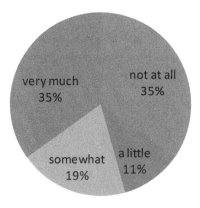

Fig. 6. Importance of avatar resemblance

How important for you that your friends' avatar resemble them?

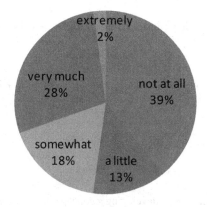

Fig. 7. Importance of peers' avatar resemblance

References

1. Dalgarno, B., Lee, M.J.W.: What are the learning affordances of 3-D virtual environments? British Journal of Educational Technology 41(1), 10–32 (2010)
2. Dickey, M.D.: Three-dimensional virtual worlds and distance learning: Two case studies of Active Worlds as a medium for distance education. British Journal of Educational Technology 36, 439–451 (2005)
3. Linden Research. Second Life grid survey region database (2012), http://www.gridsurvey.com/ (retrieved July 01, 2012)
4. Warburton, S.: Second Life in higher education: Assessing the potential for and the barriers to deploying virtual worlds in learning and teaching. British Journal of Educational Technology 40(3), 414–426 (2010)

A High-School Homeschooling Education Model Based on Cloud Computing

Jordan Valdespino, William Zuhlke, and June Wei

College of Business
University of West Florida
11000 University Parkway, Pensacola, FL 32514, USA
{jtv2,wez2}@students.uwf.edu,
jwei@uwf.edu

Abstract. This paper aims at developing a conceptual model for homeschooling education at a high-school level by using cloud computing technologies. Specifically, a data flow model was developed to show how cloud computing can be adopted in home-schooling education. Then, a set of usability solution items were derived based on breaking down each flow in the data flow model. The findings from this paper will be helpful to system developers and education system decision makers when making decisions on homeschooling systems development.

Keywords: homeschooling, cloud computing, education.

1 Introduction

Homeschooling is an approach to education that has been taking place for generations. Robert Kunzman mentioned that the homeschoolers is more than two million in the United States (2012). More children are being taught at home now than ever before. States and parents have been at odds about insuring "quality of education" and parents' rights to supply that education themselves. While some states require strict control and monitoring that require parents to report the progress of the student others don't require reporting to the state. (Sparks, 2012) Questionable school ratings, poor funding, and safety issues have made homeschooling more appealing.

Colleges today have made concessions from the traditional entrance requirement, recognizing that homeschooled students may not have traditional transcripts and entrance exams scores. (Callahan, Callahan. 2004) While these concessions help, home-schooled students still face disadvantages when applying to many universities. Hence, a well-designed education service system is required to fill in the gap between public education and homeschooling education without the encumbrance of undesired regulatory intervention. In this paper, we offer a cloud-computing based bridge that allows

A.A. Ozok and P. Zaphiris (Eds.): OCSC/HCII 2013, LNCS 8029, pp. 216–221, 2013.
© Springer-Verlag Berlin Heidelberg 2013

parents to educate their children at home and be assured that future opportunities will be available to the student.

Literature review on cloud computing showed that the cloud computing technology has been widely to assist decision making via a cloud computing environment (Brynjolfsson, Hofmann & Jordan, 2010; Miller and Veiga, 2009; Peng, Zhang, Lei, Zhang, Zhang, & Li, 2009). Cloud Computing is one of those pieces of technology that is useful to almost everyone, but the implementation of it in schools depends on the grade level, and the size of the school itself. With a majority of cloud computing being used for colleges more than high schools, the purpose of this paper is to bring cloud computing to the high school level homeschooling.

The format of this paper is organized as follows: Section 2 presented a conceptual data flow model for high-school homeschooling education. Section 3 derived a set of usability features based on the flows in the developed conceptual data flow model. Section 4 presented discussions and conclusions.

2   High-School Homeschooling Education Services Model

A high-school homeschooling education model is developed and illustrated in Figure 1. This model is developed by using the data flow diagramming. A cloud computing based system stores the information of all courses. To support the courses, we will be utilizing the services of teachers to create learning videos on a variety of subjects. Once that is complete, a simple form will be made to allow for new students and let the guardians pick the proper method to teach them. The scope of the system will be purely for high school levels (9-12), with material that can be used to prepare for college. After the completion of the 12th grade the customer/student, he or she will be adequately prepared for college and have a high school diploma (through being home schooled) but be no different. With the implementation of this system, the guardians of the kids using our system will have complete control of how they teach without outside intervention.

In Figure 1, the primary components of the model consist of an internet connected device for the user to access the system; a Registration process, which creates a Login account as well as a financial transaction. The Manage Financials procedure produces the customer receipt and handles internal and external financial processing, including Bank and Teacher Payment; while the Login process records usernames, passwords, and a course list in the Login Data Store and allows access to the courses the student is enrolled in. The Courses Data Store is a compiled list of all the courses offered. To create the courses, we begin with state certified Teachers that are selected by Advantage Education Services to deliver the course criteria and record lecture videos to complement the written course

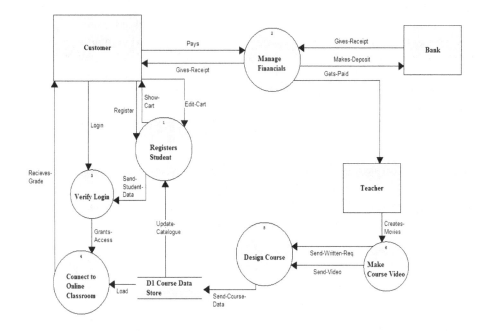

Fig. 1. High-School Homeschooling Education Services Model

material. The components "Create Videos" and "Compile Course" will file the courses in the Course Data Store. Once the student begins a class, periodic Grades are sent to the account administrator.

3   Features in High-School Homeschooling Education Services

Based on the top-down system analysis approach, a set of features were further decomposition based on flows in Figure 1. The produced set of features is presented in Table 1.

These developed features in Table 1 were given to experts for validation. Based on the comments from these experts, Table 1 was modified. A final validated table was constructed based on feedbacks from experts.

Based on the features developed in Table 1, a prototype system was developed. In the system analysis phase, the process modeling such data flow diagrams were used to construct users' required features in Table 1. This prototype system was constructed by using the Visual Basic.net for menu driven user interfaces and Microsoft Access for database management.

Table 1. Decompositions of information flows

Information Flow	Feature
Customer Payment	Guaranteed the student placement in courses. Chose a variety of payment options. Customer input Name/Address/Number of Children.
Customer Invoice	Customer gave a receipt of registration. Received payment (mail or e-mail).
Shopping Cart Alterations	Customers put classes in shopping cart. Removed classes. Payment checkout confirmation. Class selection confirmed.
Viewing Shopping Cart	Class selection viewed.
Customer/Guardian/Student Registration	Customer/Guardian ID number created. Gave an account. Gave a Student ID number. Input registration information. Received e-mail and text message confirmation for new account.
Customer Login	Customer login to the system.
Student Graded Material	Real-time entry of data.
Catalogue Update	Input of Course ID number. Course description. Course material needed. Course requirements.
Registered Student Data	Allowed access to cloud course site. Given access to attend and participate in classes.
Customer is Granted Access to the Online Classes	Used to have the student input homework assignments and view class materials.
Bank Gives a Receipt for the Deposited Money	Real time receipt of amount of money in bank account.
Bank Collects Deposited Money	Money deposited is secure. Money available for withdrawal.
Teacher Receives Payment	Gave a portion of the customer payment to teacher for services provided.
Video/Movie is Created	Allowed for student view. Used for educating on a certain topic. Created based on school and state requirements.
Written Course Requirements	Used to make sure the video is up to par. Used to make sure the customer believes the courses will educate the student.
Completed Video Sent	Real time entry.
Send Course Data	Real time entry.
Loading Courses	Selected course moved from Data Store to Online account. Allowed the customer to view the selected class list (chosen by the customer).

4   Database Design Using Microsoft Access

Microsoft Access was used to analyze the entities and relationships among these entities. The Entity-Relation (ER) diagrams were developed in Figure 2. Then, a set of relations were mapped in the design phase and database was implemented in Visual Basic.net. The sample tables included are Class, Course, Guardian, Grade, Login, Semester, Student, Video, and Written Material. The Guardian and Student tables contain the personal information about both the guardian and the student. The Login table allows the Guardian access to the grades and class registration, the Login table also allows the student access to the course work.   There are three forms titled: Guardian, Login and Student which allows new customers to be input into the system. One report is in the database named, Guardian Login Report, which gives you a list of the guardians with their usernames and passwords.

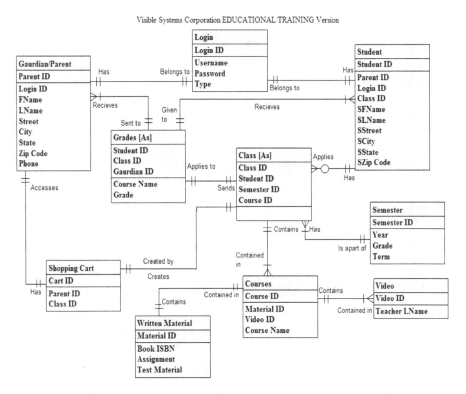

Fig. 2. Entity Relation Diagram for High-School Homeschooling Model

5   Conclusions

This paper developed a high-school homeschooling model for educational services based on cloud computing technologies. Specifically, it first presented a conceptual model based on data flow diagramming. Then, a set of usability features for educational services for high-school homeschooling were derived based on the developed model. Finally, a prototyping system was developed based on this set of features.

The major findings from this study are: First, this study builds the gap by utilizing cloud computing technologies so that high-school homeschooling students can access and receive high-level education services anytime and anywhere. Second, the set of features developed in this study can help to develop high-tech homeschooling education systems.

The future study involves the system evaluation including usability testing. Moreover, the factors impacting on users' adoption of the homeschooling systems will be studied.

References

1. Brynjolfsson, E., Hofmann, P., Jordan, J.: Economic and business dimensions cloud computing and electricity: beyond the utility model. Communications of the ACM 53(5), 32–34 (2010)
2. Callahan, D.W., Callahan, L.B.: Looking for engineering students? go home. IEEE Transactions on Education 47(4), 500–501 (2004)
3. Hollingworth, S., Mansaray, A., Allen, K., Rose, A.: Parents' perspectives on technology and children's learning in the home: social class and the role of the habitus. Journal of Computer Assisted Learning 37(4), 347–360 (2011)
4. Kunzman, R.: Education, schooling, and children's rights: The complexity of homeschooling. Education Theory 62(1), 75–89 (2012)
5. Miller, H.G., Veiga, J.: Cloud computing: Will commodity services benefit users long term? IT Professional 11(6), 57–59 (2009)
6. Peng, J., Zhang, X., Lei, Z., Zhang, B., Zhang, W., Li, Q.: Comparison of several cloud computing platforms. In: Proceedings of International Symposium on Information Science and Engineering (ISISE), Shanghai, China, December 26-28, pp. 23–27 (2009)
7. Sparks, S.: 'Hybrid' home-teaching options grow in popularity. Education Week (37), 16 (2012)

Adult Learners and Their Use of Social Networking Sites

Yuanqiong (Kathy) Wang and Jessica Arfaa

Towson University, Dept. of Computer & Information Sciences, Towson, MD 21252
ywangtu@gmail.com, jessicaarfaa@yahoo.com

Abstract. The goal of this study was to explore the benefits associated with incorporating social networking functionalities within an adult's learning experience. Which social networking sites do they use most frequently? What are the intended purposes of their use? What kind of experience do adult learners have when utilizing social networking services? Why or why not are adult learners using the services provided by the social networking sites? This paper reports a survey conducted among adult learners to identify the answers for the above questions. We believe that the findings from this survey will contribute to understanding future learning design expectations and arrangements.

Keywords: Social Networking, Adult Learner, Education.

1   Introduction

Social networking services, such as Facebook and Google+, have flooded mainstream media with their ability to collaborate with many interrelated individuals and organizations. In recent years, the services provided by these sites and their concepts have been leveraged as a supplement for communication in the academic world.

Educators are always looking for new ways to convey information. Conventional digital methods, especially those that Fernando [1] note as "webinars, flash demos, and animated-to-death PowerPoint slides," have become commonplace in today's information deliverance in academia. Newer applications in the Web 2.0 world, such as social networking sites, blogs, and wikis, have caught the eye of academia for its framework of information and collaboration.

Educational institutions are weighing in on the benefits of web-based social networking applications, as they offer robustness and compatibly with diverse platforms. In addition, these institutions are incorporating social networking theories within education, based on the benefits of enhanced collaboration. With these advancements, these new methods of information deliverance not only open windows of opportunity, but also create challenges for many learners.

The purpose of this article is to report the preliminary findings of a study we conducted among adult university students. We developed a survey to identify the most frequently used social networking services (SNS) among students, and reasons for which they use SNS. We believe these findings will contribute to the understanding of future learning design expectations and arrangements.

A.A. Ozok and P. Zaphiris (Eds.): OCSC/HCII 2013, LNCS 8029, pp. 222–229, 2013.
© Springer-Verlag Berlin Heidelberg 2013

This paper is divided into five main sections. Following the brief introduction, we first review related literature on adult learner and social networking services. We then present the research design in detail. Section 4 presents the results and findings from the survey. The directions for future research is presented at the end.

2   Literature Review

2.1   Participation in Higher Education

Education can be divided into, but not limited to, three types: basic, secondary, and tertiary. For the purpose of this research, basic is defined as primary school, elementary school, middle school, and junior high school. Secondary is defined as high school, prep school, and vocational school; post-secondary is defined as college and vocational colleges; and tertiary is defined as education beyond college, including graduate school, post graduate school, and professional school [2]. Within this paper, secondary and tertiary will be held synonymous (definition and statistics) with the term "higher education."

Adult learners "constitute a majority of students in higher education" [3]. Over the decades, there has been a noticeable increase in enrollment of adult learners in higher education.

2.2   Adult Learners

The adult learner's plethora of needs and motivations to earn a higher education has increased the rate of enrollment in colleges and universities. According to US Department of Education[4], from 2000 to 2010, the enrollment of students below age 25 increased by 34 percent, while students 25 and over increased 42 percent. Future projections for 2010 to 2020 show an 11 percent increase in enrollments for students under 25, and a 20 percent increase in enrollments of students 25 and over. Vocational courses were dominated by 45 to 64 year olds, following 25 to 34 year olds. 52 percent of graduate students were enrolled part time.

Many researchers have tried to define the characteristics of adult learners [5][6]. The classification of learners enrolled in higher education can be disseminated into many categories, such as gender, enrollment status, and age. Dean [6] separates this distinction into the following criteria, where a person can meet one or all of the criteria to be considered an adult: (1) physical development and maturity, classifies an adult in their physiological milestone of growth and age; (2) legal age-related definitions, describing an adult by governing laws; (3) the social roles defined by society's perceived notion of responsibilities that transition a child to an adult; and (4) internal factors which describes mental development stages achieved.

Advancements in technology, along with the ease of user interfaces, have changed the usage of computers from a novelty to daily life. Although there is progress, there are still many users, notably adults, who are not comfortable transacting online.

Badke [5] agrees that there are barriers that can inhibit an adult learner's progress, and concurs the transition of analog to "the digital world requires a whole new way of thinking.

Within this study, we refer to an adult learner as age 34 years or older. Traditional students are defined in two age brackets, 16-21 and 22-34 due to their small gap in continuous years enrolled in secondary to post-secondary school. This paper will focus on the experience of adult learners.

2.3   Social Networking Sites

Social networking site usage has grown in the number of users, the dollar amount of revenue, and the number of enhanced features and applications offered. According to Alexa.com [7], a website that tracks web traffic, the top 10 websites on the Internet include search engines and online collaboration tools. Examples of these sites include online encyclopedias, such as Wikipedia; media collaboration sites such as YouTube; and social networking sites such Facebook, Google+, and Twitter. Facebook ranks second and Twitter places the tenth for the most popular websites visited.

Social networking applications promote online interaction and communication by providing features such as free or low cost profile space, facilities for uploading content (e.g. links, photos, music), messaging in various forms, and the ability to make connections to other people. The types of relationships found on social networking sites include, but are not limited to,   friendships, professional, academic, and location [8].

2.4   Social Networking Sites in Academia

The growth in higher education in conjunction with the changing student population requires an evaluation of the instructional methodologies provided to potential students. In the past, classrooms took place face-to-face in a physical classroom. However in recent years classrooms have progressed from an invasive analog scheme to a digital one, and institutions have begun to supplement courses with learning management systems and have since then, begun to supplement LMS' with online collaboration tools, such as Facebook.

Integrating classrooms with social networking applications can be seen as beneficial to students. Liccardi et al [9] note that the social interaction within an online framework can help university students share experiences and collaborate on relevant topics. Lockyer and Patterson [10] suggests that social networking sites provide informal learning, because of the ability to share ideas, provide peer feedback, and engage in critical thinking. But will the learners really use these SNS for learning purposes?

3   Survey and Participants

A survey questionnaire was created to collect respondents' past experience of SNS. The questions are grouped into four main parts: Demographics, Work Experience,

Computer Experience, and Social Networking Experience.   Within Social Networking Experience, questions regarding the participants' general social network usage, reasons of using the social network sites, and experience in using social network sites for informal learning and formal learning.

The survey was distributed online to adult learners in several accelerated undergraduate classes at a mid-Atlantic university. Students were asked to submit the questionnaire on a voluntary basis. At the end, 43 completed questionnaires were received. Among 43 participants, 40 (93%) were female. Participants' ages range from 23 to 54 with the average being 38. The majority of participants (33, 76.7%) were part-time students, 39 (90.7%) were employed full-time at the time of the survey. Participants have been employed between one year and 30 years with the average of 7. The majors of the participants varied, including nursing, business, and computer science. 13 participants reported that they have never enrolled in a hybrid or distance learning course in the past. The majority (25, 58.1%) of participants rated themselves as intermediate computer users, while 16 (37.2%) were basic users who only knows how to surf the internet and some light word processing. The majority (38, 88.4%) of the participants reported to using a computer daily. 40 (93%) reported to have at least one social networking site account, such as Facebook, LinkedIn, Twitter, etc. For the ones that did not have a social networking account, they either do not know how to use it or not have time for it.

4   Results and Discussions

Among all the participants who reported to have social networking accounts, we've asked them to list all the sites that they have accounts with. The majority of them reported to have been using Facebook (36, 90%) followed by Google+ (12, 30%), Twitter (7, 17.5%), other social networking sites (5, 12.5%), and LinkedIn (4, 10%). When being asked about the frequency of using the sites, Facebook still takes the lead with 27 (67.5%) reported using it the most frequently. Even though some students reported to have a Twitter account, none of them reported to use it frequently.

When being asked about the reason of using social networking services, the majority of the participants reported to have been using it for sharing of opinions, for personal socialization, or widening their perspective in some way. Table 1 below shows the descriptive statistics of the reasons for using social networking services.

In addition to the general reasons of using social networking services, participants were also asked to indicate whether they are using different website for different purposes. For example, LinkedIn has been promoted as a social networking mainly for professionals while Facebook has been viewed more for creating/maintaining personal connections. Will the participants also view these different services as defined by the site itself? Ten (40%) of the participants chose Facebook and Google+ while only 5 (20%) selected LinkedIn as their choice for understanding business environment. Google+ has also been selected as the top choice (9, 42.9%) to "better your job prospects" with Facebook and LinkedIn tied in the second place, while no one selected

Table 1. Types of Content

	SA	A	N	D	SD
Understand business environment	1 (2.5%)	8 (20%)	15 (37.5%)	8 (20%)	8 (20%)
Create an id and sense of belongings to a community different from your real life	0 (0%)	12 (30%)	10 (25%)	11 (27.5%)	7 (17.5%)
Better your job prospects	3 (7.5%)	13 (32.5%)	8 (20%)	8 (20%)	8 (20%)
Keep yourself updated on current events	8 (20%)	21 (52.5%)	3 (7.5%)	1 (2.5%)	7 (17.5%)
Be part of a formal discussion forum	4 (10%)	16 (40%)	9 (22.5%)	5 (12.5%)	6 (15%)
Entertain yourself	11 (27.5%)	22 (55%)	4 (10%)	1 (2.5%)	2 (5%)
Stay in touch with family/friends/contacts you see a lot	17 (42.5%)	19 (47.5%)	1 (2.5%)	1 (2.5%)	2 (5%)
Make plans with your friends/contacts	10 (25%)	20 (50%)	3 (7.5%)	4 (10%)	3 (7.5%)
Build opinions	4 (10%)	11 (27.5%)	13 (32.5%)	6 (15%)	6 (15%)
Make new friends/contacts	4 (10%)	17 (42.5%)	6 (15%)	8 (20%)	5 (12.5%)
Stay in touch with family/friends/contacts you rarely see in person	15 (37.5%)	24 (60%)	1 (2.5%)	0 (0%)	0 (0%)
Flirt with someone	2 (5%)	3 (7.5%)	9 (22.5%)	11 (27.5%)	15 (37.5%)
Share opinion for educational purpose	1 (2.5%)	19 (47.5%)	9 (22.5%)	5 (12.5%)	6 (15%)
Share opinion for work purpose	1 (2.5%)	15 (37.5%)	9 (22.5%)	7 (17.5%)	8 (20%)
Share opinion for political purpose	3 (7.5%)	7 (17.5%)	10 (25%)	14 (35%)	6 (15%)

Twitter for this purpose. To keep updated on current events, the majority reported to use Facebook (22, 66.7%) and Google+ (17, 51.5%). Facebook also was selected as the top choice for formal discussion forum, entertainment, stay in touch with others, and make plans with friends. When being asked whether they would share opinions with others for educational, work, or political purpose, the majority also selected Facebook followed by Google+. Even though some participants have accounts on multiple social networking sites, they are not utilized equally. The use of the social networking sites are not always corresponding to the established image of the service provided. Even though Google+ is a relatively new platform for social networking, it has gained popularity among adult students.

Seventeen (42.5%) reported that they have used social networking service to get informal learning by posting questions to solicit help from others. The reasons for not using it for this purpose ranged from "never thought of it", "never needed help", "wanted to keep question private", to "did not know it was allowed", "did not think would get a correct response", and "don't think social network is appropriate". 10 (43.5%) reported that they would like to try getting help through a social network if the question is related to their study.

For the ones that reported to have solicited help through social network, Facebook was their first choice. However, most of the questions they posted were not education related. The majority of them reported that they would likely to do it again in the future. They have reported getting help through a social network was fun, helpful while also noted that it sometimes may not receive well-constructed responses.

When being asked their preference of using social networks to share opinions for class related purposes, instead of posting questions on their own wall, they prefer more by asking questions to the instructor directly, check updates posted by the instructor, share resources found online with others, or using a group page for a group project.

For those who reported that they prefer not to use a social networking site for learning purposes, 22 (51.2%) reported to prefer not to mix their studies with personal life, while 3 (7%) think social networking is a waste of time, or don't have an account and don't intend to create one.

5   Conclusions and Future Work

This article explores the reasons of using networking sites, benefits realized by adult learners by utilization of social networking sites, and potential ways to incorporate learning activities through social networking for adult learners. Over the past decades, the participation of adults enrolled in higher education has increased due to psychological, technological, and environmental reasons. These drives, along with others, have changed what we know of the traditional student.

Many adults find themselves enrolled in programs where technology is the primary mode of information deliverance and collaboration. For many of these adult learners whom have not been enrolled in school for a long period of time, have difficulty with the transition from a traditional to a blended or purely online classroom. Traditional students are advantageous because they have had technology embedded in their daily lives. However, many adult students are not natives of technology, and find the transition from an analog to digital lifestyle challenging.

Although social networking has been popular for its entertainment and networking value, many schools and instructors have embarked on supplementing their courses with social networking sites; taking advantage of the online collaboration tools and additional functionalities. This survey confirmed that although adult learners may not be expert users of computers, but may start getting into the arena. In addition, some adult learners have realized the potential benefit of "networking" by not only simply reading from others posts but solicit help from others as well. Moreover, it also indicates the potential of incorporating social networking for learning purposes.

Although many adult learners indicated their willingness of using social networking for learning purposes, there is still some resistance. For example, some respondents were concerned about the mix of study and their personal life, while some regard social network as a "waste of time" or simply don't want to create one account just for this purpose. It could be suggested that adult learners need to balance their work, home, and study while having the responsibly of financing their own studies. With this accountability, adult learners may not want the burden of using a social networking site when they have other priorities. Therefore, when designing social networking activities in classrooms (hybrid or distance learning), it is important to consider alternative approaches. In addition to their lifestyle, adult learners may not be as technologically savvy to use these types of sites, as Lockyer and Patterson [10] suggest lecturers may have to play a considerable technical support role in helping students who are new to such technologies.

 The preferences collected in the survey also suggests that the incorporation of social networking in the learning process may focus on building the community within the class while have the potential to extend to outside world with the instructor's control. Students prefer to get information from the instructor or communicate with the instructor within a specific area (e.g. an established group).

The fact that adult learners in this survey view Facebook and Google+ as the sites for getting business information and establish connections rather than LinkedIn, suggests that they may view social networking sites differently from what the sites promotes. How to attract users to create an effective social network remains a question for the designer of SNS. In addition, companies may want to think about establishing and the maintenance of their presence on those sites.

Although participants expressed their willingness to utilize SNS for getting help from others, they have also identified potential problems associated with this kind of activities -- how to control the quality of the answers. If we ever encourage students' use of SNS for informal learning -or get to help from others- how do we ensure the quality and creditability of the answers? Educate students on how to evaluate the quality and creditability of the work is needed. Future work should involve the design of potential activities based on the findings from this study and assess if students with social networking site usage in their classrooms performed better than students that did not have a social networking site integrated in their course.

In conclusion, this study explored the adult learner's use of social networking sites, the reasons of using/not using the social network, and potential ways of using social networking sites for educational purposes. However, this survey had a relatively low response. Future studies in getting larger samples of the adult learner's opinion and a comparison between the adult learner and traditional students is needed.

References

1. Fernando, A.: Baby steps in Web 2.0 education. Communication World 25(2), 8–9 (2008)
2. Wikipedia contributors: Higher Education. Wikipedia, The Free Encyclopedia, http://en.wikipedia.org/wiki/Higher_education (accessed: December 2012)
3. West, L.: Beyond Fragments: Adults, Motivation and Higher Education, p. IX. Taylor & Francis LTD (1996)
4. Department of Education: National Center for Education Statistics Fast Facts (2012)
5. Badke, W.: Information Literacy Meets Adult Learners. Online Magazine.Net 32(4), 48 (2008)
6. Dean, G.: An introduction to adult learners: Nothing is for sure. Fieldnotes for ABLE Staff, pp. 1–11 (2004)
7. Alexa: Top 500 Companies, http://www.alexa.com/topsites (accessed: December 2012)
8. Mitra, A., Bagchi, S., Bandyopadhyay, A.: Design of a Data Model for Social Network Applications. Journal of Database Management 18(4), 29–79 (2007)
9. Liccardi, I., Ounnas, A., Pau, R., Massey, E., Kinnumen, P., Lewthwaite, S., Midy, M.: The role of social networks in students' learning experiences. In: Proceeding ITiCSE-WGR 2007 Working Group Reports on ITiCSE on Innovation and Technology in Computer Science Education, pp. 224–237 (2007)
10. Lockyer, L., Patterson, J.: Integrating Social Networking Technologies in Education: A Case Study of a Formal Learning Environment. In: Proceedings of the 2008 Eighth IEEE International Conference on Advanced Learning Technologies, ICALT 2008, pp. 529–533 (2008)

Part III
Society, Business and Health

The Influence of Social Networking Sites on Participation in the 2012 Presidential Election

Rachel F. Adler[1] and William D. Adler[2]

[1] Northeastern Illinois University, Department of Computer Science, Chicago, Illinois, USA
R-Adler@neiu.edu
[2] Johns Hopkins University, Department of Political Science, Baltimore, Maryland, USA
williamadler@gmail.com

Abstract. Social networking sites are gaining in popularity, and candidates for president have been getting more involved in these online platforms. In order to examine whether a presidential candidate's presence on social networking sites influences people's political participation, we conducted a survey asking users a series of questions related to their social networking involvement, political involvement, and political involvement on social networking sites, specifically with regard to the 2012 presidential election. Our results indicate that despite being politically minded, these users do not use Facebook for political reasons and a candidate's online presence does not influence their decision on how to vote.

Keywords: Social Networking Sites, Elections, Facebook.

1 Introduction

Tens of millions of people are using Social Networking Sites (SNS). From 2005 to 2009 the number of Internet users who use SNS quadrupled [1]. Businesses, celebrities, and politicians can utilize this to their advantage. For instance, politicians now have a new method through which they can reach out to large numbers of people in a relatively inexpensive way [2]. However, the effectiveness of using SNS in this way for political gain is still a matter of debate.

A growing literature discusses the connections between SNS and political participation. Studies have examined how candidates for office use their public pages [3-5]; how those pages create space for political discourse [6]; whether SNS are altering basic democratic values [7]; and whether SNS encourage people to become politically active[8-13]. In one notable recent study, a 61 million person experiment of Facebook users was conducted to see if political messages would mobilize people to be politically engaged. They concluded that the messages affected political behavior online and offline [14].

Others, however, have argued that the high hopes surrounding the possibilities of online political discussions have not yet been fulfilled [15]. There is, so far, no consensus in the existing literature on whether or how offline and online political activities influence each other, with some studies seeing a direct connection and

A.A. Ozok and P. Zaphiris (Eds.): OCSC/HCII 2013, LNCS 8029, pp. 233–239, 2013.
© Springer-Verlag Berlin Heidelberg 2013

others separating the two. Clearly much work on understanding the impact of the Internet on politics remains to be done [16].

We propose here to extend this literature by studying how SNS did or did not influence individual participation in the 2012 presidential election. We attempt to determine whether a candidate's presence on social networking sites affect decisions about political participation in the 2012 presidential election. Understanding this potential connection has profound implications for the study of this emerging technology to political candidates, citizenship, and democratic life. To the extent that such activities on behalf of candidates are not effective, it raises questions about the usefulness of SNS to politicians and whether SNS should be utilized in a different manner.

In this paper, we describe a survey conducted of Facebook users to determine whether SNS influenced decisions related to the 2012 presidential election. To accomplish this, we selected Facebook as an example of a SNS and conducted a survey of Facebook users to obtain their views on their SNS involvement, political involvement, and political involvement with regard to SNS.

2   Methodology

In order to examine how SNS impacted political activity in the 2012 presidential election we conducted a survey of Facebook users. Participants were recruited through SNS such as Facebook and Twitter. The survey was open for responses beginning October 10, 2012 and closed the evening before Election Day on November 5, 2012. One hundred and thirty one participants (55 male and 76 female) completed the survey. All participants were required to be at least 18 years of age and have a Facebook account.

2.1   Questionnaire

In addition to demographic questions (such as age, gender, education level, ethnicity, and political party affiliation), our survey was constructed into three main categories. These are:

— I SNS Involvement - Participants were asked their primary and secondary reasons for using SNS as well how often they tended to go on Facebook.
— II Political Involvement - Participants were asked a series of political questions to determine whether they were politically active, such as how often they discussed political events and the presidential election and whether they paid attention and stayed informed about the presidential election.
— III Political Involvement on SNS - This section asked participants to rank whether they strongly agree or disagree with a series of statements, such as whether a candidate's presence influences their decision on how to vote or to contribute to a campaign, or whether their friends' opinions on Facebook influence their opinions regarding candidates.

3 Results

3.1 SNS Involvement

In order to determine how involved the participants were on the SNS, we examined Facebook usage. The breakdown for participants and their level of usage can be seen in the second row of Table 1. Seventy five percent of the participants checked Facebook at least a few times a day and 90% at least once a day. This demonstrates that our sample consists of users who are frequently on Facebook.

Table 1. Frequency of Facebook Usage and Political Discussions

	Number of Participants (Percentage of Participants)				
Survey Responses	*At least a few times a day*	*About once a day*	*At least a few times a week*	*Once a week*	*Less than once a week*
How often do you check Facebook	98 (75%)	19 (15%)	11 (8%)	0 (0%)	3 (2%)
How often do you discuss political events	41 (31%)	35 (27%)	25 (19%)	15 (11%)	15 (11%)
How often do you discuss the 2012 presidential election	29 (22%)	39 (30%)	32 (24%)	20 (15%)	11 (8%)

*Figures don't add up to 100% due to rounding

3.2 Political Involvement

When examining the political responses, it appears quite clear that the subjects were politically active. For example, a majority of the participants discussed political events and the presidential election at least once a day, while over 75% discussed them at least a few times a week (see Table 1, rows 3 and 4).

In addition, we asked two questions based on Kushin and Yamamoto's [17] four-question scale for political involvement. Using a 5-point Likert scale we asked participants to rank from Strongly Disagree to Strongly Agree the following statements: (1) *I pay attention to information about the election for president* and (2) *I like to stay informed about the election for president*. Over 80% of the participants agreed with both of the statements. The results suggest that the participants who completed the survey can generally be considered politically active.

3.3 Political Involvement on SNS

Using a 5-point Likert scale, participants were asked a series of questions pertaining to their political activities on Facebook, both in general and with regard to the presidential election. Participants did not tend to use Facebook for political reasons and candidates' active presence on the site did not seem to impact their final vote choice. Over 80% disagreed with the statements "A presidential candidate's active presence on Facebook affects my decision on how to vote" and "A presidential candidate's active presence on Facebook affects my willingness to donate to his/her campaign." In fact, no user answered "Strongly Agree" for either of these two statements.

Furthermore, in order to discover whether friend's political activities and comments over Facebook can influence SNS users, we asked participants whether they agreed with these statements: (1) *I often change my mind based on my friends' political opinions on Facebook* and (2) *I often change my mind based on my friends' opinions on presidential candidates on Facebook.*" Over 80% of participants disagreed with these statements.

Despite these users being politically minded and frequently on their SNS, our results indicate that they do not use Facebook for political reasons. In fact, the primary reason given for using Facebook was pleasure, as shown in Table 2. Only two people stated they used Facebook primarily for political purposes and just eight listed it as a secondary reason.

Table 2. Reasons for Checking Facebook

	Number of Participants				
Survey Responses	*Pleasure*	*Political Reasons*	*Work/ School Related*	*Other*	*No Secondary Reason**
What is your primary reason for checking your Facebook page?	121	2	1	7	
What is your secondary reason for checking your Facebook page?	8	8	27	14	74

*Note: This option was only provided for the second question.

4   Discussion

It seems that although the participants frequently used Facebook and were also considered generally active politically, Facebook is not the locus of their political activity. Indeed, what candidates for the presidency did or did not do on their public pages seemed to have little impact on individuals' votes or on their willingness to donate to the candidates. In addition, their views on candidates were not influenced by others' Facebook remarks. The impact of social networks on political participation was quite limited.

These findings stand together with some findings in the previous literature on the impact of SNS on political participation. Like Baumgartner and Morris [9], as well as Kushin and Yamamoto [17] and Larsson [15], who found that users of SNS were no more likely to engage in political participation, we see SNS as holding much promise but delivering little in terms of real-world impact on people's political activities. It is true that Bode [10] found that interacting with a Facebook community increased the likelihood of offline political participation. However, we would suggest those results may be limited by the specific demographic targeted in that study (namely, college undergraduates) which creates very little space between its offline and online behaviors. Other demographics, which grew up without SNS, may see their Facebook community as distinct from their offline social activities. Our study group also consisted of a highly educated, politically motivated sample, which may be less likely to be influenced by others.

The results of the massive experiment conducted by Bond et al. [14] are compelling, given the large sample targeted. They found that political messages sent on Facebook did cause those targeted to become more active in politics, to be more likely to vote, and more likely to influence their friends to participate in politics as well.

The results of our study may stand in contrast because our data are self-reported and rely on individuals' recollections of their actions, or alternatively because the questions we asked elicited more direct information about how SNS users interacted with the candidates for office. The Bond et al. [14] study did not directly examine how candidates could increase Facebook users' likelihood to vote for their campaigns.

Our findings may indicate more limited possibilities for targeted messaging by any specific campaign. In other words, it is not clear whether politicians on SNS will necessarily get the results they desire to increase voter turnout or donations.

4.1   Limitations

One limitation in this study is that subjects were recruited to participate in this study through statuses on social networking sites (such as Facebook and Twitter). Therefore, the survey respondents consisted of followers and followers of followers of the authors. Therefore, we suggest caution when applying these findings to other populations.

Another limitation is that the survey reflects individuals' perceptions about whether or not they were influenced, which may or may not equal the degree to which participants were actually influenced. While people's views may not be influenced by SNS overall, it may have impacted them subtly without them being aware of it.

5   Conclusion

We conducted an experiment to determine the effects of candidates' presence on SNS. One hundred and thirty one people responded to our study and our results indicate that even for people who are politically active the activities of presidential candidates on Facebook does not affect their willingness to vote or donate to the candidate. Facebook is not the locus of their political activity. Furthermore, their friends' political or presidential views do not influence their political opinions.

Future research directions include examining the degree to which members of different political groups respond differently to messages received through Facebook or other social networking sites. If Democrats are earlier adopters of this new area of technology, their response to the candidates' actions may differ significantly from non-Democrats.

References

1. Lenhart, A.: Adults and social network websites. Pew Internet & American Life Project (2009), http://www.pewinternet.org/~/media/Files/Reports/2009/PIP_Adult_social_networking_data_memo_FINAL.pdf.pdf (retrieved March 1, 2013)
2. Gueorguieva, V.: Voters, MySpace, and YouTube: The impact of alternative communication channels on the 2006 election cycle and beyond. Social Science Computer Review 26(3), 288–300 (2008)
3. Robertson, S.P., Vatrapu, R.K., Medina, R.: Off the wall political discourse: Facebook use in the 2008 U.S. Presidential election. Information Polity: The International Journal of Government & Democracy in the Information Age 15(1/2), 11–31 (2010)
4. Haynes, A.A., Pitts, B.: Making an impression: New media in the 2008 presidential nomination campaigns. PS: Political Science and Politics 42, 53–58 (2009)
5. Williams, C.B., Gulati, G.J.: Social networks in political campaigns: Facebook and the congressional elections of 2006 and 2008. New Media and Society 15(1), 52–71 (2013)
6. Robertson, S.P., Vatrapu, R.K., Medina, R.: The social life of social networks: Facebook linkage patterns in the 2008 U.S. Presidential election. In: Proceedings of the 10th Annual International Conference on Digital Government Research: Social Networks: Making Connections between Citizens, Data and Government, pp. 6–15 (2009)
7. Swigger, N.: The online citizen: Is social media changing citizens' beliefs about democratic values? Political Behavior (forthcoming)
8. Conroy, M., Feezell, J.T., Guerrero, M.: Facebook and political engagement: A study of online political group membership and offline political engagement. Computers in Human Behavior 28(5), 1535–1546 (2012)
9. Baumgartner, J.C., Morris, J.S.: Myfacetube politics: Social networking web sites and political engagement of young adults. Social Science Computer Review 28(1), 24–44 (2010)
10. Bode, L.: Facebooking it to the polls: A study in online social networking and political behavior. Journal of Information Technology & Politics 9, 352–369 (2012)
11. Vitak, J., Zube, P., Smock, A., Carr, C.T., Ellison, N., Lampe, C.: It's complicated: Facebook users' political participation in the 2008 election. Cyberpsychology, Behavior, and Social Networking 14(3), 107–114 (2011)

12. Bode, L., Vraga, E., Borah, P., Sha, D.: A new space for political behavior: Political social networking and its democratic consequences. Journal of Computer-Mediated Communication (forthcoming)
13. Vesnic-Alujevic, L.: Political participation and web 2.0 in Europe: A case study of Facebook. Public Relations History 38(3), 466–470 (2012)
14. Bond, R.M., Fariss, C.J., Jones, J.J., Kramer, A.I., Marlow, C., Settle, J.E., Fowler, J.H.: A 61-million-person experiment in social influence and political mobilization. Nature 489(7415), 295–298 (2012)
15. Larsson, A.O.: "Rejected bits of program code": Why notions of "politics 2.0" remain (mostly) unfulfilled. Journal of Information Technology & Politics 10(1), 72–85 (2013)
16. Farrell, H.: The consequences of the internet for politics. Annual Review of Political Science 15, 35–52 (2012)
17. Kushin, M.J., Yamamoto, M.: Did social media really matter? College students' use of online media and political decision making in the 2008 election. Mass Communication and Society 13(5), 608–630 (2010)

Teaching about the Impacts of Social Networks: An End of Life Perspective

James Braman, Giovanni Vincenti, Alfreda Dudley, Yuanqiong Wang,
Karen Rodgers, and Ursula Thomas

Towson University
Dept. of Computer & Information Sciences
Towson, MD 21252
{jbraman,gvincenti,adudley,ywang}@towson.edu,
{kholmes,uthomas}@students.towson.edu

Abstract. As the use of various social networking technologies increase, so does the importance of understanding the long term implications for users in the context of end of life. Users post many digital artifacts online for many reasons, such as for storage, construction of their digital identity, communication, etc. Often these posts and uploads inadvertently build the digital legacy of the user. In this paper, we discuss the impacts of social networking and the construction of an online identity from an end of life perspective. The authors discuss the importance of education as an essential element for preparation and understanding of this topic. A survey of college social network users is also reported along with a discussion on their feedback.

Keywords: Social Networking, End of Life, Death, Education, Thanatechnology.

1   Introduction

Many are using social networks for a plethora of reasons: staying in touch, finding new friends, reading news, status updates, just to name a few activities. The use of various social networking tools has been on the rise for some time, and trends suggest that this increase will continue [1]. Although participating in these social platforms are now commonplace, the implications of using these technologies in terms of the future are often not clear or not even considered. In this paper, we discuss the impacts of social networking and the construction of an online identity from an end of life perspective. We also report some preliminary insights from a survey of college age social network users as a step to gain a better understanding on how people feel about this topic. This paper focuses on the need for educating digital native students about these issues, as they will be the content creators of significant digital legacies and online identities through long-term usage of social networks.

Content is added to our social networking sites (SNS) such as comments, pictures, videos, links and, also replied comments to and from, other "friended" users,

A.A. Ozok and P. Zaphiris (Eds.): OCSC/HCII 2013, LNCS 8029, pp. 240–249, 2013.
© Springer-Verlag Berlin Heidelberg 2013

and are aggregated to create the "profile" of an individual. These bits of data can also be thought of as "Narrative Bits" of information, or "narbs", which describe a user and their interactions over time [2]. "The identity of an individual is eventually constructed by the combination of narbs that are available on a social networking site where different kinds of narbs work together to produce the composite narrative of a person at any moment in time" [2]. Others have referred to this combination of interactions and information joined on social media as one's "digital soul" [3]. This is also true with other social technologies where text and media are not the primary mode of interaction. Over time, these chunks of information become our digital legacy. The entirety of our online identity is what remains after we are physically gone. This digital legacy is what many other users, friends and family members will remember of us once we are no longer living. It is therefore important to consider this fact, in order to be mindful of what is posted online and to also actively protect certain digital artifacts if the intent is to bequeath information, software, media or other digital content to friends, family or other users. We are interested in the implications of social network usage from a legal and ethical perspective in the context of end of life [4]. In this paper, we focus on an educational perspective by teaching and preparing users so as to be better equipped for future planning. There are many questions to consider in regards to content, individual "branding" or online identity. In other words, upon a user's death, what happens to the information? What were the wishes of the user in the event of their death? Is the culmination of posts, pictures, and status updates over a life time, the online legacy the user intended to leave behind? Additionally, what are the legal ramifications of the deceased user's information?

Many educators are already aware of the need to teach proper Internet etiquette or "netiquette". This can include teaching students about appropriate language use, online professionalism, email usage, and many other respectful online behaviors [5]. With the rise of online and web based forms of interaction in modern society, knowing how to act in a responsible way online will be an important social norm for the future. Instances of employees losing their job due to posts on Facebook, or potential employers not hiring someone due to compromising photographs, and the development of social networking policies for employees illustrate the impact of SN usage on our real lives. Also related to online behaviors, the effects of cyber bullying have been gaining attention in recent years. While negative consequences of improper online behavior have promoted education for better online usage, it is educators that have taken an important role at raising awareness and prevention. Similarly, educators can play a key role at raising awareness about the long term effect of SNS usage, when it comes to digital content and that of our digital legacy. While many of these netiquette ideas are helpful, the death of a user is often something that is not often considered. We feel that raising awareness through additional education is needed, but first we wanted to better understand the perception of this topic from current users. In order to gain insight on how users of social networks considered this topic, a survey was administered to college age students and is discussed in the next section.

2   Research Methodology

To begin to understand students' viewpoint on social network usage from an end of life perspective, we developed a brief survey. We wanted to understand how college age SN user's viewed the topic and to also gain insight on the types of content posted online, and if preparation of digital information had been considered. We also wanted to investigate what the final wishes of the person might be. Our current focus has primarily been on SNS, but we are also considering other online content in relation to virtual worlds, which also fit into the category of SNS in the context of how one communicates and forms relationships and identity. Boyd & Ellison describe a social network defines a web-based social networking site as a service that allows users to: "(1) Construct a public or semipublic profile within a bounded system (2) articulate a list of other users with whom they share a connection, and (3) view and traverse their list of connections and those made by others within the system" [6, pg 211]. These main points also true from a virtual world perspective.

A survey was distributed to two undergraduate classes at a Mid-Atlantic university. One of the classes is a new seminar course, titled "Virtual Worlds and Society: Impacts of Online Interaction", consisting of students in their first year of undergraduate education, the other is an upper level computer science class in artificial intelligence,, consisting of seniors in their last semester of undergraduate classes.

To gain immediate feedback on this topic from students and their perceived considerations on SNS usage, many discussions have taken place in the seminar course. The main focus of the course is on virtual worlds, but topics related to SNS are often discussed. Initial observations and discussions from students have been positive with their realization that a need does exist to consider these facts and to protect digital information for long term usage if SNS will be a technology used in mass for many years to come. Many students expressed that they had never considered this topic, while several had, due to their own experiences with friends and family members passing away, while their SNS remained active and online. Some students expressed a desire to have their SNS memorialized in the event of their passing, while a majority wanted their online presence deleted. Several methods were discussed as to preparation, such as creating and maintain a final status update, including certain aspects into estate planning, and about several websites that provide services for digital content management, specifically related to end of life. The survey was distributed to this class after the discussion. In the section below we report on the combined data from both classes.

3   Survey Results

3.1   Demographics

In both classes combined there were 51 students with 41 students that responded to the survey, for an 80.4% response rate. The average age for the responding students was 21.3 years old. This included 15 females and 26 males. In the seminar course, the declared majors for the students varied greatly, with the most frequent majors being art and design, exercise science and family studies. Several students in the class were listed with an undeclared major of study. In the artificial intelligence course 21 students listed their major as computer science and the remaining three were information systems majors.

3.2   Results

When responding to the question regarding the average amount of hours students generally spend online each day;   12 students (29.3%) reported they spend 1-3 hours online, 17 students (41.5%) reported 4-6 hours spent online, 11 students (26.8%) reported spending 7-9 hours online, and 1 (2.4%)   student noted that they spend more than 9 hours online each day. There were no students that reported they spend no time online or that they were unsure for the approximate time spend online. This survey did not specify how students were connecting to the internet or what they considered was being online or connected.   When being asked if they have a profile on a social networking site and which sites they maintained a profile (multiple responses are allowed), 39 (95.1%) students noted that they do indeed have a SNS profile. The remaining 2 students (4.9%) noted that they do not have a SN profile. For these two respondents, their data was not used in further data calculations where the survey question required having a social networking presence (i.e. question 3 and 4).   For the sites that they have accounts with, respondents listed Facebook 29 times, Twitter 15 times, tumblr 3 times, instagram 2 times, and LinkedIn once. Nine of the respondents did not list where they had a social networking site.

In terms of types of information users generally post on their social networking site, five generalized categories were listed in the survey as options for this question; users were asked to list content if they chose "Other".   Table 1 below describes the frequency of the choices. Users could select multiple options.

Table 1. Types of Content

Choice	Total
A. Pictures	33
B. Text based posts	33
C. Video	15
D. Music or other audio	9
E. Other	2
Content Listed for Choice E.	Links, Articles, Software

Users were asked to rank the importance of the content that they post on their social networking profile, from "Not at all important" to "Highly important". From the respondents, one student had no response (n=40). The majority of the respondents (21) thought the content was somewhat to extremely important. Table 2 describes the frequency of responses from both classes.

The survey also asked participants if they knew anyone that had died, but their social networking profile is still present / active after the person's death. From the students, 24 (58.6%) reported "Yes" and the remaining 17 (41.4%) reported "No". When asked "Would you want your social networking page to remain active if you were to pass away?", 10 (24.4%) students responded "Yes" and the remaining 31 (75.6%) responded "No". The next question asked about the types of digital assets that they currently have online (or on a personal computing device) that need to be protected after their death (if any). For this question, more than one option could have been selected. Photos, personal information, and documents are the ones being selected the most frequently. Table 3 lists the responses from both classes for this question.

Table 2. Content Ratings

Rating	Total
A. Not at all important	8
B. A Little important	11
C. Somewhat important	12
D. Very important	7
E. Extremely important	2

Table 3. Digital Assets that need Protecting

Category	Total
A. Photos	27
B. Documents	15
C. Music	9
D. Video	7
E. Intellectual property (i.e. things that you or others have created)	9
F. Personal Information (i.e. tax documents, addresses, financial data etc.)	18
G. Other	4 reported "nothing"
H. No Response	3

Table 4 below describes the responses for both groups when responding to whether they would want their digital content to be deleted, preserved with some restrictions or remain the same after their death. Participants were asked if they did choose option B to preserve their content with restrictions, to list what restrictions they would want.

For this question, 5 students noted that they would only want family to be able to have access, 2 students did not have any restrictions listed, 1 student noted that they only wanted certain people to view/access the content, 1 reported that they didn't want everyone to have access, 1 wanted no one to be able to sign into any accounts, 1 wanted only a spouse to be able to access, 1 student noted that financial information should be removed but remain active, and 1 noted that his/her account should remain active, but no one should be able to access it. The remaining 4 students that chose option B in that group did not report a restriction.

The survey also asked if they have files or digital content that they would want erased so no one would know about the content. From the students 9 (22%) responded "Yes" and 32 (78%) responded "No". In the questionnaire, students were also able to list the content that they would want erased. This included: Facebook posts, photos, messages, chat logs and status updates. One person wanted everything deleted. When being asked whether they would want a virtual memorial when they pass away, 12 (29.3%) responded "Yes" in favor of a virtual memorial, while 27 (65.9%) responded "No", and 2 (4.8%) students had no response. It was optional, for participants to comment on their options for this question. Some comments from participants that were against virtual memorials include: *"I think it is good enough having a real memorial. I wouldn't want to burden someone in creating a virtual memorial for me"; "I'd rather have a real memorial if at all"; "I don't want to be remembered as just a Facebook profile"; "Because my family doesn't use a lot of social network-ing"; "I may be remembered in the wrong way"*. Some comments from participants that were for virtual memorials include: *"I have a lot of online friends who I'm very close to"; "It might be nice for friends to remember me by"; "It would be Memora-ble"; "I think it's pretty cool". "I feel like it would be nice for my friends and family to have something to remember me by"*.

Table 4. Content Preservations

Choices	Total
A. Deleted	21
B. Preserved with restrictions	17
C. Remain the same (where anything could happen with access)	3

As part of the study we wanted to examine if participants had any legal or other informal documentation that expressed their final wishes in terms of end of life preparation. This was asked as part of Question #11, but did not specify if this re-garded only digital content. Only 1 (2.4%) responded "Yes" while the remaining 40 (97.6%) responded "No". Participants were asked to rate the statement "When it comes to virtual memorials on SNS how would you rate your feelings" using a scale from Disrespectful to Respectful and also from Not Important to Important. We have treated this scale as Likert scale because of the large deviation to see how the opinions are actually distributed across the board. Close to half of the participants (19) were neutral on this statement for both scales, while majority of the remaining participants thought it was respectful but not important to have virtual memorials. Table 5 below lists the frequency of responses. The lower the rating relates to a stronger feeling towards disrespectful and it being not important to consider. Fol-lowing with Table 6, it describes participants rankings related to the question which asked to choose a statement that best identifies a position on the moral/ethical obli-gations of digital assets after death. Majority of the participants (25) felt it is some-what to extremely important.

Table 5. Rating For Importance and Respectfulness

Rating	Frequency		Rating	Frequency
Disrespectful			Not Important	
1	1		1	7
2	3		2	8
3	19		3	20
4	12		4	6
5	6		5	0
Respectful			Important	

Participants were then asked if they had considered the importance of protecting online content in case of one's death before taking the survey. 11 (26.8%) students reported "Yes" and 30 (73.2%) responded "No". As it relates to another future project, they were asked "Would you want a permanent memorial to represent you in a virtual world?". A memorial in a virtual world, would be some type of permanent or semi-permanent 3D structure or representation unlike a memorialized page on a SNS. Students taking the survey were all familiar with virtual worlds. Seven students (17.1%) responded "Yes" while 32 (78.0%) responded "No" and 2 students (4.9%) noted that they were unsure. Participants were then asked to rank on a Likert scale, their feelings in three categories as it related to virtual memorials on SNS. Close to half of the respondents were neutral on this topic, while majority of the remaining participants thought it was respectful but unimportant. Participants were evenly divided on whether it is creepy to set up a virtual memorial.   Table 7 lists the results from that question.

Table 6. Moral/Ethical Position Related to Digital Assets after Death

Choice	Total
I cannot assess my position on this issue	11
I don't feel capable and knowledgeable in stating a moral/ethical issue	3
I feel that morality/ethics is somewhat important	11
I feel that morality/ethics is very important	12
I feel that morality/ethics is extremely important	4

When being asked "Have you ever conducted an online or virtual "funeral" before deleting a profile or account?" All students (100%) responded "No" to this question. However, during class discussions previous to the survey, students had expressed hearing about a virtual funeral taking place in the World of Warcraft for a user who died in real life. The following question asked "Do you feel that more education on this topic is important?". The majority of the students, 30 (73.2%) reported "Yes" and 11 reported "No" (26.8%). The final question in the survey was an open ended question that only asked if they had any other thoughts or comments about the topic overall. Table 8 lists several comments that were reported.

Table 7. Rating for Virtual Memorials

Rating	Freq.	Rating	Freq.	Rating	Freq.
Disrespectful		*Not Important*		*Creepy*	
1	2	1	8	1	4
2	3	2	9	2	10
3	17	3	19	3	13
4	13	4	5	4	9
5	6	5	0	5	5
Respectful		*Important*		*Not Creepy*	

Table 8. General Comments

Comments
"People should be more aware of what to do with all their online data after they pass"
"I rarely use my SNS so it's hard to say I care about its contents. I prefer to stay connected in person or over the phone"
"Leaving a will that instructs loved ones about digital data sounds important'"
"Online friendships can be very powerful. An online friend man never meet you once in person, but that doesn't mean they will be any less affected by your death"
"I think it is important to honor someone who has passed. It has to be respectful though. I personally have written on someone's Facebook page that has passed. It helps release emotions"
"I would like to know more about it and the process of doing a virtual memorial"
"I feel like everyone should know about it and have precautions in case of an accident, but I also feel like a virtual memorial could be a little much"
"I feel that posting pictures, videos and memories of the person that passes away on their SNS is a nice way of remembering them. I feel that it should be able to remain there for as long as possible. It may be the only way that some people have to remember that person"

4   Discussion

There seems to be a significant need of addressing issues such as this during the college years. The matter regarding death and arrangements for one's virtual identity is really a composite view of technological, legal, social and ethical perspectives which converge into an often new perspective for most students. Anecdotally we have observed that students who received an exposure through in-class discussions seem to be slightly more aware about the importance of such arrangements. From the survey however, we can see that students do have some varying opinions regarding this topic. It is clear that the students had multiple presences on several SNS and posted a wide array of content. While most posting of content seem to be primarily text based content and photographs, this may change as more applications and services are being ported to the cloud, allowing more content to be stored online. Although many ranked their online profile as being only somewhat important, many spend large amounts of time online and interacting with other users on SNS. While some viewed their digital content as having importance that needed some preservation and/or protection, others did not seem to care what would happen to their content if something were to happen to them.

We feel that the results of this survey are helpful at gaining insight on how some college students feel about their content and in general, what they would want to happen in terms of their content. As noted by the question regarding the importance of protecting online content in case of one's death, many students had not previously considered protecting their digital content in the context of this topic. From this preliminary survey, we observed that the majority of the students are active on one or more SNS and spend time online each day. Most of their SN profiles contain several types of content with pictures and text based posting being the most popular. The students for the majority noted they did know of other people that had died and where the deceased's page was still active. However, for their own content, the majority expressed that they wanted their own page be deleted and not active in the case of their death. Many other students did want their information persevered but with restrictions. With observing that many in our survey noted that they do not have any estate planning related to SN usage along with the fact they do want their content restricted or deleted, this topic needs additional research to help user protect content. Only 26.8% of those responding had considered the importance of protecting their own content in the event of their death. Additionally when asked about this topic, 73.2% agreed that additional education was indeed needed.

Education about proper planning is essential for protecting your digital content and/or your digital legacy. There are several key questions that one can ask as they are posting or storing any content online, such as: 1. Is this content something I'm alright with if it becomes part of my digital legacy?, 2. Is this content something that should be protected if something were to happen to me? and, 3. If this content should be protected, how can it be protected? Also, as part of our overall digital estate planning, there are a few more general question we may want to ask ourselves as well, such as: 1. Are my overall wishes for my digital content known?, 2. Can my final wishes for my digital content / online identity be carried out? and, 3. For the data I want to have protected or bequeathed, can my estate executor access my content?

Although this was a preliminary survey, it was helpful as a first step at gaining insight on the perception of college-aged users on this topic and to identify the need for additional education on this matter. In future studies we plan on focusing on certain questions more in-depth and to ask questions related to specific content and usage. This could include asking about specific time spent on their SNS, how they access the content, the frequency of posting and if they intend to use or maintain a profile online throughout their lifetime.

5   Conclusions

Although not a pleasant topic, protecting one's digital assets in the event of one's death is of a particular concern that deserves more attention and potentially affects every user with a digital presence. We believe that educating today's students whom will be using SNS in an abundant number of ways need to consider long-term implications. As we move to a more digital way of life, more protection and education of preparedness is needed. We hope that through this project, we can make more people aware of how to prepare as well as further understand current perceptions related to SNS usage.

As part of our future work, we are in the process of collecting more data from several more surveys as well as expanding our initial user model. We are also working towards extracting interaction details and comments from public profiles of individuals that are known to be deceased in order to see how other users interact with the content of these pages, how long they stay active, and what types of content remain on these profiles. With more of content being transitioned into electronic formats, it is of ever growing importance to protect this content and our own content for the future.

References

1. Arno, C.: Worldwide Social Media Usage Trends in 2012. Search Engine Watch (2012), http://searchenginewatch.com/article/2167518/Worldwide-Social-Media-Usage-Trends-in-2012 (retrieved)
2. Mitra, A.: Creating a Presence on Social Networks via Narbs. Global Media Journal 9(16) (Spring 2010)
3. Paul-Choudhury, S.: Digital Legacy: The Fate of your Online Soul. New Scientist, issue 2809 (2012), http://www.newscientist.com/article/mg21028091.400-digital-legacy-the-fate-of-your-online-soul.html (retrieved December 28, 2012)
4. Braman, J., Dudley, A., Vincenti, G.: Death, Social Networks and Virtual Worlds: A Look into the Digital Afterlife. In: Proceedings of the 9th International Conference on Software Engineering Research, Management and Applications (SERA), Baltimore, MD, USA, August 10-12 (2011)
5. Berk, R.: Top 12 Be-Attitudes of Netiquette for Academicians. The Journal of Faculty Development 25(3), 45–48 (2011)
6. Boyd, D., Ellison, N.: Social Network Sites: Definition, History, and Scholarship. Journal of Computer-Mediated Communication 13, 210–230 (2008)

The Effects of Navigation Support and Group Structure on Collaborative Online Shopping

Yihong Cheng[1], Yanzhen Yue[1], Zhenhui (Jack) Jiang[1, 2], and Hyung Jin Kim[1]

[1] Dept. of Information Systems, National University of Singapore, Singapore, 117418
[2] National University of Singapore (Suzhou) Research Institute, 377 Lin Quan Street,
Suzhou Industrial Park, Jiang Su, P.R. China
yihong.c.nus@gmail.com,
{Yanzhen,jiang,kimhj}@comp.nus.edu.sg

Abstract. As a new paradigm of e-commerce, collaborative online shopping fulfills online consumers' needs to shop with close ones in a social and colla-borative environment. While previous e-commerce research and practice mainly focus on consumers' individual shopping behavior, a recent trend is for con-sumers to buy things together online. This study proposes two new types of navigation support and investigates how different types of navigation support influence consumers' collaborative online shopping experience. Specifically, their impacts on consumers' coordination performance and perceived useful-ness are assessed by comparing two types of extant navigation support in a lab experiment. Meanwhile, the moderating role of the group structure of collabora-tive consumers is also assessed.

Keywords: Collaborative Online Shopping, Navigation Support, Group Struc-ture, Ease of Uncoupling Resolution, Perceived Usefulness.

1 Introduction

While previous e-commerce research and practice mainly focus on consumers' indi-vidual shopping behavior, a recent trend is for consumers to buy things together online. In this study, we look at this emerging phenomenon, collaborative online shopping (COS), defined as the activity in which a consumer shops at an online store concurrently with one or more remotely-located shopping partners [20]. COS pro-vides collaboration support for consumers to search and evaluate products together. On one hand, collaborative online shopping enables consumers to share and exchange their opinions about products; on the other hand, it fulfills online consumers' needs to shop with close ones in a social and collaborative environment.

In spite of the evident demand for consumer collaboration, COS is not well sup-ported by current e-commerce platforms [1]. Most of the e-commerce websites are designed for solitary use. Collaborative online consumers have to use their web browsers independent of each other, leading to ineffective communication and discus-sion due to lack of contextual information about each other's focus [3,6]. To better

A.A. Ozok and P. Zaphiris (Eds.): OCSC/HCII 2013, LNCS 8029, pp. 250–259, 2013.
© Springer-Verlag Berlin Heidelberg 2013

support consumers' collaborative product search and evaluation, we attempt to propose new designs to solve the problem.

Since a prominent feature of COS is to facilitate collaborative product search, it is important to design appropriate navigation mechanisms that helps collaborative consumers navigate to the same products of their interest to establish a common referential context for the collaborative product evaluation and discussion. Two types of navigation support were investigated in prior studies [20], namely separate navigation and shared navigation. While the former only allows each user to view and control his/her own separate browser, the latter enables both collaborative users to synchronize their browsing paces so that one can always know what the other person is looking at. Prior research has found that although shared navigation is in general better than separate navigation in terms of collaborative product search, shared navigation leads to unexpected uncoupling problems when the two collaborators do not well coordinate with one another.

To solve this problem, we propose two new types of navigation support: separate navigation with location cue and split screen navigation. In the separate navigation with location cue condition, each user is provided with a clickable visual location indicator, which displays his/her partner's real-time location information. The user can navigate to the web page that his/her partner is viewing by clicking on the location cue. Split screen navigation divides the browser into two separate screens, with one screen controlled by one user and the other screen instantly displaying the current web page his/her partner is viewing. These two navigation support designs are empirically evaluated against separate navigation and shared navigation in this study.

Another purpose of this study is to investigate the moderating role of the group structure of collaborative shoppers. It is commonly observed that consumers may shop with others in two forms of group structure: (1) 'co-buyers' structure [2], e.g., two individuals buy a birthday gift together for their common friend; and (2) 'buyer/advisor' structure [18,20], e.g., one individual buys a skirt for herself, and she invites her friend to offer advices on product selection. It has not yet been empirically investigated whether or not the group structure of collaborative shoppers affects the effectiveness of different types of navigation support, and if so, to what extent.

This paper is organized as follows. The next section reviews previous literature and theoretical foundations, followed by the proposed research model and hypotheses. After that we demonstrate the research method and report the analysis results. The last section concludes with discussions of the implications and future research directions.

2   Literature Review and Theoretical Foundations

Collaborative online shopping could be considered as a kind of real-time distributed collaboration, in which physically distant shopping partners collaboratively search for product alternatives of interest at the same time. Hence, we discuss two theories on situational awareness and dual task interference to provide the theoretical foundations for the exploration of effects of navigation support and group structure on collaborative online shopping consumers' experience.

2.1   Situational Awareness Theory

Situation Awareness (SA) is generally defined as "the perception of the elements in the environment within a volume of time and space, the comprehension of their meaning and the projection of their status in the near future" [6]. Situation awareness includes more than attending to information, but also the integration of multiple pieces of relevant information to the person's goal [7]. SA plays an important role in various collaborative activities to reduce effort and increase efficiency for the activities of collaboration [8].

With the help of SA, people are able to keep an updated understanding of other people's interaction with their shared workspace, which in turn guides people's ensuing behavior. In contrast, without situation awareness, the ease and naturalness of collaboration will be lost, making remote collaboration awkward and inefficient as compared to face-to-face work [8]. Prior studies suggest that collaborators must attain and maintain reciprocal awareness of shared activity to coordinate effectively [3].

2.2   Dual Task Interference Theory

Dual-task interference refers to the situation where people perform two or more activities concurrently [16]. As the main theoretical underpinning for dual-task interference, "bottleneck" model assumes that individuals have limited cognitive capacity. Cognitive capacity is scarce mental resource [14], thereby when individuals perform two tasks at the same time, competition for the same cognitive resource may occur, leading to less cognitive capacity for each task and impaired task performance.

Prior empirical studies in IS have suggested that in a GSS system, participants who experience dual-task interference process less information (poorer performance) than participants working on a single task [10]. Similarly, in the collaborative online shopping context, it is quite common for shopping partners to search for product information on their own while scrutinize other's activities for discussion, implying a high possibility to experience dual-task interference.

In this study, the effects of the two new types of navigation support (i.e. separate navigation with location cue and split screen navigation) are assessed by comparing with the extant separate navigation and shared navigation.

3   Research Model and Hypotheses Development

Information search has been considered as an important stage for web-based consumer decision making [15]. In information search stage, consumers actively collect information to make potentially better purchase decisions [17], whereas insufficient information search may lead to detrimental decision performance [12,19]. In this study, perceived ease of uncoupling resolution (defined as the extent to which consumers perceive that resolving the uncoupling occurred during the collaborative shopping process would be free from effort) and perceived usefulness (refers to the extent to which a particular type of navigation support is expected to help

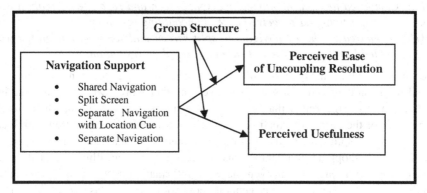

Fig. 1. Research Model

collaborative consumers to conduct product search together and accomplish their shopping goals) are included as dependent variables correspondingly to represent the two critical elements in the collaborative online shopping process.

The research model is proposed as shown in Figure 1.

3.1   Perceived Ease of Uncoupling Resolution

Uncoupling has been defined by Zhu et al. [20] as the state in which collaborative shoppers lose coordination with their shopping companions. According to situation awareness theory, situation awareness can reduce effort, increase efficiency and reduce errors for the activity of collaboration [8]. In the context of collaborative online shopping, the availability of awareness of shopping partners' current navigation state enables collaborative consumers to understand each other's contextual cues, and thus is likely to reduce coordination effort to resolve various uncoupling. Comparing with separate navigation, split screen and separate navigation with location cue provide more situation awareness via the shared screen and location cue. Accordingly, collaborative consumers would be aware of their partner's current focus of attention and ensure a shared referential base for discussion to facilitate the resolution of occurred uncoupling.

In shared navigation condition, shopping partners' web page navigations are always synchronized in the screen level. Collaborative shoppers are aware of each other's search path as well as the information that has been processed by their partner. When uncoupling occurs, collaborative shoppers may communicate with each other to pinpoint the location of the information on the current screen that both of them are looking at, or go back to a specific information based on the search path that they have experienced together, thus decreasing the effort to resolve uncoupling when compared to split screen and separate navigation with location cue. Therefore, we propose,

H1a: Compared to separate navigation, split screen and separate navigation with location cue leads to higher perceived ease of uncoupling resolution.

H1b: Compared to shared navigation, split screen and separate navigation with location cue leads to lower perceived ease of uncoupling resolution.

When using separate navigation with location cue, shopping companions' common ground has been confined to a web page level. In other words, what they are sharing is actually a web page, rather than a screen as in split screen condition, which makes the pinpoint of the target information more difficult in separate navigation with location cue than in split screen. In addition, the identical location cue information received by both shopping companions may further generate an illusion that they are looking at the same product, or even the same information at the same time. Consequently, this misinterpretation may generate confusion and increase effort when they try to resolve the occurred uncoupling. Therefore, we propose

H1c: Compared to separate navigation with location cue, split screen navigation leads to higher perceived ease of uncoupling resolution.

3.2   Perceived Usefulness

Davis [5] suggested that the most important determinant of technology adoption is perceived usefulness. In the context of collaborative online shopping, perceived usefulness refers to the extent to which a particular type of navigation support is expected to help collaborative consumers to conduct product search together and accomplish their shopping goals.

One of the major facilitator for collaborative online shopping is to establish a common referential context for the product information sharing and discussion. Compared to separate navigation, separate navigation with location cue and split screen navigation enable collaborative consumers to be more aware of the contextual information regarding what product their partners are currently examining. By clicking on the location cue bar (with separate navigation with location cue) or switching their attention to the shared screen side (with split screen navigation), consumers could navigate to the target product page and access the same information shared by their partners without much effort. In other words, the accessibility of target information displayed on partners' screen is greatly enhanced with the help of location cue and split screen. While providing situational awareness to collaborative consumers, separate navigation with location cue and split screen also allow them to search for products in parallel, rather than tightly bounded in the same screen, as the case in shared navigation condition. As a result, this may encourage more efficient information search, and consequently render a higher perceived usefulness. Therefore, we propose

H2a: Compared to separate navigation, split screen and separate navigation with location cue leads to higher perceived usefulness.

H2b: Compared to shared navigation, split screen and separate navigation with location cue leads to higher perceived usefulness.

As split screen navigation provides more situation awareness than location cue, which alleviates the effort to explain to each other about which information being viewed, collaborative consumers will have more cognitive resource to search for and scrutinize new product information with split screen. Therefore, we propose:

H2c: Compared to separate navigation with location cue, split screen navigation leads to higher perceived usefulness.

3.3   Moderating Effects of Group Structure

The concept of group has been frequently studied in the context of computer-mediated collaboration as well as real time distributed collaboration [11, 18]. In this study, we apply the concept of group structure which is defined as an indication of the role combination among group members. Specifically, we identify two forms of group structures, namely, "co-buyers" and "main buyer/opinion giver". In co-buyers structure, all group members are the direct beneficiaries of a product or products collaboratively purchased. In contrast, in main buyer/opinion giver structure, there is only one direct beneficiary (i.e. main buyer) of the product, with opinion giver providing suggestions to the products of interest by main buyer.

According to Pashler [16], dual task interference refers to the situation where people need to perform two or more activities concurrently. Prior research on dual task interference has indicated that dual task interference significantly reduces people's information processing and decreases task performance [4].

Dual task interference is more likely to occur when shopping companions are formed in co-buyers structure. The reason is that, in co-buyers structure, both shopping partners are inclined to actively and collaboratively engage in product information search and evaluation process. While searching products of interest by themselves, they are also required to attend to the products information suggested by their partners. Thereby, they are forced to split their limited cognitive resources between different sub-tasks. The frequent switch between information processing task of the product of interest by themselves and information processing task of the product of interest by their partners makes the cognitive resources rather rare. Consequently, split screen is better than separate navigation with location cue in easing the effort to resolve the uncoupling when it occurs, and search more efficiently for product alternative information.

On the contrary, in the main buyer/opinion giver structure, both individuals focus on one single task, i.e. evaluating the product of interest only by the main buyer, resulting in much cognitive resources saved for both main buyer and opinion giver. Therefore, the use of split screen versus separate navigation with location cue is unlikely to cause significant differences in perception of ease of uncoupling resolution and perceived usefulness.

H3a: The superiority of split screen navigation over separate navigation with location cue in terms of perceived ease of uncoupling resolution will be less prominent when the group is formed in a main buyer/opinion giver structure as compared to a co-buyers structure.

H3b: The superiority of split screen navigation over separate navigation with location cue in terms of perceived usefulness will be less prominent when the group is formed in a main buyer/opinion giver structure as compared to a co-buyers structure.

4   Research Method

The hypotheses proposed in the present study were tested through a laboratory experiment with a 4×2 full factorial design (i.e., 4 types of navigation support ×2 types of group structure). The four types of navigation support include: (1) separate navigation, (2) separate navigation with location cue, (3) split screen navigation, and (4) shared navigation. Each person who volunteered was asked to invite a friend to attend the experiment together with him/her, to emulate a real shopping context. A total of 74 dyads were recruited from a major public university campus and randomly assigned to the eight treatment conditions.

The two subjects in the same dyad were allocated in two different rooms. They were asked to visit a website to book a hotel room collaboratively with the assigned navigation support, as if both of them (co-buyers structure) or only one of them (main buyer/opinion giver structure) need(s) to stay in for their/his coming overseas trip. After finishing the hotel searching and selection, the subjects completed questionnaires and were paid $15 each as participation reward.

The questionnaires items (using 7-point Likert scale) were generated based on a review of the previous information systems and marketing literatures. Where previously tested measures were not available, we developed items based on the construct definition and description. Three faculty members and eight PhD students were invited to discuss the phrasing of the items to ensure that the items had at least content validity.

5   Data Analysis

5.1   Manipulation Check

No significant differences were found between subjects randomly assigned to each of the eight experimental conditions with respect to age, gender, online shopping experience and social intimacy. All these evidence indicate that participants' demographics were quite homogeneous across different conditions.

A notable difference between co-buyers structure and main buyer/opinion giver structure is observed (F = 91.5, p<.001) by asking the following questions:

> *The entire hotel booking process was primarily dominated by only one of us.*
> *Both of us contributed equally to lead the hotel search process.*

Therefore, the manipulation check for group structure was successful.

5.2   Hypotheses Testing

Analyses of variances (ANOVA) were conducted in hypotheses testing. Corresponding results are shown in Tables 1-3.

Table 1. ANOVA Summary: Perceived Ease of Uncoupling Resolution

Source	df	Mean square	F	Sig.
Navigation Support	3	.295	.384	.765
Group Structure	1	.008	.011	.917
Navigation Support * Group Structure	3	2.201	2.868	.043 *

Table 2. ANOVA Summary: Perceived Usefulness

Source	df	Mean square	F	Sig.
Navigation Support	3	4.019	4.189	.009 *
Group Structure	1	.413	.431	.514
Navigation Support * Group Structure	3	.802	.836	.479

The results in Table 1 indicate that H1a, H1b, and H1c are not supported. H3a was further tested by only considering separate navigation with location cue and split screen. It shows the significant interaction effect exists (F=4.489, Sig.=.041) , and thus H3a is supported (Figure 2).

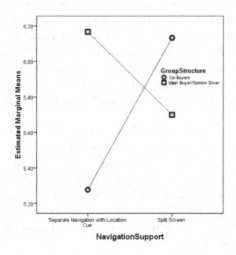

Fig. 2. Results on Perceived Ease of Uncoupling Resolution

Table 3. Tukey Multiple Comparisons of Perceived Usefulness

Group A	Group B	Mean difference (A-B)	Sig.
Separate Navigation	Separate Navigation with Location Cue	-0.801	0.067
	Split Screen	-0.787	0.083
	Shared Navigation	0.031	0.999
Separate Navigation with Location Cue	Separate Navigation	0.801	0.067
	Split Screen	0.013	0.999
	Shared Navigation	0.832	0.053
Split Screen	Separate Navigation	0.787	0.083
	Separate Navigation with Location Cue	-0.013	0.999
	Shared Navigation	0.818	0.066
Shared Navigation	Separate Navigation	-0.031	0.999
	Separate Navigation with Location Cue	-0.832	0.053
	Split Screen	-0.818	0.066

The results in Table 2 and Table 3 show that H2a and H2b are marginally supported, while H2c, and H3b are not supported.

6   Conclusions

This study proposes two new types of navigation support and examines their effects on consumers' perceived ease of uncoupling resolution and perceived usefulness. The findings show that 1) separate navigation with location cue and split screen leads to higher perceived usefulness than separate navigation and shared navigation; 2) there's significant interaction effect between navigation support and group structure, i.e. the superiority of split screen navigation over separate navigation with location cue in terms of perceived ease of uncoupling resolution will be less prominent when the group is formed in main buyer/opinion giver structure as compared to a co-buyers structure.

This study opens new directions for future research on collaborative online shopping. For example, this study only looks into a two-shopper situation which may limit its contribution to a relative small scope. In real life, it is natural that people tend to shop in groups of more people. Future study may consider collaborative shopping group with more than two people. In addition, there may be some other variables that could also moderate the effects of navigation support, such as trust between the collaborative shoppers, implying that different types of navigation support may have distinct effects in various situations.

Acknowledgement. The authors thank Singapore Ministry of Education for their financial support (Project number: MOE2009-T2-1-062).

References

1. Benbasat, I.: HCI Research: Future Challenges and Directions. AIS Transactions on Human-Computer Interaction 2(2), 16–21 (2010)
2. Bettman, J.R., Johnson, E.J., Payne, J.W.: Consumer Decision Making. In: Robertson, T.S., Kassarjian, H.H. (eds.) Handbook of Consumer Behavior. Prentice Hall, Englewood Cliffs (1991)
3. Carroll, J.M., Rosson, M.B., Farooq, U., Xiao, L.: Beyond being aware. Information and Organization 19, 162–185 (2009)
4. Chewning, E., Harrell, A.: The effect of information overload on decision makers' cue utilization levels and decision quality in financial distress decision task. Accounting, Organizations and Society 15(6), 527–542 (1990)
5. Davis, F.D.: Perceived Usefulness, Perceived Ease of Use, and User Acceptance of Information Technology. MIS Quarterly 13(3), 319–339 (1989)
6. Endsley, M.R.: Toward a Theory of Situation Awareness in Dynamic Systems. Human Factors 37(1), 32–64 (1995)
7. Endsley, M.R., Garland, D.J. (eds.): Situation awareness analysis and measurement. Lawrence Erlbaum Associates, Mahwah (2000)
8. Gutwin, C., Greenberg, S.: A descriptive framework of workspace awareness for real-time groupware. Computer Supported Cooperative Work 11, 411–446 (2002)
9. Helson, H.: Adaptation-Level Theory. Harper & Row, New York (1964)
10. Heninger, W.G., Dennis, A.R., Hilmer, K.M.: Individual Cognition and Dual-Task Interference in Group Support Systems. Information Systems Research 17(4), 415–424 (2006)
11. Katz, A., Te'eni, D.: The Contingent Impact of Contextualization on Computer-Mediated Collaboration. Organization Science 18(2), 261–279 (2007)
12. Keller, K.L., Staelin, R.: Effects of Quality and Quantity of Information on Decision Effectiveness 14(2), 200–213 (1987)
13. Mennecke, B.E., Valacich, J.S.: Information is what you make of it: The influence of group history andcomputer support on information sharing, decision quality, and member perceptions. Journal of Management Information Systems 15(2), 173–197 (1998)
14. Navon, D., Gopher, D.: On the Economy of the Human Processing System. Psychological Review 86, 254–284 (1979)
15. O'Keefe, R., MeEachern, T.: Web-Based Consumer Decision Support Systems. Communication of the ACM 41, 71–78 (1998)
16. Pashler, H.: Dual-Task Interference in Simple Tasks: Data and Theory. Psychological Bulletin 116(2), 220–244 (1994)
17. Schmidt, J.B., Spreng, R.A.: A Proposed Model of External Consumer Information Search. Journal of the Academy of Marketing Science 24, 246–256 (1996)
18. Sniezek, J.A., Buckley, T.: Cueing and Cognitive Conflict in Judge-Advisor Decision Making. Organizational Behavior and Human Decision Processes 62(2), 159–174 (1995)
19. Tan, C.H., Teo, H.H., Benbasat, I.: Assessing screening and evaluation decision support systems: A resource-matching approach. Information Systems Research 21(2), 305–326 (2010)
20. Zhu, L., Benbasat, I., Jiang, Z.: Let's shop online together: An empirical investigation of collaborative online shopping support. Information Systems Research 21(4), 872–891 (2010)

Building and Sustaining a Lifelong Adult Learning Network

Ken Eustace

Charles Sturt University, Australia
keustace@csu.edu.au

Abstract. What happens when a group of co-learners engage in a continuous lifelong learning community in the context of rapid changes in both the use of ICT in learning and the curriculum?

This paper describes a longitudinal study from 1995 to 2010 into the design and use of Information and Communications Technology (ICT) in an adult e-learning community operating at Paideia University - one of the world's first 'virtual' universities, based in The Netherlands. Working in partnership with Charles Sturt University in Australia, the Paideia study began at a time when all universities were seeking to understand the virtual university model and to discover which path to follow as learning and teaching online was about to change the adult learning landscape. The underlying theoretical framework of social constructivism, was supported at Paideia by its original 'virtual university' curriculum model for dialogue and peer learning techniques. The participants in this study shared a unique desire to seek alternative ways to learn beyond what was offered by conventional practice and universities.

Keywords: action research, alternative adult e-learning, comparative education, complementary education, curriculum modeling, ethnography, human-computer interaction (HCI), information and communication technology (ICT), interdisciplinary interaction, multi-user object-oriented domain (MOO), massive open online course (MOOC), online community, peer learning, RITA model, social constructivism, transnational education, Web 4.0.

1 Introduction

Since the 1990s, the educational value of virtual communities and the popular paradigm of the virtual university model [11] in adult learning was a driver of change in the adult distance learning everywhere, particularly in Australia [2], [4], [7]. The learner-centred design of ICT facilities for adult e-learning [23] was part of that change [3], [9], [20] and presented many problems associated with building and sustaining online adult learning communities, The problems included teachers excited about using new ICT and takings risks by moving away from a prescriptive curriculum; developing ICT efficacy (digital literacy) [8] among learners; handling the technical and management issues [14] surrounding global course development [12] and internationalization or transnational education; understanding the socio-cognitive

A.A. Ozok and P. Zaphiris (Eds.): OCSC/HCII 2013, LNCS 8029, pp. 260–268, 2013.
© Springer-Verlag Berlin Heidelberg 2013

processes [1], [14] involved; cultural interaction; virtual university models [11]; curriculum renewal and learning about new ICT media that was emerging on the horizon.

In a report to the Australian Council for Educational Research on ICT trends in education in 2008, [33] concluded that more effort in research was required on the effects of ICT upon collaboration and the successful use of virtual communities on learning.

One of the reasons for this gap in the literature was the time, cost and effort needed to build and sustain an effective lifelong online adult learning community. This is much longer in most cases than a semester long unit of learning, which is too short to observe and interpret the results, as found in this study. It takes time to build digital literacy, and the developmental steps in socialization, cultural awareness, alliance building and trust before all members of a team can be effective in contributing to the success of virtual communities in learning.

Changes in e-learning and professional practice drive the need for evaluative research by academic staff of their own online teaching practice. The ICTed Project findings [24], under recommendations 4 and 9, in particular, suggested studies like this thesis are required in order to improve interaction with the outside world through longitudinal and retrospective evaluation of e-learning innovation and dissemination. The ICTed Project also recommended that all ICT educators needed to evaluate their own teaching and learning practices and that each university consider supporting a limited number of ICT e-learning environments.

Since the release of the Web in 1991, university learning and teaching embraced the development of an ideal 'virtual university model' in many formats. The literature on the andragogy needs of adult learners, suggested that an effective ICT-based learning environment or Learning Management System (LMS) must be interactive, learner- centered [13] and support self-direction in adult learners [5], [6]. It was Paideia University that pioneered the operation of a virtual university in 1993 just as the World-Wide Web (WWW) began.

Paideia University [16] began in 1973 as a type of 'school without walls' offering 'peer to peer' support and then renewed its curriculum model and went online on the Web in 1993, registered as an Education Foundation (Stichting) in Amsterdam. Paideia offered arts degrees via peer interaction with a global e-learning perspective and desire for local action. Undergraduate and Postgraduate interdisciplinary studies in Liberal and Policy Studies were the core curriculum. Development of a blended learning and research model through lifelong peer interaction began via the Web in 1995 with ICT and research support from Charles Sturt University (CSU)) in Australia.

1.1   Background

Paideia held the belief that the regular infusion of new media and interfaces not only supported the social constructivist theory [1], [31] but also developed an interest and self-efficacy with ICT among the learners that in turn, motivated and enhanced their social learning experiences together. All participants could use ICT facilities to extend and be part of the holistic and conventional adult learning practices and be free to free explore and share the new ICT learning experiences offered by being online topgether. The research specifically targeted how ICT facilities could be used to support social constructivism in a lifelong adult e-learning community.

A collaborative learner-centred design approach [13] was used at Paideia to develop the e-learning environment using open or community source software applications available via the Internet such as the social virtual reality pioneer server software-lamdaMOO [10] and AussieMOO [17], hosted at Charles Sturt University. This meant that the development of self-efficacy with ICT was a fundamental competency requirement for all participants. This collaborative learner-centred design approach at Paideia University contrasted with the top-down conventional institutional approach represented by its partner Charles Sturt University. The involvement of participants in a collaborative design approach also allowed for a more detailed study of their interactions, relationships and processes via ethnography.

While retaining the values of conventional study and using new ICT, Paideia University in 2013 is still providing a small scale e-learning and blended research experience via social constructivism [1], [18], [31]. Paideia University still strives to be a leader among universities providing an alternative life-long-learning opportunity to people throughout the world. Such an alternative pathway in higher education is not rivaled by the development of the Massive Open Online Courses (MOOCs) but would look to include the MOOC platform [25] as another innovation to consider in its own operation and growth.

2   Methodology

The key question being investigated was about educational value of ICT in collaborative learning:

What are the facilities in an e-learning environment that support social constructivism?

This evaluative research used a hybrid methodology by combining and applying both ethnography and action research methods [22] to the e-learning environment as Ethnographic Action Research [30]. This study demonstrated that it was a useful methodology for collaborative design of an e-learning environment with the ICT as an enabler of an effective and sustainable learning community or network. The research also examined the patterns of change that the use of new technology had upon the andragogy, learning theory, curriculum model and the holistic educational value of the ICT facilities in supporting learning and knowledge building through social constructivism. Data was collected over fifteen years (1995-2010) using three ethnographic action research cycles in this continuous study of the online learning community at Paideia University. A focus group was formed to guide e-learning environment development, participant progress and change over time. The results included interpreted cases and arguments presented as ten key findings about how the ICT facilities in an e-learning environment support social constructivism theory and its mechanisms. Those ICT facilities supporting peer-learning interaction, dynamic curriculum models and social constructivism were at the core of building and enabling an effective e-learning community and lifelong learning network. Virtual communities take longer to build and sustain beyond the length of time in a normal unit of work (course or subject) and exhibit a five-year pattern for cyclical changes to the ICT facilities and the curriculum model in use.

3   Research Findings

During the 15-year study, the curriculum model changed three times almost at the same time as the community moved to a new ICT e-learning environment. Unlike a semester unit, a lifelong learning community will tend to renew itself in a 5-year cycle of curriculum change and use of ICT.

Table 1. The Cyclic Pattern of Changes in the Lifelong E-learning Environment

ICT trends in E-learning	E-learning environment changes	Year
Computer conferencing (CMC)	IRC and Website in Amsterdam	1994
Virtual worlds and social virtual reality [10], [17]	AussieMOO [17]; PAIDEIA-L mailing list and Website in Amsterdam	1995
Web and multimedia	enCore MOO interface and ZOPE	2000
Web 2.0 and Integrated learning environments [19]	MOODLE [15] and Website as one integrated tool (blogs, forums, Podcasts)	2005
Social Media and MOOC [25]	Yammer, Google+, Class2Go	2010+

The RITA model using four enablers to describe an ICT supported social constructivist lifelong learning community was proposed (Fig. 1). It is based on a deeper understanding of four concepts: Relevance, Involvement, Technology and Acceptance [29]. The role of Technology in enabling social constructivism via development of self-efficacy with ICT, peer learning techniques, acceptance of learner-centred control of ICT facilities is part of the learning agenda of curriculum model. Feedback from informants indicated the role of Involvement by reflection and interpretive practice, also at the core of the model. These enablers are coupled to an understanding of the cognitive and social/situational context of participants [1], [23] and the importance of self-efficacy with ICT in scaffolding regular engagement with each other. This model is important as a guide to others educators keen to shift the e-learning focus to peer learning techniques and develop an online community or learning network that allows all participants to co-learn and act as "associates in practice" in Vygotsky's Zone of Proximal Development [31]. The RITA model supports a similar paradigm where relevance of the curriculum model, social presence and the co-creation of knowledge by participants is connected to professional practice as suggested by [21].

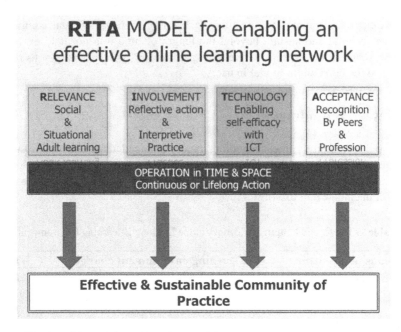

Fig. 1. RITA model: enablers for a social constructivist learning community

4   Conclusions

Table 2 lists the results into ten key findings that encapsulate and define what it means by the term "adjacent learners", to co-learn in the moment and be associates in practice as a lifelong online learning community.

Table 2. The TEN key findings on how ICT supports social constructivism

1. The 'RITA model for enabling an effective online learning network' is based on an understanding of the cognitive, social/situational contexts education through continuous or regular engagement with ICT facilities and described how effective online learning communities and social constructivism can operate over the time and space dimensions of e-learning (lifelong learning).
2. The study revealed a 5-year Pattern for Cyclical Change in the ICT e-learning environment and facilities for interaction and curriculum renewal. Five types of open source ICT tools and three co-existing curriculum models were identified and used and all required scaffolding.
3. 'MOO Wizards' operate in the Zone of Proximal Development (ZPD) [31] by scaffolding learners with virtual world building, interface design, user training and support.
4. ICT facilities that develop rapid self-efficacy with using ICT e-learning environments (supporting digital literacy) are a fundamental learning path within each curriculum model through both self-directed and group-directed discovery.

5. Time together with other members: Online communities take longer to build, sustain and reach full potential than the length of a regular semester or 12-week unit of learning as a course or subject.

6. The educational and research value of the learning journey research approach for interpretive practice in learning and teaching is a rewarding and reflexive experience for scholarly research;

7. Online communities discover and use the new modalities offered by the networking of individual personal learning networks via use of social media.

8. Effective evaluation of participants is by continuous peer assessment of ePortfolios; efficacy with ICT; contributions made to the dialogue; project work and action. This is open and subject to moderation by external benchmarks.

9. The dynamic curriculum models are complementary to the traditional adult learning practices. Paideia University supports improvisation and the asymptotic nature of learning within multiple disciplines as all participants seek to operate as 'Associates in Practice' in a blended learning and blended research model [27-28].

10. Higher education institutions are less resistant and supportive towards letting go over control and access for teachers and students to the new ICT and social media that pushes education towards the RITA model for a richer and context-based, social/situational learning environment.

The findings and conclusion also offer a historical narrative of ICT in higher education over that period and proposed a curriculum model for enabling effective online learning networks in the future. The methodology can be described as interpretive research, as a learning journey by all participants. The original Paideia has been transformed in recent years into a lifelong independent co-learning network [21], [26] and continues operating as Border Studies, and is the resulting non-traditional, inter-professional lifelong learning community or network that was built and sustained over a period of fifteen years.

5   Discussion

A successful online learning community takes shape as a woven tapestry over time. To build and sustain a unique online learning community or social learning network like Paideia University since 1994 required weaving together new ICT interfaces and metaphors, stages of development of the e-learning environment, use of the appropriate mechanisms of social constructivism, changing curriculum models, digital literacy and self-efficacy with online learning and participant action.

Such integrated longitudinal development is part of the process of building and sustaining a lifelong social learning network, so all educators or those self-organized adult learners seeking to build their own social learning networks for their semester course or similar short courses may not achieve a desired level of efficiency and sustainability in such as a limited time frame. Social media has quickly infused, renewed and re-engineered professional practice online.

The World-Wide Web is almost 25-years old with Web 2.0 described as the 'social Web'. Web history has its own lessons for change in adult e-learning since the original Web of information to the social, semantic and data Web metamorphosis in more recent times. The Web Science Trust [32] supports the future development of open data analytics and interdisciplinary involvement in its development. If Web 4.0 exists then it must be the Interdisciplinary Web.

The path to an effective and sustainable learning network in universities is at the program or degree level over several years. This research showed that online learning communities require nurturing and can be sustained beyond the use of new ICT, course boundaries or borders and grow further into a lifelong learning journey for participants. Paideia University is now a Blended Research University that represents a holistic model for the way adult learning should occur in a digital age by using interdisciplinary research teams and Web technology to enhance global learning and research practices.

References

1. Bandura, A.: Social cognitive theory of mass communication. In: Bryant, J., Oliver, M. (eds.) Media Effects, 3rd edn., pp. 94–124. Routledge, New York (2009)
2. Bates, A.W.: International distance education: cultural and ethical issues. Distance Education 22(1), 122–136 (2001)
3. Beldarrain, Y.: Distance Education Trends: Integrating New Technologies to Foster Student Interaction and Collaboration. Distance Education 27(2), 139–153 (2006)
4. Berge, Z.: Interaction in post secondary Web-based learning. Educational Technology 38, 57–61 (1999)
5. Bower, M., Hedberg, J.G., Kuswara, A.: A framework for Web 2.0 Learning Design. Educational Media International 47(3), 177–198 (2010)
6. Bruckman, A.: Community Support for Constructionist Learning, Computer Supported Collaborative Work. The Journal of Collaborative Computing 7, 47–86 (1998)
7. Bullen, M.: Review of Distance learning in higher education: institutional response for quality outcomes. Quarterly Review of Distance Education 3(1), 107–109 (2002)
8. Bullen, M., Morgan, T., Qayyum, A.: Digital Learners in Higher Education: Generation is Not the Issue. Canadian Journal of Learning and Technology 37(1) (2011), http://www.cjlt.ca/index.php/cjlt/article/view/550
9. Cowie, B., Jones, A.: Teaching and Learning in the ICT Environment. In: Saha, L.J., Dworkin, A.G. (eds.) International Handbook of Research on Teachers and Teaching, pp. 791–801 (2009)
10. Curtis, P., Nichols, D.A.: MUDs Grow Up: Social Virtual Reality in the Real World Xerox PARC, Palo Alto, USA (1993), http://www.file//parcftp.xerox.com/pub/MOO/papers/MUDsGrowUp.txt(accessed July 10, 1995)
11. D'Antoni, S. (ed.): The Virtual University Models and messages: Lessons from case studies (2004), http://www.unesco.org/iiep/virtualuniversity/home.php

12. Dean, A.: E-learning: Invention, Innovation, Implications: Towards a Manifesto. E-JIST 2(5) (2002)
13. De Troyer, O.M.F., Leune, C.J.: WSDM: A user-centered design method for web sites. In: Proceedings of the Seventh International World Wide Web Conference, Brisbane, Australia, April 14-18 (1998)
14. Dillenbourg, P.: Some technical implications of distributed cognition on the design of interactive learning environments. Journal of Artificial Intelligence in Education 7(2), 161–179 (1996)
15. Dougiamas, M., Taylor, P.C.: Moodle: Using learning communities to create an open source course management system. In: Proceedings of ED-MEDIA 2003: World Conference on Educational Multimedia, Hypermedia & Telecommunications, Honolulu, June 23-28 (2003)
16. Eustace, K.: Paideia: the virtual university? A case study. In: Proceedings of The Virtual University Symposium, University of Melbourne, Melbourne, November 21-22 (1996)
17. Fellows, G., Fellows, J., Fellows, M., Eustace, K.: Welcome to AussieMOO: an educational and social hub for distance education (1994), http://farrer.csu.edu.au/amoo (accessed February 12, 2005)
18. Gulati, S.: Constructivism and emerging online learning pedagogy: a discussion for formal to acknowledge and promote the informal. In: Proceedings of the Annual Conference of the Universities Association for Continuing Education - Regional Futures: Formal and Informal Learning Perspectives, Centre for Lifelong Learning, University of Glamorgan, April 5-7 (2004)
19. Harris, A.L., Rea, A.: Web 2.0 and Virtual World Technologies: A Growing Impact on IS Education. Journal of Information Systems Education 20(2), 137–144 (2009)
20. Kahn, T. M.: Designing virtual communities for creativity and learning (1998), http://www.designworlds.com/articles/VirtualCommunities.html
21. Katernyak, I., Ekman, S., Ekman, A., Sheremet, M., Loboda, V.: eLearning: from social presence to co-creation in virtual education community. Interactive Technology and Smart Education 6(4), 215–222 (2009)
22. Kemmis, S., McTaggart, R.: The Action Research Planner, 3rd edn. Deakin University, Geelong (1998)
23. Knowles, M., Holton III, E.F., Swanson, R.A.: The adult learner: The definitive classic in adult education and human resource development, 6th edn. Elsevier, Burlington (2005)
24. Lynch, J., Collins, F.: Teaching ICT - the ICE-ed project: the report on learning outcomes and curriculum development in major university disciplines in Information and Communication Technology. Higher Education Division, Department of Education, Training and Youth Affairs. Canberra (2001)
25. Norvig, P.: Peter Norvig: The 100,000-student classroom, TED Conferences (2012), http://www.ted.com/talks/peter_norvig_the_100_000_student_classroom.html
26. Peters, O.: The Transformation of the University into an Institution of Independent Learning. In: Evans, T., Nation, D. (eds.) Changing University Teaching: Reflections on Creating Educational Technologies, pp. 10–23. Kogan Page, London (2000)
27. Picciano, A.: Blending with Purpose: The Multimodal Model. Journal of the Research Center for Educational Technology (RCET) 5(1), 4–14 (2009)
28. Rovai, A., Jordan, H.: Blended Learning and Sense of Community: A Comparative Analysis with Traditional and Fully Online Graduate Courses. The International Review of Research In Open and Distance Learning 5(2), Article 5.2.2 (2004), http://www.irrodl.org/index.php/irrodl/article/view/192

29. Selim, H.M.: Critical success factors for e-learning acceptance: Confirmatory factor models. Computers & Education 49, 396–413 (2007)
30. Tacchi, J.A., Slater, D., Hearn, G.N.: Ethnographic Action Research: A User's Handbook. QUT ePrints Archive (Australia) (2003),
    http://eprints.qut.edu.au/archive/00004399/
31. Vygotsky, L.S.: Mind in Society. Harvard University Press, Cambridge (1978)
32. Web Science Trust (2013), http://webscience.org/
33. White, G.: ICT Trends in Education, Australian Council for Educational Research (2008),
    http://research.acer.edu.au/digital_learning/2

City 2.0 and Tourism Development

Karim Fraoua and Christian Bourret

Equipe Dispositifs d'Information et de Communication à l'Ere Numérique (DICEN)
Conservatoire national des arts et métiers, Université Paris-Est
77454 Marne-la-Vallée
France
fraoua@univ-mlv.fr

Abstract. Carefully cities have to evolve in order to help tourist during their travel. The huge use of web 2.0, must force the cities to be more and more implied in this area. The role of referenced website and those of community manager will be greater in the future and contributes to the attractiveness of the territories. Nowadays, the social web is obviously essential strategy in information retrieval or gathering during holidays preparation and will be more and more important to help travellers during the travel.

Keywords: tourist, visitor, marketing, website, city, attractiveness.

1 Introduction

The idea of this paper is to help the whole community of tourism to make travel more and more pleasant. Two ideas will emerge from this work, one is creating community managing in the official website of the city gathering of course all the information, undeniably useful to tourists such as places to visit, train schedules or bus, the location of the taxi station etc. For this purpose, we can imagine a wifi born located in some place of the city where the tourist can be connected and the map of the area should be presented. This free connection, could help the tourist during his visit, furthermore the use of mashup approaches using different techniques are affordable nowadays. The approach of developing these technologies by official website is to respond to a new behavior of tourist when they are visiting the cities, they are in needs of more information since they are optimizing their time during their holidays and in order to make their vacation more happiest which is their goal and those of the city. We know that the words of mouth are efficient to incite other tourist to visit the city. The new way to the transmission of this mode of communication is electronic and named the web 2.0

In fact, they want to relate their holidays to others, if they have spent a well moments, and if the city was in a positive role to help them during their holiday. The majors problems encountered during the holidays are well known as the place to visit, in some cities, they face to the cost of things since they don't know the fair prices, the bus or train timetable, the location of taxi station and the rules of the city. One of the

A.A. Ozok and P. Zaphiris (Eds.): OCSC/HCII 2013, LNCS 8029, pp. 269–277, 2013.

advantage offered by the city 2.0 is that appears as an official website which can grow reliability of the site [1] in the eyes of tourists who will use the services offered by the city under the control of community manager.

Nobody can deny that nowadays the use of Web 2.0 has become commonplace [2]. Citizens use more the collaboration fields and the interaction with others through new connected tools, that can be mobile phones, digital tablets, or other tools since the wifi signal is available everywhere, this will allows an easily use of these technologies and the participation process. Social media have changed the way of many people how they get information about news on in their communities, and global events [3]. They provide new ways to share information and to interact with others. Social media tools are designed to facilitate social interaction and diffusing information through society for the creation of new contents including blogs, wikis videos, music, pictures and podcasts with more and more louder weight and social networking sites such as facebook [4].

The social web is a phenomenon defined by connecting people to each other in an area without border which has become the digital space or digital territories. Users work together to share information verified or unverified, under declared or avatar identity, not hesitating to rate any services including hotels [5] and sharing experiences with other members. Generally, social networks are used to afford various types of activity whether commercial, social or some combination of the two. We analyses technological mediation through electronic word-of-mouth and involvement factors related to virtual dissemination of travel narratives on the behavior of other tourists. Moon [6] indicate the major role of interaction between people which could permit a higher expected outcomes.

2   City 2.0

The goal of e-government portals is to provide public information [7, 8]. This portals use classical design of website such menus, different links to another interesting website, connecting to intra or extra search engine and some of them use multimedia tools such as video, audio, forums or maps named Mashup techniques [9], all these effort are made to provide valuable data and information to citizens through different tools as Tablet, mobile phone.

The introduction of Web 2.0 tools and the use of new platforms such as mobile devices and social media permit a new mode of communication and participation and more and this collaboration between the city and local actors, creating the potential for a new local e-governance model for the back-office side, which will permit to update the information offered to the visitors [10]

The web has great potential for promoting regional tourism. An effective website can reach global audiences, being accessible every time and from any place. The apparition of collaborative tools such as wikis and blogs for the first category and a real-time interface such instant messaging tools like a social web. In fact Web 2.0 is considered as second generation of Internet-based services, where the social networking websites take more and more places, wikis, communication tools, and folksonomies permits to share knowledge or to enhance online collaboration.

The city must be very careful when they design the folksonomies or a social tags [11] used by the visitors. Indeed the visitor coming from different country, the community manager has to be aware about the terms used by tourist since they don't have the same cultural approach and they may confuse some terms. In this way, during the collaborative creation, one must for evidence annotate and categorize content. Indeed, where the ontologies and metadata is generally created by expert using special vocabulary [12] , the novice use free words. To manage this controlled website, we can consider that the best issues are is to encourage visitors to develop terms selected from rigid terms. We must remember that this vision is a scientific approach web. Ontology is a representation of concepts with a domain and the relationships between those concepts [13]. It is a shared conceptualization of a domain, which is in our case a tourism domain where the concept is easily shared. It is certainly a complex and complicated task but it is necessary so that the city can offer a quality service especially for tourists who do not tend to leave their accommodation.

Web 2.0 has revolutionized the way people communicate across the Internet. Web 2.0 has transformed the Web into an environment enrich user experiences by allowing them to share a different formats of shared concept and information using a variety of data formats, as text, video, map, music and so on.   The web 2.0 facilitate the interaction between multiple users whatever their location and their culture, leading to creation of a new shared concept through the collaboration and sharing of information.

The websites that introduce online web 2.0 services is considered as successful, the huge use of twitter or facebook are now considered as evident by users to interact with the portals, and it will be very important to the city to promote different part of the city as a tools of web territorial marketing to enhance experience of the tourist and growing the activities of local industries. This design of the network, taking advantage from the new sociology of citizens in general, improving relationships, create new connections, and enable public officials to deliver more complete information [14].

Social web account can be a very interesting tool to deliver a hot news or to send messages with news, warnings, emergency response, from the community manager during a disaster during the typhoon at Taiwan [15] or in the case during the storm in New York city. The use of facebook could connect visitors with officials of tourism or other visitors to share information or a good plan to help others.

In a final comment, we suggest that municipality can incorporate comment boxes or modern tools within the portals to gather opinions of visitors, in order to improve the quality of service provided. The main objective is to create new design of city 2.0 through a website including all the modern tools with a clear web 2.0 strategy and a general perspective of interaction between visitors and the city and other official agency related to the domain.

2.1   Collaborative Process with Local Players

The cities, since they are visited by tourist, and whatever their situation versus economy of tourism must collaborate with local actors of tourism whatever they are, hotels, cafes, restaurants, museums, ...The role of the cities must be greater than observed, they have to play a central role in the collaborative process of tourism development like in marketing process through their presence in the web 2.0 sphere.

In the tourism industry, the goal of actors is to enhance the tourist pleasure during their visit. These may push them to work together to reach this goal sharing experiences on a common issue, as the official city website, exchanging ideas and expertise [16] by combining knowledge [17]. The government agencies play a key role in this development, aggregating other actors in such activities devoted to visitor, through general politics of tourism of the cities.

The official or government's representations as municipalities websites is a central components of public information sharing networks, which include the cities and non-official actors collaborating, and sharing information. This cooperation between different actors around this project could be a new model of territorial intelligence about creating value for a visitor. This new basis of work of actors on digital network is very important.

The notion of centrality is a key concept in the question of collaborative process through the network. It refers to the position within the network that an individual organization has. The conclusion about this position is who to lead others across the information process. The central occupation permits a great role or power of influencer on others and may coordinate the action of others or influence their opinion [18]. It will have in the network's coordination functions.

Gray and al. [19, 20, 21] indicates clearly the definition of theories about collaborative processes. He suggests that collaboration can be defined as a process that combines many actors who must share decision making process among key actors about the future of that domain

Nevertheless it must observe the behavior of the anonymous participation during the web 2.0 cooperation or collaboration. Indeed, impunity of anonymity that the new technologies allow can lead to harmful behaviors result in immediate reaction due to unmet expectations. When free space is not regulated by law, it is the war of each against all, as Hobbes said [22]. The reason is considered as individual and never collective. People act by instinct and passion, the tourist will always thinks reasonably that his holiday could be better, and it is the role of official to lead them to the better and not to the worse.

3   Mashup Exploration in Tourism Design

A mashup, is a new approach of construction of a web page, or web application, that combines data, presentation or functionality from many   sources in order to afford to the web user a new services in the same web pages. A huge google services are offered nowadays to the developers to integrate google map into the web pages. In the same way, many tools are offered from IBM technologies to enterprise development that will enhance the web 2.0 uses [23]. The simple use of these techniques allows developing this web site more easily.

It is considered by Maness and al. [24] that the hybrid of two or more technologies or services will create a new enriched service. For example, a new mapping of crime density is developing using this approach. It consist to present existing information in new ways. The Chicago Police Department publishes a situation of crimes in the city in their local bulletin using this model and shows the crimes that have taken place within the city, and their approximate location [25]. This is a clearly example a benefit use of this mashup-approach by the city and the new "paradigm" of the web 2.0 to the citizen 2.0. The impact of the mashup design on the life of citizen is still under discussion specially the impact on social life and behavior of citizen in general [26].

These new uses of disparate elements in a website are very efficient and it corresponds to the expectation of web user nowadays. You have to imagine the utility to the tourist of a website that contain both places to visit through a map of the location near tourist localization and each of these sites has been rated by other visitors, the site of transport as bus stops, the schedules, taxi stations, trains. We can add for every site to visit the rate obtained by the other visitors or the number of tourist who have visited this site. It will be very incentive from the front-office point of view and it help community to understand why the other site is bad rated or less visited, from the back-office point of view.

There is no doubt that we are in a new phase of consumption of tourism activities, it is still necessary that the tourist is encouraged to visit the city and barriers related to the danger perceived by visitors to be abolished. This will allow the possibility to create a new economic value into all the territories.

The creation of economic value around territories will certainly add value for all stakeholders involved in the project in the city. We explained above that the collaborative process is a great tool for creating values with the involvement of all local stakeholders.

4   Sociology of Modern Tourist

In general, the citizens over the world are increasingly relying on social media for communication with their family, friends, colleagues, businesses and unknown users who share some of their value, concern or interest. The utilization of electronic social media is growing also in a consumer practices and are very relevant to a tourism area, since it is the sector who are more faced to electronic commerce. The influence of electronic social media on holidaymaker's information sharing is a part of our normal practices today when we decide a trip. The tourists are more and more involved in developing and sharing of virtual content. The information shared by tourist information system in relation to interaction aspects of social media, in a context of holiday choices is very important in the life of tourist [27]. In conceptualization point of view, the social media spaces as a novel, unprecedented and revolutionary entity permits the emergence of a new entities in a modern sociology of tourism as the tourist 2.0, the virtually or electronic borders of exchange finally don't constitute barriers, it was initially feared to see people do not sharing these spaces, as a chatroom, these digital domains along cultural lines to systematize and deepen understanding of future citizen. Merely, we admit that there is dominant cultural dimension of Web 2.0 spaces that constitute the new paradigm of informed and connected citizen utilitarian-driven, aesthetic-driven, context-driven and value-driven.

The study of classical of tourist profiles is a recurring subject in the research on tourism socio-behavioral. Historically, two general groups are distinguished by Wahlers and Etzel [28]. They found that there is an adventurous group, looking for innovative holiday who have an aversion for the so called structured holidays and another group who likes structured and enriched holidays and who prefers packaged and organized vacations. This adventured group of tourist is a high sensation seekers [29], moreover male adventure tourists tended to be higher sensation seekers than females. These groups of novelty seeking tourists perceived international tourism to be less risky than classical class of tourist seeking tourists.

In general some perceived risks associated with tourism, such as food and cultural difference, places to visit, cultural heritage might actually attract the novelty seeker due to their information level and to the neuroeconomics approach which let us to understand more the notion of the risky part due the information level and the huge uses of amenities and services offered by the city as the transports.

Cohen defines a new classes of tourists from a sociological perspective [30], where Plog works of classifying and explaining tourists from a psychological approach [31]. Plog distinguish mainly two groups of traveler: psychocentrics and allocentrics, who travel extensively and tend to be adventurous in their tourism choices [32]. The psychocentrics avoid uncertainty and risk, they prefer to travel as part of a group as they feel that being with others gives them a sense of safety and security and prefer destinations with well-developed amenities.   Allocentrics prefer travelling in general alone and visit places that are less visited. The results of Plog shows clearly the segmentation of these different tourists profile with 20 % of the population classified as allocentrics or near allocentrics, and 80% from mid-centrics to psychocentrics.

This above explanation about the social profile of tourist is very important in order to understand to whose this new design of the city 2.0 is dedicated and to whom effort must be made to convince them to visit the city and to explain through the web 2.0 that the risk is low, considering that barrier of income is crossed. From apparition of the web and all related items as the web 2.0, the tourists are more informed and the latest classification can be discussed. The notion of information, as predicted by game theory can reduce or even disappear completely the feeling of risk due to the uncertainty for the tourist. This may lead on the emergence of two novel groups of tourist, those who are informed and the not well informed or risk averse group who prefer gather their information generally from one channel as the travel agencies.

The modern travelers are generally more cultivated due to their implication into their travel preparation and organization, by searching information among the web. Whatever the social level of tourist profile, the use of web in general and social web in particular is now admitted as a source of information. This social observation corresponds to the way of life of the majority of urban population in tourist-sending countries. There is actually a real demand from tourists for access to reliable information. The website of city devoted to the visitors have a real potential for responding to the needs in real time for more effective improved public safety and security or for critical events that can be identified.

5   Game Theory and Neuroscience View on Participative Web

The game theory can assess the behavior of individual versus a decision-making under a rational process [33]. The user having many perspectives, can decide the wellness, as a key factor of his choice process, other utility factors can drive this process as the financial aspect named a reward. The reward as well as the mental system is engaged in economic decision-making.

Neuroeconomics is an interdisciplinary discipline dedicated to investigate in the field of economic-related behavior by using neuroscientific methods [34]. Thus, neuroeconomists examine nowadays in details in the neural correlates what motivate agent or player during his decision-making process. It is admitted that reward and social interaction or biases are central concepts in this discipline. The appearance of neuroimaging tools permits to correlate more easily the brain activities and the considered human behavior as the result of a process of decision-making, weighting costs and benefits of actions to maximize utility (formal or ordinal utility). The problem is that these unmeasured feelings and preferences influence decision-making. One aspect of the neuroeconomic approach is to understand how it can be relevant to this study since the decision of tourist to use or not the structure of the city implies a social behavior in addition to economic classical aspect of reward, so thus regarding to as social decision-making

This let us conclude that the use of official website must be fair and shows the reality of the city to the tourist. It must push the tourist in a social interaction, this implies to understand more deeply the role of neuroeconomy in a social decision-making. Neuroimaging studies have provided further evidence for emotion-based rejection of unfair offers [35].

A social decision-making context leads to examine the effect of expectations, with emotional aspects. In the domain of social decision-making which is closer to the tourism domain, since the tourist are subject to social decision during his holidays in a unknown city, which growth the degree of uncertainty of partner behavior, Delgado and al. [36] using Game Theory and functional neuroimaging explain how the information learned about a partner can greatly influence the decision behavior when paired with the partner, this second partner can be considered as the website of the city. What that neuroscience can bring to neuroeconomics and what impact on the user behavior of web 2.0 in particular when visiting a city. In fact, we can understand that the human behavior is not rational in a first point of view. The situation becomes very complex to understand the reaction of visitors versus the information system in order to make it efficient. The goal is to encourage tourists to use it and allow them to visit several places in the city.

We don't miss that they are under the influence of affective mechanisms, which often play a decisive role in action. These processes have been shaped by evolution of our modern society, things evolve from a cultural point of view, but also through social or normative aspects. Thus, decision-making will be influenced by mechanisms dedicated to social interaction and not only by mathematical mechanisms. By this way, the modern tourist decides sometimes over his economic self-interest and use services that seems not a good investment for him.

6   Conclusion

This work shows that the sociology of tourists has changed in the recent years, they are more connected and drowned in a flood of information continuity process? continues. This information is also impacted by rumors including the use of web 2.0. This new space allows individuals to respond instantly to any event or situation, flooding the space by opinion justified or not.

The appearance of the city in the world of tourists can disseminate information in a clear and credible perspective. However it is still necessary that this space is actually the expression of opinion under the control of a community manager who meet issues and concerns of visitors. This will also be promoted by policies marketing through wifi terminals dedicated to the dissemination of information along the city indicating the places to visit near the terminal, such as museums, cafés, restaurants, ...

References

1. Carter, L., Bélanger, F.: The utilization of e-government services: citizen trust, innovation and acceptance factors. Information Systems Journal 15, 5–25 (2005)
2. Allen, M.: What was Web 2.0? : Versions as the dominant mode of internet history. New Media & Society (July 6, 2012)
3. Qualman, E.: Socialnomics: How Social Media Transforms the Way We Live and Do Business. John Wiley & Sons (2010)
4. O'Reilly, T.: What Is Web 2.0: Design Patterns and Business Models for the Next Generation of Software. Communications and Strategies 65, 17–37 (2007)
5. Jeong, M., Jeon, M.M.: Customer Reviews of Hotel Experiences through Consumer Generated Media. Journal of Hospitality & Leisure Marketing 17(1-2), 121–138 (2008)
6. Moon, M.J.: The Evolution of E-Government among Municipalities: Rhetoric or Reality? Public Administration Review 62(4), 424–433 (2002)
7. Chang-Lee, K., Kirlidog, M., Lee, S., Lim, G.G.: User evaluations of tax filing web sites: A comparative study of South Korea and Turke. Online Information Review 32(8), 842–859 (2008)
8. Xue, S.: Web usage statistics and Web site evaluation: a case study of a government publications library Web site. Online Information Review 28(3), 180–190 (2004)
9. Dobrev, B., Stoewer, M., Makris, L., Getsova, E.: E-MuniS — Electronic Municipal Information Services - Best Practice Transfer and Improvement Project: Project Approach and Intermediary Results. In: Traunmüller, R., Lenk, K. (eds.) EGOV 2002. LNCS, vol. 2456, pp. 199–206. Springer, Heidelberg (2002)
10. Kavanaugh: Government Information Quarterly 29(4), 480–491 (2002)
11. Pirolli, P., Kairam, S.: A knowledge-tracing model of learning from a social tagging system. User Modeling and User-Adapted Interaction, 1–30 (2013)
12. Sugumaran, V., Storey, V.C.: Ontologies for conceptual modeling: their creation, use, and management. Data & Knowledge Engineering 42(3), 251–271
13. Gruber, T.: What is an Ontology. Encyclopedia of Database Systems 1 (2008)
14. Ballejos, L.C., Montagna, J.M.: Identifying interorganisational networks: a factor-based approach. International Journal of Networking and Virtual Organisations 7(1), 1–22 (2010)

15. Huang, C.M., Chan, E., Hyder, A.: Web 2.0 and Internet Social Networking: A New tool for Disaster Management?-Lessons from Taiwan. BMC Medical Informatics and Decision Making 10(1), 57 (2010)
16. Vernon, J., Essex, S., Pinder, D.: Collaborative policymaking: Local Sustainable Projects. Annals of Tourism Research 32(2), 325–345 (2005)
17. Bramwell, B., Lane, B.: Collaboration and Partnerships in Tourism Planning. In: Bramwell, B., Lane, B. (eds.) Tourism Collaboration and Partnerships: Politics, Practice and Sustainability, pp. 1–19. Channel View Publications, Clevedon (2000)
18. Rowley, T.J.: Moving beyond dyadic ties: A network theory of stakeholder influences. Academy of Management Review 22(4), 887–910 (1997)
19. Gray, B., Wood, J.D.: Collaborative Alliances: Moving from Practice to Theory. The Journal of Applied Behavioral Science 27, 3–22 (1991)
20. Gray, B.: Conditions facilitating interorganizational collaboration. Human Relations 38(10), 911–936 (1985)
21. Gray, B.: Collaborating: Finding common ground for multiparty problems, San Francisco (1989)
22. Hobbes, T.: Leviathan, The Matter, Form and Power of a Commonwealth Ecclesiastical and Civil (Published April 1651)
23. Lanubile, F., Ebert, C., Prikladnicki, R., Vizcaíno, A.: Collaboration tools for global software engineering. IEEE Software 27(2), 52–55 (2010)
24. Maness, J.M.: Library 2.0 theory: Web 2.0 and its implications for libraries. Webology 3(2) (2006)
25. http://gis.chicagopolice.org/
26. Curran, K., Murray, M., Norrby, D.S., Christian, M.: Involving the user through Library 2.0. New Review of Information Networking 12(1-2), 47–59 (2006)
27. Egger, R.: Theorizing Web 2.0 Phenomena in Tourism: A Sociological Signpost. Information Technology & Tourism 12(2), 125–137 (2010)
28. Wahlers, R.G., Etzel, M.J.: A Consumer response to incongruity between optimal stimulation and lifestyle satisfaction. In: Hirschman, E.C., Holbrook, M.B. (eds.) Advances in Consumer Research 12, pp. 97–101. Association for Consumer Research, Provo (1985)
29. Gilchrist, H., Povey, R., Dickinson, A., Povey, R.: The sensation seeking scale: Its use in a study of the characteristics of people choosing 'Adventure holidays'. Personality and Individual Differences 19(4), 513–516 (1995)
30. Cohen, E.: Who is a tourist? a conceptual clarification. The Sociological Review 22(4) (1974)
31. Plog, S.: Why destination areas rise and fall in popularity. The Cornell Hotel and Restaurant Administration Quarterly 14(4), 55 (1974)
32. Plog, S.: The power of psychographics and the concept of venturesomeness. Journal of Travel Research 40(3), 244 (2002)
33. Hargreaves Heap, S.P., Varoufakis, Y.: Game theory. A Critical Introduction, London und New York (1995)
34. Sproten, A.N.: Developmental Neuroeconomics: Lifespan Changes in Economic Decision Making (2013)
35. Sanfey, A.G.: Expectations and social decision-making: biasing effects of prior knowledge on Ultimatum responses. Mind & Society 8(1), 93–107 (2009)
36. Delgado, M.R., Frank, R.H., Phelps, E.A.: Perceptions of moral character modulate the neural systems of reward during the trust game. Nature Neuroscience 8(11), 1611–1618 (2005)

Looking Back at Facebook Content
and the Positive Impact Upon Wellbeing:
Exploring Reminiscing as a Tool for Self Soothing

Alice Good, Arunasalam Sambhantham, and Vahid Panjganj

University of Portsmouth, PO1 3AE, UK
alice.good@port.ac.uk

Abstract. The premise of this paper is to explore the potential of reminiscing in facilitating self soothing. The research presented looks at people's activities on Facebook and whether these particular activities impact upon their perceived sense of wellbeing, furthermore, whether specific Facebook activities enable a self –soothing effect when feeling low in mood. A survey was distributed amongst Facebook users. The results from the study appear to indicate that in comparison to other Facebook activities, looking back upon photos and wall posts in particular, could have a positive impact upon wellbeing. Additionally, the results indicate that people who have mental health problems, experience a more positive impact upon their wellbeing when looking at photos and wall posts, than those who did not have a history of mental health issues. The results from the research presented here contribute towards the viability of developing a mobile application to facilitate positive reminiscing.

Keywords: Wellbeing, Facebook, Reminiscing, Social Networking.

1   Introduction

The use of technology in promoting 'well being' has enormous potential, as has been seen through the varied applications developed and utilized over recent years. These include social networking sites, discussion forums, virtual environments such as Second Life and more recently phone apps. Indeed, since the advent of Web 2.0 technologies in 2004, there has been an increase in the use of social networking sites and other applications that enable online communities, which facilitate support for people with mental health problems, or people who simply require occasional emotional support. Social networking sites and discussion forums, are reported to have decreased the sense of 'feeling alone' for people with mental health problems (Neal & McKenzie, 2010; Patti et al, 2007). Facebook usage in particular, is reported to increase a sense of wellbeing amongst its users. The aspects of wellbeing relate to the fact that users were more easily able to form relationships, provide companionship and emotional support, and feel more positive after reading status updates (Hampton et al, 2012; Mauri et al, 2011; Burke et al, 2010; Toma, 2010).

A.A. Ozok and P. Zaphiris (Eds.): OCSC/HCII 2013, LNCS 8029, pp. 278–286, 2013.
© Springer-Verlag Berlin Heidelberg 2013

The research presented here looks more closely at the extent to which Facebook can impact or improve upon wellbeing. The focus of this paper is to then look specifically at users' interactions on Facebook, and evaluate whether specific interactions, namely looking back upon wall posts and photos, has any impact upon positive wellbeing. The theory behind the research is linked to positive reminiscing, and how this process can impact upon emotional wellbeing. The results from the study will inform the viability of a mobile application which would enable users to store 'favourite' photos and notes. The rationale being, that facilitating the means for people to easily access their 'favourite things', could potentially increase a sense of wellbeing, particularly among those people who have some history of mental health issues. The research is not claiming that such a tool could cure any mental health issues, but rather that it could serve as a tool to promote self soothing in times of low mood. This research should be considered more as an exploratory study, given the small number of participants, and therefore the results should be viewed as indicative and also as a prelude to further research.

2   Social Networking and Wellbeing

The Internet has changed peoples' lives in many aspects, including social and health (Van de belt et al., 2010) and wellbeing. Social Network Sites have been described as a consequence of these changes, which introduced a new way of communication among people (Ross et al., 2009; Cheung & Lee, 2010). Social Network Sites (SNS) are indisputably popular. Facebook was listed as the most visited website, with 800,000,000 unique visitors in a "double click ad planner" report by Google (2013), having reached a billion users in September 2012 (Business Week, 2012). Online Communities are the main active areas in which applications such as Facebook can impact upon a positive sense of wellbeing.

Many people prefer to utilize the wide spectrum of ICT applications to facilitate support, as opposed to face-to face support. For example, face-to-face support groups are often difficult to schedule and are limited in manner of time and location. Moreover, many people with psychiatric problems can experience difficulties accessing these support groups (Taylor & Luce, 2003). In contrast, online support groups and forums are much more accessible, particularly given the growth in smart phones providing ubiquitous access. Studies by Van Uden-Kraan et al (2008) highlight the fact that users within these support groups not only receive support, but are also able to advise and share their own experience, which could potentially provide psychological well-being for the patient. Shepsis (2010) reports interactions made by participants, as more frequent and with higher level of candor comparing to the traditional (offline) methods. These findings are supported by earlier studies, which suggest online communities are a potential option for emotional support (Van Uden-Kraan et al, 2008) and as a consequence, can positively enhance wellbeing

The behavior and type of activities within these SNS provide a new social experience, which can be deeper than traditional ways of socializing, as well as impacting positively upon wellbeing. Examples of this firstly include the way these SNSs facilitate establishing and maintaining pre-existing relations (Greenhow & Robelia, 2009; Ross et al., 2009; Bargh & McKenna, 2004). Secondly, they make available virtual support groups and communities for social purposes, which make it possible for users to establish new connections around their shared interests or situations (Greenhow & Robelia, 2009; Kamel Boulos & Wheeler, 2007). Thirdly, the ability of virtual environments to facilitate emotional support, and the possibility for individuals to feel comfortable with having deeper personal conversations about their problems, beyond face-to-face limitations and restrictions (Hampton et al, 2012; Ross et al., 2009). Finally, the increased sense of self esteem which is enabled (Mauri et al, 2011; Burke et al, 2010; Toma, 2010). All these factors contribute towards a person's sense of wellbeing. Other aspects of Facebook which may have some impact upon wellbeing could include looking at photos and wall postings, particularly where this activity relates to positive reminiscing.

2.1   Positive Reminiscing and Self Soothing

Looking at meaningful photos is a traditional method used in therapies to promote improved mood. For example, Reminiscent Therapy (RT) is a popular method used in promoting positive mood and well being, and reduces the sense of feeling alone for people with dementia. It involves using meaningful prompts, including photos, music and recordings, as an aid to remembering life events (Norris, 1986). Some research states that it has been useful in reducing depression (Scogin F & McElreath, 1994) as well as being an important tool to facilitate socialization. Whilst it has been predominantly utilized in people with dementia, there could be scope for applying the theory of RT in other mental health conditions, particularly where depression and general low mood are common. This could potentially induce a 'self soothing' process which could lend itself well to people who struggle with day to day living as a result of low mood, or indeed who experience the occasional 'off-day'. The act of 'self soothing', that is calming us down, is in fact one of the hardest things to do when you have mental health problems. Yet the capability to be able to calm oneself down, to essentially self soothe, would be advantageous to people with mental health problems, and could potentially prevent problems from escalating, if only by means of a distraction.

3   Method

The research presented here is specifically interested in whether activities that relate to reminiscing, impact upon emotional wellbeing. A study was designed to look at people's activities on Facebook and whether these specific interactions impact upon wellbeing. In addition, it seeks to understand whether there is any indication that looking back at photos and wall posts is beneficial to people with mental health problems. This is based upon the theory that positive reminiscing has been shown to promote a sense of positive wellbeing in people with dementia (Norris, 1986; Scogin F & McElreath, 1994). The research then presents the following two hypotheses:

H1. Looking at 'wall posts' and photos shared on Facebook improves mood.

H2. People who have experienced mental health problems will experience a greater 'self soothing' effect, from looking back at wall posts and photos, than those who have not experienced mental health problems.

Facebook users were invited to complete an online survey, hosted by Survey Monkey (www.surveymonkey.net), an online survey hosting site, and was conducted in December 2012. The study was facilitated by Facebook. The researchers used their personal and University profile pages to post the link to the survey on their Facebook pages, which also included a brief explanation of the purpose of the study. The target demographic included young people of University age, as well as friends and friends of friends of the researchers. A total of 144 attempted the survey, with 135 fully completing it.

4   Results

The research instrument gathered information on the following areas:

1. Demographics and other descriptive data that included: frequency of accessing Facebook and whether participants owned a smart phone, as well as history of mental health problems.
2. Activities on Facebook that make people feel better, including frequency of usage.

4.1   Demographics and General Facebook Usage

Demographic data was collected on gender and ownership of smart phones. The survey sought to identify whether participants had experienced any degree of mental health problems. This item is particularly relevant, given that the research endeavors to compare results of the study between those that have, and those that have not, experienced mental health problems. This is in relation to whether there is any indication that people, who have experienced some degree of mental illness, derive a self soothing effect from looking at photos and wall posts. 39% of the participants stated that they had experienced mental health problems previously. The data can be seen in Table 1 below.

Data was also collected and measured on the frequency of Facebook usage and behavior of participants, in relation to accessing Facebook via their phones, as shown in Table 2 below. Individual items were ranked using Likert scale, ranging from 1=strongly disagree to 5=strongly agree. The scales are presented by taking the mean value of items where the lowest possible value equals 1 and the highest possible value equals 5. The results show that 86% of participants access Facebook more than once a day. The mean values show a tendency towards regularly accessing Facebook via phones (mean value = 3.51), with a significant majority ensuring that they always carry their phones with them (mean value = 4.63). Participants tend to also use Facebook as a distraction tool (mean value = 3.09).

Table 1. Demographics (N=134)

	Mean or % (n)	
Age	34	
Gender		
Male	54.5%	(73)
Female	45.5%	(61)
Experienced mental health issues 39%	(53)	
Owns a smart phone	80%	(110)
Always carries phone with them	94%	(106)

Table 2. Summary Statistics for Facebook Use

Items	Mean or %
Uses Facebook more than once a day	86%
I regularly access Facebook on my phone	3.51
I like being able to stay in touch with Facebook on my phone	3.28
I do not like to use Facebook on my phone	2.45
I prefer to use Facebook on my phone (than via desktop PC/iPad/other)	2.42
I always carry my phone with me	4.63
I use Facebook as a distraction tool	3.09

4.2   Facebook Activities and Their Impact Upon Wellbeing

In this section, we explore the following hypothesis:

H1   Looking at 'wall posts' and photos shared on Facebook improves mood.

Data was collected on participants' behavior on Facebook and the extent to which they participated in each activity. Individual items were ranked using a 5 point scale. 1= not at all; 2= a few times; 3= sometimes; 4= frequently and 5= almost always. The scales are presented by taking the mean value of items where the lowest possible value equals 1 (not at all) and the highest possible value equals 5 (almost always). The percentage of participants that have indicated at least 'sometimes' for each activity is also shown in Table 3 below. The results suggest that reading wall posts as the activity most frequently performed (mean value = 3.76) and playing games as being the least frequently performed (mean value = 1.54). 86% of participants stated that they read wall posts frequently, compared to 16% of participants who played games regularly. Whilst looking at photos isn't an activity carried out as frequently as reading wall posts, the data does indicate that this is an activity carried out more frequently than playing games; updating status and using messenger.

Data was then gathered on which Facebook activities helped participants in improving their mood, when feeling low. Results can be seen in table 4 below. Participants were finally asked about the ease of accessing favourite photos and posts, which can be seen in table 5. Individual items were ranked using Likert scale, ranging from

1=strongly disagree to 5=strongly agree. The scales are presented by taking the mean value of items where the lowest possible value equals 1 (strongly disagree) and the highest possible value equals 5 (strongly agree).

Table 3. Summary Statistics for Frequency of Facebook Activities

Items	Mean	%
Looking back on wall posts	3.76	86
Playing games	1.54	16
Updating your status	2.56	50
Looking back at photos posted on your wall	3.24	75
Using Facebook messenger	2.86	56
Looking back at photos you have previously posted	2.62	54

The results suggest that the three highest activities that improve mood when feeling low are: looking back on wall posts (mean value = 3.07; looking back on photos previously posted (3.13) and looking at photos others have posted (mean value = 3.14). Looking back on wall posts is shown to be the most significant activity in improving mood. Results of the data also show that a significant number of participants are not able to locate favourite wall posts and photos, yet would like to be able to do so.

Table 4. Summary Statistics of Facebook Activities that improve mood

Items	Mean	%
Looking back on wall posts	3.07	76
Playing games	2.04	32
Updating your status	2.73	58
Looking back at photos posted on your wall	3.14	73
Using Facebook messenger	2.91	64
Looking back at photos you have previously posted	3.13	71

Table 5. Summary Statistics ease in accessing favourite photos and posts

Items	Mean	%
It is not easy to locate my favourite photos I have posted	3.07	75
I would like to be able to access these photos	3.42	88
It is not easy to locate favourite photos others have posted		
I would like to be able to access these photos.	3.35	84
	3.45	86
It is not easy to locate my favourite wall comments	3.43	85
I would like to be able to access these wall comments	3.47	86

These results correlate with the previous results, shown in table 4, where the data indicates that looking at photos and wall posts, does impact positively upon wellbeing.

4.3   The Self Soothing Effect of Facebook Activities on People with Mental Health Issues

In this section, we explore the following hypothesis:

H2: People who have experienced mental health problems will experience a greater self soothing effect from looking back at wall posts and photos, than those who have not experienced mental health problems.

In table 4 above, mean values related to the self soothing effect of each Facebook activity were presented. The results showed that looking back at photos and wall posts promoted increased self soothing, when feeling low in mood. These were compared to other activities, including updating status, playing games and using Face book messenger. Further to this, the research sought to evaluate whether there was any significant difference in the effect of self soothing facilitated from looking back at photos and wall posts on Facebook, specifically between people who have experienced mental health problems and those that have not. As already stated previously, this is based upon the theory that positive reminiscing has been shown to promote a sense of positive wellbeing in people with dementia (Scogin F & McElreath, 1994). A positive significant difference with the group of participants indicating a history of mental health problems would lend further validity to the the theory. A two sample t-Test, for difference of the population means (equal variances) was applied, to see whether there was any significant difference between the two groups; in relation to the self soothing effect that looking back upon wall posts and photos has, when feeling low in mood. Group A represents participants who have never experienced mental health problems. Group B included participants who have indicated that they have previously, or currently, experience mental health problems.

The null hypothesis predicted that there will be no significant difference between the mean values of the two groups. As in the previous results, individual items were ranked using Likert scale, ranging from 1=strongly disagree to 5=strongly agree. In all three activities, the P value is less than 0.05; therefore the null hypothesis can be rejected. These results indicate that looking back on wall posts and photos, previously posted or which others have posted has more of a self soothing effect upon those that have experienced mental health problems, than those that have never experienced mental health problems. This then further contributes to the validity of reminiscent type activities facilitating self soothing for people who are experiencing low mood.

Table 6. Looking back at wall posts; comparison of self soothing effect

Activity: Looking back at wall posts	Group A	Group B
Mean	2.90625	3.29787234
Variance	0.943452381	0.909343201
P(T<=t) one-tail	0.01835153	
t Critical one-tail	1.658953459	

The scales are presented by taking the mean value of items where the lowest possible value equals 1 (strongly disagree) and the highest possible value equals 5 (strongly agree).

Table 7. Looking at photos others have posted; comparison of self soothing effect

Activity: Looking back at photos others have posted	Group A	Group B
Mean	2.90625	3.446808511
Variance	0.975198413	0.948196115
P(T<=t) one-tail	0.002486147	
t Critical one-tail	1.660234327	

Table 8. Looking back at photos I have posted; comparison of self soothing effect

Activity: Looking back at photos I have posted	Group A	Group B
Mean	2.96875	3.333333333
Variance	1.014880952	1.24822695
P(T<=t) one-tail	0.038979616	
t Critical one-tail	1.661051818	

5   Discussion

In considering the original research questions, the results of the study do indicate that activities involving reminiscing have a positive impact upon wellbeing. Moreover, looking back on photos and wall posts was seen to provide a greater self soothing effect, when participants were feeling low in mood, than other Facebook activities. This is further supported in that a significant number of participants were not able to easily access 'favorite' wall posts and photos, and yet would like to be able to do so. In addition, the activity of looking back on photos and wall posts was carried out more frequently by participants than other activities, such as playing games, updating status and using messenger. This suggests that the activity of looking back upon photos and wall posts is a popular activity, as well as having a positive impact upon emotional wellbeing.

To further explore the theory of which Facebook activities were deemed to promote self soothing, we examined whether participants who have experienced mental health problems were able to derive a greater sense of self soothing from looking back on photos and wall posts, than those participants who have never experienced mental health problems. For each of these reminiscent type activities, the statistically analyzed results suggest a positive indication towards the potential of self soothing derived. In spite of the positive results, there are shortcomings in this research, given the limited number of participants. Whilst statistical analysis was enabled with the number involved, the results can really only be viewed as indicative. Further research is necessary to evaluate the self soothing effect of reminiscent type activities.

The research presented here, is part of a larger study, exploring the potential of mobile applications that facilitate self soothing for different user groups (Good et al, 2012), particularly by incorporating reminiscent type (RT) therapy. Based upon RT, the application would contain meaningful memorabilia including photographs and notes. Essentially, this memorabilia would be 'favorite' items that could be easily accessible and potentially promote positive mood. The significance of this research is therefore in the development of an application which can facilitate self soothing and subsequently improve a sense of wellbeing.

References

1. Burke, M., Marlow, C., Lento, T.: Social Network Activity and Social Well-Being. In: ACM CHI 2010: Conference on Human Factors in Computing Systems, pp. 1909–1912 (2010)
2. Cheung, C.M.K., Lee, M.K.O.: A Theoretical Model of Intentional Social Action in Online Social Networks. Decision Support Systems 49(1), 24–30 (2010)
3. Good, A., Wilson, C., Ancient, C., Sambhanthan, A.: A Proposal To Support Wellbeing in People With Borderline Personality Disorder: Applying Reminiscent Theory in a Mobile App. In: The ACM Conference on Designing Interactive Systems (2012)
4. Greenhow, C., Robelia, B.: Old Communication, New Literacies: Social Network Sites as Social Learning Resources. Journal of Computer Mediated Communication 14, 1130–1161 (2009)
5. Hampton, K., Goulet, L., Marlow, C., Rainee, L.: Why Most Facebook users get more than they give. Pew Internet (2012)
6. Kamel Boulos, M.N., Wheeler, S.: The emerging Web 2.0 social software: an enabling suite of sociable technologies in health and healthcare education. Health Information and Libraries Journal 24, 2–23 (2007)
7. Mauri, M., Cipresso, P., Balgera, A., Villamira, M., Riva, G.: Why Is Facebook So Successful? Psychophysiological Measures Describe a Core Flow State While Using Facebook. Cyberpsychology, Behavior & Social Networking 14(12) (2011)
8. Neal, D.M., McKenzie, P.J.: "I Did Not Realize So Many Options Are Available": Cognitive Authority, Emerging Adults, and e- Mental Health. Library & Information Science Research (2010)
9. Norris, A.D.: Reminiscence with Elderly People. Winslow, London (1986)
10. Ross, C., Orr, E.S., Sisic, M., Arseneault, J.M., Simmering, M.G., Orr, R.R.: Personality and Motivations Associated With Facebook Use. Computers in Human Behavior 25(2), 578–586 (2009)
11. Scogin, F., McElreath, L.: Efficacy of Psychosocial Treatments for Geriatric Depression: A Quantitative Review. Journal of Consulting & Clinical Psychology 62, 69–74 (1994)
12. Taylor, C.B., Luce, K.H.: Computer- and Internet-Based Psychotherapy interventions. Current Directions in Psychological Science 12, 18–22 (2003)
13. Toma, C.: Affirming the Self Through Online Profiles: Beneficial Effects of Social Network Sites. In: Proceedings of the SIGCHI Conference on Human Factors in Computing System. ACM, New York (2010)
14. Van De Belt, T.H., Engeleni, L., Berbent, S.A.A., Schoonhoven, L.: Definition of Health 2.0 and Medicine 2.0: A Systematic Review. Journal of Medical Internet Research 12(2) (2010)
15. Van Uden-Kraan, C.F., Drossaert, C.H.C., Taal, E., Lebrun, C.E.I., Drossaers-Bakker, K.W., Smit, W.M., Seydel, E.R., Van de Laar, M.A.F.J.: Coping With Somatic Illnesses in Online Support Groups. Do the Feared Disadvantages Actually Occur? Comput. Human Behav. 24, 309–324 (2008)

User-Centered Investigation of Social Commerce Design

Zhao Huang and Morad Benyoucef

Telfer School of Management, University of Ottawa
55 Laurier Avenue East, Ottawa, ON K1N 6N5, Canada
zhuan2@uottawa.ca, benyoucef@telfer.uottawa.ca

Abstract. Evidence from relevant studies indicates that social commerce can benefit from a user-centered design. This study explores users' perception and preferences of social features implemented on current social commerce websites, focusing on two major categories of social commerce platforms. Results point to a number of important social features, such as the "Comment" button, allowing users to provide feedback, and encouraging users to respond to comments made by others. We also present and discuss the differences in user preferences of social features between the two social commerce platform categories. By considering the user perspective, this study aims to help business organizations develop successful social commerce systems.

Keywords: Social commerce, Social media, Social design, User-centered design, User preferences.

1   Introduction

The widespread use of social media applications, such as blogs, forums, social networks and wikis is an opportunity for the emergence of a new business model called social commerce [1]. Social commerce generally refers to online commercial applications that harness social media and Web 2.0 technologies. It supports social interactions and user-generated content to assist users in their decision making and acquisition of products and services in online marketplaces and communities [2]. Recently, social commerce has been rapidly proliferating, driven not only by the popularity of social media, but because user participation, one of the key elements of social media applications, has a significant impact on business. For example, Threadless.com uses an online community to encourage users to submit ideas about T-shirt designs and the best designs are selected as a part of products. This way of doing commerce stimulates product development, captures market trends and even increases sales [3]. As a result, thousands of social commerce websites are being created and made accessible to a large audience of users [4]. However, challenges for social commerce design remain high. One such challenge stems from the fact that social commerce is being developed in two major ways, yielding two categories of social commerce applications. The first one is based on e-commerce websites that leverage social media features; the second is built on social network websites that offer e-commerce features [5]. Such diversity, among other challenges, increases the need for

A.A. Ozok and P. Zaphiris (Eds.): OCSC/HCII 2013, LNCS 8029, pp. 287–295, 2013.

understanding the complexity of social commerce design. In addition, social commerce involves and relies on user participation. Without considering the users' point of view in informing social commerce design, social commerce may not have the wide consumer acceptance that researchers and practitioners claim it deserves.

Therefore, this study takes a user-centered approach in investigating the design of social commerce platforms. We focus on specific social commerce websites selected from the two main social commerce categories, identifying their important and less important social design features. We also present and discuss significant differences in user preferences towards social features between the two categories of social commerce. The paper is structured as follows: Section 2 briefly reviews related work on social commerce. It is followed by a presentation of the research instruments and procedure in Section 3. Section 4 reports on and discusses the study results. Finally, conclusions are drawn and future studies are recommended in Section 5.

2   Related Work

Social commerce is defined as commerce activities mediated by social media [5]. However, Stephen and Toubia [6] depict a more comprehensive definition where social commerce is a form of online social media that allows users to participate actively in the marketing and selling of products and services in online marketplaces and communities. Evidence from previous studies indicates that there is no unique definition since this concept can be explained from marketing [7], computing [8], and users' perspectives [9]. In spite of the various definitions, it can be argued that social commerce is a subset of e-commerce [10], even though some believe that social commerce is an evolution of e-commerce [5]. One major difference between e-commerce and social commerce is that the e-commerce user is usually perceived as isolated, disconnected from his community, and conducting an individual act. In addition, e-commerce usually allows a one-way information flow from business to users, where the user may find it difficult to send information back to the e-commerce [8]. But the interaction between users and social commerce differs significantly because social commerce is perceived as the interaction of a community of users and potential users with online commerce services and applications. Such interaction allows users to express their preferences and share recommendations with members of their communities, potentially affecting their purchase decision making and behaviors [2].

Kim and Park [10] further claim that social commerce fosters rich social interactions and user contributed content to facilitate the online buying and selling products. This significantly supports users' purchase behavior in terms of searching for products, acquiring feedback, and disseminating word-of-mouth referrals. Similarly, Kim and Srivastava [11] examined the influence of social media design in e-commerce on user purchase decision making. The study found a set of important social design features that help users make better decisions, including providing feedback, rating reviews and chatting with friends online. On the other hand, leveraging social media tools can have a profound impact on business applications and strategies. For instance, social media increases user power, transforming online marketplaces from product-oriented to user-centered platforms [12]. Likewise, Serrano and Torres [13] found that using social media makes significant improvements in the social and collaborative capabilities of business processes.

Existing empirical research investigated the business needs [14], examined the service quality [19] and analyzed the marketing requirements [7] of social commerce design, while granting little attention to the users' perceptive. It can be argued that failing to understand users and their needs will keep social commerce from reaching its potential. Moreover, social commerce can be developed in two major directions: one brings e-commerce to social network platforms; the other brings social media to e-commerce platforms [5]. This diversity may call for implementing different social features on different social commerce websites. In other words, users may have different preferences of social features between the two social commerce categories.

To this end, this study aims to explore users' perceptions of social commerce design, identifying the important social features on specific social commerce websites and revealing differences in user preferences of social features between the two categories of social commerce websites. By doing so, we hope to contribute to user centered deign of social commerce.

3   Methodology

To conduct this study, an online survey was employed with the purpose of capturing users' perception and preferences of social features on social commerce websites. The survey was developed based on a conceptual model for social commerce design [2], which identifies four core design elements, namely "Individual", "Conversation", "Community", and "Commerce". Individual refers to providing a sense of self identification and user awareness, such as offering a personal profile or presenting an activity profile. Conversation relates to offering a diversity of interactions among users in order to build peer communities. Community is an aggregation of user groups, which forms the network power and produces social effects. Commerce is a set of commercial functionalities that engage users in various services and applications provided by online businesses. Guided by these key elements, we developed social design criteria by leveraging recent social media studies (e.g., [7]) and e-commerce studies (e.g., [11]). Based on these criteria, associated social design features were selected and grouped into the corresponding social commerce design elements. Finally, survey questions were developed.

Four social commerce websites were selected as representatives of current social commerce systems: Amazon and Groupon, which represent e-commerce systems that incorporate social media applications, and Facebook Starbucks and Facebook Green Day, which represent social network platforms that incorporate e-commerce applications. In total, 280 participants took part in our social design feature assessment survey. 70 participants were assigned to each target social commerce website. All participants are assumed to have good knowledge of social media applications and relevant experience using a social commerce website. Each participant followed the same assessment process consisting of: (1) a free review of the assigned website; the

(2) completing the online questionnaire. The free review allows participants to study the target social commerce website (in case they are not familiar with its functionalities), or, if they choose to, focus only on the specific social design features found on the website.

4   Discussion

4.1   Important and less Important Social Design Features

Table 1 shows a set of important social design features that have been found on the target social commerce websites. The most common ones are that the websites provide the "Comment" button, allowing users to give feedback; the websites allow users to respond to comments made by others, and the websites offer rewards to users. These common features are meant to encourage user generated content and user distribution of that content, which motivates social connection and collaborative interaction among users. This can have the effect of transforming online marketplaces into social, user-centered environments, where users can interact with more people and use their knowledge and experiences to support each other in achieving their expected service outcomes [15].

Moreover, important social features have been identified on each specific social commerce website. For example, on Amazon, the most important social feature is that the website allows users to provide product reviews. On Groupon, the social feature of "Wish-Lists" creation was identified as the most important. Likewise, the social feature of providing the "Like" button which allows users to express what they like was found to be the most important on Facebook Green Day. These findings suggest that different social commerce platforms have different sociability requirements. Hence organizations need to consider their business objectives and implement relevant strategies that are congruent with, or suited to different social design features as well as to the goals of the organization [16]. For example, if the primary concern of the organization mainly focuses on commercial services provision (e.g., e-commerce-based websites), then social features design should emphasize more on encouraging user participation and providing quality website services to support all user purchase activities. Nevertheless, if a business intends to develop social network websites (e.g., Facebook-based websites), then social design features in relation to developing user conversation and building brand communities should be paid more attention.

Some less important social design features have also been identified on each target social commerce website (see Table 2). As shown in the table, the least important social feature on Amazon consists of branded online applications, such as social games. On Groupon, the feature of reporting user activity through notifications is identified as the least important. Similarly, allowing a group of users to buy products together, and providing flash sales are found to be the least important social features on Facebook Starbucks and Facebook Green Day respectively. These findings may imply that although a variety of social design features become available for social

Table 1. Important social design features

Amazon			
Important social design features	Mean	SD	Significance
Allowing users to provide product reviews	1.92	0.75	T=-5.693, P=0.000
Proving the "Comment" button	2.10	0.77	T=-3.516, P=0.001
Offering rewards to users	2.11	0.76	T=-3.413, P=0.001
Allowing users to rate other people's reviews	2.15	0.78	T=-2.872, P=0.005
Allowing to respond to comments made by others	2.17	0.79	T=-2.700, P=0.009
Providing product recommendations	2.20	0.83	T=-2.269, P=0.026
Allowing experts to give advice on what to buy	2.21	0.82	T=-2.158, P=0.034
Providing the "Send" button	2.24	0.74	T=-2.074, P=0.042
Groupon			
Proving the "Comment" button	1.76	0.55	T=-8.882, P=0.000
Allowing users to provide product reviews	1.83	0.70	T=-6.113, P=0.000
Allowing users to create "Wish-Lists"	1.93	0.80	T=-4.290, P=0.000
Allowing to respond to comments made by others	1.94	0.77	T=-4.281, P=0.000
Offering rewards to users	1.97	0.76	T=-4.064, P=0.000
Providing the "Like" button	2.04	0.80	T=-3.093, P=0.003
Allowing a group of users to buy products together	2.04	0.78	T=-3.165, P=0.002
Providing flash sales	2.06	0.84	T=-2.796, P=0.007
Allowing experts to give advice on what to buy	2.06	0.93	T=-2.552, P=0.013
Providing product recommendations	2.13	0.76	T=-2.339, P=0.022
Facebook Starbucks			
Allowing to respond to comments made by others	1.87	0.53	T=-6.920, P=0.000
Providing the "Comment" button	1.89	0.64	T=-5.532, P=0.000
Offering the "Like" button	1.91	0.61	T=-5.624, P=0.000
Offering rewards to users	2.01	0.89	T=-2.818, P=0.006
Allowing users to provide product reviews	2.03	0.76	T=-3.150, P=0.002
Facebook Green Day			
Providing the "Like" button	1.76	0.73	T=-6.751, P=0.000
Providing the "Comment" button	1.79	0.61	T=-7.682, P=0.000
Allowing to respond to comments made by others	1.79	0.65	T=-7.147, P=0.000
Allowing users to chat with people	1.87	0.70	T=-5.681, P=0.000
Providing a community to interact with users	1.93	0.62	T=-5.634, P=0.000
Timely updating social activities (i.e. recent posts)	1.99	0.73	T=-4.129, P=0.000
Offering rewards to users	2.03	0.72	T=-3.691, P=0.000
Announcing online and offline social events to users	2.13	0.77	T=-2.347, P=0.022

commerce websites, it is not enough to simply clone social design features from one website to another. In fact, there is a need to understand the social design features and characteristics of social commerce websites, and ensure that social design features meet the needs of social commerce websites. By doing so, organization can efficiently harness various social features and derive value from them.

Table 2. Less important social design features

Amazon			
Less important social design features	Mean	SD	Significance
Providing branded online applications, social games	3.21	1.02	T=6.467, P=0.000
Presenting information about user recent activities	3.00	1.15	T=4.196, P=0.000
Reporting user activity through notifications	2.77	1.00	T=2.955, P=0.004
Allowing users to chat with people	2.75	0.90	T=3.009, P=0.004
Sharing product review on social networks	2.73	0.98	T=2.647, P=0.010
Allowing users to co-browse online store together	2.63	0.83	T=2.134, P=0.036
Groupon			
Presenting information about user recent activities	3.47	1.16	T=8.127, P=0.000
Providing branded online applications, social games	3.23	1.03	T=7.154, P=0.000
Reporting user activity through notifications	2.80	1.08	T=3.540, P=0.001
Allowing users to chat with people	2.79	0.99	T=3.754, P=0.000
Providing its storefronts on social networks	2.60	1.01	T=2.139, P=0.036
Allowing users to create own conversation topics	2.57	0.80	T=2.384, P=0.020
Facebook Starbucks			
Presenting information about user recent activities	3.27	1.04	T=7.633, P=0.000
Allowing a group of users to buy products together	2.77	0.93	T=4.084, P=0.000
Allowing users to co-browse online store together	2.71	0.93	T=3.574, P=0.001
Providing its storefront on other social networks	2.51	0.83	T=2.010, P=0.048
Facebook Green Day			
Presenting information about user recent activities	3.31	1.00	T=8.088, P=0.000
Providing flash sales	3.01	0.97	T=5.753, P=0.000
Allowing users to co-browse online store together	2.86	0.82	T=5.195, P=0.000
Allowing a group of users to buy products together	2.80	1.04	T=3.630, P=0.001
Sharing product review on social networks	2.73	0.88	T=3.614, P=0.001

4.2   Social Design Feature Preferences

Our analysis also indicates that there are significant differences in user preferences towards some social design features between the two social commerce categories (see Table 3). More specifically, the social features of providing product recommendations, allowing experts to give advice on what to buy and why, and "Wishlists" creation, are more favored by participants who used e-commerce-based websites than those who used Facebook-based websites. Conversely, the features of allowing users to chat with other people, providing an online community to interact with users, and offering online and offline events to users are more preferred by participants who used Facebook-based websites than those who used e-commerce-based websites.

Table 3. Preference differences of social design features

Social design features	E-commerce-based		Facebook-based	
	Amazon	Groupon	Starbucks	Green day
Providing product recommendations	2.20(0.83)	2.13(0.76)	2.31(0.89)	2.43(0.81)
Significance			F=7.689, P=0.000	
Offering experts advice on what to buy	2.11(0.82)	2.06(0.93)	2.16(0.82)	2.21(0.96)
Significance			F=10.884, P=0.000	
Allowing users to create "Wish-lists"	2.21(0.89)	1.94(0.83)	2.51(0.92)	2.54(0.89)
Significance			F=8.112, P=0.000	
Allowing users to chatting with people	2.75(0.90)	2.79(0.99)	2.21(0.93)	1.87(0.70)
Significance			F=11.730, P=0.000	
Providing online community to interact with users	2.44(0.95)	2.40(0.92)	2.14(0.78)	1.93(0.62)
Significance			F=4.271, P=0.001	
Offering online-offline events to users	2.48(0.71)	2.44(0.87)	2.24(0.73)	2.13(0.77)
Significance			F=2.667, P=0.022	

These results may signal that although the two categories of social commerce websites have utilized social features to facilitate the online buying and selling of products and services, the goals of users' visit to these websites are significantly different. Actually, users visit e-commerce-based websites primarily for purchasing products. However, users go to Facebook-based websites with the purpose of communicating and information sharing. These implications also echo the view of other social commerce studies, such as Marsden [18], which indicates that the essence of using social media tools on e-commerce (e.g., Amazon and Groupon) is to help people connect where they buy, whereas, the essence of utilizing commercial features on social media platforms (e.g., Facebook Starbucks and Facebook Green Day) is to help people buy where they connect. Therefore, it is important for business organizations to understand the characteristics of different social commerce categories, and develop appropriate social commerce platforms to support users' needs.

5   Conclusion

Evidence from previous studies indicates that social commerce design is facing big challenges in developing user centered social commerce websites. This research explores social design features by conducting an empirical study, with an emphasis on two categories of social commerce websites. We identified a set of important and less important social design features on the target social commerce websites, the most important ones being the "Comment" button provision, allowing users to give feedback; encouraging users to respond to comments made by others, and offering rewards to users; while the least important feature consists of presenting information about users' recent activities. In addition, users' preference differences towards social features with regards to the two social commerce categories have been identified. Each social commerce website has its own business objectives so it is important to understand these objectives when developing social commerce. In this way, companies with different objectives can achieve their desirable social commerce design outcomes. Moreover, addressing the user perspective in social commerce design can provide concrete prescriptions for developing more user-centered social commerce websites that may be expected to increase user participation and the volume of sales by aligning with the needs of the users.

There are limitations to this study. For example, we only selected four social commerce websites, which may provide a limited insight into social design feature identification. Further studies may select a larger social commerce sample as well as other social network–based platforms (e.g., Twitter). In addition, as indicated by Kim and Park [10], users' perception significantly influences their interaction with social commerce. Hence, future research may investigate users' preferences and their performance with social design features in order to better understand their needs in terms social commerce design.

References

1. Liang, T.P., Turban, E.: Introduction to the Special Issue Social Commerce: A Research Framework for Social Commerce. International Journal of Electronic Commerce 16(2), 5–14 (2011)
2. Huang, Z., Benyoucef, M.: From e-commerce to social commerce: A close look at design features. Electronic Commerce Research and Applications (2013), http://dx.doi.org/10.1016/j.elerap.2012.12.003
3. Huang, Z., Yoon, S.Y., Benyoucef, M.: Adding Social Features to E-commerce. In: The 5th Annual Conference on Information Systems Applied Research, New Orleans, Louisiana (2012)
4. Tredinnick, L.: Web 2.0 and Business. Business Information Review 23(4), 228–234 (2006)
5. Curty, R.G., Zhang, P.: Social commerce: Looking back and forward. Proceedings of the American Society for Information Science and Technology 48(1), 1–10 (2011)
6. Stephen, A.T., Toubia, O.: Deriving Value from Social Commerce Networks. Journal of Marketing Research XLVII, 215–228 (2009)
7. Constantinides, E., Fountain, S.J.: Web 2.0: Conceptual foundations and marketing issues. Journal of Direct, Data and Digital Marketing Practice, 231–244 (2008)
8. Lee, S.-H., DeWester, D., Park, S.R.: Web 2.0 and opportunities for small business. Springer (2008)
9. Kang, J., Park-Poaps, H.: Motivational Antecedents of Social Shopping for Fashion and its Contribution to Shopping Satisfaction. Clothing and Textiles Research Journal 29(4), 331–347 (2011)
10. Kim, S., Park, H.: Effects of various characteristics of social commerce (s-commerce) on consumers' trust and trust performance. International Journal of Information Management (2012), http://dx.doi.org/10.1016/j.ijinfomgt.2012.11.006

11. Kim, Y.A., Srivastava, J.: Impact of social influence in e-commerce decision making. In: Proceedings of the Ninth International Conference on Electronic Commerce, New York, NY, USA, pp. 293–302 (2007)
12. Wigand, R.T., Benjamin, R.I., Birkland, J.L.H.: Web 2.0 and beyond: implications for electronic commerce. In: Proceedings of the 10th International Conference on Electronic Commerce (2008)
13. Serrano, N., Torres, J.M.: Web 2.0 for Practitioners. IEEE Software (2010)
14. Liang, T.P., Ho, Y.T., Li, Y.W., Turban, E.: What Drives Social Commerce: The Role of Social Support and Relationship Quality. International Journal of Electronic Commerce 16(2), 69–90 (2011)
15. Murugesan, S.: Understanding web 2.0. The IEEE Computer Society (2007)
16. Kietzmann, J.H., Hermkens, K., McCarthy, I.P., Silvestre, B.S.: Social media? Get serious! Understanding the functional building blocks of social media. Business Horizons 54(3), 241–251 (2011)
17. Kim, D.: Under what conditions will social commerce business models survive? Electronic Commerce Research and Applications (2012),
    http://dx.doi.org/10.1016/j.elerap.2012.12.002
18. Marsden, P.: Social commerce: Monetizing social media. SYZYGY Deutschland Gmbh, Germany (2010)
19. Lee, J., Cha, M.S., Cho, C.: Online Service Quality in Social Commerce Websites. In: Khachidze, V., Wang, T., Siddiqui, S., Liu, V., Cappuccio, S., Lim, A. (eds.) iCETS 2012. CCIS, vol. 332, pp. 335–351. Springer, Heidelberg (2012)

Effects of Sharing Farmers' Information Using Content Management System

Tomoko Kashima[1], Shimpei Matsumoto[2], and Tatsuo Matsutomi[1]

[1] Kinki University
1 Takaya Umenobe, Higashi-Hiroshima City, Hiroshima, 739-2116, Japan
[2] Hiroshima Institute of Technology
2-1-1 Miyake, Saeki-ku, Hiroshima 731-5193, Japan

Abstract. In recent years, new business models for agricultural markets have appeared. Under this perspective, we develop a new information system for urban markets to facilitate the transactions. Both sides, consumers and farmers, require certain information from markets about agricultural products. For example, consumers may make requests about the exact information of agricultural products or their safety, while farmers may want to make requests about the information on how to boast their produce. Under the considerations of such requirements at the markets, which may be conflicting, we propose a new information system to assist in the negotiation between parties.

1 Introduction

In recent years, the number of agricultural-product markets is over the number of convenience stores in Japan. However, many farmers are experiencing a lot of problems nowadays. Farmers are rapidly aging because young people who get a agricultural job are decreasing in number. Consumers worry about the safety of the food which Farmers produce because the problem of the quantity of the agricultural chemicals used for agricultural products And, there is also a growing concern that the Trans-Pacific Partnership(TPP) has a negative influence on domestic agriculture. These problems could be a big opportunity to try and change domestic agriculture in Japan by introducing IT. We have already developed a Menu Recommendation System which gathers data on what people like to eat, and with that data, it can make automatic recommendations for an individual[9]. This idea can also be applied in developing the Agricultural Information System for urban markets, for the benefit of farmers and the local agriculture in Japan. This system will provide information on what agricultural products are in demand by analyzing consumer consumption and market trends. With this information, the farmers can have a better idea of what crops to prioritize. This can also help stabilize the economic sustainability of farming by improving farm management. With the system at work, it will reduce oversupply and undersupply of certain agricultural products, and the stable supply-demand relationship will prevent the underpricing of agricultural products and help in stabilizing market prices.

A.A. Ozok and P. Zaphiris (Eds.): OCSC/HCII 2013, LNCS 8029, pp. 296–303, 2013.

2 Present Conditions of Japanese Gricultural

A long time ago, the Japanese agricultural system was by the self-sufficiency which makes agricultural products by itself and is eaten by itself. The agricultural products to need were created as needed. The farmhouse created agricultural products and consumers bought agricultural products directly by development of the food system. Next, agricultural products were sold from Central Wholesale Market from farmhouse to retail, and were sent to consumers. Consumers' opportunity to get to know the place-of-production information on the purchased agricultural products decreased from such change. Also at the restaurant, a customer's opportunity to get to know the detailed information of the foods used for a menu decreased. Similarly, a farmhouse's opportunity to acquire consumers' information decreased. For example, the customer needs the information what kind of products they want to buy and how season they want to get the products.

The problem of food attracted attention since about 2000. Consumers changed to become interested to food of secure and safe. Consumers began to ask for getting to know how and where agricultural products were made. Consumers came to get interested also in quantity of the agricultural chemicals of agricultural products and growing information of agricultural products. If such information about food were released to the public, a menu has added value. For example, we think that the quantity of agricultural chemicals and the information on a place of production become important. The foods of the bastard size may also be needed at a restaurant.

Many researchers did systems development and have proposed from various viewpoints [8], [5], [3].The agricultural problem is tackled also in countries other than Japan. The food safety management system in Korea is largely managed [4].The Agri-food Safety Information System planned to be upgraded continuously by connecting practical safety management information and by constructing Emergency Warning System and Crisis Coping System which can be used to promptly cope with situation when a food accident occurs. The agricultural extension system in Tanzania has faced many problems [1], [6]. Moreover, farmers has a problem of reduction in income. Farmers are pressed for the need for change from the old selling method. The Farmers need to plan and grow the agricultural products which consumers regard as wanting rather than need to create without a plan. The Farmers need to investigate best-selling agricultural products in advance, and need to sell them in a store. However, there is a big problem here. The problem is the physical distance between consumers and farmers. Now, many of sales information of Farmers is not managed. The Farmers have not acquired a customer's sales trend.

Jensen expressed whether improvements in information impact market performance [2]. When information is limited or costly, agents are unable to engage in optimal arbitrage in fishery and agriculture. Between 1997 and 2001, mobile phone service was introduced throughout Kerala, a state in India with a large fishing industry. Using microlevel survey data, they showed that the adoption of mobile phones by fishermen and wholesalers was associated with a dramatic reduction in price dispersion, the complete elimination of waste, and near-perfect adherence to the Law of One Price.We think

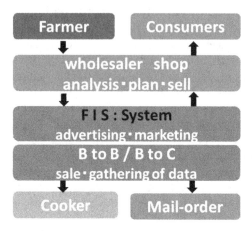

Fig. 1. Configuration of the Farmers Information System

farmers release information and sharing information leads to the stability of the prices of agricultural products from this case.

In addition, IT-related company has begun entry in agriculture [7]. They are applied for agriculture using a clud-computing. They have focused on introducing the latest technologies (sensors, wireless networks and Cloud computing), radically revising approaches to agriculture and conducting business feasibility studies to make a hypothesis model of Cloud services that truly contribute to agriculture.

However, it is very difficult for farmers to build the large-scale system which has a network all over the country. Therefore, it is difficult for farmers to share information mutually. Moreover, it is very difficult for local farmers to do the same measure as a major company. In this research, we consider those problems, and we aims at the configuration of the farmers information system which can be used also in district agriculture(Figure1).

3   Problem and Solution

We think there are three problems about agricultural management. The first problem is stabilizing agricultural management. If the quantity of production is unstable, market prices would also be unstable. If supply and distribution is indefinite, the income of a farmer is also indefinite, thereby making it difficult to recruit the younger generation to engage in farming. This particular problem means that the farming industry workforce is not infused with new laborers while the existing farmers become older. In 2010, the percentage of farmers aged 65 and over was 62percent. The average age of farmers is 66 years old. The income that farmers make today is only half of what a farmer makes 20 years ago. The area of agricultural land which is not being used and cultivated is continuously increasing. The farming experience and wisdom of the expert farmers are not being put to good use and because there is no one to inherit their knowledge of farming. If the farmers do not adjust their farming schedule to fit the demand of consumers, they automatically loose that sales opportunity. It is then very important that the farmers take into consideration what the consumers really want, to avoid not being able to sell their products or worse, sell it for a very low price. Farmers should focus on producing products that has actual consumer demand. They have to adjust their farming schedule in a way that by the time they harvest, their product is actually sought upon by consumers. For example, the farmers should only plant watermelons just in time for the summer, when it is popular.

The next problem is the unstable supply of agricultural products. Long term storage of certain agricultural products just to maintain a steady supply is difficult to do because some agricultural products have short shelf life. This problem makes it impossible for farmers to supply market demands for certain periods of time. Sometimes, certain environmental phenomenon, like the weather, affects the planting, harvesting and even delivering goods to the market difficult. Our goal is to design a system that will provide farmers information on when to plant so that the harvesting can be synchronized with actual market demands. To accurately approximate the time between the planting preparations up to the time of harvest, information on rate of seedling growth before planting, growing information and shipping time approximations until the product reaches the markets, will be used make a planting prediction. This information is then disclosed to the public via the web. This way, ordinary consumers, the food service industry, the farmers and other sectors than can benefit from this information may have access. The information on which agricultural products the Farmers can supply and be made available to the market at a given time, may be known buy prospective buyers and consumers alike. If this is so; consumers and buyers can plan their purchases in advance. The food service industry can also take advantage of this information by being able to plan ahead the kind of food they can serve on the menu during that certain period. This system will give both farmers, consumers and the food industry sufficient time to prepare and make necessary adjustments and preparations.

The last problem is that worth of agricultural products is cheap, even though Farmers grew the agricultural products carefully. It is necessary for the farmers to provide the consumers the information related to the production of the products. Consumers are interested with the process because they need to be secure that the products they are buying are of good quality and that they were grown carefully. This agricultural information system would include pictures of the actual farmers and their farms, information on growing practices and methods will also be included, along with the information on what type of chemicals or fertilizers were used in growing the products, or what type of preservatives were added to the products, if ever there was any. The objective of the system is to provide consumers information that cannot be known by simply looking at the products. This information can be considered as a value added to the products, thereby resulting to better acceptance of the products and better market prices.

4   Farmers Information System

This system is a system which connects farmers, a customer, and a sales store. The system has some pages. Farmers disseminate the information on agricultural products.

Fig. 2. FIS's Top of System   **Fig. 3.** FIS of Input Form

The system can perform an information input simply. For example, a farmer only sends the photograph taken by the cellular phone by e-mail. The system can exhibit what kind of agricultural products farmers are making. The system can exhibit the date of scheduled harvest of agricultural products. Moreover, farmers can display relief on web by displaying the photograph of products. The photograph and comment which contributed are immediately displayed on a system. Consumers can peruse the page of farmers. Consumers can also write a comment to the photograph and comment which farmers posted. They can peruse the cooking method of the purchased vegetables. Moreover, they can post the dish of boast built using the purchased vegetables. A grocery store has a duty which gives the information of farmers to consumers. Many information gathers for a system. The information is printed by paper like a newspaper. Consumers can see the information on a system with a personal computer or a cellular phone. However, it is also effective to distribute information to the consumers who came to the store in paper. The new information in a system is published by paper.

Figure2 and Figure3 shows the details of a system. There are some functions in the system. A function summarizes the new information on a system to one sheet. The information on one sheet becomes like a newspaper. At the store, shop assistant can give the newspaper to customers who do not see the web site. The other function posts the information on the Farmers and agricultural products which the store obtained. The shop assistant can post easily from a cellular phone or a personal computer. New information is displayed on this space(Figure2). This space is posted by Farmers, consumers, seller, sommelier of vegetables, etc. The other function is information effective in consumers and the master chief of a restaurant. Consumers can know that agricultural products are raised safely. The master chief of a restaurant can know the

64.16% New Visitor
247 Visits

35.84% Returning Visitor
138 Visits

Fig. 4. Visitor of FIS

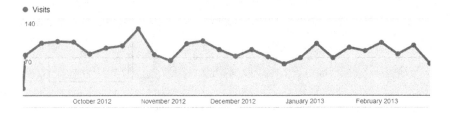

Fig. 5. Audience over view of FIS

information on the agricultural products harvested next, when creating a menu. Farmers who checked this web site can acquire various information. Usual, there was no opportunity for Farmers to get to know how the agricultural products which he raised are eaten by consumers. Farmers become an opportunity to get to know consumers' comment over agricultural products. The information is useful for next cultivation for Farmers. A system has a page of Farmers, a page of information sending, a page of a recipe, an event page, etc. other than a top page. The detailed information of the agricultural products into which each agricultural products raise the page of Farmers is displayed. The page has the harvest time and the amount of agricultural chemicals of agricultural products. The calender with harvest information can be known visually.

5   Results

We report the results of analysis of the system about the visitor. Figure4and Figure5 show the percentage of visitors and new visitors of the system. In this period, SEO and listing advertising measures have not done. New visitors accounted for approximately 65% in spite of not doing the advertising. Figure6 lets you see where visits originate. Location is derived from mapping IP addresses to geographic locations. A figure shows that there are most visits from Kobe which is an enforcement place of this study. As an attention point, many visiting places to the 2nd are Shibuya in Tokyo distant from Kobe. The good effect of transmission of information has shown up.

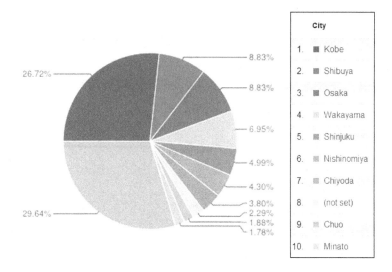

Fig. 6. Ration of Total Visit Region

6   Conclusion

In this paper, farmers information system for carrying out a remedy to three problems was proposed. The problem about the present agriculture was shown in this paper.Solution was proposed to those problems and the support system was developed. The structure which connects Farmers, consumers, and a store was built. The solution of the problems takes much time. However, this system will be useful for a problem solving.

As future works, the authors will support social activities towards the applications for marketing and policy planning by understanding customer's attributes and activities from stored data through the operation in the real worksite. This study hopes to construct a business support model for restaurants considering some external factors from the viewpoint of entire optimization, but the local improvement only for mall. To achieve this objective, a simulation model is needed to be constructed. The authors are planning to make a computational model based on the game theory which enables to examine the changes of overall benefit depending on collaborative relationships between restaurants.

References

1. Mattee, A.Z.: Reforming Tanzania's Agricultural Extension System: The Challenges Ahead. African Study Monographs 15, 177–188 (1994)
2. Robert, J.: The Digital Provide: Information (Technology), Market Performance and Welfare in There South Indian Fisheries Sector. The Quarterly Journal of Economics 122(3), 879–879 (2007)
3. Miyasaka, J.: Modelling and Optimization for Agricultural Production Systems. The Institute of Systems, Control and Information Engineers 54(4), 138–143 (2010)

4. Oh, L.K., Yeonghwan, B., Kei, N.: Construction and Management Status of Agri-Food Safety Information System of Korea. Journal of the Faculty of Agriculture 55, 341–348 (2010)
5. Hashimoto, M., Utsumi, T., Yukimatsu, K.: Networking System for Large Rice Field Using Independent Power Supply System and Long Distance Wireless LAN. Agricultural Information Research 16(1), 9–21 (2007)
6. Masawe, J.L.: Farming System and Agricultural Production among Small Farmers in the Uluguru Mountain Area, Morogoro Region, Tanzania. The Center for African Area Studies 13, 171–183 (1992)
7. Hori, M., Kawashima, E., Yamazaki, T.: Clud Computing Applied for Agriculture and Other Fields. FUJITSU 61(3), 314–320 (2010)
8. Hoshi, T., Shiozawa, E., Shinma, K., Takaichi, M., Firufuji, M.: Development of an Application Program for Field Servers to Acquire and Leverago Production History Information in Protected Horticulture. Agricultural Information Research 16(1), 1–8 (2007)
9. Kashima, T., Matsumoto, S., Ishii, H.: Decision Support System for Menu Recommendation Using Rough Sets. International Journal of Innovative Computing, Information and Control 7(5), 2799–2808 (2011)

Untangling the Web of e-Health:
Multiple Sclerosis Patients' Perceptions of Online Health Information, Information Literacy, and the Impact on Treatment Decision Making

Anna L. Langhorne[1], Patrick Thomas[2], and Laura Kolaczkowski[2]

[1] University of Dayton, Department of Communication. Dayton, Ohio
[2] University of Dayton, Department of English. Dayton, Ohio
{alanghorne1,pthomas1,lkolaczkowski1}@udayton.edu

Abstract. Social media have changed how patients, caregivers and physicians produce, manage and use information when making medical treatment decisions. Because Multiple Sclerosis (MS) patients rely on online information to self-educate about treatment options, it is important to determine whether online decision-making tools are reliable and useful given patients' knowledge of their disease and varying information literacy skills. Therefore, this study investigates the online search practices, perceptions, and usability of web-based information among MS patients. Perceptions of MS patients are measured by a questionnaire administered to a convenience sample of MS patients. Their online search practices are evaluated to determine the kind of information sought and used. Second, online search behaviors and needs are examined for trends related to MS disease type, stage and severity. Third, the relationship between online search behaviors and perceived impact on patient-neurologist communication is examined. Recommendations are offered for improved patient-neurologist communication and the development of inclusive treatment decision-making tools.

Keywords: Information seeking, decision making, information usability, information literacy, web navigation, Web 2.0, Multiple Sclerosis, patient communication.

1 Introduction

For over a decade, Web 2.0 technologies and the social networks they enable have brought about significant changes in the ways medical information is produced and exchanged. Similarly, the development of "Health 2.0," "eHealth" and "Medicine 2.0" as global phenomena points to the ways that access to social networks within which health-related information is exchanged has become increasingly important to patients and physicians. Of particular importance for the practice of medicine by health professionals as well as the experiences of diseases among patient populations

A.A. Ozok and P. Zaphiris (Eds.): OCSC/HCII 2013, LNCS 8029, pp. 304–312, 2013.
© Springer-Verlag Berlin Heidelberg 2013

is the use of internet-based health information for the purpose of making course-of-treatment decisions. Despite this significant context in which to investigate physician- and patient-user informational needs, research in fields as diverse as information architecture, cyber informatics, health sciences, and human-computer interaction have largely overlooked the needs of Health 2.0 participants within the context of medical treatment decision-making, offering instead a vast amount of research focusing on health-related Web 2.0 tools, their affordances, and design [1], as well as Web 2.0 tool use for general health educational purposes, training health professionals, or on-going collaboration among medical specialists [2]. Less evident in Health 2.0 informatics research are population-based accounts of patients' online search practices and perceptions of web-based health information, particularly with attention to the specific contexts that motivate information search practices relevant to patient-users (i.e., searching for a health provider, initial self-diagnosis, or, in the case of the present study, to make treatment decisions). Underlying the questions regarding use of internet-based health related information is a concern for information access. Indeed, the types of health related information patients to which many patients have access is no longer determined solely by physicians, patients search for health related information online in different ways, and patients value different kinds of information based on their own experiences of their diseases [3], and the types of information patients access is only part of the information available to patients. Prior to any accurate rendering of information usability within Health 2.0 participant populations is the examination of those populations' perceptions of and practices locating online health related information.

As part of a larger investigation of patient, neurologist, and caregiver perceptions and use of web-based health information and the role of web-based health information in making treatment decisions, this article details a pilot study investigating one Health 2.0 participant population's internet search practices and perceptions of online health related information; namely, Multiple Sclerosis (MS) patients located in Southwestern region of the state of Ohio, in the United States. The MS patient population presents a unique case in which to examine perceptions of and practices locating web-based health information. With no known cure for MS and often trial-and-error methods of selecting among treatment options [4], a diverse set of symptoms and lengthy diagnostic process [5], a wide range of disease types – the relation between which is still contested [6], a varied set of drug treatment and complementary therapy options, and, as a central nervous system disease, highly idiosyncratic sets of treatment side effects, MS patients must negotiate a particularly large set of considerations when making course-of-treatment decisions. Yet, MS patients have long been considered a well-informed patient population, although informational needs have been found to differ depending on patients' length of diagnosis [7], [8]. In this study, we ask the following questions: what sources do MS patients consult when searching for MS-related information online, and with what frequency? What kinds of information do MS patients search for online? And what are patients' motivations for searching for MS-related information online? Through an examination of the MS patients' search practices and the types of and frequency with which online sources are consulted, the data presented in this report can lead to better understandings of the factors that influence patients' perceptions of MS-related online information.

Central to the analysis of patient perceptions of online health information is an examination of the types of health related information patients seek. Prior research examining patients' self-education suggests that the types of information patients seek are related to variables of patients' disease type, stage, and severity [9], [10]. Despite this, prior research within MS clinics suggests that while many MS patients report using web-based information to prepare for an initial consultation, online information searches correlative to disease severity and type were less apparent among patients post-diagnosis [11]. This apparent contradiction suggests that information searching online is variable across different diseases; for patients with a chronic diseases like MS, information types will likely differ across time. Understanding the relationship between information needs and perceptions of web-based MS-related information within the context of treatment decision-making must likewise account for patients' already existing informational schema and the ways in which prior knowledge of their disease impacts patients' motivations for online information searches.

A guiding supposition concerning the study of patient perceptions of online MS-related information is that patients' self-reports of search practices are indicative of the qualities of information patients require to make course-of-treatment decisions. Consequently, it is important to consider the role of patients' information literacy when examining search practices as a way to account for how perceptions of online MS-related information are formed out of and in response to the information patients are able to retrieve from online sources. Patients' perceptions of online information invoke judgments concerning the validity, reliability, comprehensiveness, accuracy, currency, and personal relevance of web content [12], [13], [14]. These judgments concerning information attributes rely on individual patients' subjective positions toward the content they are able to access. It is for this reason that information literacy is a fundamental indicator of patients' online search practices. However, overwhelmingly, research on the relationship between information literacy and patients' informational needs has failed to define "information literacy" despite several claims about its role in patients' access to and perceptions of medical information [15], [16] even in the context of medical treatment decision-making [17]. By "information literacy," we do not mean to suggest a particular set of autonomous skills all users might employ in the process of searching for information online. On the contrary, information literacy – and the kinds of online search practices different kinds of information literacy allow – is a social practice [18], highly contextual and localized ways of working with online information, and these practices vary according to the kinds of information for which internet users search, the domains in which information is used, and change over time [19]. Viewing information literacy as a social practice provides a conduit between patients' informational needs, how they search for these informational needs online, and the ways in which patients construct their perceptions of web-based MS information.

Related to information literacy, the examination of patient demographics, such as participant internet access (including the tools through which patients access the internet and the reliability of internet connectivity these tools provide, such as mobile devices or desktop computers, as well as the location of these devices through which patients access web-based information, like workplace, community, and home environments) is particularly relevant to the study of online search practices. These demographic questions provide an important framework for understanding patients' use of online information and the material conditions in which patients' search practices are carried out.

To better understand MS patients' search practices, the online sources patients rely on for MS-related information, and patients' motivations for engaging in these search practices, we designed a quantitative study to measure MS patients' information needs and generate initial data about how patients carry out their online searches. In the following sections, we detail the study's design and discuss initial results pertaining to MS patients' information sources, frequency of visitation to these sources, and purposes for engaging in online information searches.

2   Methodology

2.1   Questionnaire

The pilot questionnaire comprised six parts: background health information related to MS, types and frequency of information resources used, online interactivity, relationship of information and healthcare management, information usability, demographics, and instrument feedback. These questions attempted to quantify how patients with MS search, perceive, and use online information resources for healthcare decision-making. Many questions were developed to bridge the information usability, healthcare satisfaction, and patient-physician communication literatures.

The instrument included a variety of question types, including nominal, ordinal, interval, and ratio-level measures. A total of 65 measures were used: 13 open-ended, 2 contingency, 25 multiple choice, and the remaining were matrix. The instrument yielded categorical and numerical data as well as qualitative information.

A web-based survey on www.fluidsurveys.com was used to facilitate ease of completion and future assessment of large patient populations. A complete copy of the questionnaire and a detailed description will be available from the researchers when the current data collection effort and instrument validation are complete.

2.2   Sample

The participants comprised patients with Multiple Sclerosis in the southwest Ohio region of the United States. The participants were recruited from a convenience sample of self-identified MS patients who regularly participate in ongoing research activities and MS physical therapy programs offered through the home institution's Doctor of Physical Therapy Program and Center for Neurology. One hundred sixty-nine patients were invited to participate in the study. Email invitations were distributed using FluidSurveys.com invitation feature. Due to the pilot nature of this study, no incentives were available to encourage participation. The sample size was 39 and the response rate was 23%.

Approximately 65% of respondents were aged 45–64 years of age. Twenty-four percent were male and 76% were female. Fifty-six percent had a 4-year post-secondary degree and 67% accessed the internet multiple times per day from home.

3   Results

The data were cleaned, processed, and imported into SPSS. For the purposes of this article, only the descriptive statistical analyses are reported. Results from the correlation, regression, and cluster analyses will be shared in a future article.

3.1   Background Health

Participants were asked what form of MS they have. Sixty-nine percent reported Relapsing-Remitting type. In terms of general health, 82% indicated they are in good to very good health; however, 82% gauged the status of their MS as fair to good. The strong majority (95%) reported that they are under the care of a neurologist for their MS treatment, and 68% of respondents visit their neurologist twice per year.

3.2   Information Resources and Information Practices

Table 1 summarizes answers from a questionnaire item that asked what source was consulted first during a most recent need for MS-related information.

Table 1. First source consulted most recently for MS-related information

Source	Average percentage
Neurologist	45
Book	3
Health-related website	26
MS Organization	13
MS Online Discussion Board	3
A family member with MS	0
A non-diagnosed family member	0
A peer/friend with MS	8
A non-diagnosed peer/friend	0
Other	3

Participants were asked to cite the source they would consult the next time MS-related information is needed. Only two categories increased: 54% selected neurologist and 36% would use a health-related website. The remaining categories decreased or remained the same. In terms of online sources, participants infrequently consulted formal MS organizations and discussion forums (See Tables 2 and 3.).

Table 2. Online visitation of MS organizations

Organization website	Daily	1x/wk	2-3/mo	1x/mo	<1x/mo	Never
www.nmss.org	0%	3%	18%	21%	45%	13%
www.msassocation.org	0%	0%	11%	18%	47%	24%
www.msfocus.org	0%	0%	5%	16%	50%	29%

Table 3. Online visitation of health discussion forums

Forum	Daily	1x/wk	2-3/mo	1x/mo	<1x/mo	Never
Everyday Health (www.everydayhealth.com)	3%	3%	0%	3%	16%	76%
MS-related Facebook Groups	5%	11%	3%	3%	5%	74%
MedHelp (www.medhelp.org)	0%	0%	0%	5%	21%	74%
MS Connections (www.msconnection.org)	0%	0%	8%	24%	29%	39%
MS World (www.msworld.org)	0%	3%	3%	8%	18%	68%
Patients Like Me (www.patientslikeme.com)	0%	3%	0%	5%	21%	71%
This Is MS (www.thisisms.com)	0%	0%	0%	0%	11%	89%
WebMD (www.webmd.com)	5%	3%	18%	11%	39%	24%

Regarding the MS-related topics for which participants search online, the majority conducted inquiries less than once per month (See Table 4.). Participants were asked to rate the importance of various reasons for online MS-related searches. Primary reasons for many participants included preparation, interpretation, supplementation, and investigating (See Table 5.).

Table 4. Frequency of online search for MS-related information

Information topics	Daily	1x/wk	2-3/mo	1x/mo	<1x/mo	Never
Disease-Modifying Drugs	0%	3%	13%	3%	71%	11%
Treatments for MS symptoms	0%	3%	18%	8%	71%	0%
Alternative/Complementary Therapies	0%	0%	16%	8%	61%	16%
Side Effects of Treatment or Drugs	0%	0%	3%	24%	68%	5%
Emerging Research	3%	0%	13%	29%	42%	13%
Patient Advocacy issues	3%	0%	8%	16%	47%	26%
Peer-Groups/Patient to Patient Support	3%	5%	3%	21%	39%	29%
MS Health Services Providers	0%	3%	0%	11%	53%	34%
Neurologist Credentials	0%	0%	0%	3%	55%	42%
Caregiver Credentials	0%	0%	0%	5%	18%	76%

Table 5. Motivation importance of online search MS-related information

Motivation	Extremely Important	Important	Neutral	Low Importance	Not at Important	N/A
To prepare for an upcoming doctor's visit	18%	37%	13%	18%	13%	0%
To interpret a doctor's response	13%	45%	21%	5%	11%	5%
To supplement the information provided by a neurologist	11%	61%	8%	11%	5%	5%
To find how other people are dealing with a specific MS-related problem	8%	47%	18%	3%	16%	8%
To research MS drug options available	16%	47%	11%	21%	3%	3%
To learn about emerging new treatment options (alternative drug therapies, clinical trials, etc.)	21%	37%	18%	11%	8%	5%
To look for alternative treatment options (physical therapy, acupuncture, etc.)	16%	32%	24%	13%	11%	5%
To find out how other people are managing their MS	8%	37%	24%	13%	8%	11%
To evaluate my neurologist's credentials	3%	8%	26%	11%	24%	29%
To evaluate caregivers' credentials	0%	8%	13%	5%	18%	55%

4   Future Research and Limitations

As a pilot investigation, the limitations of this study include participant population size. The use of convenience sampling limits the participant population to MS patients located in a particular geographic region. In addition, the use of a web-based questionnaire limits MS patient participation to those with access. Future work in this study will provide multiple methods of access for patient participation, including the use of print questionnaires and face-to-face participant recruitment.

The data reported here also provide preliminary results regarding patients' perceptions of web-based MS health information through indirect measures of patients' self-reports of the source types and frequencies with which online sources are accessed. These data offer initial understandings about patients' perceptions of web-based information, yet further research examining the qualities of web-based MS information patients search for can be augmented by qualitative means. A mixed methods design, employing methods such as interview protocol or simulated internet searches, as well as revision of the current survey instrument, will enable the study of patients' perceptions through complementary measures. Including these complementary measures can also lead to developmental heuristics for use among patients, caregivers, and physicians of varying disease types.

Additionally, within the context of the deliberative process in which course-of-treatment decisions are made, it is necessary to not only expand the participant base among MS patients beyond the geographical limitations of the pilot study, but also to consider the perceptions and practices of online MS-related information among other constituencies involved in the MS treatment decision-making process; namely MS caregivers (both professional and non-professional), and neurologists specializing in MS.

Finally, more data is needed to consider larger questions raised by this study; for example, how is web-based MS related information used within treatment decisions? Does this information play a significant role in the deliberative process for treatment decisions, or is the role of online information ancillary to physician-supplied information? And how can patients' perceptions of web-based health information be used to design better health information systems? The questions raised by this preliminary investigation demand attention if health professionals are to understand how to mitigate the use of web-based health information in professional practice.

5   Conclusion

This article presented the results of a survey of 39 patients with MS from the southwest region of Ohio. The purpose was to understand different aspects of MS patient online search practices and how various information sources are perceived. Descriptive statistics were reported to identify the general patterns of online information seeking in terms of source types and frequencies of visitation to these sources, as well as patients' motivations for engaging in online searches. Results indicate that patients prefer neurologist-supplied information, but also frequent health-related websites. The specific sites patients visit vary significantly according to both type (MS organization's sites, general health websites, social networking sites) and frequency. Contrary to prior research, participants in this study rarely search for caregiver credentials online, and more frequently search for drug treatment side effects and emerging research. Similar to prior research, patients' motivations for searching MS-related information online include preparation for upcoming doctor's visits. Patients also indicated searching for drug therapies, new treatment options, and emergent new alternative therapies. Further research is required to understand the role of MS patients' search practices within MS treatment decision-making.

References

1. Harland, J., Bath, P.: Assessing the Quality of Websites Providing Information on Multiple Sclerosis: Evaluating Tools and Comparing Sites. Health Informatics J. 13(1), 207–221 (2007)
2. Hughes, B., Joshi, I., Wareham, J.: Health 2.0 and Medicine 2.0: Tensions and Controversies in the Field. J. Med. Internet Res. 10(3), 3:22 (2008)
3. Henwood, F., Wyatt, S., Hart, A., Smith, J.: 'Ignorance is Bliss Sometimes': Constraints on the Emergence of the 'Informed Patient' in the Changing Landscapes of Health Information. Soc. of Health & Illness 25(6), 589–607 (2003)

4. National Multiple Sclerosis Society, http://www.nationalmssociety.org/about-multiple-sclerosis/what-we-know-about-ms/who-gets-ms/epidemiology-of-ms/index.aspx

5. Schäffler, N., Köpke, S., Winkler, L., Schippling, S., Inglese, M., Fischer, K., Heesen, C.: Accuracy of Diagnostic Tests in Multiple Sclerosis – A Systematic Review. Acta Neurol. Scand. 124(3), 151–164 (2011)

6. Frischer, J.A., Bramow, S., Dal-Bianco, A., Lucchinetti, C., Rauschka, H., Schmidbauer, M., Laursen, H., Soelberg Sorensen, P., Lassmann, H.: The Relation Between Inflammation and Neurodegeneration in Multiple Sclerosis Brains. Brain 132(5), 1175–1189 (2009)

7. Stewart, D., Sullivan, T.: Illness Behavior and the Sick Role in Chronic Disease: The Case of Multiple Sclerosis. Soc. Sci. Med. 16(15), 1397–1404 (1982)

8. Baker, L., Conner, J.: Physician-Patient Communication from the Perspective of Library and Information Science. Bull. Med. Libr. Assoc. 82(1), 36–42 (1994)

9. Houston, K.T., Allison, J.J.: Users of Internet Health Information: Differences by Health Status. J. Med. Internet Res. 4(2), e7 (2002)

10. Rice, R.: Influences, Usage, and Outcomes of Internet Health Information Searching: Multivariate Results from the Pew Surveys. Int. J. Med. Inform. 75(1), 8–28 (2006)

11. Hay, M.C., Strathmann, C., Lieber, E., Wick, K., Glesser, B.: Why Patients Go Online: Multiple Sclerosis, the Internet, and Physician-Patient Communication. Neurologist 14(6), 374–381 (2008)

12. Berland, G.K., Elliot, M.N., Morales, L., Algazy, J.I., Kravitz, R.L., Broder, M.S., Kanouse, D.E., Muñoz, J.A., Puyol, J.-A., Lara, M., Watkins, K.E., Yang, H., McGlynn, E.A.: Health Information on the Internet: Accessibility, Quality, and Readability in English and Spanish. J. Amer. Med. Assoc. 285(20), 2612–2621 (2001)

13. Eastin, M.: Credibility Assessments of Online Health Information: The Effects of Source Expertise and Knowledge of Content. J. of Comp. Mediated Comm. 6(4) (2001)

14. Diaz, J.A., Griffith, R.A., Ng, J.J., Reinert, S.E., Friedmann, P.D., Moulton, A.W.: Patients' Use of the Internet for Medical Information. J. Gen. Intern. Med. 17(3), 180–185 (2002)

15. Birru, M.S., Monaco, V.M., Charles, L., Drew, H., Njie, V., Bierria, T., Detlefsen, E., Steinman, R.E.: Internet Usage by Low-Literacy Adults Seeking Health Information: An Observational Analysis. J. Med. Internet Res. 6(3), e25 (2004)

16. Paasche-Orlow, M.K., Taylor, H.A., Brancati, F.L.: Readability Standards for Informed-Consent Forms as Compared with Actual Readability. N. Eng. J. Med. 348(8), 721–726 (2003)

17. Kim, S.P., Knight, S.J., Tomori, C., Colella, K.M., Schoor, R.A., Shih, L., Kuzel, T.M., Nadier, R.B., Bennett, C.L.: Health Literacy and Shared Decision Making for Prostate Cancer Patients with Low Socioeconomic Status. Cancer Invest. 19(7), 684–691 (2001)

18. Street, B.: Literacy in Theory and Practice. Cambridge University Press, Cambridge (1984)

19. Barton, D., Hamilton, M.: Literacy Practices. In: Barton, D., Hamilton, M., Ivanič, R. (eds.) Situated Literacies, pp. 7–15. Routledge, London (2000)

Supporting Social Deliberative Skills Online: The Effects of Reflective Scaffolding Tools[*]

Tom Murray[1], Lynn Stephens[1], Beverly Park Woolf[1],
Leah Wing[3], Xiaoxi Xu[1], and Natasha Shrikant[2]

[1] School of Computer Science
[2] Commination Dept.,
[3] Legal Studies Dept.
University of Massachusetts, Amherst, MA
tmurray@cs.umass.edu

Abstract. We investigate supporting higher quality deliberations in online contexts by supporting what we call "social deliberative skills," including perspective-taking, meta-dialog, and reflecting on one's biases. We report on an experiment with college students engaged in online dialogues about controversial topics, using discussion forum software with "reflective tools" designed to support social deliberative skills. We find that these have a significant effect as measured by rubrics designed to asses dialogue quality and social deliberative behaviors.

Keywords: E-participation and e-democracy, Empathic online communities, Communication and deliberation skills, scaffolding.

1 Introduction

A key human capacity is the ability to negotiate situations involving differing opinions where a resolution of ideas is sought, e.g., in dispute resolution, collaborative problem solving, knowledge building, and civic deliberation processes. The need for this deliberative capacity is seen in all realms of human activity from international politics, to collaborative work, to mundane familial squabbles (Gastil & Black, 2008; Spragens, 1990; Kögler, 1992; Toulmin, 1958). Conflict and difference too often result in unsatisfactory outcomes that can be attributed to insufficient skill, or an inability to bring existing skills to bear in difficult situations. Throughout the various contexts mentioned above many of the same underlying skills and capacities are called for. For example, Jordan et al. (2013) propose two important skill sets for skillfully addressing "complex societal issues, such as gang-related crime, deteriorating residential areas, environmental problems, long-term youth unemployment, [and] racist violence" (p. 34.). These skills are "complexity awareness" and "perspective

---

* This research was funded by an award from the NSF #0968536, "The Fourth Party: Improving Computer-Mediated Deliberation through Cognitive, Social and Emotional Support." Any opinions, findings, conclusions or recommendations are those of the authors and do not necessarily reflect the views of the funding agency.

A.A. Ozok and P. Zaphiris (Eds.): OCSC/HCII 2013, LNCS 8029, pp. 313–322, 2013.

awareness." Our work involves studying how such skills can be supported in online deliberation and collaboration.

Participants engaged in extended collaborative knowledge-building or problem solving eventually encounter moments of tension in which they are challenged to understand each other's perspectives and opinions. These moments are microcosms of and foreshadow key moments in the social and civic life of adults writ small and large. Both the literature on creative problem solving and the literature on civic deliberation emphasize the importance of having diverse perspectives represented in collaborative processes, but scholars often do not acknowledge the skillfulness needed to work productively with these differences.

We use the term "social deliberative skills" (SD-skills) to indicate the capacity to deal productively with heterogeneous goals, values, or perspectives, especially those that differ from ones own. SD-skill includes social perspective taking, meta-dialogue, social inquiry, systems-thinking (complexity thinking), and self-reflection. Though the teaching/learning/support (including computer-based support) of these related skills have been researched intensively, the prior research does not adequately address some key challenges in building mutual understanding and mutual regard when interlocutors encounter the disequilibrium of diverse perspectives. This research makes an incremental contribution in this area.

2   Background

One of the goals of education is to produce competent national and global citizens capable of participating in democratic self-governance and capable of wrestling with the difficult questions and dizzying array of information and opinion they face in our technologically advanced society. Engaging with others on complex topics requires not only learning the relevant facts and concepts and making logical inferences, but also engaging with the perspectives and opinions of others who may not share one's views or goals. Doing so requires skills that can be systematically supported (King & Kitchener, 1994; Rosenberg, 2004; Herzig & Chasin, 2006; Holman et al., 2007).

We differentiate our research from others that focus on *argumentation*, which aims to help learners generate logical, well-formed, well-supported explanations and justifications (Andriessen et al., 2003, Baker et al. 2007), usually framed in objective rather than intersubjective terms. That is, they are about finding the right answer or the most efficient and effective solution to a technical or scientific question—but don't adequately address the specific moments of deliberation or collaboration where opportunities for mutual understanding and mutual recognition arise.

Our research draws on prior studies of higher order skills in: social metacognition (Lin & Sullivan, 2008; Joost et al., 1998), reflective judgment and epistemic skill (King & Kitchener, 1994; Kuhn, 1999, 2000; Winne et al., 2006), social perspective-taking and empathy (Desiato 2012; Dahlbert 2001), and perspective seeking and question asking (Graesser et al., 2008).

Prior studies of computer-based support of higher order skills are directly applicable to our research on SD-skills (a subset of higher order skills). Researchers are developing educational software that scaffolds metacognitive and higher order skills including inquiry skills, metacognition and self-regulated learning skills, and reflective reasoning skills (see White et al., 1999; Puntambekar & du Boulay, 1997; Azevedo et al., 2004; Linn, 2000), and evaluations indicate that such support can be quite successful (Baker et al., 2007; Suthers et al., 2001; Scardamalia, 2003). There has also been significant R&D in systems to support argumentation skills (Baker et al., 2007; Suthers, 2008; Scheuer et al., 2010). These studies indicate that under ideal conditions technological scaffolding in the form of prompts, awareness tools, and feedback can improve metacognitive skills, epistemological understanding, and other higher order thinking skills, though studies differ on the enabling conditions necessary for such improvement (Reiser etl all 2001; Suthers et al. 2001; Soller et al. 2005).

3   Method

For the online discussions we used the Mediem deep dialogue discussion forum software created by Idealogue Inc. (see Figures 1, 2).[1] In addition to standard (semi-threaded) discussion forum features, Mediem has a number of features intended to support deeper engagement and reflection (based in part on the designers' many years experience with members of the National Coalition on Dialogue and Deliberation).

Hypothesis. Participants were put in three experimental groups: 1) the "Vanilla" (control) group using only plain discussion forum features; 2) the "Sliders" group using a slider tool to rate opinions; and 3) the "Reflective tools" group using tools designed to support meta-dialogue, good question asking, and self-reflection (described below). The primary research hypothesis was that the features intended to support SD-skills, i.e. in groups 2 and 3, would be shown to do so based on hand coding of participant posts. We are also interested in relationships among skill use, posting activity, response relationships, and survey results.

Mediem Features. Mediem has been used in a number of dialogue contexts including interfaith discussions among college students. Figure 1A shows the Mediem home screen, with sections listing Dialogues ("Conversations"), Opinion Sliders, Participants, and Resources. Each section lists items that can be expanded for full view. Dialogues are semi-threaded discussion forums with additional features mentioned below. Normally participants in open-ended discussion will propose their own dialogue topics and "set the table" for a conversation by specifying certain parameters (number of participants, demographic information, etc.) and inviting others to join; however, in our study we used pre-determined dialogue topics entered by the facilitator. The Participants section shows participant profiles, and the listing can show graphical indications of demographic and other participant information. The Resources section allows participants to upload documents and links related to the conversation. We did not use the Participants or Resources features for this study.

---

[1] We worked with Idealogue to create an API for exporting the data from the dialogue (posts and other user actions) for our monitoring and data analysis. We also worked with them to build additional customization features supporting experimental trials.

Fig. 1. A, B: Mediem Home Screen and Sliders

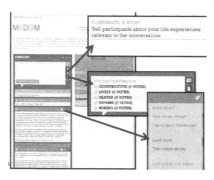

Fig. 2. Mediem Reflective Tools

The Mediem software was chosen for our study because it has a number of features designed to support deeper reflection and engagement. Figure 2 illustrates the expanded view of a Conversation (Dialogue), showing three such features illustrated separately. The discussion is viewed in the "Timeline" with most recent activity on top. Participants type their thoughts in the empty box at the top and submit. The Timeline shows posts and also other events (resources posted, conversation ratings, etc.) in temporal order. Posts are replied to using the arrow-shaped button above a post. To the left on the screen are tools for viewing participants, sliders, stories, and resources associated with the particular Conversation.

Figure 2 shows the three reflective tools used in the "Reflective tools" group. First is the Story feature, which gives participants a special place to say how the issue at hand relates to them personally, including relevant background information about themselves and "what is at stake" for them in the issue. Second is the Conversation Thermometer, a meta-dialogue tool that allows participants to rate (vote on) the quality of the conversation at any time. The choices can be customized by the administrator. Third is the Contribution Tag feature, which allows participants to give brief comments on other's contributions. It provides a fixed vocabulary similar to the sentence starters (or locution openers) used in other dialogue software, but the tags remain attached to the target post rather than starting a new post (see Soller, 2001).

The software includes an Opinion Slider, a polling feature used in the "Sliders" group, shown in Figure 1B. (As with Conversation topics, participants usually set up their own Opinion Slider questions, but ours were pre-defined for the classroom dialogues.) Sliders are thought to provide a motivational, brainstorming, and group-awareness function similar to Student Response Systems ("clickers"), which draw attention to differences, similarities, and diversity of opinion within the group as a whole. The slider gives a summary view of where participants stand on an issue.

Participants and Discussion Questions. Twenty six students in a college Alternative Dispute Mediation class discussed two topics (one each week over two weeks) in moderated discussions using Mediem. Students were randomly broken into three discussion groups of 8-9 members each, with all groups given identical questions. The activity was a required assignment that was part of the course and students were given class credit based on participation alone (not the content of participation). They were required to post at least once every day. In a prior class session students had brainstormed interesting and controversial topics for this activity. The discussion topics chosen were 1) Trayvon Martin killing in Florida, and 2) Gun Control.

Facilitation. We employed the service of experienced facilitators. To keep the control and experimental groups comparable, the facilitators were asked to keep their interventions to a minimum, and if they made an intervention in one group to do something similar, or at least something of similar length, in the other groups. Facilitator #1 facilitated all three groups during the Trayvon Martin discussion (week #1) and facilitator #2 facilitated all three groups during the Gun Control topic (week #2).

Data Collected and Analyzed. The three groups had similar numbers of students participating in the discussions (Vanilla 9, Sliders 8, Reflective Tools 9). There were 8 males and 14 females ranging in undergraduate grade level from sophomores to seniors, with one non-degree student. All text from student posts was collected; in addition, "reply" connections between posts were collected. Data were collected on Slider, Story, Conversation Tag and Thermometer use in the groups where these features were offered. All subjects were given a post-survey including 18 questions using a 5-point Likert "agree...disagree" scale.

Coding. Text of student posts was divided into segments and coded by two independent coders using a coding scheme developed by our group that focuses on social deliberative skills and other indicators of dialogue quality. Our coding scheme has 42 categories, 17 of which indicate deliberative skill. This scheme synthesizes prominent frameworks found in the literature (Black et al., 2011; Stromer-Galley, 2007; Stolcke et al., 2000) and adds codes for dialogue quality specific to SD-skills (Murray et al., in preparation). Cohen's Kappa Interrater reliability measure for this coding scheme is 71%, (76% agreement) averaged over five dialogue domains we have used it in(this level is considered "good" (ref) and is particularly good given the complexity of our coding scheme). For this classroom data that is the subject of this paper the interrater agreement is 77% and the Cohen's Kappa is 72%.

For this experiment, 7 codes were singled out for data analysis: *Intersubjectivity*: perspective awareness, perspective taking or question asking; *MetaTopic*: Birds eye or systemic view of the topic (related to complexity or systems thinking); *MetaD*: Meta-dialogue, discussing the quality of the dialogue and proposing changes to its structure;

Appreciation: Gratitude, affirmation of another's idea or situation); *Apology:* noting and/or taking responsibility for one's errors; and *Source Referencing*: mentioning a source for a fact or idea. A Total-SD-Skill score was computed for each segment by adding the scores of the seven skill measures for that segment. An average Total-SD-Skill score per segment was then computed for each student in each discussion.

Students who posted fewer than 5 times for both topics combined are excluded from statistical comparisons. Also, preliminary analysis revealed several issues with the Sliders group sufficient to lead us not to include this group; we compare only the Vanilla and Reflective tools groups.[2] Students in these two groups who met the criteria for inclusion happen to be balanced in total number and in gender, though not in grade level. Although the individual codes included in the study had been determined to show no effect due to grade (within-group ANOVAs ranging from $p = 0.25$ to $p = 0.78$), due to the difference in distribution of juniors and seniors, we continue to include grade as a potential factor in correlations.

4   Results

In this section we will report on: (1) the main question of whether the group using reflective tools showed higher (total and subskill) skill levels than the control (Vanilla) group; (2) look for possible relationships between SD skill scores and gender, post size and frequency, post reply statistics, tool use statistics, and survey results. Participation and basic statistics for the Vanilla and Reflective Tools groups:

- The data set over the two groups contains 241 posts and 516 segments; for an average of 15.06 posts for each student over both topics ($SD = 7.45$).
- The mean words per post was 53.60 ($SD = 42.12$) and the mean characters per post was 299.40 ($SD = 241.95$).
- We found no significant relationship between the number of posts and the length of posts among participants.

The average student skill scores as percentage of each student's segments were:

Intersub	Meta_D	Meta_Topic	Apology	Apprec.	Fact_Src	Src_Ref
25.08%	0.88%	5.51%	0.22%	1.30%	0.28%	1.20%

The main results of the study include   (see Stephens et al. 2013 for more detail):

- A main effect between Total-SD-Score and grouping, $F(1, 14) = 6.89$, $p = 0.02*$, $d = 1.46$ (a very large effect) in favor of the Reflective Tools group. Thus our main hypothesis was confirmed.

---

[2] In the Sliders group one student failed to follow instructions (did not use the sliders). This student dominated the discussion, contributing over a third of the total posts. Two other students in this group did not post enough to be included in the analysis. One student wrote a note to the facilitator claiming that one student in this group seemed overly critical and not respectful, which affected her feeling of safety.

- A significant relationship between Intersub and grouping, $F(1, 14) = 4.81$, $p = 0.05*$, $d = 1.05$ (a large effect) in favor of the Reflective Tools group. Intersub was strongly correlated with Total-SD-Skill, indicating that most of the effect of Total-SD-skill comes from the Intersub subskill. There was no significant relationship between any of the other subskills and group.
- ANOVAs revealed no difference due to gender on the Total-SD-Skill score or on any of the subskills except for Appreciation, where females scored higher, F (1, 14) = 5.59, p = 0.03. Six females had at least one segment coded Appreciation; none of the males did.
- From the survey, there was some positive correlation between Total-SD-Skill and self-reported Engagement (r = 0.44) and Learning (r = 0.21). These results conform to our intuitions that those exhibiting more skill would find the experience more positive, though we cannot infer causation in either direction.

Next we look more closely at two phenomena: the use of the reflective tools, and the reply structure among participants.

Student Replies to Each Other. The number of contributions that reply to (or refer to) other contributions is one indicator of a robust deliberation (Stromer-Galley, 2007; Suthers 2008). We analyzed several quantitative metrics related to this phenomenon. Our hypotheses were: 1. students with higher skill (especially the intersubjective code); 2. students showing positive survey opinions would post more replies; 3. the reflective tools would support more replies.

- The average number of posts per student that were explicit replies to posts of another student (Replies_by_me) were 10.59 (*SD* = 3.41), about 71%.
- The average number of replies each student received (Replies_to_me) was 10.35 (*SD* = 6.86).
- There was a correlation between Replies_by_me and Replies_to_me: R = 0.8284. In other words, students who replied more to posts of their fellow students received more replies in return.
- There was no main effect on Replies-by-me or Replies_to_me due to experimental group and no significant relationship between Replies_by_me or Replies_to_me and grade level within either group.
- There was no significant difference between genders in the numbers of Replies_by_me or Replies_to_me within the Reflective Tools group. However, within the Vanilla group, females replied to others significantly more often than males, t = 2.68, p = 0.04*; females replied more than twice as often as males.

In summary, our hypothesis that reflective tools would support more replies was not supported. A majority of the posts were replies to other posts and were replied to in turn; students who replied more to posts of their fellow students received more replies in return; and, interestingly females in the Vanilla group replied to the posts of others more than twice as often as did the males within that group.

Use of Reflective Tools. The reflective tools group had at their disposal a set of three tools that constitute innovations over what is offered by most discussion forum software: the scaffolded post comment tool, a discussion temperature rating, and a story tool where participants could write personal stories about the topic (see Figure 2). We hypothesized that there would be a positive relationship between the amount of tool use and evidence of social deliberative skill (presumably because making use of the scaffolding supports bringing skills to bear in the dialogue, but causation can not be inferred from the data). This hypothesis was confirmed in finding a positive correlation between intersubjective speech acts and total tool use (R=.54) and dialogue temperature tool (R=.85) (this was for the Trayvon topic, as discussed below).

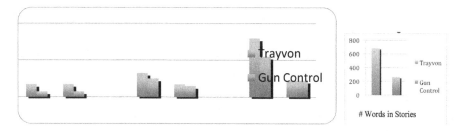

Fig. 3. A: Reflective tool use vs. topic; B: story words vs. topic

The amount of tool use is shown in Figures 3a and b. For this analysis we separated the data by discussion topic because we noted more tool use in the first topic, Trayvon Martin. As can be seen, students posted less in their stories, used the discussion temperature tool less, and posted fewer comments for the second topic (Gun Control). We believe this could have been due to several factors: the novelty and motivation to do this homework task could have worn off after the first topic; the Trayvon topic was more specific (involved specific people) and could have been related to more easily than the Gun control topic; Trayvon was salient from recent news reports; the second topic was facilitated by the less experienced facilitator. In general, the participation levels in the reflective tools group were acceptable but not particularly high. This concurs with the average survey Engagement rating, 4.0 in a 1-5 scale. This analysis also highlights the potential large effects of choice of topic and other context variables on measures of student deliberation and problem solving.

5   Summary

Internet-based social and technological innovations usually support increasing *quantities* of information and connectivity (e.g. the growing WWW, number of FaceBook friends, number of email and text messages per day) without supporting—and sometimes sacrificing—its *quality*. We join those calling for research and development of online systems that support communication and information quality, specifically, supporting more reflective thinking, deliberative dialogue, and mutual understanding in communications. This study suggests that simple scaffolding features can increase skillful deliberation online. We found a significant effect with (very) large effect size of reflection tools as supportive scaffolding for SD-skills.

Our attempts to use text classification to automate SD-skill assessment lead to only modest results, and we are working on further machine learning models for SD-skill classification, with earl encouraging results (Murray et all 2012; in submission; Xu et al. 2013). We are also developing a Facilitators Dashboard for visualizing deliberative dialogue properties and showing the visualizing the results of real-time automated analysis. Identifying methods for gently and broadly scaffolding SD-skills in online deliberation could impact many contexts: knowledge-building, situated learning, civic engagement, and dispute resolution.

References

1. Andriessen, J., Baker, M., Suthers, D. (eds.): Arguing to Learn: Confronting Cognitions in *Computer-Supported Collaborative Learning Environments*. Kluwer, Dordrecht (2003)
2. Azevedo, R., Guthrie, J.T., Seibert, D.: The role of self-regulated learning in fostering students' conceptual understanding of complex systems with hypermedia. Journal of Educational Computing Research 30(1), 87–111 (2004)
3. Baker, M., Andriessen, J., Lund, K., van Amelsvoort, M., Quignard, M.: Rainbow: A framework for analyzing computer-mediated pedagogical debates. International Journal of Computer Supported Collaborative Learning 2(2-3), 315–357 (2007)
4. Black, L., Welser, H., Cosley, D., DeGroot, J.: Self-Governance Through Group Discussion in Wikipedia Measuring Deliberation in Online Groups. Small Group Research 42(5), 595–634 (2011)
5. Gastil, J., Black, L.W.: Public deliberation as the organizing principle in political communication research. Journal of Public Deliberation 4(1), 3 (2008)
6. Graesser, A., McNamara, D.: Computational analyses of multilevel discourse comprehension. Topics in Cognitive Science 3(2), 371–398 (2010)
7. Graesser, A., Vasile, R., Zhiqiang, C.: Question classification schemes. In: Proc. of the Workshop on Question Generation (2008)
8. Herzig, M., Chasin, L.: Fostering dialogue across divides: A nuts and bolts guide from the Public Conversations Project. The Public Conversations Project, Watertown (2006)
9. Holman, P., Devane, T., Cady, S.: The change handbook: The definitive resource on today's best methods for engaging whole systems. Berrett-Koehler, San Francisco (2007)
10. Jordan, T., Andersson, P., Ringnér, H.: The Spectrum of Responses to Complex Societal Issues: Reflections on Seven Years of Empirical Inquiry. Integral Review 9(1) (February 2013)
11. King, P.M., Kitchener, K.S.: Developing reflective judgment: Understanding and promoting intellectual growth and critical thinking in adolescents and adults. Jossey-Bass (1994)
12. Kögler, H.H.: The power of dialog: Critical hermeneutics after Gadamer and Foucault. MIT Press, Cambridge (1992)
13. Kuhn, D.: A Developmental Model of Critical Thinking. Educational Researcher, 16–25 (March 1999)
14. Kuhn, D.: Metacognitive Development. Current Directions in Psychological Science 9(5), 178–181 (2000)
15. Lin, X., Sullivan, F.: Computer contexts for supporting metacognitive learning. In: Voogt, J., Knezek, G. (eds.) International Handbook of Information Technology in Primary and Secondary Education, pp. 281–298. Springer Science+Business Media, LLC (2008)
16. Linn, M.C.: Designing the knowledge integration environment. International Journal of Science Education 22(8), 781–796 (2000)

17. Murray, T., Woolf, B., Wing, L., Shipe, S., Shrikant, N.: A manual coding scheme for social deliberative skills and other attributes related to dialogue quality (in preparation)
18. Murray, T., Woolf, B.P., Xu, X., Shipe, S., Howard, S., Wing, L.: Supporting social deliberative skills in online classroom dialogues: Preliminary results using automated text analysis. In: Cerri, S.A., Clancey, W.J., Papadourakis, G., Panourgia, K. (eds.) ITS 2012. LNCS, vol. 7315, pp. 666–668. Springer, Heidelberg (2012)
19. Murray, T., Xu, X., Woolf, B.P.: An Exploration of Text Analysis Methods to Identify Social Deliberative Skills (in submission, 2013)
20. Puntambekar, S., du Boulay, B.: Design and development of MIST—A system to help students develop metacognition. J. Educational Computing Research 16(1), 1–35 (1997)
21. Reiser, B.J., Tabak, I., Sandoval, W.A.: BGuILE: Strategic and conceptual scaffolds for scientific inquiry in biology classrooms. In: Carver, S.M., Klahr, D. (eds.) Cognition and Instruction: Twenty-Five Years of Progress, Erlbaum, Mahway (2001)
22. Scardamalia, M.: Knowledge-building environments: Extending the limits of the possible in education and knowledge work. In: DiStefano, A., Rudestam, K., Silverman, R. (eds.) Encyclopedia of Distributed Learning, pp. 269–272. Sage Public, Thousand Oaks (2003)
23. Scheuer, O., Loll, F., Pinkwart, N., McLaren, B.M.: Computer-supported argumentation: A review of the state-of- the-art. Int. J. of Computer Supported Collaborative Learning 5(1), 43–102 (2010)
24. Soller, A., Martínez-Monés, A., Jermann, P., Muehlenbrock, M.: From Mirroring to Guiding: A Review of State of the Art Technology for Supporting Collaborative Learning. I. J. Artificial Intelligence in Education 15(4), 261–290 (2005)
25. Spragens, T.A.: Reason and Democracy. Duke University Press, Durham (1990)
26. Stephens, L., Murray, T., Shrikant, N., Wing, L., Xu, X., Woolf, B.P.: An evaluation of online forum features supporting social deliberative skills: Preliminary results (submitted to AIED, 2013)
27. Stolcke, A., Ries, K., Coccaro, N., Shriberg, J., Bates, R., Jurafsku, D., et al.: Dialogue act modeling for automatic tagging and recognition of conversational speech. Computational Linguistics 26(3), 39–373 (2000)
28. Stromer-Galley, J.: Measuring Deliberation's Content: A Coding Scheme. Journal of Public Deliberation 3(1) (2007)
29. Suthers, D.D.: Empirical studies of the value of conceptually explicit notations in collaborative learning. In: Okada, A., Buckingham Shum, S., Sherborne, T. (eds.) Knowledge Cartography, pp. 1–23. MIT Press, Cambridge (2008)
30. Suthers, D.D., Connelly, J., Lesgold, A.M., Paolucci, M., Toth, E.E., Toth, J., Weiner, A.: Representational and advisory guidance for students learning scientific inquiry. In: Forbus, K.D., Feltovich, P.J. (eds.) Smart Machines in Education: the Coming Revolution in Educational Technology, pp. 7–35. AAAI Press, The MIT Press, Cambridge, MA (2001)
31. Toulmin, S.E.: The uses of argument. University Press, Cambridge (1958)
32. White, B., Shimoda, T., Frederiksen, J.: Enabling students to construct theories of collaborative inquiry and reflective learning: computer support for metacognitive development. International J. of Artificial Intelligence in Education 10, 151–1182 (1999)
33. Xu, X., Smith, D., Murray, T., Woolf, B.: Analyzing Conflict Narratives to Predict Settlements in EBay Feedback Dispute Resolution. In: Proceedings of the 2012 International Conference on Data Mining (DMIN 2012), Las Vegas (July 2012)

Part IV
Designing and Developing Novel On-Line Social Experiences

A LivingLab Approach to Involve Elderly in the Design of Smart TV Applications Offering Communication Services

Malek Alaoui and Myriam Lewkowicz

Troyes University of Technology. Tech-CICO, UMR STMR 6279 12, rue Marie Curie
CS42060 10004 Troyes Cedex -France
{malek.alaoui,myriam.lewkowicz}@utt.fr

Abstract. Aging is a new step of life with a lot of changes that could be related with physical, cognitive and social frailties. Rather than addressing autonomy and dependency issues for which a variety of assistive technologies has been designed, our aim is to define how ICTs could alleviate elderly loneliness, in order to cope with their social frailty. We make the hypothesis that TV is a good medium for this purpose and we design Smart TV applications dedicated to foster the social interaction among elderly. We adopt a living lab approach, which assure us of an early engagement of the end-users.

Keywords: Elderly, Online communities, Design, Living lab, Smart TV.

1 Introduction

Nowadays, elderly are encouraged and are willing to stay at home as long as possible, rather than entering institutional care. This issue has been addressed in several research initiatives focusing mainly on the development of a variety of assistive technologies. From our point of view, ageing well cannot be reduced to physical and cognitive frailties and technologies have to tackle the quality of life of the elderly by improving their psychological well-being and self-esteem.

Extensive research has established the strong relationship between social isolation and health. Even, recent studies have showed that the lack of social relationships influences the risk of mortality for aging people [1]. Older adults may be particularly vulnerable to social isolation and diminished social network because of transitions from work, loss of a spouse, and the onset of illnesses that limit social participation. Older adults with poor or weak social networks are 60% more likely to develop cognitive decline due to isolation or high stress levels caused by the death of a spouse [2]. Social isolation and the gradual reduction of the mobility and autonomy lead older people to depression, which could have a fatal impact on their health and longevity.

A.A. Ozok and P. Zaphiris (Eds.): OCSC/HCII 2013, LNCS 8029, pp. 325–334, 2013.

This paper charts a work in progress in the frame of the European AAL project FoSIBLE[1]. This project aims at providing technological support for social interaction among elderly people.

In the following, a description will be given of our research context and issues, the adopted design methodology and the involvement of elderly people in the design process. We explain user sampling and how interviews were done in France (the end-user association which is one of the partners of the FoSIBLE project is French). User requirements are presented in the form of result synthesis and design implications. We conclude by describing the derived services and perspectives to adapt usability testing to suit our selected participants.

2   Online Communities and Social Support among Elderly People

Interacting with other people, participating in groups and social relationships are critical to people's well-being [3] [4]; social relationships support social well-being directly as well as indirectly by increasing self-esteem [3]. Social engagement, which refers to making social and emotional connections with people and the community [5] is increasingly being seen as critical to health and general well-being of elderly [6].

A means of fostering social interactions and enhancing social connectedness is to make use of technologies that enable individuals to access information and to communicate with others. In particular, providing individuals with the opportunity to use the Internet may be one means of reducing social isolation because it offers the opportunity to increase contact with others, to communicate with new social groups and to pursue old or new interests—in essence, to reconnect with the world in a new way. This, in turn may have a positive impact on psychological health [7]. Research results emphasize the potential of modern technology to help reducing the risk of social isolation and compensating disabilities [8][9]. This body of work has shown the potential of these services to enable older adults to keep in touch with their social network and to improve their quality of life.

So, contrary to some critics addressed to the Internet, it does not pull people away from face-to-face contact, making them less sociable, less able to relate to other people. In contrary, virtual communities could help promoting social inclusion among elderly [10]. Online community involvement encourages greater social contact via other means, especially face-to-face and telephone. In fact, the engagement in the online community increases the involvement of the members in the offline community [11]. Moreover, older adults friendships have been found to contribute to psychological well being of older adults in more positive ways than family relationships [12]; elderly participating in age-designated online communities appear to value personal recognition, along with the opportunity to learn from peers, and to interact socially with members of their peer group. By asking their peers in forums and chat groups, they may readily get access to the help they need.

---

[1] Fostering Social Interactions for a Better Life of the Elderly.

Many online communities involving elderly have been studied. One of the largest virtual communities for elderly is the Australian GreyPath, which offers various available options, such as forum, blogs and chat rooms. In interviews [13], members of GreyPath frequently expressed feeling like they belong to this community of people who share their life experiences and with whom they could discuss things relevant to their age group. The assumption is that perceived friendliness will have a positive effect on the elderly's attitude toward using a social platform.

3   Research Issues

Within the FoSIBLE project, our researches are devoted into creating services for elderly by rethinking the use of well-known existing technologies and to broaden their scope to be more affordable by older people.

The questions that arise are related to the role of technologies to cope with social isolation and are methodological:

1. Could we consider the development of innovative services based on an interactive Smart TV platform as a solution for elderly' social isolation issues? In general, elderly are reluctant to use computers and most of them consider computers as a working tool rather than a communication media [14]. We suppose that TV is a good alternative for the elderly reluctance about using computers. Moreover, knowing that their relatives are watching the same program than them could be a good opportunity to start a discussion whereas it is not always obvious for them to start an interaction, as they may be afraid to disturb.
2. Acknowledging that it is technically possible to develop online applications for social interaction among older people will the feelings of mutual trust and of belonging be sufficient to build virtual community among elderly who are used to face-to-face interactions?

We can find excellent ergonomic guidelines to support the design of interfaces for the elderly and to help developers in building applications for interactive television [15], [16]. The use of these guides provides a real added value in terms of accessibility, however it does not reflect the functional needs of the future users and it is not focused on sharing among different stakeholders. Thus, designers do not have any tool allowing them to focus on the social aspects of interactive television applications, even if there is recent research that attempts to provide answers to this issue, including Geerts and Grooff [17], who introduced heuristics to support the social practices through interactive television services. It is essential for our research to have effective methods to interact with elderly end-users and to collect data on their needs concerning relationships. Then, how could we adapt the established user-centred methods for developing innovative applications for elderly people accessible via TV? More precisely, how these methods could be adjusted to allow us to effectively gather the expected needs of the elderly in terms of social interaction[18]? Having in mind that a real-life experiential environment allows all stakeholders to concurrently consider both the performance of a service and its adoption by users at the earlier stage of research and development, we have adopted a Living Lab approach.

4   A Living Lab Approach for User Centered Innovation

Direct and autonomous involvement of the future users in the technical design of functionality and in their evaluation is needed to promote a more proactive role by bringing ideas from their experience, practices desires and frustrations. Such participation ensures that a broad range of interests, needs, and values are addressed in the design work. For so doing, we are adopting a living lab approach. It will allow us to put the users' perspective at the forefront of every design decision. The real challenge of adopting a living lab approach consists in involving all the stakeholders in the design process by taking into account the micro-context of their everyday contexts for discovering emerging scenarios, usages and behaviors. A living lab approach is particularly promising due to the opportunity it gives to try out, and obtain user feedback on services at different levels of development, where relatively large numbers of users may be involved in the innovation process.

We have established a small-scale living lab. Services access was given to a relatively small number of users and the feedback loop between users and designers is made as short as possible. Such approach will enable us to learn from older people what functionality and attributes are important to them, what motivates them to use a product or service, and what factors would hinder the usability, as well as to conceptualize how parts of older people's lives could be improved by the use of technology. It is also important to be aware of the context provided by older people's lives, and to discover when technology should be introduced and when its introduction would have a negative effect on the older person's quality of life.

4.1   Involving Elderly in the Design Process

Older people are frequently perceived and portrayed as being resistant to technology. In fact, some of them are willing to accept novel digital technologies into their lives. The issues that arise with acceptance do so because the ways in which older people construct their decision to use or not use these technologies are fundamentally different to the ways younger adults do.

Designing digital technologies for older people is not simply a matter of addressing the immediate consequence of the most obvious functional impairments. In practice, the designers are ill equipped to design technologies for older people [19]. Inappropriate design is a mechanism through which society disables people with impairments by ignoring them.

End-Users Selections Process

For the selection of the potential end-users, we organized a meeting which took place on the conference room of Les Arcades (the end-user organization which participates in the FoSIBLE project), in Troyes (North- East of France). The participants received an invitation letter from Les Arcades, announcing the purpose of the FoSIBLE project. During this meeting, we presented the project. Two brochures were made for this occasion and given to the participants. One gives a general overview of the project and the other includes a set of usage scenarios of social television, so that participants can get an idea on some potential opportunities for using the system that we intend to design.

The involvement of the end-users is based on voluntary participation. Ten volunteers were recruited, eight women and two men aged between 65 and 90 years. Two Participants were never married and the others are widowers and do have children and grandchildren. Almost of the participants do not suffer from chronic physical disability except one who suffers from arthritis affecting her hands and feet. Four of them are basic computer and Internet users.

The volunteers did not feel isolated and so not really convinced that the project objectives are related to their situation and directly relevant to their interests. But, they stated that they were widely interested in new technologies and defining services which could be helpful for the future. Understanding an older person's interaction with a design depends on the older person showing realistic levels of motivation and this was a consideration in recruiting our volunteers.

Two of the participants quitted the project before the in-house rollout. One because of family issues with their children and the second was afraid not to be able to perform the experience. She argued that she is ok with her TV and does not want a new one.

A Set of Personas
Personas [20] are user archetypes whose goals and behavior patterns are well understood. Personas help to visualize and imagine the typical and realistic usage workflow and environment of the real user. Design for the archetype conduct to satisfy the broader group of people represented by that archetype. We defined a set of personas from the first series of semi-interviews with the participants [21]. Their description includes behavior patterns, goals, skills, attitudes, and environment, with a few fictional personal details to bring the persona to life. Such detailed persona is a key to the suppression of any tendency for the developers to usurp or distort the real end-user lead to the situation where developers make products solely based on their own interpretation of the older person's needs, a solution that can be ineffective and patronizing.

4.2   The Existing and Expected Use of TV
The interviews revealed the picture of the daily activities and current use of existing technologies in the daily life of our participants. The obtained information also provided us with design implications and user requirements.

TV as a Communication Device
Face to face social interactions mostly take place in societies, and especially in Les Arcades. The research confirms that certain relationships appear to reduce subsequent

loneliness: going to church, volunteering, seeing friends or neighbors, and talking with them on the phone. Interviewees expressed needs in relation to the use of their TVs to allow sharing real-life moments: grandchildren making them drawings, sharing comments during watching their favorite programs and also after (water cooler effect) instead of doing it on the phone. For those who have friends at the retirement house, they would appreciate to communicate with them through television (as they say TV is the main occupation in the retirement house). The idea of communicating with other people than family or friends to discuss various topics (television programs, shared interests) seems also good opportunity from their point of view.

Features have also been proposed like recording broadcasts or movies in order to share them afterwards, and searching for information. We also note that participants focus on sharing and communicating about their activities rather than around the TV programs.

Reflecting the situation that many of the elderly had to give up their former hobbies, it would be interesting to offer them media supported possibilities to help in doing this hobby again. This could be constructed as some coaching activities or by virtualizing the hobby, for example online book club. By those activities we could build up social communities which could lead to a better social integration of the elderly.

TV for Collective Activities

In terms of cooperative activities, our interviewees proposed some very interesting features that would be useful in their daily lives and would help them feel better:

- They would appreciate to learn things on television and to share their comments and impressions with others – for instance exchanging recipes during or after a cooking course. They would also like to exchange reading tips and to share advices.
- They would enjoy participating to dedicated and tailored sessions on television (e.g. yoga), and especially virtually attending to sessions at the same moment than their friends from Les Arcades.
- They would enjoy virtually sharing games (crosswords, sudoku, bridge) with their relatives and friends.
- They would like to benefit from on-line poems written by one of their friends.

Another participant also mentioned the importance of common interests. For example, a support group for those suffering from a health issue, or for informal caregivers.

Usability Issues

Participants expressed the need for more accessible and less complicated interfaces than computers. About control interface, participants who do not have disabilities think using a keyboard would be possible but not very practical. They would prefer a digital tablet with digital pen, even if they find that the voice control is also a simpler interface than the keyboard. The digital control interface could be used for collective games as crosswords, puzzles or sudoku, and to exchange drawings with small children. For the participant suffering from arthritis, the digital tablet with digital pen is also difficult to use.

Given mentioned requirements results, we here summarize the translation of the collected data from the study into functionalities by having in mind present technology possibilities and expressed user needs.

4.3   Prototypes and Derived Functionalities

Applications implementing expressed needs by our users are developed on a smart TV platform. Smart TV[2] is a set of web-based services running on an application engine installed in digital TV connected to the Internet. A Smart TV application is a special type of widget that is implemented on a browser and runs on the TV screen. Viewing an application is very much like viewing web pages using a web browser on an ordinary PC. Screen resolution, hardware specifications and remote controller make differences between applications and web pages. An application is a web page consisting of HTML, CSS and JavaScript. The smart TV service makes possible to extend the functions of the TV, so that users can obtain useful information and interesting contents on their TV screen.

Combining the possibilities offered by this technology and the collected data from the end-users, we have identified that the following services would be helpful for the elderly:

- Awareness services through the use of a "buddy list"
- Synchronous communication services: being able to chat with some "buddies" when looking at the same TV show.
- An asynchronous communication service taking the form of integrated clubs organized by interests. Thus, new communities of interest could arise which are able to build or expand their knowledge collaboratively.

The users access the platform by widgets. The background is slightly transparent so the image of the TV program can still be visible. On this platform users will be able to use a tablet PC (figure 1) as an additional terminal to navigate on the TV menu, but also to enter text. The tablet can additionally be used to display messages, when the TV is switched off or to be able to read messages in another room (e.g. read a recipe sent by a friend in the kitchen).

When looking at a TV show, the user can decide if one of these three widgets should appear: "Online Friends", "Chat", and "Participate in clubs".

When the user selects "Online Friends" using the tablet or the blue button of the remote control, s/he will be able during the TV program to see a buddy list with all the friends who are watching TV at that time, with the channel information and their

---

[2] http://www.samsungdforum.com

Fig. 1. Tablet Interface for Entering Text

recent activities on the platform. "Chat" can be opened and closed via the tablet or the red button on the remote control. It allows sending short messages to the online friends for instance to initiate a discussion when watching a TV program. The messages are typed on the tablet.

"Participate in Clubs" is launched using the yellow button of the remote or the tablet. It shows the list of existing clubs (yoga, philo cafe, cooking, poetry, reading ...). After entering a club, one can comment or create a new topic by using the tablet. For example, in the reading club, one can browse existing reviews, comment them or add a new one (figure 2)

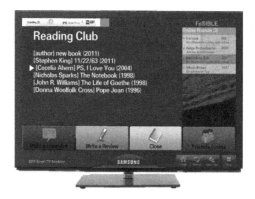

Fig. 1. Browsing Reviews in the Reading Club

5   Next Step –Evaluating the Proposed Services

In order to get a deeper understanding on how users perceive the developed services, and according to the living lab approach that we have adopted, we have planned evaluation at home of the elderly, during one year, together with design iterations.

Our participants are enthusiastic and enjoy the opportunity to provide their perspectives and influence. However, incorporating them in the evaluation process involves taking into account their doubts or anxiety about their ability to successfully perform or complete the activities.

Participants are now equipped at home with the FoSIBLE system and we are still working on the evaluation protocol. Information about the capabilities, limitations, and needs of older adults will be collected during this evaluation phase.

6   Conclusion

Monitoring is a solution for older people to be able to live in their environment as long as possible, especially for those suffering from disabilities related to age or diseases. However, we believe that we need to take into consideration social isolation due to loss of relatives and weak social network as a factor contributing to depression and may have negative impacts on the general health status. For that, we would like to allow elderly to interact online using the devices they already have at home.

We are iteratively designing SmartTV applications to support socially oriented activities for older people. They are actually being developed and the InHouse rollout started this month and will last six months. Rollout includes TV, Tablet, and the Integrated Widgets. The analysis and evaluation of the use of this platform being designed in a user-centred approach will help us to answer our research issues.

Acknowledgment. This work was partly funded by the European Community and the National Research Agency (ANR) through the AAL 169 program (FoSIBLE Project No. ANR-09-AALI- 002-04).

References

1. Holt-Lunstad, J., Smith, T.B., Layton, J.B.: Social Relationships and Mortality Risk: A Meta-analytic Review. PLoS Med 7(7) (2010)
2. Seeman, T.E.: Social ties and health: The benefits of social integration. Annals of Epidemiology 6(5), 442–451 (1996)
3. Crossley, A., Langdridge, D.: Perceived Sources of Happiness: A Network Analysis. Journal of Happiness Studies 6(2), 107–135 (2005)
4. Schueller, S.M., Seligman, M.E.P.: Pursuit of pleasure, engagement, and meaning: Relationships to subjective and objective measures of well-being. The Journal of Positive Psychology 5(4), 253–263 (2010)
5. Victor, C., Scrambler, S., Bond, J., Bowling, A.: Being alone in later life: loneliness, social isolation and living alone. Reviews in Clinical Gerontology 10, 407–417 (2000)
6. Tomaka, J., Thompson, S., Palacios, R.: The relation of social isolation, loneliness, and social support to disease outcomes. Journal of Aging and Health 18, 359–384 (2006)
7. Mellor, D., Firth, L., Moore, K.: Can the Internet Improve the Well-being of the Elderly? Ageing International 32(1), 25–42 (2008)
8. Czaja, S.J., Charness, N., Fisk, A.D., Hertzog, C., Nair, S.N., Rogers, W.A., Sharit, J.: Factors predicting the use of technology: Findings from the Center for Research and Education on Aging and Technology Enhancement (CREATE). Psychology and Aging 21, 333–352 (2006)
9. Cornejo, R., Tentori, M., Favela, J.: Ambient Awareness to Strengthen the Family Social Network of Older Adults. Computer Supported Cooperative Work (CSCW), 1–36 (2012)

10. Burmeister, O.K.: Virtuality Improves the Well Being of Seniors through Increasing Social Interaction. In: Berleur, J., Hercheui, M.D., Hilty, L.M. (eds.) HCC9 2010. IFIP AICT, vol. 328, pp. 131–141. Springer, Heidelberg (2010)
11. Kavanaugh, A.L., Patterson, S.J.: The Impact of Community Computer Networks on Social Capital and Community Involvement. American Behavioral Scientist 45, 496–509 (2001)
12. Nussbaum, J.F.: Friendship in Older Adulthood. In: Hummert, M.L., Wiemann, J.M., Nussbaum, J.F. (eds.) Interpersonal Communication in Older Adulthood: Interdisciplinary Theory and Research. Sage Publications (1994)
13. Burmeister, O.K., Foskey, R., Hazzlewood, J., Lewis, R.: Sustaining Online Communities Involving Seniors. The Journal of Community Informatics (2012)
14. Lehtinen, V., Näsänen, J., Sarvas, R.: "A little silly and empty-headed": older adults' understandings of social networking sites. Paper presented at the Proceedings of the 23rd British HCI Group Annual Conference on People and Computers: Celebrating People and Technology, Cambridge, United Kingdom (2009)
15. Carmichael, A.: Style Guide for the Design of Interactive Television Services for Elderly Viewers. Independent Television Commission. Winchester, UK (1999)
16. Dickinson, A., Arnott, J., Prior, S.: Methods for human computer interaction research with older people. Behav. Inf. Technol. 26(4), 343–352 (2007)
17. Geerts, D., Grooff, D.D.: Supporting the social uses of television: sociability heuristics for social tv. Paper presented at the Proceedings of the 27th International Conference on Human Factors in Computing Systems, Boston, MA, USA (2009)
18. Eisma, R., Dickinson, A., Goodman, J., Syme, A., Tiwari, L., Newell, A.F.: Early user involvement in the development of information technology-related products for older people. Universal Access in the Information Society 3(2), 131–140 (2004)
19. Lindsay, S., Jackson, D., Schofield, G., Olivier, P.: Engaging older people using participatory design. Paper presented at the Proceedings of the 2012 ACM Annual Conference on Human Factors in Computing Systems, Austin, Texas, USA (2012)
20. Cooper, A.: The Inmates Are Running the Asylum. Macmillan Publishing Co., Inc. (1999)
21. Alaoui, M., Lewkowicz, M., Seffah, A.: Increasing elderly social relationships through TV-based services. Paper presented at the Proceedings of the 2nd ACM SIGHIT International Health Informatics Symposium, Miami, Florida, USA (2012)

The Role of the Community
in a Technical Support Community: A Case Study

Donald M. Allen[1] and Thomas Schneider[2]

[1] Cisco Systems, Inc., Technical Services, Colorado Springs, USA
donallen@cisco.com
[2] Cisco Systems, Inc., Technical Services, Zurich, Switzerland
thschnei@cisco.com

Abstract. Resource tagging has become an integral and important feature in enabling community users to easily access relevant content in a timely manner. Various methods have been proposed and implemented to optimize the identification of and access to tags used to characterize resources across different types of social web-based communities. While these user-focused tagging methods have shown promise in their limited application, they do not transfer well to internal business applications where the cost, time, tagged content, and user resources needed to implement them is prohibitive. This paper provides a case study of the process, tools, and methods used to engage users in the development and management of a tag taxonomy (folksontology) used to characterize content in an internal technical support community in the Cisco Global Technology Center.

Keywords: component; tag, taxonomy, folksonomy, social community, folksontology, case study.

1   Introduction

Cisco launched an internal technical support community to enhance support and troubleshooting collaboration among 3500 support engineers across eight primary technical centers, as well as numerous other smaller technology groups around the globe. The focus of the internal support community (called TechZone) is to replace the historical standard of practice using internal email mailing lists to post questions and request assistance from experts. The use of the mailing lists relied heavily on the submitter's knowledge of the mailers associated with specific technologies and the willingness of the email list members to respond to those requests. This type of interaction led to poor predictability of when and whether a response would be received. In addition, different support engineers would repost the same requests when they encountered the same problem at a later time.

One goal of the support community is to provide a better structure for posting requests for assistance; to make submission targets more obvious; and to prove a mental

A.A. Ozok and P. Zaphiris (Eds.): OCSC/HCII 2013, LNCS 8029, pp. 335–344, 2013.

model of the technologies and the semantics of the technology hierarchy. Cisco has thousands of products and services that are supported by the Cisco Technical Services group, each with its own vocabulary to describe the product, its features, and the types of problems encountered by customers using it. This issue is similar to large retail and community support web sites where web site structure and navigation is important to guiding users to the correct location and obtain product support. User enabled support communities are common on the internet. Companies and end user communities establish them to facilitate the sharing of configuration and troubleshooting lessons learned among community members. The business impact on a company when a user fails to post to the correct discussion board or does not receive a correct and timely response via this type of free service is minimal since the user is getting what he paid for. When a company, such as Cisco, uses the same user support community to assist support engineers who are in turn assisting paying customers the impact to the company could be considerable. Cisco considered it paramount to address the navigability of the over 290 support communities supported in TechZone in order to ensure proper posting and facilitate timely response. A number of product hierarchies exist within Cisco to support various business activities associated with designing, developing, manufacturing, and selling products. None were deemed applicable since our support organizations were not consistently organized around products. This paper describes how Cisco employed collaborative tools to enable target users of the community support system to construct and manage the navigational structure of the internal support site.

A second goal of the development of the support community is to capture the knowledge developed during discussion posts and convert it into content available to other engineers to avoid future repetitive posts. Various enhancements were made to the community application to improve access to the available content. The enhancements required a quality of content characterization (metadata) which was not available from the content in the system.   Tagging is common among content rich web sites (e.g. Flickr, Delicious) to improve resource (e.g. pictures, websites) access. In order to maximize content "findability" and to move the organization to a common support-focused vocabulary, the development team worked with the internal support community using social collaboration tools to develop an augmented folksonomy[1] to improve content access. The logic, tools, and processes that were employed in this effort will be described below. Three efforts within the overall implementation effort are discussed in the paper:

1. Definition of the discussion board navigational model,
2. Identification of the structured vocabulary (folksonomy) used to characterize the discussion posts and knowledge content in support of timely and accurate access.
3. The design and development of a tool to enable members of the community to self-manage the structured vocabulary.

---

[1] A folksonomy is a system of classification based on the activity of sorting information into categories based on the consensus of the users of the information.

2   Tags, Taxonomies, Folksonomies and Labels

Web sites such as Delicious (formerly del.icio.us) and Flickr and the research associated with their use demonstrates the importance of augmenting user supplied content with tags as a method to improve user access [1-2]. The emergence of folksonomies [3], including user-created and managed tag sets, demonstrates the efficacy of utilizing tag taxonomies to further enhance user content accesses [4] and to provide additional structure to the deployed tag set. The majority of the research around collaborative tag assignment and tag taxonomy focuses on two areas. The first focus is on the assignment of tags involving the collaboration of a group of content reviewers. Their goal was to assign the appropriate tags to a piece of content [1]. The second area of focus is on the application of computational logic to large, pre-tagged content data set with the goal of surfacing tag-relatedness in support of identifying tag navigational hierarchies [5,9] or tag presentations in the user interface (e.g. tag clouds). Both methodologies require specific resource availability. Collaborative tagging requires the availability of users who can review content and assign the appropriate tags, while algorithmic analysis requires the availability of large data sets, in terms of tag content, in order to characterize tag usage.

Note: Cisco utilized *Social Support Online Community* software licensed from Lithium to implement the TechZone support community. The Lithium software provides both a tag and label infrastructure for annotating content (discussions and articles). The tag system is consistent with the community-based unmanaged, informal functionality common to Web 2.0. The label infrastructure utilizes an administrator controlled folksonomy system [1]. In order to avoid confusion between the two terms in this paper and to be consistent with prior research, the term tag is be used in place of labels.

The application of existing research methods to the TechZone support community is problematic. As noted earlier there are 290 separate communities within TechZone: in essence a community of communities. Each community targets a specific technology and contains discussions and articles focused on that technology. The TechZone underlying infrastructure supports a document library of articles developed to address specific product problems and solution. An analysis of the available articles was conducted during the development of the new tag taxonomy. At the time of the analysis, the one year old site contained over 6,000 articles. The number articles per community ranged between 4 and 233, with an average of 21 articles per community. A detailed analysis of the tag utilization revealed that on average only 2.7 tags were assigned per article with a range between 2 and 22. Considering that the system required that at least one tag be assigned to an article prior to publication and that required tag was automatically assigned based on the content type of the article (e.g., How-to, Troubleshooting, etc.), users were assigning fewer than 2 tags to characterize an article. Applying established tag refinement methods to the available data set was considered impractical. Collaborative tagging would require the time and coordination of support engineers across the globe whose job responsibilities preclude such an effort; moreover, there was no management buy-in to the process. The existing data set is not sufficient within each communities to apply the techniques used in prior research since the since tag sets would need to be community-specific (a tag used in the Security Firewall community would not necessarily be applicable in the TelePresence Call Control community).

A hybrid, targeted folksontology [6] approach was taken to construct a tag taxonomy that identified the common tags across communities as well as those that would be specific to a single or subset of communities. A folksontology combines the distributed, community driven tag set with the disambiguated, hierarchical and formality of a taxonomy. Our approach involved technical leaders from each of the different technologies (e.g. IP Telephony, LAN Switching, etc.) who worked together using collaboration tools to construct the set of communities and associated list of tags targeted to their technology. Technical leaders were paired with a taxonomist to augment that tag set with structure and additional metadata to improve overall utility of the resulting tag set [4]. This approach accommodated the rollout plan of new technology to the different groups (which included training, communications, and content migration) while at the same time afforded the construction of a tag taxonomy that included tags common across technologies (e.g. install, configure, troubleshoot) as well as those specific to the technology (e.g. AAL2 Trunking, ASR5000).

2.1   Tag-Zation with Representation

Kiu and Tsui [7] identified two problems associated with constructing and using taxonomies traditionally constructed by taxonomists and/or domain experts: 1) the disconnection between the terms identified by the "experts" and those employed by the vocabulary users and 2) the difficulties involved and costs associated with keeping the taxonomy up-to-date. Kiu and Tsui's propose the application of computational algorithms and data mining techniques to address these issues. We chose a more user-centric design approach, one that actively engaged representatives of the user communities and gave them ownership of the tag taxonomies (to their taxonomies) in order to address the disconnection and update problems.

In order to provide direct control of the tag taxonomy to members of the community, we designed and implemented an application to enable the technology community representatives to manage the tag set (additional information about the Label Manager can be found in the corresponding section later in this document). Previous research on the use of controlled vocabularies versus social tagging demonstrates some advantages to using controlled vocabularies in terms of content retrieval [8].

In order to address the issues of tag differentiation, group think tendencies, and relevant tag availability, we decided to provide richer information about a tag to enhance the end user's access to and understanding of a tag. In addition, there was an interest in expanding the application of the tag taxonomy into other areas of the business. One area of interest is in the streamlining of the flow between the creation of a customer support case, the content in TechZone available to address the case and the support engineers with the knowledge and expertise to provide assistance. A single, common vocabulary to characterize a support case, content, and support engineer knowledge provides a foundation for automation.

The need to share and exchange the tag taxonomy within Cisco and with Lithium and a desire to base our development on industry standards led us to select the Simple Knowledge Organization System (SKOS). SKOS provides a standard method to represent knowledge organization using the Resource Description Framework (RDF) [11]. The SKOS schema provided the foundation for many of the metadata elements needed to support tagging. The table below identifies the tag metadata used:

Table 1. Tag metadata used

Attribute	Description
ID	System generated unique ID
Preferred Tag	Tag that will be used by the system when presenting the tag to the user
Definition	Text describing the tag – could include an expanded acronym
Scope Note	Text describing the context (technology or sub technology) where the tag is intended to be used
Alternate Tags	Set of tags that are equivalent to the preferred tag such as synonyms and expanded acronyms
Hidden Tag	Set of tags that are equivalent to the preferred tag but are not displayed to users (e.g. project code names)
Category	Specialize grouping of tags based on their similarity, used to make user tag access easier – Activity, Content Type, Environment, Feature, Miscellaneous, Problem, Cisco Product, Third-Party Product, and Protocols & Standards
Communities	Set of support communities where the tag has a strong affinity
Broader/Parent	Set of tags that have a more general definition than the tag (the parent in a parent-child relationship)
Narrower/Child	Set of tags that have a more specific definition than the tag (the child in a parent-child relationship)

Tag metadata is used by the search, filter, and tag assignment components in the UI to improve the overall usability of tags in the following ways:

- Tool tips presented when a user moved the mouse pointer over a tag displayed the tag description and the broader and narrow information if present.
- The preferred, alternate and hidden tags are used during search and when assigning tags to content.
- Tag category and the broader/narrower attributes are used display the tags in a hierarchy component used for filtering and assignment.
- The community attribute is reserved for future use (see the Future Plans section).

3   Support Community Identification

3.1   The Process

A participatory design approach [10] was utilized during the construction of both the community structure and the tag set. A design team was established for each of the major technology areas. Each design team consisted of experts from the technology group, a program manager, a developer, and human-computer interaction expert (who also played the role of the taxonomist). Each technology design team completed the following process:

1. Held a kickoff meeting in which the overall process was discussed along with deliverables and timelines.
2. Trained technology experts on the social community application which included the different capabilities they were expected to configure (community hierarchy, tags, etc.).
3. Seeded a pad in Etherpad [13] with a template which included instructions and an example structure to follow.
4. Established a schedule with checkpoints for group review.
5. Mapped the community to existing problem code taxonomy to facilitate system-to-system data exchange. This step was purposefully sequenced after the group constructs the community hierarchy in order to prevent the existing structure from influencing how team organizes the community.
6. Identified the set of tags to characterize the content for each of the identified communities (details of this process are provided in the Tags and Taxonomy Process section of this document).

3.2   Lessons Learned

Using Etherpad to collect the community structure proved to be a good method for collaboration among the team members. The ubiquitous access to the pad enabled users across different geographic locations and time zones to collaborate on the building and refinement of the community structure. A signification shortcoming however was the inability to provide comment or the reasoning behind a change or suggested change. Typically these kinds of discussions migrated to email and became unavailable to some of the team members.

4   Tag and Taxonomy Identification

4.1   The Process

The support community structure developed during the initial phases of a deployment was used as the framework onto which the tags were identified and organized. The following process, similar to the one used for the community structure, was used: a kickoff meeting, followed by training, interim checkpoint meetings, and a finalization meeting. The goal of the training was to educate the design group on how the users in the support community would leverage the tags to search for and filter content. The training also provided some general guidelines and heuristics for identifying relevant tags. We wanted to avoid being too prescriptive in terms of the number of tags we were expecting and avoided providing hard and fast rules that needed to be followed. Our desire was to have the design teams identify the tags most used for folks in their organization to characterize their questions (discussion posts) or to find the solutions to their problem (articles).

4.2   Tag Identification Guidance

The following guidance was provided as part of the technologist training:
When to add a new tag

- Tag does not exist or new tag is not an alternate to an existing tag
- Existing tags do not provide the differentiation needed

When to use acronyms versus words

- Acronyms should be used when they are the common method of identification
- Do not create new acronyms, only use established ones

Using single word versus multiple word tags

- A tag should not combine object and action
- Multi-word tags should be composed of words that are unable to stand alone (Active Directory) and identify the intended target
- Avoid using existing tags in new multi-word tags (categories and product names are the exception)

When to modify an existing tag

- Changes to shared tags (used by other dictionaries) should be negotiated where it makes sense

Use the lemma/headword as a tag

- Other forms should be alternate tag (configure – configuring)

Differentiate noun and verb version of a headword

- Example - Install (verb) and Installation (noun)

How to identify product model numbers

- Avoid the use of model numbers without qualifier (e.g., "7921 IP Phone" instead of "7921")

4.3   Tag Identification

The technology representatives collaborated in the identification of the tags using the Etherpad created to construct the community structure. When the community structure was complete, reviewed and agreed upon, the Etherpad was versioned and all subsequent changes to the finalized tag set were either communicated to the Taxonomist for update or were created using the Tag Manager application (see below for more details). We found that some groups migrated to other tools to identify their tags (such as Microsoft Excel) in order to better track common versus community-specific tags.

4.4   Role of the Taxonomist

During the early phases of the technology rollouts to Tech Zone the Taxonomist played an active role to ensure that the proposed tags followed the guidelines presented during training to preserve the integrity of the tag metadata.   There was a propensity demonstrated by some groups to combine product and activities together into a single tag (e.g. "Configure ASR500") and for acronyms to be added without the corresponding expanded version.   Additional tag refinement was required in the Activity category in order to differentiate the task being performed versus situations where the task had already been performed (e.g. installing a router versus configuring an installed router).

5   Tag Infrastructure

As noted earlier many social communities have moved toward tag hierarchies primarily driven by computational analysis of tags or user collaboration to create tag taxonomies.   Cisco lacked the body of tagged content and the business justification for user collaboration (i.e. the cost associated with engaging support engineers by taking them off the work queue).   Our decision was to develop a tag taxonomy infrastructure that could support our tag metadata, hierarchical needs and would integrate into an existing user interface of the deployed support community web application. We worked with Lithium for approximately a year to get the infrastructure in place in Social Support Community (Lithium) and to design and implement an application to manage tags (Cisco - see the next section).

5.1   Tag Management

A tag management application (representative self-managed tag taxonomy) was developed to provide the technology representatives a tool to create, edit, and update the shared tag set used within the support communities.   The application included the ability to search for tags as well as to filter the tag set based on community and tag category.   In order to address the need for tags that are specific to certain technologies, a user is able to add tags to communities they have permission.   To support common tags users are able to associate exiting tags to their communities.   The application supports user entry of all of the metadata described above.   A number of usability enhancements were added to prevent users from entering duplicate tags either as single or multiple word tags.

The Tag Management application is a web-based application deployed via Apache HTTP server and Apache Tomcat. The internal data representation of the tag taxonomy is based on the Resource Description Framework (RDF) which is based on the W3C standard to describe metadata [11], provide an interoperable taxonomy exchange format, and can easily be merged with other Cisco ontologies. The Sesame [12] infrastructure was used for backend storage of the tags, user access/authorization, and the storage of the community discussion board hierarch.

5.2   End User Request for Tag Changes

A technical community within TechZone is used to engage end users in the tag management process. Users can post new tag requests to the discussion board to facilitate discussion with their peers and to interact with the taxonomist and technology tag representatives. Once a change has been properly vetted the Tag Manager application is used to update the tag set and push the update to TechZone.

6   Future Plans

6.1   Automatic Tagging

Ideally technology could be used to automatically assign the tags to content or to suggest tags to the user based on an algorithmic analysis. We are currently evaluating natural language processing capabilities that might be able to enable this. We suspect having a controlled tag vocabulary will make this processing a bit easier; however, some degree of specialized logic (such as considering context) will be required to ensure the user is not overburden with spuriously relevant tags. We hope to report on this work in the future.

6.2   Existing System Integration

As with any large, established company there are a number of existing systems that might benefit from understanding the mapping of the TechZone tags into their workflow. A couple of efforts currently underway include: 1) Automating the association of tags in a legacy document publishing system used in the external publication of content to Cisco's public site to streamline moving TechZone articles to that site, and 2) Integrating the use of the TechZone tag set into our customer case reporting and management tool to enable the cross communication between the two systems more efficient.

6.3   Tag Lifecycle Management

As other researchers have noted, in order to maintain the freshness and relevancy of a tag set it is important to analyze the use of tags within the system. To efficiently perform this analysis tools are needed that can map historical tag utilization against product lifecycle for both Cisco and Third Party products. Understanding tag usage as it relates to the evolution of a product (initial introduction, updates, and end-of-life) is critical to effectively manage product tags. It will not be enough to look at simple tag utilization to understand the usefulness of a tag; evaluations must be done in context. Combining the data and the product lifecycle will be a challenge.

The role of a tag taxonomist in the tag management process is one we must explore and resolve. The breadth and depth of product, feature, and problem knowledge required to manage such a large content domain is too large for a single person to undertake. Adopting a hybrid model combining the skills of the technology specialist sand taxonomists appears to provide a viable approach; the details of that relationship have yet to be sorted out.

7   Conclusions

This paper described a process and an application developed that addresses the requirement to develop a tag taxonomy in a business environment where neither the content needed to algorithmically identify neither tags nor the business justification for engaging community users in the tag identification process were present. The material presented proposed a method for engaging technology experts in the tag identification process as well as in the maintenance of the tag taxonomy. Monitoring and analysis of the use of tags in TechZone and the tag maintenance activities of the technology experts should provide insight into the efficacy of this approach.

References

1. Robu, V., Halpin, H., Sheppard, H.: Emergence of Consensus and Shared Vocabularies in Collaborative Tagging Systems. ACM Transactions on the Web (TWEB) 3(4), 14:1–14:34 (2009)
2. Heymann, P., Garcia-Molina, H.: Collaborative Creation of Communal Hierarchical Taxonomies in Social Tagging Systems. Stanford Info Lab Technical Report (2006)
3. Hammond, T., Hannay, T., Lund, B., Scott, J.: Social Bookmarking Tools A General Review. D-Lib Magazine 11(4) (2005)
4. Trattner, C., Körner, C., Helic, D.: Enhancing the Navigability of Social Tagging Systems with Tag Taxonomies. In: Proceedings of the 11th International Conference on Knowledge Management and Knowledge Technologies. ACM, New York (2011)
5. Astrain, J.J., Echarte, F., Córdoba, A., Villadangos, J.: A Tag Clustering Method to Deal with Syntactic Variations on Collaborative Social Networks. In: Gaedke, M., Grossniklaus, M., Díaz, O. (eds.) ICWE 2009. LNCS, vol. 5648, pp. 434–441. Springer, Heidelberg (2009)
6. Van Damme, C., Hepp, M., Siorpaes, K.: FolksOntology: An Integrated Approach for Turning Folksonomies into Ontologies. In: Proceedings of the ESWC Workshop "Bridging the Gap Between Semantic Web and Web 2.0" (2007)
7. Kiu, C., Tsui, E.: TaxoFolk: A hybrid taxonomy–folksonomy structure for knowledge classification and navigation. Expert Systems with Applications 38(5), 6049–6058 (2011)
8. Golub, K., Moon, J., Tudhope, D., Jones, C., Matthews, B., Puzon, B., Nielsen, M.: En-Tag: Enhancing Social Tagging for Discovery. In: Joint Conference on Digital Libraries (JCDL), pp. 163–172. ACM Press, New York (2009)
9. Simpson, E.: Clustering tags in enterprise and web folksonomies. HP Labs Technical Reports, HPL-2007-190, pp. 222–223. AAAI Press, Palo Alto (2008)
10. Ehn, P.: Scandinavian Design: On participation and Skill. In: Schuler, D., Namioka, A. (eds.) Participatory Design, Principles and Practices, pp. 41–78. Lawrence Erlbaum Associates (1993)
11. SKOS Simple Knowledge Organization System, http://www.w3.org/2004/02/skos/
12. openRDF.org, http://www.openrdf.org/about.jsp
13. Etherpad, http://etherpad.org/

Experiences by Using AFFINE
for Building Collaborative Applications
for Online Communities

Mohamed Bourimi and Dogan Kesdogan

Information Systems Institute,
University of Siegen, Germany
bourimi@wiwi.uni-siegen.de, kesdogan@uni-siegen.de

Abstract. Continuous problems and deficits in developing complex and
ever-changing (software) systems led to agile methods, e.g. Scrum. Nevertheless, the problem of considering a plethora of different functional as well
as nonfunctional requirements (N/FRs) remains unsolved and gains in
importance when engineering state-of-the-art software. The current tide
of approaches aims at handling every single NFR by an individual process integrated into Scrum, yielding a process complexity which can not
be handled properly. Scrum-based AFFINE[1] was designed explicitly to
provide an alternative solution to over-complex design- and development-
processes and still considering all kinds of NFRs early enough in the
process. In this paper, we discuss collected findings by using AFFINE in
various projects dealing with the development of software for user-centered
online communities towards some evidence of its suitability.

Keywords: Agile Software Process, Nonfunctional Requirements Engineering, Security and Usability, User Experience, Scrum, AFFINE.

1 Motivation

Applications, covering many collaboration measures and social aspects for many
important areas of our professional and leisure life activities, are increasingly
used in our information society. Technical support for this is mainly provided
through different kinds of collaborative applications also known as groupware.
Software systems and applications supporting collaboration are considered as
socio-technical systems in the Human-Computer Interaction (HCI), IT Security,
and Computer Supported Collaborative Work (CSCW) research fields [1–3][2].
Shneiderman et al. state in [1] that most computer-based tasks will become collaborative because most work environments have social aspects. From a general
software engineering (SE) point of view, the socio-component is related to human

---

[1] Agile Framework For Integrating Nonfunctional requirements Engineering.

[2] Due to the multidisciplinary nature of our contribution and difficulty to consider
related work from each research field, we cite in the following one representative
work from each research community for argumentation completeness.

A.A. Ozok and P. Zaphiris (Eds.): OCSC/HCII 2013, LNCS 8029, pp. 345–354, 2013.
© Springer-Verlag Berlin Heidelberg 2013

factors (developers, end-users etc.) and their influence on Information Systems and Information Technology (IS/IT) projects is significant from various perspectives (i.e. development and management perspectives). The inherent involvement of the (non-deterministic human) socio-component makes the significance and impact of human factors in the development of collaborative applications more crucial than in other IS/IT projects. The ultimate goal of any IS/IT project is to efficiently reach the following aims:

1. reducing costs by optimizing resource allocation,
2. minimizing product delivery failure risk (increasing so opportunity of success), and
3. reaching end-users/customers satisfaction by ensuring good product quality and User eXperience (UX).

Researchers from various fields recognized that solutions of static nature cannot satisfy changing needs, e.g., requirements emerging from the usage of a software system. With respect to collaborative applications, different agile approaches promise better consideration of changing requirements and of human factors. They at least strongly and constantly early involve end-users and better react on uncertainties in the development process (e.g. difficulties related to requirements elicitation, negotiation, etc.). Thus, various user-centered and participatory design methodologies with different degrees of agility are increasingly adopted today when building sophisticated groupware solutions. Furthermore, various human factors related issues arise due to the adopted agility, e.g., between users' and developers' needs. Such needs remain mostly neglected in our opinion and have to be better considered. Agile development is believed to help in reaching these aims, even evidence is still investigated for different project aspects. SE practitioners agree on the need of evidence supporting this believe and state the rarity of studies confirming it. Lack of evidence is the most-cited criticism against agile development methodologies even they are gaining importance.

In this paper, we report on experiences of agile development for building collaboration software with AFFINE [4] by handling nonfunctional requirements (NFRs) at different levels (i.e. management and development level) and avoiding the complexity within the process thereby. The remainder of this paper is structured as follows: Problem analysis is addressed in the following Section. Section 3 presents AFFINE's design while Section 4 discusses first collected experiences by using it for building collaborative applications for online communities. Section 5 concludes our contribution.

2   Problem Analysis and Statement(s)

Recently, agile method(ologie)s such as Extreme Programming (XP) and Scrum are becoming popular in industrial and academic fields. They are used in order to better match changing requirements and human factors[3] in the development of

---

[3] Human resources constitute an average of 70% of SE projects costs. *"Project management issues (costs, time, schedule) are often considered as non-functional requirements as well"*, however, at the project organizational/management level [5].

groupware (e.g., [6]). Scrum as an agile framework [7] is experiencing a wide acceptance nowadays [8]. It provides explicit support for addressing human factors related issues in its framework, as shown in recent studies, over the influence of human factors on IS/IT projects [9, 8]. However, practitioners of agile methodologies stress, that adequate support for NFRs is not provided (e.g., it is not easy to consider NFRs in user stories). With respect to Scrum, Ambler states in [10] that *"Scrum's product backlog concept works well for simple functional requirements, but as I described in 'Beyond Functional Requirements on Agile Projects' (www.ddj.com/architect/210601918), it comes up short for nonfunctional requirements and architectural constraints."* [SIC]. In this respect, the identified gap of properly considering NFRs in agile methods is the main reason preventing the adoption of agility in the security (requirements) engineering area for instance. Indeed, a systematic literature review shows explicit reserve [11]. This is originating from various factors i.e.: (i) the nature of security oriented research targets to be formal as possible in order to assess traceability of requirements, their completeness etc., and (ii) security requirements engineering methods were designed and mostly used with classical software life cycle processes (e.g. waterfall or V model cf. Fig. 1) with expected slots for assurance and risk analysis techniques etc., thus being not easily portable or even suitable to agile methods [12] (at least without further research [13]). However, recently one also can notice an emerging need for more investigation with respect to the suitability of agility for security, especially to spare costs while ensuring earlier consideration of security requirements. Figure 2 depicts a suggestion made by some practitioners[4] from the industrial field on how to extend an agile process (Fig. 2-a) to consider security best practices (Fig. 2-b).

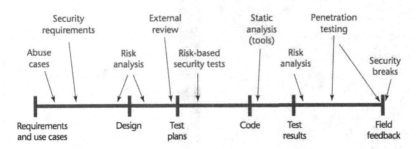

Fig. 1. Software security best practices within a sequential process (from [12])

In contrast to usability, such reserve against agility cannot be noticed in the HCI community. In fact, usability engineers and UX experts tend to ask for agility since it supports earlier involvement and tests while developing the

---

[4] Agile and Secure: can we do both?
http://jazoon.com/portals/0/Content/ArchivWebsite/jazoon.com/
jazoon09/download/presentations/7102.pdf (Last access: March 2013).

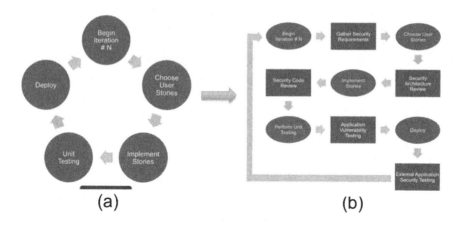

Fig. 2. Suggested extension of an agile process to integrate security practices (by Jason Li and Jerry Hoff)

intended product. However, one can state that most of software and requirements engineering method(ologie)s and development processes followed in each research community are going their own way for dealing with their NFR of importance.

For instance, Lee et al. presents an integrated approach known as eXtreme Scenario-based Design (XSBD) towards agile UX. Figure 3 (a) depicts the "curse of complexity" when trying to extend the basic Scrum scheme (lower part) with

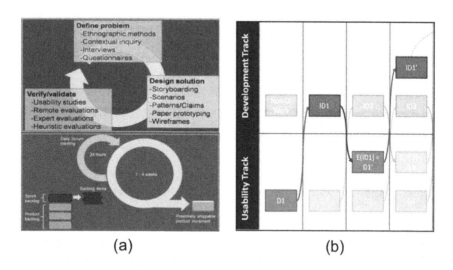

Fig. 3. Usability best practices integrated into agile Scrum (from Lee's Tutorial Materials at CHI'12 and [14])

different sub-processes for the plethora of different methods addressing NFR (upper part) in analysis, design and implementation phases for complex systems. Based on further experimentation and comparative analysis they also currently try to address XSBD usage for distributed teams by considering time factors in the process [14] (cf. Fig. 3-b).

We argue that, while the first tide of ignoring NFRs mostly took place at the level of addressing them as *"add-ons, often postponed, not considered as system-wide properties"*[5] etc., the current tide is doing it at the level of studying their consideration and integration in agile method(ologie)s and processes (and mostly contemplated separately from other (N)FRs as shown above for security and usability people). From both presented extensions of agile processes above (in each example), it is obvious that the consideration of all (N)FRs is a crucial task and one can ask him/herselfs the following questions:

- How could a consideration/integration of all NFRs look like in agile methods? What will be the resulting scheme of the steps to be followed in the resulting method(ology) or process?
- How much best practices from each *"NFR" Engineering* field should be adopted and explicitly addressed? Who will decide that (by considering that in the same research community different directions exist, mostly not harmonizing with each other)? Which effect has the nature of the product to be developed on such decisions (e.g. critical safety products will surely follow established and well-proven processes)?
- Will the resulting method(ology), process etc. then still be applicable and by whom (in terms of qualifications)? How much will such an adoption cost?

3   AFFINE's Design and Its Suitability for Our Purposes

The result of our research for answering related issues to the previously listed questions is reflected in AFFINE [4]. AFFINE's main targets consist of *simultaneously* addressing previously cited deficits by:

1. conceptually considering NFRs early in the development process,
2. explicitly balancing end-users' with developers' needs, and
3. proposing a reference architecture providing support for NFRs in order to overcome conceptual lack of guidance and support for efficiently fulfilling NFRs in terms of a software architecture in general.

The nature of our (collaborative) scenarios and prototypes/products to be developed, implies earlier consideration of privacy and (multilateral) security along with other competing NFRs, such as usability and social/group awareness throughout the whole software life cycle process. In our case this nature demands an agile way of development. We do this exemplarily in AFFINE by extending Scrum to enforce their earlier consideration at development as well as management level. Choosing Scrum is not just based on mentioned arguments above

---

[5] As stated by Santen for Security in [15] and which remains true for all NFRs.

such as selected practitioners' experiences and empirical studies (e.g. [16, 9, 8]), but also on own positive experiences in other projects. Constitutive requirements for AFFINE were gathered based on a detailed analysis of existing work from various research fields (i.e. HCI, CSCW, Security, and SE) as well as based on experiences from various projects on designing and implementing groupware systems or applications needing privacy and (multilateral) security consideration in general.

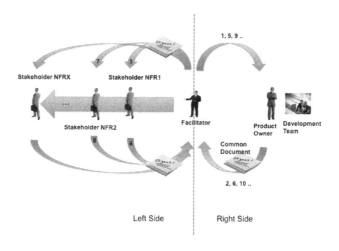

Fig. 4. The big picture of the Scrum-based AFFINE (from [4])

In summary, Scrum was chosen due to its high tailorability, its support for human factors consideration[6], not only at the level of development but also at the management level, and its increasing adoption in industry as well as positive first-hand management experience with Scrum. Nevertheless, even though Scrum is helping in overcoming many issues in this respect, some of the important phases need to be specified more sharply as this is the case for requirements engineering/gathering in it (cf. [16]). E.g. the usage of a common document[7] in AFFINE (s. Fig 4) helps in better eliciting requirements and keeping track of changes (e.g. traceability of change requirements, decisions for solving conflicts for a given design among NFRs, etc.). The consideration of NFRs best practices is ensured by explicit involvement of experts in the respective iterations. While in our case, Scrum defines the coarse agile production process, experts still have the chance to integrate their wished practices while developing the product (in the requirements engineering phases, i.e. gathering, elicitation and negotiation).

---

[6] In contrast to other agile approaches, Scrum supplies the support for agile project management in general. XP, e.g., primarily focuses on development aspects [7].

[7] Agile methodologies tend to avoid documentation. However, many extensions in different research fields suggest recently to rethink such practice.

Choosing the necessity as well as degree of accuracy is delegated to them and ne-gotiation as well as conflict solving mechanisms are defined in AFFINE (refer to [4] for how AFFINE is executed, e.g. follow numbering in Fig. 4 for a perfect iter-ation without breakdowns that could result from conflicts among stakeholders). Furthermore, we suggest a concrete mapping of NFRs by using Service-Oriented Architectures (SOA) and Aspect-Oriented Programming (AOP) techniques (fol-lowed since 2006 in our group for this kind of socio-technical software).

4   Experiences by Using AFFINE

We used AFFINE in various projects from 2009 until now to investigate some evidence about its suitability for building collaborative applications. The most important ones are the iAngle[8] and iFishWatcher[9] projects which deal with support for online mobile communities. The iAngle project itself emerged as a spin-off from the EU project PICOS[10] that dealt with privacy and identity man-agement in mobile communities. PICOS followed a user centered and scenario based proceeding for eliciting the gathered needs and requirements (such as user stories, interviews and questionnaires) for three different mobile communities (Taxi Drivers Community, Angling Community, and Gamer Community). The Angling Community is built by recreational anglers who explore water bodies and coastal areas, to an extent that is unattainable by scientific projects. They spend enormous time and effort investigating fish communities. The PICOS and iAngle location-based services (LBS) scenarios are of collaborative nature which means, that they presume the interaction of the community members (i.e. en-tering watercourses and fishing spots, rating those spots, etc.). The prototypes implemented various LBS scenarios such as "Sharing Fishing Sites" with dif-ferent use cases like "Show Fishing Spots" and "Add Fishing Spots"; as well as "Localizing Contacts around Me". Various functional extensions followed with the time and are reflected in the results listed on the respective websites.

The iAngle project was started at the University of Siegen after PICOS lab and user trials which took place on the 27th/28th November 2009 in Vienna and 12th/13th December 2009 in Kiel. Lab and user trial tests were conducted by members of the Center for Usability Research & Engineering in Vienna and Leibniz Institute of Marine Sciences in Kiel. While the iAngle and iFishWatcher projects strongly followed AFFINE, PICOS played a big role in designing it as well as unintentionally comparing it with classical SE processes. A full descrip-tion of the results goes beyond the scope of this paper. The interesting point is that stakeholders who observed the development process described it as fol-lows:"The process methodology followed for the Picos project during development was different within the teams: One team, referred to as the AFFINE-team, fol-lowed the AFFINE framework described in this paper. The other three software development teams followed traditional software engineering methods such as the

---

[8] http://www.uni-siegen.de/fb5/itsec/projekte/iangle/index.html

[9] http://www.ifishwatcher.org/news.php

[10] http://www.picos-project.eu

waterfall model". The AFFINE team was responsible for developing LBS as well as communication functionalities for the Angler Community for the first prototype. This includes also the design of the graphical user interface (UI). A single document containing these scenarios and related use cases was then circulated. The development team involved 3 developers and a product owner as well as a facilitator. This document used UML for further eliciting the requirements and provided first UI prototypes. After this, the document was circulated to the end-users again, then to the privacy and usability stakeholders and so on. A PICOS Platform stakeholder, responsible for integration, was only contacted if missed functionality had to be supported. At a given time, the usability stakeholders introduced a sophisticated click dummy to reach better prototyping. The AFFINE team oriented further UI work to fulfill the click dummy UIs. However, the agile method followed, corresponded not to standard Scrum.

The three projects primarily focused on the evaluation of usability and privacy/security, involved usability experts formulated their observations with respect to AFFINE as follows: *"The expert usability evaluation for the different prototypes was carried out through heuristic evaluations. Usability problems and security aspects were assessed by criteria relevant for usability and guidelines. The reviews from the expert evaluations were communicated via multiple channels such as emails or telephone conferences including small reports. A general observation is that reaction to changes was faster in the AFFINE team than in the other teams in the case of PICOS. Moreover the AFFINE team actively asked for usability feedback during implementation, which made the process even more proactive and faster. Considered from a usability expert perspective in PICOS, the usability feedback for the AFFINE team approach was more focused and delivered in small portions. This approach reliefs the usability reviewer from evaluating hundreds of screens and enables them to focus on certain aspects. Besides the expert evaluations, end-users are additionally directly integrated in the project through lab and field tests. The results will be communicated and influence a second phase of development. The review for lab and field tests is not of a quick nature as it is more complex to set up lab tests with real end-users and gain results. Therefore quick usability reviews are more suitable for agile approaches such as AFFINE."*

They also stated that: *"The AFFINE approach allowed the integration of HCI instruments such as usability expert evaluations during the whole development process while considering privacy and security as well. Usability expert evaluations are very suitable to solve the ad-hoc problem solving needs inherent to agile methods. Generally this approach is more successful insofar as, the sooner NFR problems (such as usability and privacy problems) are detected, the less cost sensitive are the changes. This is even more important, as deficits in usability and UX have great impact on privacy issues as well. E.g. it is a well known fact, that good usability and UX are important factors for trust .. the team implementing the AFFINE process achieved better results regarding usability, user experience and privacy on the interface level than teams implementing following a traditional software engineering process. The AFFINE framework requires involving*

NFRs such as usability, user experience or privacy throughout the development process; therefore they have been an integral part from the beginning of the development process. The framework itself incorporates several small cycles that assures all stakeholders to be included. The AFFINE-team reacted instantly to the feedback given by the usability team and used it for further implementation .. In general, design for usability and for privacy have to be an integral part from the beginning of the project, and the agility, flexibility and rapidness of AFFINE meets the aims of reacting to changes very quickly. Especially in projects in the context of NFRs, appropriate agile methods to overcome these challenges are beneficial in direct comparison to traditional approaches.". The iAngle and iFishWatcher projects involved under- and post-graduate students from the University of Siegen and partner institutes (in addition to Germany, from Spain and the Philippines). These students were introduced to AFFINE (and Scrum). Stakeholders in both projects are listed on the websites (i.e. students who participated and performed tasks under supervision of experts for usability, privacy and security as well as SE experts). In the case of iAngle/iFishWatcher, the same PICOS Angling Community was involved. The sprints were very short (5 to 6 days), however, not continuos due to restrictions in academic settings. In general, the evaluation with all experts stated that also this kind of distribution of work was still conform to Scrum and reached at the end very good acceptance.

5   Conclusions and Future Work

The AFFINE framework incorporates several short cycles which assure that all stakeholders are included and that reaction on needed changes can happen in an agile way. To be accurate, the core assumption of this contribution is based on the following: (i) AFFINE is suitable for the development of collaborative applications which could profit from agility due to their complex nature, (ii) AFFINE provides an empirical framework that is powerful enough to handle the problems of early and adequately (according to experts) addressing NFRs without making the process of production complex, and (iii) experts' involvement helps in meeting (i) and (ii) in a multilaterally and qualitatively acceptable manner for all stakeholders within the project. Without (iii) the reader might imagine which process will emerge, if stakeholders are simultaneously extending a process to meet their best practices within their community of interests. Currently we are in the process of analyzing collected data for AFFINE (also in other projects, e.g. the EU funded di.me project) and preparing the results for more accurate scientific dissemination in respective communities (e.g. Empirical SE, Security and Usability Requirements Engineering conferences etc.). Further, we introduced the AFFINE method to practitioners in workshops. A first resonance showed the simplicity of understanding and performing AFFINE-based exercises (e.g. in form of simulation or in different projects works). In summary, first experiences promise great suitability of AFFINE for future work of multidisciplinary nature (HCI and IT Security/Privacy communities in this contribution). Further efforts will focus on the questions listed above and that still need answers and evidence.

Acknowledgments. Thanks are due to Thomas Barth, Eva Ganglbauer, Joerg M. Haake, and Bernd Ueberschaer (in alphabetical order) as well as all people who contributed with design or development activities related to AFFINE.

References

1. Shneiderman, B., Plaisant, C.: Designing the User Interface: Strategies for Effective Human-Computer Interaction, 4th edn. Pearson Addison Wesley (2005)
2. Cranor, L., Garfinkel, S.: Security and Usability. O'Reilly Media, Inc. (2005)
3. Gross, T., Koch, M.: Computer-Supported Cooperative Workspace. Oldenburg (2007)
4. Bourimi, M., Barth, T., Haake, J.M., Ueberschär, B., Kesdogan, D.: AFFINE for enforcing earlier consideration of nFRs and human factors when building socio-technical systems following agile methodologies. In: Bernhaupt, R., Forbrig, P., Gulliksen, J., Lárusdóttir, M. (eds.) HCSE 2010. LNCS, vol. 6409, pp. 182–189. Springer, Heidelberg (2010)
5. Cremers, A.B., Alda, S.: Organizational requirements engineering (ch. 9) (2010), http://www.iai.uni-bonn.de/III/lehre/vorlesungen/SWT/RE05/ slides/09_Nonfunctional%20Requirements.pdf (last accessed, February 2013)
6. Schümmer, T.: A Pattern Approach for End-User Centered Groupware Development. Schriften zu Kooperations- und Mediensystemen - Band 3. JOSEF EUL VERLAG GmbH, Lohmar - Köln (August 2005)
7. Schwaber, K., Beedle, M.: Agile Software Development with Scrum, 1st edn. Prentice Hall PTR, Upper Saddle River (2001)
8. França, A.C.C., da Silva, F.Q.B., de Sousa Mariz, L.M.R.: An empirical study on the relationship between the use of agile practices and the success of scrum projects. In: Proceedings of the 2010 ACM-IEEE International Symposium on Empirical Software Engineering and Measurement, ESEM 2010, pp. 37:1–37:4. ACM, New York (2010)
9. Li, J., Moe, N.B., Dybå, T.: Transition from a plan-driven process to scrum: a longitudinal case study on software quality. In: Proceedings of the 2010 ACM-IEEE International Symposium on Empirical Software Engineering and Measurement, ESEM 2010, pp. 13:1–13:10. ACM, New York (2010)
10. Ambler, S.: Complex requirements on an agile project. Online (2008)
11. Salini, P., Kanmani, S.: Survey and analysis on security requirements engineering. Comput. Electr. Eng. 38(6), 1785–1797 (2012)
12. McGraw, G.: Software security. IEEE Security and Privacy 2, 80–83 (2004)
13. Beznosov, K., Kruchten, P.: Towards agile security assurance. In: Proceedings of the 2004 Workshop on New Security Paradigms, NSPW 2004, pp. 47–54. ACM, New York (2004)
14. Lee, J.C., Judge, T.K., McCrickard, D.S.: Evaluating extreme scenario-based design in a distributed agile team. In: CHI 2011 Extended Abstracts on Human Factors in Computing Systems, CHI EA 2011, pp. 863–877. ACM (2011)
15. Santen, T.: Security Engineering: Requirements Analysis, Specification, and Implementation. Habilitation, Fakultät Elektrotechnik und Informatik, Technische Universität Berlin (2006)
16. Ambler, S.: Beyond functional requirements on agile projects. Dr. Dobb's Journal 33(10), 64–66+ (2008)

Context Management for RFID-Based Distributed Interaction Spaces

Pedro G. Villanueva, Félix Albertos, Ricardo Tesoriero, Jose Antonio Gallud,
Antonio Hernández, and Víctor M.R. Penichet

University of Castilla-La Mancha
Escuela Superior de Ingeniería Informática de Albacete
Campus Universitario s/n, 02071 Albacete, Spain
{pedro.gonzalez,jose.gallud,ricardo.tesoriero}@uclm.es

Abstract. Information system management in distributed interaction spaces is
not an easy task because the information should be contextualized in the space
it is being manipulated in order to keep it consistent and coherent to the users.
For instance, museum visitors usually have difficulties to associate the information provided by an electronic guide while they are moving inside the building.
The association/contextualization of the information to a physical space is not
an easy task. This article presents the system of management of contextual information CAIM to solve this problem from the management point of view, allowing managing virtual contexts, and from the point of view of the end user.
CAIM assures that the information is provided with coherent and consistent
manner in the different contexts from distributed interaction spaces. The article
shows a case of use study and an evaluation of CAIM system implemented by
means of technology RFID.

Keywords: HCI, Virtual Contexts, Evaluation.

1   Introduction

Every day the scenarios are more common where several users participate simultaneously to make tasks in common, with great variety of personal devices and interactive screens. This tendency does that the use of the new paradigm of distributed interaction scenarios is becoming increasingly important and is moving to the traditional
interaction scenarios.

There are a great variety of distributed interaction scenarios. Next, some of them
are enumerated like for example the work meetings scenarios: WallShare [1], i-Land
[2], Connectable [3]; e-learning scenarios: MPrinceTool [4], Co-Interactive Table [5];
tourist and cultural scenarios: Interactive EcoPanels RFID [6], etc. This work is centered in a concrete type of scenarios, the scenarios where through interactive panels,
provided with technology RFID, certain contextual information referring to these
panels or referring to the environment is shown to the users.

A.A. Ozok and P. Zaphiris (Eds.): OCSC/HCII 2013, LNCS 8029, pp. 355–364, 2013.
© Springer-Verlag Berlin Heidelberg 2013

The paradigm of the distributed interaction spaces entails a series of problems. One of them is that these spaces consume or generally make use of information that must be available in a set of devices that lodge the user interfaces. In addition, a typical problem that we can be found in this type of scenarios is to detect the change between contexts, so that the information shown the user is coherent with the context.

Some problems also affect the administrators of the resources, for example when it must associate the objects with the RFID tag that are made generally on a plane of the surroundings, instead of in this way making it in-situ on the own objects, causing possible errors at the time of associating them. Another problem with the administrators is at the time of making the maintenance of the labels. Until now we worked with the identifier of label RFID, therefore whenever a label was replaced, the data base had to be updated in the server and offline devices have to be updated.

System CAIM puts solution to these problems from the point of view of the management and from the point of view of the end user, allowing the management and consumption of contextualized information.

The document is structured of the following way. In this section an introduction to the problem is made and the proposal appears briefly, later is made a review by some related works. In section 3 the proposed system is described, next in section 4 considers a case of study that is evaluated in section 5, in the section 6 we present a discussion, concluding finally with results in section 7.

2   Related Work

In this section we will see some works related to the system that we propose. We have identified a series of works that they have in common the RFID technology and interactive panels for the provision of services, and works designed to computerize the cultural spaces offering multimedia information to users. Finally, a concept that we consider is slightly related to context management such as Content Management Systems.

Interactive EcoPanels RFID [6] is a collaborative and context-sensitive application attached to the concept of social software. Its main purpose is to allow users to share opinions and ideas related to the environment, using simple natural gestures and sensitive panels with RFID technology. Another interesting project is Smartmaps [7] consisting sensorised map using RFID technology, through which the user interacts via gestures with your mobile device. Within the field of video games there are interactive games based on RFID to improve care in children with TDAH and people with intellectual disabilities [8, 9]. In the environment of cultural spaces can be found works as GUIMUININ, which allows anyone through your mobile device to know where is located and through its location receive multimedia information. Similar works are Cyberguide [10], Guide [11], Smart Sight Tourist Assistant [12] e Irreal [13]. The Context Management Systems (CMS) [14] allow you publish, edit and modify multimedia content which is then accessible by users. Our Context

Management Systems shares certain features with the CMSs. Of all the works mentioned none of them faces the challenge of context management in distributed interactive spaces and that is where our proposal takes interest.

3   Management Context in Distributed Interaction Spaces

In this section is presented the context management in distributed interaction space scenarios. Abstraction of the context is one of the challenges that are facing the administrator or Manager of the spaces that you want to provide information, is the create locations that enable you to organize different information containers so that they are consumed by users. Depending on the conceptual model used, the Manager of the space will have different options for modeling different containers.

Here is proposed the use of a conceptual model for the description of containers of information which is completely abstract. Within the framework of our proposal, we introduce the notion of context in order to model any physical entity or not. In this way you can model any distribution manager need, without being limited to combining contexts and nest them. Administrators will benefit since the organizational abstraction will allow them to use any desired distribution, without having to be tied to previous assumptions or predefined objects. It provides flexibility and consistency to the created models. Users are also benefit thanks to the abstraction of contexts. It offers a navigation control according to the context that ensures that information displayed at all times correspond to informative containers that the user is consulted. Systems that provide information to users, for example in museums, are often based on the fingering of a code. This process can lead to errors. The use of the RFID system combined with the management of contexts makes the system information displayed to the user that corresponds according to their physical location at all times.

3.1   Device-Independent and Centralized Information Management Protocol

The establishment of a protocol for the management of flexible information, enabling your update and handling of quick and convenient way to properly is essential to achieve an improvement over existing systems. To achieve that the system fits to the described parameters, has established a protocol for the management, updating and consumption of information.

First of all, taking advantage of the capabilities of writing of RFID tags, has been established in make the association between the multimedia resources (images, text, video and audio) and containers of information, RFID tags. In earlier proposals the information was directly related to the ID of the tag. This identifier must be present in the database of the application. Through our proposal, if realized a substitution of a label, the only action that is performed is the partner resource again through a simple and straightforward action. In the same way, if you decide change resources associated with an RFID tag, simply replace them with a natural gesture, in a simple way.

The second, designed a protocol for information management that allows the independent Association of the RFID tag, discussed earlier, but which also allows that the management, distribution and updating of information is conducted in such a way that it meets the desired objectives, simplicity and flexibility. The Protocol establishes the structure of the information that is stored within the data space, write RFID tag memory. This structure can be seen in Figure 1.

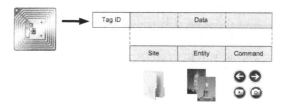

Fig. 1. Information management protocol in RFID tags

The site represents the context that you want to model, representing anything likely to contain other contexts or entities. The entity represents an object within the site, which will have associated text, image, audio or video resources. The last field of the structure, is used to select the type of media (text, image, audio or text) that you want to display within the entity, as well as the navigation (next or previous) among them. Note that the Protocol is independent of the label ID.

3.2   Generalization of the Context Management Protocol

The way in which we can abstract the context to describe the units of information is explained in section 3.1. Later in section 3.2 has been proposed the Management Protocol the context implemented RFID technology with the aim of facilitating your understanding on a specific technology.   This section aims to be a generalization of the context management protocol to facilitate its implementation on other similar to the RFID technologies that could do a similar job. Examples of these technologies include the QR [15], ISO/IEC 15426-1 [16] and NFC bar code [17].

The Protocol establishes that regardless of the technology used by each entity or command should have a mark or label to allow storing certain information and that it can be read later. The stored information will be as follows depending on whether a command or entity. If entity, the information store is composed of 13 digits (5-digit code for the site + 5-digit code of the entity + 000 which represents the neutral command). If command, the information store is composed also-13 (5-digit code for the site + 00000 representing the neutral entity + 3-digit command code).

Command codes are the following: 000 = neutral command (indicates that this is an entity and not a command), 001 = show text, 002 = show image, 003 = show video 004 = show audio, 011 = next, 012 = previous.

Explained the generalization of the protocol you can easily see how to detect a change of context (site) is trivial, simply it is necessary to compare the latest site code read with new site code that is read.

4   Prototype CAIM: Manager of Virtual Spaces

For higher compression system will happen to explain a series of important concepts used in the platform, relating to the creation and management of Web management platform of virtual system contexts CAIM virtual contexts, as well as the process of partnership between the different virtual contexts and multimedia resources.

The term "Site" is that use hereafter to refer to different virtual contexts. A site can be any space that you want to manage and contain within other sites. For example in a Museum, would be the main site Museum, this site would have sites children could be Sala1, Sala2 and Sala3, within Sala1 can have another site that is Vitrina1, etc.

A site in turn can contain one or many "entities". An entity will be the logical representation of the physical RFID tag that represents a point of information of the interactive panel, i.e. after its adaptation to physical and real space will be a 'hot zone' interactive panel. Each entity is associated with one or more multimedia resources, resources can be in text, image, audio or video. For example the Museum site has a welcome entity which is a panel that is in the entrance of the Museum.

The term "resource" we mean different multimedia resources that will finally play users. Resources will be associated to the corresponding entities.

CAIM system consists of three applications: two mobile applications and a Web application. The first is the final application which users consume the different multimedia resources of interactive panels. Everything will work through gestural interaction, i.e., if a user wants to view the images of an area of the pane, you must follow the steps that are shown in Figure 2. Step A is to hold the device to the area label which we wish to obtain information, in step B approach the device resource type which in this case will be image and finally in step C approach the device the "following" tag to navigate to the next resource.

Fig. 2. Process to consume information panels. (a) select the location on the map, (b) select the type of resource to display and (c) navigate to the next resource.

The other mobile application of the system is the part of administration of interactive panels. From your mobile device administrators of cultural space will connect to the Web management system platform and can manage all of the panels of their cultural space in a fast and easy way. Once the administrator has downloaded and updated files from the management application, he can see the elements. The next step will be through this mobile application reconfiguring interactive panels of their space. The association is written in the memory of the RFID. In addition, this mobile device management application will allow the administrator change easily interactive panels commands tags, simply bringing the device to the corresponding label. Figure 3 shows the process. In step A place the device on the label that you want to manage, and in step B indicates the entity or the command.

The third application that is part of the CAIM system is the system management Web platform. This Web-based platform allows you to manage simultaneously different cultural spaces in an independent way.

For the better understanding of the complete project, in following Figure 4 you can see an example of interactive panel to be used in the system. As we can see, the panels are divided into entities and commands. In this example the site would have two entities.

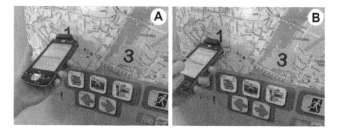

Fig. 3. Process of association of resources with the panels. (a) select the location on the map to manage and (b) indicate the entity or the command that you want to associate.

Fig. 4. Interactive Panel based on RFID

5   Case Study

The objective of this section is to make a practical example using the developed system. For this we will use a real scenario, as is the city of Cordoba. The objective is to give extra information to tourists in three areas of public interest in the city such as the tourist office, the Cordoba Mosque and the Roman Bridge together with the Calahorra Tower.

In this case as the scenario is a city, in which we must computerize three points of tourist interest, we are going to have to locate interactive panels in which users can consume multimedia resources from the environment in which they are found in these three city areas. For this example we will create a simple virtual structure, we will have a main site, called "Cordoba panels" ("paneles de Córdoba"), which will encompass 3 sites, "Tourist Office" ("Oficina de Turismo"), "Mosque" ("Mezquita"), "Roman Bridge" ("Puente Romano"). Once we have list the structure of Sites, the next point is to associate different Entities (hotspots of the interactive panel) we need to each site.

After you associate the entities to the sites it is necessary to associate various multimedia resources to each entity and finally select the main site that we want and to carry out the process by which leaves a compressed file on the server with all directories and resources you need to manage the real space, according to the protocol.

6   Proposal Evaluation

The resources needed for the collection of information have been the following:

Participants. Among the users selected for the experiment we find two types: among eight users, four of them were experts and the remaining users had no experience on these topics. Ages have ranged between 18 and 35 years. None had seen before the application to evaluate, therefore all departed from the same conditions.

Tasks. Tasks were designed to cover all the main functions of the system. Task 1: Login. The user must authenticate to the Web management platform, with a user name and password given. Task 2: Create virtual structure of cultural space. The user must go to the Site Administration, and create a primary site. Then, the user must add three sites. Task 3: Creation of entities. User must associate the necessary entities to the sites created previously. Each site must contain two entities, which will represent an interactive panel with two "hotspots" at each site. Task 4: Assign Resources. Each entity must have at least one resource from text, image, audio and video. Task 5: Generate content. The user must enter the area of content generation, select the created Site and press the button to generate content. Task 6: Close Session. Once the user has generated contents, ends the session by clicking the "Logout".

Location and users' profile. The evaluation was carried out in the building I3A at the University of Castilla-La Mancha. Expert evaluators observed participants. We clarified to users that it was not measured their ability, but the ease of use of the system on which they had to perform each of the tasks proposed. We also informed to them about the basic concepts on know to make use of the management platform. In addition, we also explained the association between the different panels of real space with virtual entities of the system. We also explained to them the proposed tasks for the session, and the environment to be used to carry them out. Evaluators gathered relevant data such as: time used, mistakes, if they could do the task or not, etc. Once finished all tasks, we provided them with a questionnaire, called reduced SUMI, 10 questions and is thanked them for their participation. They were also asked to provide us a comment about the usability or any aspect.

Here are the results obtained after the experiment. The metrics necessary for the analysis have been: the time and the completeness of the tasks, the frequency of errors and user satisfaction.

Effectiveness

Task completeness: Completed tasks are those in which the user achieving to perform what he/she asks for each task. Tasks that have not finalized their implementation are considered not completed. We can highlight that all users found the tasks very simple to perform, fast and affordable to all types of users. Only one user was unable to complete the Task 5, by internet connection problems.

Frequency of errors: The frequency of errors is calculated by measuring the errors made by users. Since all users have done all tasks correctly, we will highlight some aspects as possible error that may have delayed the purpose of the task. The user confuses the visual metaphors. Occasionally they cannot understand all virtual space structure to manage. When you add different entities from the entity add form, the feedback is not adequate in some cases, because the confirmation message "Entity successfully added" is maintained, which means that a user is not sure if the entity has been added.

Efficiency

Average task time: It is measured in minutes and gives us the average temporary efficiency obtained when performing tasks. These data are the time medium that has taken 8 participants for each task and will determine the productivity and efficiency offered by the system. The task times (from Task 1 to Task 6) where the following: 0,11 minutes; 1,06 minutes; 1,88 minutes; 4,60 minutes; 0,08 minutes and 0,03 minutes.

Results show that the four task has been that more time has consumed. This is because each entity has associated different multimedia resources, and this entails more time than the other tasks. Remaining tasks are performed in less time.

Satisfaction

In the test done to measure the user satisfaction have been provided ten statements and three possible answers; agree, undecided and disagree. They were numbered in the following way: 1 -> Agree, 2 -> Undecided, 3 -> Disagree. After analyzing in detail the results we have calculated the proportional value of each statement, below all twenty-five statements will be explained.

1. This software responds too slowly to inputs. Of those surveyed, 87.5% are in disagreement with the statement and 12.5% replied that is undecided. This means that the system responded quickly to the demands of users.
2. I would recommend this software to my colleagues. 75% of users would recommend the software to colleagues against 25% who was undecided.
3. The instructions and prompts are helpful. 50% of users think that the instructions and dialogues are useful, compared with 37.5% which are undecided and 12.5% were disagreement with this statement. This means it would be advisable to improve them.
4. This software has at some time stopped unexpectedly. 87.5% of the people who used the software found that it worked quite fluently. But 12.5% met with little fluidity at some point.

5. Learning to operate this software initially is full of problems. 75% of respondents felt that it is very easy to learn to use the program. However, 25% were undecided. The statement showed that we get a program intuitive and easy to use.
6. I sometimes don't know what to do next with this software. The results were that 25% of users felt indecisive something using the application, compared to 75% at all times able to react to tasks required.
7. I enjoy the time I spend using this software. 75% of users enjoyed the session, however there were 25% undecided. This means that none of the tested users had tense or frustrated with the software.
8. I find that the help information given by this software is not very useful. Most users think that the information was useful to 75%, compared with 25% that they were undecided if the information given was useful or not.
9. If this software stops it is not easy to restart it. 87.5% of respondents did not have to restart the session, because they had no problem. 12.5% had to restart the session and they seemed that it could restart easily.
10. It takes too long to learn the software functions. 100% of users did not take hardly anything to learn the software commands.

7   Conclusions and Future Work

The scenario of interaction in which a user interacts with more than one device to perform same task is known as distributed interaction space. The profusion of mobile devices like tablets and smartphones, operating together with traditional desktop or portable systems thank you Internet services, make up this new distributed environment of interaction.   One of the most pressing problems that appear in the distributed interaction spaces is how to manage the context of information that the system provides to the user based on, for example, of its geographical location. The issue occurs when the system is not able to manage the change of context as the user moves, causing that this can be lost to receive information that does not match your current location. This article proposes the system Cayman as a solution for the management of contexts in spaces of interaction distributed to maintaining coherence and consistency, both the interaction and information. CAIM system solves the problem both from the point of view of the user who consumes the information, as the responsible administrator associate digital resources to the different locations. CAIM system can manage distributed both physical and virtual spaces. Tests with users, as well as provide information for improving the system, confirm that the adopted solution solves effectively providing contextualized according to the physical location information.

References

1. Villanueva, P.G., Gallud, J.A., Tesoriero, R.: WallShare:A Collaborative Multi-pointer System for Portable Devices. In: PPD 2010: Workshop on Coupled Display Visual Interfaces, Rome, Italy, May 25 (2010)
2. Streitz, N.A., Geißler, J., Holmer, T., Konomi, S., Müller-Tomfelde, C., Reischl, W., Rexroth, P., Seitz, P., Steinmetz, R.: i-LAND: an interactive lndscape for creativity and innovation. In: Proc. CHI 1999, pp. 120–127 (1999)

3. Tandler, P., Prante, T., Müller-Tomfelde, T., Streitz, N., Steinmetz, R.: ConnecTables: Dynamic coupling of displays for the flexible creation of share workspaces. In: Proc. of 14th ACM Symp. on UI Software and Tech., UIST 2001, pp. 11–20. ACM Press, New York (2001)

4. Fardoun, H., Villanueva, P.G., Garrido, J.E., Sebastián, G., Romero, L.: Instructional m-Learning System Design Based on Learners: MPrinceTool. In: Fifth International Multi-Conference on Computing in the Global Information Technology, ICCGI 2010, pp. 220–225 (2010)

5. Guía, E.D.L., Lozano, M.D., Gallud, J.A., Tesoriero, R., Penichet, V.M.R.: Co-Interactive Table: a New Facility to Improve Collaborative Meetings. In: MobileHCI 2010, Lisbon, Portugal, September 7-10, ACM (2010)

6. Tesoriero, R., Tebar, R., Gallud, J.A., Penichet, V.M.R., Lozano, M.D.: Interactive ECO-Panels: Paneles Ecológicos Interactivos basados en RFID. In: Lozano, M.D., Gallud, J.A. (eds.) Proceedings IX International Congress of Person-Computer Interaction 2008, pp. 155–165. University of Castilla-La Mancha, Albacete (2008) ISBN: 978-84-691-3871-7

7. Romero, S., Terosiero, R., Villanueva, P.G., Gallud, J.A., Penichet, V.M.P.: Sistema interactivo para la gestión de documentos georeferenciados basado en rfid. In: Interacción 2009, X Congreso Internacional de Interacción Persona-Ordenador (2009)

8. Guía, E.D.L., Lozano, M.D., Penichet, V.M.R.: New Ways of Interaction for People with Cognitive Disabilities to Improve their Capabilities. In: Proc. of 2nd Workshop on Distributed User Interfaces in conjunction with CHI 2012, Austin, Texas, USA, May 05 (2012) ISBN: 84-695-3318-5

9. Guía, E.D.L., Lozano, M.D., Penichet, V.M.R.: Stimulating Capabilities: A Proposal for Learning and Stimulation in Children with ADHD. In: Interaction Design in Educational Environments (IDEE 2012), ICEIS, Wrocław (Poland) (June 2012)

10. Long, S., Aust, D., Abowd, G., Atkeson, C.: Cyberguide: Prototyping context-aware mobile applications. In: CHI 1996 Conference Companion, pp. 293–294. ACM (1996)

11. Davies, N., Mitchell, K., Cheverst, K., Blair, G.: Developing a Context Sensitive Tourist Guide. Technical Report Computing Department, Lancaster University (March 1998)

12. Yang, J., Yang, W., Denecke, M., Waibel, A.: Smart sight: a tourist assistant system. In: 3rd International Symposium on Wearable Computers, San Francisco, California, October 18-19, pp. 73–78 (1999)

13. Butz, A., Baus, J., Kruger, A.: Augmenting buildings with infrared information. In: Proceedings of the International Symposium on Augmented Reality, ISAR 2000, pp. 93–96. IEEE Computer Society Press (2000)

14. Ulrich, A.M., Thomas, P.: Professional Content Management Systems: Handling Digital Media Assets. John Wiley & Sons (2004) ISBN:0470855428

15. ISO/IEC 18004:2006: Information technology. Automatic identification and data capture techniques. Bar code symbology, QR code

16. ISO/IEC 18092:2004 Information technology – Telecommunications and information exchange between systems – Near Field Communication – Interface and Protocol (NFCIP-1). ISO (retrieved December 11, 2011)

17. ISO/IEC 15426-1:2006: Information technology – Automatic identification and data capture techniques – Bar code verifier conformance specification – Part 1: Linear symbols

A Three-Level Approach to the Study
of Multi-cultural Social Networking

Yifan Jiang and Oscar de Bruijn

Manchester Business School East, Booth Street East, Manchester, M13 9PL, UK.
{Yifan.Jiang,Oscar.deBruijn}@mbs.ac.uk

Abstract. This paper firstly introduces three levels of research on online social networking and the corresponding three levels of research on multi-cultural social networking in our project: individual level, interaction level and consequence level. Our studies on multi-cultural online social networking through these three levels are then presented in more detail, ranging from the discussion of previous cross-cultural research at each level, to the research designs and main findings of our studies. Lastly the combined results from the three studies are discussed to achieve an overall picture of this phenomenon.

Keywords: Social Networking, Cross-cultural, Social Capital.

1 Introduction

According to Boyd and Ellison [3], social networking sites are *"web-based services that allow individuals to 1) conduct a public or semi-public profile within a bounded system, 2) articulate a list of other users with whom they share a connection, and 3) view and traverse their list of connections and those made by others within the system"*. Social networking sites therefore allow users to build up and manage their online social networks, to present themselves, to view other users' presentations and to interact with other users through networked connections. Not surprisingly, social networking research to date has focused on three levels corresponding to these features of social networking sites: 1) individual level (e.g. self-presentation [19], privacy concern [1]); 2) interaction level (e.g. network analysis [5], motives and use of social networking sites [8], [16], [18]); and 3) consequence level (e.g. social capital [9], [10]).

Social networking sites have been popular with university students (e.g. Facebook), but have also been introduced in large global organizations (e.g. IBM Beehive). Such communities typically contain people from many different nationalities and cultures, and the many multi-cultural connections existing in these offline communities may be mirrored in those connections on social networking sites. In order to determine the nature of multi-cultural social networking, attention should be directed towards the three different aspects, or levels of social networking research, mentioned above. Firstly, for the individual level, how do cultural differences influence the way individuals present themselves and perceive others? Secondly, for the interaction

A.A. Ozok and P. Zaphiris (Eds.): OCSC/HCII 2013, LNCS 8029, pp. 365–374, 2013.

level, how do cultural differences influence the nature of social interactions? Thirdly, for the consequence level, how do the previous two combine to determine the benefits of multi-cultural social networking?

In our project, different research methods were applied to examine three levels of research. Study one focused on the individual level of multi-cultural social networking, by investigating through experiments, the effects of cultural differences on the perception of online presentations [14]. Participants were asked to make judgments about personality and interaction desirability of the presenters. Study two, which focused on the consequence level, used the concept of social capital to measure cross-cultural social networking effectiveness. A combination of survey research and interview research was applied in order to quantitatively establish the existence of the relationships between cross-cultural social networking and social capital, and then qualitatively examine the nature of those relationships [15]. Finally, study three examined the interaction level of multi-cultural social networking. It explored factors that influence users' decisions on whether and/or how much effort was place upon each type of social networking, through interview analysis. The factors identified were tested in an experiment.

In this paper we explain why such a multi-level approach is needed and provide examples of studies into multi-cultural social networking that we conducted at each of these different levels. By combining the studies' findings, as opposed to focusing on just a single aspect, we gain a more comprehensive insight into the phenomenon.

2   Three Levels

This section outlines our studies at three levels, by following and contributing to the existing literature.

2.1   Individual Level

Cross-cultural research on online social networking has addressed the area of self-presentation at the individual level. De Angeli [7] compared the differences of online presentation between British and Chinese students on one of the early social networking sites – Windows Live Space - through three aspects: effort, communication style and self-disclosure. She found that Chinese people put more effort into the presentations of their personal spaces because they are more concerned about the results of their presentations perceived by the audience. Secondly, Chinese users tended to be more polite and formal in their virtual space presentations, whereas British users tended to be more open and direct. Lastly, British users were more likely to disclose their individuating information, whereas Chinese users disclosed more social-related information.

These cultural differences found in online social networking can be linked to the cultural differences suggested by previous cultural theories. For example, the differences in communication styles and self-presentation styles reported in De Angeli's [7] research, is similar to Hall's [12] low context and high context culture theory, which suggests that in the former culture, people need to speak explicitly and follow a direct communication style; whereas in the latter, people do not need to communicate explicitly as they rely more on the context (the culture) to explain. One reason for this is that people from a high-context culture tend to live interdependently with others and as such, through the development of a common understanding, are able to understand others better. This is in contrast to people from a low-context culture, who want to make everything clear and straightforward, in order to let others understand their real needs. Secondly, people from a high-context culture may be more considerate of other people's feelings and reactions towards what they say, making some speech implicit.

As De Angeli's [7] study suggested that cultural differences did exist in the self-presentation in online social networking between presenters from different cultures, and that these differences are well connected with previous cultural theories, the following research questions were constructed for our study. Firstly, do cultural differences in online self-presentation affect audiences' perception of the presenters? Secondly, do people from different cultural backgrounds have different ways of perceiving other people's online self-presentation? We focused upon cultural differences in perception of others in online social networking at this level, because this may affect users' further interactions in cross-cultural social networking context. Our study [14] hypothesized that cultural differences in presentation styles would affect the viewers' perception of the presenters. It was also hypothesized that viewers from different cultural backgrounds tend to focus on different cues (i.e. verbal cues and non-verbal cues) of self-presentation when building up their perception. To test these hypotheses in an experiment, two specially constructed online blog styles of a typical British and a typical Chinese person were created, reflecting different presentation styles in verbal content. These blogs were designed based on the cultural differences suggested by previous cross-cultural studies ([12], [13], [20]). The content of blogs reflected seven cultural characteristics that were summarized from these studies describing the cultural differences between Western and Eastern cultures (e.g. direct and indirect; long- and short-term relationship orientation; social equality and hierarchical). Cultural differences suggested by cross-cultural online communication research were also addressed in the blog design. For example, people from a Western culture like to use the word "I", whereas people from an Eastern culture like to use the word "we" when describing their activities [24]. In addition to the two blogs, two profiles were created: one with a Chinese name and an East Asian face; the other with a British name and a Caucasian face, reflecting non-verbal content. The two blogs and two profiles were combined to make four different personae of Windows Live Space homepages presenters: two congruent combinations (i.e. Chinese style blog and Chinese, British style blog and British profile); and two incongruent combinations (i.e. Chinese style blog and British profile, British style blog and Chinese profile). 40 Chinese and 40 British participants were invited to view these personae and rate their perceptions via the interpersonal attraction scale (social attraction, physical attraction and task attraction) [22] and the source credibility scale (trustworthiness, caring and competence) [21].

The results showed that differences in presentation styles of blogs did affect viewers' social perception. Moreover, British and Chinese viewers tended to pick up upon different cues when judging other people's online self-presentation. Chinese viewers were more sensitive to the verbal content, as they tended to judge the personae with Chinese style blogs as being more caring and more socially attractive (i.e. the viewers would like to be friends with the presenter). These perceptions revealed Chinese users' preference of interacting with people from their own cultural group; however, Chinese viewers judged the personae with British style blogs as having higher competence. On the contrary, British participants tended to focus more upon the non-verbal content when perceiving other people's online self-presentation. Based upon their perception, British viewers gave the personae with a British profile higher scores in competence, compared to the personae with a Chinese appearance. One surprising result was that the incongruent combination of the personae with a Chinese profile and a British style blog, scored higher on task attraction (i.e. the viewers would like to work with the presenter). From the participants' answers towards the question - where do they think the persona they viewed is from - most participants regarded this persona was from Hong Kong or a British Born Chinese. This may explain why participants thought this persona was most attractive to work with, because these groups of people tend to have a higher level of cross-cultural engagement. If this is true, it could be seen that when people form their perception of others online, they may trigger a stereotype perception, based on their experience.

2.2   Consequence Level

Although cross-cultural research on social networking sites through the individual level is in its infancy, none of previous research has addressed cross-cultural research regarding the consequence (or benefit) of social networking through the concept of social capital. According to Bourdieu [2], Coleman [6] and Putnam [23], social capital is generated from networked relationships (or social networks) and can bring benefits to the actors who keep the relationships (or that lies in the networks). From a network point of view, there are two types of social capital: bridging social capital and bonding social capital. A bonding network tends to be denser (i.e. most actors are connected with each other) and closer. It usually contains homogeneous groups of people [23], and it is easier to share understanding, build social norms and store trust. With higher levels of trust and understanding, actors should be more likely to share limited resources and provide substantive support to other actors within the network. This is because they should have a greater level of confidence that other actors who benefit from them can pay back their effort in the future [6]. Furthermore, it would be easier for actors to use these connections to enable mobilization [26]. These benefits mentioned above are associated with bonding social capital. A bridging network tends to be sparser (i.e. only few actors are connected) and more open. It usually contains more heterogeneous groups of people [23]. It is easier to develop new connections through bridge connections for previous unknown connectors [4]. Moreover, this is a greater opportunity to diffuse reciprocity, disseminate and receive new information [26]. These benefits are associated with bridging social capital. Granovetter [11] argued that relationship strength could be distinguished as strong ties and weak ties according to interaction frequency, and the levels of trust and intimacy. Strong ties are more likely to offer the benefit of bonding social capital, whereas weak ties are more likely to provide the benefits of bridging social capital.

Williams [26] developed scales to test online social capital based on the concept of bridging and bonding social capital, in order to test the effectiveness of online interactions. This online social capital scale contains ten items for bonding social capital and ten items for bridging social capital. Ellison and colleagues [9] examined the relationship between Facebook use and the amount of social capital perceived by student users. They adapted Williams' [26] scales, and included a dimension called maintained social capital, in order to assess one's ability to maintain relationships with previous inhabited friends (e.g. classmates after graduation). Their results showed all three forms of perceived social capital were positively associated with intensive Facebook use. Steinfield and colleagues conducted a similar study [25]. They also applied the concept of bridging and bonding social capital to measure various dimensions of organizational social capital, and they examined the use of an internal social network site for employees in an enterprise. They found all forms of social capital were positively associated with the intensity of social networking use. These results provided evidence that using social networking sites could help people not only to maintain a larger network with heterogeneous contacts (bridging social capital), but also to well maintain and deepen their friendships with existing strong connections (bonding social capital). These studies illustrated that social networking is associated with social capital, however it is still unknown whether this is the case for cross-cultural social networking because of differences in building social relations that exist across cultures [17]. It appears therefore a study looking at this area by linking cross-cultural social networking and social capital is necessary to contribute to cross-cultural social networking research at the consequence level.

Our research of this level followed previous research ([25], [9]) on social capital and social networking. Being interested in cross-cultural Facebook interactions among student users in an international university campus, the first concern was whether cross-cultural Facebook interactions exist, and secondly whether these interactions were associated with users' perceived increase of online social capital. By adapting Williams' [26] and Ellison and colleagues' [9] scales, a cross-cultural social capital scale was devised for measuring users' perceived amount of bridging, bonding and maintained social capital from their cross-cultural online networks. In a survey study of 100 British and 100 Chinese university students, participants were asked to rate these scales, in addition to answering questions about their general Facebook use and intensity of cross-cultural Facebook interactions. Regression analysis results suggested that intensive cross-cultural Facebook interactions were positively associated with all three forms of cross-cultural online social capital, especially bridging and bonding cross-cultural online social capital. One cultural difference was that British users reported a lower amount of perceived cross-cultural bonding social capital than Chinese users. These results were further explored through a follow-up interview study in order to understand why users could perceive the increase of cross-cultural bridging and bonding online social capital, as well as why British users tended to perceive less cross-cultural bonding social capital.

The interview study asked 15 British and 15 Chinese interviewees who participated in the survey study to report their interactions with different kinds of cross-cultural relationships on Facebook and what benefits they received through these activities. Three Facebook interaction types emerged from the interview analysis: observing (i.e. view other people's information or activities without giving a response or further interactions); communicating (i.e. one-to-one communication via the public Facebook walls or private chat); and grouping (i.e. interact with more than one friend through Facebook groups or Facebook walls). These emerging interaction types mainly correspond to Facebook functionality. Moreover, four types of bridging social capital benefits were found (i.e. broaden views, enlarge friend circle, get new resources, and diffuse reciprocity); in addition to three types of bonding social capital benefits (i.e. receive access to limited resources, obtain substantive support, and mobilizing solidarity). The ones who provided these benefits to interviewees were distinguished according to relationship strength: strong ties and weak ties. The results suggested that all Facebook interactions with all relationship types in cross-cultural Facebook interactions can provide bridging social capital benefits. However, cultural differences did exist in British and Chinese interviewee reports of their cross-cultural bonding social capital. British interviewees only reported one way of receiving one benefit of cross-cultural bonding social capital (e.g. mobilizing solidarity through grouping with cross-cultural strong ties); whereas Chinese interviewees reported a few ways of receiving two benefits of cross-cultural bonding social capital (e.g. getting substantive support through communicating with cross-cultural strong ties; and acquiring access to limited resources through both communicating and grouping with cross-cultural strong ties).

2.3   Interaction Level

At the interaction level, cross-cultural research on online social networking has addressed the general motivations behind and the usage patterns of social networking. Kim and colleagues [17] compared the motives for and usage patterns on social networking sites between American undergraduate students in the US, and Korean undergraduate students in Korea. They found five common motives for using social networking sites in general: seeking friends, social support, entertainment, information and convenience; these were similar between the two sample groups. Nevertheless, they found differences in usage patterns. American users tended to put more effort into establishing casual relationships (e.g. through common experience), making the size of their online social networks larger than their Korean counterparts. Korean users however were more likely to use social networking sites to maintain existing close relationships for obtaining social support.

The differences in motives and usage patterns of social networking reported in their [17] study, correspond to the cultural differences mentioned by previous cultural theory. For example, Markus and Kitayama's [20] self-construal theory suggests that the interdependent selves (i.e. usually people from Eastern culture) tend to define themselves through their role and relationship with others, whereas the independent selves' self-concept (i.e. usually people from Western culture) is grounded in autonomy and uniqueness; other people are still important to them, but mainly for social comparison. The difference in self-construal affects people's interactions with others, with the former being more likely to consider other people's feeling and needs when making their decisions as well as rely more on other people's social support; and the latter tending to be more independent with less concern or constraint from other people.

As Kim and colleagues [17] compared American and Korean social networking users' general motives and usage patterns, our study at this level focused more upon the factors affecting users' decision-making when they perform activities on social networking sites. The analysis started from reviewing interview answers of British and Chinese interviewees towards the following questions: What did users do with friends on Facebook; why users did these actions on Facebook? The categories emerged from this interview analysis were similar to those reported in our consequence level study: three types of Facebook interactions (i.e. observing, communicating, grouping), four types of bridging social capital benefits (i.e. broaden views, enlarge friend circle, get new resources and diffuse reciprocity), three types of bonding social capital benefits (i.e. get substantive support, access to limited resources and mobilize solidarity), two types of relationship strength (i.e. strong ties and weak ties), and three types of Facebook communication content (i.e. self-disclosure, information exchange and support).

Relationship strength was the first factor that affected users' decision on how much and what type of Facebook interactions they perform with online friends. British interviewees tended to observe and communicate with strong ties; however the relationship strength did not affect their grouping behaviors. Chinese interviewees reported that they tended to communicate and group with strong ties; however the relationship strength did not influence their observing behaviors.

This study also found that social capital benefits were not only the consequences of social networking use (as suggested by our study at the consequence level), but also the drivers of social networking use (as the second factor that affect users' decision on social networking activities). For example, when British interviewees explained why they group with weak ties in addition to their strong ties, they answered the aim was to enlarge their friend circle - a typical bridging social capital benefit. Similarly, when Chinese interviewees explained why they observe their weak ties through social networking in addition to their strong ties, they answered the aim was to broaden views and get new resources - typical bridging social capital benefits. Furthermore, Chinese interviewees seemed to be affected more by bonding social capital benefits. For example, in order to get substantive support from their strong ties, they tended to put effort towards supporting their strong ties through communicating and grouping.

In order to check the reliability of these results, an experimental study to test the interaction patterns that had emerged through the interview analysis was conducted. In this experiment, types of social capital benefits, types of relationship strength and the nationality of participants were designed as independent variables. Types of Facebook interactions and content of Facebook interactions were measured as dependent variables. Types of social capital benefits and types of relationship strength were manipulated based on the subcategories that had emerged from the interview analysis, through descriptions in scenarios. The scenarios basically described a group of British friends or Chinese friends with either strong or weak tie relationships with the audience, and the potential bridging or bonding social capital benefits that can be generated from interacting with the group of friends on Facebook. 80 British and 80 Chinese participants were asked to read the scenarios and rate how likely they were to choose different interactions with these friends in the scenarios, compared to their normal activities on Facebook. The experiment examined both cross-cultural relationships (e.g. when Chinese participants read the scenarios about their British friends) and in-cultural relationships (e.g. when Chinese participants read the scenarios about their Chinese friends) in this setting. The experimental study confirmed most of the results from the interview analysis. In addition, the experiment results suggested that Chinese participants were more likely to observe and communicate with their cross-cultural weak ties, which seemed to bring bridging social capital benefits to them (according to our study at the consequence level).

3   Discussion

Combining the three levels, our studies in which British and Chinese social networking users were systematically compared, suggest that cultural differences exist in different levels. At the individual level, cultural differences in self-presentation styles affected the audiences' perception of the presenters. British and Chinese users had tended to focus on different cues when perceiving other users' online self-presentations (the former focus on non-verbal content; the latter pay more attention to the verbal content details). At the consequence level, the case study on Facebook showed cross-cultural social capital (especially cross-cultural bonding and bridging social capital) was positively associated with cross-cultural social networking. However, British participants perceived a lesser amount of bonding social capital from cross-cultural social networking. Further interview analysis revealed that all kinds of social networking interactions (i.e. observing, communicating, grouping) could help users obtain the benefits of bridging social capital (e.g. acquiring new information and diffusing reciprocity); however only communicating and grouping with strong relationships brought different aspects of bonding social capital benefits to British and Chinese users. For instance, communicating and grouping helped Chinese users receive substantive support and access to limited resources; whereas grouping with strong relationships helped British users mobilize solidarity. The cultural difference at the consequence level is that British users perceived less amount of bonding social capital from cross-cultural online social networking in terms of both quantity and quality. Lastly, at the interaction level, three main factors may influence users' decisions regarding multi-cultural social networking interactions: (a) relationship strength - although both British and Chinese users tend to communicate mostly with strong relationships, they have differences in observing and grouping with different relationships. British users tend to observe mostly strong relationships and group with all relationships, whereas Chinese users tend to group mostly with strong relationships and observe all relationships; (b) perceived benefit of social capital - only bridging social capital benefit affected British users' decision, whereas both bridging and bonding social capital benefits motivated Chinese users; and (c) users' cultural background.

The advantage of researching cross-cultural social networking in different levels is that a fuller picture of the observation is created. Our study of the consequence level suggested there was a strong link between how much people invest in cross-cultural Facebook interaction and how much cross-cultural social capital they perceive as having in their cross-cultural friend networks on Facebook. It provided clearer evidence of causal links between different Facebook interactions with cross-cultural friends and obtaining the benefits of social capital. Our study of the interaction level suggested that social capital benefits may not only be the consequence, but also the drivers of Facebook interactions. Combining the results from the two levels, it is likely that as people experience the actual benefits of social capital from online social networking with friends, they will become more confident about a link between the intensity of Facebook interactions and their perceived online social capital. This confidence will motivate them to invest more in certain Facebook interactions, both in terms of time and emotion, thereby completing a reinforcement loop (Fig 1).

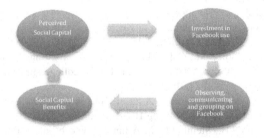

Fig. 1. Reinforcement Loop of Facebook Interactions and Online Social Capital

References

1. Acquisti, A., Gross, R.: Imagined communities: Awareness, information sharing, and privacy on the Facebook. In: Golle, P., Danezis, G. (eds.) Proceedings of 6th Workshop on Privacy Enhancing Technologies, pp. 36–58. Robinson College, Cambridge (2006)
2. Bourdieu, P.: Forms of Capital. In: Richardson, J.G. (ed.) Handbook of Theory and Research for the Sociology of Education, pp. 241–260. Greenwood Press, Westport (1986)
3. Boyd, D., Ellison, N.B.: Social network sites: Definition, history, and scholarship. Journal of Computer-Mediated Communication 13(1), 210–230 (2008)
4. Burt, R.S.: The network structure of social capital. Research in Organizational Behaviour 22, 345–423 (2000)
5. Catanese, S., De Meo, P., Ferrara, E., Fiumara, G., Provetti, A.: Crawling Facebook for social network analysis purposes. In: Proc. of the International Conference on Web Intelligence, Mining and Semantics (WIMS 2011), p. 52. ACM, Sogndal (2011)
6. Coleman, J.S.: Foundations of Social Theory. Harvard University Press, Cambridge (1990)

7. De Angeli, A.: Cultural variations in virtual spaces design. AI & Society 24, 213–223 (2009)
8. DiMicco, J., Millen, D.R., Geyer, W., Dugan, C., Brownholtz, B., Muller, M.: Motivations for social networking at work. In: Proceedings of the 2008 ACM Conference on Computer Supported Cooperative Work (CSCW 2008), pp. 711–720. ACM Press, New York (2008)
9. Ellison, N.B., Steinfield, C., Lampe, C.: The benefits of Facebook "friends:" Social capital and college students' use of online social network sites. Journal of Computer-Mediated Communication 12(4), 1143–1168 (2007)
10. Ellison, N.B., Steinfield, C., Lampe, C.: Connection Strategies: Social capital implications of Facebook-enabled communication practices. New Media & Society 13(6), 873–892 (2011)
11. Granovetter, M.: The strength of weak ties. American Journal of Sociology 78(6), 1360–1380 (1973)
12. Hall, E.T.: Beyond culture. Doubleday, New York (1976)
13. Hofstede, G.: The cultural relativity of organizational practices and theories. Journal of International Business Studies 14, 75–89 (1983)
14. Jiang, Y., de Bruijn, O., De Angeli, A.: The Perception of Cultural Differences in Online Self-presentation. In: Gross, T., Gulliksen, J., Kotzé, P., Oestreicher, L., Palanque, P., Prates, R.O., Winckler, M. (eds.) INTERACT 2009. LNCS, vol. 5726, pp. 672–685. Springer, Heidelberg (2009)
15. Jiang, Y.F., de Bruijn, O.: (to appear)
16. Joinson, A.N.: Looking at, Looking up or Keeping up with People?: Motives and Uses of Facebook. In: Proc. CHI 2008, pp. 1027–1036 (2008)
17. Kim, Y., Sohn, D., Choi, S.M.: Cultural difference in motivations for using social network sites: A comparative study of American and Korean college students. Computers in Human Behavior 27(1), 365–372 (2011)
18. Lampe, C., Ellison, N., Steinfield, C.: A Face(book) in the crowd: social searching vs. social browsing. In: Proc. CSCW 2006, pp.167–170 (2006)
19. Lampe, C., Ellison, N.B., Steinfield, C.: A familiar Faceb(book): Profile elements as signals in an online social network. In: Proceedings of the SIGCHI Conference on Human Factors in Computing Systems, pp. 435–444. ACM Press, New York (2007)
20. Markus, H.R., Kitayama, S.: Culture and the self: Implications for cognition, emotion, and motivation. Psychological Review 98, 224–253 (1991)
21. McCroskey, J.C., Holdridge, W., Toomb, J.K.: An instrument for measuring the source credibility of basic speech communication instructors. The Speech Teacher 23, 26–35 (1974)
22. McCroskey, J.C., McCain, T.A.: The measurement of interpersonal attraction. Speech Monographs 41, 261–266 (1974)
23. Putnam, R.D.: Bowling Alone: The Collapse and Revival of American Community. Simon & Schuster, New York (2000)
24. Setlock, L.D., Fussel, S.R., Neuwirth, C.: Taking it out of context: collaborating within and across cultures in face-to-face settings and via instant messaging. In: Proceedings of the 2004 ACM Conference on Computer Supported Cooperative Work (2004)
25. Steinfield, C., Di Micco, J.M., Ellison, N.B., Lampe, C.: Bowling online: social networking and social capital within the organization. In: Proceedings of the Fourth International Conference on Communities and Technologies (C&T 2009), pp. 245–254. ACM, New York (2009)
26. Williams, D.: On and off the "net": Scales for social capital in an online era. Journal of Computer-Mediated Communication 11(2), 593–628 (2006)

Towards Visual Configuration Support for Interdependent Security Goals

Fatih Karatas, Mohamed Bourimi, and Dogan Kesdogan

Chair for IT Security, Privacy and Trust,
University of Siegen,
57076 Siegen, Germany
{karatas,bourimi}@wiwi.uni-siegen.de, kesdogan@uni-siegen.de

Abstract. This work investigates visual support for easing the configuration of interdependent security goals. The interdependent nature of security goals did not receive sufficient attention in related work yet. A formal approach to adequately model interdependent security goals are *multi-criteria optimization problems* which can be solved either exactly or heuristically. This however depends on the question if the user is able to articulate his/her preferences regarding security goals. Furthermore, heuristic approaches confront users with possibly unlimited alternative configurations where each solution is equally well. In order to support users in the process of articulating preferences and selecting a suiting alternative, we provide visual facilities at the level of the user interface. The need for handling such issues emerged from the analysis of the EU funded di.me project which explicitly requires that such configurations are carried out by lay users. We present an approach tackling these issues by means of visual concepts triggering a service selection in the background which respects the interdependence of security goals. We concretely discuss the application of our approach by addressing a scenario concerned with deployment decisions in the di.me project.

Keywords: Interdependent Security, Decision-support, Preference Articulation, Trade-off Visualization, Security and Usability, User Experience.

1   Introduction

The majority of applications, processing data of users offer security settings for ensuring different levels of protection depending on the user's needs. This is mostly supported for instance by respective wizards in the user interface (UI). Security preferences are seen as quality attributes and the usability of provided wizards strongly affects the user experience (UX). Indeed, usability is a prerequisite for security [1][1] and UX is related to *every aspect of the user's*

---

[1] The inherent interplay between usability and security with respect to easing security configuration in general was realized as early as 1883 by *Kerckhoffs* who formulated it as his sixth principle for building secure systems [2]. An english translation of the original french article can be found at http://www.petitcolas.net/fabien/kerckhoffs/index.html#english .

A.A. Ozok and P. Zaphiris (Eds.): OCSC/HCII 2013, LNCS 8029, pp. 375–384, 2013.
© Springer-Verlag Berlin Heidelberg 2013

interaction with a product, service, or company that make up the user's perceptions of the whole[2][SIC].

Supporting visual configuration of interdependent security goals did not receive sufficient attention in related work yet. Since these kind of security objectives can either strengthen, weaken or implicate each other, respective visual configuration facilities should reflect emerging trade-offs resulting from this interdependence i.e. at the level of the respective application's UI. To our best knowledge, the only application tackling this issue is described in [3] for SSONet system. The solution does however not address any kind of user feedback at the level of the UI. The foundation of our approach is a model to describe interdependent security goals, formulated as *multi-criteria optimization problem.* Problems of this class are characterized by the circumstance, that they can usually only be solved heuristically. Exact solutions can only be obtained (if at all) if users articulate their preferences with respect to the objectives. Otherwise the result is a possible unlimited set of solutions where each solution represents an equally well compromise with respect to the objectives. In order to support users in the process of articulating preferences and selecting a suiting alternative, we provide visual facilities at the level of the UI. To our best knowledge, this kind of facilities were not proposed in the field of interdependent security configuration yet.

The rest of the paper is structured as follows. Section 2 introduces the EU funded di.me project which forms a test bed for the approach presented here. Consequently the requirements analysis in section 3 is based on this project. Section 4 presents our approach for tackling the issues discussed above as well as the implementation in di.me and Section 5 concludes the paper. It should be noted that along the whole paper, we concretely discuss the application of our approach by having in mind a scenario concerned with deployment decisions in the di.me project.

2   Target Community and Use Case

The EU funded project di.me[3] specifies a platform incorporating user-control deeply in design: a private service (PS) and userware offer a central user node in a decentralized network connecting to other user nodes or external services, like social networking platforms, through distinct identities [4,5] (cf. Figure 1). This node integrates all personal data in a personal information sphere, including user interests, contact information, and social network services. Intelligent features further guide user interactions within the digital sphere, illustrated by context-aware access control, trust and privacy advice, or organizing their personal information sphere [6,7].

---

[2] According to Usability Professionals Association's (UPA) Glossary:
http://www.usabilitybok.org/glossary
[3] http://www.wiwi.uni-siegen.de/itsec/projekte/dime/index.html.en

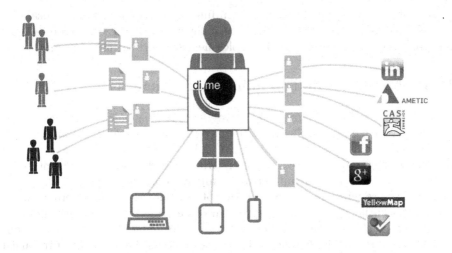

Fig. 1. The big picture of di.me

One of the main objectives of the di.me userware is to be under full control of end users, which implicates enabling them to be able to host the userware on any trusted node they state as secure enough for their usage purposes (e.g. on a desktop PC at home which is accessible via the Internet). With this, the deployment of the PS onto cloud infrastructures was required as cloud computing (CC) as a facility for the deployment of user-controlled servers is a growing trend[4]. Furthermore, various industrial[5] partners explicitly required supporting this feature along with enabling di.me to support multi-user/multi-tenant hosting[6]. In the case of di.mes' industrial partners, the end-user carrying out the deployment task is the administrator at the respective company. Because of this, di.me has to support lay as well as experienced users in performing the CC deployment by considering ease of configuration (incl. consideration of interdependent security goals). For meeting our gathered requirements, we proposed in [8] a solution, which is formed by an "Environment for secure cloud applications by adaptable virtualization and best practice consideration" or ESCAVISION for short. ESCAVISION is the core of our approach and supports lay as well as experienced users in considering security best practices. The requirements gathering, elicitation and negotiation process followed the AFFINE methodology involving all stakeholders (i.e. end-users, experts, developers) and enforcing the earlier

---

[4] One main cause is the high availability and various cost-reducing factors in comparison to own hosted PSs.

[5] i.e. industrial partner interested in di.me exploitation later.

[6] One of the main objectives of di.me is to evaluate developed concepts with a large set of users. This technical/infrastructural challenge led to the discussion if the userware should not be extended to multi-user/multi-tenant support for trusted communities, e.g. a family or friends servers.

consideration of functional as well as non-functional requirements (i.e. usability and security) in an agile way [9,10]. In the following, we analyze the requirements and present our approach with the deployment support scenario in mind.

3   Preliminaries and Requirements Analysis

As mentioned before, security objectives are interdependent and can either strengthen, weaken or implicate each other [3] (see Figure 2). As an example consider anonymity and accountability. A high level of anonymity makes it hard to account single events to certain users while a high degree of accountability makes it hard for users to upkeep their anonymity. Thus anonymity and accountability are mutually weakening each other. Because of the interdependent nature of security objectives, the problem of determining the security level of applications such as service compositions can be formulated as multi-criteria optimization problem [11,12]. The basic idea is to assess the influence of technical as well as organizational factors such as encryption algorithms and admission control policies on security objectives. These objectives can thus be formulated as interdependent objective functions (for further details, the interested reader is referred to [11]).

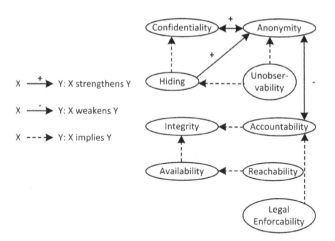

Fig. 2. Correlation of protection goals (from [3])

A challenge remains solving multi-criteria optimization problems. Usually such problems have a set of optimal solutions where each solution represents a compromise with regards to the objective functions. Depending on the question if the decision maker is allowed to articulate her preferences before (*a priori*), during (*interactive*) or after (*a posteriori*) performing the search algorithm, it is possible to employ either exact algorithms or heuristic approaches [13].

In this paper we focus on *a priori* and *a posteriori* approaches as one of the design goals of our prototype (see next section as well as [11]) was to determine near-optimal solutions with minimal user-interaction.

Articulation of preferences *a priori* or *a posteriori* has however also effects on the exploration of the search space. While approaches with *a priori* articulation of preferences allow for finding exact solutions, they restrict the search space. On the contrary, approaches with *a posteriori* articulation of preferences are heuristic but allow for exploring the search space without limitation.

Another issue is the selection of the solution which best fits the decision-makers needs. As stated above, each solution of a multi-criteria optimization problem represents a compromise with regards to the single objective functions. Therefore it is not possible to automatically decide which solution is "the best". Instead, decision-makers need to decide, based upon the trade-offs of each solution which one fits their needs best. This can however become hard in the face of numerous objective functions.

Supporting decision-makers in the process of (a) preference articulation and (b) selecting the solution which best fits their needs thus yields the following requirements:

1. Decision-makers need facilities to articulate preferences *a priori* as well as *a posteriori* (**R1**).
2. Consequences of preference articulation by means of received solutions (exact vs. heuristic) and search space exploration need to be communicated to decision-makers (**R2**).
3. Decision-makers need support to better evaluate the trade-offs of single solutions (**R3**).

4   Approach

In this section we will present our concepts for tackling the requirements identified above. The concepts are illustrated with a prototypical implementation within the Service Selection Workbench (SSW). The SSW is a tool for determining secure service compositions for given workflows. It was first introduced in [11] which provides more information about the tool. In this paper we will focus on the selection facilities and how decision-makers are supported visually for the di.me deployment scenario introduced in section 2. For di.me we apply workflows with one task to find a suiting deployment option offering security facilities that match user requirements. While from a service composition point of view, di.me is less interesting, the issues described in section 3 still apply. The typical sequence of tasks in service selection is as follows:

1. The user formulates requirements for each protection goal.
2. If desired, the user can express preferences regarding protection goals.
3. A service selection is performed by solving a multi-criteria optimization problem with the user requirements being the constraints. If the user articulated

preferences in step 2, the problem can be solved exactly. Otherwise a predefined number of heuristic solutions (e.g. 10) is determined.

4. The user selects from the determined solutions the one which best fits her preferences.

4.1   Preference Articulation (R1)

We concentrated on two methods for *a priori* preference articulation, namely weighting of objective functions and lexicographic ordering of objectives (see Figure 3). The decision-maker must specify, which kind of *a priori* preference articulation she prefers (if any). Weighting of objective functions is straightforward. Decision-makers can enter a real value $w \in [0,1]$ for each objective function where the sum of all weightings must be ≤ 1. For ordering functions, decision-makers are provided with buttons next to each objective function. The rule is that the highest function is optimized first. The result set of the first function represents the input for the second and so on. In order to give decision-makers a visual feedback of the relevance of each objective function in the order, objectives are automatically colored according to their rank from green to red.

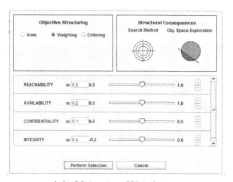
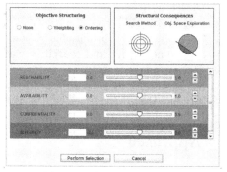

| (a) Objective Weighting | (b) Lexicographic Ordering |

Fig. 3. Different methods for preference articulation

4.2   Communication of Structural Consequences (R2)

As already mentioned, preference articulation *a priori* leads to exact solutions at the cost of search space restrictions. On the other hand, heuristic approaches allow for searching the search space more thoroughly. In order to visualize these structural consequences to decision-makers, we implemented a view showing icons depending on the problem structure (see the upper right corner in both screenshots in Figure 3).

Currently we take effects on search method (see Figure 4) and search space exploration (see Figure 5) into account as these apply on each optimization problem. Other effects such as primal degeneracy which only apply to certain classes of optimization problems [14], were not included (yet).

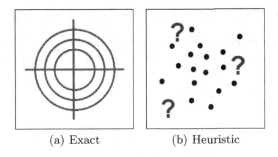

(a) Exact   (b) Heuristic

Fig. 4. Icons for visualizing search method properties

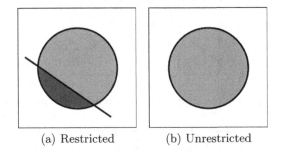

(a) Restricted   (b) Unrestricted

Fig. 5. Icons for visualizing search space exploration

4.3 Trade-Off Visualization (R3)

In order to communicate the trade-offs regarding different protection goals, we employ metaphors for visualization. A sample metaphor which we prototypically implemented is a house on a hill with a sun shining above the scenery. Depicted in Figure 6 is the metaphor representing user-requirements for single protection goals. Depending on the security model employed, the single elements of the metaphor need to be mapped to a protection goal. For the widely used CIA model of security (*Confidentiality, Integrity* and *Availability*), a possible mapping is shown in Table 1. As mentioned in section 1, the result of service selection is a set of function values for each alternative. These function values are used to construct a visualization for each composition alternative on the basis of $\delta_k = pf_k - r_k$ where pf_k is the function value of protection goal k for the current alternative and r_k the user requirement for protection goal k. If $\delta_k \neq 0$, the corresponding metaphor element is being altered to reflect this difference. E.g., if integrity is less than required ($\delta_k < 0$), the smile of the sun turns over to a sad face. If it's higher ($\delta_k > 0$), the smile gets even brighter. Figure 7 shows two examples for service composition alternatives with different than required security properties. Alternative 1 offers better confidentiality than required, but less integrity and availability. Alternative 2 offers better integrity and availability than required but less confidentiality.

Table 1. Sample mapping of protection goals to metaphor elements

Protection Goal	Metaphor Element
Confidentiality	*Jalousies in the windows*
Integrity	*Smile of the Sun*
Availability	*Hill steepness*

Fig. 6. Metaphor representing user-requirements for protection goals

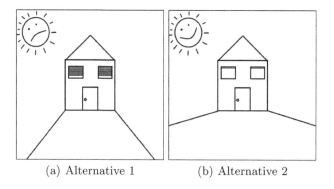

(a) Alternative 1   (b) Alternative 2

Fig. 7. Alternative service compositions with different security properties

4.4   Deployment Scenario from di.me

The deployment scenario is concerned with creating a di.me PS at the instance of a few mouse-clicks and deploying it on almost any cloud infrastructure. After logging in at the website of di.me, the user can configure her di.me PS by selecting required features from a list. Next, a personalized ISO is created which then can be deployed on cloud infrastructure[7]. Integrating our proposed approach with the current state of the deployment scenario would require the steps in section 4

---

[7] A demo video for an adapted CRM usage of this scenario is available at: http://www. uni-siegen.de/fb5/itsec/projekte/dime/dime-cloud-deployment-setup.avi

to be executed after the ISO creation step. For each selection option, identified by the selection algorithm, a metaphor would be generated in order to visualize the trade-offs of that particular solution. Finally, the solution with the metaphor which attracts the user most, would be selected and deployment of the di.me, PS would be performed.

5 Conclusion and Future Work

In this paper, we investigated visual support for easing the configuration of interdependent security goals. The need for handling such issues emerged from the analysis of the EU funded di.me project with requirements for carrying out such configurations by lay users for supporting a scenario concerned with deployment decisions. Our analysis yielded the following three requirements: (i) Articulation of preferences *a priori* and *a posteriori*, (ii) communication of consequences of preference articulation on obtained solutions in terms of search method properties (exact vs. heuristic) as well as search space exploration (partial vs. unlimited) and (iii) visualization of trade-offs of single solutions with metaphors. For each requirement we presented an approach to tackle the respective issue, namely: (i) *a priori* preference articulation by weighting or lexicographically ordering security objectives, (ii) communicating structural consequences by showing icons in a view and (iii) by presenting the user metaphors (e.g. a scenery with a house on a hill) to visualize trade-offs of single solutions. To our best knowledge, there is no work proposing similar facilities in the field of interdependent security configuration. Future work will focus on continuing the implementation of the proposed approach by following AFFINE and evaluating it with end-users as well as experts. Another direction of future work will be implementing facilities for articulating preferences *a posteriori*.

Acknowledgments. This work has been partially supported by the German Federal Ministry of Education and Science (BMBF) under grant no. 13N10964 in the project ReSCUe IT which is jointly conducted together with the French Agence Nationale de la Recherche (ANR). Parts of this work are also supported by the digital.me EU FP7 project, funded by the EC(FP7/2007-2013) under grant agreement no. 257787. Thanks are mainly due to Sophie Wrobel and Marcel Heupel for their contributions to this work.

References

1. Cranor, L.F., Garfunkel, S.: Security and Usability: Designing Secure Systems That People Can Use. O'Reiley (2005)
2. Kerckhoffs, A.: La cryptographie militaire. Journal des Sciences Militaires IX, 5–38 (1883)
3. Wolf, G., Pfitzmann, A.: Properties of protection goals and their integration into a user interface. Computer Networks 32, 685–699 (2000)

4. Scerri, S., Gimenez, R., Herman, F., Bourimi, M., Thiel, S.: digital.me towards an integrated Personal Information Sphere, (June 2011),
http://d-cent.org/fsw2011/wp-content/uploads/fsw2011-digital.me-towards-an-integrated-Personal-Information-Sphere.pdf

5. Thiel, S., et al.: A requirements-driven approach towards decentralized social networks. In: Park, J.J., Leung, V.C.M., Wang, C.-L., Shon, T. (eds.) Future Information Technology, Application, and Service. LNEE, vol. 164, pp. 709–718. Springer, Heidelberg (2012)

6. Heupel, M., Fischer, L., Kesdogan, D., Bourimi, M., Scerri, S., Hermann, F., Gimenez, R.: Context-aware, trust-based access control for the di.me userware. In: 2012 5th International Conference on New Technologies, Mobility and Security (NTMS), pp. 1–6 (May 2012)

7. Bourimi, M., Rivera, I., Scerri, S., Heupel, M., Cortis, K., Thiel, S.: Integrating multi-source user data to enhance privacy in social interaction. In: Proceedings of the 13th International Conference on Interacción Persona-Ordenador, INTERAC-CION 2012, pp. 51:1–51:7. ACM, New York (2012)

8. Karatas, F., Bourimi, M., Barth, T., Kesdogan, D., Gimenez, R., Schwittek, W., Planagumà, M.: Towards secure and at-runtime tailorable customer-driven public cloud deployment, pp. 124–130 (March 2012)

9. Bourimi, M., Barth, T., Haake, J.M., Ueberschär, B., Kesdogan, D.: AFFINE for enforcing earlier consideration of nFRs and human factors when building socio-technical systems following agile methodologies. In: Forbrig, P., Bernhaupt, R., Forbrig, P., Gulliksen, J., Lárusdóttir, M. (eds.) HCSE 2010. LNCS, vol. 6409, pp. 182–189. Springer, Heidelberg (2010)

10. Bourimi, M., Kesdogan, D.: Experiences by using AFFINE for building collaborative applications for online communities. In: HCI International 2013, Parallel Sessions. HCII 2013 (to appear, 2013)

11. Karatas, F., Kesdogan, D.: A flexible approach for considering interdependent security objectives in service composition. In: Proceedings of the 28th Symposium on Applied Computing (ACM SAC), pp. 1919–1926 (2013)

12. Karatas, F., Heupel, M., Bourimi, M., Kesdogan, D., Wrobel, S.: Considering interdependent protection goals in domain-specific contexts: The di.me case study. To be published in the Proceedings of the 10th International Conference on Information Technology - New Generations (2013)

13. Cohon, J.L., Marks, D.H.: A review and evaluation of multiobjective programing techniques. Water Resources Research 11(2), 208–220 (1975)

14. Dantzig, G.B., Thapa, M.N.: Linear Programming 2: Theory and Extensions. Springer (2003)

Composites Ideas in COMPOOL Immersion: A Semantics Engineering Innovation Network Community Platform

Niki Lambropoulos[1], Panayota Tsotra[2], Ilias Kotinas[1], and Iosif Mporas[1]

[1] Wire Communications Laboratory, Dept. of Electrical and Computer Engineering
[2] Applied Mechanics Laboratory, Dept. of Mechanical Engineering and Aeronautics
University of Patras, 26504, Rion-Patras, Greece
`nlampropoulou@wcl.ee.upatras.gr`, `tsotra@mech.upatras.gr`,
`{ikotinas,imporas}@upatras.gr`

Abstract. Nowadays, organisations and companies collaborate towards interoperable solutions difficult to derive in one closed research and development department. Currently, such concepts started to be implemented within User Innovation Networks, opening a new collective, productive space for the individual and the inter-community collaboration. Also the emergence of Internet platforms that enable and support collaborative innovation research anchored in WEB 03 semantic technologies generate new challenges and opportunities in a period of crisis. Based upon these ideas, COMPOOL Web 3.0 Collaboration Platform is an innovative collaboration research proposal, focusing on developing partnerships between governmental organisations, academia and industry to produce new composite materials based on disruptive and incremental open innovation. COMPOOL 's main aim and functionality is to synthesize and manage ideas from different disciplines so to reduce time execution as well as high costs and risks associated with technologies in composites research and development. The proposed COMPOOL platform uses Semantic Analysis, Human Computer Interaction Immersive Experience and User Innovation Networks aiming at real micro- and macro-scale industrial implementations for out of the box problem solving within diverse industries, as for example, aerospace, automotive, construction, wind energy and sports.

Keywords: Human Computer Interaction, Composites, User-Innovation Networks, User Experience, Computer Mediated Communication, E-research with Communities, Community Based Innovation.

1 Introduction

Nowadays, in several occasions, companies experience difficulties in solving problems and turn to user communities for solutions. For example, The Deepwater Horizon oil spill disaster was an oil spill in the Gulf of Mexico on the BP-operated Macondo Prospect, and is considered as the largest accidental marine oil spill in the history of the petroleum industry. As BP could not solve the problem immediately, the researchers turned to user communities for solutions. Innovation network community platforms

A.A. Ozok and P. Zaphiris (Eds.): OCSC/HCII 2013, LNCS 8029, pp. 385–394, 2013.
© Springer-Verlag Berlin Heidelberg 2013

now serve communities of special interest; if for innovation, they can provide a revolutionary model where industry, academia, non-profit organizations, along with government organisations, collaborate to rapidly deliver solutions, new technologies and innovative capabilities. Such networking for research and development purposes can involve universities, research institutes and industry approaching artificial or mixed material such as composites from different point of view, e.g. engineering, physics, chemistry etc. In this way, by providing an open environment to support idea generation and management, the collaboration space, methods, tools and techniques can be used to support direct dialogue and inquiries from and with the industry.

Composite materials are a rapidly developed field gaining new applications almost every day [1]. Composites consist of two or more materials with significant different properties which remain separate and distinct within the finished structure, however, with superior properties compared to its parts. Research in this field is interdisciplinary and can be found in chemistry, engineering, mathematics, physics etc or fields that seem to be completely irrelevant to composites engineering. Consequently, immediate and associated responses to such needs finding the right expert is of high importance and in some cases the solution is not the obvious. In other words, an expert can be found in faculties not directly connected to the composite world. Due to the fast growth and the complexity of these applications, industries are often facing severe problems that need fast solutions directly implemented within authentic environments.

Bringing ideas into applications and reality is based on the open innovation model[2] and user innovation networks in particular. Engaging users from different backgrounds speeds up the problem solving process faced by the industry via the rapid and agile development of composite applications in situ. Semantic Web 3.0 technologies can provide a solution to this problem by bringing together experts from governmental, industrial and academic organisations on Semantic Analysis Engineering Platform. Web 3.0 is about:

- Data, metadata, semantic search and facilitating interoperability by including semantic content in web pages.
- Encouraging and enabling users to find, share, and combine information
- Create meaningful connections between the data, legible and meaningful (understandable) by the machine.

User Innovation Networks (UIN) has been considered the open innovation model for this century as it functions entirely independently of manufacturers. Networks can be built up horizontally – with actors consisting only of innovation users (more precisely, "user/self-manufacturers") [3][4]. Free and open source software projects are examples of such networks. Some users have sufficient incentive to innovate and some other users to voluntarily distribute their innovations. If the innovation products are at low or no cost they can compete with commercial ones. The benefits are related to the identification and development of something that is missing in the market and distributed within the networks and beyond.

2   Immersive Experience Design for Innovation Communities

Immersive eXperience (iX)[5][6], as with User Experience (UX), is the creation of immediate, deeply immersive, meaningful and memorable learning experience. Thus, it is appropriate, satisfying, successful, and related to humane values, also directed towards the specific learning objectives for each course or session. User eXperience (UX) is a person's perceptions responses resulting from use and/or anticipated use of a product, system or service.

iX is focused on supporting users' natural curiosity and reasoning, individual interests, drives and opening up the space for their reasoning including aligning several aspects of diverse information. These factors can be explicit such as cognitive, learning, social and pedagogical, and implicit such as metacognitive, affective and conative such as curiosity. This is the exact reason why iX is best suitable for COMPOOL, a platform to support disruptive innovation and not only.

These directly affect inductive/deductive reasoning preferences and thus, choices on directions learners make on learning pathways, leading to tailor-made, targeted and constructive anywhere-anytime learning as well as motivating and engaging in teamwork. Consequently, an attractive and efficient 3D iX environment provides customisable control and immediate feedback. Such functionalities can challenge the learners by providing creative flow conditions with enhanced awareness and sensitivity about specific needs, excitement, enthusiasm and joy found in imaginative and innovative activities.

Curiosity is the desire to know, based on knowledge or experience that motivates exploratory behaviour; furthermore, curiosity is activated when there is the feeling of lacking knowledge for a subject of interest. Such needed information is substantial and capable of increasing subjective feelings of competence, in our case technological and digital competencies. Therefore curiosity also serves as an intrinsic motivational and activation factor. Intrinsic motivation is an internal state typified by a strong desire to engage and interact with the environment with stimuli. It is reinforced by interest and enjoyment, a willingness to initiate and continue autonomous behaviour, and prompts an individual to engage in activity primarily for its own sake, because the individual perceives the activity as interesting, involving, satisfying or personally challenging. There are specific immersive factors, conditions and associated iX Design attributes that enable and enhance the user's engagement and activity on platforms that require such actions.

Immersive Factors

1. Clear goals as challenge level and skill high level
2. Concentration and focused attention
3. Loss of feeling
4. Distorted sense of time
5. Direct and immediate feedback
6. Balance between ability level and challenge
7. Sense of personal control over the situation or activity
8. The activity is intrinsically rewarding, so there is an effortlessness of action
9. Lack of awareness of bodily needs
10. Absorption into the activity.

iX 10 Design Attributes

1. Common purpose: Have a clear & focused purpose
2. Powerful Presence – Co-Presence: Intimacy (closeness) as the interpretation of the degree of interpersonal interactions[8]; Immediacy (directedness) as psychological

distance[9]; The degree of salience (stands out) of the other person in a mediated communication and the consequent salience of their interpersonal interactions[10][11]; The degree by which a person was perceived as real in an online conversation[12].

3. Engagement Factors: Perception via the senses; Action via the body/kinaesthetic – physical body functions; Emotion via the heart – emotional & instinctual nature functions; Cognition via the mind – rational consciousness functions; Co-creativity via imagination & intuition – higher consciousness thinking functions; Be in a state of constant flow;   Connect with each other

4. Virtual Collaboration: Team knowledge building; Creating creativity: Users' generated context provides the background for new collaboration; Collect-relate-create-donate[13]; Participatory problem solving; Social innovation

5. Zone of Proximal Flow (ZPF) is the area where flow occurs within the zone of proximal development[6], that is the peer-to-peer gap of knowledge and potential development. In this way learners' interest and engagement counteract the anxiety experienced in the creative flow.

6. Connectedness: Direction, Motivation, Activation; Knowledge, Understanding, Meaning; Skills, Competencies; Flow, Activities; Trust, Belonging; Learning, Sharing, Co-creation; Consciousness, Inter-Connectedness

7. Engagement in Compelling & Memorable Activities

8. Sense of Belonging

Immersive Taxonomy. When building User Innovation Networks design and development of an organically evolving community is needed. The following diagram depicts the evolution process enabling the community members to inform, share, relate and create new ideas for composites coming from diverse backgrounds.

Figure 1 proposes the detailed transition from the individual contribution to the collective intelligence outcomes based on the evolving sense of contributing into the innovation community. This is possible by starting from small talks and mere information to sharing experience and creating common dreams.   As such, active engagement serves the community purposes based on trust and belonging so to be open for sharing and co-creating in a spiral fueled by common inspiration.

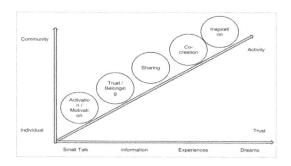

Fig. 1. COMPOOL Innovation Community Immersive Taxonomy [6]

3   COMPOOL: The Composites Pool Open Innovation Environment

COMPOOL platform design and development supports open community collaboration for disruptive and incremental innovation by enabling idea generation and management, problem solving, and solutions and innovation development of advanced composites. COMPOOL brings together associated communities such as governmental, academic and industrial stakeholders. The process starts with the stakeholders' registration, profiling and requirements submission and identification. Then collaboration and mixing ideas ignites integration and development of diverse teams, project/program definition which, by using COMPOOL tools, leads to project development and innovative solution application. COMPOOL is built on a Semantic Ontology and Semantic Analyses techniques and language enquiries for intelligent ideas and solutions search to support Disruptive and Open Innovation Management.

The COMPOOL platform is based upon WEB 3.0 technologies and shares common characteristics with intranet platforms, web portals, social networks, wikis and VIEs. Its basic framework consists of a shared information space that supports sharing and discovery of information among users. The space is comprised of a number of technical standards and platforms interconnected in a network within boundaries of group of people and topics. All communication goes through a web-browser using the TCP/IP and HTTP protocols. Thus any client application can be a part of the platform as long as the browser is the primary client interface. The platform provides a variety of functionalities to its users in order to promote user engagement, information sharing, data discovery and more importantly incentives for idea sharing and innovation. The underlying structure includes components that support WEB 3.0 technologies like the Semantic Analysis (LSA/ESA), ontology building, summarization and user adaptation. COMPOOL also supports different user categories having diverse roles and backgrounds to reach information and perform tasks in a personalised manner.

The Underlying Information Architecture. Researching the suitable Information Architecture (IA) of a Collaboration environment is of great importance. Effective information architecture enables people to step logically through a system confident they are getting closer to the information they require. Lacking a suitable Information flow increases the risk of creating great content and functionality that no one can ever find. The proposed Information Architecture is based on the fact that the content is not going to be created by a group of administrators or content authors, but it will be mostly supplied by distributed research teams and their members in a collaborative and contributing manner. However, the distributive character of the user base makes the decision of the suitable information containers much more difficult. Two questions are the most prominent in this decision process: i) what is important and for whom? ii) What has to be accessible and for whom?

The Information Architecture of the system needs to answer sensibly these two questions for the largest part of the users possible. The proposed platform uses a "Pull" (or self-subscribe) rather than a "Push" model for the Information flow and the Notification system, in order to fulfil the above issue. That means, that each user selects what is important for him and thus reaches it with less effort (the "Push" model is available in some functions as well, but that does not reflect the general philosophy of the platform). This mechanism is implemented using "Spaces" and subscriptions. The content is enclosed in respective Groups called "Spaces" that subscribed users use to access and post information. These groups are routinely created by users around the topic of their interest, area of expertise or even around an idea. The access control to these groups is user defined and thus both public and private groups co-exist in the platform.

The user navigation is supported by a hybrid combination of hard-coded and system-generated links. The hard-coded navigation menu includes a global top-level navigation block, which provides entering users with access to spaces, topics, materials, stakeholders and events, and a per-space menu block, which guides users to group-specific content like documents, wikis, diagrams, Q&A, bibliography lists and group meet-up events. Additionally, the system auto-generates an always evolving navigation system based on the semantic analysis of subjects, documents, terms and users.

The same underlying models built by the semantic analysis components are available to a custom search engine which further aid user find related information and contacts. Finally, the navigation and search systems are further adapted according to each user's trained user profile.

Basic Functionalities

1. User Registration: The user registration is the first logical step for a new user to start using the platform. It provides access to the platform, private access to personal data and subscribed groups and finally it allows the system to create a personalized user profile in order to adapt its behaviour and appearance. The next logical step is the creation of a user profile. Users may select one of the following categories or templates, when building their profile: Stakeholder, Manufacturer, Researcher, and Student. This aids the user discovery and provides the necessary initial information to the system to adapt its information architecture to the logged in user.

2. Stakeholder identification and discovery: COMPOOL users, upon completion of their personal profile, may add specific details about their area(s) of interest, their knowledge/expertise, their working domain and other personal notes which are indexed and available to stakeholder listings and searches. The discovery of related stakeholders is then facilitated by a filtering and searching form, which additionally uses underlying models built with the semantic analysis of user shared content.

3. Spaces: A *space* is a virtual content container created and used by users with common interests. Spaces can be public (i.e. accessible by every user) or private (accessible only to members). The content in public spaces is parsed and semantically analysed by the back-end learning algorithms in order to build globally accessible ontologies and is available to global searches and navigation. Private spaces can be managed by either the space owner (creator) or by other people who are given further access granting privileges.

4. Dashboard: The results from the back-end semantic analysis along with traditional content metrics are displayed in summary pages called dashboards. Two types of dashboards exist: the global dashboard and the space dashboard. The global dashboard lists personalized trending and popular content, related users and topics fetched by public and user-subscribed spaces. The space dashboard summarizes recently posted, updated or discussed content, exclusive into this specific space.

5. Spaces collaboration features: Several collaboration facilities are available in order to support different user needs, team structures and content types. The main collaboration facilities are:

   a. Documents and comments: Documents are online content containers stored directly into the platform database. Ordinary files can be uploaded and added as attachments to a document permitting desktop file exchange between users. Documents can be further categorized in hierarchical containers called "Books". This allows for the hierarchical organization of related content and files. Documents do not support collaborative editing, thus they better serve the need for personal knowledge sharing. However, a commenting system is available and thus feedback can be provided by partners to the content author.

   b. Wikis: Unlike documents, which do not support collaborative editing of content, wikis may be edited by more than one user, allowing thus the building of documents based on community rather than just personal knowledge. Wikis are supported by full version control so that content can survive human mistakes or vandalism.

   c. Questions and Answers: This facility supports the posting of user questions which other experts from similar or different areas of expertise may answer.

   d. Projects and Task Tracker: Spaces may facilitate also the building of projects among subscribed users. Projects are subdivided in tasks and a ticketing system, named "Task tracker", supports the delegation of tasks and monitoring of their progress.

   e. Micro-blogging: Inspired by the advent of social networks, spaces support also the need of short, informal and highly interactive conversation fulfilled by a micro-blogging facility, accessible to all the members of a specific group.

   f. Bibliography listing: Publications related to materials, composite materials and manufacturing may be shared using the bibliography section. Users may either post their own publications or other interesting publications useful for the members of the group.

   g. Surveys and questionnaires: User initiated surveys appear to be very useful to idea holders in order to reveal and extract patterns from stakeholder interests and discover trends in industry and related markets. Thus, a survey building and sharing facility is incorporated in COMPOOL available to all users of a specific group. Surveys may be publicly shared with people with no user account in order to get greater user feedback.

h. 2D/3D Virtual canvas. In several cases, complicated ideas may be better explained in a 2D/3D vector canvas rather than on paper, especially in the field of composite materials research, the geometrical structure of which is one of the most important factors. Ready-made objects and pattern structures are available in order to aid in rapid prototyping of ideas. Users may also create reusable objects. Moreover, 2D and 3D models can be collectively built and edited by authorized users, thus building better models based on community knowledge and experience.

i. Meet-ups and events: The members of a space may schedule local meet-ups or annual global meetings in order to get in touch and further discuss their ideas and projects. This facility is further supported by a personalized calendar which is automatically generated for each user. Users may also search and discover meet-ups in public groups, filtered by distance, subject and date.

6. Building learning material: COMPOOL supports also the creation of learning material for students or even experts in order to support lifelong learning. Users may use the aforementioned spaces facilities in order to create courses which may consist of books, presentations, videos and 3D interactive models. Online exercises may also be created using the available survey/questionnaire facility.

7. Innovation support: COMPOOL builds on several features to support user innovation and encourage the exchange of ideas among researchers and other stakeholders.

j. An idea sharing facility is separately built which is based on a collection of assets like documents and 3D models and a copyright holding agreement signed between the owner and the contacted stakeholder.

k. Researchers or industry representatives may search and discover publicly shared, related innovative ideas.

l. Users may navigate the auto-generated ontology and discover posted information about the related materials and their industry applications.

m. Idea holders may reach and contact manufacturers through the stakeholder discovery form.

n. Community innovation is supported by the collaborative features of "spaces"

8. Notifications and external communication: The semantic analysis and user adaptation models may be used to provide useful timely information to the subscribed users. A summarization module, builds lists with recent information related to each user which are made available either through e-mail as a personalized newsletter or using syndication feeds (RSS).

9. Desktop client: A desktop client may be used in order to support immersive multisensory stimuli for the 3D interactive and collective model building facility. The desktop client is required in order to access native drivers not available to a browser client and also achieve better performance through the usage of additional system APIs.

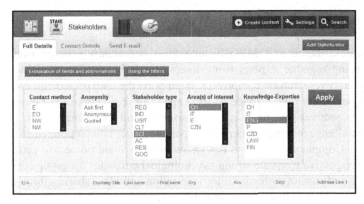

Fig. 2. A view of the stakeholder identification and discovery facility

Using the aforementioned facilities, the user engagement is significantly enhanced, since users feel members of a community, participate in private and open discussions and use tools which promote safe and rapid exchange of their ideas. As mentioned above, beyond the user facilities aiming to achieve innovation and immersive experience (iX), an underlying back-end system is utilized to support the semantic analysis and language enquiries of submitted content. The methods used are described in the following section.

3.1   COMPOOL Semantics

Computing semantic relatedness between terms or documents of natural language texts requires access to common-sense and domain-specific world knowledge, based on similarities to documents of a reference corpus, this is the ontology. It can be used to reason about the entities within that domain and may be used to describe the domain and renders shared vocabulary and taxonomy. Latent and Explicit Semantic Analysis (LSA & ESA): LSA is a technique to analyse relationships between a set of documents and terms they contain by producing a set of concepts related to documents and terms. LSA assumes that words that are close in meaning will occur close together in text. ESA represents the meaning of texts in a high-dimensional space of concepts derived from Wikipedia.

LSA and ESA have never been used for semantic similarity problems towards the identification of right experts, ideas and/or solutions. Therefore new Human Collective Intelligence semantic similarity algorithms need to be invented for COMPOOL.

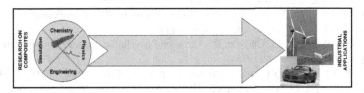

Fig. 3. COMPOOL diverse innovation community to support industrial innovation

4   Conclusions and Future Work

This paper described the COMPOOL innovation community open environment aiming at bringing together experts from diverse fields in order to facilitate industrial interdisciplinary research on composites. It supports the unexpected and creative solutions everyday users may provide to the experts in the composites field to enhance multiple perspectives and diversity for disruptive and open innovation. In order to achieve users' engagement, Immersive eXperience (iX) is incorporated into the common Human Computer Interaction design and development process to provide a multisensory perspective to create strong psychological attributes for groups creative flow engagement and sustain enthusiasm for inspiration and ideas sharing through an innovation community development organic process.

COMPOOL is based on a semantics engineering approach; users' engagement is anchored in a number of Web 3.0 functionalities and semantics engineering creating strong vibrations to remember.

References

1. Tsotra, P., De Verclos, O., Howland, D.: New Generation of Paste Adhesives for Aerospace and Wind Turbine Blade Bonding. In: The Composite Symposium 2009, TU München, Germany (2009)
2. von Hippel, E.: Horizontal innovation networks- by and for users. MIT Sloan Working Paper No. 4366-02, http://opensource.mit.edu/papers/vonhippel3.pdf
3. Chesbrough, H.W.: Open Innovation: The New Imperative for Creating and Profiting from Technology. Harvard Business School Press, Boston (2005)
4. Lambropoulos, N., Kampylis, P., Bakharia, A.: User Innovation Networks and Research Challenges. In: Ozok, A.A., Zaphiris, P. (eds.) OCSC 2009. LNCS, vol. 5621, pp. 364–373. Springer, Heidelberg (2009)
5. Lambropoulos, N., Mystakides, S.: Learning Experience+ within 3D Immersive Virtual Environments. In: The Proceedings of the Federated Conference on Computer Science and Information Systems, FedCSIS 2012, Wrocław, Poland, September 9-12, pp. 857–862 (2012)
6. Lambropoulos, N., Reinhardt, P., Mystakidis, Σ., Tolis, Δ., Danis, Σ., Gourdin, A.: Immersive Worlds for Learning eXperience+: Engaging users in the zone of proximal flow in Second Life. In: EADTU Conference, Paphos, Cyprus, September 27-28 (2012)
7. Vygotsky, L.S.: Mind in Society. Harvard University Press, Cambridge (1978)
8. Argyle, M., Dean, J.: Eye-contact, distance and affiliation. Sociometry 28, 289–304 (1965)
9. Wiener, M., Mehrabian, A.: Language within language: Immediacy, a channel in verbal communication. Appleton-Century-Crofts, New York (1968)
10. Dourish, P., Bellotti, V.: Awareness and Coordination in Shared Workspaces. In: Proceeding of ACM CSCW Conference, pp. 107–114 (1992)
11. Short, J.A., Williams, E., Christie, B.: The social psychology of telecommunications. John Wiley & Sons, New York (1976)
12. Meyer, K.A.: The web's impact on student learning. T. H. E. Journal 30(10) (2003)
13. Shneiderman, B.: Leonardo's Laptop: Human Needs and the New Computing Technologies. The MIT Press, Cambridge (2002)

Supporting Distributed Search in Virtual Worlds

Hiep Luong, Dipesh Gautam, John Gauch, Susan Gauch, and Jacob Hendricks

University of Arkansas Fayetteville, AR 72701, U.S.A
{hluong,dgautam,jgauch,sgauch,jhendric}@uark.edu

Abstract. As three-dimensional (3D) environments become both more prevalent and more fragmented, the need for a data crawler and distributed search service will continue to grow. By increasing the visibility of content across virtual world servers in order to better collect and integrate the 3D data, we can also improve the efficiency and accuracy of crawling and searching by avoiding both the crawling of unchanged regions and the downloading unmodified objects that already exist in our collection. This helps to lower bandwidth usage during content collection and indexing, and for a fixed amount of bandwidth, maximizes the freshness of the collection. This paper presents a new services paradigm for virtual world crawler interaction that is co-operative and exploits information about 3D objects in the virtual world. By analyzing redundant information crawled from virtual worlds, our approach decreased the amount of data collected by crawlers, kept search engine collections up to date, and provided an efficient mechanism for collecting and searching information from multiple virtual worlds.

Keywords: Virtual World, Distributed Search, Data Crawling, Bandwidth.

1 Introduction

Search engines revolutionized the way we discover information in the World Wide Web. It seems natural that search would also vastly improve how we can discover and use information hidden in virtual worlds. Hence we have a need for virtual world crawlers, programs that automatically collect object data from virtual world servers. This object data is often text embedded in texture images, note cards, and chat messages that is triggered by avatar proximity or action. This means that a virtual world crawler must 'touch' the object before collecting its information. In other words, crawlers are expected to move around and approach objects in a region being explored. Traveling in a region, a crawler may encounter objects that have already been collected by previous crawls. When a crawler collects redundant object data, a crawler needlessly consumes bandwidth.

Our goal in this work was to explore a more efficient and exhaustive method of collecting content from virtual worlds. In this paper, we investigate the potential bandwidth savings that a collaborative crawling approach could achieve. In addition, this collaborative approach could be used to direct a crawler to a list of unvisited

A.A. Ozok and P. Zaphiris (Eds.): OCSC/HCII 2013, LNCS 8029, pp. 395–404, 2013.

regions or a region in the virtual world that has a high rate of change. We developed a focused crawler allowing us to collect data from Second Life and/or OpenSimulator virtual worlds. Once we gathered the data, we explored how frequently content changes in different regions and built a model of the rate of change in virtual worlds. With this model in mind, we have proposed an architecture that could allow the crawler to collect new or unvisited objects in a virtual world. Our empirical experiments using data from Second Life servers have shown that proper management of data redundancy based on our proposed architecture can decrease bandwidth traffic.

In this paper, we begin with a summary of related work on crawling data in virtual worlds. Then, we introduce our crawler architecture and present methods to evaluate data redundancy and bandwidth consumption savings during the crawling process. Next, we report our experimental results for this approach and discuss the impact of our work. The final section presents conclusions and discusses our ongoing and future work in this area.

2   Related Work

This section describes related work on crawling data in virtual world and efforts to support crawlers in exploring objects in 3D environment.

Crawlers for the WWW aim to collect exhaustive, fresh content from the WWW while minimizing bandwidth utilization. Cooperative crawlers incorporate methods that exploit information about web pages such as creation dates, update dates, file size and request frequency for each object of a website [2]. In [3], Chandramouli et al. designed a collaborative architecture in which web servers combine information from web logs and the file system to keep track of page creation, deletion, and modification. This information was available to web crawlers via a web service. They showed that, with this collaborative architecture, the crawler could discover new and valuable pages with reduced server traffic.

Interoperation among several virtual world environments remains a major challenge. The lack of interoperation on several current and possibly future virtual worlds is the main constraint on the growth of virtual worlds. Several researchers have been working to mitigate this constraint. Bell et al. [1] introduced VWRAP (Virtual World Region Agent Protocol) which addresses the problem of interoperability for a family of current and future virtual worlds, while [8] proposed an architecture and protocol for decentralizing multiuser virtual environments in which multiuser applications can exchange user agents and assets.

Among the current virtual worlds, Second Life[1] and OpenSimulator (OpenSim)[2] are the two most active worlds and have the most subscribers. There are two existing search services for Second Life and broader virtual worlds. The official Second Life search relies on the internal content database and does not extend to emulator worlds. The second service appears to rely on a combination of avatar crawlers and indirect database access for OpenSimulator worlds. OpenSimulator worlds can be connected

---

[1] http://secondlife.com/
[2] http://opensimulator.org/wiki/Main_Page

to by any Second Life client, but can also be hosted separately and combined into ad hoc grids to form separate virtual worlds.

There has been some work on exploring virtual worlds. Researchers have created a framework to collect avatar-related data using Linden Scripting Language (LSL) [10]. In [8], a crawler is used to collect spatial data of a user in Second Life in order to reveal relationships between behavior of real world humans and avatars in the virtual world.

Crawling data in virtual worlds is an essential task for the development of a distributed search service for 3D environments. Eno et al. ([4], [5] and [7]) demonstrated that virtual worlds could be effectively crawled with an autonomous agent that behaves like a normal human. They emulated a client protocol with an intelligent crawling agent to mimic normal user behavior. Their crawler   navigates a region through an expanding spiral survey path[4]. In other work [6], Eno et al. examined landmarks and the picks to analyze the link between the regions. Their results showed that regions in the virtual world are linked similarly in pages of the flat web. Although they primarily studied regions within Second Life, they detected evidence of existence of a denser link structure on virtual world sites hosted in OpenSimulator.

In other work, Varvello et al. [9] analyzed Second Life's scalability, popularity, staleness of objects and quality of the user experience based on counting the objects in various regions at different points of time. However, staleness may not be accurately assessed merely by counting the number of objects. In our work, not only did we take the number of edited objects at different points of time into account, but we also compared the identities of the objects to get a count of unique objects. In this paper we focus on calculating the bandwidth required when regions are repeatedly crawled completely, including the collection of stale objects, and contrast that with the bandwidth needed by a collaborative architecture modeled on [3], a web service that publishes information about the virtual world's updates to the crawler.

3 Our Approach

Our goal is to estimate the amount of redundant data collected by a traditional crawler that repeatedly revisits regions and downloads all of the objects it can access. To do this, we developed a crawler that visited sample regions and analyzed the data collected, week by week, to identify any changes within that region. We then estimate the amount of data redundancy in this collection and describe a new architecture that would avoid the collection of redundant data, reducing bandwidth and the time necessary to update a search service's database. This section describes our virtual world crawler and the methods we used to identify redundant data as well as potential bandwidth consumption savings.

3.1 Overview

This section describes an overview of our proposed architecture that would support search across distributed virtual worlds by incorporating a collaborative crawler.

We have developed a search engine collection system that includes a knowledge base and indexing programs to store the collected data in addition to crawler software that gathers the content collection. The content collection is done by a set of virtual world client emulators interacting with the virtual world servers such as Second Life, OpenSim, etc. As the content is discovered, it is added to both a metadata database and an inverted index structure for query retrieval.

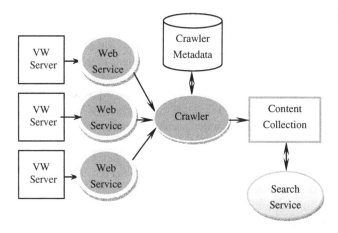

Fig. 1. Proposed System Architecture Overview

Unlike the web service paradigm proposed by [3] for flat web, we propose the development of a web service for each virtual world server such that each server shares object metadata in XML format with a collaborative crawler (Fig. 1.). The crawler then exploits this metadata information to identify the objects that have been added or modified since its last visit and focus on collecting only those objects. As another benefit, if the metadata also includes information about deleted objects, the crawler can remove those from the search engine's content collection, increasing the collection's accuracy. The crawler can also save metadata about the rate of change per region so that future crawls can target fast-changing regions more frequently.

As a first step to this, we developed a traditional crawler that visits regions and downloads all of the objects it can find. By repeatedly visiting sample regions, we develop a model of the rate of change of objects in different regions (additions, modifications, and deletions) so that we can estimate the potential benefits of our proposed architecture.

3.2   Collaborative Crawling in Virtual Worlds

We have developed collaborative crawler agents designed to collect user-generated content in Second Life and related virtual worlds. The crawling system architecture contains different components that are dedicated to crawling, coordination, and storage tasks. Specifically, the server manager starts the crawling tasks by assigning specific regions to crawl for individual agents. Then, it keeps track of completed and queued regions as well as the status of the crawler in each region. The coordination layer consists of a server management program that coordinates individual crawlers and includes components for duplicate detection and queue management for the entire virtual world. Once the data is collected from each region, it is saved by the storage layer that includes both database storage and searchable index storage for the architecture [4].

When a crawler instance is assigned to explore data from a specific region, it will attempt to teleport to that region. When the crawler agent teleports successfully to a region, it begins storing object positions as they are automatically sent from the server. Scripts associated with objects are triggered when the crawler agent begins moving around the region to come into close proximity or touch the object.

Though more objects were discovered when the crawler agent moves near the object, the number of objects collected did not improved significantly with navigating the region when compared to the number of objects collected while standing at the landing area of the region. So, instead of navigating the region of interest, we sent the crawler to the landing area and let it to rotate around. For our preliminary experiment, we have selected 100 different regions from Second Life virtual world and let our crawler harvest data from these regions over several weeks. The data crawled were stored in the database.

3.3   Data Redundancy

The main issue for any information crawler is avoiding the collect of data that has already been downloaded. This creates unnecessary Internet traffic and wastes search engine resources during page collection and indexing.

In the virtual worlds, given the increased time necessary to physically navigate the 3D environment, it is particularly important to avoid collecting redundant data and to prioritize collecting the newly added objects or modified objects. We calculate the data redundancy collected by traditional crawling techniques by counting the common objects between two crawler collections, divided by the total number of unique objects collected by either crawl.

$$DR = \frac{UC}{TC} * 100$$

where UC is the number of unchanged objects which are crawled in a region, and TC is total number of objects crawled from that region. The average data redundancy is calculated using the average UC and TC values over all regions that are crawled.

3.4   Bandwidth Consumption Saving

In this section, we present a measure that estimates the potential savings in bandwidth consumed by the crawler using the proposed architecture. The bandwidth consumption savings metric is defined as follows:

$$BS = \frac{TC - UC}{TC} * 100$$

with UC and TC are defined in the above section. This bandwidth consumption saving value represents the percentage of savings that a crawler can achieve by avoiding the collection of redundant data.

4   Experiments

Our crawler has the task of interacting with the virtual world environment to collect content. It has been built using the OpenMV library available from Open Metaverse. This C# library provides the Second Life client emulation functionality necessary to connect to a Second Life server, move around, and interact with other objects or avatars. Multiple instances of the crawler connect to the virtual world at one time, coordinating their activities through the Server Controller. We have designed a test scenario that would determine the effectiveness of our crawler and help us characterize different classes of objects that are found in Second Life regions.

4.1   Data Collection

Our first task was to select regions to crawl. Initially, a list of regions is obtained by configuring our crawler to teleport to random Second Life regions from a seed region. From 300 regions selected from Second Life servers, we calculated the normalized number of objects crawled and the normalized time rate of collecting objects from each region (Fig. 2). The smallest regions took only a few minutes to be crawled while the largest regions required several hours to visit. Most of the regions among the 300 took from 6 to 12 minutes to crawl. In order to experiment with average sized regions, we excluded 100 regions including smallest and largest regions, and randomly selected half of the remaining 200 regions to obtain our final set of 100 regions.

In order to see how effectively the crawler captures objects in the virtual world, we launched the crawler with the same input parameters four times in four consecutive weeks. We started the crawler in a fixed time of the week (Thursday at 9:00AM) and saved data crawled for each week. Among 100 experimental regions, there were 3 regions from which the crawler was unable to collect objects; therefore we report our results over 97 regions. Table 1 shows a summary of data crawled over four weeks. For each snapshot, we report the total number of objects crawled. We then compare object records from consecutive crawls and calculate the number of objects added, deleted, modified and unchanged during each snapshot. Notice that the number of objects added and the number of objects deleted are relatively consistent from snapshot to snapshot, and are roughly 33% as large as the total number of objects crawled. The number of objects with modified attributes is also consistent from snapshot to snapshot, but these values are less than 2% of the total number of objects. Finally, the number of unchanged objects is roughly 66% of the number of objects crawled.

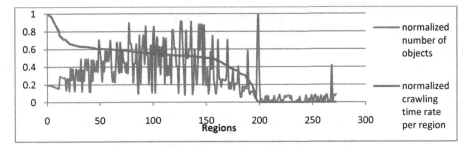

Fig. 2. Selection Second Life regions for experiments

Table 1. Data collection from 4 weeks

	#Objects crawled	#Objects added	#Objects deleted	#Objects modified	#Objects unchanged
Week 1 snapshot	490,850	0	0	0	0
Week 2 snapshot	486,294	157,492	162,048	5,627	323,175
Week 3 snapshot	481,313	154,860	159,841	8,074	318,379
Week 4 snapshot	449,729	136,653	168,237	8,293	304,783

4.2   Evaluation

Data Redundancy. Our goal with this experiment was to get a sense of how much redundant information is collected during each region crawl. Fig. 3 represents the data redundancy reported over four weeks. The DR_W2 curve shows the data redundancy between weeks 1 and 2. Similarly, the DR_W3 and DR_W4 curves show the redundancy between weeks 2 and 3, and between weeks 3 and 4. In all three cases, the redundancy values for each region have been sorted in decreasing order. Fig. 4 combines the data redundancy over four weeks, plotting the average data redundancy for each region crawled over the 4-week experiment. Notice that the median value for data redundancy is roughly 66%, which is consistent with the data in Table 1.

For each crawl, we also calculated the number of new objects that are created, the number of objects deleted, and the number of objects that are modified. In Table 2 we illustrate how the total number of objects changed is distributed in each week. TC_W2 is the total number of objects changed between week 1 and 2 for selected regions. Similarly, TC_W3 and TC_W4 are the total number of objects changed between week 2 and 3, and between week 3 and 4 respectively. We present the main percentile values at the 25th, 50th and 75th positions in order to see how the number of objects varies over four weeks.

Bandwidth Savings. A main advantage of our approach is its ability to analyze the data redundancy and decrease the amount of bandwidth used by crawlers. Fig. 5 represents the average bandwidth consumption saving for the whole data collection over four weeks.

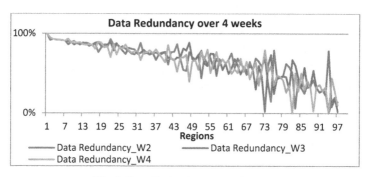

Fig. 3. Data Redundancy over 4 weeks

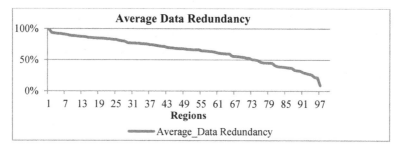

Fig. 4. Average Data Redundancy

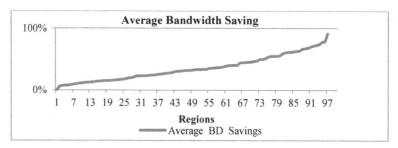

Fig. 5. Average Bandwidth Saving

Table 2. Percentile of number of objects changed over 4 weeks

Percentile	TC_W2	TC_W3	TC_W4
25th	4,138	4,119	4,072
50th	1,815	2,012	2,172
75th	1,324	1,213	1,287

5   Discussion

After investigating the data collected from our four weekly crawls of 100 regions of Second Life we have analyzed in detail the number of objects added, deleted and modified in each region. Using this information, we calculated the bandwidth savings that would be provided by our proposed architecture. Table 3 shows a summary of the 25th, 50th, and 75th percentile values of bandwidth saving over four weeks. These values are very consistent from week to week. The bandwidth savings for the 25th percentile region averaged 48.50%, which indicates that roughly ½ of the objects in these regions remain unchanged from week to week. The 50th percentile region had an average bandwidth saving of 31.70%, which is a significant drop from the 25th percentile region. Finally, the 75th percentile region only had a bandwidth saving of 16.37%, which is only 1/3 of the 25th percentile value.

Table 3. Percentile of bandwidth savings over 4 weeks

Percentile	Saving Week 2	Saving Week 3	Saving Week 4	Average Saving
25th	45.86%	46.31%	49.70%	48.50%
50th	29.61%	30.14%	31.45%	31.70%
75th	15.16%	14.89%	16.50%	16.37%

According to our investigation, the crawler seemed to collect redundant data over the weeks because many of the objects in a virtual world, objects like chairs, trees, towers and buildings, are static. On the other hand, the crawler failed to collect certain data, particularly data pertaining to dynamic objects. Dynamic content such as sand boxes, avatar outfits, billboards and some robots may appear at a place and time only to disappear at another time. Similarly, when the crawler moves, some objects are missed because they are far away from the crawler avatar, not in the range of visibility. Of course another reason that the crawler failed to collect data about some object is that the object has actually been removed from the region.

6   Conclusions

The goal of our research was to implement and validate an intelligent crawler that collects data from virtual worlds. We have demonstrated that crawler performance can be significantly enhanced in terms of bandwidth consumption savings. Our approach to reduce bandwidth usage was to avoid redundant object collection.

We have shown that there is typically a considerable amount of data redundancy in crawling virtual worlds. This can lead to unnecessary bandwidth usage if this redundant data is collected by a crawler. Our approach was empirically tested using data we collected from Second Life servers that contain different kinds of objects in virtual worlds. The experimental results showed that our approach's ability to analyze the data redundancy in crawling potentially helps to reduce resource consumption of the collection process by downloading only unvisited and newly added content.

Our future work includes research into appropriately weighting objects and using interactive content that could guide the crawler to collect more useful object data, while avoiding previously collected objects. We also plan to extend the search function with flexible input parameters to create search service more appropriate for virtual world environments.

Acknowledgements. This research is supported by the NSF grant number 1050801 - III: EAGER: Mapping Three-Dimensional Virtual Worlds.

References

1. Bell, J., Dinova, M., Levine, D.: VWRAP for virtual worlds interoperability [Standards]. IEEE Internet Computing 14(1), 73–77 (2010)
2. Buzzi, M.: Cooperative Crawling. In: Proceedings of First Latin American Web Congress (LA-WEB 2003), pp. 209–211. IEEE Computer Society, Washington, DC (2003)
3. Chandramouli, A.: A co-operative web services paradigm for supporting crawlers. Ph.D. dissertation, Univ. of Kansa, Lawrence, KS, USA (2007)
4. Eno, J.: An Intelligent Crawler For A Virtual World. Ph.D. dissertation, Univ. of Arkansas, Fayetteville, AR, USA (2010)
5. Eno, J., Gauch, S., Thompson, C.: Intelligent Crawling in Virtual Worlds. In: Proceedings of the 2009 IEEE/WIC/ACM International Joint Conference on Web Intelligence and Intelligent Agent Technology (WI-IAT 2009), vol. 3, pp. 555–558. IEEE Computer Society, Washington, DC (2009)
6. Eno, J., Gauch, S., Thompson, C.: Linking Behavior in a Virtual World Environment. In: Proceedings of the 15th International Conference on Web 3D Technology (Web3D 2010), pp. 157–164. ACM, New York (2010)
7. Eno, J., Gauch, S., Thompson, C.: Searching for the Metaverse. In: Spencer, S.N. (ed.) Proceedings of the 16th ACM Symposium on Virtual Reality Software and Technology (VRST 2009), pp. 223–226. ACM, New York (2009)
8. La, C.A., Michiardi, P.: Characterizing User Mobility in Second Life. In: Proceedings of the First Workshop on Online Social Networks (WOSN 2008), pp. 79–84. ACM, New York (2008)
9. Varvello, M., Picconi, F., Diot, C., Biersack, E.: Is there life in Second Life? In: Proceedings of the 2008 ACM CoNEXT Conference (CoNEXT 2008), Article 1, p. 12. ACM, New York (2008)
10. Yee, N., Bailenson, J.N.: A method for longitudinal behavioral data collection in second life. Presence: Teleoper. Virtual Environ. 17(6), 594–596 (2008)

A Consideration of the Functions That Support to Find New Friends in Social Games

Kohei Otake[1], Tomofumi Uetake[2], and Akito Sakurai[1]

[1] School of Science for Open and Environmental Systems, Keio University, 3-14-1 Hiyoshi,
Kohoku-ku, Yokohama-shi, Kanagawa-ken 223-8522, Japan
kohei_otake@hotmail.co.jp, sakurai@ae.keio.ac.jp
[2] Graduate School of Business Administration, Senshu University, 2-1-1 Higashimita Tama-ku
Kawasaki 214-8580, Japan
uetake@isc.senshu-u.ac.jp

Abstract. Recently, social games have attracted considerable attention. Building a relationship with other players can heighten the enjoyment derived from these games. However, many users play social games only with their fixed friends. There are functions to assist users to find friends in social games and SNS, but the existing functions are not simple enough to find friends easily. In our previous research, we proposed methods of reducing the barrier that hinders making contact with unknown users. In this study, we propose a function to facilitate finding new friends using these methods.

Keywords: Social Games, Community forum, Network Analysis, Visualization.

1 Introduction

Social networking services (SNSs) are growing in popularity. SNSs are web-based online services that build and reflect the social networking among people. Typical SNSs in Japan include Facebook, Mobage, mixi, and GREE. Their business model of these SNS companies is based on a large membership count, and online advertising through their website is a major source of revenues. Therefore, it is very important for SNSs to attract large number of users. In this situation, social games have also been attracting attention [1][8]. Interesting social games can bring together many users, which is why SNS companies are aggressively introducing these social games.
Social games have following two special features:

— They are easy to play and the contents are simple.
— They can be enjoyed more by building a relationship with other players.

Social games leverage the player's social network [2]. For example, FarmVille, a farm training game developed by Zynga in 2009, is a very simple and easy game. Players can share information and their experiences with like-minded people and friends. At the height of its popularity, this game had more than 100 million players. Therefore, in social games, playing with like-minded people and friends is just as important as

A.A. Ozok and P. Zaphiris (Eds.): OCSC/HCII 2013, LNCS 8029, pp. 405–411, 2013.
© Springer-Verlag Berlin Heidelberg 2013

any other aspect of the game. Therefore, it is important for social game developers and SNS companies to provide functionalities that can support ways to find like-minded people and friends easily [7].

Usually, there are two ways to contact unknown users in a social game. One way is through a search function to find friends, which is provided by the game. However, it is difficult to connect with unknown users using this function because it does not provide sufficient information to communicate with the other users. Another way is by joining a (formal or informal) community forum provided by the SNS. We think that this is a very good way to start new relationships, because it includes a large amount of information. However, this is not enough to find good like-minded people and friends easily in a social game.

There has been a lot of research about the different aspects of the SNS [3][4][5]. For example, there has been research focusing on the structure of large-scale friend networks [5], analysis of network structures [10][11], and growth models of SNS[12]. Moreover, there has been research on small-scale SNSs (Regional SNS) that pays attention to the relationships between friends, and studies the network analysis using active users and an active link that changes dynamically [13]. Therefore, the research on social games offered by large-scale SNS has stopped only at the research on a characteristic business model from the height of the novelty.

2   The Purpose of Our Research

Social games have attracted a lot of attention in recent years. They have also ex-panded the market size and now serve as a major attraction of the SNS. Moreover, we think that social game is an effective tool to make new friends. We focus on this fea-ture of social games. We think that it is necessary to examine how to effectively exhi-bit the search functions in social games. In this study, we focus on social games, and consider and propose functions to find new friends easily.

We focused on "Bandit Nation," a famous Japanese social game on Mobage (a leading Japanese SNS). The "Bandit Nation" players have two aims, becoming the leader of the banditry, and collecting treasures by stealing them from the other play-ers. Players can also register other users as their companions, to enable exchange of items and treasures. Most users are, therefore, playing a game in cooperation with their friends. Therefore, this game is more enjoyable when played along with many companions. Hence, it is important for the SNS site to offer functionalities to increase the number of users who play together.

3   Problems of Existing Functions Offered by SNS and Social Games

At first, we carried out surveys (251 users) and interviews (15 users) in order to iden-tify the problems associated with social gaming. The two main questions we asked were:

- What kind of social games do you play?
- What kind of people do you play with?

From the responses to the questionnaires, we found that many of users did not make new friends through social games. They were playing social games with other users already known to them. They felt social games were enjoyable, but found it difficult to make new friends. Therefore, we interviewed social game players (15 people) about this difficulty. From these interviews, we found that many players were apprehensive when they made contact with unknown users. In addition, we identified the following two important problems:

1. It is difficult to find new friends, because there are many users who have a wide variety of similar personal information.
2. Many players of social games who want to expand their friend lists do not know the kind of information needed to connect with unknown friend candidates.

Social game players wanted to increase the number of friends they play with, but they found it difficult to make new friends using the existing search function. The existing function does not lower the barrier while contacting unknown users and are insecure. Therefore, we proposed functions that support finding new friends easily. Our functions used two methods to solve the two important problems. First, we examined the visualization method using the user information to solve the former problem (it is difficult to find new friends, because there are many candidates who have a wide variety of personal information). Second, we examined the specifying and extraction methods that should be shared among users to solve the latter problem (Many players of social games who want to expand their friend lists do not know the kind of information needed to connect with unknown friend candidates). Our function proposed combining these two methods.

4   Proposal of the Functions That Support Finding New Friends in Social Games

4.1   The Outline of Our Proposal System

We propose functions that support finding new friends using a player's personal information. Our proposed function has the following two features:

- We offer a network diagram using the information about games, game categories, and communities the player belongs to so that the relationship between the players can be made out easily.
- We extract information about manners, merits, and communication from large amount of information in the bulletin board and offer them so that the player can contact the friend candidates easily.

In our previous research, we examined the visualization method which uses player's personal information [6]. When visualizing in the social games community, it became clear that using the information on a game titles, game categories, and communities is an effective strategy to visualize the social games community. We also examined specifying and extraction methods [5]. The results of this analysis show that the following three elements -Manner, Merits, and Communication- have been important criteria for contacting unknown players from the bulletin board, in addition to basic attributes such as their status and conditions for which a partner is asked. We built the function combining these methods. The outline and the example are shown in Fig.1 and 2.

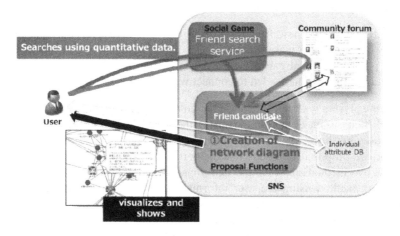

Fig. 1. The Outline of Our Proposal System

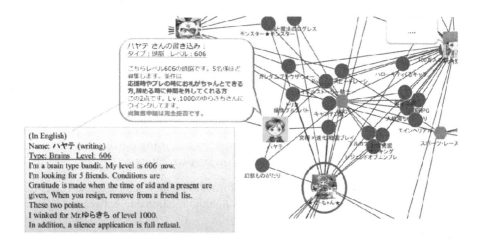

Fig. 2. Example

The development environment is shown below.

— Visualization was performed using CytoScape[1], a Java-based software for network analysis.
— Specifying and extraction are performed by KHCoder[2], a software for text analysis.

Our proposal function has the following steps:

1. Using friend search service of a social game and bulletin board of an SNS, a friend candidate is selected based on the quantitative data.
2. Individual attributes are added to the elected friend candidates.
3. Write-in contents are added to the elected friend candidates.
4. Using the information in 2 and 3, a network diagram is created.
5. There are represented as a network diagram, and users can identify the relation between a candidate and themselves.

A visualized network diagram follows the following rules (table 1).

Table 1. The rule used in the case of visualization

Item names	Note
Player node	large gray triangle
Candidates of friends (cf) node	small triangle
Friends' candidates' friends node	large circle
Community node	small ellipse
Game title node	small square
Game category node	small diamond
Paths to communities and games from cf	black path
Paths to friends from cf	gray path
Paths to game categories from cf	black and dots path
Paths to game categories from Game	gray and dots path

Our function used two methods (visualization method and specifying and extraction method) in order to solve the two important problems described in section 3.

5   Experimental Evaluate

We got 11 subjects to use the function. The subject's attributes are as shown below:

— Eleven men and women (6 men, 5 women) aged 20 to 25-year-old.
— The average time that the experiment took was 28 minutes.
— The average play years of a social game was 15 months.

---

[1] http://www.cytoscape.org
[2] http://khc.sourceforge.net/en/

Subjects evaluated the existing functions and proposed function in five steps about the following two points:

- A friend candidate's appropriateness
- The time of the candidate sorting takes.

Each evaluation result is shown below.

Table 2. Evaluation about existing function and proposal function

Common evaluation criteria	Bulletin board	Random search	Proposal function
A friend candidate's appropriateness	3.8	2.5	4.4
The time of the candidate sorting takes.	2.4	4.6	4.2

From these results, it is seen that the proposed function is excellent compared with existing functions.

6   Conclusion and Future Subject

In this paper, we focused on social games provided in SNS. First, we identified the problems of finding new friends in social games. There are two important problems: "It is difficult to find new friends, because there are many candidates who have a wide variety of personal information" and "Many players of social games who want friends do not know what kind of information is needed to get contact from unknown friend candidates smoothly". Social game users want to play with friends, but they find it difficult to make new friends using existing functions because of security fears and their reluctance to contact with unknown users. Then, we proposed functions for finding new friends easily on the basis of a visualization method, along with specifying and extraction methods. We found that the performance of the proposed functions is superior to that of existing functions. We believe that the use of the proposed functions can enable users to expand their friend network.

In the future work, we will implement a support system with our proposed functions and evaluate it in actual use.

References

1. The annual On-line Game industry report in 2009, 2010, 2011 (in Japanese)
2. FGH : Famitsu game hakusho 2010, 2011, enterbrain (in Japanese)
3. Matsuo, Y.: Individuals and Collaboration in Web2.0 Environments. Information Processing Society of Japan 47(11) (2006) (in Japanese)
4. Adami, L.A., Buyukkokten, O., Adar, E.: A Social Network Caught in the web. First Monday 8(6) (2003)
5. Yuda, K., Ono, N., Fujiwara, Y.: Structural Analysis of Human Network in Social Networking Services. Information Processing Society of Japan 47(3) (2006) (in Japanese)

6. Otake, K., Uetake, T.: Consideration for community activation in social games. The Japanese Society for AI (2011) (in Japanese)
7. Otake, K., Uetake, T.: Consideration of the function to find friend in social game. In: IARIA COLLA 2013 (2013)
8. Nojima, M.: Why do people buy things why do not form. NTT Shuppan Sha (2008) (in Japanese)
9. Kamada, T., Kawai, S.: An algorithm for drawing general undirected graphs information. Processing Letters 31, 7–15 (1989)
10. Fujio, T., Ken, I., Kenichiro, I.: Analysis of Network of Regional SNS. IEICE technial report, AI2008-22 108(208), pp. 33–38 (2008)
11. Yutaka, M., Yuki, Y.: How Relations are Built within a SNS world – Social Net-work Analysis on Mixi. Transactions of the Japanese Society for Artificial Intelligence Technical Report AI 22, 531–541 (2006)
12. Ken, I., Fujio, T., Kenichiro, I.: Proposal for a Growth Model of Social Network Service. In: Proceedings of Web Inteligence and Intelligent Agent Technology, pp. 91–97 (2008)
13. Ryuuichi, Y., Fujio, T., Kenichiro, I.: Analysis of user behavior in SNS. IEICE, AI 108(456), 69–74 (2009)

Group Recommender Systems as a Voting Problem

George Popescu

École Polytechnique Fédérale de Lausanne, Switzerland
Systemic Modeling Laboratory (LAMS), BC 167, 1015, Lausanne, Switzerland
george.popescu@epfl.ch

Abstract. Nowadays, technology allows for a better understanding of user needs through system design (recommender system) methodologies that position the individual at the center of all his actions. In this paper we start by reviewing the state of the art in both individual and group recommender systems technologies. On this ground we cluster the main characteristics of recommender systems with respect to the tasks they perform, the methods they employ and the issues they address. The other theoretical part we rely on is derived from social choice theory and voting. The main objective of this paper is to highlight the role of voting in group recommender systems, more precisely discussing several voting methods together with their characteristics. Our main contributions focus on: reviewing the state of the art literature related to voting in GRS, proposing an innovative and transparent voting mechanism and highlighting the current development of our music recommender system, GroupFun.

Keywords: Behavior, Social choice, Game Theory, Group Decision Making, Incentives, Preference Aggregation, Recommender Systems, Voting.

1   Introduction

Online recommendation technology, for instance, offers the possibility of understanding users' preferences after just a few clicks. In addition, the interaction of various online services can offer a more precise user decision model and propose products that might interest him. Another dimension explored in recommender systems in recent years is the use of social resources to elicit users' preferences and reduce individual effort. Thus, individuals can benefit from excellent recommendations through their network or group of friends. The ubiquitous nature of recommender systems in online commerce websites suggest this new approach helping users make effective decisions, filtering information and allowing companies to increase their revenue through product promotion by targeting an entire group rather than a single, isolated individual.

A (individual) recommender system is a system which, through an information filtering technique, attempts to recommend information items - e.g.: music, movies, TV programs, videos on demand, books, news, images, web pages, research papers etc.) which are likely to be of interest to a single user. In individual recommender systems the more effort a user puts in stating his preferences the more accurate recommendations

A.A. Ozok and P. Zaphiris (Eds.): OCSC/HCII 2013, LNCS 8029, pp. 412–421, 2013.
© Springer-Verlag Berlin Heidelberg 2013

he will obtain. The challenges associated with recommender systems focus on the lack of data: they need a lot of information to effectively make recommendations. Furthermore, recommender systems are "biased towards the old and have difficulty showing new": the issue of changing data. Also, users' preferences change over time. This change cannot be very precisely measured and predicted.

In group recommender systems (GRS) the challenges are a lot more complex: e.g. users do not need to interact with the system more and still obtain group-satisfying recommendations. Their preferences need to be understood by the recommender following social rules. Also, users need to have an incentive for stating their preferences truthfully for the entire group. Research in the game theory field provides mechanisms for truthful preference elicitation. Recommender systems, on the other hand, have been used for solving social choice issues such as: information adaptation, preference aggregation and automated negotiation. They offer the potential for substantially improving preference aggregation and elicitation.

Understanding group recommenders issues relate to the interaction between the system and the users. However, applications of game theoretic methods to group recommenders are still an open research area. The development of such theoretical consideration and applications is a research priority for the social group recommender systems and human computer interaction research fields. Findings in this field are related to truthful preference elicitation, recommendation understanding and user adoption.

The significance of the current article is two folded: on the one hand we discuss theoretical concepts grounded in game theory such as incentives for truthful preference elicitation and voting strategies for influencing a group decision, and, on the other, we showcase on implementation of a truthful voting scheme implemented in our Facebook application. In GroupFun, users can contribute music to their group and rate each other's songs while seeing others' ratings. Through this design we can measure the extent to which some users are more individualistic trying to get their songs voted to the top of the playlist whereas others are more group oriented, giving "fair" ratings. The results mentioned in this paper have an impact in dynamic online environments when users vote (and change their votes) numerous times. Instead of competing for the desired outcome we shown how a probabilistic voting scheme can help users state their preferences truthfully. Using a simple algorithm we have defined an incentive-compatible scheme in which scores are interpreted as probabilities.

2   Recommender Systems and User Preferences

The way an individual recommender system works is that typically it compares a user profile to some reference characteristics, and tries to predict the 'rating' that a user would give to an item they had not yet considered based on these characteristics which may belong to the information item (the content-based approach) or the user's social environment (the collaborative filtering approach) (McCarthy et al. 1998).

A group recommender system is a recommender system aimed at generating a set of recommendations that will satisfy a group of users, with potentially competing interests. The challenges associated with this simple statement deal with: considering how to record and combine the preferences of many different users as they engage in simultaneous recommendation dialogs (Jameson, 2004).

Recommender systems are widely extended in most online applications and platforms. They help users reach the items they want instead of searching them online by finding out which might be of interest to the user. Social networks can be of help in the sense that one's friends can decide which items may be recommended for someone else through means of sharing the same interests. Furthermore expertise can be both useful and not: sometimes the experts' approvals do not reach the mass. From an economic point of view 2/3 of Netflix rented movies are due to recommendations, 38% of Google News clicks are due to recommendations and 35% of Amazon's sales are due to them also (Adomavicius et al. 2010). On the internet everything can be recommended under the generic name of "item": music, books, news, advertisements, cloths, programming code, friends, cafes, restaurants, etcSocial Choice Theory

Social choice theory is a theoretical framework for measuring individual interests or welfares as an aggregate towards collective decision (Chevaleyre et al. 2007). Social choice theory and decision-making theory are strongly connected. Much advancement in both fields contributes to the success of the other field: social choice deals with evaluation of methods for collective decision-making while decision making helps putting decisions into practice for maximizing social welfare. When extending individual decision-making or set of preferences to a group or collective decision making process one needs to take into account far more preference levels and intensities related to the field of choice in order to maximize a common welfare state, payoff or satisfaction function (Gruenfeld 2006, Hastie and Kameda 2005).

The main challenges discussed in the social choice literature are related to: social filtering, group formation, strategy-proofness, unconditional privacy, satisfaction measurement (Masthoff 2005, Masthoff 2006), coalition formation, recommendation collaboration and negotiation (Chevaleyre et al. 2007).

Jameson (2004) explores the challenges for group recommender systems while finding the response to four novel research issues: "What benefits and drawbacks can member preference specification have, and how can it be supported by the recommender system?", "How can the aggregation procedure effectively discourage manipulative preference specification?", "How can relevant information about suitability for individual members be presented effectively?" and "How can the system support the process of arriving at a final decision when members cannot engage in face–to–face discussion?"

Jennings et al. (2001) examine the space of negotiation opportunities for autonomous agents with the purpose of defining automated negotiation prospects, methods and challenges Negotiation is presented as the best method for management and resource sharing in a multi-agent environment. It also evaluates negotiation key techniques and presents some major challenges for future automated negotiation research. The general negotiation framework is modeled on the basis of agreements and proposals. The space between negotiation acceptance (agreement) and refusal opens the discussion for efficiency and effectiveness.

3   Voting in Recommender Systems

Recommender systems have emerged in the mid-1990s when forecasting theories and information retrieval algorithms have linked this domain with social choice modeling. The most basic formulation of a recommender system is that of aggregating a set of user preferences – which can be either implicit or explicit – into a common social welfare function which would maximize the satisfaction of all users. For online applications especially voting is one of the most common used ways for users to manifest their preferences. Ratings can come after users' interaction with the system or by interpreting his/her preferences as extract of personal data. Once votes are submitted the recommender system should come up with solution corresponding to the highest scored items. The difficulties encountered by such a system are numerous: the number of users, their preferences, cold start or initial recommendation, complex interpretation of preferences, utility statements, fact and desirability, etc. Voting difficulties relate back to: number of votes, user interaction, voting scale, which items to be displayed first, voting estimation for non-voted items, voting differences in interpretation across users, lack of an absolute framework, etc.

In recommender systems utility is typically represented through users' votes or ratings. The central problem of voting in recommender systems is connecting rated items with unrated ones. Through their nature, group recommendation systems aim at recommending items that are most relevant for the common interest of a group of users. In most cases voting mechanisms assume that users rate all (or some) items in order to identify the item (or a group if items) that suits the preferences of all group members. This represents a very strong assumption since it is mostly desirable that users should do the least of effort while expecting that the recommender system will know their common preferences. So the above assumption proves as not being feasible in sparse rating scenarios which are very common in the field of recommender systems. Compared with other decision mechanisms such as negotiations, coalitions and actions, voting is a very common and easy framework for helping users reach a common output. It becomes desirable to determine the winning item(s) while using a minimal set of the group members' ratings, under certain assumptions of the voting mechanism of the recommender system. Voting can be a very computationally costly mechanism thus yielding the need for effectiveness. Heuristic algorithms prove to be extremely useful in scenarios depending on user interest and their effort: minimizing the number of user required ratings, for instance.

4   GROUPFUN

GroupFun is a Facebook application available at the address http://apps.facebook.com/groupfun/ and hosted at EPFL.

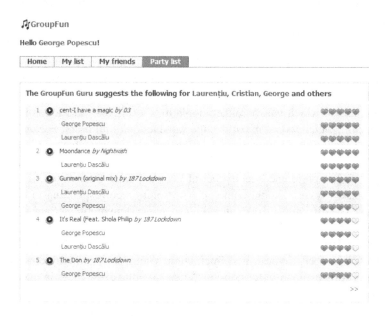

Fig. 1. "Party list" tab in GroupFun

4.1   Home

The "Home" page contains the visual identify of the GroupFun and three playlists: Top 8 GroupFun, Christmas and Lausanne Party. Three entities are samples of what GroupFun can have as output, as shown above.

4.2   My List

Users can create their own playlist from a number of 10.000 songs. After the playlist is created, the user can rate the songs, as in the figure 2. The music player, soundmanager, can help the user to take the right decisions. The user can edit his/her playlist and add/remove songs from the playlist.

4.3   My Friends

The user can invite his/her friends to use the application and check their activity: they accepted or not the invitation and what are their music preferences. In the implementation, we used the standard Facebook request fb:multi-friend-selector, customized with 6 maximum invitations and 5 friends per column. The activity of user's friends is available, in case that he/she wants to check their music preferences. This feature increases the interaction within a group of friends, as some users can rate the songs already rated in the system. A preview is available in the figures below.

4.4   My Scrobbler

Using the Last.fm music recommender system called "Audioscrobbler", we imported users data into GroupFun by taking advantage of the profile of each user's musical taste after recording details of the songs the user listens to, either from Internet radio stations, or the user's computer or many portable music devices. This information is transferred to Last.fm's database ("scrobbled") and then scrobbled again into Group-Fun. The profile data is then displayed on the user's profile page.

4.5   Party List

Users can express their preference related to the songs from the event playlist. For the "Party list" page, we implemented two recommendation algorithms and the output is a common playlist, based on the preferences of all the users.

5   Voting Mechanism

The motivation of this research was to find a preference elicitation and aggregation method for a group deciding on a joint outcome. Two criteria are important for developing this method: it must maximize the group satisfaction, and it must encourage users to state their preferences truthfully so that group satisfaction actually corresponds to satisfaction of user preferences. This problem is a general instance of social choice and often modeled as a voting problem. We let A be the set of all users and S the set of all possible outcomes that can be rated. In a group music recommendation setting, the outcomes are songs s_i to be selected in a joint playlist. We let each user a_j submit a numerical vote $score(s_i, a_j)$ for each song s_i that reflects its preference for that song. These votes are given as ratings, for example 4 out of 5 stars, and normalized so that the scores given by each user sum to 1. We then assign a joint score to each song that is computed as the sum of the scores given by the individual users:

$$score(s_i) = \sum_{a_j \in A} score(s_i, a_j) \tag{1}$$

To choose the songs to be included in a playlist of length k, a deterministic method is to choose the k songs with the highest joint rating. This is a generalized plurality rule. However, this method is not truthful: consider a user who very much likes a song X that is certainly not liked by anyone else, but also has a second best song Y that many others like. This user has no interest to give a high vote for X, since X will never make it into the k songs with the highest joint score. Instead, she should give a stronger vote to Y, which actually has a chance to make it into the selection. In fact, a famous result in game theory, the Gibbard-Satterthwaite theorem, shows that there does not exist a truthful deterministic voting method. However, we note that this theorem does not apply to non-deterministic methods where the choice includes a random element. Consider for example the random dictator rule: we randomly pick one of the users with equal probability, and let this user decide the next song to be chosen. Once chosen, the user knows that her choice will be included, so she will report it truthfully even if it is not very popular among other users.

5.1   Voting Algorithm

As a method for choosing a joint playlist, we thus propose a method we call the probabilistic weighted sum (PWS) that is equivalent to the random dictator rule: we iteratively choose each of the k songs randomly according to the probability distribution:

$$p(s_i) = score(s_i) \Big/ \sum_{s_i \in S} score(s_i) \tag{2}$$

To illustrate how PWS works, we consider the following example. In the table below, user1, user2, and user 3 represent group members. The score distribution for each of the candidates is displayed in the respective row, and the joint scores are shown below.

Table 1. An example of three users and 6 candidates using PWS

User1	Song 1: 0.1	Song 2: 0.3	Song 3: 0.2	Song 4: 0.1	Song 5: 0.1	Song 6: 0.2
User2	Song 1: __	Song 2: 0.1	Song 3: __	Song 4: __	Song 5: 0.4	Song 6: 0.5
User3	Song 1: 0.4	Song 2: 0.2	Song 3: __	Song 4: 0.2	Song 5: __	Song 6: 0.2
Total score	Song 1: 0.5	Song 2: 0.6	Song 3: 0.2	Song 4: 0.3	Song 5: 0.5	Song 6: 0.9

For a playlist of size 2, the plurality rule would always choose songs 6 and 2, and User3, who prefers song 1, would have no interest to vote for that song. After normalizing the total scores by the sum of the scores, we obtain the following probability distribution for the set of outcomes.

| Probability | Song 1: 0.16 | Song 2: 0.2 | Song 3: 0.1 | Song 4: 0.06 | Song 5: 0.16 | Song 6: 0.3 |

It would choose the playlist by choosing one song after another using this probabilistic distribution. Compared to other social choice based algorithms, PWS is incentive compatible. That is, it is to the best interest of the individual to reveal his/her preferences truthfully. It is in fact equivalent to a random dictator method, where the dictator will choose a song randomly with the probabilities given by its degree of preference – a reasonable method since nobody wants to hear the same song over and over again. This is because the probability of a song si to be chosen can be written as:

$$p(s_i) = score(s_i) \Big/ |A| = \sum_{a_j \in A} \frac{1}{|A|} score(s_i, a_j) \tag{3}$$

or, in other words, the probability of choosing user aj times the normalized score that user aj has given to song si. And indeed, User3's preference for song 1 yields a significant probability that this song will be included in the playlist.

Advantages of PWS Compared with Other Methods

- Users are free to choose as many or as few songs as they like
- Users can easily rate each song and the system will turn it to utility score
- Ratings are updated permanently

- The algorithm is computationally simple
- Incentive-compatible truthful property is observed

Disadvantages

- Difficult to quantify rating differences between distinct users. The weights given by each user cannot be compared with the ones given by another.
- Self-selection effect: most popular songs will receive most votes (not ideal if long tail distribution is desired).

5.2   Evaluation

More than 100 users have tested our system during various pilot tests and experiments organized by uploading and rating music in a small group. Here we report only the results concerning the role of the probabilistic weighted sum algorithm in music recommendation. We planned and carried out an experiment in which 24 individuals evaluated 4 algorithms under the name of Alg1 (Deterministic Weighted Sum), Alg2 (Probabilistic Weighted Sum), Alg3 (Least Misery) and Alg4 (Probabilistic selection).

The results highlighted in the chart and table below together with users comments and inputs are very fruitful for our development of the probabilistic weighted sum algorithm. With colored lines are presented all of the users' ratings (due to space concerns we include only 8 users' ratings) and with a dashed black line the average of all results (16 recordings). We notice a favorable trend for the first two algorithms. The least misery one is less preferred in general by all members compared with the first two whereas the random or probabilistic selection received the least scores.

The last row in the table shows that the average scores for PWS and DWS are very close: 3.625 for the first one and 3.875 for the second one. Given the fact that in our

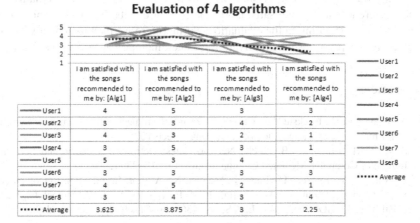

Evaluation of 4 algorithms

	I am satisfied with the songs recommended to me by: [Alg1]	I am satisfied with the songs recommended to me by: [Alg2]	I am satisfied with the songs recommended to me by: [Alg3]	I am satisfied with the songs recommended to me by: [Alg4]
User1	4	5	3	3
User2	3	3	4	2
User3	4	3	2	1
User4	3	5	3	1
User5	5	3	4	3
User6	3	3	3	3
User7	4	5	2	1
User8	3	4	3	4
Average	3.625	3.875	3	2.25

Fig. 2. Evaluation of algorithms

experiment users did not have the time to experience the advantages of PWS in many voting sessions we find this result very encouraging for future research. Moreover, we note that none of the users gave a score lower than 3 (out of 5) for PWS and DWS. Other 2 algorithms received very low ratings. Out of the reasons mentioned by our users favoring PWS we report: serendipitious and non-popular music recommendations, transparent information of other members' ratings and discovery effects.

6   Conclusions and Future Work

Recommender systems have known significant improvement in the past years. Many of them have been due to voting protocols and the fact that the system could understand better users' preferences. The work proposed in this paper is strongly connected to dynamic online environments in which users vote and change their votes numerous times. Instead of competing for the desired outcome we have shown how a probabilistic voting scheme can help users state their preferences truthfully. Using a simple algorithm we have defined an incentive-compatible scheme in which scores are interpreted as probabilities. The static and the dynamic cases further contributed to measuring user preference for the deterministic case.

This advances previous work carried on for understanding the voting mechanism as well as its dynamics and user choice. Users are free to state their preferences individually as well as modify them according to some group dynamics factor and intermediate common decision. In real-life examples the two cases presented are very frequently encountered and numerous applications stated in the beginning denote the need for adaptive group recommender systems. GroupFun is one of these systems designed for users to spend the least amount of time stating their preferences and be able to reach the common music playlist goal.

Future work will consider best ways for allowing group members to interactively achieve common outcomes that they are willing to consume. By studying user interaction in a group recommender system we will be able to match group dynamics with music preferences and group satisfaction for a set of events. Fairness is another study point worth investigating in the evaluation. Furthermore we plan to deduct what inspirational process produces user motivation for deciding upon a specific playlist.

References

1. Adomavicius, G., Bockstedt, J., Curley, S., Zhang, J.: Impact of Recommender Systems on Consumer Preferences: A Study of Anchoring Effects (2010)
2. Boyd, D.M., Ellison, N.B.: Social Network Sites: Definition, History, and Scholarship. Journal of Computer-Mediated Communication 13, 210–230 (2008)
3. Chevaleyre, Y., Endriss, U., Lang, J., Maudet, N.: A Short Introduction to Computational Social Choice. In: van Leeuwen, J., Italiano, G.F., van der Hoek, W., Meinel, C., Sack, H., Plášil, F. (eds.) SOFSEM 2007. LNCS, vol. 4362, pp. 51–69. Springer, Heidelberg (2007)

4. Crossen, A., Budzik, J., Hammond, K.J.: Flytrap: Intelligent Group Music Recommendation. In: Proceedings of the 7th International Conference on Intelligent User Interfaces, Intelligent Information Laboratory, Northwestern University, USA (2002)
5. Gruenfeld, D.H.: Group composition and decision making: How member familiarity and information distribution affect process and performance. Organizational Behavior and Human Decision Processes 67(1) (2006)
6. Hastie, R., Kameda, T.: The robust beauty of majority rules in group decisions. Psychological Review 112, 494–508 (2005)
7. Jameson, A.: More than the sum of its members: Challenges for group recommender systems. In: Proceedings of the International Working Conference on Advanced Visual Interfaces, pp. 48–54 (2004)
8. Jennings, N., Faratin, P., Lomuscio, A., Parsons, S., Sierra, C., Woodridge, M.: Automated negotiation: Prospects, methods and challenges. International Journal of Group Decision and Negotiation 10(2), 199–215 (2001)
9. Kay, J., Niu, W.: Adapting information delivery to groups of people. In: Proceedings of the First International Workshop on New Technologies for Personalized Information Access at the Tenth International Conference on User Modeling, Edinburgh (2005)
10. Kerr, N.L.: Group performance and decision making. Annual Reviews Psychology 55, 623–655 (2004)
11. Lang, J.: Some Representation and Computational Issues in Social Choice. In: Godo, L. (ed.) ECSQARU 2005. LNCS (LNAI), vol. 3571, pp. 15–26. Springer, Heidelberg (2005)
12. Masthoff, J.: Group modeling Selecting a sequence of television items to suit a group of viewers (2004)
13. Masthoff, J.: The pursuit of satisfaction Affective state in group recommender systems. In: Ardissono, L., Brna, P., Mitrović, A. (eds.) UM 2005. LNCS (LNAI), vol. 3538, pp. 297–306. Springer, Heidelberg (2005)
14. McCarthy, J.F.: Pocket Restaurant Finder: A Situated Recommender System for Groups. Accenture Technology Labs (2002)
15. McCarthy, J.F., Anagnost, T.D.: MUSICFX: An Arbiter of Group Preferences for Computer Supported Collaboration. In: Proceedings of the 1998 ACM Conference on Computer Supported Cooperative Work. Center for Strategic Technology Research, Accenture (1998)
16. Pennock, D.M., Horvitz, E., Giles, C.L.: Social Choice Theory and Recommender Systems: Analysis of the Axiomatic Foundations of Collaborative Filtering. In: Proceedings of the Seventeenth National Conference on Artificial Intelligence, pp. 729–734. AAAI Press (2000)
17. Ricci, F.: Decision making and recommender systems (2009)

Social Media: An Ill-Defined Phenomenon

James White[1], King-wa Fu[2], and Braeden Benson[1]

[1] Center for Advanced Communications Policy, Georgia Institute of Technology, USA
[2] Journalism and Media Studies Centre, University of Hong Kong, Hong Kong
{ James.White,braeden}@cacp.gatech.edu, kwfu@hku.hk

Abstract. This paper questions whether and to what extent social media matches its many presumed desirable attributes, through references to social media in the United States and China, and in light of data that indicates that social media use tends to be dominated by a small group of elite users and driven by conventional forces. It concludes with implications for policy development.

1 An Ill-Defined Phenomenon

The promises of social media are many. "Everyone is a media outlet" proclaims Shirky's *Here Comes Everybody* (2008). A list of common descriptive features of social media includes interactive, user-generated, collaborative, shared, social network and rapid information dissemination (Kaplan & Haenlein, 2010). This paper questions whether and to what extent social media does or can realize the positive potential embedded in such a catalog of presumed desirable attributes.

Scott states that "there isn't a hard- and fast- definition of social media that everyone agrees on" (2007, 64), with the consequence that "there seems to be confusion among managers and academic researchers alike as to what exactly should be included under [the term social media]" (Kaplan & Haenlein 2010, 60). Cohen (2011) found some of his respondents defined social media by their platform and outputs, and others by the interactive communications they enable. Greenstein identifies this as a basic dichotomy in approaches to the term, that not only is social media the "technologies (people use to) share content, opinions, insights, experiences, perspectives, and media," but that social media is also the "practices" by which people share content (Cohen, 2011). We can discern two basic approaches: to consider social media as a wide range of "interactive digital tools" (Fraustino et al, 2012) or platforms; or to focus on the mode of social media, the way its content happens and is used, "to the interaction of people and also to creating, sharing, exchanging and commenting contents in virtual communities and networks" (Ahlqvist et al, 2010).

Lack of a widely accepted definition of the term social media[1] muddies the communications waters, as does a frequent conflation of social media with the much larger concept of social network, which has widespread acceptance in the sociological

---

[1] See also FEMA 2012, Lindsay 2011, Xiang & Gretzel 2010.

A.A. Ozok and P. Zaphiris (Eds.): OCSC/HCII 2013, LNCS 8029, pp. 422–431, 2013.

literature. This is especially true when communication is urgent, for example in the origination and dissemination of alerts and warnings at the time of an emergency, or when the subject is in some way controversial. In short order, legal, political and social issues arise. Exemplar areas of concern include privacy, credibility, security, free speech, trust and censorship.

The definitional confusion reflects a wider debate in the literature, between those who depict the "inexorable rise (of social media)... while legacy media are still in decline" (O'Connor, 2012: 259), and others like MacKinnon (2012) and Carr (2010) who warn about the need to govern the new technologies and to pay attention to what may be lost as well as what is gained through such technology. In short, the contrast is between the potential of social media as technologies, and the cultural, economic, historical and social settings that provide their context.

Evaluating social media becomes problematic without this context, epitomized in the debacle of the initial offering of shares in Facebook in May 2012, which dropped by 45 percent in value in the first five months. In part, this was a reflection of uncertainty about the worth, effectiveness and impact of the social media phenomenon, in turn signaling confusion over the meaning of the term. For example, can impact be measured with a yardstick other than subscriber base? Is effectiveness to be measured by the means, the tools of social media (e.g., which platforms should be considered, in what priority, for which audience?) or by the mode of delivery, whether a push (publishing) or a pull (not only receiving information, but also actively soliciting input from the public) or a relay (passing on information)?

The problem is compounded when social media goes international. In authoritarian China, for example, "social" and "media" are terms loaded with alternate meanings. In the view of government, Chinese social media are likely to be defined and contextualized as a mixture of user-generated contents, a variety of social networks (layered on top of physical social networks), and social control. In terms of the Chinese user, another layer of meaning is suggested by the underlying idea of social networking, the potential for development of a civil society parallel to or beyond that mandated by communist party control.

Further, the mechanics of social media can differ. The Chinese equivalent of Twitter is *Sina Weibo,* which claims registered user figures comparable to Twitter's 500 million (Cooper, 2013). *Weibo* is a direct translation of the word "microblog"; however, *weibo* is more of a Twitter-Facebook hybrid than a pure Twitter clone. Like Twitter, *weibo* allows users to post and share short messages with 140 characters or less, and allows users to "follow" another user or to repost (or "retweet", in Twitter parlance) another user's post to one's own readership. There are important differences, however, including the capability to repost a post with one's post as a separate entity on *weibo* (Twitter allows only 140 characters for the retweeted post and user comment together), and the fact that the nature of the Chinese language is such that each "character" is potentially an ideogram, with embedded meaning, so that a Chinese post translated into English could be many sentences long. These differences change the dynamics of conversation on *weibo* systems to make them more like a dialog, as *weibo* also organizes threaded comments for individual posts.

The purpose of this paper is to focus on the frequent mismatch between the promise of social media (as captured in some of the citations above) and the reality as shown through observation and research. Consequently we are primarily interested in describing social media in terms of communications processes, the practices rather than the technologies, and in focusing on various characteristics that are commonly attributed to them. We broaden the consideration of social media from the technological means (the platforms) to the manner of communication itself. [2]   In part this is for the practical reason that the social media technologies and platforms are so remarkably diverse. For example, Fraustino proposes a categorization schema of ten different social media types, illustrated with 26 separate social media examples, all American. We choose to focus on characteristics of two of the types identified by Fraustino: microblogs (American examples: Tumblr, Twitter; Chinese examples: *Sina Weibo*, *Tencent Weibo*) and social/professional networking (American examples: Facebook, Google +, LinkedIn, MySpace; Chinese examples: *Renren, Kaixin*).

2   Characteristics of and Differences from Common Perceptions

In the following sections we discuss and question some common perceptions of social media.

2.1   Participation

Over the past decade, the notion that the Internet has opened up the public sphere to increased participation has been widely shared (see Benkler, 2006; Kline & Burnstein, 2005; Dahlberg, 2001). More recently the nature and extent of that participation has come under scrutiny. Starting in 2009 Bakker carried out a representative survey of more than 2,000 Dutch people to determine their use of "participatory media" defined as "blogs, Twitter, discussion forums, social networks and comment sections of blogs and news sites," in order to ascertain who actively engaged in political discussions or contributed content to online forums. Bakker found a major imbalance between the active and the passive audience, a division between those who consume and those who actually contribute content. For example, very few (6%) contributed to social media political discussions. And they were the usual suspects: already engaged in such discussions, often male and usually highly educated (Bakker, 2013).

2.2   Interactivity

The above findings reinforce a number of studies into the phenomenon of participation inequality (see Nielsen, 2006) and reflect negatively on another social media shibboleth, the notion that social media represent bi-directional communication, i.e. interactivity, especially in contrast to the traditional media which are seen as one-way communication. As Bakker indicates, this seems to be overstated – only a small group

---

[2]   The authors chose not to emphasize the question of content, due to space considerations.

of social media users are actively speaking while most are primarily listening. One quantitative indicator is the percentage of lurkers among users, representing the proportion of social media users who follow the posts but never contribute. Nielsen describes the 90-9-1 rule, that 90% of users are lurkers, 9% contribute from time to time, while 1% are heavy contributors, with some social media, such as blogs and Wikipedia, being even more heavily skewed (Nielsen, 2006). In China, a recent *Sina weibo* study revealed that 57% of 30,000 randomly sampled *weibo* accounts have nothing in the timeline, indicating that this group of users did not write anything at all (Fu & Chau, 2013). These findings suggest that even if social media have considerable potential to empower human interpersonal communication, only a minority of users exploits that potential. Most communication among social media users, whether in the U.S. or in China, is unidirectional – like broadcasting. They also bring into question other characteristics commonly attributed to social media, such as the ideal of a collaborative space for users – this may be the exception, not the rule, especially in the case of microblogs, where only a small percentage of the messages are original, and most are retweets (Yu et al, 2012) – and of sharing, when in fact this may be the exception, not the rule (ibid).

2.3   Homophily

Even if social media users do manage to interact with each other, i.e. social networking does take place, they are likely to share pre-existing similarities. Similarity breeds connection, in the phenomenon known as homophily or "Birds of a feather flock together" (McPherson et al, 2001). Both Twitter and *Sina Weibo* share in this behavior, with the Chinese social media site users having especially pronounced homogeneity, and also being notably more hierarchical in structure, with users tending to follow those at a higher or similar social level (Chen et al, 2012).   At worst, this serves to polarize opinion development or reinforce the segregation of user communities. Conover et al (2011) found a "highly segregated partisan structure" in their analysis of political communication on Twitter during the 2010 U.S. congressional midterm elections (Conover et al., 2011), although interestingly this applied to the retweet network (in which users are connected if one has rebroadcast content produced by another), not to the user-to-user mention network (in which users are connected if one has mentioned another in a post, including the case of tweet replies).

2.4   Rapid Information Dissemination

The speed of social media is a given, and of great importance in countries like China, where users engage in a constant game of cat-and-mouse with the authorities. Bakker points out that, contrary to his general finding that there is limited political use of online participatory media, in countries with low levels of press freedom, participation in online social networks is relatively high (Bakker, 2013: 36). Tufekci & Wilson (2012) describe social media, in particular Facebook, as key news sources which the government could not easily control at the time of Egypt's Tahrir Square protests in 2011, and as playing a vital role as facilitators of protest participation. However rumor enjoys the same advantage. During the Hurricane Sandy disaster, the Federal Emergency Management Agency (FEMA) had to set up a rumor control center on their website to counteract the large amount of misinformation provided on social networks.[3] Hill (2012) identified one individual microblogger as being particularly prominent in the spreading of false information, made more problematic by the fact that some of his tweets were true. However social media itself was used to quickly separate the false from the accurate (ibid).

In China, reliable information is scarce, official sources are not seen as trustworthy, and the public information system is not well-developed. The Chinese government has developed a long track record of hiding sensitive and controversial information, leading to a popular tendency to discount government information but place relatively higher trust in unofficial information sources, which may partly explain some recent cases in China when rumors went viral on *Sina Weibo*. Examples include stories of "Tanks in the streets of Beijing"[4] at the time of the sudden fall of a party leader, Bo Xilai, and fears of radiation from the tsunami-damaged Fukushima Daiichi nuclear-power complex in Japan reaching Chinese coastal cities, leading to residents in Shanghai to stock up on iodine pills.[5] Especially during a crisis, trust is an overarching mediating factor in the information exchange involving the authorities and the people and both traditional and social media in credibility-seeking, no matter whether it is situated in American or Chinese settings (White & Fu, 2012).

3   Old Media, New Media: How Much Has Changed?

The proudest claim of social media may be that they have opened up the public sphere to voices that otherwise would be ignored. The following case history from China suggest that while this claim may be true in part, the amplification effect from other, traditional media still makes a major difference.

After Xi Jinping was elected to be General Secretary of the Chinese Communist Party in November 2012, the identities of a number of corrupt Chinese officials were revealed by journalists and by citizens who disclosed evidence, photos, and video on *Sina Weibo*. The posts were retweeted massively and discussed openly, and for the most part were not censored by the authorities. It remains unknown whether the relative lack of censorship was deliberate or coincidental.

The Journalism and Media Studies Center team collected samples of more than 20 such incidents about corrupt Chinese officials from November to December 2012. Their results showed that online versions of the traditional media (including Sina.com, Southern Metropolis Daily, People's Daily, and Phoenix TV) remain major

---

[3]   http://www.fema.gov/hurricane-sandy-rumor-control.
[4]   "Rumor, Lies, and *Weibo*: How Social Media is Changing the Nature of Truth in China." http://www.theatlantic.com/international/archive/2012/04/rumor-lies-and-weibo-how-social-media-is-changing-the-nature-of-truth-in-china/255916/
[5]   "China Fights Fears and Rumors of Japan Radiation." http://blogs.wsj.com/chinarealtime/2011/03/16/china-fights-fears-and-rumors-of-japan-radiation/

sources of information amplification, even though the first *weibo* associated with an incident was often contributed by individual microbloggers. This challenges another oft repeated characteristic of social media, that it is undermining the status and the impact of traditional media (Clark & Aufderheide, 2009).

As an illustration of the observation that the individual microblogger relies on other high-follower-count microbloggers (such as the social media presence of traditional media) to get their message across, the following is a striking example. On March 4, 2012, a *weibo* was posted from a *weibo* account named "旸旸旸" ('旸' means sun in Chinese) on the day before the opening of the National People's Congress 2012 in Beijing. Account "旸旸旸"'s profile picture reveals that she is a Beijing-based young woman with 609 followers. The *weibo* read "Luxury Brands in Two Meetings" and featured photos of the luxury name brand goods worn by attendees [Figure 1]. This post was retweeted 7,040 times when it was published at 10:52am.

Fig. 1. Illustration of Chinese congress members wearing luxury brand name goods

The retweets were collected and the time trend pattern of posting and mode of message diffusion analyzed. Figure 2 displays the hourly time trend of the retweets, in which two major spikes – sudden increases in the numbers of retweets – occurred at 1 p.m. and 5 p.m. on the same day.

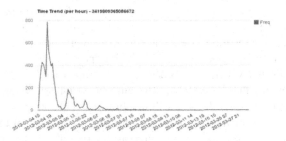

Fig. 2. Time Trend (per hour)

An analysis of the ten highest retweets from microbloggers revealed the frequency of retweets originating directly from their accounts, i.e. out degree in a network graph. Besides the original poster, 旸旸旸, who was ranked as first, the second and the fourth top retweeted microbloggers were 凤凰网围观 (551) and 鳳凰網歷史 (87) . Both accounts belong to online branches of Phoenix Television (凤凰卫视), which is a commercial television broadcast channel in mainland China.

In Figure 3, the diagram presents the microbloggers' retweets generating a network connected by retweets (arrows) between users (nodes). Nodes 551 and 87 form the "epicenters" of the two major clusters of retweets that help propagate the original post to a larger and broader network of microbloggers. This exemplifies the significant role of the online presence of traditional media in *weibo* message diffusion, indicating that social media alone may not be sufficient to distribute information from an individual to the society at large. Social media may be user generated, but often it is the megaphone provided by the mainstream media that let's the user voice be heard.

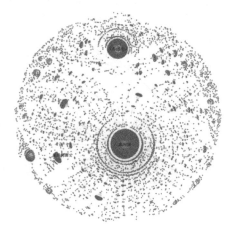

Fig. 3. "Broadcasting" social media

3.1   Developing Trust

Finally, on a more positive note, the real promise of social media may lie in a different direction, that of credibility, trust building and information prioritization. White and Fu (2012) proposed "trust" as a key variable in their iterative credibility seeking model of the communication process at times of emergency and consequently called for the inclusion of new forms of mediated interpersonal communication, including social media, in that verification process. They emphasized the importance of such communications for the disconnected (because of social or economic circumstances) or disadvantaged (such as people with disabilities). This suggests a direction where the promise of social media might be realized. In their analysis of the real-time use of social media in an actual emergency situation (the presence of an armed intruder on a college campus), Tyshchuk et al (2012) found that Twitter played an important role in the warning and verification process. Gilbert and Karahalios (2009) built a predictive model that mapped social media data from Facebook to tie strength, with implications for privacy controls, message routing, and friend introductions.

4   Implications for Policy Development

The expectation is that social media will empower people, allowing them to express opinions and to contribute to the formation of public discourse on a variety of social platforms. The OECD foresees that such modes of online participation can establish a new avenue for enriching political discussion and societal debates, potentially increasing diversity of opinions and promoting pluralism (OECD, 2007). Many countries around the world have initiated e-government activities, including the United States. In 2009, President Obama committed to "creating an unprecedented level of openness in Government" by working to "establish a system of transparency, public participation, and collaboration" (The White House, 2009). The push for open government promoted many government agencies "to [develop] and [expand] their presence via social media technologies with several agencies using social media such as Facebook, Twitter, Flickr, and YouTube for various purposes, depending on mission and goals" (Bertot et al, 2010).

We argue for caution in evaluating such expectations. The optimism that is regularly associated with social media may be built on an ill-defined, misconceived, and technologically deterministic conception, which in some cases contrasts with reality. This apparent reality gap can have significant policy implications, for example, the notions of participation inequality and homophily, as described above, can undermine the potential of social media for promoting pluralism or may even encourage its opposite. Fake information and distrust in the social media message may discourage diversity of opinions and de-motivate people from participation, and can have a serious negative impact on the use of social media at times when it could be particularly valuable, such as disasters and emergencies, or for those whose communications needs are acute, such as people with disabilities.

We should also leave room for caution when gauging the impact of social media. Social media create massive data sets collected from the virtual world's user profiles, content, and usage activities. These are extensively extracted, analyzed, and manipulated in the hope of better understanding "real world" problems, such as disease surveillance or the recovering and analysis of censored social media posts in China (Fu, Chan, & Chau, 2013). Too often such data mining is done in the services of overtly political or commercial ends, and we might do well to heed the warnings of boyd & Crawford (2012), that "given the rise of Big Data as a socio-technical phenomenon, we argue that it is necessary to critically interrogate its assumptions and biases."

Finally, attention is due to what has always been a challenge for media, whether new or old, that of censorship. Internet censorship is no longer a policy restricted to authoritarian states like China, but also exists, by different means, in democratic societies. As noted by Bambauer (2013, 1):

> Internet censorship has evolved. In Version 1.0, censorship was impossible; in Version 2.0, it was a characteristic of repressive regimes; and in Version 3.0, it spread to democracies who desired to use technology to restrain unwanted information. Its latest iteration, Version 3.1, involves near-ubiquitous censorship by democratic and authoritarian countries alike.

The internet and social media are global, and that is the stage on which censorship policy as applied to social media is being developed. While social media in China is avowedly censored, employing a "distributed, heterogeneous strategy for censorship that has a great amount of defense-in-depth" (Zhu et al, 2013:11), to date, specific attempts at censorship in the West have been isolated, and controversial. At the time of riots in English cities in August 2011, Prime Minister Cameron announced to Parliament talks with companies including Twitter and Facebook to discuss actions that could limit their reach, as social media were widely used to co-ordinate the riots across the country (Scotsman, 2011), but apparently those actions did not occur. While political censorship of the Internet in the West will always be contentious (but as various reactions to Wikileaks show, not beyond consideration), a greater concern may be corporate self-censorship. For example, while China has recently implemented a real name registration system for all Internet users, companies like YouTube and Google, have expressed interest in requiring the disclosure of real identities to minimize trolling, so that if a user wants to post an Android app review, a public Google+ account, i.e. the user's name, is required. Early research into the impact of real identity requirements imposed on Chinese microbloggers is not encouraging, as it suggests that the new policy might already have stopped some microbloggers from writing about social and political subjects (Fu et al, 2013).

References

1. Ahlqvist, T., et al.: Road-mapping the societal transformation potential of social media. Foresight 12(5), 3–26 (2010)
2. Bakker, T.: "Chapter 2: The people still known as the audience." From Citizens as political participants: The myth of the active online audience? Dissertation. Faculty of Social and Behavioral Sciences, University of Amsterdam (2013)
3. Bambauer, D.: Censorship v3.1. IEEE Internet Computing (2013), http://doi.ieeecomputersociety.org/10.1109/MIC.2013.23 (retrieved)
4. Benkler, Y.: The Wealth of Networks. Yale University Press, New Haven (2006)
5. Bertot, J.C., et al.: Social Media Technology and Government Transparency (2010)
6. Boyd, D., Crawford, K.: Critical questions for big data. Information, Communication & Society 15(5), 662–679 (2012)
7. Carr, N.: The Shallows. W.W. Norton, New York (2010)
8. Chen, Z., Liu, P., Wang, X., Gu, Y.: Follow whom? Chinese users have different choice. arXiv preprint arXiv:1212.0167 (2012)
9. Clark, J., Aufderheide, P.: Public Media 2.0: Dynamic, Engaged Publics. Center for Social Media, American University (2009)
10. Cohen, H.: 30 Definitions of Social Media (May 9, 2011), http://heidicohen.com/social-media-definition/ (retrieved)
11. Conover, M.D., Ratkiewicz, J., Francisco, M., Gonçalves, B., Flammini, A., Menczer, F.: Political polarization on twitter. Paper presented at the Proc. 5th Intl. Conference on Weblogs and Social Media (2011)
12. Cooper, D.: Sina Weibo passes 500 million user mark, how's your site coming along? Endgadget (2013), http://www.engadget.com/2013/02/21/sina-weibo-500-million/ (Posted February 21, 2013)
13. FEMA: Social Media for Natural Disaster Response and Recovery. Federal Emergency Management Agency (2012)

14. Fraustino, J., Liu, B., Jin, Y.: Social Media Use During Disasters. Final Report to Human Factors/Behavioral Sciences Division, Science and Technology Directorate. U.S. Department of Homeland Security. START, College Park, MD (2012)
15. Fu, K.W., Chan, C., Chau, M.: Assessing Censorship on Microblogs in China: Discriminatory Keyword Analysis and Impact Evaluation of the "Real Name Registration" Policy. IEEE Internet Computing PP(99), 1 (2013)
16. Fu, K.W., Chan, C.H.: Analyzing Online Sentiment to Predict Telephone Poll Results (2013), http://www.ncbi.nlm.nih.gov/pubmed/23374168
17. Fu, K.W., Chau, M.: Reality Check for the Chinese Microblog Space: a random sampling approach. PLOS ONE (2013), http://www.plosone.org/article/
18. Gilbert, E., Karahalios, K.: Predicting Tie Strength With Social Media. In: CHI 2009, Boston, Mass, April 4-9 (2009)
19. Granovetter, M.: The strength of weak ties. American Journal of Sociology 78(6), 1360–1380 (1973)
20. Hill, K.: Hurricane Sandy, @ComfortablySmug, and The Flood of Social Media Misinformation. Forbes (2012),
    http://www.forbes.com/sites/kashmirhill/2012/10/30/hurricane-sandy-and-the-flood-of-social-media-misinformation/
21. Kaplan, A., Haenlein, M.: Users of the world, unite! The challenges and opportunities of Social Media. Business Horizons 53(1), 59–68 (2010)
22. Kline, D., Burnstein, D.: Blog! How the newest media revolution is changing politics, business and culture. CDS Books, New York (2005)
23. MacKinnon, R.: Consent of the Networked. Basic Books, New York (2012)
24. McPherson, M., Smith-Lovin, L., Cook, J.: Birds of a feather: Homophily in social networks. Annual Review of Sociology 27, 415–444 (2001)
25. Mosco, V.: The Political Economy of Communication. Sage, London (1996)
26. O'Connor, R.: Friends, Followers and the Future. City Light Books, San Francisco (2012)
27. OECD: Participative web and user-created content: Web 2.0, wikis and social networking (2007), http://www.sourceoecd.org/scienceIT/9789264037465 (retrieved)
28. Scotsman: Riots: David Cameron threatens Twitter 'shut down' (August 11, 2011)
29. Scott, D.M.: Social Media Debate. EContent 30(10), 64 (2007)
30. Scott, P.: Why you can't judge a social network by its number of users (2012),
    http://sociable.co/social-media/why-you-cant-judge-a-social-network-by-its-number-of-users/
31. Shirky, C.: Here Comes Everybody. Penguin, New York (2008)
32. The White House: Transparency and Open Government (2009),
    http://www.whitehouse.gov/the_press_office/TransparencyandOpenGovernment (accessed October 10, 2012)
33. Tufecki, Z., Wilson, C.: Social Media and the Decision to Participate in Political Protest: Observations from Tahrir Square. Journal of Communication 62, 363–379 (2012)
34. Wardell, C., Su, Y.S.: 2011 Social Media Emergency Management Camp: Transforming the Response Enterprise. CAN Analysis and Solutions (2011)
35. White, J., Fu, K.: Who Do You Trust? Comparing People-Centered Communications in Disaster Situations in the United States and China. Journal of Comparative Policy Analysis: Research and Practice 14(2), 126–142 (2012)
36. Xiang, Z., Gretzel, U.: Role of social media in online travel information search. Tourism Management 31, 179–188 (2010)
37. Zhu, T., Phipps, D., Pridgen, A., Crandall, J., Wallach, D.: The Velocity of Censorship: High-Fidelity Detection of Microblog Post Deletions. Cornell: arXiv:1303.0597[cs.IR] (2013)

Searching Emotional Scenes in TV Programs Based on Twitter Emotion Analysis

Takashi Yamauchi[1], Yuki Hayashi[2], and Yukiko I. Nakano[2]

[1] Graduate School of Science and Technology, Seikei University, Japan
[2] Department of Computer and Information Science, Seikei University, Japan
dm126222@cc.seikei.ac.jp,
{hayashi,y.nakano}@st.seikei.ac.jp

Abstract. Twitter is a social networking service (SNS) that is specifically used to report the user's current status and what is going on in the presence of the user. One interesting new trend on Twitter is to tweet while watching a TV program. This paper proposes a method of analyzing emotions expressed in tweets. Our method assigns the emotional polarity values to tweets based on the dependency analysis as well as morphological analysis. The results of emotional analysis are used in indexing scenes in TV program viewer, and each scene is characterized with the emotions expressed in tweets posted at that time. This viewer allows users to search a TV program by referring to other Twitter users' emotional impressions for each scene.

Keywords: Twitter, emotion analysis, exploring TV programs.

1 Introduction

In recent years, the number of users for social networking services (SNSs) has been rapidly increasing. Twitter is one of the most popular SNSs and specifically used in reporting the user's current status and what is going on around the user. One interesting new trend on Twitter is to tweet (i.e., to send a message on Twitter) while watching a TV program. Users send their program-related tweets to exchange their opinions and share their feelings about impressive scenes. Such usage of Twitter enhances the users' enjoyment of the TV program together with other Twitter users.

However, people do not always watch TV programs when they are on the air. People frequently record the programs and watch some of them later by searching and selecting interesting ones. For these purposes, video-viewing supporting functions have been developed. As a basis for such systems, it is important to develop automatic video-indexing technologies that pick up important and/or interesting scenes and mark them. Previous indexing technologies determine the indexes by processing audio-visual signals, such as colors and textures of the visuals, and the loudness of the sound. However, with such methods, the opinions of the audience are not considered. Based on this background, we have proposed an emotion-based scene indexing method that characterizes scenes and assigns emotional indexes to scenes by analyzing

A.A. Ozok and P. Zaphiris (Eds.): OCSC/HCII 2013, LNCS 8029, pp. 432–441, 2013.

Table 1. Emotion polarity dictionary

	joy	anticipation	anger	disgust	sadness	surprise	fear	trust
cute	8	0	0	0	0	0	0	6
grateful	10	0	0	0	0	0	0	7
fearful	0	6	0	0	0	4	10	0
enviable	0	0	3	8	6	6	0	0
(´･ω･`)	0	0	0	0	9	6	6	0
(･∀･)	10	8	0	0	0	0	0	0

emotional expressions embedded in program-related tweets [16]. However, our previous method simply uses morphological information, and does not take account of the relationship between morphemes. Therefore, our previous method does not properly handle negation, and the negation of positive feeling is interpreted as positive. In this study, we improve our method by adding a dependency analysis in Japanese and considering the syntactic structure in interpreting emotions in Japanese tweet messages. Then, we use the result of emotion analysis in indexing scenes.

2 Related Work

Various video-indexing techniques have been proposed that variously utilize colors and textures in graphics [1,9], style of camera operation, sound type and loudness, subtitles, and features of human faces [5, 8,12]. On the basis of these techniques, video-viewing interfaces have been proposed, such as those that identify interesting scenes based on the visual characteristics of the video [3], search scenes [13,15], and show the digest of the program [4].

For TV programs indexed using Twitter, Nakazawa et al. [10] proposed a method to determine the climax of a TV program by looking at a histogram of tweets related to the program. In addition, they showed that it is useful to analyze the content of tweets when identifying the factors that trigger the climax. This research is different from these studies in that it focuses on analyzing emotions expressed in tweets, and it uses the results of TV program indexing, which allows the users to search a TV program by referring to other users' opinions on Twitter.

3 Emotional Polarity Dictionary

3.1 Emotion Model

To analyze the emotional characteristics of tweets, an emotion model needs to be defined. In this study, we employ Plutchik's model of emotion [11], which classifies eight primary human emotions: anger, fear, sadness, disgust, surprise, anticipation, trust, and joy.

3.2   Emotional Polarity

We selected 112 emotional words from the WordNet-Affect and translated them into Japanese. We also selected 116 emoticons, such as (・ ∀ ・), from the Japanese Emoticon dictionary. To collect emoticons that are frequently used in Japanese tweets, we randomly chose 2,000 tweets and selected emoticons that were used multiple times.

The emotional polarity values for 8 types of emotions were assigned to each emotional word and emoticon based on the 11-point scale ratings by human annotators. Examples of emotional polarity values are listed in Table 1. For instance, "cute" and "grateful" have strong polarities for positive feelings such as joy and trust. On the other hand, "enviable" has a strong polarity for negative feelings such as disgust and sadness. For emoticons, (・ ∀ ・) has a strong polarity for positive feelings such as joy and anticipation.

3.3   Expanding Emotional Words Using WordNet

Since the number of annotated emotional words (112 words) was insufficient, we added additional emotional words using the Japanese WordNet thesaurus [2]. As a result, we increased the number of emotional words in the dictionary to 2,278 words. Moreover, we assigned emotion polarity values to these words using the similarity produced by WordNet. For example, the similarity between "liking" and "favoritism" is 0.08, and "liking" has an emotion polarity value 8 for the joy dimension. In this case, by multiplying the value of "liking" (8) by the similarity value (0.08), 0.64 is assigned to "favoritism" as the emotion polarity value for joy.

4   Twitter Emotion Analysis System

The process of our Twitter emotion analysis system is shown in Fig. 1. First, tweets related to a TV program are retrieved from the Twitter server. The emotions expressed in the tweets are then analyzed. The results of the analysis are visualized as a graph that displays the temporal changes in emotion polarity values. Components consisting this system are shown in Fig. 2. In the following subsections, we will explain the process of each component in further detail.

4.1   Collecting Tweets from the Twitter Server

First, the tweet collection module collects tweets. We used the Java API Twitter4j [14]. The Twitter server accepts requests at a rate of up to 350 requests per hour from a single account. Therefore, our system can send a request to the Twitter server every 10.3 s. We collected tweets by specifying the time and search queries. In the current system, the search queries need to be specified by users because useful words for retrieving specific tweets differ depending on the TV program.

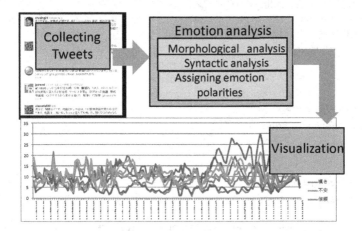

Fig. 1. System architecture

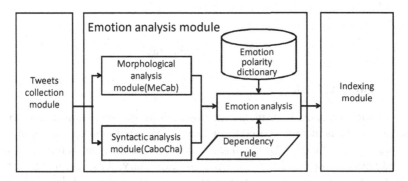

Fig. 2. Processing flow

4.2   Linguistic Analysis

Collected tweets are analyzed in the morphological analysis module and the syntactic analysis module. As the morphological analysis module, we use the MeCab [6] Japanese morphological analyzer. This module splits the sentence into morphemes and outputs a list of words and their morphological information, such as part of speech information and the original form. Emoticon is treated as a special punctuation mark, and is also processed as a morpheme.

To take into account of the dependency relations between words, syntactic information is necessary. For this purpose, we use Cabocha [8] as the syntactic analysis module. The dependency relations are used in calculating the weight to each emotional word which is identified based on the morphological analysis.

```
<?xml version="1.0" encoding="UTF-8"?>
<root>
    <wordset>
            <cluster name="JOY">
                        <word>楽しい</word>
                        <word>嬉しい</word>
                        <word>面白い</word>
            </cluster>
            <cluster name="EMPHASIS">
                        <word>すごく</word>
                        <word>とても</word>
                        <word>非常に</word>
            </cluster>
    </wordset>
    <grammar>
            <rule word="JOY" relation="EMPHASIS" type="forward" value="1.5" />
            <rule word="かわいい" relation="ない" type="backward" value="-0.5" />
            <rule word="だけど" relation="null" type="sentence" value="1.2" />
    </grammar>
</root>
```

Fig. 3. Dependency rules

4.3   Emotion Analysis

In the emotion analysis, first, the morphological information obtained from the morphological analysis module is used to find emotional words and emoticons in a tweet, and assign the emotional polarity value to each tweet. If the general form of a word is matched with an entry in the emotion polarity dictionary, the emotional polarity values of the entry are assigned to the tweet (Examples are shown in Table 1). If multiple emotional words and emoticons are found in a tweet, the sum of the emotion polarity values is calculated. To avoid an undesirable effect of the number of emotion words on the values, the values are normalized using the following equation:

$$e'_i = \frac{e_i}{e_{max}}$$

In this equation, e_i indicates the emotion polarity value for the i-th dimension in the eight-dimensional model before normalization, e'_i indicates the value after normalization, and e_{max} indicates the maximum value among the eight dimensions. Thus, the maximum value for e'_i is 1.

After assigning the emotion polarity values, dependency rules are applied to the results of syntactic analysis. The rules are defined in XML format. Dependency rules can be added and customized by the users. Thus, the users can create their own rules that fit to a specific genre, such as dramas and music shows.

Fig. 3 shows a set of example rules in XML. A set of words is defined by "cluster" tag, and a set of word clusters is indicated by "wordset" tag. For example, the JOY cluster consists of "楽しい (joyful)", "嬉しい (pleased)", and "面白い (interesting)",

ちょっと-D
悪い-D
流れだったけど、---D
PERSON>岡崎</PERSON>が-D
ゴール。
途中-D
消え気味だった<u>けど</u>-----D
最後は---D
<u>すごく</u>-D
よかった！

Fig. 4. Result of syntactic analysis

and the EMPHASIS cluster consists of "すごく (tremendously)", "とても (very)", and "非常に (extremely)". In addition, dependency rules are defined in "grammar" tag. The "word" attribute indicates the target word or a target wordset. The relation attribute specifies the dependency relations, such as emphasis and negation. The "type" attribute specifies the dependency type. In this example, three types dependency types are defined; forward dependency, backward dependency, and sentence level dependency (modifying the whole sentence). The "value" attribute indicates the weight and its polarity.

The first rule in Fig. 3 is an example of adverbial modification using forward dependency. In this grammar rule, if a word is included in JOY cluster and modified by an adverb included in EMPHASIS cluster using forward dependency, its polarity value is multiplied by 1.5. The second rule is a negation rule. If the word label is "かわいい (cute)" and a negation relation "ない" is expressed using backward dependency, then the emotion polarity value of this word is multiplied by -0.5, which means that the emotion polarity of this message is changed. The third rule is an example of sentence level dependency. In this rule, when a contradictory conjunction "だけど" modifies the whole sentence, the emotion polarity values in this sentence are multiplied by 1.2.

4.4   Example of Emotion Analysis

Fig. 4 shows an example of syntactic analysis. In this tweet, the morphological analysis extracts two emotional words; "bad (悪い)" and "good (よい)". The syntactic tree shown in Fig. 4 indicates that "bad (悪い)" is modified by "little (ちょっと)", and "good (よい)" is modified by "tremendously (すごく)". In addition, a contradictory conjunction "but (けど)" modifies the second half of the sentence. If the rules in Fig. 3 are applied to this example, emphatic adverb strengthens the emotion polarity value for "good", and weakens the emotion polarity value for "bad". In addition, "but (け

ど)" also strengthens the value for "good". As a result, the emotion polarity value for "good" becomes most salient in this tweet message.

4.5   Visualizing Emotion Polarity Values

The latest 100 tweets are retrieved from the tweet database every 10 s, and the sum of their emotion polarity values is used to characterize a scene for 10 s. The weight for each tweet is determined according to the elapsed time after posting the tweet. The weight is calculated by the following equation:

$$weight = \frac{1}{\dfrac{(current\_time - posting\_time)(\sec)}{10} + 1}$$

Each emotional polarity value is multiplied by the weight. Thus, the closer the time that the tweet was posted to the current scene, the more the tweet affects the emotion values for that scene. The impact becomes smaller with time. Fig. 5 shows the output of the emotion analysis mechanism. It shows the change in emotion polarity values over time. In the graph in Fig. 5, where joy is represented by a thick blue line, there is a clear peak at the graph's second half, at a time period corresponding to a scene where the hero proposes marriage to the heroine.

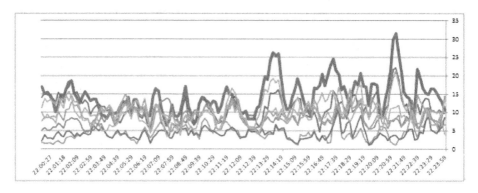

Fig. 5. Estimated emotions displayed in graph format

5   Preliminary Evaluation

We created a simple rule set for adverbial modification using forward dependency, negation relation with backward dependency, and checking whether the modified word is actor's name or the program title. We expect that the last rule is useful for distinguish emotional expressions for a TV program from that for an actor.

We collected 300 tweets for variety shows, and counted the number of times that our dependency rules are applied. The rules were applied to 30% of the collected tweets, and the emotion polarity values for these tweets were properly modified by applying the dependency rules. This suggests that such a simple rule set is effective in emotional analysis at least for 30% of the tweets if the users define appropriate rules for their target genre.

6   Prototype of a Scene Exploring System

Finally, we propose a scene exploring user interface that implements the proposed method. Fig. 6 shows the snapshot of the system. This interface consists of four panels: Movie, Twitter, Graph, and Timeline. The Movie panel plays a recorded TV program. The Twitter panel shows a list of tweets posted relating to the program. The Graph panel visualizes the emotion polarity values. In this example, the values for sadness and joy are displayed. Finally, the Timeline display provides another type of visualization for the emotion polarity values; the x-axis indicates the time, and the y-axis indicates the intensity of the feeling. The Movie panel is synchronized with the Graph and Timeline panels. Therefore, as the movie is played, the Graph and Timeline panels are updated to show the current status. In addition, when a user clicks anywhere in the Timeline panel, the movie jumps to the scene at the time.

The presented interface may support the user in exploring TV programs in two ways. First, by viewing the Timeline panel, the user can find a peak for a feeling in which he is interested. The user can then watch the most interesting scene by clicking on the peak in the Timeline panel. Another way of using this interface is to watch the graphs as they update while also watching the TV program; in this way, users are able to both see how other users feel while watching a specific scene, and share that feeling with other users.

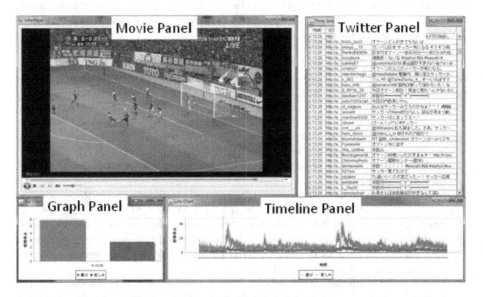

Fig. 6. Snapshot of the scene exploring system

7   Conclusion and Future Work

This study proposes emotion analysis method in Twitter. Our method assigns the emotional polarity values to tweets based on the dependency analysis as well as morphological analysis. The results of emotional analysis are used in indexing scenes in TV program. In this system, the users can freely define the dependency rules. A preliminary evaluation showed that the dependency rules improve the emotion analysis at least 30% of tweets if the users define appropriate rules for a given genre.

As a future direction, the emotion analysis mechanism needs to be improved by adding functions that can handle colloquial expressions and unknown words. Since the users send their message after watching a scene, there is a time lag between the time that the user watched the scene and that the tweet was sent. It is necessary to diminish the time lag. Moreover, while the dependency rules can be created by the users, it would be preferable if default dependency rules are provided for each genre. To define the default rules, it is necessary to investigate what rules are necessary in what genres.

Acknowledgements. This work was partially funded by a MEXT Grant-in-Aid for Building Strategic Research Infrastructures.

References

1. Akutsu, A., Tonomura, Y., Hashimoto, H., Ohba, Y.: Video Indexing using Motion Vectors. In: Proc. VCIP 1992, pp. 522–530 (1992)
2. Bond, F., Baldwin, T., Fothergill, R., Uchimoto, K.: Japanese SemCor: A Sense-tagged Corpus of Japanese. In: The 6th International Conference of the Global WordNet Association (GWC 2012), Matsue, pp. 56–63 (2012)
3. Christel, M.G., Huang, C.: Enhanced Access to Digital Video through Visually Rich Interfaces. In: Proc. of ICME 2003, MD-L5.1, pp. 21–24 (2003)
4. Hashimoto, T., Shirota, Y., Mano, H., Iizawa, A.: Prototype of Digest Viewing System for Television. Trans. of IPSJ 41(SIG3) (TOD6), 71–84 (2000)
5. Intille, S.S., Bobick, A.F.: Closed-world Tracking. In: Proc. of ICCV 1995, pp. 672–678 (1995)
6. Kudo, T., Yamamoto, K., Matsumoto, Y.: Applying Conditional Random Fields to Japanese Morphological Analysis. In: Proc. of EMNLP 2004, pp. 230–237 (2004)
7. Kudo, T., Matsumoto, Y.: Fast Methods for Kernel-Based Text Analysis. In: ACL 2003, Sapporo, Japan (2003)
8. Miyamori, H.: Automatic Annotation of Tennis action for Content-based Retrieval by Integrated Audio and Visual Information. In: Bakker, E.M., Lew, M., Huang, T.S., Sebe, N., Zhou, X.S. (eds.) CIVR 2003. LNCS, vol. 2728, pp. 331–341. Springer, Heidelberg (2003)
9. Nagasaka, A., Tanaka, Y.: Automatic Video Indexing and Full-video Search for Object Appearances. In: Proc. of the IFIP TC2/WG 2.6 Second Working Conference on Visual Database Systems II, pp. 113–127 (1991)
10. Nakazawa, M., Erdmann, M., Hoashi, K., Ono, C.: Social Indexing of TV Programs: Detection and Labeling of Significant TV Scenes by Twitter Analysis. In: Proc. of AINA Workshops, pp. 141–146 (2012)

11. Plutchik, R.: The Emotions, pp. 109–112. Univ. Pr. of Amer. (1991)
12. Smith, M., Kanade, T.: Video Skimming and Characterization through the Combination of Image and Language Understanding Techniques. In: Proc. of CVPR 1997, pp. 775–781 (1997)
13. Sumiya, K., Munisamy, M., Tanaka, K.: TV2Web: Generating and Browsing Web with Multiple LOD from Video Streams and Their Metadata. In: Proc. of ICKS 2004, pp. 158–167 (2004)
14. Twitter4j: http://twitter4j.org/ja/index.html
15. Uchihashi, S., Foote, J., Girgensohn, A., Boreczky, J.: Video Manga: Generating Semantically Meaningful Video Summaries. In: Proc. of MULTIMEDIA 1999, pp. 383–392 (1999)
16. Yamauchi, Y., Nakano, Y.: A Scene Explorer for TV Programs Based on Twitter Emotion Analysis. ICIC Express Letters 6(12), 3069–3075 (2012)

Sentiment Classification of Web Review Using Association Rules

Man Yuan[1,2], Yuanxin Ouyang[1,2,*], Zhang Xiong[1,2], and Hao Sheng[1,2]

[1] School of Computer Science and Technology, Beihang University,
100191 Beijing, P.R. China
[2] Research Institute of Beihang University in Shenzhen,
518000 Shenzhen, P.R. China
{ym,oyyx,xiongz,shenghao}@buaa.edu.cn

Abstract. Sentiment Classification of web reviews or comments is an important and challenging task in Web Mining and Data Mining. This paper presents a novel approach using association rules for sentiment classification of web reviews. A new restraint measure AD-Sup is used to extract discriminative frequent term sets and eliminate terms with no sentiment orientation which contain close frequency in both positive and negative reviews. An optimal classification rule set is then generated which abandons the redundant general rule with lower confidence than the specific one. In the class label prediction procedure, we proposed a new metric voting scheme to solve the problem when the covered rules are not adequately confident or not applicable. The final score of a test review depends on the overall contributions of four metrics. Extensive experiments on multiple domain datasets from web site demonstrate that 50% is the best min-conf to guarantee classification rules both abundant and persuasive and the voting strategy obtains improvements on other baselines of using confidence. Another comparison to popular machine learning algorithms such as SVM, Naïve Bayes and kNN also indicates that the proposed method outperforms these strong benchmarks.

Keywords: Association rule, sentiment classification, text categorization.

1 Introduction

Sentiment Classification, also referred as Polarity Classification or Binary Classification, aims to determine whether the semantic orientation of the given text is positive or negative. The rise of social media such as blogs and social networks as well as e-commerce suppliers such as Amazon and EBay has fueled interest in sentiment analysis. Automatic detection and analysis of consumer reviews or comments from the Web holds great promise for customer research, business intelligence, recommendation system and Smart City applications which need the human feedback analysis. As the number of Web reviews for any product (movies,

---

* Corresponding author.

A.A. Ozok and P. Zaphiris (Eds.): OCSC/HCII 2013, LNCS 8029, pp. 442–450, 2013.

e-commerce, social network content etc.) grows rapidly, it is hard for a potential consumer to make informed decision when reading hundreds of reviews on a single product, and if he/she reads part of the reviews, he/she may get a biased view point. For manufactures or online shopping sites, it also requires great effort to manage and keep track of the large scale review dataset. So, sentiment classification is becoming a challenging and interesting topic in text mining area.

Effective sentiment classification relies on multiple disciplines, such as machine learning, natural language processing, linguistic, statistic etc. One of the main methodologies for sentiment classification is to treat sentiment classification as a special case of Text Categorization [1], which has been a well studied field in the last few decades. Comparing with text categorization, the difference in sentiment classification is that the predefined labels only include "positive", "negative" and sometimes "neural", rather than the topics. Comparative studies demonstrated that these general techniques provide strong baseline accuracy for sentiment classification and outperforms other method based on lexicon analysis.

Pang [2] firstly tried to classify movie reviews into positive/negative by using several supervised machine learning methods: Naive Bayes, Maximum Entropy and SVM. In their following work [3], they added in subjectivity detection with minimum cuts algorithm to avoid the sentiment classifier from dealing with irrelevant "objective" sentences. As reported in their work, the classification performance of product reviews is worse than that of normal topical text categorization. One of the main difficulties is that people typically use both positive and negative words in the same review. In analyzing political speeches, [4] exploited the argument structure found in speaker reference links to help determine how a members of congress would vote given their congressional floor speeches. The method in [5] used bag-of-words, Part-Of-Speech information and sentence position as features for analyzing reviews, representing reviews as feature vectors. In [6], the problem of attributing a numerical score (one to five stars) to a review is presented using Naïve Bayes and SVM.

Among all the text categorization method, there is still a lack of investigation on sentiment classification based on association rules. Association rule based classifiers (associative classifier) originate from association rule mining task of data mining. Since association rules reflect strong associations between items and includes more underlying semantic and contextual meaning than individual word, it has been developed within the text mining domain in different aspects [7] [8] [9].

In this paper, we investigate the association rules in sentiment classification problem. The motivation is to the convert this general classification approach into a binary and special domain classification problem. The main contributions of this work involve: first, we introduce the AD-Sup metric to extract discriminative frequent term sets and eliminating terms with no sentiment orientation which contain close frequency in both positive and negative reviews; Second, optimal rule set is generated to abandon the redundant rules to construct classifier; Third, in rules matching phase, we propose a new metric named Maximum Term Weight and a multiple metric voting scheme to solve the problem when matched rules are not applicable or not confident enough.

2   Proposed Method

The proposed method includes four steps: (1) Data pre-processing and feature selection; (2) Frequent term set extraction and rule mining; (3) Mining optimal classification rules; (4) Predicting test review with multiple metric voting.

Before extracting frequent term set, feature selection is conducted for dimension reduction using Information Gain (IG) [10]. In this study, the magnitude of dimensions is reduced from 10^5 to 10^3. An important reason that makes feature selection essential is that the number of frequent term sets extracted from single terms grows exponentially when the input terms increase. So, the input number of single terms must be restricted to a reasonable scale.

2.1   Frequent Term Set Extraction

In text mining issues, each document d in $D = \{d_1, d_2, \ldots d_n\}$ is treated as a transaction and the set of terms $T = \{t_1, t_2 \ldots t_m\}$ contained in D corresponds to the items set. A term set S in T is frequent if $Sup(S) \geq min\text{-}sup$. The $min\text{-}sup$ constraint of term set is a key measure for frequent sets extraction because it determines the scale and quality of the selected frequent sets. When applied to text mining problem, the concept of support count corresponds to Document Frequency (DF). However, support count cannot be simply substituted by DF because DF only measures the occurrences and this is not sufficient to differentiate the discriminative effect of the frequent term sets. To solve this problem, our previous work proposed a new metric Average Deviation Support (AD-Sup), considering the distribution discrepancy of term sets in each class. Assume the documents set have n classes $\{class_1, \ldots class_i, \ldots class_n\}$ and let FS denote the term set and t is the term in FS, AD-Sup can be formulated as :

$$AD\text{-}Sup(FS) = \frac{\sqrt{\sum_{i=1}^{n} \{Sup(FS)_i - Ave(Sup(FS))\}^2}}{Ave(Sup(FS))} \tag{1}$$

The expression of AD-Sup (1) can be deemed as a modified support deviation, where $Sup(FS)_i$ means the local support of FS in class i and $Ave(Sup(FS))$ denotes the average value of $Sup(FS)$ in all the classes. The frequent term extraction procedure is implemented using Apriori strategy [8]. After obtaining all the frequent term sets (FS), AD-Sup restraint is used to select the frequent features. The selected FS will involve more term sets that are not only frequent but distributed unevenly in different classes.

2.2   Optimal Rule Mining

Following the extraction of frequent term sets, an association rule is an implication denoted by $X \Rightarrow Y$, where both X and Y are subset from a frequent set. For classification problem, the consequent of the rules are class labels. However, it suffers the following problem:(1) the confidence and support restraint is not always suitable for any mining pr paper problem;(2) the number of association rules are usually too large which makes the pruning quite challenging;(3) the vast amount of association rules involve much redundant information. To overcome these obstacles, many interesting metrics and pruning strategies have been proposed to find "optimal rules". There is no standard definition for "optimal rules". This paper utilizes a similar strategy close to [11]:

Definition (optimal association rule set): A rule set is optimal with respect to an interestingness metric if it contains all rules except those with no greater interestingness than one of its more general rules. Given two rules $P \Rightarrow C$ and $Q \Rightarrow C$ where $P \subset Q$, the latter is more specific than the former and the former is more general than the latter.

2.3   Predicting Sentiment Class by Association Rules

For general association rule based classification, the classifier is a collection of selected rules using different rule matching strategies. However, for sentiment classification, these strategies may fail to predict correctly in some cases. Given covered rule sets with positive and negative classification rules, following examples are hard to judge the sentiment: First, the covered positive rules have the highest confidence but the difference with that of the negative rules is quite small, while the number of negative rules is much more than that of the positive rules. In this case, the test review should be negative rules but it will be predicted to be positive. Second, the number of covered rules and the max-confidence of rules are both equal. Third, the situation can be more complicated, where the negative rules have a higher confidence with a little priority than the positive but besides the highest confidence rules, comparing other covered rules, the positive rules are more persuasive.

To overcome these obstacles, borrowing the ideas of democratic regime, we propose a new association rule based class predicting method by a voting scheme of the following metrics. The class label of test review will be determined by a combination of voting score.

$$Score(test\_review_i) = \sum_0^m Vote(metric_j) \tag{2}$$

The vote on a metric is 1,-1,or 0 depending on the different metric value on covered positive rules (PR) and negative rules (NR). Vote(metirc$_j$)=1 if metric$_j$(PR)>metirc$_j$(NR), and respectively, if metric$_j$(PR)<metirc$_j$(NR), Vote(metirc$_j$)=-1, if metric$_j$(PR)=metirc$_j$(NR), Vote(metirc$_j$)=0. The assigned class label depends on whether vote score of metrics is a positive number or negative number.

The metrics that are evaluated here include:

Definition 1 (Max-conf): the highest confidence value of covered rules.

Definition 2 (Cover-len): the number of rules in the covered rule set.

Definition 3 (Minor-conf): the average confidence of covered rules excluding the highest one.

All the above 3 metrics can be obtained by counting the recorded value generated in the rule mining procedure. However, sometimes there is no promising rule with a high confidence in the covered rules. When the Max-conf is not very high or the Max-conf in PR and NR are very close, it is hard to predict if it belongs to any category. To solve this problem, we propose a new metric named MTW (Max Term Weight):

Definition 4 (MTW): Maximum Term Weight, the average term weight of each rule clusters in covered rules. In this paper, we use the information gain (IG) of each term obtained in the frequent term set mining procedure for its weight. A rule cluster is a collection of rules which contains the same term. Given a covered rule set, the algorithm to get max term weight can be described as follows:

```
Algorithm 1: MTW metric generation
Input: single term set (TS) in descending order
    For each term T_i in TS:
        If covered rule set is not empty
            For each rule in covered rule set:
            If(Rule_j contains T_i )
            Add Rule_j to rule cluster(RC_i);
            Set:weight(RC_i)=GetTermWeight(T_i);
            Delete Rule_j in covered rule set;
            end If
            end For
        end If
        end For
```

$$\text{Return: } Average(\sum_{i}^{k} weight(RC_i))$$

The motivation of MTW is to make use of discriminative measurement of single terms contained in the covered rules. Besides IG, similar measurement like TF*IDF and χ^2 are also applicable here.

3   Experimental Results

In this paper, Multi-Domain Sentiment Dataset [12] is used for experimental evaluation. This dataset contains product reviews taken from Amazon.com from many product types (domains). We selected four domains of this datasets: DVD, Book, Kitchen and Electronic. Each domain contains 1000 positive and 1000 negative reviews. All the above reviews are pre-processed by stemming and stop-word elimination. The evaluation is conducted through 3-folds cross validation.

3.1   Frequent Term Sets Extraction

The frequent term sets extraction starts from the selected single terms by IG. The first scan generates frequent term sets with two terms and these double term sets are used as the input term sets for the candidate-generating algorithm. Then the iteration starts until no candidate is selected to be frequent term set. In this paper, input number of single terms is set to be 600 and *min-sup* is 2%.Table 1 reports more details of selected terms and extraction results. The top single terms are ranked by its IG value, followed by the frequent term sets by support count and refined term sets by AD-Sup. Note that the stemming changes the form of the words and makes the stemmed terms appear to be different from the real words. On Electronic dataset, all the top 5 frequent term sets by *min-sup* contain word "i". They are selected due to their high occurrences, but "i" is a common pronoun without discriminating value. We can observe similar results in all the four datasets. Contrarily, term sets selected by AD-Sup contain more sentiment oriented words and also have better consistency with the most important single terms. A *min-AD-Sup* threshold is then used to prune these un-discriminative term sets before mining classification rules.

Table 1. Top Single term and frequent term sets in Electronic and Kitchen dataset

Top5 terms	Frequent termSets	Refined Term Sets	Top5 terms	Frequent termSets	Refined Term Sets
great	us/i	terribl/i/	easi	num/my	return/time/first/
return	work/i	refund/i	return	my/so	worst/ever
excel	i/get	worst/i	great	num/so	wast/monei/do
price	i/all	return/i/bui	love	my/time	wast/monei/even
wast	i/when	wast/work	disappoint	my/get	wast/monei/what

We set *min-conf* as 50% in this experiment to extract classification rules. Table 2 lists the top classification rules of the two datasets.

Table 2. Top positive (Pos) and negative (Neg) rules for Electronics and Kitchen dataset

Pos Rules	Neg Rules	Pos Rules	Neg Rules
excel/price	terribl/i	easi/so/love	wast/monei
perfect/i/us	refund/i	easi/num/love	return/product
perfect/us	return/bui	easi/great/love	return/bui
price/good/well	worst/i/	love/dishwash	return/again
great/perfect	support/call	best/so/can	worst/ever

3.2   Sentiment Prediction Using Multiple Metric Votes

Figure 1 is the F_1 value comparison of classification result on the four dataset. To demonstrate the effectiveness of the metric voting method, we select two baseline algorithms: the Single Rule tries to match the maximum confidence rule of the covered rules set, and the Multi-Rules compares maximum confidence + average confidence value. The results show that in all the four datasets, our strategy outperforms the other two baselines. The maximum improvement of 2.8% was obtained on DVD. On each dataset, all the algorithms were implemented with different *min-conf*. The results also prove that 50% is the best *min-conf* to generate classification rules. When the *min-conf* increases to 70% and 80%, the performance declined rapidly because the number of rules decreases to a very little scale and makes too many test documents covered by none of the rules.

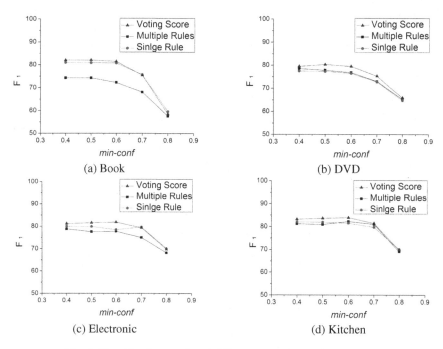

Fig. 1. Classification results of different strategies on four datasets

Table 3. Classification results vs. other classifiers : F_1 (%)

Dataset	SMO	LibSVM	NB	kNN	Voting Score
Book	77.1	81.8	77.7	66.6	82.1
DVD	78.7	76.0	77.1	66.4	80.3
Electronic	82.5	75.6	73.5	67.4	81.9
Kitchen	82.1	81.9	75.6	58.5	83.9

Table 3 summarizes the classicization results of the proposed method comparing with other popular machine learning classifiers. SVM, Naïve Bayes (NB), kNN are well studied text document classifiers with very good performance track in many previous researches. SVM was implemented with two algorithms, LibSVM and SMO.

In three of the four datasets, the F_1 value of multiple metric voting strategy surpassed the other four benchmark algorithms, except for Electronic where the result of our method is very close to SMO.

4   Conclusions

This paper has presented a novel approach using association rules for sentiment classification of web reviews. To extract discriminative frequent term sets, a new restraint measure AD-Sup was used which considers more on the term set distribution on different sentiment classes. The experiment results on multiple domain reviews from real web sites demonstrated that AD-Sup was an effective metric to eliminate terms with no sentiment orientation which contain close frequency in both positive and negative reviews. An optimal classification rule set was generated which abandons the redundant general rule with lower confidence than the specific one. In the class label prediction procedure, we proposed a new metric voting scheme to solve the problem when the covered rules are not adequately confident or not applicable. The final score of a test review depends on the overall contributions of four metrics. To demonstrate the effectiveness of the voting strategy, we compared the classification performance with different baselines of using confidence and the result shows 50% is the best min-conf to guarantee classification rules both abundant and persuasive, and the voting method obtains improvements on all the four datasets. We also compared the proposed method with popular machine learning algorithms such as SVM, Naïve Bayes and kNN. The result also shows that our strategy is effective and outperforms the other strong benchmarks. Since this research focused on binary classification, our future work will concentrate on a further optimization and the extension to multiple label classification problem.

Acknowledgements. We are grateful to Shenzhen Key Laboratory of Data Vitalization (Smart City) for supporting this research. This work was also supported by National Natural Science Foundation of China (61103095), International S&T Cooperation Program of China (2010DFB13350) and National High Technology Research, Development Program ("863" Program) of China (2011AA010502) and Fundamental Research Funds for the Central Universities

References

1. Sebastiani, F.: Machine Learning in Automated Text Categorization. ACM Computing Surveys 34(1), 1–47 (2002)
2. Pang, B., Lee, L., Vaithyanathan, S.: Thumbs up? sentiment classification using machine learning techniques. In: ACL 2002 Conference on Empirical Methods in Natural Language Processing, pp. 79–86 (2002)
3. Pang, B., Lee, L.: A sentimental education: Sentiment analysis using subjectivity summarization based on minimum cuts. In: The 42nd Annual Meeting of the Association for Computational Linguistics, pp. 271–278 (2004)

4. Thomas, M., Pang, B., Lee, L.: Get out the vote: Determining support or opposition from Congressional floor-debate transcripts. In: ACL 2005 Conference on Empirical Methods in Natural Language Processing, pp.327–335 (2006)
5. Baccianella, S., Esuli, A., Sebastiani, F.: Multi-Facet Rating of Product Reviews. In: Boughanem, M., Berrut, C., Mothe, J., Soule-Dupuy, C. (eds.) ECIR 2009. LNCS, vol. 5478, pp. 461–472. Springer, Heidelberg (2009)
6. Prasad, P., Vasudeva, V.: Published Supervised Learning Approaches for Rating Customer Reviews. Journal of Intelligent Systems 19(1), 79–94 (2010)
7. Mahgoub, H.: Mining Association Rules from Unstructured Documents. In: The 3rd International Conference on Knowledge Mining, pp.167–172 (2006)
8. Thabtah, F.: A review of associative classification mining. The Knowledge Engineering Review 22, 37–65 (2007)
9. Han, J., Cheng, H., Xin, D., Yan, X.: Frequent pattern mining: current status and future directions. Data Mining and Knowledge Discovery 15, 55–86 (2007)
10. Forman, G.: An Extensive Empirical Study of Feature Selection Metrics for Text Classification. Journal of Machine Learning Research 3, 1289–1305 (2003)
11. Li, J.: On Optimal Rule Discovery. IEEE Transactions on Knowledge and Data Engineering 18(4), 460–471 (2006)
12. http://www.cs.jhu.edu/~mdredze/datasets/sentiment

Author Index